Truth for Today
Commentary

An Exegesis & Application of the Holy Scriptures

Psalms 1–50

Eddie Cloer, D.Min.

Resource □
Publications

2205 S. Benton
Searcy, AR 72143

Truth for Today Commentary
Psalms 1—50
Copyright © 2004 by Resource Publications
2205 S. Benton, Searcy, AR 72143

All rights reserved. No portion of the text of this book may be reproduced in any form without the written permission of the publisher.

ISBN: 0-945441-47-9

Scripture taken from the NEW AMERICAN STANDARD BIBLE®, © Copyright 1960, 1962, 1963, 1968, 1971, 1972, 1973, 1975, 1977, 1995 by The Lockman Foundation. Used by permission. (www.Lockman.org)

Contents

Preface   vii

Abbreviations   ix

Hebrew Transliteration   xi

Introduction: A Book of Jewish Songs and Prayers   1

Book I: Psalms 1—41   33
- Psalm 1: The Blessed Life   35
- Psalm 2: Opposing God and His Anointed   46
- Psalm 3: A Morning Cry   57
- Psalm 4: An Evening Prayer   67
- Psalm 5: Bringing the Day to God   77
- Psalm 6: Sick Because of Sin   88
- Psalm 7: The Pain of Slander   97
- Psalm 8: The Majestic Name of God   108
- Psalm 9: God and the Nations   119
- Psalm 10: Why Do the Wicked Go Unpunished?   131
- Psalm 11: Faith or Flight   143
- Psalm 12: God's Answer to Evil   153
- Psalm 13: When God Is Silent   165
- Psalm 14: Man's Inhumanity to God   174
- Psalm 15: Who Can Dwell in God's Presence?   185
- Psalm 16: God: The Supreme Good   195
- Psalm 17: A Prayer for Protection   209
- Psalm 18: A Song of Thanksgiving   221
- Psalm 19: A Mirror of God's Magnificence   245
- Psalm 20: Before the Battle   258
- Psalm 21: Praising God for the Victory   269
- Psalm 22: Overwhelmed but Trusting in God   281
- Psalm 23: Satisfied with God   298
- Psalm 24: Celebrating the Presence of God   311
- Psalm 25: Piety Portrayed   324
- Psalm 26: Living with Integrity   341
- Psalm 27: An Antidote for Fear   354
- Psalm 28: Praying in a Crisis   368

Psalm 29: God and the Storm	383
Psalm 30: When a Disaster Has Passed	396
Psalm 31: "Into Your Hand I Commit My Spirit"	408
Psalm 32: The Fruit of Repentance	427
Psalm 33: Let Us Praise Him!	441
Psalm 34: "The Lord Has Been Mindful of Me"	456
Psalm 35: Evil Returned for Good	471
Psalm 36: Good or Evil: Which?	489
Psalm 37: Do Not Fret About the Wicked	502
Psalm 38: "Grace Greater Than My Sin"	525
Psalm 39: God and the Meaning of Life	539
Psalm 40: The Ever-Present God	554
Psalm 41: Hope in the Midst of Suffering	569
Book II: Psalms 42—72	583
Psalm 42: Thirsting for God	585
Psalm 43: "Bring Me to Your Temple"	599
Psalm 44: In the Absence of Mighty Works	606
Psalm 45: An Ode to a Beautiful Wedding	621
Psalm 46: "A Mighty Fortress Is Our God"	634
Psalm 47: Our God: The King of Kings And Lord of Lords	646
Psalm 48: God and the City of God	657
Psalm 49: God or Gold	670
Psalm 50: True Religion Before God	684
A Final Word	701
Have You Heard . . . About Truth for Today?	703

Preface

The psalms have been at the center of worship for both the Jews and the Christians since they were first written. They were sung (or chanted) in the temple and synagogue worship of the Jews. They were on the lips of Christians as they worshiped, "speaking to one another in psalms and hymns and spiritual songs, singing and making melody with [their] heart[s] to the Lord" (Eph. 5:19).

Kyle M. Yates said, "When I approach the Psalms, I feel the impulse to say, 'Take off your shoes for you are standing on holy ground.'"[1] The Bohemian reformer John Hus went to the stake to be burned alive reciting Psalm 31. Girolamo Savonarola (1452–98) awaited death in Palazzo Vecchio in Florence by composing a meditation of Psalms 31 and 41. The Puritans sang psalms as they crossed the sea to freedom from religious tyranny. The third book published in America was the Bay Psalm Book in 1639. The Constitutional Convention began with the reading of Psalm 127:1:

> Unless the Lord build the house,
> They labor in vain who built it;
> Unless the Lord guards the city,
> The watchman keeps awake in vain.

Eddie Cloer has done a masterful job in writing this first of three commentaries on Psalms. His comments on the text and his applications are carefully written. As the first Old Testament volume to be published in the commentary series, it will be a blessing to all who read it.

I have known brother Cloer for many years. We served as colleagues on the Bible faculty of Harding University. Since my retirement, I have worked daily with him and with the staff of Truth for Today World Mission School and Resource Publica-

---

[1] Kyle M. Yates, *Preaching from the Psalms* (New York: Harper and Brothers, 1948), ix–x.

tions. Eddie has the heart of a preacher. This is clearly seen in the penetrating applications he makes to each of the Psalms. I thank him for his scholarship and for his love for the Lord and His church.

Don Shackelford, Th.D.
Associate Old Testament Editor

Abbreviations

OLD TESTAMENT

Genesis	Gen.	Ecclesiastes	Eccles.
Exodus	Ex.	Song of Solomon	Song
Leviticus	Lev.	Isaiah	Is.
Numbers	Num.	Jeremiah	Jer.
Deuteronomy	Deut.	Lamentations	Lam.
Joshua	Josh.	Ezekiel	Ezek.
Judges	Judg.	Daniel	Dan.
Ruth	Ruth	Hosea	Hos.
1 Samuel	1 Sam.	Joel	Joel
2 Samuel	2 Sam.	Amos	Amos
1 Kings	1 Kings	Obadiah	Obad.
2 Kings	2 Kings	Jonah	Jon.
1 Chronicles	1 Chron.	Micah	Mic.
2 Chronicles	2 Chron.	Nahum	Nahum
Ezra	Ezra	Habakkuk	Hab.
Nehemiah	Neh.	Zephaniah	Zeph.
Esther	Esther	Haggai	Hag.
Job	Job	Zechariah	Zech.
Psalms	Ps.	Malachi	Mal.
Proverbs	Prov.		

NEW TESTAMENT

Matthew	Mt.	1 Timothy	1 Tim.
Mark	Mk.	2 Timothy	2 Tim.
Luke	Lk.	Titus	Tit.
John	Jn.	Philemon	Philem.
Acts	Acts	Hebrews	Heb.
Romans	Rom.	James	Jas.
1 Corinthians	1 Cor.	1 Peter	1 Pet.
2 Corinthians	2 Cor.	2 Peter	2 Pet.
Galatians	Gal.	1 John	1 Jn.
Ephesians	Eph.	2 John	2 Jn.
Philippians	Phil.	3 John	3 Jn.
Colossians	Col.	Jude	Jude
1 Thessalonians	1 Thess.	Revelation	Rev.
2 Thessalonians	2 Thess.		

ASV	American Standard Version
KJV	King James Version
NASB	New American Standard Bible
NEB	New English Bible
NIV	New International Version
NKJV	New King James Version
NRSV	New Revised Standard Version
RSV	Revised Standard Version

HEBREW TRANSLITERATION

Studying the Word of God in the original languages brings out more fully the richness of the biblical texts. This series attempts to incorporate a healthy number of Greek and Hebrew words that help clarify the passages under investigation. Although translating and transliterating are difficult tasks with any language, Hebrew poses a particular challenge. First, it is an old language, and spelling and pronunciation have evolved over time. Second, there are multiple methods for transliterating Hebrew words into English. Therefore, the editorial committee has discussed how we will transliterate Hebrew, and we have adapted our own method for the series. It is assumed that not all of our readers will have a working knowledge of Hebrew. Our system attempts to present a transliteration that will simplify pronunciation and assist in word studies. In order to accomplish this, we have applied the following rules throughout the commentary.

Rule 1. No difference is indicated by the hard/soft pronunciation of "Begad Kapath" letters: תתפפככ דדגגבב. The meaning of a word is not affected by whether or not these letters are hard or soft.

Rule 2. When the *Daghesh Forte* indicates a doubling of consonants, the letter is doubled in the transliteration.

Rule 3. The Tetragrammaton (יְהוָה) is transliterated *YHWH* and written "Yahweh" in the text. Since the original vowel pointings are unknown for this word, they have been left out when it appears in the commentary, thus forming יהוה.

Rule 4. The transliteration distinguishes between ה when used as a consonant and ה when used as a vowel letter to lengthen the vowel *Qamets*.

Rule 5. The vocalized *sheva* is indicated by ᵉ.

Rule 6. Since the word "torah" (law) is a commonly known word, the ת that begins this word is transliterated as *t* rather than *th*.

Examples of transliterated words:

לְדָוִד, *lᵉdawid*; חַטָּאִים, *chatta'im*; תּוֹרָה, *torah*; אַשְׁרֵי, *'ashrey*; and אִישׁ, *'ish*

Consonants

There are twenty-three consonants in the Hebrew text. They are listed below by name, Hebrew symbol, and transliteration.

Name	Hebrew	Transliteration
Aleph	א	'
Beth	ב	b
Gimel	ג	g
Daleth	ד	d
He	ה	h
Vav	ו	w
Zayin	ז	z
Heth	ח	ch
Teth	ט	t
Yodh	י	y
Kaph	כ ך	k
Lamedh	ל	l
Mem	מ ם	m
Nun	נ ן	n
Samekh	ס	s
Ayin	ע	'
Pe	פ ף	p
Tsadhe	צ ץ	ts
Qoph	ק	q
Resh	ר	r
Sin	שׂ	ś
Shin	שׁ	sh
Tav	ת	th

Vowels

The vowels in Hebrew are used more for determining the form of a word rather than the root meaning. We have tried to differentiate between these vowels to help guide their pronunciation and grammatical function. They are listed here by name, Hebrew symbol, and transliteration.

Name	Hebrew	Transliteration
Qamets	ָ	a (long)
Patach	ַ	a (short)
Tsere	ֵ	e (long)
Segol	ֶ	e (short)
Hireq Yodh	ִי	i (long)
Hireq	ִ	i (short)
Qamets Yodh	ָי	ay
Segol Yodh	ֶי	ey
Tsere Yodh	ֵי	ey
Holem	ֹו	o (long)
Qamets-Hatuph	ָ	o (short)
Shureq	וּ	u (long)
Qibbuts	ֻ	u (short)
Hatep-Patach	ֲ	a
Hatep-Segol	ֱ	e
Hatep-Qamets	ֳ	o

Suggested Hebrew Grammar Books

For further study of the Hebrew language, we recommend the following books:

Kelly, Page H. *Biblical Hebrew: An Introduction Grammar*. Grand Rapids, Mich.: Wm. B. Eerdmans Publishing Co., 1992.

Pratico, Gary D. and Miles Van Pelt. *Basics of Biblical Hebrew Grammar*. Grand Rapids, Mich.: Zondervan, 2001. This book includes an interactive CD-ROM.

Seow, Choon Leong. *A Grammar for Biblical Hebrew*. Nashville: Abingdon Press, 1987.

Weingreen, J. *A Practical Grammar for Classical Hebrew*, 2d ed. New York: Oxford University Press, 1959.

INTRODUCTION
A BOOK OF JEWISH SONGS AND PRAYERS

Perhaps it would not be too great an exaggeration to say, as others have said, that the Book of Psalms is contained in the Old Testament and the Old Testament is contained in Psalms. This unique book provides a restatement (in devotional literature) of the full, dynamic message of the Old Testament. James Luther Mays wrote, "The Book of Psalms is a virtual compendium of themes and topics found in the rest of the Old Testament."[1] Athanasius called the Psalms "an epitome of the whole Scriptures."[2] Basil believed that the book comprises a detailed summary of the theology of the Bible.[3] Martin Luther referred to the Psalms as constituting "a little Bible," containing in various forms the entire range of the teachings of the Scriptures.[4]

Because of the breadth of the book's coverage of the Old Testament and its personal nature, Theodore H. Robinson said,

---

[1] James Luther Mays, *Psalms*, Interpretation: A Bible Commentary for Teaching and Preaching (Louisville, Ky.: John Knox Press, 1994), 1.

[2] Athanasius, an Alexandrian writer (c. A.D. 293–373), in his *Ad Marcellinum*, wrote, ". . . in the words of this book the whole human life, its basic spiritual conduct and as well its occasional movements and thoughts, is comprehended and contained."

[3] Basil, a Cappadocian scholar (c. A.D. 329–379), said that the Book of Psalms "foretells coming events; it recalls history; it frames laws for life; it suggests what must be done; and, in general, it is the common treasury of good doctrine, carefully finding what is suitable for each one" (Basil, *Homily* 10, 1, 2).

[4] Martin Luther (A.D. 1483–1546) wrote, "It might well be called a little Bible. In it is comprehended most beautifully and briefly everything that is in the entire Bible." Martin Luther, *Luther's Works*, 35:254.

The Hebrew Psalter . . . has ministered to men and women of widely different races, languages and cultures. It has brought comfort and inspiration to the sorrowing and to the faint-hearted in all ages. Its words have shown themselves to be adaptable to the needs of people who have no knowledge of its original form and little understanding of the conditions under which it was produced. No other part of the Old Testament has exercised so wide, so deep, or so permanent an influence on the life of the human soul.[5]

The praise of God is the dominant idea of this book, a fact that convinced W. O. E. Oesterley to describe Psalms thematically as "the grandest symphony of praise to God ever composed on earth."[6]

ITS USE IN THE NEW TESTAMENT

The Book of Psalms is quoted in the New Testament more often than any other Old Testament book. The "Index of Quotations" in *The Greek New Testament* lists 414 quotations and allusions found in the New Testament that are drawn from it.[7] The second most quoted book by New Testament writers, Isaiah, has 369 quotations and allusions in the New Testament; thus Psalms is used 45 more times than Isaiah by New Testament penmen. Furthermore, 83 of the quotations and allusions from Psalms are found in the writings of Paul, which means that about one-fifth of his quotations from the Old Testament come from Psalms. In addition, some of the key quotations from the Old Testament by our Savior are passages from Psalms (for example, see Mt. 27:46).

---

[5]Theodore H. Robinson, *The Poetry of the Old Testament* (London: Gerald Duckworth and Co., 1947), 107.

[6]W. O. E. Oesterley, *The Psalms: Translated with Text-Critical and Exegetical Notes* (London: S.P.C.K., 1939), 593.

[7]*The Greek New Testament*, 4th rev. ed., ed. Barbara Aland, Kurt Aland, Johannes Karavidopoulos, Carlo M. Martini, and Bruce M. Metzger (Stuttgart: United Bible Societies, 1998), 895–96.

INTRODUCTION

Undoubtedly, the use of Psalms in the New Testament witnesses to the significance of this book. This fact further confirms the truth that Peter, Paul, and others of the New Testament Era read the Psalms, memorized them, and quoted them in establishing the evidence for their faith in God and Christ.

ITS HISTORY

Through God's divine inspiration and providence, the Book of Psalms grew into a final collection over a period of approximately one thousand years. Its compilation is similar to a hymn book made of songs that were written over several centuries and were gathered by an editor into its final book form.

The 150 psalms that constitute the book were songs, supplications, wisdom pieces, or devotional thoughts for the children of Israel. Numerous internal references are given to praise, prayer, walking with God, and the worship of God. Hence, as one reads the Psalms, he is actually looking into the songs, guidelines for living, and prayers that were sung, meditated upon, and prayed by the devout believer in the Old Testament Age.

ITS TEXT AND VERSIONS

All of the psalms were originally written in Hebrew. The majority of the translations of Psalms are based upon the "Masoretic text," which is abbreviated as MT. The latest edition of this text is found in the *Biblia Hebraica Stuttgartensia* (1967–77) which is based on the *Leningrad Codex* manuscript (B 19a) that is held in the Russian Public Library in St. Petersburg, Russia (formerly known as Leningrad). This most recent edition of the Hebrew text includes in its apparatus references to the Dead Sea Scroll discovery of 1947. A footnote in it claims that this manuscript was copied by Aaron ben Moses ben Asher in A.D. 1008. In the case of the Book of Psalms, Paul C. Kahle collated B 19a, the *Leningrad Codex*, with two other Leningrad manuscripts.

As is apparent, the extant manuscripts of the Masoretic text are comparatively late. We do not have an early Hebrew consonantal text, a text that consists of consonants without vowels. Excluding the Dead Sea fragments and scrolls from consideration, the earliest complete manuscript has the vowels that were added by the Masoretes in the 700–800s.

The oldest and the most important Old Testament version is the Septuagint (LXX), a Greek translation of the Old Testament, which was completed in Egypt about 150 B.C. Of the three oldest manuscripts of the Septuagint, only *Codex Sinaiticus* (a fourth century A.D. manuscript) contains all of the Psalms.

Among the other, later Greek versions that are helpful to the textual critics are those of Aquila, Theodotion, and Symmachus. Of value also are the Syriac version (called the Peshitta) and the Targum (in Aramaic), which is more of a paraphrase than a version. A final version of importance is the Vulgate or Latin version by Jerome from the Hebrew text (A.D. 487–488).

A succession of discoveries in the area of the Dead Sea from 1947 to 1956 have been of great assistance in establishing the text of the Old Testament. Being the oldest textual witnesses discovered to date, they take us back almost one thousand years beyond any manuscripts we had. Thirty fragments to date of the Psalms have been recovered, one of which is a large Psalm Scroll that contains forty-one psalms from the last third of our Book of Psalms (basically, Ps. 101—147). Furthermore, four Bible commentaries containing psalm texts have been discovered. In all probability, the Qumran community had more copies of the Psalms than any other biblical writings. Apparently, they had a keen interest in reading the psalms.

These thirty psalm texts and the four Bible commentaries found at Qumran plus three psalm texts that have been discovered at other sites in Israel constitute the oldest textual readings that we have. With but few exceptions, they are in general and basic agreement with the biblical text that we had before they were found.

INTRODUCTION

ITS WRITERS

Who wrote the psalms? According to the subtitles that stand before the psalms in the Hebrew Bible and in our translations, they were written by several authors. Seventy-three seem to be ascribed to David,[8] twelve in some way to Asaph (50; 73—83; see 1 Chron. 15:17; 16:5), eleven in some way to the sons of Korah or some descendants of Korah (42; 44—49; 84; 85; 87; 88; see Num. 16; 26:11; 1 Chron. 9:19), two are related to Solomon (72; 127), one to Heman the Ezrahite (88; which is also attributed in some way to the "sons of Korah"), one to Ethan the Ezrahite (89), and one to Moses (90).

Within the subtitles David is identified with the writing of all of the psalms in Book I, with the exception of 1, 2, 10, and 33. This fact may mean that Book I was the first collection. Perhaps it was brought together by David himself.

Legitimate questions have been raised in recent years concerning the subtitle references to the Davidic authorship (לְדָוִד, $l^e dawid$). The Hebrew preposition l^e can be translated "for," "belonging to," "to," "by," "of," or "concerning." If any of these alternate translations are used, the subtitles would not be advocating a Davidic authorship but only a connection of some kind to David. (In the discussion of each superscription in this commentary, the possible meaning for l^e is stated as "of," "by," "for," or "to" David.)

However, a three-part response to these questions can be given. First, the background of the psalms, the Old Testament, pictures David as having unusual musical abilities (1 Sam. 16:15–23; 18:10; 2 Sam. 1:17–27) and as being a composer of music (Amos 6:5). Second, the Old Testament relates that David, king of Israel, created the temple guilds of singers and musicians (1 Chron. 6:31–32; 15:16). In other words, the evidence we have indicates that writing psalms and songs was a large part of David's life. Third, the New Testament writers speak of David as the author of several psalms (see, for example, Acts 2:25–28;

---

[8]Ps. 3—9; 11—32; 34—41; 51—65; 68—70; 86; 101; 103; 108—110; 122; 124; 131; 133; 138—145.

4:25, 26). Our Lord Himself attributed many psalms to David (see Mt. 22:43–47; Lk. 20:42). It follows then that where the New Testament gives a specific confirmation of Davidic authorship of a psalm, one should consider the matter settled.

As time passed, other psalms were added to David's collection, and an editor (maybe Hezekiah or Ezra) grouped them into books. Psalms, in the final analysis, should be seen as a collection that was written at different times by different inspired authors.

ITS TIME FRAME

The most recent psalm was written almost 2,500 years ago, while the oldest psalm was written maybe 3,500 years ago. From the writing of the oldest psalm to the writing of the most recent is a wide time-gap. When we read and meditate upon a piece of literature that was written 2,500 to 3,500 years ago, we wonder if it could speak effectively to us in the twenty-first century.

While circumstances have changed and people have changed, amazingly the psalms have remained relevant. People in all ages have found their own emotions, struggles, and prayers voiced in them. Is this fact not proof of the divine inspiration of the Book of Psalms?

When God wrote His revelation, He spoke to His people in ways and thought-forms that related to their own unique world. However, through the power of the Spirit, He presented a revelation to them that had the properties of timelessness and continued relevancy, and thus His revelation speaks to us and to every succeeding generation with power and force. We can be assured that these Old Testament psalms will express the desires of spiritual hearts until our Lord returns.

ITS DATE

Some of the psalms were composed after the time of David. Psalm 137, for example, was written during the Exile. One or two of them were written after the exile. Psalm 126 speaks of "the fortunes of Zion" as having begun to be restored, which brings the time of writing to the end (or near the end) of the exile.

Hence, based upon the evidence supplied within the psalms themselves, the present collection was not arranged as we now have it until after the Exile. David himself may have begun a formal collection and arrangement of them, and Ezra or some other inspired man must have been the final editor or arranger.

The total book is an end-product of a process of writing, collecting, and arranging that covered over a thousand years. The writing range stretches from Moses' time to David's time to Ezra's time, with the book we now have culminating in its final form around 500 B.C. We should therefore view the Psalms as a living, open book, growing and being collected during much of the Old Testament period.

ITS FIRST READERS

The psalms were composed initially for the Israelite nation. Consequently, some of them, like Psalms 137 and 150, are not appropriate for the Christian to pray as an actual prayer as he lives under the last will and testament of Jesus Christ in the Christian Age. Although we learn valuable lessons from each psalm, some of them were designed to give the devout Israelite specific guidance for worship in the unique context of the Old Testament. Most of the psalms, however, express timeless truths that are appropriate for any Christian to pray, even though they were written long ago, during a pre-Christian time.

ITS PLACE IN THE OLD TESTAMENT

Our English Old Testament—due to the influence of the Greek and Latin translations of the Old Testament—is divided into five divisions: Law, History, Poetry, the Major Prophets, and the Minor Prophets. Psalms appears in the third division as the second book of Poetry. These divisions have remained constant because of their topical nature and practical usage.

However, the Hebrew Bible has only three main divisions: the Law, the Prophets, and the Writings. In most of the ancient manuscripts, Psalms is the first book of the Writings. In Luke 24:44, our Lord referred to the writings as "the Psalms," apparently because the Book of Psalms—as the first and longest book of the division—had become a convenient title for the whole division.

ITS OUTLINE

In the Hebrew text, as well as in most ancient versions, the Book of Psalms is divided into five books, each terminating with a doxology. The last psalm of the book (150) forms a concluding doxology to the last collection and to the whole of the Psalms. The five parts are as follows:

1. Book I (1—41)
2. Book II (42—72)
3. Book III (73—89)
4. Book IV (90—106)
5. Book V (107—150)

A Jewish *Midrashic* commentary on the Old Testament Scriptures compares these five books to the five books of Moses: "Moses gave the Israelites the five books of the Law, and to correspond to these David gave them the Book of Psalms containing five books."[9] Perhaps then the collection was divided into five books to parallel Moses' five books of the Law.

Within the body of Psalms, other groupings are detected such as the "Songs of Ascents" (120—134). Psalms from earlier collections are seen, but some of them are broken up and scattered throughout the book.

The psalms are not arranged according to subject matter or type; rather, each psalm possesses its own individuality, manifesting its own special theme and style.

---

[9]*Midrash* on Ps. 1:1.

INTRODUCTION

ITS TITLE

The Hebrew Bible entitles the entire collection of psalms "The Book of Praises" (*seper t^ehillim*), or simply "Praises" (*t^ehillim*). The title in the Greek Bible is sometimes *Psalmoi* (songs) and sometimes *Psalterion* (a collection of songs). The Vulgate followed the title of the Septuagint (LXX) with *Liber Psalmorum*, and from this we have derived the title in the English Bible, "The Book of Psalms" or "The Psalms."

ITS SUBTITLES

About three-fourths of the psalms, or 116, have subtitles or superscriptions. Thirty-four of them are without subtitles and are usually referred to as "orphan" psalms. An example is Psalm 33. Sixteen psalms have subtitles that contain no name in the ascription. The subtitle in Psalm 66 is an example of this.

Their Location
In the Hebrew Bible, the subtitle is the first verse. Most English translations place the subtitle at the beginning of the psalm, between the number of the psalm and the text, so that it will be regarded by the reader as separate from the psalm itself. Consequently, the subtitles are presented more like headings in our English Bibles.

Their Function
Five types of information may be found in a subtitle. First, it may possibly tell about *the author*. As already noted, one of six specific names are given in the various superscriptions.

Second, it may suggest *the historical occasion behind the psalm*. Fourteen psalms contain this type of information (3; 7; 18; 30; 34; 51; 52; 54; 56; 57; 59; 60; 63; 142). Each describes David in some circumstance, and David is always referred to in the third person (or as "he").

Third, the subtitle may indicate *the melody or tune to which the song was to be sung*. The problem with these references to tunes is that we do not know them today. For example, Psalm

22 was sung to the melody of "To the Doe of the Morning," and Psalm 45 was sung to the melody of "Lilies."

Fourth, the subtitle may describe the psalm's *function or character*. For example, *mizmor* may mean "sung with stringed instruments," and *maskil* may mean "a song of special skill" (like an anthem). Hints concerning the musical setting or performance of the psalm may also be included. In them guidance "to the chief musician" is given, such as *"Neginoth," "Nehiloth," "Alamoth," "Sheminith,"* or *"Gittith."* All of these notations are probably references to the musical instruments or the type of singing to be used in connection with the rendition of the various psalms.

Fifth, the subtitle may even point to *the use of the psalm*. For example, Psalm 30 was for "the Dedication of the House," Psalm 92 was "for the Sabbath day," and Psalms 120—134 have been named "The Songs of Ascents," which may have been used during the journeys to the temple for worship.

Their Value

What value do these subtitles have for us? Some scholars see them as canonical, that is, inspired; but we have no evidence that they were ever part of the original text of the psalms. Other scholars say that they have no value and that they should be ignored. They assume that the titles resulted from later Jewish additions to the psalms, arguing that these superscriptions are nothing more than the titles and chapter headings that were added by copyists and/or translators in the early history of the Bible. Their value, they say, would depend upon the accuracy of the scholarship that produced them. Still others say that the subtitles are noncanonical but provide reliable, early tradition.

The superscriptions are hoary with age. Translators of the Septuagint found them attached to the psalms. However, they were so obscure in meaning even to these translators that they were able to understand only a little more than their general import.

In light of these facts, the best approach to take toward the subtitles seems to be the last view. They should be seen as uninspired, very old, and reliable enough to be worthy of the Bible student's consideration. The rule of interpretation might be stated as follows: They should be allowed to inform the reader of the psalm, but the reader should not bend the interpretation of the psalm unnaturally to make it conform to the implications of the subtitle.

ITS LOFTY THEMES

Gleason L. Archer, acknowledging the tremendous diversity of the Psalms, concluded that "the 150 Psalms composing this collection cover a great variety of themes, and it is difficult to make any valid generalizations. Personal response to the goodness and grace of God is the best theme."[10]

In brief stretches they move us from the highest joy to the deepest grief, transporting us in a single bound from incredibly short poems (like 117, with 2 verses) to extremely long ones (like 119, that has 176 verses).

Their content is remarkably free from references to the particular events that brought them into being. They stand as little islands of devotional literature, sometimes almost entirely detached from the circumstances out of which they grew. As one reads them, he finds himself wanting to know more than what is said about the men who wrote them and the unique environments that surrounded the writers.

Every human emotion is expressed or touched upon somewhere in the book. All deep feelings and pervasive thoughts, including slight references to the sexual emotion (45), appear somewhere in the Psalms. Each psalm is new and refreshing, expressing the feelings we have had or are having. The reader might say, "Whoever wrote this piece has lived in the same kind of world and in the same kind of body in which I live. He has experienced the same emotions, frustrations, joys, and tears that I have known."

---

[10]Gleason L. Archer, *A Survey of Old Testament Introduction* (Chicago: Moody Press, 1964), 424.

ITS PURPOSES

The Book of Psalms is so multifaceted, so broad in the topics discussed, that designating one purpose for the book is difficult. It is more of a devotional handbook than anything else. To use the words of Edward J. Young:

> The Psalter is primarily a manual and guide and model for the devotional needs of the individual believer. It is a book of prayer and praise, to be meditated upon by the believer, that he may thereby learn to praise God and pray to Him.[11]

The psalms were written for different reasons and in different settings. Some originated in northern Israel (90); some originated in southern Israel (48:2, 11, 12). Some celebrated military successes (18), and others called upon God for victory in war (20). Some were cries for help in individual or national crises (137). Some were written by individuals who were stricken with severe illnesses (38). Some were penitent cries for forgiveness (51).

A unique characteristic of the earlier part of the book is that the laments outnumber the praises. As one moves toward its end, praise overtakes lament until, in the last part of the book, he sees a continuous, exploding anthem of praise. Beyond question, a paramount intention for the gathering of the psalms was that they might be used in the private and public worship and serve as meditations for the devout Israelite.

Although the psalms were composed for different purposes, one could say they all teach one basic spiritual lesson: We are to trust in God regardless of our circumstances. The writers may be in the worst of difficulties; they may not know what to do, but they know where to look, they know where to go for their help. They remind us of King Jehoshaphat, who, when he found himself in the valley of absolute despair, cried to God, "Nor do

---

[11]Edward J. Young, *An Introduction to the Old Testament* (Grand Rapids, Mich.: Wm. B. Eerdmans Publishing Co., 1949), 299.

we know what to do, but our eyes are on You" (2 Chron. 20:12).

ITS LITERARY STRUCTURES

The principal features of Hebrew poetry are not so much rhyme and rhythm as they are parallelism and figurative language. One cannot properly interpret it without understanding the special literary qualities that make it what it is.

Parallelism

In 1753 Robert Lowth, as a result of a careful study of the nature of Hebrew poetry, began stressing the recognition of parallelism in connection with the interpretation of poetical texts. He saw parallelism as a fundamental literary structure of Hebrew poetry, a style of writing in which one line is parallel to the next line in some way. He identified synonymous, antithetic, and synthetic types of parallelism.[12]

Today, biblical scholars usually go further with the concept of parallelism by referring to not only synonymous, synthetic, and antithetic, but also to climactic and emblematic.

Synonymous parallelism is an immediate repetition in the second line of the thought presented in the first line. An idea is stated in the first line and then repeated in the next line in almost—but not necessarily—synonymous words. Numerous examples of this type of parallelism are seen in the Psalms, and the structure is one of the easiest to recognized.

> Hear this, all peoples;
> Give ear, all inhabitants of the world (49:1).
>
> O God, do not remain quiet;
> Do not be silent and, O God, do not be still (83:1).
>
> Why do the nations conspire,
> and the peoples plot in vain? (2:1; RSV).

---

[12]See Robert Lowth, *Lectures on the Sacred Poetry of the Hebrews*, 3d ed., trans. G. Gregory (London: Thomas Tegg and Sons, 1835).

Synthetic parallelism is a structure in which the second line completes the thought of the first line. Some scholars, like Tremper Longman, contend that this is not a parallelism at all, but just a completion of the sentence.[13] Consider this example from Psalm 3:

> I was crying to the LORD with my voice,
> And He answered me from His holy mountain (v. 4).

Antithetic parallelism expresses a thought by contrasting opposites. A single idea is expressed positively and negatively in the same sentence. This form of parallelism is particularly frequent in Proverbs.

> A soft answer turneth away wrath:
> but grievous words stir up anger (Prov. 15:1; KJV).

Climactic parallelism is seen when several lines are used to move the reader forward to an obvious, important conclusion. An example of this is Psalm 29:1, 2:

> Ascribe to the LORD, O sons of the mighty,
> Ascribe to the LORD glory and strength.
> Ascribe to the LORD the glory due to His name;
> Worship the LORD in holy array.

Emblematic parallelism employs figurative language in the following line(s) to convey the thought of the first line, or vice versa. We see this type of parallelism in Psalm 1:3:

> He will be like a tree firmly planted by streams of water,
> Which yields its fruit in its season
> And its leaf does not wither;
> And in whatever he does, he prospers.

---

[13]Tremper Longman III, *How to Read the Psalms* (Downers Grove, Ill.: InterVarsity Press, 1988), 99.

Chiastic Structure

Another type of parallelism that is often recognized is the *chiastic* arrangement. Sometimes called *inverted parallelism*, it involves grammatical structures that are repeated in reverse order. An a-b-b-a order of thought is used. It is sort of a synonymous parallelism repeated in the reverse. The name of this poetic device derives from the Greek letter *chi*, which is written with two crossing lines (χ). A clear sample of this parallelism is seen in Psalm 51:1 in the KJV:

a—Have mercy upon me, O God,
b—according to thy loving-kindness:
b—according unto the multitude of thy tender mercies
a—blot out my transgressions.

Acrostic Poetry

The *acrostic* poem is probably more familiar than any of the other styles of Hebrew poetry. In this poem the first word of each line or verse begins with a different letter of the Hebrew alphabet until the entire alphabet has been used (9; 34; 37; 119).

Sometimes the writer did not use the complete acrostic design. He may have changed a letter or two, or he may have chosen to repeat a letter or two. Psalm 119 is the most extended and most complete acrostic poem in the Book of Psalms. It has eight verses for each letter of the alphabet. Twenty-two letters, multiplied by eight verses each, equals the 176 verses.

ITS POETIC NATURE

Hebrew poetry does not emphasize rhyme, as is the case with English verse, but it does stress ideas. Each line is divided into two parts, usually having an equal number of accented ideas in each part. It can have two, three, or four stressed ideas in each half of the line. The exceptions are the funeral dirge and the more elegant pieces of poetry that may have three stressed ideas in the first half of the line and two stressed ideas in the second half.

ITS LITERARY IMAGERY

Another exciting feature of Hebrew poetry is the figurative images that are used in it. It abounds with exaggerated language and colorful word pictures. For example, God is described as a shield, a fortress, a rock, a storm cloud, a shepherd, a warrior, an archer, a chariot rider, a king, and much more. We encounter literary imagery in all parts of the Bible, but it is especially plentiful in the books of Poetry.

Unless we recognize the figurative language that is used in the Psalms and understand how to interpret such language, we will not know how to read and apply the Psalms. Just as one must take a different approach to the interpretation of Revelation (because of its apocalyptic character), even so one must read the Psalms with a special grasp of the function of figurative language.

Especially prominent in the Psalms are the figures of speech known as personification, simile, and metaphor.

Personification attributes human characteristics to something nonhuman. Goodness and mercy cannot run after us as a human being can. The sea cannot reach out and grab us. The mountains and hills cannot skip like a calf. However, these figurative expressions are relatively common in the psalms.

Simile is a comparison made using the word "like" or "as." It presents an explicit word picture.

> As the deer pants for the water brooks,
> So my soul pants for You, O God (42:1).

With this simile the psalmist compares himself to a thirsty deer eagerly looking for water. He is desperately searching for the satisfaction that comes from worshiping God. The simile type of comparison is easily spotted because of the presence of the word "like" or "as."

A *metaphor* also makes a comparison, but the comparison is implicit. It is made without using "like" or "as."

INTRODUCTION

The LORD *is* my shepherd,
I shall not want (23:1; emphasis added).

A metaphor communicates a more vivid image than a simile because it is factually stated and draws the comparison more closely.

Numerous other literary devices are used in the psalms. Here is a list of some of them:

Alliteration: a repetition of a letter or sound (44:7).
Apostrophe: the personification of an inanimate object in a direct address (50:4).
Ellipsis: the omission of a thought or word that must be filled in from the previous line to complete the meaning (12:3).
Hendiadys: the use of two expressions that are understood as one thought (107:10).
Hyperbole: the use of appropriate literary exaggeration (40:12).
Inclusion (or inclusio): the use of the same statement or phrase at the beginning and at the end of a sentence or paragraph (70:1, 5; 106:1, 48).
Irony: an actuality that is pictured with its opposite (118:22).
Litotes: an understatement that is used to convey the converse (51:17).
Merismus: two expressions that are combined to express totality (49:2).
Metonymy: meaning that is expressed by a vivid comparison (18:2).
Repetition: the recurrent use of a word or phrase to emphasize a theme (29:1, 2).
Synecdoche: the use of a part to represent the whole (7:3; 52:4).

Literary imagery adds to the beauty of the Book of Psalms.

ITS INTERPRETATION

Likely no book of the Bible has been studied as thoroughly as has the Book of Psalms. In an introduction of this kind, only brief references can be made to the detailed studies of psalmic scholarship, confining us to touching upon the past and current major trends of the interpretation of it.

Past and Present Interpretative Directions

The Book of the "Second Temple"
Led by Julius Wellhausen, source critical scholars in the nineteenth century spoke of the Book of Psalms as "the hymn book of the second temple."[14] They meant by this phrase that only a few, if any, of the psalms in the Book of Psalms were written by David, and that any Davidic psalms that might be in it had been rewritten and adapted for use in the services of the second temple long after its construction by Zerubbabel and his fellows. They were further persuaded that the majority of the psalms we have were produced by the temple personnel to be used by priests and the religious community of the Jews in connection with the life of the second temple.

Although this understanding of the psalms has carried considerable influence, the case for it has now lost much of its credibility because the view has not been able to stand the test of thorough investigation. Psalms studies have recognized that the psalms we have could not have been written as late as these critical scholars envisioned. In addition, the claim that the majority of the psalms were written during the Greek period of history flies into the face of the clear testimony of history and the New Testament writers.

The Classification by Genre
Later, Hermann Gunkel (1862–1932), in his publications of his study of the Psalms, drew his attention to the character of

---

[14]Julius Wellhausen, *The Book of Psalms: A New English Translation* (New York: Dodd, Mead, and Co., 1898), 163.

each psalm.¹⁵ He concluded that clues are found within the psalms concerning their purpose and the circumstances that brought them into existence. Through his study of the mood, the vocabulary, and the other components of each psalm, he divided the psalms into different genres or groupings.

One of Gunkel's conclusions was that a psalm should not be considered a purely literary production of a certain writer—for he postulated that a long history lay behind each psalm. Much of the material in the Book of Psalms, he said, was first an oral piece and then later was written down and became a literary composition, receiving a permanent place in the canon of Hebrew poetry.

The psalms, he insisted, were associated at the beginning of their existences with religious rites. When they were written down for continued use, they were cast into forms of liturgical literature or were designed primarily to fit into the structures of public worship. Later in the life of the psalm, he surmised that some Israelite may have adapted them either for his own personal use or for the use of other Israelites.

The views of Gunkel were ingenious and have exerted much and lasting influence upon psalm studies. His emphasis has brought new and valid ideas to the study of the background of each psalm, but most agree that he carried his analysis to an extreme. Although he did succeed in getting the religious world to turn its attention to the different types of psalms, he provided little evidence for his ultimate argument.

The Book of Enthronement Psalms

A student of Gunkel's, Sigmund Mowinckel (1884–1965), being convinced that form analysis and genre classification of the Psalms was a sound technique to use in understanding them, gave himself intensely to this type of study.¹⁶ He concluded that forty-three Psalms were related to the worship ritual and were

---

¹⁵Hermann Gunkel, *The Psalms: A Form-Critical Introduction*, trans. Thomas M. Horner, Facet Books Biblical Series, vol. 19 (Philadelphia: Fortress, 1967).

¹⁶Sigmund Mowinckel, *The Psalms in Israel's Worship*, trans. D. R. Ap-Thomas (New York: Abingdon, 1962).

to be interpreted in terms of the worship offered at the sanctuary by the Israelite community.

Through comparative studies of Babylonian literature, he conjectured that the most important cultic celebration of Israel was the annual New Year's Festival. In the autumn, he imagined, a celebration at the temple—similar to the annual enthronement of Marduk the chief deity of the Babylonians—took place during which Yahweh was enthroned as the universal King amidst much worship. For Mowinckel, the New Year's Festival became the most important of Israel's festivals. As an application of this, he saw reflected in the Psalms Israel's enthroning Yahweh anew each year in a celebration similar to Babylon's.

This approach to the Psalms was more fanciful than evidential. The stubborn fact is that there is no evidence in the Old Testament for such a New Year's ritual. H. C. Leupold has said, "Never has so elaborate a superstructure been built on so minimal an amount of evidence."[17]

The Festival of Renewal

Continuing in a similar vein of research, Artur Weiser proposed that Israel had a covenant festival that originated among them before the monarchy. The festival was celebrated at the beginning of the religious New Year in the autumn, he contended. The core feature of this festival was the renewal of the Sinaitic covenant and the re-enactment of the salvation-history of the nation. In his view, this covenant commemoration provided the setting for most of the psalms.[18]

The Old Testament does picture times of renewal and recommitment to the covenant that God had made with His people (Josh. 8:30–35); however, it does not give any evidence of an annual festival of this kind. While it is likely that the major Israelite festivals formed the background not only to numerous national psalms but also to many of the psalms of the individual,

---

[17]H. C. Leupold, *Exposition of the Psalms* (Columbus, Ohio: The Wartburg Press, 1959; reprint, Grand Rapids, Mich.: Baker Book House, 1969), 12.

[18]Artur Weiser, *The Psalms*, The Old Testament Library, trans. Herbert Hartwell (Philadelphia: Westminster Press, 1962), 27–28.

an annual, national festival of a covenant renewal is never seen in the Old Testament. The three pilgrimage festivals were likely the only occasions when multitudes of the Israelites had an opportunity to worship at the temple in Jerusalem.

The Royal Zion Festival

Somewhat similar to Weiser's hypothesis, Hans-Joachim Kraus championed a view which he called the Royal Zion Festival.[19] According to Kraus, this festival, which revolved around the election of David as the king of Jerusalem, played an important role in the writing of Psalms. Likewise, he saw in it the background setting for *many* of the psalms.

Although the anointing of a new king was always a highly elaborate occasion for Israel, the Old Testament shows this occasion to be the backdrop for only a *few* psalms. To expand the background of a few psalms into a major festival that occurred each year, a festival that served as a circumstance of origin for most of the psalms, would not be justified by the inspired, historical evidence that we have.

A Liturgical Use Only

A growing tendency among scholars today is to see a liturgical use behind all the psalms in the Book of Psalms. This presupposition is adopted by the interpreter, who then searches for the particular public worship service that gave rise to the psalm.

Clearly, some of the psalms were written for the setting of community worship, but an across-the-board deduction that all of them were is unwarranted by a fair assessment of their contents. The truth is, the psalms were written in various circumstances, and in most cases it is very difficult for us to determine their exact milieu or *Sitz im Leben* (their life situation). The tremendous variety alone within the Book of Psalms is sufficient reason for our being skeptical of any approach to the study of the psalms that begins with the assumption that one must find a public liturgical origin to each psalm.

---

[19]Hans-Joachim Kraus, *Theology of the Psalms*, trans. Keith Crim (Minneapolis: Augsburg, 1986).

The Basic Rules

How, then, should the Christian interpret a psalm? What is the most basic and practical way of understanding them?

Obviously, the psalms should be seen as devotional literature—as guides to worship, personal mediation, and daily walking with God for the Israelite. Whether an individual psalm was written for the public worship of God or for a private meditation is hard to ascertain. Whether a psalm was written for private consideration and later adapted by an inspired person for the public worship or some other situation is also difficult to determine. It is best, therefore, for us to take each psalm on its own merit—using it for whatever its contents urge and demand.

Three basic rules of interpretation will be faithful friends as we study the Book of Psalms in this commentary. First, we will seek to reconstruct from its contents the setting of the psalm. We will envision—without intentionally stretching the text—the purpose for which that particular psalm was written. Using the clues of the text to guide us, we will try to see circumstances, or life in general, through the eyes of the writer.

Second, we will observe the psalm's structure and literary imagery, taking special note of the types of parallelism that are found in the psalm. Any figurative expressions will be carefully analyzed in light of its historical context.

Third, we will try to capture the mood of the psalm. For example, is the psalm a lament, a hymn, or an expression of confidence?

ITS LITERARY GENRE

Applying these rules will require that we recognize the different types of psalms. The type of literature found in Psalms is Hebrew poetry, but the sub-types within this larger genre can be classified under seven different headings.[20]

---

[20]Longman, 23–35.

INTRODUCTION

The Hymn Psalm

The hymn psalm begins with a call to worship, continues with a list of reasons for worshiping God, and then closes with a call to worship. It adheres to this format/pattern rather rigidly, but exceptions will be found. Its dominating characteristic is that it is almost continuous in its expression of praise to God. Psalm 113 is an example:

> Praise the LORD!
> Praise, O servants of the LORD.
> Praise the name of the LORD (v. 1).

The Lament Psalm

The lament psalm is generally defined by its mood of calling upon God for help out of a trying situation. As a type of complaint to God or a cry to God, its arrangement frequently has the following stages:

> Invocation;
> Plea to God for help;
> Complaints;
> Confession of sin or an assertion of innocence;
> Curse of enemies (imprecation);
> Confidence in God's response;
> Hymn or blessing.

The writer may have been troubled by his own thoughts and actions. His words may complain about the actions of others or even express frustration with God Himself. An example that quickly comes to mind is Psalm 22. Notice the first two lines:

> My God, my God, why have You forsaken me?
> Far from my deliverance are the words of my groaning (v. 1).

The Thanksgiving Psalm

The thanksgiving psalm begins in a similar way to a hymn of praise. However, it is usually a response to an answered lament, which is typically followed with an account of salvation.

An example is Psalm 30:1:

> I will extol You, O LORD, for You have lifted me up,
> And have not let my enemies rejoice over me.

The Remembrance Psalm
The remembrance psalm does not have a specific historical reference other than the fact that it may refer to a major period or event in history, like the Exodus or the Davidic dynasty. These psalms usually make reference to a special victory given by God in the past. Psalm 18 surveys all of God's victories and closes with the following summation:

> He gives great deliverance to His king,
> And shows lovingkindness to His anointed,
> To David and his descendants forever (18:50).

The Confidence Psalm
Tone and content are the main characteristics of the confidence psalm, with feelings of trust dominating the whole psalm. The writer is expressing belief in God's goodness and power. Any one of the following psalms will provide a good sample: 11, 16, 23, 27, 62, 91, 121, 125, or 131.

The Wisdom Psalm
The wisdom psalm, a teaching psalm, gives a concrete description of how God wants the believer to live. A contrast may be given between the way of the righteous and the way of the wicked. Psalm 1 is a prime example.

The Royal Psalm
The royal psalms are about kings. Sometimes they focus on the earthly king (20; 21); sometimes they depict God as the King (47:7); and sometimes they speak of the Messiah, the coming King (2).

INTRODUCTION

ITS USE FOR THE CHRISTIAN

An Old Testament Book

While reading the psalms, the Christian must keep in mind that they were written initially in the Old Testament period for Old Testament people. Without this awareness he would not know how to apply fully the Psalms to the Christian's life today. For example, offering sacrifices to God is a major emphasis in the Psalms. New Testament guidance teaches us that these references do not relate to the Christian. We know that Jesus, the Son of God, offered His blood for our sins, once for all time, and that our salvation rests upon His "once-for-all-time" atoning sacrifice at the cross. Christian discernment must be exercised in the use of the Psalms so that they may have their proper spiritual impact upon the Christian.

A Book of Praise and Thanksgiving

Since the psalms comprise expressions of worship and thankfulness to God and since they continually describe a righteous man's walk with God, much of their content can be easily carried over to the Christian Age. However, a good safeguard to use in interpreting a psalm is to find a New Testament passage which assures us that the teaching of the psalm should be appropriated by the Christian in this dispensation. If the teaching given in the psalm is for a Christian, the New Testament will confirm it.

A Book About Walking with God

With the above being said, we can further say that the psalms should be experienced, not just read. Psalms is more of a devotional book than a history book, more of a songbook than a lawbook. Someone has said that this book was meant to be read on one's knees.

How can we experience them? *First, they can serve as a guide in teaching us to think about God.* Some may find it rewarding to read them thoughtfully for a while and then write one's own psalm. One can ask, "How has this psalm taught me to think about God?" The psalms reflect the beauty and meaning of walking with God. While we are absorbing and meditating upon them, we find that they clarify the desires of our hearts and help us to visualize what communion with God really means.

Second, they help in our struggle of learning to pray. One Christian man said that he did not know how to pray. He could not come up with the right words to express what he wanted to say to God. A friend of his advised him to use the psalms as a primer for his thoughts. He said to him, "You cannot say everything within them in prayer to God, but much of them you can pray. Read a psalm aloud, and then go back over that psalm looking for phrases that you as a Christian should be praying to God. After thinking about them, pray those phrases in your own words to God." The man was impressed with the suggestion, followed it, and found it to be a wonderful time of communion with God. He said that he prayed much of the night.

APPLICATION

When Faith and Reality Meet

Walter Brueggemann has proposed that one can view the psalms from the three levels of faith.[21] These three plateaus are really three stages of growth in understanding and trust.

The first level might be called *orientation*. This level place is the solid ground of our beliefs—that God created all things, that He has given us His will, that His kind wisdom surrounds us, that He protects His own, and that He is in charge of our well-being. When one stands on this plateau, he puts all his weight on the basic beliefs held by all true believers.

The second level can be called *disorientation*. Tragedy comes. It could come in the form of enemies, physical disease, financial calamities, or something else. Our world suddenly is turned upside down. We are disoriented. In bewilderment, we are tempted to ask, "Where is God when I need Him?" Or, in the secret palace of our souls, we may wonder, "Is God really going to protect His own? Where is the peace that I have heard so

---

[21]Walter Brueggemann, *The Message of the Psalms* (Minneapolis: Augsburg, 1984).

much about?" It is then that we must come to level three.

The third level is *reorientation*. We face our crises with faith, and in the crucible of suffering we are forced to see that God's ways are not our ways. We learn that in faith we must hold on to God when we cannot see Him holding on to us. He is the same Almighty God that we have always believed Him to be, but we are brought to a new level of understanding about Him—He is not going to put us in an utopia because we believe. Faith in Him will not be a passport to an isle of paradise; we must walk with God in a real world of suffering and pain. Sometimes we see His obvious works—His great deliverances, and sometimes we must trust in Him when He works behind the scenes, behind the screen of the great unknown. Stepping up to this level, we find that He has not forsaken us even though—when our minds are clouded by the dark mist of struggle—it may appear to us that He has.

The challenge comes when we must move from disorientation to reorientation. If we get stuck in disorientation, if we are captured by confusion and become cemented in doubt, we will never rise to the highest level of understanding that God wills for all of His children. Pity the child of God who never ascends to a rugged faith, a reoriented faith, that trusts when it cannot touch, that believes when it cannot see, that feels the mercy and mighty acts of God when surrounded by the misery and misfortune of a sin-laden world.

Bringing Our Problems to God

The lament psalm provides a practical pattern for our calling upon God for help. Suppose you are in the whirlpool of disaster: How do you pray about it? How do you bring your petition to God?

First, cry out for help. Our prayers in such a situation may be summarized by two words "Lord, help!" The request is short and to the point. We are simply telling God that we need Him.

Second, recount what God has done. Voice to Him your gratefulness for what He has done for you in the past. You may even describe what God has done for all those who believe.

Third, picture your distress. Go into detail. Lay your problem before Him. Literally, talk it over with God, describing your feelings and fears.

Fourth, express your trust in God. You are a believing, trusting child of His. Tell Him so. Furthermore, you know that He will never fail His own, for He is full of lovingkindness.

Fifth, petition Him for deliverance. Make known to Him the desires of your heart. What do you want Him to do? Tell Him you do not know what is best for you, but you will state what you understand that you need.

Sixth, praise Him. You know who He is. You know what He will do. You know that He is trustworthy and faithful. Praise Him for what He has done, is doing, and will do. Praise Him for the promises that He has given all those who believe.

A pattern like this is used in the psalms. It is the language one uses when he prays with faith in God in difficult situations.

How to Say "Thank You" to God

One can use the pattern of the praise psalm in expressing gratitude and thankfulness to God. Suppose you want to come to God and simply praise Him; how do you do it? One way is to follow the praise format in the psalms.

First, proclaim your thankfulness. Express your adoration, praise, and reverence for Him. He is God, and we need to acknowledge in prayer who He is.

Second, summarize His wonderful acts. You may want to list in your prayer the saving acts of God in the Scriptures. The story line of the Bible is what God has done for His children.

Third, remember in your prayer how He has blessed you. Recount how God has saved you, provided for you, and made promises to you.

Fourth, express to Him the promises that you have made to Him. Perhaps you will want to mention the resolves that you made when you became a Christian or the resolutions you made when God delivered you from trouble.

Fifth, praise Him for revealing to us who He is. Two of the greatest gifts He has given to us are the Scriptures and the Savior. They join together in telling us what God is like and what He has done for those who trust in Him.

INTRODUCTION

Assistance in Prayer

A sister-in-law of mine was afflicted with cancer and lingered in that illness for a long time before her death. Toward the end, a gospel preacher came to see her and asked her if she wanted to talk about anything. She said, "Yes, I'm worried about my last few hours. I'm afraid that I won't be thinking clearly and won't know how to pray. Would it be all right for me to write out a prayer to my God now and put in it what I will want to say to God just before I meet Him? Then, when my last hour comes and I can't think the way I would like to think or say to Him what I want to say to Him, I can say, 'God, You know what I'm trying to say to You and don't have the ability now. You can see my prayer on that piece of paper that I wrote out when I was more myself, when I was thinking more clearly. Hear that prayer, God, as I come into Your presence." The preacher got some paper, and they wrote out her prayer. I do not know if my sister-in-law used that prayer as she was dying, but she was prepared in case she needed it.

What Do We Learn from the Psalms?

The heart of the Book of Psalms is the pilgrimage of walking with God day by day. Each psalm is different and unique, separate and distinct from all the others—but at the same time each one participates in this common theme of fellowship with God.

In our study of Psalms, what do we learn about living in the presence of God?

First, we will see that a daily relationship with God can be a reality. The psalms grow out of the life experiences of real people who are undergoing trials and difficulties common to all people. These hymns, prayers, words of wisdom, and anthems of praise were written to show the beauty, the joy, and the struggle of being one with God regardless of the situation.

Second, we will observe that walking with God can only happen through obedience. Knowing God is not just sentimentalism; it is spirituality through submission. His Word is not ignored, but it is held dear and regarded as the only true guide for living in this world.

Third, we learn that being in God's company requires discipline and perseverance. Over half of the psalms are laments, plaintive cries for help. Genuine faith pursues a true relationship with God. When horrible circumstances disturb us, we may ask God "Why?" but we continue to pray and trust in Him.

Fourth, we are made to realize that walking with God is based upon trust, not sight. We will not always be able to see His hand. God does not always work visibly before us; He often works behind the scenes, quietly fulfilling His purposes. We may not know what He is doing, but we believe that He is faithful to us.

Fifth, we are confronted with the truth that being a friend of God involves praise, prayer, and thanksgiving. Regardless of the situation, praise and thanksgiving are appropriate. We are to fight our battles with the prayer of praise. Beyond what we see and what the world says, we know that God is good and will never forsake His children.

Sixth, we will be gripped by the truth that walking with God is the highest goal of life. Living each moment in His blessed fellowship is the *summa bonum,* the highest good, of our existence. Living in God's presence should be a greater ambition for each of us than going to heaven, for the glory of heaven is being with God.

Seventh, we will see that walking with God involves community. In one sense, one does not walk alone with God. He is part of a family of people who trust in God. The one who trusts in God, who thinks and prays for the entire family of believers, is one with them; and he delights in worshiping God with them.

Eighth, we will observe that dwelling with God imparts to us the character of compassion for others. One cannot be with God without taking on, to some degree, His traits. He is full of loving-kindness, and those who walk with Him will imbibe and exhibit this grace to the people around them—expressing it to their families, their friends, the strangers they meet, and even the enemies they may have.

Ninth, we will see that being in the presence of God enables us to see God all around us. We note that behind the thunder clap is the hidden power of God. To us, the lightning shoots out from His fingers. The majestic mountains do not just represent the magnificence of nature, they stand as unanswerable testimonies to the goodness of God. The stars are more than heavenly bodies

INTRODUCTION

to be studied; they are His preachers that proclaim His glory to anyone who will look at them. Walking with God sharpens our vision to the glory of God that surrounds us.

These psalms come to life out of the crucible of suffering. In the main, they were given birth by the fiery fingers of pain, misunderstanding, disappointment, and grief. The servants of God who wrote them had seen the raw side of life intimately; but they never permitted the darkness of pain to hide the face of God. The intention behind all 150 of the Psalms is to provide a guide to sing, to mediate upon, and even to pray as we walk with God regardless of the circumstance in which we may be.

True Religion Summarized

We often see the religion of the Bible summarized in a verse or two. In the Old Testament, for example, we see this truth in Ecclesiastes 12:13, 14: "The conclusion, when all has been heard, is: fear God and keep His commandments, because this applies to every person. For God will bring every act to judgment, everything which is hidden, whether it is good or evil." In the New Testament we see it in James 1:27: "Pure and undefiled religion in the sight of our God and Father is this: to visit orphans and widows in their distress, and to keep oneself unstained by the world." These summaries were never meant to cover every detail of God's plan for mankind. They were only intended to give us the gist, where we could see in a glance the basic elements of His religion.

Another summary of the religion of the Bible can be seen by reducing the entire Book of Psalms to a few basics. The gist is something like the following: Religion is putting one's trust in God, faithfully obeying Him, praying to Him in sunshine and shadow, and praising and worshiping Him because of His blessings and because of who He is.

Here then are four fundamental aspects of God's will for mankind.

Trusting in God. The psalms of this book put us into every type of situation we can imagine and under every type of problem one can conceive. The answers to all of life's difficulties are not always revealed in these writings; however, the appropriate response for every circumstance is always given: Trust in God regardless. God is in charge of His world, and in the end He will make all things right.

Obeying God. Faithfulness to God is part of the covenant God made with His people. No one is ever excused from obedience. In tragedy or triumph, every member of the covenant is to be loyal to God and express it in following His precepts.

Praying to God. Obedience is more than slavish conformity; it results in communion with God. It involves praying to and living with God. In happiness, daily life, trial, and death, prayers are made. It is not a time of burdensome duty; it is a sweet and exquisite fellowship. The Christian's life is undergirded with the presupposition that God hears the prayers of His children.

Praising and worshiping God. He praises God for what He has done for him; he worships God because of who He is. He finds this activity as natural as the night turning to day. Whether he is going to the temple for the offering of sacrifices or whether he is engaged in private prayers and worship, his life is immersed in the activities of praise and worship; he is surrounded by them.

So, according to the Psalms, when religion is boiled down to a line or two, the religion of the Bible—God's religion—its sum is trusting in God, obeying God, praying to God, and praising and worshiping God.

In light of these truths, let us ask ourselves, "Are we religious?"

BOOK I
PSALMS 1—41

David is the only author mentioned in the subtitles in Book I (Ps. 1—41). Thirty-seven psalms of the forty-one are ascribed to David, identifying him as the author or the subject. Four psalms have no titles (1; 2; 10; 33) and thus have no name ascription.

Of the five books that make up the Book of Psalms, this book is the second longest collection, with Book V being a little longer.

There does not seem to be any special order in the arrangement of this collection. Each psalm has its own individual message and must be treated as a separate entity. A number of titles contain historical references that relate the psalms to events in David's life, but these uninspired headings do not suggest any chronological order.

Book I, along with Books IV and V, has been called a Yahwistic collection because the name more commonly used for God is Yahweh, whereas the name used for God in Book II is Elohim. By count, Book I uses the name Yahweh 278 times and Elohim only 49.[1]

This book is thought by many to be the original collection of psalms; maybe it was even brought together by David himself. Over time, as the Holy Spirit so chose, other psalms or collections were added until the final Book of Psalms came into being.

---

[1]This count is given by *Accordance,* 5.6.1 [CD-ROM] (Altamonte Springs, Fla.: Oak Tree Software, 2002).

Psalm 1
The Blessed Life

The Superscription: None.

This beginning psalm provides an introduction to the entire Book of Psalms. Perhaps it was selected from existing psalms as a prologue to the Book of Psalms, or maybe it was written purposefully as an introduction to the book.

Because of its connection with the psalms that follow in Book I, David is thought to be the author. Clearly a psalm of wisdom, with similarities to sections of the Book of Proverbs, its main purpose is to instruct the reader about the good life. It was not necessarily written to be sung in the assembly.

As a psalm of wisdom, it first extols the virtues of the righteous life by presenting in express statements the superlative nature of that life; then, in the second half of the psalm, the God-fearing life is contrasted with the wicked life. It concludes by picturing—by implication—two roads from which the people of the earth must choose: the path to blessedness or the road to cursedness.

Jeremiah 17:5–8 contains a similar, expanded contrast between the righteous and the wicked:

> Thus says the Lord,
> "Cursed is the man who trusts in mankind
> And makes flesh his strength,
> And whose heart turns away from the Lord.
> For he will be like a bush in the desert
> And will not see when prosperity comes,

But will live in stony wastes in the wilderness,
A land of salt without inhabitant.
Blessed is the man who trusts in the LORD
And whose trust is the LORD.
For he will be like a tree planted by the water,
That extends its roots by a stream
And will not fear when the heat comes;
But its leaves will be green,
And it will not be anxious in a year of drought
Nor cease to yield fruit."

When this passage is compared to Psalm 1, we notice that in Jeremiah's contrast the wicked are mentioned first and then a reference is made to the righteous. The beatitude of Jeremiah's psalm appears near the middle, while the one in Psalm 1 is at the beginning.

THE DESCRIPTION OF THE RIGHTEOUS
(1:1–3)

**¹How blessed is the man who does not walk in the counsel of the wicked,
Nor stand in the path of sinners,
Nor sit in the seat of scoffers!
²But his delight is in the law of the LORD,
And in His law he meditates day and night.
³He will be like a tree firmly planted by streams of water,
Which yields its fruit in its season
And its leaf does not wither;
And in whatever he does, he prospers.**

In the first half of this psalm, the good person is described negatively, positively, and in terms of the consequences for deciding to be righteous. He is portrayed by what he does not do, by what he does, and by what results from his actions.

Verse 1. The opening words begin a beatitude regarding righteous living with the words **How blessed is the man**. It is one of twenty-six beatitudes that are scattered throughout the Psalms.[1] The Hebrew word for "blessed" is אַשְׁרֵי ('ashrey), a word always used in reference to humans, never in regard to God.

"Blessed" means "happy" or "a state of complete and full prosperity." The Hebrew word is plural and could actually be thought of as declaring that the righteous person enjoys "happinesses." H. C. Leupold has called attention to the special meaning of the plurality of the word:

> The Hebrew expresses the superlative by a plural of intensity: "happiness of the man." This gives the statement the force of an exclamation, which would be very nearly approximated by: "O how very happy is the man!" For the plural ('ashrey) literally means the full measure of the happy circumstances.[2]

The point is that the righteous life is rewarding and fulfilling; it is the way of true happiness.

A threefold progressive parallelism is used to describe the righteous life from a negative viewpoint, highlighting what the righteous person *avoids*. "Man" (אִישׁ, 'ish) here is not gender specific and could be translated "person" or "anyone."

The perfect verb forms are used—"has not walked," "has not stood," and "has not sat." These perfects express what has not been his practice in the past and what is not now his practice in the present. He is in a blessed state because he has been firm and resolute—over time—in his righteous living.

The righteous man **does not walk in the counsel of the wicked**. He has not listened to the "counsel" (עֵצָה, 'etsah) or guidance given by the wicked on how to live his life. The Hebrew word for "wicked" is רְשָׁעִים (r*e*sha'im), a word that depicts lawless men who bow to no authority and submit only to their own desires. Like the Chaldeans, they make up their own laws and submit to no others (Hab. 1:7).

---

[1] Ps. 1:1; 2:12; 32:1, 2; 33:12; 34:8; 40:4; 41:1, 2; 65:4; 84:4, 5, 12; 89:15; 94:12; 106:3; 112:1; 119:1, 2; 127:5; 128:1, 2; 137:8, 9; 144:15; 146:5.

[2] H. C. Leupold, *Exposition of the Psalms* (Columbus, Ohio: The Wartburg Press, 1959; reprint, Grand Rapids, Mich.: Baker Book House, 1969), 34.

The godly man does not **stand in the path of sinners.** The "sinners" (חַטָּאִים, *chatta'im*) are those who totally miss the mark. They are in the pathway of habitually violating the will of God. Disobedience has become the nature of their lives. When the wicked man has extended an invitation for the righteous man to join him in his rebellious life, the righteous man has faithfully spurned his solicitation.

The man who has God's favor does not **sit in the seat of scoffers**, in the settled position of the defiant and cynical person. He will not be found in the assembly of the acid tongues, in the circle of the critics who mock at holy things and good living. The "scoffers" (לֵצִים, *letsim*) are people who have reached a stage of confirmed opposition to righteousness. They sit and sneer. All reverence has left them. With vulgar lips, they disdain what is proper and right.

Each phrase of this verse is a step downward toward the committed life of sin. Comments that minimize the progression have not been convincing. We see degrees here: listening to the thinking, accepting the thinking, and living the thinking. The righteous man does not heed the counsel, enter the path, or sit in the seat. He refuses the words of the wicked, the lifestyle of the sinner, and thus he never reaches the cemented state of the scoffers.

The person who desires to lead a righteous life, therefore, avoids this path, these people, and this pursuit of evil. His decision about such wicked ways was made in the past, and he remains unshaken in his resolve.

Verse 2. The psalm now turns to what the righteous man *does*: The writer says **his delight is in the law of the Lord.** The positive side of the righteous man is seen in what he appreciates. "His delight [חֵפֶץ, *chepets*] is in" the things of God, especially the sayings and teachings of God. Instead of contemplating evil, the righteous man is absorbed with the "law" (תּוֹרָה, *torah*) of God. "The law of the Lord" is synonymous with the "words of" or "instructions of" Yahweh. The Greek word for *Torah* is *Nomos* (νόμος). Jesus used it for the five books of Moses, Genesis through Deuteronomy (Lk. 24:44), but at another time He applied it to the whole Old Testament (Jn. 10:34). The word

Torah had a limited use when this psalm was written, referring only to the early part of the Old Testament; but later it grew into a larger use, as more Old Testament books were written.

He **meditates** (יֶהְגֶּה, *yehgeh*) or muses on God's Word. He perhaps even ponders it by reading it aloud or murmuring it to himself. He gives his life to God's Word, for he thinks about it by **day and night.** He does not think of it only once in a while; it fills his mind continually as he contemplates what God has said and how he can honor His words. With this description, the writer affirms that the faithful person—in thought and actions—is anchored in the Word of God.

Verse 3. To what then is the righteous man analogous? The psalmist says **he will be like a tree firmly planted by streams of water.** The consequences of the righteous life are put in the form of a comparison. He says the one who yields daily to God's will is like a "tree firmly planted" and growing by channels or "streams of water." For that tree, water is always available and abundant, ever near in a never-ending supply. Nothing could be more attractive to a citizen of arid Palestine than a constant source of water. His illustration would have great appeal to the first readers.

This tree **yields its fruit in its season.** "In its season[s]" (in the times of fruit bearing), it will be productive because of its ample resources. The tree is perpetually draped in lively green, for **its leaf does not wither.** The point of this figure is that the godly man, because of the sustenance he receives, has a robust spiritual life and naturally emits the fruit of a good life.

The reader is constrained to weigh and ponder the blessings that the good man enjoys. He is like a tree, alive and vibrant. The word for "planted" suggests that he has received special attention and has stability. His location—by canals or streams of water—indicates that he has available resources for life and growth that are more than sufficient. His leaf does not wither, for he is radiant with spiritual health. He brings forth fruit during the seasons of fruit bearing because he enjoys natural and perpetual fertility.

The phrase **In whatever he does, he prospers** reflects the spiritual success that God wills for each righteous man to have. In whatever circumstances he finds himself, *he* will prosper. His surroundings may be less than desirable sometimes, but he—the man—will always excel as God's man through God's favor upon his life.

A CONTRAST WITH THE WICKED
(1:4, 5)

⁴The wicked are not so,
But they are like chaff which the wind drives away.
⁵Therefore the wicked will not stand in the judgment,
Nor sinners in the assembly of the righteous.

Verse 4. The wicked are not so, for their lives and futures are the opposite of God's design for real life. The writer does not consider the apparent successes of the wicked and the apparent failures of the righteous: He is contemplating the overall outcome and character of righteous living as opposed to the internal and final result of the way of wickedness.

The illustration used is a winnowing of grain in the evening. At the threshing floor where the chaff was beaten from the wheat, the wheat and chaff would be tossed into the air, and evening breezes would separate them from each other, allowing the heavier wheat to fall to the floor and the chaff to be blown away.

The good person is like a tree; the wicked, without root and fruit, are like worthless **chaff**, that is dead, good for nothing, empty, weightless, and **the wind drives** [it] **away**. The tree can withstand the winds, but the chaff is scattered into oblivion.

Verse 5. In light of these facts, a **therefore** appears. The wicked **will not stand in the judgment** of life and certainly not in the judgment of eternity. The judgments that everyone must face will knock them down. Life will eventually break them, for their approach to life is flawed. It follows then that if they cannot stand up under the blazing light of the judgment of life, they cannot even begin to find approval before the bar of God.

In the community of believers in the Old Testament world, assemblies would often be convened for worship and other important matters. Obviously, the wicked had no place **in the assembly of the righteous.** They were not a part of it, had no appreciation of it, and had no influence in it.

Thus the writer of this psalm lists for us the failures and inadequacies of the wicked. He says that the wicked are worthless, cannot stand before the judgments of life, and will not be permitted to stand in the convocations of the righteous.

THE LORD'S ULTIMATE JUDGMENT (1:6)

⁶**For the L**ORD **knows the way of the righteous,
But the way of the wicked will perish.**

Verse 6. The reason the righteous prosper is "the LORD knows" their way. The word for "knows" is יֹדֵעַ (*yode'a*), which means to know intimately. It does not mean to be simply aware of someone's existence. **The L**ORD **knows the way of the righteous** means that God shows special concern for and gives special attention to those who are living godly lives. The word used for "know" is a participle and carries the idea of a continual knowing. The Lord puts a shield around His people and preserves them. He loves and blesses them. He knows the righteous in the sense that He cares for and looks after them.

The way of the wicked will perish, for this way has the seeds of destruction within it. Ruin will inevitably come to any who take this road of life.

"The wicked" live without God and head down the way to destruction. They have chosen to live by their own rules and must suffer the consequences of their choices.

God and life will judge the wicked. They will ultimately perish in life and in eternity. However, God watches over the righteous, approving of them, and guiding them; the righteous walk with God, are known by God, and have His favor.

This psalm has moved from a beautiful beatitude to an appropriate implication: People either live for God or eventually will forever wish they had.

APPLICATION

The Whole of Life

Arthur G. Clarke has noticed that Book I contains three beatitudes that go in three directions and cover almost the whole of life.[3]

Psalm 1:1 is about *the obedient person, which is a God-ward view*. This individual meditates upon God's Word and lives by its precepts. His relationship with God is predicated upon his submission to God's will.

Psalm 32:1 is about *the forgiven person, which is a self-ward direction*. He comes to God in penitence, giving God a humble and contrite heart, allowing God to forgive him of his sin. He is a product of God's grace.

Psalm 41:1 is about *the compassionate person, which is a man-ward movement*. He has allowed the goodness of God to permeate him and flow out to others. As he has walked with God, he has taken on His attribute of lovingkindness.

Here is the totality of life—obedience, forgiveness, compassion; God, self, and others. We cannot serve others until we are right with God, we cannot be right with God until He forgives us. We cannot serve others aright except with a heart of compassion. The big priorities of life are piety, penitence, and pity.

Which Will It Be?

The challenge of Psalm 1 is that we must decide about the way we will live: wisely or foolishly, righteously or wickedly.

A man cannot walk along two roads at the same time; he cannot get in his car and drive off in two directions. When a ship sinks, two lists are posted: one list of survivors and another of the lost. Likewise, the world is made up of only two groups: the righteous and the wicked. Every person must choose which group he will join. We will either live under God's divine care, or we will eventually fall from life and pass into judgment—and, like all wicked people, perish.

---

[3]Arthur G. Clarke, *Analytical Studies in the Psalms* (Kilmarnock, England: John Ritchie, 1949), 26.

Why Should We Be Righteous?

The implication of this psalm is that the believer in God should lead a righteous life, choosing deliberately and confidently the way of true living.

The main question answered by the psalm is "Why should we aspire to have the good life?" To say it another way, "What is there about this way of living that should attract us?" Three reasons are given in this psalm.

Because of the happiness such a life brings (vv. 1, 2). A beatitude is announced: The righteous one will have the fullness of God.

Because of the prosperity such a life enjoys (vv. 3–5). The righteous one is analogous to a leafy, fruitbearing tree. He will be verdant with the life of God, productive, and receiving God's prosperity.

Because of the approval such a life receives (v. 6). In various ways, God will place His "well done" judgment over a righteous person's life. For example, God shows His approval by giving numerous blessings to the righteous.

Sin's Downward Trend

The journey pictured in verse 1 involves the progression of believing, behaving, and belonging. The progression could be pictured as persuasion, practicing, and a settled position. This verse is a parallelism to be sure, but it is more of a progressive parallelism than a synonymous one.

Notice carefully the journey.

We *look* at sin. "What harm is there in just looking?" we ask.

Soon the look turns to *listening* as we give heed to its appeals and charming invitations. "I need to know both sides of life. It is merely an academic exercise," we say.

Listening eventually leads to *learning* sin's ways. We become street-wise. Before we know it, we become experts in evil—knowledgeable about its types, attractions, and experiences.

Little by little, we grow to *love* it. Slowly, with a power like steel cables, it wraps its cords around our hearts.

Finally, in death's grasp, we sit down in the company of evil and *live* the life of sin.

The Righteous and the Word of God

An old saying is that the righteous person is "Bible-bred, Bible-led, and Bible-fed."

We are born into Christ by the Word. We began with the Word, allowing it to bring us to the new birth (1 Pet. 1:23).

We are guided by the Word in living for Christ. We cannot know God's will except through His Word. He does not guide us through supernatural intervention but by scriptural instruction.

As we feed on the Word, we are made to grow in Christ. The Christian life is one of growth in the Word (1 Pet. 2:1, 2; 2 Pet. 3:18). Without milk, a baby dies; without the Word, a Christian deteriorates.

Therefore, one who does not "live in the Word" simply does not and cannot know the life of God.

Like a Tree

One of the best ways to communicate truth and beauty is by a simile or metaphor; this psalm does this with unforgettable vividness. How is the righteous man like a tree?

To begin with, *he has stability.* He has been planted near the streams of water. The winds, waves, and violent circumstances of life cannot uproot him or shake him from his life in God.

Furthermore, *he has sustenance.* All the resources that he needs are available to him. In Christ he is complete, possessing all spiritual blessings. He does not need more blessings; he just needs to use wisely the blessings that he has.

Finally, *he has success.* He brings forth his fruit in the seasons of fruitbearing. His leaves do not wither. He will prosper in whatever he does.

What more could anyone desire? Who would want to be anything but "a tree planted by the rivers of water"?

Evaluating the Wicked

How are the wicked portrayed by this psalm?

They are outside God's plan. They are like chaff. They are lifeless, valueless, and pointless; and they are burned or blown away by the winds of circumstances and judgment. In the fulfillment of God's great, eternal plan, the wicked mean nothing to God and in the end mean nothing to mankind.

They are ineffectual. When their lives have been lived, they will find that they cannot stand up under the demands of life and will fall before the judgment of man and God. The wicked are hollow shells parading as human beings.

They are clearly destined for destruction. They have no future. One of the certainties of life is that the wicked are going to perish. They live on "Doomed Street" in the "City of Destruction"— whether they know it or not.

The Prosperity of the Righteous

This psalm says of the righteous man, "And in whatever he does, he prospers." This is a beautiful promise, but what does it mean?

First, it does not mean that *the righteous will always live in favorable circumstances.* Job, Daniel, Paul, Peter, and John are witnesses to this fact. The ultimate illustration is Jesus. He enjoyed the prosperity of God as He hung on a cross in shame.

Second, the promise does not mean that *every enterprise in which he engages will succeed.* Noah failed in winning the world with his message; Jeremiah did not succeed in saving Jerusalem; and Paul did not preach without serious persecution.

Third, Romans 8:28 in the KJV has, "All things work together for good." Some manuscripts read, "God causes all things to work together for good." "All things" have never and will never work together for good; but *God* has always, and will always, make all things work together for the good of those who love Him.

Finally, this phrase means that *the righteous will prosper in all that they do.* They are trusting in the Lord and abiding in His will. God will see that they prosper, regardless of their circumstances and difficulties. Daniel grew with God even though he was thrown into the lion's den; the three young Hebrew men prospered even though they were thrown into the fire.

God promises that the righteous will prosper, and He will keep that promise regardless of what the world determines to say or do about it!

Psalm 2

Opposing God and His Anointed

The Superscription: None.

The Davidic authorship of this psalm has been divinely attested. In Acts 4:25, Peter stressed that the Holy Spirit spoke the psalm by the mouth of David.

The first psalm in the Book of Psalms appealed to each individual to choose the righteous life; this psalm calls upon each nation to recognize God as the true God and to trust in Him. Together, these two psalms form a fitting introduction to the entire Book of Psalms—one addresses the individual and the other beseeches the nation.

Even though an earthly king is the principal topic of this royal psalm, the earthly king prefigures a greater King, the antitype Jesus Christ, thus giving the psalm a messianic character. This view of the psalm is confirmed by the New Testament's application of the psalm to the Messiah in five places (Acts 4:25, 26; 13:33; Heb. 1:5; 5:5).

When a new king came to the throne, the surrounding nations were likely to take advantage of his inexperience in leadership and try to take over his nation. Land-hungry national powers watched for opportune times—like the changing of the power of the throne—to subjugate other nations and bring them under their domain.

A similar event probably prompted the writing of this psalm. A new king had been or was being placed upon the throne of Israel. This man was God's choice; consequently, he had God's protection. Ignorantly, the other nations were plotting against the new king of God's people. They wanted to throw off any prior relationship with Israel and subdue it to their advantage.

Through this psalm, a reminder was given to any would-be conquerors that they would have to do battle with God, the true power behind the throne, if they came against Israel.

WHAT THE NATIONS ARE DOING
(2:1–3)

¹Why are the nations in an uproar
And the peoples devising a vain thing?
² The kings of the earth take their stand
And the rulers take counsel together
Against the LORD and against His Anointed, saying,
³ "Let us tear their fetters apart
And cast away their cords from us!"

Verse 1. Pictured first in the psalm in the form of two questions is the plotting of the surrounding Gentile nations (vv. 1–3). These peoples are in an **uproar** or tumult (רָגְשׁוּ, *rogshu*); they are astir with the clamor of putting together their battle plans. Four words are used synonymously to describe the evil powers around Israel who are getting set for war—**nations, peoples, kings,** and **rulers.**

They are **devising** or plotting through serious meditation. The same word that is found in 1:2, יֶהְגּוּ (*yehgu*), is used here. In Psalm 1 the righteous man meditates on the Torah; in this psalm the pagan kings and rulers meditate on the taking of Israel. They plan and muse—surely even thinking aloud—over their strategy for war.

David is amazed that any nation would dare come against God's anointed in light of the power of God that stood behind him. What these nations are doing is described as **a vain thing,** a useless attempt. The word for "vain" is רִיק (*riq*), a word that conveys emptiness or vanity. The very idea that a group of kings would dare to come against God!

Verse 2. The writer says that these nations are "devising," counseling **together**, and taking a stand **against** God and **His Anointed**. God had put or was putting a king in place, and they are preparing to oppose this coronation perhaps with force.

The Lord's "anointed" (מָשִׁיחַ, *mashiach*), His chosen one, is the central subject of this psalm. Samuel illustrates the anointing of a king as he is brought into office with his anointing of Saul to be Israel's first king. Samuel was told to anoint him secretly and then make known that Saul was God's choice. At an appropriate time, Samuel poured a flask of oil on Saul's head, declaring, "Has not the Lord anointed you a ruler over His inheritance?" God had set him apart to lead the people as His earthly representative (1 Sam. 10:1).

Ritualistic anointing is found throughout the Old Testament: Anointing was used to consecrate objects, such as an altar (Ex. 29:36), the ark (Ex. 30:26), and the tabernacle (Lev. 8:10). It was used to consecrate priests (Ex. 28:41), prophets (1 Kings 19:16), and kings (1 Sam. 10:1, 16:3; 1 Kings 1:39; 2 Kings 9:6). Such a ritual symbolized the setting aside of the thing or person to the service of God.

The word "anointed," as used in verse 2, refers to this coronation of a king as he comes to the throne. The word "Messiah" derives from this Hebrew word. "Christ" has the same meaning in Greek.

In a far greater sense, in the form of a type and antitype, Jesus, God's anointed Son, the Messiah, is being prophesied. This view is confirmed by the way this passage is used by inspired men of the New Testament days (Acts 4:25, 26; 13:33; Heb. 1:5; 5:5).

Thus the nations are failing to observe a significant truth: Any rebellion against this king would be a blatant rebellion against God since He put him on the throne.

Verse 3. The rulers are saying to one another, **"Let us tear their fetters apart and cast away their cords from us!"** Whatever relationship they have known with Israel they do not want anymore. Whatever binds them to Israel, whatever cords tie them to Israel, they will break and cast from them.

WHAT GOD DOES (2:4–6)

⁴He who sits in the heavens laughs,
The Lord scoffs at them.
⁵Then He will speak to them in His anger
And terrify them in His fury, saying,
⁶"But as for Me, I have installed My King
Upon Zion, My holy mountain."

Verse 4. David describes the almighty One who sits enthroned in the heavens, the true Ruler, as reacting with laughter to the plot of the nations. He **laughs** (שָׂחַק, *śachaq*) and **scoffs** (לָעַג, *la'ag*) at what these nations are thinking and planning (see Ps. 37:13; 59:8). His power is so far beyond the strength of any earthly king or kings that it is comical to watch their feeble attempts to overthrow His king (vv. 4, 5). God is amused at their child's play, laughing at their antics in divine derision. With highly figurative language, the writer pictures God as acting with the emotions characteristic of a man.

Verse 5. God will **speak to them in His anger.** If they persist, they will feel the brunt of His wrath. When God speaks, His power will decimate them. He will send the kings who plotted against His anointed into confusion; He will **terrify them in His fury,** as He brings down His judgment upon them. He will act with devastating might in behalf of His king.

Verse 6. David pictures God as speaking and telling of what He has done, by portraying God as saying that He has placed His king in office on Zion. He **installed** him; hence, his kingship has the hand of God upon it.

Zion, a prominent hill of Jerusalem, had become a synonym for Jerusalem and is used as an appellation for Jerusalem thirty-seven times in Psalms. This city was the place where God had chosen to put His name. In the words of this verse, Zion was God's **holy mountain,** and no one, not even a nation or a confederacy of nations, could disturb what He had done.

WHAT THE KING SAYS (2:7–9)

⁷"I will surely tell of the decree of the LORD:
He said to Me, 'You are My Son,
Today I have begotten You.
⁸Ask of Me, and I will surely give the nations as Your inheritance,
And the very ends of the earth as Your possession.
⁹You shall break them with a rod of iron,
You shall shatter them like earthenware.'"

Verse 7. This section of the psalm tells, in the king's words, how God has chosen him. He says, **"I will surely tell of the decree of the LORD."** The king will announce what God has decided and done. The decree is likely a reference to the promise God made to David in 2 Samuel 7:11–16 (see also 1 Chron. 28:6).

God has adopted (**begotten**) this chosen one as His king, an adoption that occurred on the day of the king's enthronement. He has put this king in place as His earthly leader. This affirmation prefigures God's sending the true and final King, Jesus, His divine Son, into the world.

Verse 8. God said, the king says, that He will give **the nations as** [an] **inheritance** to His king, and He will make his territory reach out to **the very ends of the earth**. The king whom God anoints will have more power and possessions than the other kings could imagine.

Verse 9. In figurative, idealized language, words that suggest the strength and power of the king's rule, the Lord says that the king will **break** [all enemies] **with a rod of iron**. Three rods of power are referred to in the Old Testament: the shepherd's rod, the king's scepter, and the punishment rod. This "rod of iron" is undoubtedly a figurative reference to the king's scepter. It was made of the strongest metal and would have the greatest strength. He would use it in subduing the enemies of the kingdom. With this rod, he could shatter his enemies like the breaking of fragile **earthenware** or clay pottery. He could smash a nation as a strong man could break a frail, delicate piece of pottery (v. 9). In other words, God's king, His anointed one, would have total dominion over the whole earth.

Israel never fully enjoyed the complete domination that David mentioned, but this lofty, spiritual description conveys the strength, greatness, and universal character of God's blessings upon David and Israel. Even further, it shows in prophecy the wide, universal dominion of the coming Messiah (v. 8).

WHAT THE NATIONS SHOULD DO
(2:10–12)

¹⁰Now therefore, O kings, show discernment;
Take warning, O judges of the earth.
¹¹Worship the LORD with reverence
And rejoice with trembling.
¹²Do homage to the Son, that He not become angry, and you perish in the way,
For His wrath may soon be kindled.
How blessed are all who take refuge in Him!

Verse 10. Who the Lord is, the greatness of His power and sovereignty, demands a **therefore**. The nations should **show discernment** (or wisdom) about God and His kingdom. They are to **take warning** by receiving instruction and exercising discipline. All the authorities of the earth ought to use good sense and recognize the true authority of God. Failure to do so would be an act of stupidity and would bring ruin to them, regardless of the power, position, or provisions they might have.

Verse 11. What response should the nations make to God? They are to give Him **reverence**. They are to **worship** the Lord with godly respect and faithful service. The word for "worship" (עֲבַד, *abad*) can also be translated "serve." They are to acknowledge Him as the true God and do His bidding. They are to **rejoice** before His greatness with **trembling**. This phrase, probably synonymous with the preceding phrase, suggests that they are to own Him by submission as their God and King.

Verse 12. The nations, however, must understand that they cannot honor God unless they honor the king He has chosen. They are to recognize His **Son** as the true King by giving **homage** to him.

The Hebrew admonition is "Kiss the son" (נַשְּׁקוּ־בַר, *nashshᵉqu bar*). The KJV and ASV chose to be literal in their translations and rendered the phrase with the simple "Kiss the Son." The KJV capitalized "Son" (suggesting deity) while the ASV did not. Other translations (such as the NASB) have chosen to handle the expression interpretively and have translated it "Do homage to the Son" or something similar.

Bar (בַּר) is the Aramaic word for "son" while *ben* (בֵּן) is the Hebrew equivalent. Why the writer used the Aramaic word here and the Hebrew word in verse 7 is a debated question. If "kiss" is figurative for "give homage to," then the basic idea of the expression is that of physically honoring the chosen one as the king. For example, after Samuel anointed Saul as the first king, he kissed him in recognition of what he had become (1 Sam. 10:1).

The writer further says that those who rebel and incite the fury of this King will **perish** in their undertakings. No one can stand against His **wrath**. He is endowed with the power of God, and His wrath can quickly be put into action.

In light of all the forgoing facts, the kings of the earth should resolve to take "refuge in Him," that is, in God. By their submission to God, the power behind this throne would become to them a secure place of safety.

In the concluding line, the basic truth as to how the nations are to view God is put in the form of a "beatitude": **How blessed are all who take refuge in Him!** This beatitude is the second one in the Book of Psalms. The first psalm begins with a beatitude; this second psalm ends with one. In other words, all nations should say, "Oh, the multitude of blessings that come to those who put their trust in God!" The nations are to seek "refuge" (חָסָה, *chasah*) in God. They are to find their comfort, peace, and protection in Him.

The final truth of this psalm declares that the only refuge *from* God is a refuge *in* God. Sensible men and nations will acknowledge this truth!

PSALM 2

APPLICATION

Putting Trust in God

The heart of this psalm is a description of the Lord, the true Ruler, and why we should trust Him (vv. 10–12). Based on His majestic attributes, we are urged to *put our faith in the almighty God of Israel*. To do so is sensible; not to do so is foolish. The appeal for us to believe in God is made from two perspectives.

First, we are to do so *because of His invincible power* (vv. 4, 5). No nation or any group of nations can stand against Him successfully. How futile to attack Gibraltar with a toy gun; to try to overthrow God would be the height of insanity!

Second, we should trust Him *because of His supreme sovereignty* (vv. 6–9). He is the only true God. In reality, He controls all peoples, kings, and nations. Any attempt to stand against Him is the vain aspiration of the frail creature seeking to oppose his almighty Creator.

Pagan Traits

We see characteristics of the worldly mindset in verses 1 through 3. The implication is that whoever possesses these traits cannot succeed.

First, *arrogance* is implied. The surrounding kings would like to take over the Lord's kingdom. Can you imagine? Who would dare to do battle with God?

Second, there is *greed*. Their actions are compelled by a desire for more. Not being satisfied with what they have, they destroy another to add to their possessions.

Third, there is *insensitivity*. A heartless attitude has come out. They do not care for others or for what others have; the only thing that moves them is the expansion of their territory. Their philosophy is not "Live and let live"; it is "Live and get all you can!"

Then, there is *irreverence*. Can you picture a group of kings or a king daring to fight against God? This God they are talking about, the almighty Creator of all things, is not just another king!

"Today I Have Begotten You"

The king of Israel saw his coronation as a day of becoming God's special representative on earth. It was a sacred time that was somewhat like adoption, a time of divine selection. In a sense, God was owning him as His son.

From the viewpoint of the New Testament, something far deeper is addressed in this verse. We know of two times in the life of Jesus when He was claimed as God's Son by an audible voice from heaven: at His baptism (Mt. 3:17; Mk. 1:11; Lk. 3:22) and at His transfiguration (Mt. 17:5; Mk. 9:7; Lk. 9:35). Furthermore, Paul said that God chose Him as His Son in a figurative way at His resurrection from the dead (Acts 13:33; Rom. 1:4). A total of three times the phrase "today I have begotten You" is found in the New Testament, and each time it is used in reference to Jesus (Acts 13:33; Heb. 1:5; 5:5).

We must not fail to see the messianic overtones in this phrase in Psalm 2. King David perhaps thinks he is writing about himself or some other king of Israel, but in truth he is writing of the greatest King, Jesus Christ, who was chosen to be God's Son for the salvation of mankind.

Looking at Jesus Christ

How shall we view Jesus? He was and is *the Son of God forever*. Paul said that He was on an equal plane with God the Father (Phil. 2:5).

He is *the Son of God incarnate*. He did not have to wait to become the Son of God; He was God's Son at birth! The angel told Joseph that He was to be the Savior of mankind (Mt. 1:21).

He is *the Son of God acknowledged*. God the Father chose to make known His Son at His baptism, transfiguration, and ultimately for all time at His resurrection (Rom. 1:4).

How Shall We View God?

According to this psalm, the appropriate response that nations and individuals are to make to God is fourfold:

First, there is reverence (v. 11). We are to bow down before Him in holy worship. He is God, and there is no other God besides Him.

Second, there is rejoicing in His greatness (v. 11). Those who put their trust in Him need not fear His judgment. He loves His children and will sustain them and protect them.

Third, there is recognition of His Son as the true King. The King, Jesus, is the King God has chosen. We come to God through Him.

Fourth, there is a resolution to take refuge in Him (v. 12). He is the only true refuge that there is. Pity the person or nation who tries to find a refuge in anything or any haven other than God!

Surely, no one can so view God in this fourfold manner and not be determined to become a Christian.

Becoming a Blessed Nation

This psalm closes with a beatitude concerning the nation that puts its trust in God. How will such a nation be blessed? The preceding part of the psalm delineates the blessings that will come to a nation that believes in the Lord.

Such a nation will have *God's power*. God is behind the king that He has put into office, and He will be behind any nation that surrenders to His will.

Furthermore, the nation that trusts in God will have *His protection*. Anyone who comes against God's king will have to fight against God.

Third, it will have *God's providence*. God said that He would give His king expansion and dominion. His rule will reach out to the ends of the earth.

Let us choose to be "one nation under the favor of God."

God and the World

What kind of relationship does God sustain with His world?

To begin with, we see that *He has a work going on in this world*. He places His king on the throne and stands behind him. He is involved with what is going on in the world.

It should be observed further that *He will not be intimidated by the disobedient nations of the earth*. He laughs at their little plots and plans. His purposes will not be foiled by them.

He brings about the success of His king. He will give him dominion over all the earth.

Finally, *He invites all nations to put their faith in Him.* He will bless and provide for those who take refuge in Him.

God and Our Basic Needs

The Bible contains three great promises that answer to a person's greatest fears. Found in the Patriarchal, Mosaical, and Christian Ages, they are brought out from one end of the Bible to the other. All Christians believe in these three assurances to some degree, or they have simply missed the heart of the Scriptures. God has said, in effect, "If you walk before Me in faith, I will make a pledge to you in the form of three promises."

First, He says, *"I will guide you."* One of our major fears is ignorance. God has asked His people to walk by faith in Him in every dispensation. His revelations have not been the same for each age, but His promise has. He has given us His will, telling us how to worship Him, how to live before Him, and what to do for Him.

Second, He says, *"I will protect you."* Another of our greatest fears is insufficiency. If He does not deliver us from difficulties, He will sustain us in them. He told Abraham, "I will bless those who bless you, and I will curse those who curse you" (Gen. 12:3). He told Moses, "I will go before you and drive the enemy out." He told Paul, "Do not be afraid, I will be with you" (Acts 27:24).

Third, He says, *"I will provide for you."* Yet another fear is that we must face invincible foes, the foes we cannot do anything about, such as disease, decay, and death. God says, "I am going to take care of you." He gives His people what they need to do what He wants as long as He wants them to do it. He does not satisfy our greed, but He does meet our needs.

Shame on us for fretting! We have no reason to worry. If we are anxious, something is out of kilter in our thinking and in our faith. Either we do not believe that God will fulfill His promises, or we are not His people in practice.

Psalm 3
A Morning Cry

The Superscription: A Psalm of David, when he fled from Absalom his son. With a prepositional prefix attached to the name David, usually translated **of David** (לְדָוִד, *l^edawid*), the title advocates that David is either the author, is related to the psalm in some significant way, or is the subject of the psalm. The Hebrew preposition can mean "of," "by," "for," or "to." This is the first of seventy-three references to David in the superscriptions in the Book of Psalms.

Furthermore, the title says that it is **a Psalm** (מִזְמוֹר, *mizmor*), a term indicating that this composition is a prayer, a song, or a writing for worshipful meditation. In addition, the heading describes the probable historical setting of the psalm with the phrase **when [David] fled from Absalom his son.** The awful trial thought to be behind this psalm is that of David abandoning Jerusalem due to one of the worst rebellions of his life (2 Sam. 15—18), the mutiny created by his son.

While these superscriptions are not inspired, they are extremely old. They precede the Greek translation of the Old Testament Scriptures (the LXX) that was completed around 150 B.C., for this translation had these superscriptions with some variations at the beginning of each psalm. The Hebrew texts that we now have use them as the first verse of the psalm.

Obviously, we should not bend the psalms to fit the descriptions and affirmations given in these headings; but because of their age, we would probably not go far afield if we regard them as fairly reliable guides in understanding the background of the psalms.

In the case of this psalm, nothing in the psalm contradicts the Davidic authorship suggestion or the subtitle's clue regarding the historical background.

This morning cry is a lament/prayer that calls upon God

for protection. The writer is in a treacherous and dangerous situation; thus, from his dark valley of difficulty, he is coming to his God in an earnest petition for help as he begins the day.

To capture the spirit of the psalm, picture David leaving Jerusalem, his capital, as a beaten, broken king. The glory of his kingdom has been wrestled from him by hands that have turned cruel and rebellious—not by a vicious foreign power, but by one of his own household, his son. He has all but lost his kingdom, and he is in grave danger of being executed. His enemies—those who are joining in the rebellion—rise up around him as an overwhelming flood.

His death is sought by many. As he hurries out of Jerusalem, nightfall overtakes him and wraps a protective cloak of darkness around him. Worn out from the worst disaster that he has ever known, weary from gathering what he could and abandoning his palace, he lies down in the crevice of a rock, in a cave, or in a clump of trees for needed rest. Before his eyes close in sleep, he speaks to God in prayer, committing to Him his life, his kingship, and his army. A few hours later, he greets the day with this psalm/prayer. Perhaps he writes it and then prays it; maybe he prays it and then writes it; maybe later he looked back on this scene and wrote about what he had prayed; or maybe an inspired witness wrote it about what David did and said.

The psalm is divided into four parts: a complaint (vv. 1, 2), a consideration of the strength of God (vv. 3, 4), a trusting calmness (vv. 5, 6), and a call for God to help him (vv. 7, 8).

Although it is classified as a lament psalm, it does not follow the normal lament pattern in every detail.

THE COMPLAINT (3:1, 2)

>¹O LORD, how my adversaries have increased!
>Many are rising up against me.
>²Many are saying of my soul,
>"There is no deliverance for him in God." Selah.

Verse 1. The writer's life-threatening circumstance has

turned his mind to his only source of salvation; he begins his prayer with a plea for deliverance, addressing God out of his desperation, **O Lord.**

The writer believes that a host of enemies has surrounded him. He calls them his "adversaries" (צַר, *tsar*), a term that sums up all of those who are threatening and opposing him. They are foes to David and opponents of God, as the later verses indicate. Their number was small at the beginning, but it has rapidly grown and is continuing to mushroom. With amazement, fear, and trembling, he declares, **How my adversaries have increased! Many are rising up against me.** He uses "many" or "great" (רַבִּים, *rabbim*) twice in this psalm to depict his plight (vv. 1, 2). The numbers begin to intimidate him.

Verse 2. He says, **Many are saying of my soul, "There is no deliverance for him in God."** These enemies are speaking disparagingly to his "soul," seeking to discourage his spirit, his spiritual life, his confidence in God. Tauntingly, they say, "There is no deliverance for him in God." The Hebrew word that is translated "deliverance" (יְשׁוּעָה, *yᵉshuʻah*) is a word that is often translated "salvation." The enemies declare in their hatred that his God cannot save him. They know that the writer believes in God and walks with Him, and their words are intended to be arrows of derision, sent out to pierce his heart with the poison of hopelessness and despair. They mean that they do not believe his God is strong enough to help him, does not wish to help him, or has rejected him because of his sin.

Thankfully, he does not listen to these negative voices. He refuses to regard his situation as hopeless, for he knows that God is his helper. Belonging to God, he is confident that his God will not abandon him. Thus, throughout the rest of the psalm, he sings of what God has done for him and what God can and will do for him in his present crisis.

Selah is seen for the first of its seventy-one times in the Book of Psalms. It is found in only one other book of the Old Testament, appearing three times in Habakkuk 3. The word is usually at the end of a stanza or at the end of a major thought. Even though the word's meaning is obscure, it must be a musical term meaning something like, "Pause and think about this thought."

A CONTEMPLATION OF HIS GOD
(3:3, 4)

³But You, O LORD, are a shield about me,
My glory, and the One who lifts my head.
⁴I was crying to the LORD with my voice,
And He answered me from His holy mountain. Selah.

Verse 3. Pressed hard by the troubles around him, he turns to the God who has blessed him in the past. He says, **But You, O LORD, are a shield about me**. His solace comes from the memory of God's faithfulness. His comfort rests squarely upon God's lovingkindness, not upon his feelings or circumstances.

For example, he says that God is his "shield" (מָגֵן, *magen*). A shield was a wooden frame covered by leather or pieces of some kind of metal and would protect a man from the arrows, spears, and swords of the enemy. In a spiritual sense, God is providing protection for David. He encircles him with His presence, power, and providence. The preposition "about" (בַּעַד, *ba'ad*) is a strong one, meaning to be surrounded, to be engulfed, to be immersed in. God is covering him up with His divine, invincible shield of His promises and power.

Furthermore, God is his **glory** (כָּבוֹד, *kabod*). By doing God's will, David is a reflection of the holy splendor of God. He knows that whatever glory or honor he has received was a gift from God. David's throne was given to him by the Lord. His renown, popularity, abilities, opportunities, and thus his successes, are acts of grace and kindness from the hands of God. Were David placed back on the throne, he would become a reflection of God's royal majesty once again.

Therefore, God is David's encourager. He says He is **the One who lifts** [up his] **head.** Those times come when no one other than God can elevate our spirits. Every time David has been disappointed in men and events, he has been built up by his God.

Now David needs God's inspiration and support more than ever before. He has lost everything—even his family. He knows that God can raise him up from his condition of having fallen on the ground as before a judge in disgrace and defeat.

Verse 4. He has prayed in the past, and God has heard him. He says, **I was crying to the LORD with my voice, and He answered me.** Now, like then, he is looking to God to give him deliverance from those who seek his kingdom and his life. An opposing army is mounting by the minute. To whom can he turn? Only God can be his source of help.

He has prayed, and God has answered him **from His holy mountain.** The imperfect tense is used to show that the action is incomplete—God has answered him and will answer him. The "holy mountain" was Jerusalem, the place where God reigned among His people.

A TRUSTING CALMNESS (3:5, 6)

⁵**I lay down and slept;**
I awoke, for the LORD sustains me.
⁶**I will not be afraid of ten thousands of people**
Who have set themselves against me round about.

Verse 5. David relates what he had done: **I lay down and slept.** Emphasis is used with an emphatic "I." With the conviction that God would care for him, he closed his eyes and went to sleep. It takes strong faith to sleep when imminent dangers lurk in the shadows around us, but such was the faith of this man. Since God has been his Deliverer, he could testify to His kindness: **I awoke, for the LORD sustains me.** As he awakes from his sleep, he finds that God is sustaining him again as He had continually done in his other trials. Once again, the word "sustains" is in the imperfect tense which suggests that God has sustained him and will again sustain him. God is doing for him in this crisis what He has done for him in the past—and what He always does for His people.

Verse 6. What kind of confidence has his praying instilled in him? In the assurance that should belong to every faithful follower of God, he says, **I will not be afraid of ten thousands of people who have set themselves against me round about.** God's watch-care through the previous night inspires David to engage the coming day with the bracing truth that God will deliver him though he may be attacked by "ten thousands" (רְבָבָה, *r*ᵉ*babah*) of enemy warriors. The word is "myriads" of enemies. It is usually translated "ten thousands." We must remember that the gravity of a situation should not be assessed by counting the number of fierce attackers standing around in battle array. Our condition can only be evaluated by whether or not we have invited God's power into it. Is God with us or not? Will *God* fight for us, or will *we* do it? In Judges 6, only two made a majority: God and the sword of Gideon!

God has been David's support and stay. In the dark and frightening valleys, he repeatedly prayed to God, and God heard him. Continually he has been saved—not by the sword, an army, or human strategy; the almighty One has been his salvation. Deliverance has been given so often that he can say that God "sustains" him.

A CALL FOR HELP (3:7, 8)

⁷**Arise, O LORD; save me, O my God!**
For You have smitten all my enemies on the cheek;
You have shattered the teeth of the wicked.
⁸**Salvation belongs to the LORD;**
Your blessing be upon Your people! Selah.

Verse 7. In intense prayer, he urges, **Arise, O LORD; save me, O my God!** The writer asks God to "arise" and come to his aid by providing salvation (see Num. 10:35; Ps. 68:1). This phrase was Israel's war cry: When they set out to do battle with an enemy they cried, "Arise, O Lord, and scatter the enemy!"; when they returned from battle, they said, "Return, O Lord, to the people of Israel." The meaning of these phrases is that God would fight for them, and to Him would belong the glory for the victory. God lived among them, and He went before them to face all their foes.

This writer declares that the Lord will be his Commander in Chief. He has seen God fight his battles in the past: **For You**

have smitten all my enemies on the cheek; You have shattered the teeth of the wicked. He has watched as He annihilated the enemies that came against him. Smiting them "on the cheek" is an expression suggesting complete victory—conveying defeat and humiliation of the enemy.

The metaphor of shattering "the teeth of the wicked" moves the reader from a picture of military imagery to picturing the enemy as a wild animal that uses its teeth to devour its prey. The vicious lion whose teeth have been broken is reduced to a harmless animal. In overwhelming defeat, God figuratively removed the fangs of the wicked. He eliminated their ability to destroy and harm.

Verse 8. The heart of the psalm is that **salvation belongs to the Lord.** David seeks salvation from his predicament, but he knows that all praise belongs to God. His source of deliverance is God, and he freely acknowledges what God has done. The word "salvation" is the major emphasis he wants to give.

He ends his requests by remembering the Lord's people, the kingdom in which he is serving. He asks that God's **blessing be upon** all its citizens. This lament prayer does not end with David but with the people whom David has led. True spiritual prayer does not end with the needs of the one praying but with the needs of others. We may enter prayer as selfish people, thinking only of our struggles; but when the prayer ends, if we have truly prayed, we have become compassionate people who think also of the trials of others.

APPLICATION

Short and Simple

Great, genuine prayers are basically simple in form and wording. They consist of addressing God as our Deliverer, making the requests that are desperately needed, and giving thanks for the blessings that have already been given. In the Christian Age, we are asked to acknowledge the authority of Christ as we pray (Jn. 16:23). As has often been said, "We do not have faith in prayer, but we do pray in faith."

God, Our Helper and Hope

Remembering what God has done in the past will relieve our fears and give us hope for the future, even in difficulties too complex for human hands to untangle. On the basis of what God has done for us previously, what can we expect God to do in the future? How has God been our help in ages past? Let us notice what God was to David and then apply the same truths to the situations that confront us.

He is our shield (v. 3). He surrounded David with His protection, engulfing him with His care. The strength of God was encircling him and guarding him on all sides.

He is our splendor (v. 3). He allowed David to be a reflector of His glory. Whatever glory David had was a spin off from his relationship with God.

He is our encourager (v. 3). He was the One who lifted up David's head. From disgrace and fear, God raised David to a place of honor and service.

He is our sustainer (vv. 4–6). Through all the days, God had strengthened David so that he might be the king he should be. His life was undergirded by the purposes of God.

Who is God to us? He is our shield, our splendor, our source of encouragement, and our sustainer.

In Time of Need

In his time of need David turns to God in prayer (v. 7). Note his threefold petition.

He cries for God to save him. He asks for deliverance. Trouble is part of life, and all of us will one day need to pray this prayer.

He asks God to handle his enemies. God is better at this than we are. We become too emotional and filled with hatred. It is best to commit our adversaries to the Lord and commit ourselves anew to doing what is right.

He pleads for God to bless His people. We are part of a wonderful community, God's people. We should have a concern that reaches out to all who belong to God.

When you are about to be overrun by enemies, what do you say to God? What else can you say other than what David said: "Save me, deal with my enemies, and bless Your people"?

Stop and Think!

Can you imagine a darker moment than the one David was facing? Three times, he used the word "Selah" (vv. 2, 4, 8), asking the reader of this psalm to pause and think.

Think about your situation (vv. 1, 2). Look it over carefully, and see how helpless you are when you act in your own strength.

Think about God's kindness in the past (vv. 3, 4). Has God not always been faithful to you? Has He ever betrayed you or neglected you?

Think about what the Lord can do for you now (vv. 5–8). Is He not the only One who can help you? Will He not want to save you?

How do we pray in a crisis? What do we think about? We think of our need, of our gracious God, and of what God can and will do for us.

God's Watch-Care

Consider God's tender care for His children. Oh, the mystery and marvel of it!

Through His providence, He sometimes allows us to be in unusual places. Saints were in Caesar's household. Daniel was in a lion's den. Shadrach, Meshach, and Abed-nego were in a fiery furnace. Paul was tied to a whipping post. Think it not strange if you find yourself in extreme and forbidding situations.

He protects us where He has put us or has allowed us to be. No circumstance is too big or too treacherous for God. Was the furnace too hot for Him? Were the lions too vicious for Him? Were Caesar's quarters too dangerous for Him?

He pushes us on to the other places where He wishes us to be. He can use our trials to prepare us for something better and for greater service. Daniel came out of the den more trusting and more influential. The three Hebrews came out of the fire with a greater commitment to the God whom they found to be stronger than fire.

Not until eternity will we know how completely He has saved us and blessed us. Perhaps He will show us on life's other side how He used our stints in unusual places to glorify His name and to do His work.

When in Trouble

This psalm is divided into four parts: a cry for help (vv. 1, 2), a contemplation of how God has blessed David (vv. 3, 4), a calm assurance that God will care for him (vv. 5, 6), and a clear call for God to help him (vv. 7, 8). Here is a pattern we can follow when trouble comes.

When in a serious difficulty, make sure you are in God's will, and then pray for God's protection. When you pray, remember how faithful God has been. Pray in faith and thankfulness. When you pray, trust in God to provide the help that He sees that you need. Pray with confidence in the grace of God!

Sleeping in the Storm

Can you go to sleep while a storm is raging?

If you can, that may be a bad sign. Jonah, for example, went to Joppa, found a boat going to Tarshish, paid his fare, got on board, went into the innermost part of the ship, and went to sleep. He was running away from divine duty but was able to sleep.

He should have been awake straightening out matters with God, but he was taking a nap. Maybe Jonah was sleeping out of sheer exhaustion from the emotional strain of running away from God, or maybe he was totally insensitive to the whole affair. From either viewpoint, his respite in the storm was a red flag.

If you can, that may be a good sign. David was able to commit his life and kingdom to God and go to sleep even though enemies were all around him. Peter, facing execution the next day, was able to sleep between two soldiers (Acts 12:6). This kind of sleeping shows absolute trust in the kind providence of God.

If you are asleep in a storm, what kind of sleep is it—the sleep of coldness against God's will or the sleep of calmness in God's will? Are you relaxing in your sin, or are you confident in God's peace and power?

Psalm 4
An Evening Prayer

The Superscription: For the choir director; on stringed instruments. A Psalm of David. This evening prayer/song has the ascription **of** ["by," "for," or "to"] **David** (לְדָוִד, *lᵉdawid*). It is simply called a **Psalm** (מִזְמוֹר, *mizmor*). The previous prayer is for the morning, but this one seems to be a prayer offered before going to sleep; thus these two prayers are bookends for the night—one for the beginning of the night and the other one for the ending of it.

The superscription says it is **for the choir director** [לַמְנַצֵּחַ, *lamnatstseach*]; **on stringed instruments** (בִּנְגִינוֹת, *binginoth*). Apparently these instructions indicate how this prayer/song was to be sung. Stringed instruments are suggested. Instrumental music was used in worship to God in Old Testament times, just as animal sacrifices and numerous other rituals were a part of that worship; consequently, an indication is given in this heading on what instruments were to be used in the singing of the song. This part of the Psalms would not be worship instruction for the Christian. The New Testament, the authority for the new and living way, only commands singing in the worship of God in the Christian Age.

In the words of this psalm, the writer is calling upon God in the midst of deep disappointment and heartbreak. His spirit is burdened because of the cutting words that have been uttered about him. His name has been besmirched, and his reputation has been dragged in the dust of criticism. Those around him have been taught to believe the worst about him; they have chosen to listen to lies instead of the truth.

A PLEA FOR AN ANSWER (4:1)

¹Answer me when I call, O God of my righteousness!
You have relieved me in my distress;
Be gracious to me and hear my prayer.

Verse 1. Crushed by criticism, the writer cries out, **Answer me when I call, O God of my righteousness!** God is the "God of [his] righteousness," for he is confident that God knows of the integrity of his heart and is the One who will vindicate his honor. Righteousness can be bestowed, as in the case of salvation (Rom. 3:25, 26), and righteousness can be exhibited (1 Jn. 3:7), as in the case of right living. The writer believes that God sees his situation and is fully aware of the moral quality of his life. The pure eyes of his God see through the screen of the falsehoods and slander and behold his blamelessness.

He makes his appeal to God with three imperatives: "Answer me"; "be gracious to me"; and "hear my prayer." These earnest entreaties make up two synonymous lines and are parallel thoughts.

The writer calls to mind God's past mercy for encouragement in dealing with his present trial. He says, **You have relieved me in my distress; be gracious to me and hear my prayer.** Remembering how God had delivered him in other circumstances strengthens him and enables him to think properly about his current difficulty. How God has treated us is an accurate lesson on how God will treat us. When problems come, we would do well to remember how God has cared for us in the past. When David was in "distress" (צַר, *tsar*), in a small, confined place of difficulty, God had "relieved" (רָחַב, *rachab*) him and had brought him into a large, open place of freedom from harm.

He wants God to be "gracious" (חַן, *chann*) to him, or manifest favor toward him, by answering his prayer for help. God extends His grace in numerous ways to His servants—He guides them, holds them in His love, and provides for them with His sustaining presence. In this case, God is being asked by this ser-

MEDITATING OUT LOUD (4:2, 3)

²O sons of men, how long will my honor become a reproach?
How long will you love what is worthless and aim at deception? Selah.
³But know that the LORD has set apart the godly man for Himself;
The LORD hears when I call to Him.

Verse 2. Before he slips into restful sleep, in the quietness of his soul he prays for those who have made vile and caustic statements about him. He prays, **O sons of men, how long will my honor become a reproach?** He addresses his enemies as "sons of men" who have continually belittled his integrity and reputation. They have brought his honor into "reproach" (כְּלִמָּה, k*e*limmah). The ones degrading him may be people of rank and distinction.

He asks of them, **How long will you love what is worthless and aim at deception?** By their actions, they indicate that they "love" (אָהֵב, aheb) that which is "worthless" (רִיק, riq); that is, they admire the empty and the vain. They are driven by, "aim at," or seek (בָּקַשׁ, baqash) "deception" (כָּזָב, kazab) or falsehood. This motivation is wickedness gone to seed.

Verse 3. He observes—with faith—that God is always showing His strength in behalf of the godly (see 2 Chron. 16:9). He sets **apart the godly man for Himself.** His providence is dedicated to providing for and looking after those who serve Him. The word for "godly man" (חָסִיד, chasid) comes from the great Old Testament word for lovingkindness, the characteristic of God that is best defined as covenant loyalty. The godly man has taken into his personality one of the most beautiful traits of God. This man reflects the nature of God, faithfulness and loyalty, and God has separated him out of the multitudes of people for His special blessings and fellowship.

With confidence in the integrity of God, he says, **The LORD hears when I call to Him.** He is praying, as all righteous people should, with the assurance that God will respond to his prayer by coming to his rescue. One of the major truths of the Psalms is that God listens when His children pray.

A PRAYER FOR HIS ENEMIES
(4:4, 5)

⁴Tremble, and do not sin;
Meditate in your heart upon your bed, and be still. Selah.
⁵Offer the sacrifices of righteousness,
And trust in the LORD.

Verse 4. Amazingly, the writer now turns to special requests for the enemies themselves. Righteous prayers should include petitions for others, even for those who are against us. Thus he prays, **Tremble, and do not sin; meditate in your heart upon your bed, and be still.** He asks that his opposers might think of God's wrath upon the wicked and His goodness to the righteous and be constrained by such meditation to "tremble" (רִגְזוּ, *rigzu*) in humiliation and reverence before Him. Reflection leads to reverence, and reverence should bring reformation.

His prayer is a model prayer for us when we must pray for our enemies. As Jesus prayed for those who crucified Him (Lk. 23:34), and as Stephen prayed for his persecutors (Acts 7:60), this writer offers up a nighttime prayer for those who seek his harm.

His prayer for them is that they worship God and "not sin." They are to cease from being *angry* with God (according to the LXX) and thus refrain from sinning. Paul apparently quoted this phrase as he discussed anger in Ephesians 4:26. He used the phrase to teach us to deal with our anger even before we go to sleep. While this psalm is more about the relationship of enemies with God, Paul was highlighting more our relationships with other people in general.

The writer asks that the enemies "meditate" in their "hearts"

(לְבַב, *lebab*) "upon" their beds, and "be still." The phrase literally says, "Speak to your heart on your bed." He wants the wicked to lie awake at night and contemplate their ways in the secret chambers of their hearts. The evil ones need to put their hearts on God's ways. Our thoughts seem to be clearer and our consciences are sharper in the stillness of the night. Sober thinking sometimes pricks the conscience, and a hurting conscience can prompt a reconsideration of the evil that has been done. Perhaps they will be motivated to "be still" (דֹּמּוּ, *dommu*) or stop sinning long enough to contemplate their ways. These words must be a prayer for their transformation through the proper spiritual contemplation.

Verse 5. Such changes would result in their deciding to **offer the sacrifices of righteousness**. Convicted by their remorse, they might be moved to reconciliation. "May they offer the sacrifices that God requires, and may they do so with pure, righteous hearts," he is praying. We destroy enemies by making friends out of them; and even more completely, we destroy enemies by making godly people out of them. If we have enemies, let us convert them to Christ, and then they will become our friends and servants of God.

The next request must have been David's true goal in his prayer: **And trust in the LORD**. How wonderful it would be if his enemies put their faith in God! The army of evil needs to be turned into soldiers of truth who trust in God as His righteous people.

What finer prayer could be prayed for our enemies? How much better it is (for them and us) when we pray for our foes rather than castigating them with words of hatred and bitterness. Instead of retaliation, this is a prayer for reconciliation. Instead of harboring bitterness, the writer tries to pray for their salvation through the transforming power of God.

LET YOUR LIGHT FALL (4:6–8)

⁶Many are saying, "Who will show us any good?"
Lift up the light of Your countenance upon us, O LORD!
⁷You have put gladness in my heart,

> More than when their grain and new wine abound.
> ⁸In peace I will both lie down and sleep,
> For You alone, O Lord, make me to dwell in safety.

Verse 6. He says, **Many are saying, "Who will show us any good?"** Numerous ones are discouraging the psalmist from praying for his enemies just as many do the same to us. Their urgings are negative and hurtful. Unswayed, the believer knows that God's favor falls upon the gracious, forgiving, and generous person.

The writer prays, **Lift up the light of Your countenance upon us, O Lord!** Some translations (the NRSV, for example) put this phrase with the previous, negative one, presenting the text as saying, "Nothing good will happen! We will not have the light of His countenance upon us." However, it could be that this line is an appeal for God to bless the faithful with the light of His face. A similar phrase is found in Deuteronomy 33:19. Such a blessing would be synonymous with receiving God's favor. God only allows the light of His countenance, His face, to fall upon those who are pleasing in His sight.

Verse 7. He says, **You have put gladness in my heart.** He believes that the sunshine of God's presence brings more joy than the combined benevolent forces of the world. God is the One who has "put gladness" in his heart. He has a spiritual happiness, a heavenly joy. He proclaims that the trusting people have the greatest joy, even **more than when their grain and new wine abound.** The "happiness" that comes from God is an overflowing joy that is greater than material blessings, such as those benefits that come when "grain and new wine" accrue to them in abundance. The harvest time was looked upon as one of the happiest times, a time of rejoicing in the fruit of one's labors and in the gracious provisions being set aside for the future. The spiritual peace and inner life that God gives towers even above the delight of the most celebrated seasons of the year.

Verse 8. The psalm has been moving to a grand conclusion, specifically: **In peace I will both lie down and sleep.** The peace enjoyed takes in body, soul, and spirit—a complete and total serenity. It is immediate and thorough. He can turn his mind away from his cares and relax because he is in God and God is in him. He will sleep in this total security because he knows that he is in the refuge of God.

The **safety** he knows is centered in God **alone** (בָּדָד, *badad*). God sets him apart from the arrows of his enemies. He has provided him with real protection. This security is not passing—he **dwell**[s] (יָשַׁב, *yashab*) or lives in it. He does not look to this earth's goods, his friends, or his material prosperity for it—his eyes are on God alone for his protection and peace.

APPLICATION

The Gifts of Trust

Trust in God brings numerous blessings. Let us rejoice in a list of some of them.

There is *deliverance in time of trouble* (v. 1). Throughout the psalms, mention is made of this wonderful truth. God is more than an emergency bellhop who runs to our aid when we overextend ourselves. He is our Father who loves us, provides for us, protects us, and guides us.

There is *confidence that one's prayer will be heard* (v. 1). As Peter said, "For the eyes of the Lord are toward the righteous and His ears attend to their prayer" (1 Pet. 3:12).

There is *the gracious favor of God* (v. 3). God answers His people according to His lovingkindness and not according to their sins. One certainty of life is that God will be gracious to us.

There is *joy unspeakable that money cannot buy* (v. 7). The gladness that God gives transcends all earthly honors and pleasures.

There is *peace in the midst of trial* (v. 8). God does not always deliver us from the fiery furnace, but He ensures that we will be protected in it.

There is *security* (v. 8). The faithful followers of the Lord can rest with the confident hope that God is watching over them.

How attractive the righteous life is! We must not let enemies rob us of this life. Let us remember that the choice is ours, not theirs. Having prayed in truth and righteousness for those who hurt him, the writer can lie down to sleep in the peace and tranquility that the Lord gives to the righteous heart (v. 8).

See that you rest in peace tonight!

Praying for One's Enemies

How does this writer pray for his slanderers? What does he request? How should we pray for those who gossip about us?

He asks that his enemies *might think of the wrath of God and might turn from sin*. Solemn thinking will precede repentance. When people start thinking right, they will start acting right.

He asks that they *might meditate upon their beds about what they were doing*. Thinking produces meditation and meditation may bring noble resolutions.

He asks that the enemies *might turn about and offer the sacrifices of righteousness*. Jesus said that out of "the good treasure" of his heart a good man brings forth "good" things (Mt. 12:35). A change of heart brings a change of deeds.

He asks that his enemies *might come to a point of trusting in God*. Here we see the ultimate goal of the prayer: He is asking that God make faithful servants out of his enemies.

The best thing anyone can do for his enemies is to pray a prayer like this for them.

God Means More

Here, then, is the ultimate of life—knowing and walking with God.

This relationship is greater *than material riches*. An abundant harvest may come, but we see God as more precious than this.

This walk is greater *than earthly fame*. We may lose the applause of men, and we may be maligned by the evil tongues of men, but if God is with us, all is well.

This life with God is greater *than earthly comfort*. We may sleep in the crevice of a rock, but we will rest in the greatest of safety if God is with us.

True Safety

What kind of preservation and care does God give His faithful ones?

It is a complete safety. The Hebrew word for "peace" is one of completeness. It is a peace that prevails over our total being.

It is a continual safety. We dwell in it. We have it day and night. At our times of greatest vulnerability—even when we lie down to sleep—we have it.

It is the strongest safety. The refuge of life is provided by the almighty God of heaven. He is mightier than any earthly force. He knows about every enemy that we may have, and He can make dust out of any army that will ever come against us.

There is no refuge like the one God gives.

God and Our Prayers

How does God receive the prayers of those who trust in Him? Three imperatives are used in this psalm that illustrate how He looks upon them. These imperatives are synonymous, but their shades of meaning give us a little more insight into God's actions.

He will hear us. That is, His ears are open to our prayers. He is eager to give us what we seek.

He will answer them. That is, He will grant our requests if those requests are in keeping with His will.

He will be gracious to us. That is, He will give us what we need and not what we deserve. Our requests will be greeted by His lovingkindness and not by a condemnation of our failures.

The Gladness of God

What is the basic nature of the saint's joy?

His joys do not come from this world. If all earthly blessings faded away, we could still have the highest joy—the happiness of heaven.

His joys do not come from ourselves. We do not have His gladness because we are good-looking, talented, or charming. God *gives* His happiness to His faithful ones.

His joys do not come from the best circumstances. True happiness is not dependent upon what happens.

The gladness of God springs from God Himself, not from who we are or from our circumstances. We are what we are, and we have what we have because of the goodness of God.

His joy springs from our relationship with Him. Peace does not result from plenty; it comes from piety, from a holy walk with God.

Music in the Christian Age

We have noticed that some of the psalms cannot be used today exactly the way they were written, for God has different requirements in the Christian Age than He had in the Mosaical Age. For example, He used animals sacrifices in the Old Testament period, but making such sacrifices at the temple is not His will in the "last days" Age. One notices also that He commands only singing in the worship of the New Testament church.

He asks that we make melody in the heart (see Eph. 5:19). A new instrument is employed—the human spirit. There is plucking, but it is in the twanging of the heart strings.

He asks that we sing. One searches in vain for instrumental music in the worship of the church; it cannot be found. He has brought in His new covenant which is to be written on the heart (Jer. 31:31). Singing involves the personality, the soul, and the physical lips. We worship with our hearts, not with our bodies.

He asks that we offer our praise to Him through the fruit of our lips. In Old Testament times, one would offer an animal as a sacrifice; but in the New Testament, one offers himself as a living sacrifice (Rom. 12:1, 2; Heb. 13:15).

He asks that we encourage and exhort one another through singing. We are to speak to one another in our singing (Eph. 5:19). Christianity is a "one another" religion. "We love, because He first loved us" (1 Jn. 4:19).

Sing a spiritual song to God today—a song that flows from the melody of your heart, a song that you send up to God, that offers the praise of your lips, and that encourages those around you.

PSALM 5

BRINGING THE DAY TO GOD

The Superscription: For the choir director; for flute accompaniment. A Psalm of David. The title describes this psalm as a Psalm [מִזְמוֹר, *mizmor*] of ["by," "for," or "to"] David (לְדָוִד, *lᵉdawid*). In the heading, directions are also given for the choir director (לַמְנַצֵּחַ, *lamnatstseach*) to lead it "to the nehiloth" (אֶל־הַנְּחִילוֹת, *'el hannᵉchiloth*). The meaning of "nehiloth" is uncertain. It may mean for flute accompaniment, or it may even be indicating the tune that is to be used.

This beautiful composition is a prayer/song to God for the morning. The writer is thinking especially of his troubles, such as the enemies around him and how God is his protection and refuge from them.

Thus the setting is that of a righteous man, probably David, who is encircled by devious and cruel men who, for some reason, are seeking his destruction. His prayer revolves around two relationships: his life with God and his response to his enemies.

We do not know when the psalm was written or the definite circumstances about which it speaks.

CRYING OUT TO GOD (5:1–3)

¹**Give ear to my words, O LORD,**
Consider my groaning.
²**Heed the sound of my cry for help, my King and my God,**
For to You I pray.
³**In the morning, O LORD, You will hear my voice;**

In the morning I will order my prayer to You and eagerly watch.

Verse 1. Intensity characterizes the writer's supplication to God. His earnestness and depth of feeling are seen in three synonymous appeals for God to hear his prayer. He pleads, **Give ear to my words, consider my groaning,** and **heed the sound of my cry for help**. He is motivated by an anxious heart, by an inner desperation.

Verse 2. He identifies the One to whom he prays as his **King** and his **God**. The true King, the One who reigns over all things, is God. He says, **For to You I pray**. He brings his dilemma to the Supreme One, the Sovereign of the universe. He knows that the righteous are linked with the God of all creation!

Verse 3. He promises, **In the morning . . . You will hear my voice**. The day will not be permitted to begin without his talking to God. At the dawn of the day, he **will order** his prayer or lay out his plea before God. The word עָרַךְ (*'arak*) means to "prepare" or "arrange." The word "prayer" does not appear in the Hebrew text; it is supplied by the translators on the basis that the flow of thought confirms that "his prayer" is the understood subject of the sentence. He seeks to place his requests in order as one would arrange a sacrifice on an altar or as a captain would array his soldiers for battle.

After he has prayed, he says he will **eagerly watch** for an answer to be given. His resolve is expressed in one word in the Hebrew: צָפָה (*tsapah*). The word is in the intensive form, which has caused the NASB translators to add the word "eagerly" to it. He expects an answer and will wait with great anticipation for it. Prayer is not speaking into the air, but it is entering into a conversation with almighty God with intimacy and expectancy. Full belief that he will be heard characterizes his prayer.

GOD AND EVIL (5:4–6)

**⁴For You are not a God who takes pleasure in wickedness;
No evil dwells with You.
⁵The boastful shall not stand before Your eyes;**

You hate all who do iniquity.
⁶You destroy those who speak falsehood;
The LORD abhors the man of bloodshed and deceit.

Verse 4. The truth that God only hears the prayers of the righteous is the heart of this psalm. He finds no **pleasure in wickedness**, and **no evil dwells** in Him. "Evil" does not have a home with Him; it is an unwelcome guest in His presence. True prayer can only occur when a righteous person approaches the righteous God.

Verses 5, 6. The writer further prays, **The boastful shall not stand before Your eyes**. Moving from the general to the specific, he names the people who should not ask for an audience or a dwelling place with God. The "boastful," the ones who trust in their own strength, should not make such a request. Those who "do iniquity," those who cause trouble, need not apply. The people who "speak falsehood," who tell lies and mislead others, will not be permitted a place before Him. God does not admit people of "bloodshed and deceit," those who accomplish their designs by hurting or destroying others for their own personal gain.

The psalmist speaks of God possessing righteous hatred. **You hate all who do iniquity.** God combines the person doing the "iniquity" with the sin itself. From this viewpoint, God hates them.

God not only abhors "bloodshed and deceit," but He seeks to destroy it. His prayer acknowledges, **You destroy those who speak falsehood; the LORD abhors the man of bloodshed and deceit.** God does not want these twin evils to exist, and in His own ways He eliminates them. He "abhors" or despises the mistreatment of others and disdains "deceit," the misleading of others. God loves all people. He has a divine respect for them and wants each human being to be treated fairly.

THE RIGHTEOUS AND GOD (5:7, 8)

⁷But as for me, by Your abundant lovingkindness I will enter Your house,

At Your holy temple I will bow in reverence for You.
⁸O LORD, lead me in Your righteousness because of my foes;
Make Your way straight before me.

Verse 7. With an awareness of his sinfulness, the psalmist affirms the true avenue of approach to God: **But as for me, by Your abundant lovingkindness I will enter Your house.** He comes into God's presence conscious of His "abundant lovingkindness." Only on the basis of such great mercy could he possibly offer acceptable worship to God. He uses the word "lovingkindness," or "steadfast love," a word of major significance in the Psalms and in the entire Old Testament. The word is חֶסֶד (*chesed*) which the NRSV usually translates as "steadfast love" and the NIV translates as "unfailing love." Norman H. Snaith has observed that it is usually translated as "mercy" or "lovingkindness" in English versions. He commented:

> *Chesed*, in all its varied shades of meaning, is conditional upon there being a covenant. Without the prior existence of a covenant, there could never be any *chesed* at all. . . .
> . . . The original use of the Hebrew *chesed* is to denote the attitude of loyalty and faithfulness which both parties to a covenant should observe towards each other.[1]

It is as if *chesed* has within it all the great attributes of God: grace, mercy, compassion, patience, faithfulness, loyalty, and love. A true follower of God is sometimes referred to as "a lovingkindness man" instead of by the common expression "a godly man" (Ps. 4:3). He is so designated because in his walk with God he has taken on this beautiful characteristic of God.

The writer makes a promise to God: **At Your holy temple I will bow in reverence for You.** His worship involves bowing "in reverence," acknowledging the awesome presence and power of God. He is not speaking of cringing fear but of a due recognition of who God is. He would come humbly to God, rec-

---

[1] Norman H. Snaith, *The Distinctive Ideas of the Old Testament* (London: The Epworth Press, 1957), 94, 95, 99.

ognizing Him as the Supreme Ruler and himself as His servant.

Verse 8. Coupled with his vow is a petition for guidance, **Lead me in Your righteousness because of my foes.** Confused about what to do, he beseeches God to make the right way plain to him. **Make Your way straight before me,** he pleads. He wants God's way to be laid out before him where he can easily see it and walk in it. Since evil men seek his destruction, he wants to be sure that he will be pursuing God's righteous way. Minds that might have become clouded with hatred and bitterness need the way of God placed before them.

EVIL MEN FURTHER DESCRIBED (5:9, 10)

⁹**There is nothing reliable in what they say;**
Their inward part is destruction itself;
Their throat is an open grave;
They flatter with their tongue.
¹⁰**Hold them guilty, O God;**
By their own devices let them fall!
In the multitude of their transgressions thrust them out,
For they are rebellious against You.

Verse 9. Continuing his description of the evil men around him, he says, **There is nothing reliable in what they say; their inward part is destruction itself; their throat is an open grave; they flatter with their tongue.** Paul in Romans 3:13 used this portrayal, which emphasizes the foul mouth, the violent hands, and the destructive heart of the wicked person, as part of his picture of the sinfulness of the Gentiles.

The wicked are unreliable (unfaithful in speech), for "there is nothing reliable in what they say." No one can depend on what comes out of their mouths. These men have wicked hearts, for "their inward part is destruction itself." The source of their evil is the well of wickedness deep within them.

They have vile tongues. It is as if "their throat is an open grave," for when they open their mouths deadly things come out. They use their lips falsely as "they flatter [others] with their tongue[s]." They stretch the truth for their own personal profit.

Verse 10. His prayer takes on the spirit of an imprecatory prayer as he prays, **Hold them guilty, O God.** Evil demands punishment, and he calls upon God to allow the evil ones to suffer the effects of their sin. **By their own devices let them fall.** His rationale is God Himself, **for they are rebellious against You.** In their defiance, they have hurt God's cause and brought pain to innocent people. Therefore, he prays, **In the multitude of their transgressions thrust them out.** Appropriately, they should have to answer for their sins by experiencing their consequences. Perhaps this suffering is the only way that they could learn the error and evil of their rebellion.

This spirit of prayer corresponds with the spirit of the Old Testament Era. It was appropriate for a godly man to utter an imprecation (a curse-like expression) concerning the wicked (see Josh. 6). His loyalty to God and to his physical nation pitted his heart against those who would do damage to God's cause and people. Faithfulness demanded that he oppose and set himself against anyone who aggressively sought to destroy God's people or God's plan for the world. Oftentimes the only way for him to oppose such evil was to ask God to handle it with His righteous hand of judgment.

In contrast to this Old Testament attitude, because of the nature of the spiritual kingdom of the church, Jesus has instructed His followers to fight the wicked with the sword of the Spirit and grace and to leave vengeance with the Lord (Mt. 5:39, 40).

THE RIGHTEOUS MAN'S FUTURE
(5:11, 12)

> ¹¹**But let all who take refuge in You be glad,**
> **Let them ever sing for joy;**
> **And may You shelter them,**
> **That those who love Your name may exult in You.**
> ¹²**For it is You who blesses the righteous man, O LORD,**
> **You surround him with favor as with a shield.**

Verse 11. As the writer closes the psalm, he turns in his prayer to all who find security in God. He asks that the righteous may become keenly aware of their blessings and rejoice in the great grace they have received.

He says, **Let all who take refuge in You be glad.** Whoever benefits from God's protective hand should recognize what shelter he has received and pray with thanksgiving and happiness about it. He further asks that such blessed ones may **ever sing for joy.** His prayer is that they might see their blessings and continually value them and rejoice over them.

Appealing to God for these faithful ones, he prays, **And may You shelter them, that those who love Your name may exult in You.** Acknowledging our superlative gifts from His hand will result in our loving His "name" and exulting in Him, the giver of all these good things. The name of God represents God, and loving his name would be tantamount to loving God. His name is holy to the ones who love Him.

God should always be approached with praise. It is only appropriate that those who have been sheltered by God's strong arm should "exult in" or praise Him joyously. Praise is extolling God because, by His might and greatness, He has provided for His people. Prayer is not complete until God has been praised.

Verse 12. Continual praise is fitting, **for it is [God] who blesses the righteous man.** He is the source of all the wondrous, spiritual realities that have come to the faithful.

We can be sure of this one truth: God puts His favor upon the righteous person. Having experienced such grace, he can testify with confidence, **You surround him with favor as with a shield.** The "shield" is the large shield that covers almost the entire body. Two types of shields were used in Old Testament times: a small one (מָגֵן, *magen*) that could be held on one's arm and a large one (צִנָּה, *tsinnah*) that could be carried by a servant or by the soldier himself. The large one, designed to protect the entire body, is referred to here. The bountiful favors of God surround the righteous man as a protective shield covers the soldier. He puts a canopy of blessings around the righteous man which may not be visible to the physical eye, but they are present and are as real as any physical blessing.

APPLICATION

The Right Heart for Prayer
Praying to God comes out of the soil of a special kind of life.

A life of integrity. Prayer should go up from a spirit in whom there is no guile.

A life of godliness. A child should favor his parent, and a follower of God should resemble God.

A life of righteousness. The wicked man cannot know the joy of communion with God. He can mouth phrases into the air, but he cannot sincerely pray.

Prayer is a spiritual communion that occurs with the holy God who can neither sin nor be tempted to sin. He dwells in light and truth, and no one who walks in darkness can have fellowship with Him (1 Jn. 1:5).

How Do We Pray?
An outline for prayer arises here. How does one learn to pray? The best way is to listen to the praying of someone who knows God and knows how to pray. When we think about God and His grace, we will naturally talk to Him in a certain way.

We will pray with earnestness. In dire difficulties, we will understand that only God can help us. We will pray with fervency, because we know that God will hear our pleas.

We will pray in faith and purity. God is holy and asks that His people be holy. The communion of prayer grows out of trust in God and a pure life before Him.

We will pray with rejoicing, praise, and gratitude. When one talks to God, he is talking to One who has always been with him. As he opens his mouth to pray, he cannot help but think of who God is, what He has done for him, and the privilege of knowing Him and walking with Him.

Righteous prayers to the God of righteousness are the key to the day and a lock for the night.

The Great Word: God's Lovingkindness
One of the cornerstone words of the Old Testament is *chesed*, or lovingkindness. It describes the character of God. Using this

word as our answer, let us ask, "What is God like?"

He is a God of loyalty. He will always be faithful to His people. They can put their total trust in this truth.

He is a God of covenant loyalty. He will keep the covenant that He has made with us. A rainbow of promise encircles His throne.

He is a God of compassionate loyalty. His loyalty to the covenant He has made with His people is mingled with grace and mercy. His supreme kindness, however, is extended only within the sphere of His covenant.

The entire character of God can almost be summarized with this one word, "lovingkindness."

The Gain of the Righteous Man

What does God do for the righteous man?

God keeps His covenant with him. His faithfulness is expressed in a new fashion every morning. His people, as righteous people, have entered into an agreement with Him, and they rest all their hopes on His integrity.

God answers his prayers. The writer of this psalm says that he will eagerly wait for God's answers. His spirit indicates that he fully expects God to answer him. He is not presumptuous; God is complimented when His child is confident of His integrity.

God permits him to enter His house for worship. Through His lovingkindness, the righteous man can worship God and have the joy of knowing that his worship has been accepted.

God provides a refuge for him in the time of trouble. He is our shelter and rock of security.

In summary, *God surrounds the righteous like a large shield with all kinds of spiritual blessings and protection.* Actually, who can list all the benefits of serving God?

God and the Evil Man

What can be said about the evil man?

We can say that *the evil man cannot dwell in the presence of God.* A big chasm stands between God and the evil man. God does not permit him to enter into His courts.

Further, *the evil man will usually have to suffer the consequences of his sin.* Not only will he probably be punished by his sins; but if he is not penitent, he will one day be punished for his sins.

The evil man is destructive of God's cause and of innocent people. Evil men are a vile force on earth that hurts God and others.

In addition to all this, *God abhors what the evil man does.* Evil is in conflict with God's personality; and consequently, God is at war with it.

A Future with God

What does the righteous man have to look forward to if he continues his walk with God?

He will have joy. He will have a God-given inner music of the soul that will saturate his personality.

He will be sheltered by the strong arm of God. His God will provide for him, granting him His provisions and protection.

He will be surrounded by the broad favors of the Lord. The shield covered the soldier's whole body, and God's favors will cover the faithful one's whole person.

The writer was sure that the Lord would provide joy, security, and favor for the righteous man; and the same belief must undergird us.

Evil in Mankind

The writer of this psalm describes the sinfulness of man, a description that is quoted by Paul in Romans 1. How does evil show up in mankind?

It appears first in the heart. The writer says that "their inward part is destruction itself" (v. 9). Sin surfaces first in the imaginations and thoughts of the spirit.

It appears next on the tongue. "Their throat is an open grave"; "they flatter" others; "there is nothing reliable in what they say" (v. 9). What is down in the well of the heart will eventually come up in the bucket of speech.

It appears in the hands. They become men of violence and bloodshed. The wickedness of Noah's day is seen in two headings: the imagination of the heart and the violence of the hands.

Evil will attack and bring under its awful dominion the heart, the tongue, and the hands. In summary, flowing from the inner man are words, deeds, and meditations that God abhors, a life that God will not permit in His presence, and a person whom sin will ultimately destroy.

The Righteous Man's Joy

The joy of the righteous man has three dimensions.

The joy over what God has done. When we face hard trials, we find joy in contemplating what God has done for us in the past. We know that God will help us today the same way He helped yesterday (Ps. 3:3, 4).

The joy over what God is doing. God puts gladness in our hearts as we walk with Him. This joy is more precious than material gains that we might have (Ps. 4:7, 8).

The joy over what God will do. He will be our refuge tomorrow and in all the days to come. The prophets could not see clearly what was coming. However, they knew that it would be glorious, and they rejoiced in it (Ps. 5:11; 1 Pet. 1:10, 11). We can do the same.

Praying Through the Day

The Christian is told to pray "without ceasing," or continually (1 Thess. 5:17). In the Psalms special reference is made to praying at key times during the day.

In the morning. In this psalm praying in the morning is mentioned. The writer resolves to commit the day to God. He is concerned about his own safety, and he seeks God's protection for those hours ahead. Every day should begin with God. The day is fragile; we need to handle it with prayer.

At noon. Psalm 55:17 refers to praying at noon. The middle part of the day calls for prayer. We tend to relax at noon, thinking, "I have this day under control"; however, we have much yet to do, and we need our Father with us.

In the evening. Psalm 4 is a prayer that closes the day in communion with God. One should turn over the day and the coming night to God. We are never more helpless than when we are asleep. The One who "never slumbers or sleeps" is asked to watch over the writer. We need to make the same request.

Let us pray, for we need God in the morning, at noon, and at nighttime—and all the times in between!

PSALM 6

SICK BECAUSE OF SIN

The Superscription: For the choir director; with stringed instruments, upon an eight-string lyre. A Psalm of David. The heading says that this piece is **a Psalm** [מִזְמוֹר, *mizmor*] **of** ["by," "for," or "to"] **David** (לְדָוִד, *ledawid*). The overseer or leader (לַמְנַצֵּחַ, *lamnatstseach*) of music is addressed in the heading with the direction that the song is to be sung **with stringed instruments** [בִּנְגִינוֹת, *binginoth*], **upon an eight** (עַל־הַשְּׁמִינִית, *al hashsheminith*). The "eight" may be a reference to a stringed lyre or to an octave lower (such as bass voices) or something similar. These are obscure terms, and probably the best we can do is guess at their meanings.

Here is a cry of anguish, arising from the heart of a man who is ill because of sin (or sins) that he has committed. His transgression has found him out in the form of a physical malady; and in his grief, he beseeches God for mercy.

Because of its subject matter, this psalm is regarded as one of the penitential psalms. These are psalms that express repentance and sorrow over sin (see 32; 38; 51; 102; 130; 143).

We do not know the specific affliction of the writer. It could be a sickness resulting from his sin, which he regards as a judgment of God. His knowledge of evil men who hear of his ailing condition and are glad he is sick intensifies his condition. Perhaps these men wish that he would get worse or maybe even die. Three problems—discouragement, sickness, and the receiving of hate-mail—add up to a big problem.

The psalm falls into four parts: his plea for grace (vv. 1–3), the basis of his plea (vv. 4, 5), his deplorable condition (vv. 6, 7), and his confidence before God (vv. 8–10). His appeal to God is an individual lament that emerges in the latter part of the psalm into an expression of confident faith.

ASKING FOR GRACE (6:1–3)

¹O Lord, do not rebuke me in Your anger,
Nor chasten me in Your wrath.
²Be gracious to me, O Lord, for I am pining away;
Heal me, O Lord, for my bones are dismayed.
³And my soul is greatly dismayed;
But You, O Lord how long?

Sickness is not necessarily the result of a sin, as is illustrated by the Book of Job (see Job 42:7–10). However, in this writer's case, his sin has brought about his illness.

Verse 1. Since his sickness is connected with sin, the writer rightly approaches God with a plea for mercy. Thus he begins by asking for God's compassion instead of His condemnation. He says, **O Lord, do not rebuke me in Your anger.** He is asking God to show His mercy and to ease the rebuke of his soul by either removing the sickness or tempering His wrath. The additional phrase, **Nor chasten me in Your wrath,** is synonymous with the previous one and suggests that he sees God's wrath as coming down upon his sin in the form of this illness. He does not want to face the fierce wrath of God or to experience the discipline of God while He is still hot with anger. He wants God to see his remorse and deal with him as a loving father, accepting back his returning, wayward son. Seeing his sickness as chastisement from God, the writer acknowledges that he has learned from his sinfulness and is now asking for grace.

Verse 2. He describes his condition to God with this plea: **Be gracious to me, O Lord.** He sees himself drained physically, spiritually, and emotionally. Physically, he is **pining away;** that is, he is withered and languishing. He says that his **bones are dismayed.** The reference to his bones is a figurative survey of his whole physical body. He may be saying, as we do, "My body aches all over!"

Verse 3. Adding the spiritual dimension, he says, **And my**

soul is greatly dismayed. Affected by his sin, he has undergone an emotional devastation.

He asks God how long all of this will continue. **But You, O Lord how long?** This plaintive cry, "How long must I continue to suffer?" is the question that legions of sufferers have asked in the midst of their dark night of pain. This writer's query, however, may be more like, "How much discipline is enough, Lord?"

THE BASIS OF HIS PLEA (6:4, 5)

⁴Return, O Lord, rescue my soul;
Save me because of Your lovingkindness.
⁵For there is no mention of You in death;
In Sheol who will give You thanks?

Verse 4. The bottom line of the writer's plea for grace is this: **Return, O Lord, rescue my soul.** His trouble is so deep and destructive that he knows that only God can reclaim him. His trouble calls for divine surgery; God's grace is the only solution.

He bases his petition for forgiveness and life upon three important truths: his repentance, God's lovingkindness, and his intentions for the future. His repentance is never clearly stated; it is only implied. The fact that he is calling upon God for grace infers repentance. Furthermore, a penitent heart is indicated by his asking God to let him live so that he might praise Him.

He knows he cannot plead with God on the basis of his noble life or perfect qualities, for he has neither of these. Therefore, he pleads, **Save me because of Your lovingkindness.** He asks God to answer his prayer not according to his sin but according to God's wondrous grace.

He realizes that the solution to his dilemma lies only in God's forgiveness. He is fully aware of the kind of attributes that God has—great lovingkindness and marvelous grace. It is God's nature to forgive and receive sinners, and how welcome that thought is to this sinner!

Verse 5. The third basis for his plea is that God may have one more person to praise Him on earth. He says, **For there is**

no mention of You in death. "I have been to the cemeteries, and I know how silent they are! You cannot hear anyone there praising You," he is saying. He further says, **In Sheol who will give You thanks?** "Sheol" is the Hebrew word in the Old Testament for the grave. The LXX has translated שְׁאוֹל (*sh^e'ol*) with "Hades" (ᾅδης, *hadēs*), the Greek word for the place the spirit goes at death.

He pleads for God to grant him a future opportunity to serve Him. If God chooses to let him live, He will have one other person on this earth to praise and serve Him. The dead cannot praise God on earth; the grave cannot thank God among men. Therefore, if God wants someone else voicing His praise, he needs to be raised up from his sickness.

HIS DEPLORABLE CONDITION (6:6, 7)

⁶I am weary with my sighing;
Every night I make my bed swim,
I dissolve my couch with my tears.
⁷My eye has wasted away with grief;
It has become old because of all my adversaries.

Verse 6. He continues to describe his condition before God. **I am weary with my sighing.** He has groaned and ached so much that he is exhausted from it. He weeps throughout the night and makes his **bed swim** with tears. Liquid sorrow flows from his eyes continually, even while he is trying to rest. It is as if his **couch** is melting from the water of his **tears.** Poetic exaggeration is used to describe the continuation and heaviness of his grief.

Verse 7. His eyes reflect his pain and mourning. The writer says, **My eye has wasted away with grief.** That is, he has worn out his eyes from his crying. Like Jeremiah, he has cried so much that he cannot cry anymore (Jer. 9:1). His eyes have been so full of tears that they cannot function any longer. He says that his eye **has become old because of all** [his] **adversaries.** The criticism, the vicious remarks of his enemies, has so bothered him that he has wept profusely.

His enemies add to his anguish by perhaps wishing for his death. They may be using his sickness as a reason for saying that he has been rejected by the Lord. "He is dying because of his sin. God has disowned him, and he deserves it," they may be saying. Such misery that he is facing has depleted his energies and strength. He has come down to the very bottom, and he has no place to turn but to God.

HIS RESOLVE BEFORE GOD (6:8–10)

**⁸Depart from me, all you who do iniquity,
For the Lord has heard the voice of my weeping.
⁹The Lord has heard my supplication,
The Lord receives my prayer.
¹⁰All my enemies will be ashamed and greatly dismayed;
They shall turn back, they will suddenly be ashamed.**

The psalmist has prayed with confident faith and believes that God has heard his prayer. Perhaps he has seen evidence that God is answering his prayer, or in his praying he has been reminded of how gracious God is.

The song/prayer ends on a high note of assurance, on the accepted fact that God will deal with his problem or has already done so. A robust assurance of faith is evident.

Verse 8. He says, **Depart from me, all you who do iniquity**. The Lord is coming to his rescue. He has this confidence because he believes **the Lord has heard the voice of** [his] **weeping.** God has seen his tears and has heard them. The wording here must not be overlooked: "the voice of my weeping." Tears speak eloquently—not only to us, but also to God. In Psalm 56:8 the writer pleads for God to put his tears in a bottle and remember his sufferings. Nothing can be more encouraging to the suffering person than to know that God sees and hears his anguish!

Verse 9. The writer uses three expressions in verses 8 and 9 to affirm that he believes the Lord will hear his prayer: God "heard the voice of [his] weeping," **heard** [his] **supplication**, and **receives** [his] **prayer**. Each of these is part of a synonymous parallelism. Twice he uses the word "heard" (שָׁמַע, *shama'*), once in verse 8 and once here; and once he uses the word "receives" (לָקַח, *laqach*). The phrases combine to express his faith in what is happening in response to his prayers. He warns his enemies to cease their taunting and to keep their distance, for God will deliver him through His lovingkindness. Either he has seen evidence of God's hearing, or he is expressing the confidence of faith that He would. The latter must be the case. Therefore, the psalm has turned from a lament into a psalm of confidence, from a cry of pain to a song of praise.

Verse 10. He believes that **all [his] enemies will be ashamed and greatly dismayed.** Due to God's answer, these enemies will be subdued and vanquished. He has complete assurance in his heart that God will respond to his prayer and that his enemies will be rebuked for what they have done to him.

He says that his enemies **shall turn back,** and **they will suddenly be ashamed.** When they see God's glorious answer, an answer of grace and forgiveness, they will be overwhelmed with embarrassment over their wicked taunts.

APPLICATION

God's Rebuke

God has told us that He will rebuke His children when they need it (Heb. 12:8). Every faithful father does the same for his children. How does God rebuke us?

He does it through His Word. His Word is sharper than a sword and goes to our innermost being (Heb. 4:12; 2 Tim. 3:16).

He does it through other believers. We are to exhort, restore, and encourage one another (Heb. 3:13; Gal. 6:2).

He does it by allowing us to experience the consequences of our sins. The writer interprets his condition as discipline from the Lord (Ps. 6:1, 2).

Children receive the discipline of God; the unbeliever does not. Should we not be glad that God corrects us through His gracious love and brings us back to faithful service when we need it? "For those whom the Lord loves He disciplines" (Heb. 12:6).

When Sin Makes Us Sick

We may think that God wants to ignore us when we suffer because of our mistakes. The world says that God would be more inclined to say, "That serves you right!" than, "Bring your problem to Me, My child!" The psalmist believes the latter view of God.

This psalm illustrates how we need to pray when we are hurting due to our own waywardness. We must resolve to repent (vv. 4, 5), ask for grace (vv. 1–3, 6, 7), and trust in God to answer us according to His lovingkindness (vv. 8–10). Then, after praying in this fashion, we must set out to keep the promises we have made to God.

The writer prays confidently, earnestly, penitently, and sincerely. We can rest assured that when we come to God in humble repentance and contrite obedience, He will hear us.

The Plea for God's Mercy

The writer wants God's mercy, but he cannot plead for it on the basis of his own faithfulness or perfection. He can only make such a request on the basis of three truths.

The first truth is the pure lovingkindness of God. He knows God answers according to His grace and not according to sin.

Second is his repentance and sorrow for his sin. This truth is implied by the psalm. God will forgive sins when the sinner forsakes them.

The third truth is that God would have one more person praising Him on earth. If God allows him to die, He would have one less person on earth making known in joyful appreciation what He has done for sinners.

It is wonderful to contemplate what God is like, for such contemplation encourages us to walk with Him. God wants our fellowship and love. He is our father and wants to lead us to our eternal home with Him.

Sin's Poison

This psalm reminds us of how sin affects us—inside and out.

It can impact us physically. Apparently, a physical affliction because of sin is the background of the psalm. David's body was suffering the trauma of a sickness brought on by sin.

It can wreck us emotionally. His couch was swimming with tears. His spirit had been discouraged and his heart broken by what he had done.

It can affect us relationally. His enemies found the occasion of his sin to speak ill of him and further tear down his life and reputation. They might have wanted to be rid of him; and as they heard of his sickness, they rejoiced, hoping that he might die.

Sin does not favor anyone, and it exerts a destructive force on almost every part of our personalities.

Questions and Faith

A faithful servant of God may ask questions of God. He does not question God, but he does ask questions about His ways when those ways seem unclear.

Job asked God, "Why do righteous men suffer?" In his pain, he said, in effect, "I want to talk to God" (Job 13:3). Eventually, Job got his opportunity to talk to God, but God's answer was, "You will have to trust Me!" (Job 39—41).

David asked God, "How long will I have to suffer?" (Ps. 6:3). He asked this question in light of the mercy and longsuffering of God. We do not know what answer was given to his question.

Habakkuk asked God, "When will You do something about the sin that is around me?" He saw evil, and he did not see God doing anything about it (Hab. 1:3). He brought his question to God and was told that soon he would see what God was doing about it.

The questions "Why?"; "How long?"; and "When?" are questions that come to our minds when we meditate upon the ways of God. They should be expressions of faith, not of doubt.

Confidence in God

A change of mood appears toward the end of this psalm. Is it because the writer is confident that God will act in his behalf, or has he in some way already seen God's answer? It appears to be the former. The writer is rejoicing already in the answer that he knows he will receive from God. This thought makes us think of the confidence of the great, faithful ones of the Scriptures.

Abraham's confidence in God during the sacrifice of Isaac. He said to the servants, "I and the lad will go over there; and we will worship and return to you" (Gen. 22:5). He believed that God would raise Isaac from the dead in order to fulfill the promises made to him (Heb. 11:19).

Mary's confidence when told she would be the mother of the Messiah. She asked, "How can this be . . . ?" (Lk. 1:34). Her question seems to be different from Zacharias'—his was of doubt, and hers was of faith.

This psalmist's confidence in God when surrounded by enemies. He says, in effect, "You, my enemies, will be disbanded and sent on your way. You will be embarrassed over what you have done."

Why should we not be confident in God? He has never lied; He is almighty in power; He is full of lovingkindness; He is all-knowing; He has not and will not change. His love for us is a fact, not a fairy tale. Do we not believe the song, "Earth has no sorrow that heaven cannot heal"?

The Two Sides of Death

What are the two sides of death?

One can view death from earth's side—from the world of activity and relationships. The writer in verse 5 is expressing this view when he says that the grave is silent and there is no giving of thanks in Sheol. When one makes his journey to the other side, he must leave behind his work here and his relationship with God among the people of this earth.

One can view death from heaven's side—from the world of being in God's presence with the redeemed. One writer said, "Precious in the sight of the Lord is the death of His godly ones" (Ps. 116:15). We see the departure; God sees the arrival. We see a loss; God sees the gain.

When we lose a loved one, we often look at just one side of death, *our* side. We see *our* losses and pain. When we look at *that* side in addition to *our* side, we see our loved one's gain and success. Looking at *that* side will make our bearing of the grief easier and our longing for heaven more intense.

PSALM 7

THE PAIN OF SLANDER

The Superscription: A Shiggaion of David, which he sang to the LORD concerning Cush, a Benjamite. According to the title, this psalm is **a Shiggaion** [שִׁגָּיוֹן, *shiggayon*] **of** ["by," "for," or "to"] **David** (לְדָוִד, *lᵉdawid*). "Shiggaion," a unique designation, probably means something like "highly emotional." It can suggest great joy or great sorrow; in this case it conveys a supreme heartbreak. This particular form of the word occurs only here in the Old Testament. The plural form is found in Habakkuk 3:1.

The "historic" element of the superscription attempts to describes the setting behind the psalm. It says that this song is one that David **sang to the LORD concerning Cush, a Benjamite.** If this part of the title is accurate, the occasion that gave rise to the psalm is a time when slanderous charges were brought against David by a man named Cush, a Benjamite, during that period of David's life when he was being hunted by Saul (1 Sam. 24; 25). We have no additional information on this man Cush. He is not mentioned any other place in the Old Testament. The word "Benjamite" (בֶּן־יְמִינִי, *ben yᵉmini*), a tribal designation, is given as two words, "son of Jemini," and means "son of right" or "son of my right hand."

This superscription suggests a trial situation about which the psalm could have been written. Let us regard it as conveying the kind of background that must have been behind the psalm.

David was probably accused by Cush of trying to kill King Saul. The slander was groundless. On two occasions when David had the opportunity to kill Saul, he had nobly refused (1 Sam. 24:10; 26:16–21). He regarded the king as the Lord's anointed and believed that it would be wrong for him to harm him. This malicious slander cut David deeply, degrading his honor and breaking his spirit. Thus, in addition to being hounded unjustly almost daily by Saul and living as a fugitive, he was having to deal with lies that were being told about him.

The accusations were cutting and hurtful; they went deep into his heart and soul. Out of the agony of this mistreatment, out of injustice upon injustice, this psalm was written.

AN AWFUL TRIAL (7:1, 2)

¹**O LORD my God, in You I have taken refuge;**
Save me from all those who pursue me, and deliver me,
²**Or he will tear my soul like a lion,**
Dragging me away, while there is none to deliver.

Verse 1. The prayer begins with an affirmation about God: **O LORD my God, in You I have taken refuge.** A similar expression is found at the beginning of Psalms 11, 31, and 71. Earlier in his life, the writer had concluded that his real hope was in God, and he made a commitment to put his trust in Him and be under His protection. Now, acting in that relationship, he is calling upon God for assistance. His heart craves a place of comfort; he knows he will find such a place in the shelter of God.

He does not know the answer to his problem, but he knows he must lay the problem at the feet of his God. The words **Save me from all those who pursue me, and deliver me** indicate that he sees himself as being tracked by enemies and in serious trouble. We do not know who these adversaries are, but they must be men associated with Saul.

Verse 2. His heartache stems from a doubly trying situation. Saul and his men are pursuing him (1 Sam. 23). That is bad enough; but one of them, either Saul, Cush, or someone else, is especially frightening to David. He said, **He will tear my soul like a lion.** Given the opportunity, he will destroy David, as a lion tears up his prey. The lion metaphor appears frequently in the Psalms (10:9; 22:13; 35:17; 57:4). Though lions were common in Israel during biblical days, they are no longer in that region.

This terrifying enemy has great power and is cunning. David can see this man **dragging** [him] **away**, with no one around who

AN AFFIRMATION OF INNOCENCE
(7:3–5)

³O LORD my God, if I have done this,
If there is injustice in my hands,
⁴If I have rewarded evil to my friend,
Or have plundered him who without cause was my adversary,
⁵Let the enemy pursue my soul and overtake it;
And let him trample my life down to the ground
And lay my glory in the dust. Selah.

Verse 3. He follows his plea for help with a declaration of his innocence: **O LORD my God, if I have done this, if there is injustice in my hands.** . . . Deep emotion prompts his cry, "O LORD my God." A charge has been made against him, but he knows that he is free from guilt. As he claims integrity with a kind of oath formula, he is not asserting perfection; but he is saying that he is blameless regarding the accusation.

Verse 4. He uses three "ifs" to assert his blamelessness regarding the charges made: "if I have done this" (the deed of which I have been accused); "if there is injustice in my hands" (if I have treated anyone unfairly); **if I have rewarded evil to my friend** (if I have given mistreatment for kind consideration).

In connection with this last "if," he attaches an assertion: **Or have plundered him who without cause was my adversary.** The meaning of this last line is debated. It could mean, "Not only have I not injured a friend, but I have mercifully let my enemy escape from me at times." It could possibly mean, "If I have oppressed without cause him who is mine enemy. . . ." It might even mean, "If I have delivered him without cause who is my enemy. . . ." It must be that this is a line about the way David has treated Saul. If so, he is saying, "I have not plundered without cause the one who has pursued me." These remarks of self-exoneration are designed to present a conclusive case to God that he is innocent of any mistreatment of those around him.

Verse 5. In the language of poetic exaggeration, he expresses the intensity of his feelings by saying, in effect, "May I be killed by my enemy and trampled if I am not telling the truth." In a kind of oath of affirmation, he declares, **Let the enemy pursue my soul and overtake it**. He is so sure of his innocence that he invokes upon himself a violent death by the hand of the enemy if he is found to be guilty. **And let him trample my life down to the ground and lay my glory in the dust**. The destruction that David wills for himself involves not only his life but also that of his reputation. He is saying, "May my enemy not only take my life, but may he put my honor in the dust and make me die in shame."

Selah likely suggests the ending of the thought and calls for a careful noting of it. By this word, he may be insisting, "Stop and think about this."

A PLEA FOR DELIVERANCE (7:6–8)

>⁶Arise, O Lord, in Your anger;
>Lift up Yourself against the rage of my adversaries,
>And arouse Yourself for me; You have appointed judgment.
>⁷Let the assembly of the peoples encompass You,
>And over them return on high.
>⁸The Lord judges the peoples;
>Vindicate me, O Lord, according to my righteousness and
>   my integrity that is in me.

Verse 6. Using anthropomorphic language, he asks God to **arise** in His holy **anger** and act in his behalf. It is as if God has been asleep while this tragedy was taking place or sitting and indifferently watching the mistreatment of His servant. He says, **Lift up Yourself against the rage of my adversaries,** and this seems to be an even stronger expression than **Arise, O Lord**. He says, **Arouse Yourself for me; You have appointed judgment.**

The meaning is apparently this: "Awake in my behalf. Judgment is part of Your ways, and now is the time for You to render a judgment for me."

David's appeal is for God to rise up in His mighty power and take action against his enemies. The writer knows that God has not been unaware of his plight or disinterested in his trouble; this would be his figurative way of calling upon God to act in his behalf.

Verse 7. Conscious of his truthfulness, David asks God to gather an **assembly** of the righteous—from the peoples and nations of the earth—and vindicate his honor before that assembly. When the congregation has been convened, he wants God to bring him forth, and before them, judge his heart.

He asks God to come in judgment; and then he says, **And over them return on high**. This phrase means either he is to take his seat on the throne of judgment and render a verdict or he is to provide the judgment asked for and then return to His throne on high.

Verse 8. He recognizes the Lord as the true Judge of all: He is **the LORD** [who] **judges the peoples**. Therefore, he wants God to judge his heart, his **righteousness** and **integrity**. God knows his heart, and He will **vindicate** him by affirming that he has acted righteously.

His heart contains right attitudes and God's will, and thus he has an honest heart before God and mankind. However, only God can properly judge the condition of his heart; so he prays for God to do it.

A PLEA FOR EVIL TO END (7:9–11)

⁹O let the evil of the wicked come to an end, but establish the righteous;
For the righteous God tries the hearts and minds.
¹⁰My shield is with God,
Who saves the upright in heart.
¹¹God is a righteous judge,
And a God who has indignation every day.

Verse 9. He asks that **the evil of the wicked** be brought to an end and all **the righteous** be firmly planted in the way of truth. Wanting wickedness removed, he asks that the righteous be solidified through the Lord's protection, strength, and affirmation. He sees his own battle with evil as a part of the greater battle between righteousness and evil that is transpiring in the world. Having seen in his own life the wreck and ruin brought by wickedness, he prays that evil not be allowed to continue.

Where the NASB has **for the righteous God tries the hearts and minds,** the KJV says, "For the righteous God trieth the hearts and reins." In Old Testament times the heart was regarded as the organ of thought and will, and the reins (the kidneys) were considered the seat of the emotions. This phrase is a summary, figurative expression referring to a person's total being. God is the only One who can truly judge the inner being of any person. He judges or tries not only the actions but also the motives and thoughts of the heart.

Verse 10. He pictures God as his "shield" (מָגֵן, *magen*). This is the small shield that can be carried on the arm but is a mighty protection in battle. He says, **My shield is with God** or "rests with God."

Verse 11. God is the One who **saves the upright in heart** (v. 10), for he is **a righteous judge** who is fair, just, and indisputably accurate. God does possess **indignation,** but it is the kind that is appropriate and emerges from His holiness. His righteous wrath against evil is in existence **every day**. God's judicial anger against sin never rests.

BRING DOWN YOUR WRATH (7:12–16)

> ¹²If a man does not repent, He will sharpen His sword;
> He has bent His bow and made it ready.
> ¹³He has also prepared for Himself deadly weapons;
> He makes His arrows fiery shafts.
> ¹⁴Behold, he travails with wickedness,
> And he conceives mischief and brings forth falsehood.
> ¹⁵He has dug a pit and hollowed it out,
> And has fallen into the hole which he made.

¹⁶**His mischief will return upon his own head,
And his violence will descend upon his own pate.**

Verse 12. The writer makes clear in this psalm that the evil man can still repent; however, **if a man does not repent**, he will face the wrath of God.

God is ever ready to judge the wicked. The phrase **He has bent His bow and made it ready** (or fixed it) is a figurative way of saying that God stands prepared to answer sin. If the evil man does not repent or turn from his wicked way, God will sharpen His sword and cut him down. In fact, the psalmist depicts His bow as already bent to shoot arrows into him.

Verse 13. He approaches the field of battle armed and prepared. In fact, **He has also prepared for Himself deadly weapons**. His arrows are powerful and "deadly," for they are **fiery shafts**, like the fire-tipped arrows often used in fierce combat.

Verse 14. Approaching the thought from another viewpoint, David says that the wicked man will self-destruct. He uses three different metaphors. First, he says that evil comes to light through conception and birth. **Wickedness** is conceived, and the wicked man **travails** in the birth of it. **He conceives mischief and brings forth falsehood.** In his heart, he yields his intellect to do mischief, the growth process begins, and then the birth occurs, with "falsehood" being brought "forth" as the newborn child. The writer has taken the reader through the birth of a sin, which is like the sin that has affected him, the slander that has broken his heart and marred his reputation.

Verse 15. The second metaphor is that of digging a pit. The wicked man goes to great effort to entrap another: **He has dug a pit and hollowed it out**. He has made his pit deep, and it has been cleverly designed. However, one thing that he does not count on is that the pit will capture him, the one who constructed it. Haman was suspended upon the very gallows that he had built for Mordecai (Esther 7:10). With force and a powerful climax, the writer says that the wicked man has **fallen into the hole which he made** (see Prov. 28:10). Evil comes around and attacks the person who gave it birth.

Verse 16. The third figure is that of sin returning as a boomerang comes back to the one who threw it. He says that the **mischief** of the wicked man **will return upon his own head**. The violence he intends for others will come back to be his portion. Some versions (like the ASV) have, **And his violence will descend upon his own pate.** The word "pate" is an archaic word for "the crown of his head" (see the marginal reading in the NASB). The hurt he has willed for others will come down with smashing force upon the top of his head.

The self-destructive nature of sin is vividly illustrated. Perhaps no other psalm gives such an extensive picture of sin.

SINGING IN HIS TROUBLE (7:17)

¹⁷I will give thanks to the LORD according to His righteousness
And will sing praise to the name of the LORD Most High.

Verse 17. Though he has been followed, surrounded, and threatened by evil men, and though his name has been trampled in the dust by wicked designs, he praises the Lord in the confidence of faith. He gives thanks **to the LORD according to His righteousness.** When one is accused unfairly and deceptively, it brings joy to remember that God is a God of "righteousness" and truth. He will never side with evil and misrepresentation.

He also sees God as **the LORD Most High.** His might brings consolation to the righteous. "Most High" is the unique word עֶלְיוֹן (*'elyon*), which is a description/name of God that means "the exalted high One." He will praise Yahweh because He is supreme, and no other is like Him. He is the only true God.

In the midst of his trial, the writer could sing. Regardless of how dark the night is or how vicious his enemies are, the grace and goodness of God bring him hope and assurance.

APPLICATION

Godliness and Trouble
The righteous are not always free from trouble.
We have seen the wonderful hand of the providence of

God when He has graciously *delivered us from trouble*. Our breath is taken away when we contemplate what could have happened had it not been for God's help.

However, God may not spare us *from* the fiery furnace; He may choose to walk *in* it with us. God does not always *isolate* the righteous from evil in the world; He may *insulate* them from it. We are not free from physical death, but Jesus promised that death would not hurt us (Jn. 11:27). The righteous will, as Isaiah said, pass through the fire, but it will not hurt them (Is. 43:2).

We can rejoice in the Lord, for He has delivered us *from* some difficulties and He has taken us *through* other difficulties. In each case, we have been protected by His powerful hand.

The Order of Faith

We see in this psalm an order to faith. There is a line of response to believing in God.

First, there is commitment. The writer first says, "I have made You, O God, my refuge." This "making" God his refuge reveals a choice, a decision.

Second, there is calling upon God for help. "In light of the commitment I have made," the writer says, "I am calling upon You for strength during this time of trouble."

Third, there is trust or confidence. The end of the psalm expresses the confidence in God that a believer should have.

The order of faith, then, according to this psalm, is commitment, calling, and confidence.

Words That Hurt

Implied in the psalm is the truth that slander is hard to bear. False accusations bring pain and frustration. They shoot arrows into us and cripple us.

The maxim "words can never hurt us" simply is not true. When we are dedicated to honesty and transparency before God, false words about us can cut us as deeply as beatings and stonings do.

We can cut another's throat with our words. Words can be vicious missiles of destruction.

Handling Slander

What can we learn from this example to help us during those times we are slandered? Shining through the words of this psalm is the spirit that godly people can and should have when maligned by evildoers.

False accusations cause pain. David was beleaguered and broken by words. Acid words burn and scar.

Those who are slandered should take their problems to God (vv. 1, 2). God is the only real refuge. He is stronger than people's wagging tongues.

God will vindicate the righteous sooner or later (vv. 3–8). The evil ones will be found out, but the righteous will be exonerated.

The law of retribution works with exactness (vv. 9–16). The consequences of sin will hunt down sinners with precision.

In the midst of trouble, believers can sing (v. 17). Regardless of how dark the night is, we can sing about God's goodness. The attributes of God should encourage any discouraged believer.

Managing Mistreatment

Here is a short seminar for the believer on managing mistreatment.

We should put our defense in His hands. All will be brought into judgment by the Lord. He is the only true and impartial Judge.

We should remember that the wicked will self-destruct. Their evil will one day come down upon their own heads. Vengeance belongs to the Lord, not to people. God has arrows of His own that He sends forth at the wicked.

We should praise God even in the midst of our troubles because we know that God is our refuge. God is stronger than all, knows all, and is the ultimate Judge of all.

The Future of the Evil Man

Two futures await the evil man that are brought about by two types of retribution.

As a general rule, he will be punished by his sins in this life. The evil man will fall into the pit that he has dug for others.

Certainly, he will be punished for his sins by the Lord at a time of

His choosing. He has faced the judgment of his sin, but he will also face the judgment of God.

There are two courts before which the evil man must be brought: the court of his sin and the court of the righteous God. He will one day discover that evil really does not pay.

What Is Evil Like?

View carefully these three metaphoric pictures of evil.

First, evil is a horrible birth. As we picture a birth, it is usually within the confines of a beautiful beginning, but here we see a tragic ending. There is the conception, the development, and the awful coming to life of evil. Sin is born of evil parents; its life will do the work of evil. The writer names the child "falsehood." He is hurt and devastated by the child (see Jas. 1:14, 15).

Second, evil is sometimes expressed as a vicious trap, as a pit that is dug for others. The pit is something like what a hunter or trapper would use to snare a wild animal. The designer of the trap, however, has dug the pit for a person, not an animal. The pit is created to hurt, destroy, and deceive.

Third, it is a boomerang. Sin has a way of swiftly returning and landing at the feet of the person who sends it out.

God and Evil

How does God see evil? How does He act toward it?

He sees evil as a destructive force to those who live it and to those who experience the results of it. In other words, He sees evil for what it is—vicious, demeaning, and devastating. Sin is hurtful, not because it is forbidden; it is forbidden because it is hurtful.

If they do not repent, He will punish those who give birth to evil. One day the evil ones will receive their judgment. God's judgment of sin is illustrated with Adam and Eve, Jericho, the Canaanites, and the great flood. As a righteous God, He can do nothing other than condemn evil and those who embed themselves in it.

He will protect the righteous from evil if they yield to Him. He will be their refuge. Sin cannot get to us if we are hidden in God through Christ; however, it can destroy anyone who ventures out of the divine shelter.

Psalm 8
The Majestic Name of God

The Superscription: For the choir director; on the Gittith. A Psalm of David. This heading says that this is **a Psalm** [מִזְמוֹר, *mizmor*] of ["by," "for," or "to"] **David** (לְדָוִד, *ledawid*). It was obviously meant to be a hymn of praise, and it has become one of the most well-known expressions of adoration of God in the entire Book of Psalms.

The psalm is inscribed **For the choir director** [לַמְנַצֵּחַ, *lamnatstseach*]; **on** [עַל, *'al*] **the Gittith** (גִּתִּית, *Giththith*). The word, "Gittith," is also found in the headings of Psalms 81 and 84. The meaning of the term is unknown. Thought to be derived from the word "gath," it has been variously interpreted. It may indicate an accompaniment on a kind of instrument that originated in the Philistine city of Gath. It may be a Gittite melody perhaps associated with the march of the Gittite guard (2 Sam. 15:18). Since "gath" also means "winepress" in Hebrew, it may be the tune of a vintage song.[1]

Although several different types of hymns appear in the Psalms, almost all of them have a similar structure. They begin with a call to worship God, continue with an expansion on the reasons why God should be praised, and often conclude with a further invitation to worship God. This hymn follows that basic pattern by beginning and ending with an invitation to worship God (vv. 1a, 9) and by having as its body an elaboration upon the reasons why such worship should be given (vv. 1b–8).

---

[1]W. T. Purkiser, "Psalms," in *Beacon Bible Commentary*, vol. 3, *Job Through Song of Solomon*, ed. A. F. Harper, W. M. Greathouse, Ralph Earle, and W. T. Purkiser (Kansas City, Mo.: Beacon Hill Press, 1967), 158.

Hymns are easily recognized among the psalms because they are exuberant with the exaltation of the Lord from start to finish. The central thought of this hymn-psalm, its backbone theme with which it opens and concludes, is the first line: "O Lord, our Lord, how majestic is Your name in all the earth!" The psalm possibly grew out of a meditation that the writer had on a clear evening as he gazed intelligently and devotionally into the open, darkened sky. No mention is made of the sun in the psalm.

David sees the magnificent, shining array of stars, too numerous to count, with the moon glowing with a glory all its own among them. As he sits and reflects, he is swept into a silent but powerful worship service. He listens quietly and looks thoughtfully as a sermon on God is proclaimed by the star-strewn, trackless distances of space above him. What he sees impresses him with the overwhelming realization that God should be worshiped and adored.

GOD IS SUPREME (8:1)

¹**O Lord, our Lord,**
How majestic is Your name in all the earth,
Who have displayed Your splendor above the heavens!

Verse 1. His introductory words, **O Lord, our Lord**, utilize two different names for God. The first is Yahweh (יהוה, *YHWH*), the covenant name for God that was revealed to Moses, and the second is Lord (אָדוֹן, *'adon*), which suggests His position and authority. The second of these two names has the suffix "our" added to it. The One addressed, then, is the covenant God of Israel, the One whose authority and leadership are supreme, the God who is personal, almighty, and yet transcendent.

The writer ends his first line with the words, **How majestic is Your name in all the earth!** His name is the most noble, the most glorious, the most exalted name of the earth and the heavens. It should therefore be revered and respected by every human being and every living creature.

The psalmist uses "name" in a manner typical of Old Testament times. To us, a name is simply the word by which a person is designated and addressed and really nothing more. However, to the Hebrews, one's name had far more symbolism. It stood for a special personality and special quality of life. When the writer says that Yahweh's name is "majestic" throughout "all the earth," he means that God's wisdom, power, covenant-keeping nature, and goodness are seen throughout the created world. God's name, to him, stands for all His attributes. His thought must have been, "O LORD, our Lord, how gloriously You are manifested by Your creation of the world and man!"

God's exalted nature should be recognized by all because He has **displayed [His] splendor above the heavens!** It is difficult to translate this phrase into English, but the psalmist is saying something like "He has put His glory in the heavens by His creation of them; thus as they fulfill their various purposes, they reflect the wondrous nobility, grandeur, and magnificence of the hand that made them."

This first reason given for praising God, the glory of the heavens He has made, reminds us of Immanuel Kant's words: "Two things fill the mind with ever-renewed wonder and reverence . . . the star-lit heavens above me, and the moral law within me."[2]

GOD AND CREATION
(8:2)

>[2]From the mouth of infants and nursing babes You have established strength
>Because of Your adversaries,
>To make the enemy and the revengeful cease.

Verse 2. The marvelous heavens—the visible, natural revelation of God—comprise one of God's most obvious declarations of His genius and power. It is as if David is saying, "The glory, greatness, and majesty of Yahweh are splashed across the heavens like vivid shades of paint covering a canvas and creat-

---

[2]Immanuel Kant, *Critique of Practical Reason, and Other Writings in Moral Philosophy*, trans. Louis White Beck (Chicago: University of Chicago Press, 1949), 258.

ing a great masterpiece. You are the Great Artist and Your fingers are the brushes."

However, the psalm does not stop with the heavens. The writer refers further to the great and the small, the mighty and the frail. The seemingly little things, that is, the infants and nursing babes, are used as additional evidence of God's majesty. "His glory shines forth **from the mouth of infants and nursing babes**," he says. Jesus quoted this expression in Matthew 21:16, telling us that the weakest and most helpless human beings—babies—testify to the existence and character of God!

"From babies," he says, "**You have established strength because of Your adversaries**." These helpless ones bring praise to God without even being aware of what they are doing. Through their presence, their instincts and capacities for development, their abilities to learn and love, their beauty and attractiveness, their teachableness and eagerness to believe, they declare their Maker's praise. Those who oppose God, the "adversaries" of God, should read the book of evidence of His greatness presented by and through a baby.

His words **To make the enemy and the revengeful cease** emphasize that God even uses infants to shut the mouths of His critics. He creates a "sabbath of rest" (הִשְׁבִּית, *hashbith*) for their criticism. In other words, the thought of a child should lead the avenger to cease his opposition and join in the praise of God.

Pharaoh's daughter could not resist helping the crying baby Moses who was floating on the Nile in a basket. Drawing him out of the Nile, she adopted him, provided for him, and reared him in the palace, pouring upon him Egyptian luxuries and an Egyptian education (Ex. 2:6–10). The baby grew and became the one who led the Israelites out of Egyptian bondage, bringing them all the way to Sinai where God made them into His great nation. The tears of baby Moses wound up praising God through the creation of the Israelite nation!

GOD AND HIS CONCERN FOR MAN
(8:3–5)

³**When I consider Your heavens, the work of Your fingers,**

> The moon and the stars, which You have ordained;
> ⁴What is man that You take thought of him,
> And the son of man that You care for him?
> ⁵Yet You have made him a little lower than God,
> And You crown him with glory and majesty!

Verse 3. Another reason for praising God is His glory depicted in the dignity He has given to man. The writer sees God's greatness in the world above him, around him, and in the world within him.

He sees the heavens as **the work of** [God's] **fingers.** Only four other passages in the Scriptures refer to God's fingers (Ex. 8:19; 31:18; Deut. 9:10; Lk. 11:20). This terminology is simply a poetic way of referring to God's intricate, creative action.

No one can contemplate the heavens and not be motivated to ponder God thoughtfully. The psalmist says that **when** [he considers God's] **heavens, the work of** [His] **fingers,** [and] **the moon and the stars, which** [He has] **ordained** or put in place, he is overwhelmingly driven to a profound question: the question of the next verse.

Verse 4. What is man that You take thought of him? In other words, the writer is asking, What is **the son of man that** [God would] **care for him?**

He uses two designations for "man," both of which emphasize the frailty of humanity. The first is the word אֱנוֹשׁ (*ᵉnosh*), and the second is בֶן־אָדָם (*ben 'adam*) for "son of man." His point must be, "When I see the grandeur of the heavens, the magnificent stars, and the moon robed in golden light, I must ask, 'Why does God give any consideration at all to weak, frail men, who are smaller than specks of dust on His earth?'"

The KJV has, in the parallel line, "visiteth him" in the place of "art mindful of him." The word פָּקַד (*paqad*) can mean "visit," "appoint," "number," or "care for." Obviously the question is how such an almighty God could condescend to care for such feeble beings as humans. The realization that God would give special attention and consideration for mankind is profound and significant, an observation that calls for solemn meditation.

Verse 5. As he ponders this truth, the writer concludes that man is made **a little lower than God and** has been crowned **with glory and majesty!** The word employed is אֱלֹהִים (*ᵉlohim*), which is a plural word for "God," probably the plural of majesty. His point being that God has made him a little lower than Himself. The LXX has translated this word as "angels," interpreting *ᵉlohim* in light of its plurality to mean "divine beings." The KJV, perhaps following the LXX, has offered a similar translation: "For thou hast made him a little lower than the angels."

The writer of the letter to the Hebrews applied the phrase "a little lower than God" with the words "made him for a little while lower than God" (NASB) to Jesus as he declared that Jesus had become one of us, truly a man, for the suffering of death (Heb. 2:7, 9). The writer of Hebrews was quoting the LXX for his reference and thus included in the Greek text *aggelous* (ἀγγέλους) in the place of *ᵉlohim*. Neither the Hebrew nor Greek text makes any reference to time as the NASB has indicated with the phrase "for a little while." The point being made in Hebrews is that Jesus so completely identified with man in His advent, in His condescension, that He was able to experience sufferings, temptations, and even death.

The concept of man's dignity revealed in his being given rulership over the earth carries us back to the original intent in the creation of man. God said at the dawn of time, "Let Us make man in Our image, according to Our likeness" (Gen. 1:26). Only of man among all the living creatures did God say, "I have made you in My image." Making man in His image meant that God was bestowing upon him "glory and majesty." Some of the living creatures that He had made had better hearing, keener eyesight, and a sharper sense of smell; but only of man was it said that he was made in the likeness of God.

The fact that man was made a little lower than God was more amazing to the writer (and should be to us) than the starry heavens, the moon, and the glorious star-studded canopy of the night sky.

GOD AND THE RULE OF MAN
(8:6–8)

⁶**You make him to rule over the works of Your hands;
You have put all things under his feet,**
⁷**All sheep and oxen,
And also the beasts of the field,**
⁸**The birds of the heavens and the fish of the sea,
Whatever passes through the paths of the seas.**

Verse 6. As he continues to consider God, the writer is struck by another great wonder: God not only cares for man, but He has given him amazing authority and mastery comparable to what He Himself has. He made **him to rule over the works of [his] hands** [and He has] **put all things under his feet.**

Verse 7. To be specific about the rule of man, he highlights the animal kingdom: **All sheep and oxen, and also the beasts of the field.**

Verse 8. Amazingly, God, the ultimate Master of all things, has made man master of His creation—including "the beasts of the field," **the birds of the heavens and the fish of the sea,** [even down to] **whatever passes through the paths of the seas.** His crowning of man as the king of His creation is unparalleled in the bestowal of glory and honor. God has figuratively placed a crown on man's head, giving him control over all things, even giving him the earth (and perhaps beyond) as his territory and all living creatures as his subjects.

Man, a mere speck in the universe, is to be lord over the earth, using it and ruling it. God told Adam and Eve to "rule over" the animals of the field, the wild animals of the earth, the birds of the sky, the fish of the sea, and whatever else might be in the depths of the sea (see Gen. 1:28).

The description of the oversight given to man is not intended to be phrased in modern-day, scientific classifications, but it is meant only to be a general summary of the extent of the dominion that man received. Scientific understanding has extended man's rule by utilizing the laws of nature which God has established, but this extension is within the confines of the rule that God gave at the outset of time.

The wonderful truth of this psalm—a truth that should cause every human being to lift his voice in adoration of God—is that people are more important to God than matter, that they are more valuable to Him than places, and that of all His creative work man is supreme to Him. The true dignity of mankind is taught more clearly in this psalm than in any other place in the Scriptures.

ONCE AGAIN: GOD IS SUPREME (8:9)

⁹**O LORD, our Lord,
How majestic is Your name in all the earth!**

Verse 9. The psalm closes with the same refrain with which it started, an exclamation of reverent wonder: **O LORD, our Lord, how majestic is Your name in all the earth!** Can anyone improve upon this ascription of praise? Considering anew God's created world and God's concern for mankind will inspire us to think deeply about the greatness of God; and such meditation can only cause us to repeat this sentence with greater understanding and deeper emotion.

We cannot add to the majesty of His name; all we can do is proclaim it throughout the earth. God is all-glorious and nothing that we do can *embellish or increase* His glory; however, we can *reflect* His great glory in our personalities and lifestyles and *declare* it with our lips to others.

APPLICATION

Why Worship?
As the psalmist studies the vastness and beauty of the heavens and goes deeper into this worship service, he recognizes two reasons why God should be worshiped: He should be praised *for His creation of the world* and *for His creation of mankind*. To rephrase the words of Immanuel Kant: "Two things fill the

mind with ever-renewed wonder and reverence . . . the world above and man on earth beneath."

The Big Theme

This hymn is not a psalm about the importance and glory of man; it is more about the glory of God as seen in His creation of all things and in the crown He has placed upon man. After meditating on both truths, we can only burst forth in the praise of God, for the creation displays the wisdom and *power* of the Creator and the crown reflects the wisdom and *grace* of the One who has bestowed it. When we look at what God has done in the heavens, in the creation of man, and in His constant care of man, we can only praise Him!

Who Is God?

One of the most beautiful expressions concerning God is found in the first and last lines of this psalm: "O LORD, our Lord, How majestic is Your name in all the earth!" Pregnant with meaning, it gives a threefold description of God.

First, He is the covenant God. The word is "LORD," the name of the covenant God, the name given to Moses.

Second, He is the God of authority and leadership. The second word for God is "Elohim," the word for supremacy and honor.

Third, He is excellent in all His attributes. The word "name" stands for all His greatness and characteristics.

Who is God? He is the God who has entered into an agreement with us to save us, provide for us, and guide us. He is the God who is supreme in greatness and mighty power. He is truly Sovereign over all authorities and rulers. He is perfect in all His attributes. Let us worship Him!

How Is God Praised?

Three ways that God is praised are presented in this psalm.

He is praised by the glory of the heavens. He set His glory above or in the heavens. Who can see the stars without praising Him?

He is praised by the marvel of babies. Out of their innocent mouths come praise of Him. No one can look long at a baby without praising God. Even the enemies of God cannot withstand the overwhelming testimony of these little ones.

He is praised by the wisdom of His actions. He has given the rulership of his earth to frail, sinful people. This fact is a greater wonder than the starry host of heaven to the writer of this psalm. He has made mankind in His likeness but has given humans charge of the animals, fish, and all other living creatures!

"Come, Let Us Worship Him!"

The call to worship: "O LORD, our Lord, how majestic is Your name in all the earth!"

The reasons for worship: (1) He is to be praised for His creation—the stars, the moon, and the expanse of the night sky. (2) He is to be praised for His consideration of mankind. Consider how the helpless infants praise Him, and how God cares for frail human beings. (3) Praise Him for His crowning man, through His grace, with the rulership of the earth.

The call to worship: "O LORD, our Lord, how majestic is Your name in all the earth!"

God Speaks to Us?

We are reminded in this psalm of how God speaks to us.

First, He speaks through His creation, through His natural revelation. Through the heavens and the creation of mankind, He declares His strength, wisdom, and grace.

Second, He speaks through His inspired Word, through His specific revelation. The holy Scriptures tell us of His greatness, love, and instructions for salvation (2 Tim. 3:16, 17).

Third, He speaks through His Son, Jesus, through His incarnational revelation. His will for the Christian Age is bound up in the advent of Jesus (Heb. 1:1, 2).

How Should We View Mankind?

This psalm reminds us of the major views of mankind that we confront in our living and serving.

The view of mankind as weaklings, unworthy of God's consideration. When we compare the heavens and the world to mankind, we may subscribe to this view. We are ready to ask with the psalmist, "What is man that You would be mindful of him?"

The view of mankind as superhuman beings. As we look around us, we are almost constrained to say that people can do anything and are self-sufficient. When we view the accomplishments of mankind, the mastery of flight, the inventions, and the improvements in medical science, we are compelled to think that we can do almost anything. However, this view asks us to believe in humanism, the philosophy that argues that people are the center of everything. Humanism has been defined as "the practice of the absence of God."

The view of mankind as a little lower than God—the view presented in this psalm. It does not depict mankind as worthless and totally unworthy of God's care but as the superintendent of God's world. We are the caretakers appointed by God and will be held accountable for the fulfillment of His charge.

This psalm gives us the balance that God intends for us to have regarding our position in His arrangement of things. We are neither animals nor superhuman beings, neither senseless beasts nor gods who answer to no one. We are God's servants who live for God under His special care.

Seeing God's Glory

We see the glory of God all around us; in every direction we look, we behold it. Using this psalm as our springboard, let us ask ourselves, "Do I see God's glory in my world?"

In the inanimate things. The stars, moon, sun, trees, hills, and grass all proclaim the power and wisdom of God. Without tongues, they compel us to praise Him.

In intelligent life. Man is a marvel to consider. One could study the complexities of a hand for a lifetime and not exhaust its mysteries. Every part of man declares his Maker's praise.

In non-intelligent life. The living creatures fulfill the role that God gave them. The amazing balance of nature, the inexplicable character of the wildlife, and the exactness of their habitat all inspire a chorus of praise for the One who made them.

Those who do not see the glory of God all around them are surely blind or have minds that have been so numbed by the pleasures, pains, or plans of this world that their vision of what is really important has been distorted.

Psalm 9

God and the Nations

The Superscription: For the choir director; on Muth-labben. A Psalm of David. The title says that this is **a Psalm of** ["by," "for," or "to"] **David** (לְדָוִד, *l^edawid*) and contains the special instruction: **For the choir director** [לַמְנַצֵּחַ, *lamnatstseach*]; **on Muth-labben** (עַלְמוּת לַבֵּן, *'almuth labben*). The meaning of "Muth-labben" is uncertain. Perhaps it means "upon the death of the son." The phrase may refer to a tune that was known to Israel but is unknown to us.

Psalms 9 and 10 apparently go together. Perhaps at one time in the history of the Scriptures, they were combined and appeared in the Scriptures as a single psalm. Three facts suggest this possibility. First, Psalm 10 has no title, a fact that is true of only three others in Book I (1; 2; 33). Second, in other versions of the Old Testament (for example, the LXX and the Vulgate), the two are actually united and presented as one psalm. Third, both psalms participate in the same acrostic arrangement, with Psalm 9 going basically from *Aleph* to *Kaph* and Psalm 10 going basically from *Lamedh* to *Tav*.

If it is true that the two once comprised a larger psalm of thirty-nine verses (as it is presented in the LXX) which in its later history was divided into two psalms, the splitting up of the psalm has been helpful to us. This division has given us a better grasp of the thirty-nine verses because the first part—which we now call Psalm 9—pictures God and the sinning Gentile nations, while the second part—which we now call Psalm 10—raises a new question of why God does not punish the wicked.

As it now stands in the Hebrew text, Psalm 9 shows an acrostic-like arrangement with every other line beginning with successive letters of the Hebrew alphabet; however, the arrangement is not totally consistent, for some of the Hebrew letters are left out of the acrostic. The alphabetic arrangement of a psalm does not necessarily require complete conformity to the acrostic pattern as the Western mind might expect.

This psalm reminds us that, in contrast to the pagan world around us, God is always faithful to His people. The psalm weaves back and forth from praising God to asking God to deal with the writer's enemies.

"I WILL PRAISE GOD" (9:1, 2)

¹I will give thanks to the LORD with all my heart;
I will tell of all Your wonders.
²I will be glad and exult in You;
I will sing praise to Your name, O Most High.

Verse 1. The acrostic letter is א (*Aleph*).

Beginning with a hymnic expression of praise for the marvelous works of God in the past, the psalmist resolves to **give thanks to the LORD with all [his] heart.** The word for "thanks" is אוֹדֶה (*'odeh*), a word that conveys giving expressions of gratitude, praising, or acknowledging blessings. This giving of "thanks" will be done, he says, with his appreciation of the Lord springing from the totality of his "heart"—his emotions, intellect, and conscience.

He will be vocal about the Lord's great acts of grace: **I will tell of all Your wonders.** His rejoicing will involve proclaiming "all" of God's "wonders" to others. He looks upward and outward—upward toward God with gratitude and adoration and outward toward others with the news of how God has been gracious to him. He has been blessed in the past—perhaps delivered from enemies or rescued from some other trial—and he will freely tell others about it.

Verse 2. He resolves to "be glad" in God. **I will be glad and exult in You**, he says. That is, he will rejoice in God and before others over what God has done for him. He uses the word "exult" (עָלַץ, *'alats*), which means "to rejoice greatly," "to be jubilant," in God.

He says, **I will sing praise to Your name, O Most High.** He "will sing [continually of his heart's thanksgiving to God's] name." God is addressed as "O Most High" (עֶלְיוֹן, *'elyon*), a name for God that means the most exalted One. God is the Supreme One, and there is no other like Him. The writer sees God as He really is—the almighty One—and is eager to render the proper praise to Him.

WHAT GOD HAS DONE (9:3–8)

³When my enemies turn back,
They stumble and perish before You.
⁴For You have maintained my just cause;
You have sat on the throne judging righteously.
⁵You have rebuked the nations, You have destroyed the wicked;
You have blotted out their name forever and ever.
⁶The enemy has come to an end in perpetual ruins,
And You have uprooted the cities;
The very memory of them has perished.
⁷But the LORD abides forever;
He has established His throne for judgment,
⁸And He will judge the world in righteousness;
He will execute judgment for the peoples with equity.

Verse 3. The acrostic letter is ב (*Beth*).

The writer is either looking back at what God has done or is using prophetic perfects, which refer to something that is going to happen as if it already has happened. The best understanding seems to be that he is thinking of some great victory that the Lord has given to him. He says, **When my enemies turn back, they stumble and perish before You.** At the time of the victory, he saw the enemies retreat. As they reversed their field and ran, he saw them "stumble and perish" before God. It is as if His very presence caused them to wilt and melt into dust.

Verse 4. God has acted in the writer's behalf because he is God's servant, and He is in the right. He says, **For You have maintained my just cause; You have sat on the throne judging righteously.** God has defended his "just cause." In this deliverance, God has judged, as He always does, "righteously." In figurative language, he says that God is seated "on [His] throne judging righteously." As God defended His people, He was rendering a judgment. God's people can always count on God as coming down on the side of the truth and never encouraging or assisting error and sin. His judgments are fair, truthful, and impartial.

Verse 5. The acrostic letter is ג (*Gimel*).

God **rebuked the nations** [and has] **destroyed the wicked.** He has dealt with the wicked so completely and convincingly that He has **blotted out their name forever and ever.** The victory was complete, decisive, and eternal.

Verse 6. The enemy has come to **an end in perpetual ruins,** their **cities** have been **uprooted,** and **the very memory of them has perished.** These are expressions that mean that God has dealt ultimately and finally with them. They have been taken out of existence.

No enemy of the truth can defeat God, the almighty One. His foes are wiped out by His mere presence. When He judges the nations, He will judge them in truth, completely, and forever.

Verse 7. The acrostic letter is ה (*He*).

In contrast to the demise of the enemies, he says, **But the Lord abides forever; He has established His throne for judgment.** No one will escape His judgment. Time is not a factor with His verdicts, nor will He change character and act with new attributes. He "abides forever." His judgments are universal. He is the Judge of all the nations of the earth for all time and eternity.

Verse 8. The acrostic letter is ו (*Vav*).

His throne of **righteousness** and justice will never be compromised or diluted. **He will execute judgment for the peoples with equity** or impartiality. No one will be overlooked or judged unfairly, but all will be judged according to the righteous character of God.

PSALM 9

RIGHTEOUS BUT COMPASSIONATE (9:9, 10)

⁹The LORD also will be a stronghold for the oppressed,
A stronghold in times of trouble,
¹⁰And those who know Your name will put their trust in You,
For You, O LORD, have not forsaken those who seek You.

Verse 9. God, the just Judge, will also be compassionate toward those who trust in Him. **The LORD also will be a stronghold for the oppressed, a stronghold in times of trouble.** Two glorious attributes reside in the true God: strength and compassion. He will be a "stronghold" (מִשְׂגָּב, *miśgab*) to those in "trouble." This word means a "hill-fort" or "refuge" for "the oppressed" (לַדָּךְ, *laddak*) who believe in Him. David had often found a crevice of a rock to be his hiding place as he fled from Saul, and he draws this illustration from his experience to show God's protection for those who put their faith in Him.

God is the One who reaches out to us in our "times of trouble" (לְעִתּוֹת בַּצָּרָה, *leʿiththoth batstsarah*). He is a place of protection for "the oppressed," the mistreated, crushed, downtrodden, and those in the kind of circumstance in which all hope is cut off.

Verse 10. God keeps His eye on those who trust in Him. The writer has found that God will never turn away a seeking soul. He says, **And those who know Your name will put their trust in You, for You, O LORD, have not forsaken those who seek You.** To know His name is to know and experience life with Him. "Those who know [His] name" walk with God in faith and see His providence and protection. Those who have put their "trust" in God are never disappointed. They find that God has never "forsaken" those who seek to be in fellowship with Him. They may face trials during their walk, but they find that God is always their shield and strength. To "seek" God refers to making sure that nothing interferes with one's life with Him.

Circumstances may become hopeless, but people are never without hope as long as they can still trust in Him. The patient hope of faith that waits on God will find God to be faithful.

PRAISING GOD (9:11–16)

¹¹Sing praises to the LORD, who dwells in Zion;
Declare among the peoples His deeds.
¹²For He who requires blood remembers them;
He does not forget the cry of the afflicted.
¹³Be gracious to me, O LORD;
See my affliction from those who hate me,
You who lift me up from the gates of death,
¹⁴That I may tell of all Your praises,
That in the gates of the daughter of Zion
I may rejoice in Your salvation.
¹⁵The nations have sunk down in the pit which they have made;
In the net which they hid, their own foot has been caught.
¹⁶The LORD has made Himself known;
He has executed judgment.
In the work of his own hands the wicked is snared.
Higgaion Selah.

Verse 11. The acrostic letter is ז (*Zayin*).

His praise continues with an exhortation: **Sing praises to the Lord, who dwells in Zion; declare among the peoples His deeds.** The Lord's grace toward those in need should inspire a double response on the part of the righteous: the singing of the "praises" of God and the proclaiming of "His deeds among the peoples."

Verse 12. The reason for such praise is evident: **For He who requires blood remembers them; He does not forget the cry of the afflicted.** God is the avenger of blood for the righteous. He "requires blood." His law has ever been "Whoever sheds man's blood, by man his blood shall be shed" (Gen. 9:6a). This God "remembers" the afflicted by avenging them. The blood of the innocent cries to Him from the ground on which it was spilled by wicked hands (Gen. 4:10). God will, in time, settle the score with those who mistreat the innocent.

We see here the writer's personal need for God. Many hate him and are continually seeking to destroy him. God has delivered him from death's gate before, and he needs such deliverance now.

Verse 13. The acrostic letter is ח (*Heth*).

Thus his prayer is this: **Be gracious to me, O Lord; see my affliction from those who hate me, You who lift me up from the gates of death**. He makes a plea for God to be "gracious" (extend favor) to him. He asks God to behold his "affliction," for he knows that if God looks upon his difficulty, being the merciful God that He is, He will rescue him from it. His hardship, brought on by those who oppose him, is indeed serious; in fact, he refers to himself as coming to the "gates of death." He has often been only a step or two away from its entrance. He asks God to "lift [him] up" or remove him from this life-threatening situation.

Verse 14. The argument that he makes is that if God will rescue him, he will make His kindness known to others. He will praise Him in **the gates of the daughter of Zion**. This phrase "daughter of Zion" stands for Jerusalem, where God has placed His name. At those gates, he will **rejoice in** [his] **salvation**. The city gates were the places where major business activities were transacted, for they were public and in full view of the city. Thus, in the most visible location, he will rejoice in the deliverance that God provides. He urges God to move him from "the gates of death" to "the gates of the daughter of Zion" (Jerusalem), the most public place in His chosen city, where he may tell others of his victory.

If God will deliver him, He will have one more mouth to praise Him and to tell of how He delivers those who trust in Him. If God wants a witness on earth, He needs to save David, so he can be that witness.

Verse 15. The acrostic is ט (*Teth*).

He says that **the nations have sunk down in the pit which they have made; in the net which they hid, their own foot has been caught**. God sometimes allows the wicked to afflict themselves. In Old Testament times God judged men *for* their sins and *by* their sins.

Two figures are used: One is that of a hunter digging a pit that will serve to catch game. The wicked "nations" had dug a "pit," but to their surprise they fell into it themselves.

The second figure is that of a hunter's "net" or "snare" (v. 16). Once the snare has been properly set, the hunter goes on his way and forgets where he put it. Later, he passes by the place and is caught in his own snare. "Their foot has been caught" in their own trap. The snare is evil's device; the hunter is the evil nations who have become entrapped by their own sinister plans.

Verse 16. With an unusual flair, this verse ends with **Higgaion Selah.** "Higgaion" (הִגָּיוֹן, *higgayon*) is probably a musical notation representing a solemn pause of mediation. A form of it is used in 19:14 for the idea of meditation: "Let the words of my mouth and the meditation [*hegyon*] of my heart receive favor in Your sight." It appears here with "Selah." The point is, the writer is calling upon his readers to celebrate the triumph of God's judgment over the wicked. They should recognize God solemnly, and they should think about Him in reverence.

A PLEA FOR HELP (9:17–20)

¹⁷The wicked will return to Sheol,
Even all the nations who forget God.
¹⁸For the needy will not always be forgotten,
Nor the hope of the afflicted perish forever.
¹⁹Arise, O LORD, do not let man prevail;
Let the nations be judged before You.
²⁰Put them in fear, O LORD;
Let the nations know that they are but men. Selah.

Verse 17. The acrostic letter is י (*Yodh*).

Only one destination awaits the wicked individual or nation: the grave of retribution: **The wicked will return to Sheol, even all the nations who forget God.** Crop failure never occurs in connection with God's law of sowing and reaping. The righteous will reap the rewards of righteous living, and the wicked will receive the punishment they deserve. Time is no factor here. Those "nations" that do not acknowledge God and serve Him will eventually go down to "Sheol," the grave, without any hope.

Verse 18. The acrostic letter is כ (*Kaph*).

The writer expresses the confidence of faith as he says that the **needy will not always be forgotten**. Just as a day of reckoning will come for the wicked, a day of remembrance will come for those who trust in God. They may face trials now, but their day of reward will eventually come. The **hope of the afflicted** will not perish. They have not hoped in vain. God will see that their time of vindication comes.

Verse 19. In fervency of spirit he requests, **Arise, O Lord, do not let man prevail; let the nations be judged before You.** He pleads for God to show the pagan nations who is in charge, that He is really on the throne of the universe, and that He will judge the nations.

Verse 20. He asks, **Put them in fear, O Lord.** He beseeches God to put respect for His ways in their hearts. Furthermore, he says, **Let the nations know that they are but men.** He prays that God not allow the wicked to succeed in their evil, but bring them to a realization that they are "men," not God. When God confounds their evil plans and puts in their hearts the consciousness that He is the sovereign Ruler of the universe, they will understand their place.

Selah is probably used as an invitation for the reader to think profoundly about this truth.

APPLICATION

The Certainties of God

In this psalm, the writer expresses his confidence in God and His trustworthy attributes of righteousness, impartiality, and compassion. He believes that regardless of how gloomy the future may appear to be, he can count on the consistency and faithfulness of God. Therefore, he makes his appeal to God in harmony with who God is and what He is like.

He knows that God could never answer an unrighteous prayer. He also realizes that God would respond in compassion as an almighty warrior to the one who trusts in Him.

We can count on His righteousness. He will always side with truth and holiness. He will neither wink at sin nor tempt His servants to sin.

We can count on His impartiality. He will always give us a fair trial. He loves all people and would have us to come to a knowledge of His truth (1 Tim. 2:4).

We can count on His compassion. He will always respond to us with His lovingkindness, extending mercy to those who come to Him in trusting faith.

How wonderful God is! As the writer considers God's defense of His people and His relationship with the pagan nations around Israel, wonderful truths about God rush to his mind. He remembered how reliable God is, how righteous He is, and how He regards the poor.

Voicing His Praise

Verses 1 and 2 of this psalm tell us how to praise God. The word "praise" means to "give thanks for."

We will praise Him retrospectively. Looking back, we will rejoice in what he has done for us.

Praise should be given wholeheartedly. Our whole inner beings will be involved in this praising. It will not be done as an afterthought, but as a major emphasis of our lives.

We are to praise Him evangelistically. We can proclaim God's goodness to others from the experiences we have had with Him.

Praise should be gladly given. We will rejoice before Him and others in happy, joyful praise. Such praising will not be a burden to us; it will be our delight.

Praise should be given continually. It will be a daily activity. Regardless of our situations, whether we are in times of trial or triumph, we will be expressing our adoration to Him.

Praise should be given with intelligence and truth. Recognizing Him for who He really is, we will praise Him as the Most High, the Supreme One.

We need to praise Him prophetically. We have put our trust in Him, fully confident that He will fulfill every promise He has made to us.

Before His Throne

A clear picture of the judgment of God is brought before us. His temporal judgments illustrate His eternal judgments.

When He judges the nations, when He brings sinners into account, *He will judge them righteously.* He will examine them according to His holiness and truth.

He will judge them completely. No stone will be left unturned. No one, regardless of his stature, wealth, or power, will be excused from His judgment.

He will judge them eternally. His verdict will stand throughout all the ages and throughout eternity.

He will judge universally. All nations and all individuals will be judged by Him.

"For the wages of sin is death, but the free gift of God is eternal life in Christ Jesus our Lord" (Rom. 6:23).

"It is appointed to man once to die and after this, the judgment" (Heb. 9:27).

God's Righteous Wrath

Think about the nature of God's judgment. He is a God of love, but He is also a God of wrath. "Behold then the kindness and severity of God," as Paul said (Rom. 11:22).

His judgment will be righteous in its quality. We do not have to wonder about the character of it. He will officiate according to His truth and righteous nature.

It will be impartial in its execution. No one will be misjudged, overlooked, or excused.

It will be eternal in its significance. No appeals can be made, for none will be needed. His verdict will be flawless. When one leaves the judgment, he walks into his final abiding place.

Those of us who live in the Christian Age can rejoice with unspeakable joy over what the New Testament has told us. Our Savior has clothed us in His righteousness through His forgiveness and prepared us to received a welcomed "Well done."

Responding to God's Goodness

How should one respond to God's gracious acts?

With praise. God has given us numerous victories and we will acknowledge His love continually.

With public praise. In public places, we will make known God's deeds of kindness.

With humble praise. Full credit will go to the One who has gone before us. We will acknowledge Him as the great almighty One, and ourselves as His servants.

Depicting His Deliverance

How shall we describe God's deliverances?

The nations have been entrapped by their own sin. They set snares for others, and they have fallen into their own traps. God uses their own sins to confound them.

What happened to the nations is the judgment of God that comes through His permissive will. God brings His judgments through His providence; their sin captured them because of the nature of sin and because of the free moral nature that God has given to mankind.

What happened to the nations is the judgment of God that is brought about by His deliberate condemnation of sin. At the appropriate times, in His own wisdom, He chooses the destruction of nations because of His reproof of sin. In Acts 12, we see Herod dying of worms, but Luke said that an angel of God struck him (Acts 12:23).

God's wrath is a fact today—but it will be an even greater fact in eternity.

God and the Needy

This psalm reminds us that God does not overlook the oppressed, mistreated, or the poor.

His heart goes out to them. He is moved deeply by any person who is in need, but He is especially touched when one of His own is suffering.

He defends them. He is their stronghold and refuge. He fights for them and provides for them.

He sees that their day of victory will come. Their time of hope will not perish. He works to give them the springtime of life.

God's people should take on the character, compassion, and concern of God. Let us, therefore, "remember the poor" (Gal. 2:10).

PSALM 10
WHY DO THE WICKED GO UNPUNISHED?

The Superscription: None.

Three facts lead us to believe that this psalm is a continuation of Psalm 9. First, Psalm 9 ends with "Selah," which is perhaps a pause for thought. At no other place in the Book of Psalms does a psalm end with this special word. Thus, if this piece is not a continuation of Psalm 9, it would be a major exception among the Psalms. The second fact is that this psalm has no superscription. Only three other psalms in Book I are without subtitles (1; 2; 33). The introductory nature of Psalms 1 and 2 would account for their not having a superscription; however, 33 seems to share the superscription of 32. Thus, in line with the way Book I is arranged, a reasonable explanation of why Psalm 10 has no superscription would be that the superscription of Psalm 9 was intended to be for this piece as well. Third, the acrostic design seems to be continued from Psalm 9 through Psalm 10, with Psalm 9 using the letters *Aleph* through *Kaph* and with Psalm 10 using the letters *Lamedh* through *Tav*.

It must be that somewhere in the life of the initial psalm, a decision was made to divide it into two smaller psalms. The division is helpful to the reader, for it places two major discussions into two smaller pieces of Scripture, allowing the reader to understand better the total content of the two.

This psalm as a unit of Scripture has one major theme running through it: the punishment of evil. It raises an age-old question about sin in the world: "Why doesn't God eliminate evil men now?" The writer knows that sin and God are incompatible. He believes that God judges sin, but he cannot understand why God does not act immediately to judge wickedness and the wicked.

A PERPLEXING PROBLEM (10:1, 2)

¹**Why do You stand afar off, O Lord?**
Why do You hide Yourself in times of trouble?
²**In pride the wicked hotly pursue the afflicted;**
Let them be caught in the plots which they have devised.

Verse 1. The acrostic letter is ל (*Lamedh*).

The writer asks in prayer, **Why do You stand afar off, O Lord?** The picture is that of God acting in the role of an idle spectator when His help is urgently sought down in the arena of life where some real problems are being faced. The aloofness of God troubles him.

To say it another way, he asks, **Why do You hide Yourself in times of trouble?** The word for "trouble" (בַּצָּרָה, *batstsarah*) can also be translated "drought." "Where are You during my times of severe and devastating hardships?" he is saying. It appears to him that God is hiding His eyes so that He would not see the terrible strait that His servant is in. He is experiencing the silence of God.

His questions are somewhat like our saying, "Where were You when I needed You?" These lines are not accusations against God but figurative ways of asking God to come immediately to his aid.

Verse 2. While God, it seems to the writer, looks the other way and does not act during his time of need, the wicked are on the move. **In pride the wicked** [are] **hotly** [pursuing] **the afflicted**. In arrogance, the wicked are "hunting down" the poor or the weak as one would chase an animal and finally capture it. Those who are puffed up with self-importance and who are wicked in demeanor have been mistreating the poor without any interference from God.

The next phrase, **Let them be caught in the plots which they**

have devised, has been interpreted in two different ways. Was the writer suggesting that it was time for evildoers to be ensnared by their own schemes of mischief, as indicated in the NASB, ASV, and NRSV? Does he wish that the plans of the wicked would backfire and afflict them instead of the poor? Or was he saying that the poor who are pursued are caught in the plans that the wicked have devised, as indicated in the NIV? It is probably best to think of this phrase as being a wish for the wicked. The writer is praying that the wicked people will be entangled in the purposes that they have devised for the unfortunate ones.

LOOKING MORE CLOSELY
(10:3, 4)

³**For the wicked boasts of his heart's desire,**
And the greedy man curses and spurns the Lord.
⁴**The wicked, in the haughtiness of his countenance, does**
  not seek Him.
All his thoughts are, "There is no God."

The writer dissects the problem by describing the character, conversations, and conduct of the wicked. With vivid and descriptive language, he pictures pride, irreverence, unbelief, greedy materialism, false security, vile language, and the spurning of God.

Verse 3. He says, **The wicked boasts of his heart's desire** by declaring to himself that no one could foil his evil designs. The Hebrew word that is used (הִלֵּל, *hillel*) is the word for "praise." The wicked man praises the desires that he has that are literally "the desires of his soul." He brags to himself that whatever he wishes to accomplish he can do. Coming from deep within him are unworthy and atrocious plans. It has not dawned on him that God will in His own time right all the wrongs of the world.

The next word, translated "curses" in the NASB, is actually the word for "bless" (בֵּרֵךְ, *berek*), and it could be that the meaning is that the wicked "bless" or "encourage" the man who seeks to acquire gain by violence. However, the word "bless" could be an euphemism for "cursing" as it is rendered in most translations. If it is translated "curses," then the meaning is that **the greedy man**, the man who is pursuing evil as eagerly as a covetous man craves money, **curses** the Lord. This man encourages evil, and he **spurns the LORD.** He uses the Lord's name in vain, and he ignores or renounces the ways of Lord. Repentance is far from his mind, and he has actually put himself in the place of God.

Verse 4. This man **in the haughtiness of his countenance, does not seek Him.** The word "countenance" pictures the arrogance of his face which represents the totality of his approach to life—his attitude toward God, his disdain of righteousness, and his belief that he will not be called into account for his deeds.

In summary **all his thoughts** [combine to say,] **"There is no God."** As he would see it, there is no God to judge him or to motivate him to change his ways. This belief seems to pervade his entire mindset. He believes that he is free to act according to the dictates of his own mind and that no one can take him to task for his actions. He has chosen to live as if there is no God.

Here, then, is the picture: the wicked man is boastful—in his words and in his looks—about his plans and life. He is greedy or covetous, cursing the Lord and pushing Him out of his mind. He does not seek the Lord or attempt to learn how to please Him. The end result of his life is practical atheism. Perhaps he does not deny the existence of God, but he lives as though there were no God.

THE PROSPERITY OF THE WICKED
(10:5–11)

⁵**His ways prosper at all times;**
Your judgments are on high, out of his sight;
As for all his adversaries, he snorts at them.
⁶**He says to himself, "I will not be moved;**
Throughout all generations I will not be in adversity."
⁷**His mouth is full of curses and deceit and oppression;**

PSALM 10

Under his tongue is mischief and wickedness.
⁸He sits in the lurking places of the villages;
In the hiding places he kills the innocent;
His eyes stealthily watch for the unfortunate.
⁹He lurks in a hiding place as a lion in his lair;
He lurks to catch the afflicted;
He catches the afflicted when he draws him into his net.
¹⁰He crouches, he bows down,
And the unfortunate fall by his mighty ones.
¹¹He says to himself, "God has forgotten;
He has hidden His face; He will never see it."

Verse 5. The writer sees the seeming prosperity of the wicked man, and what he sees is a big problem for him. He believes that God should be doing something about it.

His ways prosper at all times, he says. The **judgments** [of God are] **on high,** that is, far removed from the wicked man. They are **out of his sight.** He cannot see them. The people, called **adversaries,** who get in the wicked man's way or try to correct him are laughed out of sight and mind. He **snorts** at anyone who would dare oppose him or teach him (see Mal. 1:13).

Verse 6. The arrogance of the wicked man is expressed in his confident statement, **"I will not be moved."** He is sure that he will not face any hardships because of his sin, either now or in the future. The **generations** to come will not bring him any **adversity,** he says to himself. He is prideful, dedicated to evil, and no truth can penetrate his heart.

Verse 7. The acrostic letter פ (*Pe*) appears to be at the beginning of this verse. This acrostic pattern is difficult to read at this point. *Lamedh* in לָמָה is the first letter of verse 7. The writer or editor(s) may have artificially kept the acrostic arrangement by making אָלָה the first word of the first line of verse 7, which would allow them to make פִּיהוּ the first word of the verse's second line and thus would give a beginning פ in the second line for the acrostic pattern. At least, this would be one explanation for the unusual design for this verse.

His corrupt heart is reflected by his tongue, for **his mouth is full of curses and deceit and oppression.** He thinks about wickedness, and he continually speaks of it. He talks of oppressing others; he is without sensitivity concerning the feelings and needs of others. **Under his tongue is mischief and wickedness.** Figuratively viewed, evil thoughts and words lie in his mouth in readiness for use.

Verse 8. The acrostic letter ע (*Ayin*) seems to be used in the last line of this verse. Once again the acrostic pattern is difficult to detect. It is the second line of this verse that begins with *Ayin*.

His sinful heart is the source of violent and wicked actions. What is down in the private places of the heart comes up in speech and deeds. He **sits** [in secret] **places of the villages** where he can implement his awful and diabolical plans. The phrase **in the hiding places he kills the innocent** is a figurative way of saying that he watches for opportunities to take advantage of innocent people—sometimes to rob them and sometimes to injure them. **Stealthily**, secretly, he watches the poor and disadvantaged, **the unfortunate**, for the right time to steal from them or abuse them.

Verse 9. His metaphor is that of **a lion in his lair**. The wicked man prowls about watching for prey to devour. **He lurks to catch the afflicted**. Like lions stalking their prey, he slips up on the poor and takes advantage of their misfortune. By mistreating the poor, the widows, and the downtrodden, he is saying, "God will not judge us. He has not even seen what we have done!" The prey he seeks is the man whom he can easily mistreat for his own gain and who would be powerless to resist his abuse.

Verse 10. To change the figure, the wicked man sets a trap for the unsuspecting poor man, and when ensnared, he comes before his prey. In godless glee, he **crouches, he bows down. The unfortunate** man has fallen into **his mighty** plans of hurting and destroying the innocent.

Verse 11. The wicked man arrogantly believes that no one, not even God, will interfere with his purposes to do evil. Three phrases are used to describe what the wicked man says to himself about God. He says, **"God has forgotten, He has hidden His face**, and **He will never see it."** The wicked man believes that he can act wickedly without having to give an account. He thinks God will forget and not notice him. God's face will be turned the other way and He will not see him, never becoming aware of his sins.

To the psalmist, it seems that the ungodly prosper all the time, as if God does not judge sin anymore. The wicked make fun of anyone who opposes them. They say, "We shall not come to any harm because of our sin." Their tongues are dedicated to evil purposes, such as cursing, lying, swearing, and overcoming others. They wait in ambush to destroy the innocent. Instead of watching for opportunities to be of service, they watch for ways to destroy others.

TOWARD A SOLUTION (10:12–15)

¹²Arise, O Lord; O God, lift up Your hand.
Do not forget the afflicted.
¹³Why has the wicked spurned God?
He has said to himself, "You will not require it."
¹⁴You have seen it, for You have beheld mischief and vexation to take it into Your hand.
The unfortunate commits himself to You;
You have been the helper of the orphan.
¹⁵Break the arm of the wicked and the evildoer,
Seek out his wickedness until You find none.

Verse 12. The acrostic letter is ק (*Qoph*).

After the writer graphically pictures the problem, he turns to the One who is the solution: God. If God is not the answer, then there is no answer.

He implores God, **Arise, O Lord**. He asks God to go into action and act in behalf of the needy. God is asked to **lift up** His mighty **hand**. As he says, **Do not forget the afflicted**, he is not implying that God has actually forgotten the downtrodden. He is asking God to remember them in the sense of coming to their aid, defending them, and delivering them. He is using figurative language to make his requests in his prayer.

Verse 13. The writer asks, **Why has the wicked spurned God?** Then he answers his own question by saying that the wicked man has told **himself** that God would not hold him accountable for his actions.

Verse 14. The acrostic letter is ר (*Resh*).

Contrary to what the wicked believe, the writer knows that God does see their meanness: He beholds all **mischief** and **vexation**, and He takes it all **into** [His] **hand** to judge it. Furthermore, the writer argues that God has always been **the helper of the orphan**. Those believing **unfortunate** ones are depending upon God and are looking to God for the divine assistance they need. God will not fail them.

Verse 15. The acrostic letter is שׁ (*Shin*).

His imprecatory petition is for God to **break the arm of the wicked and the evildoer**. He prays for Him to search out and find all the **wickedness** and destroy it. He wants God to make it so that the wicked man cannot continue in his wicked ways and will be completely removed from the earth.

THE CONFIDENCE OF FAITH
(10:16–18)

¹⁶The Lord is King forever and ever;
Nations have perished from His land.
¹⁷O Lord, You have heard the desire of the humble;
You will strengthen their heart, You will incline Your ear
¹⁸To vindicate the orphan and the oppressed,
So that man who is of the earth will no longer cause terror.

The psalm has moved from surprise at what God is doing about evil, to concern about His actions, to bold prayer for God to act, to confidence in God's faithfulness, and finally to belief that God will act in His own time. Though the psalm begins in the valley of despondency, it ends on the high plane of confidence in the integrity of God.

Verse 16. His prayer rises to the Lord who **is King forever and ever**. He is not an earthly king; He is the eternal King. He stands above all earthly kings as the heavens do above the earth. His strength is seen in the awesome reality that **nations have perished from His land**. They rise and fall at his command.

Verse 17. The acrostic letter is ת (*Tav*).

The writer knows the heart of the Lord and confidently believes that He has **heard the desire of the humble**. He sees their aspirations for relief. He will give them strength, providing for them strong hearts, the kind that they will need for their trials. He will bend or **incline** his ear so He can catch every word of their prayers, always being ready to answer them.

God in harmony with His nature will act compassionately toward the needy: He has **heard** [their] **desire**, He will **strengthen their heart**, and He **will incline** [His] **ear** to their prayers.

Verse 18. He will do all of this so that **the orphan and the oppressed** will be vindicated. Still further, the writer prays that all of this will result in a reign of peace during which no **man who is of the earth** will cause anyone else to cringe in **terror**. The picture he anticipates is the ideal, the picture that every believer yearns to see.

APPLICATION

When God Delays

As this psalm begins, the writer is wondering in prayer why God has not answered him. He is hurting, and he feels as if God is standing aloof from him.

God's delay may not be a "no" to our prayers. In His wisdom God waits until the time is right to respond to our requests. Do we not handle our children this way?

God's delay is always in our best interests. If an earthly father knows the importance of delays, why would not our heavenly Father on a much higher level know their importance?

God's delay offers us an opportunity for growth in faith and trust. Will not the God of all the earth do what is right for His children? At a time of delay, let us act in confidence and belief in God.

God loves His children and is a perfect Father toward them. He gives them what they need when they need it. His timing is perfect, and His gifts are appropriate for our personalities and our growth in faith.

God and the Wicked

How does God treat sin and the wicked?

God does not always judge sin when it is committed. We may wish for God to deal with sinners and sin immediately, but in order to protect the free moral choice of mankind and to fulfill His purpose for this world, He may wait until the Day of Judgment to make the wicked pay their accounts.

All sin is immediately condemned through God's Word, but not all sin will be brought into physical and tangible judgment until the day God chooses. We live under the guidance of God's will and we have put our trust in our Father to do what is necessary and right.

If we are called upon to endure the mistreatment of the wicked, let us face our trials with faith in God. He will strengthen us and carry us through them. Judgment Day will come for all sin and sinners, and vindication will someday come for every righteous person. Vengeance is the Lord's, and are we not glad!

We are in the world but not of it; we are part of this world but we do not belong to it.

Evil's Solution

The writer sees four truths that speak to the perplexing problem of why sinners are prospering.

First, he is aware that God sees what is going on in the world (v. 14). Nothing is a secret to Him. He is fully conscious of the success and failures of all.

Second, he knows that God has dealt with sin in the past (vv. 14, 16). Nations have been destroyed by Him; He has even destroyed the world with water as His judgment on sin.

Third, he realizes that God will not let evil go unpunished forever (v. 16). In His righteous nature, He cannot disregard sin. In His own time, He will judge it, not excuse it.

Fourth, he knows that God will strengthen those who trust in Him (vv. 14, 17, 18). If He does not deliver the righteous from oppression by the wicked, He will shelter them under His everlasting arms. If God's judgments are delayed, He will strengthen the hearts of the afflicted; and eventually, at the appropriate time, He will vindicate them.

God and sin are incompatible; they cannot coexist. God, in His own time, will destroy sin; the saint trusts in this fact.

Instruments of Sin

Several sins are mentioned in this psalm. It is helpful for us to think about these sins and make sure that we have declared war against them.

Sins of the tongue. These include such sins as vile language, cursing, and saying that God is irrelevant.

Sins of the hands. These are the sins of cheating, taking advantage of the poor, and physically hurting others.

Sins of the heart. These sins are pride, irreverence, unbelief, putting materialism over the needs of others, false security in the sense of trusting in ourselves, and spurning God.

The saint yields his members—tongue, hands, and heart—to the service of God by righteous living, faithful thinking, and godly talking.

The Journey of Faith

This psalm reminds us of our journey to confidence in God.

First, there is bewilderment at the silence of God. As the psalm begins, confusion reigns.

Second, there is concern about the progress of sin. Look at how the wicked boast about what they do. They seem to be dominating the scene and doing well.

Third, there is confidence in what God will do. Belief takes hold, and it reminds us to trust in the integrity of God.

Fourth, there is resolve about leaving the matter with God. Believers commit themselves to the realization that God will act and will act righteously.

Fifth, there is a faithful anticipation of the deliverance that God will affect. The psalm ends on the high note of confidence as is expressed in the request for God to act.

Living Without God

What is life like for those who live without God?

A warped sense of justice (v. 5). They do not see a day of judgment and a moment of accountability.

A false confidence (v. 6). They believe that people cannot possibly be moved from their chosen path and cannot be affected by their own sin.

Foul language (v. 7). God is cursed and ignored.

Perverse deeds (vv. 8–10). These are deeds that injure others for one's gain.

Disregard of accountability to God (v. 11). This attitude says that God does not see or observe what is going on in His world.

Any one of these traits spells eternal tragedy.

How Faith Acts

How does faith reveal itself in a life and heart? An idea of its role is implied by this psalm.

Those who believe recognize that God is. They are confident of His existence. One cannot please God without this type of faith (Heb. 11:3, 4).

Those who believe will see God as having the character that the Bible describes Him as having. True faith comes from His Word (Rom. 10:17). His attitudes, attributes, and nature are conveyed to us by the Scriptures.

Those who believe will have the practical confidence that God will deal with us as the Bible says He will. At the end of this psalm, the writer has worked through his lament to a confident faith that God will do what is in harmony with His nature. Look again at the latter part of Hebrews 11:4, and observe Paul's confident faith in Acts 27:25.

Psalm 11

Faith or Flight

The Superscription: For the choir director. A Psalm of David. The heading gives instruction **for the choir director** (לַמְנַצֵּחַ, *lamnatstseach*), a direction that is a frequent part of the headings that must imply that at some time and in some way the psalm was used in public worship. The title in Hebrew does not refer to this piece as "A Psalm," which is the reason that NASB has put these two words in italics in its translation. Although the psalm is ascribed to David with the phrase **of** ["by," "for," or "to"] **David** (לְדָוִד, *l^edawid*), we can only guess at its historical setting. Granting the possibility of Davidic authorship, we might imagine that the psalm grew out of David's life-threatening experiences in Saul's court.

This psalm is a beautiful affirmation of trust in God rather than a prayer. It might be called "The Song of the Steadfast Heart." The writer expresses confidence in the midst of a personal crisis. He has been advised to run from his problems by his comrades (or possibly by his own heart at a low and discouraged moment), but he responds to the advice with a dynamic declaration of faith. The psalm is clearly an expression of assurance.

David is excelling in favor with God and with the public. Saul has declined spiritually until the Spirit of God has been withdrawn from him (1 Sam. 16:14). Saul's hatred and jealousy toward David has grown until Saul, driven by the evil spirit that possessed him, has sought to kill him (1 Sam. 19:1). David has been thrust into the life of a fugitive, being constantly pursued by Saul. He knows that behind any rock or around any corner, Saul's loyalists could be waiting with daggers in their hands or arrows in their bows. Life as a fugitive means that he is continually looking over his shoulder for the deadly arrow or spear. Enemies are all around him, and at any moment he knows he could be attacked and killed. He yearns for peace as any person in his perilous situation would, but he also knows that God has put him in a special place of service for His glory and for the blessing of His people. He is determined to stay and face his difficulties in the strength of the Lord.

ERRONEOUS ADVICE (11:1–3)

> ¹In the LORD I take refuge;
> How can you say to my soul, "Flee as a bird to your mountain;
> ²For, behold, the wicked bend the bow,
> They make ready their arrow upon the string
> To shoot in darkness at the upright in heart.
> ³If the foundations are destroyed,
> What can the righteous do?"

Verse 1. The psalm begins with an announcement that God is the writer's defense from the evil forces around him. His decision regarding what to do about the danger is expressed with the words **In the LORD I take refuge.** He will not run from his problem; he will trust in the Lord as he seeks a solution to it. He knows that faith does not always go around trouble; it sometimes must go through it.

His friends are advising him to flee to a place of safety, a place of freedom from difficulty. They are saying, **"Flee as a bird to your mountain,"** or in other words, "Be like the birds during their times of disaster." When danger is near, birds fly away to the caves, crevices, or trees of the mountains where they can be safe. His friends are counseling him to employ their practice of dealing with trouble.

Verse 2. Their further encouragement is **"For, behold, the wicked bend the bow."** He is told, "Your adversaries are waiting in readiness to attack you. **They make ready their arrow upon the string."** It is as if the arrow is already in the bow, the bow is drawn at full length, and the attacker is just waiting for the opportune time to shoot. We would say, "He has his gun loaded and his finger on the trigger. He is waiting for you to come out into the clear so that he can fire." The friends continue, "They will slip up on you, for they are ready **to shoot in darkness at the upright in heart.**" They remind him that the wicked, with their killing tools in hand, are attempting to shoot him secretly (under the cover of the "darkness").

The description given by his friends or possibly his own bewildered heart indicates that David is in a difficult spot, a terrifying situation from which any man would shrink. Only a moment's reflection would convince anyone to run and hide from such a cruel circumstance.

It is difficult to tell where the quotation marks setting off what the advisers are saying should be placed. The Hebrew text does not use quotations marks as we do in English. Several translations would propose that the quotation includes verse 1b through verse 3 (NASB; NRSV; NIV). In the NEB, the quotation is just verse 2.

Verse 3. If the quotation goes through verse 3, which seems to be the better rendering, the friends of David are saying that the **foundations** of the law and order of their society are crumbling. They are being **destroyed**. This decay has doubtlessly come because of Saul's poor leadership. Due to this dissolution of the fabric of community life, his advisers are counseling that the **righteous** have not been able to do anything and will be powerless to accomplish anything in the future. Their conclusion is that staying around will be useless. They are bluntly saying, in effect, "It is time for you to abandon the ship and escape to some island that will be free from such difficulties. After all, shouldn't you seek to live a life that is free from problems?"

As dark as his predicament is, David looks at his situation from the perspective of faith. He believes that God has placed him where he is. He is in this dilemma for the noble purpose of doing God's will. His integrity and commitment to God, therefore, compel him to be faithful to his duty, even in the face of violent foes and extremely trying times. Since God is with him where he is, escaping to a cave in the mountains will not bring

God any nearer to him. He wants to do the duty assigned to him by the Lord. Therefore, the worst enemies do not scare him into running to the mountains for safety.

THE LORD IS IN CHARGE (11:4, 5)

⁴The LORD is in His holy temple; the LORD's throne is in heaven;
His eyes behold, His eyelids test the sons of men.
⁵The LORD tests the righteous and the wicked,
And the one who loves violence His soul hates.

Verse 4. God is seated in majesty on His throne in heaven. The eye of faith will see the unseen protector watching over His own rather than focusing upon the unseen foes in the darkness around him.

The LORD is in His holy temple, he says. This phrase, appearing only twice in the Scriptures, may have been quoted later by Habakkuk as he emphasized that God is the only God and added, "Let all the earth be silent before Him" (Hab. 2:20). No one has removed God from His place of rulership over the world. He is almighty, and He still reigns as the Supreme King over all people and over all the earth. "The Lord is high and lifted up; His **throne is in heaven**" is his affirmation of faith.

From His exalted position in the heavens, God surveys the affairs of mankind. Saul is not in charge; God is. Furthermore, the writer knows that God, the King of the universe, beholds the actions of people with a penetrating gaze that misses nothing. Yes, **His eyes behold** all people and all circumstances. No evil person or trying situation ever escapes His scrutiny. The phrase **His eyelids test** may be a reference to God's squinting His eyes to observe more closely the deeds of mankind. "His eyes behold" and "His eyelids test" are a synonymous parallelism.

The word for "test" (בָּחַן, *bachan*) means to examine, as one would precious metals, for the purpose of removing the impurities and dross. God allows the righteous to be placed in the fires of trial for the purposes of maturation and purification.

Verse 5. This testing is broad and comprehensive. He judges or **tests** all people—**the righteous and the wicked**. No one on earth is beyond His all-seeing gaze. He watches the godly that He may strengthen them by refining their loyalty and by delivering them when the fires of trial are too hot. He watches the wicked in order to judge and punish them. The wicked may not see Him, but He sees and judges them.

As the Lord scrutinizes "the sons of men" (בְּנֵי אָדָם, *b⁽ᵉ⁾ney 'adam*), He sees something that He despises: **the one who loves violence**. His love of righteousness presupposes the converse, His hatred of evil. God loves all people and desires that everyone be saved (2 Pet. 3:9; Jn. 3:16; 1 Tim. 2:4), but He hates wickedness. Because of who God is and the attributes of His character, we should not be surprised at the statement: "And the one who loves violence **His soul hates**." He does not just dislike violence that is energized by a malevolent and sinister motivation—He despises it. This attitude of God grows out of the nature of His righteous personality and being.

GOD AND THE WICKED (11:6)

> ⁶**Upon the wicked He will rain snares;**
> **Fire and brimstone and burning wind will be the portion of their cup.**

Verse 6. The righteous person does not have to take care of the evil ones seeking his life; God will. Assuredly, at the time of His choice, God will punish every wicked person.

Four figures are used to present the truth that God will call all wickedness into account. First, the psalmist speaks of "snares." He says that **upon the wicked He will rain snares**. The wicked will one day be caught in God's judgment even as a person is caught outside in a storm. God will pour difficulties down upon them like a watery deluge. They will, in God's time, be flooded with difficulties, especially the ordeal of divine judgment.

Second, he mentions **fire and brimstone**, a figure possibly taken from the destruction of Sodom and Gomorrah (Gen. 19:24), and used throughout the Scriptures as an expression of judgment (Deut. 29:23; Is. 30:33; Ezek. 38:22; Lk. 17:28–30, 32). The point is, the wicked will get what is coming to them, just as Sodom and Gomorrah did.

His third figure is that of a **burning wind**, a common expression to those who live in the arid desert regions. The wicked will be engulfed with the scorching, blinding, devastating winds. These winds are a metaphor for the blistering judgment of God.

The fourth figure is that of a **cup** of wrath. The "burning wind" **will be** [their] **portion**, or "their cup." The wicked will face a violent wind, or to say it with another metaphor, they will drink a "cup" of wrath. They cannot escape the coming judgment of God.

AN EXPRESSION OF CONFIDENCE (11:7)

**⁷For the LORD is righteous, He loves righteousness;
The upright will behold His face.**

Verse 7. The psalm ends with a stirring reassurance concerning the righteous. The writer gives encouragement for any distressed person with a three-pronged truth about God: what He is, what He loves, and what He promises. (1) One must remember that He is **righteous**. The foundational attribute of His character is holiness. He will never approve of evil, nor will He ever side with evildoers.

(2) An even stronger expression is **He loves righteousness**. This spiritual quality is a passion with Him—He radiates it, wants it in the world, and seeks it in His people. (3) Therefore, He promises that **the upright will** [see or] **behold His face**. Only the true of heart can walk with Him. He does not extend His fellowship to those who are evil.

For the believer, the ultimate glory is to see the face of God. The greatest gift from God is God Himself. "Behold His face" may be a figurative way of referring to an ever-increasing sense of fellowship with God. The presence of God becomes clearer as we become more like Him in godly living. Thus seeing "His face" is not a single event in eternity toward which we look (although that is true in a literal sense), but it is an ever-growing experience in this life as we draw closer to Him.

Nothing will ever change about God's character. We will not find that one day, especially during the day of our trials, God has changed and defends evildoers. However, only the righteous heart will have the benefit of His blessings and the companionship of His presence.

APPLICATION

God, the Ultimate Glory
David resolves to stand by his post of duty despite adversity. What encourages him?

He is not afraid because God is his refuge. God is around him, shielding him from any danger.

He knows that his trial will make him stronger. God does not tempt anyone to sin, but He does test the maturation of our faith.

He knows that God, at the appropriate time, as the great Avenger, will deal with the wicked. We do not have to personally punish the wicked; God is in charge of all vengeance.

David is saying, "Do not run from a fiery trial, but use it to see the face of God more clearly. Do not flee from it, but walk in it with God."

Why Stay?
Why would anyone remain in a difficult situation? The wisdom of this world would urge one to abandon hardship in search of an easier life.

David's friends plead for him to go to some secluded spot where he can rest and relax in freedom from trials. His brave response expresses his faith in God's providential care. He sees safety in steadfastness to the Lord! He tells his friends that he is staying—not because of who he is, but because of who God is.

David presents three pictures of God that give him courage in this trying circumstance.

God is a protector of those who are righteous and trust in Him. God is his refuge, and he will not be afraid of people or any circumstance.

God is the great Judge of all. No wicked person will escape His all-seeing gaze.

God is the righteous God. He loves righteousness, and He encourages and defends it.

In short, God is his refuge, the Avenger of Evil, and the tester of his soul. His response shows us how we are to think of God as we try to be faithful in difficult surroundings. God is with the righteous, not against them. He will deliver the righteous, but He will bring the wicked into judgment.

When Trials Come

In the day of trial, we always have before us three major possibilities of action. Advice is given about all three in this psalm.

We can run. This response is a big temptation. "Let us go where we will be free from difficulties," our trembling hearts may say.

We can stay and complain. We can tough it out with a sour spirit that keeps us and everyone around us upset. Such a response is a humanistic, pagan response: "I'll see this through, but I will hate every minute of it. I will stiffen my upper lip, and grimacing all the way through, I will make it."

We can stay and trust. We can recognize that God never abandons His children. He is especially near whenever His children are in trouble. No father would walk off and leave a child in pain or in a life-threatening situation. God, the perfect Father, is always standing with His children who are in distress. Those who are trying to be righteous in His sight and are seeking to walk with Him have His blessings, fellowship, presence, and protection. Furthermore, we can trust that God will be the Judge and Avenger of any enemies we may have. He watches over all people and circumstances.

What attitude shall we take when adverse circumstances seem to be engulfing us—will we flee or walk by faith with God?

Flee as a Bird?

Mary S. B. Dana used the phrase "flee as a bird to your mountain" in her spiritual song that we often sing in our assemblies.

PSALM 11

> Flee as a bird to your mountain,
>   Thou who art weary of sin;
> Go to the clear flowing fountain
>   Where you may wash and be clean.
>
> Fly, for th'avenger is near thee;
>   Call, and the Savior will hear thee;
> He on His bosom will bear thee,
>   O thou who art weary of Sin.[1]

She lifted this phrase from its psalm-setting and used it to mean that the Avenger of Sin (God) is near us and that we should flee to Jesus, the mountain in which is a clear, flowing fountain, where we can be cleansed from sin and be free from all fear.

The song pictures God as the Avenger of Sin and at the same time as the refuge, protector, and comforter of those who have been cleansed from sin. It is a beautiful song, but it has taken the liberty of using "the fleeing bird" phrase in a different way than the psalm does.

Let us remember the message of the psalm: Though David had been advised to flee from his trying situation, he refused to do so. He believed that he should stay where he was and fulfill God's will. He further believed that God would watch over him and protect him where he was.

A Special Phrase

The phrase "The Lord is in His holy temple" is found twice in the Old Testament—in this psalm and in Habakkuk 2:20.

In this psalm it suggests *the supremacy of God*. He sits above the earth, watching all the deeds of men, and He will be the final Judge of all things.

In Habakkuk 2:20, it is used to declare *the exclusiveness of God*. He is the only God, for idols are nonentities. Therefore, "let all the earth be silent before Him."

---

[1] Mary S. B. Dana, "Flee as a Bird," *Songs of the Church*, comp. and ed. Alton H. Howard (West Monroe, La.: Howard Publishing Co., 1977).

When Should We Flee?

Should we always stay and fight? No. There are times when fleeing is appropriate and even necessary. In this psalm, the writer believes that God has given him a position of responsibility and that he should not leave his post of duty without a clear directive from God. However, some examples of people fleeing are given in the Scriptures.

Flee, for the sake of your soul. Joseph fled when sin threatened him (Gen. 39:12). He saw that he did not have time to untie the knot, so he cut it and ran.

Flee, for the sake of God's will. David will later flee when God tells him to do so (1 Sam. 19:18). He is under the leadership of God, and his response to God's Word is an expression of faith. Plus, consider the other places in the Scriptures where fleeing is commanded (Gen. 19:17; 1 Kings 19:3–9; Mt. 24:16; 2 Cor. 6:17). God's will determines what people should do.

Flee, for the sake of evangelism. Paul fled when duty called somewhere else (Acts 14:5, 6). When persecution threatened his life and the lives of new converts, Paul hurried to another city to continue preaching and teaching.

Faith sometimes compels us to stay, and sometimes it commands us to flee. The decision must be made in light of the circumstance and the command of God.

PSALM 12
GOD'S ANSWER TO EVIL

The Superscription: For the choir director; upon an eight-stringed lyre. A Psalm of David. This lament psalm is described by its title as **a Psalm** [מִזְמוֹר, *mizmor*] **of** ["by," "for," or "to"] **David** (לְדָוִד, *lᵉdawid*). The superscription gives guidance **for the choir director** [לַמְנַצֵּחַ, *lamnatstseach*]; **upon an eight-stringed lyre** (עַל־הַשְּׁמִינִית, *al hashshᵉminith*). The term *al hashshᵉminith* just means "on the eighth" although the NASB has added "stringed lyre" to their translation. This portion of the title is uncertain. Some think that the two words refer to the men's voices beginning an octave lower than the women's; others think that they refer to an instrument with eight strings (perhaps a harp) even as the NASB has suggested; still others think that they refer to the eighth stage of some particular worship ritual.

This psalm was written during a time when dishonest and unscrupulous people seemed to be in the majority, and righteous people from all appearances had almost vanished from the earth. We would classify it as a community lament psalm.

An unusual feature of this song is that it first contains a prayer to God and then it gives His answer immediately following the prayer. This characteristic is found in only three other psalms in the entire Book of Psalms (60; 81; 95).

In the midst of the lament, a contrast is shown between the words of people and the words of God, between the sinfulness of mankind and the trustworthiness of God. People lie—uttering cutting words and offering vain promises; but God speaks healing words that are like pure silver and makes promises that are as sure as the foundations of the earth.

The heart of the psalm is a prayer in which the writer asks

God to put an end to the evils in his society. His petition is immediately followed by God's personal pledge to defend and sustain those who have been afflicted by the destructive words of man.

The overriding theme of this psalm is that God will care for the mistreated, even when they are surrounded by evil. The psalm progresses from a prayer (vv. 1–4) to a promise (v. 5) and then ends with a rather negative settled view of how things will be in the world (vv. 6–8).

THE PRAYER (12:1–4)

¹**Help, LORD, for the godly man ceases to be,**
For the faithful disappear from among the sons of men.
²**They speak falsehood to one another;**
With flattering lips and with a double heart they speak.
³**May the LORD cut off all flattering lips,**
The tongue that speaks great things;
⁴**Who have said, "With our tongue we will prevail;**
Our lips are our own; who is lord over us?"

Verse 1. A cry for communal salvation is being raised up to God because of the prevailing corrupted condition of the society. The plea for assistance begins with the simple request: **Help, LORD.** The word for "help" (הוֹשִׁיעָה, *hoshi'ah*) is an imperative that means "deliver" or "save." The noun form of this word (הוֹשֵׁעַ, *hoshea'*) is the name Hosea, the name worn by the first minor prophet. The supplication presupposes an awful predicament that requires a divine remedy. The writer beseeches God to come to Israel's aid, and then he proceeds to list what he wants God to do.

He laments, **The godly man ceases to be, for the faithful disappear from among the sons of men.** The main reason then for this earnest entreaty is that "the godly man" (חָסִיד, *chasid*), the trustworthy person, has almost become extinct. "The faithful" (אֱמוּנִים, *'emunim*) men have vanished from the human race. Micah was concerned about a similar tragedy in his time (Mic. 7:2). The lament is a poetic exaggeration expressing how incred-

PSALM 12

ibly hard it is for the writer to find a just person who treats others right in his community of believers.

Verse 2. What is his evidence for making such an extreme accusation? He says, **They speak falsehood to one another; with flattering lips and with a double heart they speak.** As part of his proof, he says that the people are speaking "falsehood to one another." "Falsehood" is שָׁוְא (*shaw^e*), a word that means false, empty, and vain things. Such corrupt language was a communication exchange between a man and his "friend" (רֵעַ, *rea'*). The Hebrew expression for "to one another" is "from man to friend."

In addition, he sees that people are speaking "with flattering lips." They are actually "smooth" lips (חֲלָקוֹת, *ch^alaqoth*), a metaphor for the art of saying something nice in order to get one's way or in order to gain some personal profit.

This kind of talking is done "with a double heart." The Hebrew phrase is "a heart and a heart" (בְּלֵב וָלֵב, *b^eleb waleb*). From their lips come words that evidence one kind of spirit, but their hearts are motivated by a different purpose entirely. They are "two-faced" or hypocrites. They say one thing with their lips but believe the opposite in their hearts. This type of person might be compared to the hypocrisy of a merchant who uses two weights, one for buying and one for selling (Deut. 25:13). In buying, one might use a heavy weight so that he will get much for little; in selling, a merchant might use a light weight so that the buyer would get little for much. To top it off, this crook would work the thievery with a caring face and compassionate words.

In this picture, the word "tongue" is used as a synecdoche, as a part standing for the whole. The figure represents the whole man, not just a small member of the mouth. The term "flattering lips" refers to a man, an evil soul, who misleads and takes advantage of the young, the weak, or the aged. This false way of talking has become his settled and habitual way of life.

Verse 3. The writer asks of God, **May the LORD cut off all flattering lips, the tongue that speaks great things.** His deep desire is for God to "cut off" this wickedness and put a stop to it. He asks God do something about the evil that is everywhere.

In other words, lovingkindness, trustworthiness, truthfulness, reliability, integrity, and righteousness are no longer admired as character traits and are no longer found in the people. They are not even evident in those who are part of the covenant community.

Falsehood, flattery, hypocrisy, boasting, slandering, deceiving, and cursing are for them a normal way of life. Words are no longer a way of comforting, encouraging, and teaching others; they are a means of ensnaring the unsuspecting and tripping up those unable to defend themselves.

These people brag with a "tongue that speaks great things." They have boastful spirits and they arrogantly express whatever they wish.

Verse 4. They say, **"With our tongue we will prevail."** Amazingly self-confident in their wickedness, they declare that their **lips are** [their] **own**, and that there is no **lord** or master **over** them. They believe that they can speak with impunity with their lips, that they are under no one's control, and that they will have to answer to no one.

They believe that they can do whatever they desire, say whatever they want, and be whatever they aspire to be, without any interference from God. They do not deny the existence of God, but they believe that He will not or cannot affect their lives in any way at any time. They live as though He does not exist.

Notice the types of sins that are mentioned: the sin of lying, hypocrisy, and boastful living. All three aberrations stem from hearts estranged from God.

A PROMISE (12:5–7)

⁵"Because of the devastation of the afflicted, because of
  the groaning of the needy,
Now I will arise," says the LORD; "I will set him in the safety
  for which he longs."
⁶The words of the LORD are pure words;
As silver tried in a furnace on the earth, refined seven times.
⁷You, O LORD, will keep them;
You will preserve him from this generation forever.

Verse 5. After the prayer is uttered, God immediately answers it. The psalmist records the response he receives for the benefit of the reader. God says, **"Because of the devastation of the afflicted, because of the groaning of the needy, now I will arise."** He promises to act in view of the prayer that has come up to Him. He will especially rise up in behalf of "the afflicted" and "the needy."

As is implied in the Lord's answer, the vicious tongues are especially hurtful to the poor and the disadvantaged. God has always been incensed by the predicament of "the afflicted" or the mistreated. He has heard "the groanings of the needy," and He "will arise" and bring them into **the safety** (יֵשַׁע, *yesha'*) for which they long. The word **longs** (פּוּחַ, *puach*) can also mean "panting," as a deer pants for water. The "needy" yearn for a refuge. God says that He will **set him**—this mistreated man—in the place of protection that he craves. This answer that God gives reminds us of how He heard the cry of the slaves in the furnace of affliction in Egypt and gave them deliverance (Ex. 2:24).

God says that He is going to arise and nothing on earth can prevent Him from rising up. As W. Graham Scroggie wrote, "When God arises for a man, the victory is won; and when He arises against a man, the battle is lost."[1]

Verse 6. These promises from the Lord are **pure words** (טְהֹרוֹת, *t^ehoroth*); that is, they are faithful and trustworthy. His words are like **silver** refined to perfection, **in a furnace on the earth**, so that it contains no impurities or dross.

"On the earth" may refer to where the furnace is, or it could refer to the furnace itself being made out of clay, as the NIV translates it. The purifying process is so complete that it is as if His words have gone through refinement **seven times**. The number "seven" represents completeness or fullness.

Since silver was one of the primary means of market exchange in the Near Eastern world, it was at certain times and in certain places valued above gold. God's words are like refined silver; they are dependable, for He keeps every word He speaks.

---

[1] W. Graham Scroggie, *The Psalms* (Old Tappan, N.J.: Fleming H. Revell Co., 1973), 92.

Verse 7. God says to the trusting, downtrodden people that He will **keep them** and **preserve** them throughout the future. His guarantee to "preserve" includes provisions and protection for the poor and the helpless.

God will keep His commitments. In fact, the promises of God are the most enduring things of the earth. They will reach from generation to generation. God, the eternal One, will keep the unfortunate ones from **this generation** into the next. He is the God of today, and He can be counted upon to be the faithful God of tomorrow. He will sustain the believer **forever**. His words are precious, pure, and enduring. His promises to sustain and to guard are assured by His almighty power and His unfailing love.

A SETTLED VIEW (12:8)

⁸**The wicked strut about on every side
When vileness is exalted among the sons of men.**

Verse 8. A stark realization surfaces at the end of the psalm, bringing the psalm to a conclusion on a somewhat negative note. Just as our Lord said, "We will always have the poor with us," (see Mt. 26:11) this writer implies, "We will always have the wicked with us." While we are in this world, we will have to deal with them.

He says, **The wicked strut about on every side**. He must mean that God's answer to his prayer will have to be lived out in a world where evil will continually abound. In fact, **vileness** [will even be] **exalted among the sons of men**. People will venerate it and glory in it. However, God can and will care for the righteous, even when they are surrounded by evil. He will not totally cut off the wicked, but He will shield the righteous as they live for Him in a sinful world.

During this life, we will not find a utopia or paradise that is free from the marks of evil. Much of the time, "vileness" will be honored and accepted, while righteousness will be hard to find.

APPLICATION

God and Cries for Help

God does answer our cries for help, but He will not reconstruct the world so that all evil is eliminated. Rather, He will sustain those who trust in Him even in a wicked world. In the end this psalm affirms that God will protect His own in spite of anything that evil people might do or think.

How, then, are we to live out this psalm?

We are to pray to God to deal with the sin in us and around us. This emphasis would be the main theme of the psalm.

We are to live righteous lives in the midst of wickedness. The answer lies not in joining the society of sin but in shunning it with godly living.

We are to trust God to answer our prayers. He will remove all wickedness, and He will strengthen the abused to receive His strength in the midst of a sinful and perverse country.

When You Feel Alone

At times God's great people have felt alone in their pursuit of holiness and sacred work. Micah said, "The godly have been swept from the land; not one upright man remains" (Mic. 7:2). Isaiah wrote, "The righteous perish . . . devout men are taken away" (Is. 57:1). Elijah said, "I am the only one left" (1 Kings 19:10, 14). If you feel this way sometimes, think of the following truths.

Remember that you are not alone. It may seem as if you are, but there are others who are faithfully serving.

Remember that God is with you. God and you, after all, make a majority. God plus you equals enough. He never forsakes His own.

Remember that doing God's will has never been the most popular thing. Jesus used the word "few" when he referred to the population of the S and N, the strait and narrow way (Mt. 7:13, 14). The multitudes of the earth choose the way of least resistance, the way of evil and self-indulgence.

Remember that one person has often made a big difference in the outcome of things. Noah, one man, led the way in making a new world. Paul, one man, changed the world with his missionary journeys.

Remember that you were not called to an easy life but to a cross-bearing life that will involve serving God in a world of evil. Life was not easy for Jesus, Paul, Peter, or John; and it will not be free from difficulty for us.

If He Should Answer Us

The writer laments to God in prayer, and then God gives him a specific answer to his prayer. Suppose we asked God a question in our supplications and God gave us an immediate response? We know what the answers would be to some of our questions, would we not? All we have to do is to look at the words of Jesus, His Son, for Jesus and His words compose God's basic answers to most of our prayers.

If we asked, "Lord, what about all the lost people on earth? What should we do about them?" He would answer in the words of His Son, "Go into all the world and preach the gospel to all creation" (Mk. 16:15).

If we asked, "Lord, what about all the poor people, the lonely people, and the battered people?" He would say in the words of His Son, "Feed the hungry, give a drink to the thirsty, invite in the stranger, clothe the naked, and visit the imprisoned" (Mt. 25:34–36).

If we asked, "Lord, what about the people who do not care about You? What about those who are our enemies, the ones who talk about us and misrepresent us?" He would say in the words of His Son, "Love your enemies and pray for those who persecute you, so that you may be sons of your Father who is in heaven; for He causes His sun to rise on the evil and the good, and sends rain on the righteous and the unrighteous" (Mt. 5:44, 45).

Jesus and His words are God's "Amen," His great yes to our prayers (2 Cor. 1:18, 19).

The Heart of God

By viewing God's response, we are privileged to look into

the heart of God. What kind of heart do we see?

His heart is moved by the needy people of the earth. His specific answer to this prayer accents what He wants done for the mistreated of the earth.

His heart is angered by the wickedness that especially expresses itself in taking advantage of other human beings. He is brokenhearted and moved to judgment by one man's inhumanity to another.

His heart gives special attention to those who trust in Him. He is moved to action by the prayer of the one who has faith in Him.

Through these words the Scriptures pull back the veil and give us a front row seat in observing the thinking of God. God is concerned about healing the hurts of His people, He is angered by sin, and He responds to those who trust in Him.

What Will God Do About Evil?

What does God do about evil in the world?

He grieves over it. His heart sorrows over what it does to His world and His people.

He condemns it. He has clearly registered His disapproval of it and has announced His judgment of it at different times. We can think of the flood, the destruction of Sodom, and the execution of Ananias and Sapphira, and we will see His condemnation of it.

He sends forth His Word to rebuke and correct it. We have the testimony of His Word revealing what He thinks about it and what His children should do about it.

He sends forth His children to be lights in its darkness. They are to show the world how to live and to express verbally God's will about it.

He will eventually judge and destroy it. Perhaps God will not settle His conflict with evil in the present moment. However, history is moving toward a climatic day on which all wrongs will forever be made right.

What Should We Do?

The good-versus-evil battle that rages raises questions: What should we do about evil? What has God asked us to do about it?

We are to recognize God's attitude toward it. He is our Father, and His example serves as our guidance.

We are to allow His Word to lead us in handling it. We need an objective standard to teach us.

We are to live separated lives though we are in the midst of it. We will not be perfect, but we are to be children of light, not the devil's children of darkness. A light is needed in a dark place, and our world is a horribly darkened place because of sin.

We are to rebuke it. We are not only to refuse to have fellowship with it, but we are to renounce it.

We are to rescue people from it. The church is a spiritual hospital, not a museum of saints.

We are to recognize that we will have it with us until the end. At the judgment, the devil and his cohorts will be consigned to everlasting punishment. Until then the battle will continue.

The Divided Heart
This text mentions the divided heart or the double heart (v. 2). Using this expression as a springboard, let us look at four types of divided hearts that are mentioned in the Scriptures.

First, there is the insincere heart. This would be the heart pictured by the prophet Isaiah when he said, "You speak of me with your lips but your hearts are far from Me" (Is. 29:13). Their lips speak of devotion to God, but their hearts are not wholly given to it.

Second, there is the hypocritical heart. The division of the heart is deliberate and purposeful. These people intentionally present one view with their lips, but in their hearts they intend something else.

Third, there is the occupied heart. This heart is full of other concerns. He believes in God, but he does not have time for Him. He sings and bows his head during prayer, but his heart is occupied with earthly matters.

Fourth, there is the unstable heart (Jas. 1:6–8). It is a heart that is tossed to and fro, as James said. One day it is on spiritual things, and the next day it has some other temporal devotion. It is like the wave of the sea that is tossed about by every wind that comes along. It is a heart that is half believing and half doubting.

The Lord has made it clear that He honors the person who worships Him with a consecrated heart—that is, with a heart that is not divided by a lack of interest, an evil purpose, preoccupation, or a lack of commitment.

Sins of the Tongue

Sins of the tongue can bring us down to ruin. The sins of this psalm should warn us!

The sin of flattery. This sin comes out of a double heart—the lips picture one kind of heart while an altogether different heart resides within. One is a heart that seems pleasant and good, and the other is a heart full of evil designs.

The sin of speaking falsehood to one another. This phrase could be a synonymous parallelism to flattering lips. Either way, it is the idea of not saying the truth to another person. Brethren should be able to count on brethren to tell the truth.

The sin of boastful lips. This sin grows out of a heart that does not see the need for God. Two tragedies surface here: The first is the fact that one does not believe that God is needed in his life, and the second is that he tells others about this awful belief that he has.

The tongue as a metaphor stands for one's life and words. The words originate from the heart, springing up from the thinking that is done within. With accurate precision, evil words depict an evil heart and life.

The Divine Certainties

The authentic certainties that we know emanate from God. This psalm reminds us of one eternal truth about God that we can treasure: God will defend the person who trusts in Him. The writer pleads for help from God, and God is pictured as answering him and telling him what He is going to do. We do not always know how God will do what He has said, but we can know this fact: He will act in harmony with His stated truth. He has been and always will be faithful.

God Answering Man

Jesus spoke of two men who went up to the temple to pray; and this psalm pictures two men thinking about God. One man, a trusting man, asked God for help and God answered him by saying, "I will."

The second man, a representative of impious men, said, "I do not need God. I can do what I want to do when I want to do it. God will have nothing to do with my life."

God answered the second man—by implication—by saying, "I will not preserve you, but I will preserve the one who trusts in Me. One day you will meet Me in judgment."

The Promises of God

The Spirit says that the promises of God have a special character to them.

They are pure. They are free from any falsehood. Those who know God know that His words are absolutely true.

They are proven. They are trustworthy. It is as if they have been tested in the furnace of fire seven times over. They will come to pass.

They are enduring. They are reliable, and they will carry us to and through tomorrow into the brightness of His presence. Their eternal nature is seen in their stretching without fail from generation to generation.

Life has to be built upon promises—either the promises of God or the promises of others. God's promises stand apart from all others because of their integrity.

Psalm 13
When God Is Silent

The Superscription: For the choir director. A Psalm of David. The title identifies this psalm as **a Psalm** [מִזְמוֹר, *mizmor*] **of** ["by," "for," or "to"] **David** (לְדָוִד, *lᵉdawid*) and gives the additional note **for the choir director** (לַמְנַצֵּחַ, *lamnatstseach*).

Tremper Longman has defined the lament psalm as "a cry to God from a soul who has nowhere to turn but to God."[1] This psalm fits that definition, for it is an appeal to God from a person who is going through a dark night of utter despair. In fact, this psalm is often thought of as the classic lament psalm. Having three parts, with two verses in each part, it includes a description of helplessness (vv. 1, 2), a prayer to God for deliverance (vv. 3, 4), and a concluding expression of faith in God (vv. 5, 6). However, it comprises one of the shortest lament psalms in the Book of Psalms.

The writer is a deeply troubled soul as he writes this psalm. He is passing through one of his darkest valleys of fear and hopelessness. It may be that he is in the midst of a sickness that is threatening his life; or, perhaps, he can see that he is on the verge of being hemmed in by enemies. It is possible that he is plagued by both problems—with his sickness providing an occasion for his enemies to rejoice over the possibility of his death.

While we cannot place the historical setting with accuracy, one possibility is that it was written during the period when

---

[1]Tremper Longman III, *How to Read the Psalms* (Downers Grove, Ill.: InterVarsity Press, 1988), 26.

David was a fugitive and was relentlessly hunted by Saul (1 Sam. 27:1), a trial that spanned nearly fifteen years. At least, he mentions a special enemy who is pursuing him and would find particular satisfaction in his death (Ps. 13:2, 4). If this is not the setting, thinking of this situation provides a good illustration of the kind of background that must be behind this psalm.

"HOW LONG?" (13:1, 2)

> ¹How long, O Lord? Will You forget me forever?
> How long will You hide Your face from me?
> ²How long shall I take counsel in my soul,
> Having sorrow in my heart all the day?
> How long will my enemy be exalted over me?

Verse 1. The writer begins with a plea for God to hear his prayers. He prays, **How long, O Lord?** In figurative language, he pictures God as forgetting about him and asks "how long" it will be before God answers him. God cannot forget anyone or anything; He does not have the weaknesses of humans, but it may sometimes appear to the distressed soul that God has allowed his situation to slip from His mind.

He uses "how long?" (עַד־אָנָה, *'ad-'anah*)—which in Hebrew is "until where?"—four times in four questions to express his deep heaviness of heart and his feeling of being forsaken. With his questions, he points to three relationships affected by his suffering: his relationship with God, the attitude of his own heart, and his relationship with his enemies.

He pleads, **Will You forget me forever?** He has waited a long time for God to answer him, and he is wondering how long it will take for God to respond. "Forever" could be translated "continually."

He asks, **How long will You hide Your face from me?** To the psalmist, it seems as if he were no longer in God's mind; it is as if God intentionally had turned away so that He might not have to see his peril and pain. God's face "turned toward us" is always recognized in the Scriptures as an expression of His fellowship, blessings, and approval (see Ps. 30:7; 41:12; Is. 1:15).

The worst tragedy for a believer would be for God's face to be turned away from him.

Verse 2. With great emotion the writer asks, in effect, "How long will all of this continue?" He means, "When will you step in and deal with my trouble? Will my prayers always go unheeded?"

He further asks, **How long shall I take counsel in my soul?** Apparently, he talks to himself, giving himself "counsel" (עֵצוֹת, *'etsoth*) on what to do. In the conversation going on within his heart, he reminds himself of his tremendous suffocating need. He has **sorrow in** [his] **heart all the day**. Sorrow upon sorrow floods his innermost spirit. He is burdened with pain and cannot find a solution to it. The pain is unceasing, unremitting, "all the day," an idiom that means night and day. The point is, he is experiencing nonstop suffering as he waits for God's deliverance.

Part of his pain is his enemy; and therefore, he asks, **How long will my enemy be exalted over me?** His enemy is elated at his humiliation and finds devilish delight in hounding him. It looks to him as if his enemy is enjoying a victory while he is experiencing a defeat.

"CONSIDER ME!" (13:3, 4)

> ³**Consider and answer me, O Lord, my God;**
> **Enlighten my eyes, or I will sleep the sleep of death,**
> ⁴**And my enemy will say, "I have overcome him,"**
> **And my adversaries will rejoice when I am shaken.**

Verse 3. The psalmist knows where to go to get help. He does not know the solution to his difficulty, but he knows who does. He asks that God **consider and answer** him. His address, **O Lord, my God**, indicates his personal relationship with God. He is God's servant, and he knows that God is watching over him in lovingkindness. To "consider" him would be to give special attention to him; to "answer" him would be to grant the relief from his distress.

His situation is so desperate that he sees himself as near the end. **Enlighten my eyes, or I will sleep the sleep of death,** he says. He pleads for God to deliver him from death (or a tragedy similar to it) so that he would have life once again.

God is asked to listen, weigh, and respond to his prayer. He wants God to "enlighten [his] eyes." Reddish, empty eyes symbolize sickness and sorrow (Ps. 6:7; 38:10; Lam. 5:17), and enlightened eyes suggest the revival of physical strength and the return of energy (see 1 Sam. 14:27, 29; Prov. 29:13; Ezra 9:8). When his deliverance is granted and his vitality is restored, he knows that his eyes will glisten with the laughter and joy of life and victory. He is allowing one beautiful side-effect of success—the light of his eyes—to stand for the whole victory.

Verse 4. If the psalmist is not delivered, he believes the enemy will seize upon this fact and ridicule the care God has given him. He says, **And my enemy will say, "I have overcome him"**; he argues, **And my adversaries will rejoice when I am shaken**. This rationale for his prayer is expressed by the use of פֶּן (*pen*), a word translated "or" in verse 3 and "and" in verse 4. It can also be translated "lest." In the KJV "lest" is used two times expressly and one time implicatively. He speaks of the "lest" of death (v. 3), the "lest" of defeat (v. 4), and the "lest" of ridicule (by implication, v. 4). What would God get out of assisting him? Simply this: His death would provide a basis for his enemies to rejoice over him—and through his defeat they would find a reason to claim victory over God. The implication is that his death would reflect on God, since the writer is God's servant and under His provisions. This is not what God wants. He desires servants who reflect His might, His concern for His people, and His faithfulness.

In this way, the author brings his need to God. In a simple prayer, he asks God to come and turn his dark night into a sunlit day.

"I WILL TRUST" (13:5, 6)

⁵**But I have trusted in Your lovingkindness;**
My heart shall rejoice in Your salvation.
⁶**I will sing to the L**ORD**,**

Because He has dealt bountifully with me.

Verse 5. After he prays for help, he resolves to trust in God. He affirms, **But I have trusted in Your lovingkindness**. The tone of this psalm changes from a cry to God to confidence in God, from a lament to a song, from sobbing to singing. He has assurance that God will triumphantly save him because he knows of and believes in God's love and faithfulness. He says that he will trust in God's "covenant loyalty," His "lovingkindness," and His promise to be the faithful God of His people.

We can "believe in the sun when the night is the blackest." The appropriate action to take after sincere prayer is to wait in the belief that God will do what He has promised at the right time and in the wisest way. Is there a greater One than God in whom we can place our faith?

He says that his **heart shall rejoice in** [God's] **salvation**. That is, he will rejoice in the cessation of his misery and in the removal of the opposition from enemies.

Verse 6. I will sing to the LORD, he says. He plans to be vocal about the faith of his heart, singing about how the Lord has graciously responded to all of his requests. He could rejoice **because** [God] **has dealt bountifully with** [him]. While the enemy stalks about looking for an opportunity to slay him, while the circumstances threaten to destroy him, he will sing quietly in his soul and with his lips about the grace, faithfulness, and goodness of God. The perfect place to demonstrate faith in God is in the crucible of suffering.

APPLICATION

When We Are Confused

What do godly people do when the torrents of fear and defeat sweep over their souls like the tide of the ocean? *What can we do when we do not know what to do?*

We can pray, bringing our fears and frustrations to God's throne; we can trust God to do what He deems best about our plight; we can sing in thanksgiving for His blessings, both great and small.

This psalm speaks to the storm-tossed soul, to the spirit ravaged by the forces of darkness, and to the heart that longs for hope. The fact that a believer in God is passing through a seemingly endless trial does not mean that God does not care. The reason a specific trial is not removed is hidden in the wisdom of God and may not be known until, in eternity, God vindicates every righteous sufferer.

Those of us who trust in God should not be shaken in our faith, however severe and troubling their circumstances may become. We will bring our battered lives and stormy situations before Him; we will trust Him to handle them as He sees best, and then we will go on our way singing of God's gifts of love and grace which He has showered upon us.

The Value of Prayer

Why should we pray? We can see three benefits of prayer in this psalm.

First, prayer is the divinely-ordained approach to God for those who trust in Him. Charles Hodge has said, "I don't believe in prayer . . . I believe in [God]."[2] Prayer permits special fellowship with God, an opportunity to petition God for our needs, and a time to rejoice before God over the good things He has given.

Second, prayer reminds us of what we believe about God. If we do not believe in God, we will not pray. If we do not believe that God is good, we will not pray expectantly. If we believe that God answers prayer and that He is good, we will pray and expect a gracious answer from Him.

Third, prayer ignites our noble resolves. Prayer not only reminds us of what we believe about God, but it also reminds us of what we believe our role is in living for Him. We come away from prayer more determined than ever to be faithful to our Lord. In prayer, we see God and ourselves more clearly than before.

This psalm moves from a cry of despair to a petition to a calm assurance. This movement is usually the movement that

---

[2]Charles B. Hodge, Jr., *Prayer: The Voice of Faith* (Searcy, Ark.: Resource Publications, 1996), 19.

takes place in all of us when we pray.

The Journey to Assurance

The writer makes a journey as he prays to his God, a spiritual trek that is normal and expected when one comes to God in supplication.

He puts his trust in God. He calls upon God to deliver him from his trials. By faith, he brings his anguish to God.

He resigns to allow God to answer his prayer as He deems best. He puts his trouble in God's hands with the assurance that God will answer him according to His wisdom and grace.

From this resignation, *there emerges a rejoicing in God's faithfulness.* Trust leads to gladness in who God is and what God does for those who believe in Him.

Then, there is singing. Because of who God is and because of His wonderful traits, the writer resolves that he will sing in his soul and with his lips about God's lovingkindness.

A Helpful Response

When our minds are clouded with sorrow and suffering, thinking of the nature of God, what He has done, is doing, and will do, helps us.

We can think of the past. Let us remember His faithfulness to those who have trusted in Him through the years. We can meditate upon His lovingkindness to His servants in the Bible and to us in the recent past. This will remind us of God's integrity and trustworthiness.

We can consider what God is doing now. He is busy accomplishing what He said he would do even though we may not see His actions clearly. He has not forsaken His will even though we do not see His hand with our physical eyes.

We can contemplate His promises for the future. God will not and cannot lie; therefore, one can look at His promises and see what He is going to do. His promises give us a certain picture of what tomorrow will be like.

Meditating upon God's past actions, His present actions, and His future actions makes our present problems look smaller, for we know that we will see the hand of God soon just as we have seen it in the past. Re-read Hebrews 6:13–18.

The Great Fears

The faithful followers of God usually have in their hearts four great fears. They pop up frequently in our thoughts and prayers.

There is the fear of death. We want to serve our God in this world as much as we can. In Old Testament times, the highest goal that one could envision was that of doing God's will on earth and walking with God. When our lives are cut short, we can no longer serve Him here.

There is the fear of defeat. To be overcome by an enemy of God is a big fear that we may have. We want to see victory, not failure.

There is the fear of ridicule. Following defeat would be ridicule. For the enemy to be able to say, "Look at your calamity. Your God has not been able to deliver you!" would be a horrible disaster for the person who trusts in Him.

There is the fear of bringing reproach upon our God. Behind the first three fears is this fear of disparaging the reputation of God. Death, defeat, and ridicule would dishonor our God, for we are His servants. We are under His providence. We want to spread His glory, and we never want to tarnish the righteous name of God in the minds of people around us.

The writer pleads with God from all four viewpoints as he prays. He is asking God to deliver him so that none of these fears will come to pass.

How Pain Affects Us

At least three areas of the writer's life are affected by his suffering. All of these are addressed with his questions which begin with "How long?"

His relationship with God. In his misery, he cries out, "How long before You act in my behalf?" He has not given up on God, but some people allow their disappointment over God's not acting quickly in their behalf to cause them to close their hearts to God.

His spirit. He says that daily he is filled with sorrow. He has been affected psychologically in the palace of his soul. In his innermost spirit, he is continually giving himself counsel on what to do. Confusion reigns within him. Pain throws our hearts into turmoil if we are not anchored in the ways of God.

His reputation. This writer believes that if God allows him to die, or if God permits him to go down in defeat, his enemies will gloat. Since he is God's servant, what happens to the servant reflects the care his God has given him.

When one has the perspective of faith, all three of these areas are relieved. One's relationship with God remains firm because he knows that God will act in His own time and in His own way. One's heart becomes calm even when a plan of action is not evident because he confidently believes that God will look after him. One's reputation is not in jeopardy because he has placed his reputation in the hands of God.

Why Believe in God?

Is God dependable? Is He faithful in doing what He has promised? Why should one trust in God and believe that He will answer his prayers?

We can believe it because we are praying in His will. God does not promise to bless us while we are in disobedience; but when we are walking (consistently, not perfectly) in His way, we know He will listen.

We can believe it because of His attributes. God is perfect in lovingkindness, faithfulness, and love. It is impossible for Him to lie. God cannot and will not deny Himself.

We can believe it because of His covenant loyalty. God has made promises; these promises grow out of the covenant that He has established with His people. In addition to His unchanging nature, He promises to bless and save His people. We have the double assurance that God will be faithful to us.

Yes, God will hear our prayers. The one who is walking in the light can rest in the great confidence that God will hear because of the perfection of His attributes and the covenant loyalty of His heart.

Psalm 14
Man's Inhumanity to God

The Superscription: For the choir director. A Psalm of David. This psalm and Psalm 53 are almost identical. It appears that Psalm 53 was adapted from this psalm by an inspired writer either for a special occasion of worship or for some other public use. Because Psalm 53 is a unique and meaningful variant of this psalm, the Holy Spirit chose to include it in the Book of Psalms.

The subtitle gives instruction **for the choir director** (לַמְנַצֵּחַ, *lamnatstseach*) and says the psalm is **of** ["by," "for," or "to"] **David** (לְדָוִד, *lᵉdawid*); however, the title attached to Psalm 53, its twin, adds that it is "a Maskil" (מַשְׂכִּיל) and that it was to be set to the tune of "Mahalath" (מָחֲלַת), a tune that is unknown to us.

The term "maskil" is used in the titles of twelve other psalms (42; 44; 45; 52—55; 74; 78; 88; 89; 142). It is generally thought that this term means "to instruct, to make attentive, or to make intelligent." If this interpretation is correct, these psalms are being identified as meditations that were especially designed to teach.

The NASB has referred to this piece as "a Psalm" in its translation of the title, but the two words are not found in the Hebrew. However, the NASB has placed them in italics to indicate their interpretative addition to the title.

This composition of wisdom poetry describes those who have left God out of their thoughts. The outgrowth of their foolish conclusions is shown in relation to God, their fellow man, and themselves. Their lifestyle is portrayed so vividly that Paul used parts of the description to depict the universal sinfulness of the world in Romans 3:10–12. In addition to being called a psalm of instruction (*maśkil*) by the heading of Psalm 53, it is also somewhat of a lament. Beginning with a complaint-like statement, it moves through a discussion of that lament and ends on a note of faith.

We cannot determine the setting of the psalm. Is it a depiction of the godless people of David's day? Is it a portrayal of the wicked in Israel? Could it be a reflection on the world of paganism before the flood, at the time of the destruction of Sodom and Gomorrah, or during the Babel period? We do not know.

In the main thrust of the psalm, the writer sets out to answer one question: "How is practical atheism manifested?"

THE FOOLISH ONES (14:1–3)

¹**The fool has said in his heart, "There is no God."**
They are corrupt, they have committed abominable deeds;
   There is no one who does good.
²**The LORD has looked down from heaven upon the sons of men**
To see if there are any who understand,
Who seek after God.
³**They have all turned aside, together they have become corrupt;**
There is no one who does good, not even one.

Verse 1. The psalm begins with a clear affirmation: **The fool has said in his heart, "There is no God."** This assertion claims that atheism is a matter of the heart—not of the head and not a conclusion formed because of evidence. This view of God springs from a heart devoid of righteousness. Edwin McNeill Poteat has described this unbelief as "a major prejudice, not a major premise."[1]

This type of godlessness is not a theoretical belief reached by research or honest investigation; it is a way of life that has resulted through moral default, selfish ambition, and a persuasion that God does not concern Himself with human affairs. The

---

[1] Edwin McNeill Poteat, "The Book of Psalms" in *The Interpreter's Bible*, ed. George Arthur Buttrick (Nashville: Abingdon Press, 1955), 4:278.

person described is one who has made the choice to disbelieve in God. He has declared his independence from God.

These impudent people are called "fool[s]" (נָבָל, *nabal*), a singular word that designates a class of people. Rejecting righteousness in their hearts, the foolish rush forward into a life of disobedience and wickedness. Their inner thoughts, sooner or later and in varying degrees, will erupt into a perverse, irreligious lifestyle. They are the opposite of the wise because they have deliberately closed their minds to the thoughts of God given in His divine instruction.

Having made the fundamental error of eliminating God from their world, their whole view of life has become distorted by what they have done. These people, the writer says, have become **corrupt** (שָׁחַת, *shachath*), as he compares them to milk that has turned sour and rancid. They have destroyed themselves by taking the wrong road.

The writer sees that unbelieving mankind, instead of becoming good, has become worthless. He says, **They have committed abominable deeds**. They engage in detestable words and deeds that demonstrate a total lack of regard for God. Their actions are repulsive in God's sight.

In poetic exaggeration, he describes the human race in terms of total degeneration: **There is no one who does good**. He does not see anyone who is pure in heart and who lives to do genuine good. Godliness is absent from the land.

Verse 2. As God **has looked down from heaven** [at] **the sons of men** for signs of spirituality and indications that there are people seeking Him, He sees none. He wants to know if **any** of them understand or are pursuing a relationship with Him. He finds that no one is acting wisely, and no one desires to walk with Him. The masses of the people have become oblivious to God and His will.

Verse 3. God speaks and announces His threefold judgment that grows out of what He has seen: First, He sees that **they have all turned aside**. No one is continuing in His will. They have "turned aside" to satisfy their own pleasures and to fulfill their own sinful ventures. Second, He sees that **together they have become corrupt**. When people turn from God, they turn to evil, and evil leads to degradation. Third, He sees that **there is no one who does good, not even one.** True goodness has departed from the land.

Abandoning any belief in God, these people have become depraved in nature, descending to a wicked, habitual way of living. They have evolved into people who do no good and have no desire to do any good. Alexander MacLaren said, "One who is religiously and morally wrong cannot be intellectually right."[2]

Are these words an indictment of the human race as a whole or of the large class that has denied God? Paul used quotations from this section of the psalm to prove his point concerning the sinfulness of all people in Romans 3; however, in the context of the psalm this general truth about mankind is being especially applied to the foolish ones who have chosen the way of sin, the way of practical atheism.

GOD AND THE GODLESS (14:4–6)

⁴**Do all the workers of wickedness not know,
Who eat up my people as they eat bread,
And do not call upon the Lord?**
⁵**There they are in great dread,
For God is with the righteous generation.**
⁶**You would put to shame the counsel of the afflicted,
But the** Lord **is his refuge.**

Verse 4. A sad and horrible misunderstanding of life emerges. **Do all the workers of wickedness not know?** is a question that God asks. Do not those who mistreat the decent, trusting people, know what they are doing? "Surely they do not," is the implied answer. Have they not become aware of what is happening to them? Do they not see how their thoughts and deeds have destroyed them? Do they not understand how they are hurting others?

No interest in God or in God's people can be found in their

---

[2]Alexander MacLaren, *Psalms*, Exposition of the Bible (Hartford, Conn.: S. S. Scranton Co., 1944), 3:40.

hearts. The word for "wicked" (אָוֶן, 'awen) workers might even include within it the worship of idols.

Their mistreatment of God's righteous ones is described through the vivid metaphor of "eating them up." These wicked ones have power in the community and they abuse it as they fleece the poor. Bringing people down to poverty and robbing them is characterized in the Scriptures as devouring the people themselves or as spiritual cannibalism (Mic. 3:3; Prov. 30:14). Their theology (or the absence of it) has resulted in a lack of compassion for others. It leads them to see others, even the righteous, as "things" to be used. The metaphor may also suggest that they do evil as easily as they eat bread. Corrupt as they are, sinning has become easy for them.

The people **do not call upon the Lord**[3] or ask for Him to help them to understand right from wrong. They do not see the need for God. Making the key mistake of not seeking God's guidance, they plunge themselves into willful ignorance. They should know what is true by virtue of the truth that has been handed down to them, through general revelation, and by virtue of their innate consciences; but they have rejected the light they have been given and have refused to seek further light.

Verse 5. A "dread" is mentioned; but is it a fear in the hearts of the poor because of the harsh treatment they expect from the wicked, or is it fear in the hearts of the wicked? The fact that God is present with the poor must indicate that the alarm is in the hearts of the evildoers. If the hearts of these people could be objectively observed, if their souls could be turned inside out, the fear that plagues them would be evident: **There they are in great dread**, he says. Such fear surely characterizes them because they undoubtedly know that **God is with the righteous generation.** Life without God results in terror and alarm. These people know in their hearts that God watches over the righteous. Horror seizes them because of the realization that no one wins against almighty God. James Burton Coffman wrote, "In every wicked man, there is the haunting fear, the secret dread,

---

[3]Although the NASB does not use small capital letters for "Lord" in this verse, the Hebrew word is יהוה (*YHWH*).

that, after all, God may indeed overthrow him at last in hell."[4]

The wicked know that they will eventually see how costly ignoring God has been. C. S. Lewis said, "In the end that Face which is the delight or the terror of the universe must be turned upon each of us . . . either conferring glory inexpressible or inflicting shame that can never be cured or disguised."[5]

Verse 6. The wicked have **put to shame the counsel** [or the guidance] **of the afflicted**. They have rejected that instruction and made fun of it. They look down upon it as if it were nothing but trivia. Their conduct does not, however, affect the spiritual life of the righteous, for they find their **refuge** in God. One truth that rises like a beacon of light throughout the Scriptures is that God is a stronghold for those who put their trust in Him.

THE PRAYER OF THE RIGHTEOUS (14:7)

> [7]**Oh, that the salvation of Israel would come out of Zion!**
> **When the Lord restores His captive people,**
> **Jacob will rejoice, Israel will be glad.**

Verse 7. Such a description of evil as we have seen can only constrain the righteous to wish that God would step in and wipe out all evil. The prayer of the righteous, those who are besieged by the wicked and whose hearts are worn out by seeing sin and the mistreatment of the godly all around them, is simply this: **Oh, that the salvation of Israel would come out of Zion!** They yearn for God to come forth from Jerusalem and put an end to all the chaos caused by sin. They pray, "One day soon may all see that God is righteous and good and that His ways are perfect. May it be that God's ways will be vindicated and God's mistreated ones will be delivered!"

The psalm ends with an appeal for joy and "gladness" to come to God's people. This music of the soul can come only

---

[4]James Burton Coffman and Thelma B. Coffman, *Commentary on Psalms 1—72*, (Abilene, Tex.: ACU Press, 1992), 1:91.

[5]C. S. Lewis, *Transposition: And Other Addresses* (London: Geoffrey Bles, 1949), 28.

when the LORD restores His captive people. It is difficult to tell just which captivity is being described with this phrase. The NIV rendered the word שְׁבוּת (sh°buth) as "fortunes," but "captive" is a better translation of it. Is it the bondage of sin, the Babylonian Captivity, or another oppression? It must be that the expression is simply referring to the bewilderment and hurt that is surrounding God's faithful people. They are looking for a restoration from all that they are suffering. "When the Lord delivers Israel from the sinfulness of the world, and thus leads His people out of the captivity brought upon them by evil people, joy and gladness will descend upon Jacob and Israel," seems to be their prayer. **Jacob** and **Israel** are used as synonyms for God's people.

APPLICATION

The Results of Rebellion
An awful journey can be described in only a few words—a pilgrimage from belief in God to the dark night of disbelief.

First, *a decision is made to aggressively pursue evil*. At the forefront of this choice there has to be the denial of God. The person taking this journey does not say that He does not exist in the sense that He never has existed. He says that God is unconcerned about people or that His rules are too strict. A choice is made to live without Him.

Coming out from this decision is a corrupt heart and lifestyle. He becomes sour in the big business of living. Remove God from "good," and there is only an "o" left. Remove God from the heart, and an emptiness, a vacuum, results that will be immediately filled with evil.

Proceeding from a godless lifestyle are abominable works and deeds. He has gone from bad to worse. There was a denial of God at the beginning. The heart then turned evil. Oozing out of that decayed heart came the evil works that wreck people, destroy places, and desecrate holy things.

Just as this awful journey can be related in only a few sentences, a wonderful journey, the life with God, can also be described briefly. This great life begins with an acceptance of God and continues with adherence to His will. One must choose the road he will take—the path of life or death (see Deut. 30:19; Mt. 7:24–28).

The Types of Atheists

When a person says, "I do not believe in God," we have to ask, "What kind of atheist are you?" The evidence indicates that there are three different kinds of disbelievers in God.

First, there are the intellectual atheists. They think that they have reasoned their way out of believing in God. In spite of how up-to-date and sophisticated their reasoning may sound, the Bible never excuses them. Paul uses the expression "He is without excuse" as he rebukes the Gentile and the Jew (Rom. 1:20, 21; 2:1). God has left Himself sufficient witness on earth (Acts 14:17) so that anyone will be able to conclude that He is the divine Being who provides good things for all people. The intellectual atheists may use technical terms for their reasons for denying God, but the bottom line to their argument is that they believe the world and humanity have just happened or they have somehow popped into existence from some unknown, unintelligent energy. No truly rational person can accept such a proposition. Faulty reasoning is behind such a baseless conclusion.

Second, there are the practical atheists. They do not *want* God to exist. They have set their hearts on doing evil, and, in order to maintain their ambitions and sinister desires, they have *willed* God out of existence. They have conveniently gotten rid of God so that they can pursue their thirst for evil.

Third, there are the indifferent (or functional) atheists. They are the people who simply do not think about God. They do not worship Him, pray to Him, or serve Him. They have filled their lives full of pleasure, work, or even family; and God has no place in their lives. They have neither denied His existence nor willed Him out of existence; they just *neglect* Him. They live as though He does not exist.

The worst choice anyone can ever make is to choose to live without God. A man may intellectually push God out of his life, he may will God out of existence by his practical pursuit of wickedness, or he may live without Him by being indifferent to Him.

Regardless of how he does it, he has made the single greatest mistake that a human being can make.

What God Sees

The writer pictured God coming down and observing mankind. Imagine Him coming down and looking over people today. What would He see? Would He not see what He saw then? Have people changed that much?

God saw that *they had all turned aside.* No one was eager to do God's will. They had departed from truth to satisfy their own ambitions and pleasures. Would God not see something similar now?

He saw that *together they had become corrupt.* Their hearts had become corrupt, and their deeds were abominable. From top to bottom, from desire to lifestyle, they were filled with sin. This depiction is not a picture of inherited evil, but it is a portrayal of lives gone bad because of choices to dismiss God. Would He not see the same tragedy now?

He saw that *there was no one who did good, not even one.* Genuine goodness, people pursuing what was right, could not be found. There were a few righteous people, but when the righteous ones were compared to the wicked, it was as if there were none.

We cannot choose for others, but we can choose for ourselves. May we say, "I am going to live for Christ whether or not anybody else in the world chooses to live for Him."

Turning from God

What happens when people turn away from God to go their own ways and to pursue their own pleasures?

The heart goes bad. The heart was engineered to have God's guidance and love. A heart estranged from God becomes cold, misguided, and subject to all types of evil.

The ambitions become twisted. The desires and dreams that come out of a godless heart are flawed, cruel, and sinister.

The deeds become detestable. Evil desires give birth to evil deeds. A person's conscience does not hurt even when he mistreats others, nor does he care when he destroys himself.

The disbelief of the heart usually shows up through a person hurting himself, hurting others, and certainly through the breaking of God's heart. In this psalm we have seen atheism not by a philosophical discussion but by an observance of the result of atheism as seen in disposition and deeds.

Look at What Is Ahead!
What is ahead? (v. 7). We may be surrounded by ridicule, persecution, by a distressing picture of mankind's irreverence toward God, and man's inhumanity to others; but we can always rejoice and be glad about three truths.

There is a restoration coming. One day, in His time, the wrongs will be made right, and the affairs of God will be settled. Ancient Israel knew such a time was coming, but they did not know the details of it. They believed that God would one day step in with judgment or with the coming of the Messiah. For Christians, a similar expression of hope holds true. They see the Lord coming to receive them into eternal glory.

While we wait, we have our refuge in God. He is stronger than all the forces of mankind and nature. Even death cannot hurt us. While we are under siege, we are hidden away in the rock of God. We have been promised His protection, and no power in heaven or on earth can negate His promise.

When the day of restoration comes, it will be one great time of rejoicing and gladness. We have not yet rejoiced the way we are going to rejoice. Clifton L. Ganus, Jr., has always said, "If you could take all the joys that we have experienced in this life and roll them into one big joy, you would not have a joy that is even comparable to the joy we will experience when we are received into glory."

What lies ahead for the Christian? Restoration is coming, rejoicing is coming, and while we wait for these things, God will be our refuge.

Can the Wicked Learn?
The writer pictures God as saying, "Have all the workers of iniquity no knowledge?" The implication from the question is that it is amazing that the wicked do not wake up to what they

are missing or to what they are doing. What should the wicked learn?

They should become aware *that they do not have Divine Providence working in their behalf as the righteous do.* The righteous are hidden in God even while they are mistreated by the wicked. God will seek to win the wicked to the truth, but He does not hide them in His protection as He does the righteous.

They should realize *that their prayers will not be heard.* They have not listened to God, and God says that He is not going to not listen to them. God listens to His children; however, the prayers of those in rebellion against Him come up to Him as an abomination (Prov. 28:9).

They should learn *that there is no forgiveness for the impenitent.* God will not forgive a person unless he forsakes his sins. Grace is without cost, but it is not cheap. Sin must be forsaken and the fruits of repentance must be seen.

They should recognize *that sin does not pay.* To give one's life to sin is to literally throw one's life away. Sin stains, shames, and enslaves; it damns and destroys.

They should observe *that there is no comfort for their sorrows.* God comforts His own, not the strangers who have denied Him. Without hope and without a relationship with God, they face their difficulties in human strength alone.

They should learn *that God's wisdom is higher than man's.* Through the hard knocks of sinful living, they should learn that man's wisdom is empty and destructive; God's instruction is helpful and faithful. Man's guidance is clouded by prejudice and inaccuracies; God's is perfect and righteous.

Will the wicked learn these lessons? A few do, but most do not (Mt. 7:13, 14). Many go on sinning, never accepting the facts and truths brought out by the harsh realities of sin.

PSALM 15
WHO CAN DWELL IN GOD'S PRESENCE?

The Superscription: A Psalm of David. The heading of this psalm simply says it is **a Psalm** [מִזְמוֹר, *mizmor*] **of** ["by," "for," or "to"] **David** (לְדָוִד, *lᵉdawid*). The psalm, then, is labeled by its title a Davidic psalm and is one of the most beautiful devotional pieces, describing what a worshiper should bring to worship and the character that one should have to abide with God.

To establish in our minds a major theme of this psalm, let us picture an imaginary scene: An angel stands beside the only open door of a church building in which authentic worship of God is taking place, and he is conducting a one-question interview with each person entering the building to worship. Each one is asked: "Are you spiritually prepared to worship God the Almighty?" What answers would be given to that divine interrogator? Would those going to worship know what God requires of them?

A scenario akin to this hypothetical scene is presented in this short psalm of five verses. In it the question is posed to God: "What do You require for Your worship and for one to live with You?" The psalm was most likely connected with public worship as is indicated by the superscription. Perhaps as many as thirty psalms fall into this category of worship.

WHO IS FIT? (15:1)

¹O LORD, who may abide in Your tent?
Who may dwell on Your holy hill?

Verse 1. The psalm begins with a probing query: **O LORD, who may abide in Your tent?** or, "O Lord, who is fit to dwell with You?" The parallel line adds, **Who may dwell on Your holy hill?** or, "Who is prepared to live in Your presence?" These questions are asked of God Himself in the first verse, and then the body of the psalm gives His answer, a response that should cause those reading it to search their own consciences about the worship of God.

The psalm seems to fuse together the ideas of coming to worship God and remaining in His presence. Thus the heart of the psalm is a detailed answer to the overarching questions, "Who can come and reside with God? Who can stay with Him as a continual resident?"

"Abide" (גּוּר, *gur*) or "sojourn" conveys the idea of staying as a resident alien, remaining as a person who has permanence as a result of his gracious Host. "Dwell" (שָׁכֵן, *shaken*) suggests "being a part of the family of God by moving in to become a member of His community." The psalmist is not interested in one who would like to be with God only for a brief visit and see what is in His house, one who comes as a tourist. He has in mind the person who intends to remain indefinitely in God's holy presence.

ONE WHO WALKS RIGHT
(15:2–4)

> ²He who walks with integrity, and works righteousness,
> And speaks truth in his heart.
> ³He does not slander with his tongue,
> Nor does evil to his neighbor,
> Nor takes up a reproach against his friend;
> ⁴In whose eyes a reprobate is despised,
> But who honors those who fear the LORD;
> He swears to his own hurt and does not change;

The answer to this deeper question, "Who is prepared to live in Your presence?" is given from two different viewpoints:

a positive one and a negative one. Eleven parts (not including the final affirmation) to the answer are presented, although the list of qualities is not intended to be exhaustive. It is a general portrait that is given of those who are welcome to be a guest of God and to continually enjoy His protection and hospitality. Integrity is the core trait in the list.

Verse 2. Who, then, will be admitted into God's presence and will receive the opportunity of dwelling with Him? The beginning of the positive part of that answer is this: "The one who dwells with God is the one who persistently pursues the right."

He is to possess "integrity" in three fundamental areas: thoughts, actions, and deeds. This characteristic will affect his innermost thinking, which in turn will affect his words, walk, and works.

This honest heart reveals itself in a life of uprightness. He could be characterized as one who **walks with integrity**; the habitual course of his life is that of living blamelessly before God. The word for "integrity" (תָּמִים, *thamim*) means "blameless" and is sometimes translated "perfect." It does not mean sinless perfection but rather connotes perfection in the sense of sincerely seeking to do God's will. No legitimate accusation can be brought against him. "Integrity" is wholehearted devotion to God and complete forthrightness in dealing with others.

To say it another way, the one who pleases God **works** [or exhibits] **righteousness**. This phrase may be a parallel to the phrase "walks with integrity." The idea behind the two phrases is that people who wish to have fellowship with God do what is right and speak the truth because such character springs from their very nature. Their hearts resemble God's, and their good lives flow out of the Godlike spirit living within them.

The man who **speaks truth in his heart** is the man who is absolutely sincere with himself, with others, and with God. Genuineness and transparency make up his private conversations. Telling the truth with our lips is important, but speaking the truth in our hearts to ourselves and to God is more important, for it is the fountainhead that produces all other thinking. God's requirement is truth in one's "innermost being" (Ps. 51:6, 7).

Verse 3. God looks not only at what people are and what

they do but also at what they allow and what they oppose.

The righteous man depicted in this psalm follows hard after God's heart and **does not slander** or malign others. He does not spy on others and gather morsels of gossip to spread. His tongue will not be used for vilification.

He does not do **evil to his neighbor**. "Evil" is a generic term including any kind of harm or sin. He seeks to do good to those around him; he will protect them and seek their best interests.

He does not soil his lips with that which is injurious to the reputations of others. Truth is in his heart and on his lips. He does not take up **a reproach against his friend**. Integrity is his way of life.

Verse 4. This godly person gives inspiration to others who are in the right, and he overtly discourages those who are in the wrong. He is a person **in whose eyes a reprobate is despised**. He can no more allow evil than he can personally participate in it. Anyone who has welcomed wickedness into his life can count on strong opposition from the righteous man. He will not fight wickedness with his fists, but he will oppose evil with the dedication of his heart, works, and words.

Having dedicated his life to righteousness, he stands against all evil in print, people, and public speech. He has no intentions of condoning sin. His war against wickedness and the harm that wicked people do is obvious to those who are in his circle of fellowship.

The converse is also true. The righteous man is one **who honors those who fear the** LORD. He will applaud and bid Godspeed to anyone who is seeking to show proper respect for God.

Further, he is a man who **swears to his own hurt and does not change**. He keeps his word even when he must pay a dear price to do so. When he makes a promise, he is faithful to it—even if being loyal to that promise requires a painful personal sacrifice. He believes that promises are made to be fulfilled. Naturally, if he has made an inappropriate and sinful promise, he will correct it in a righteous way that brings glory to God and keeps his integrity intact.

PSALM 15

NO INTEREST AND NO BRIBES
(15:5a)

⁵ᵃHe does not put out his money at interest,
Nor does he take a bribe against the innocent.

Verse 5a. The righteous man is careful about the use of money. Stated tersely and comprehensively, **he does not put out his money at interest.** He does not try to profit from those who are in trouble. Spirituality and generosity live in the same heart.

This statement regarding lending money should be interpreted against the background of Israelite life. In the community of Israel, money was loaned without interest to a needy brother. The Israelite was commanded not to profit from the act of helping a fellow Jew in distress. However, he could charge interest on money loaned to a foreigner (Ex. 22:25; Lev. 25:37; Deut. 23:20; Neh. 5:7; Prov. 28:8). Behind this law was the compassionate rationale that the Israelites should care for one another as an extended family. The psalmist says that the person who has favor with God is one who shows humanitarian concern for others.

The application to the Christian would be the realization that God is pleased and honored when honest and caring consideration is shown in all business dealings (see Eph. 4:28). The righteous see to it that they do not benefit from any other person's downfall. They are genuinely interested in others because of the Godlike character of their hearts.

In addition, he does not **take a bribe against the innocent.** The righteous man does not set aside the truth or his moral obligations for the sake of money. Graft in any form is tragic, but bribery that involves taking advantage of or results in the conviction of "the innocent" or guiltless is especially displeasing to God (Ex. 23:8; Deut. 10:17; 16:19; 27:25). The man of God will resist a temptation to succumb to the love of money, for to him people are more important than any kind of financial gain. He lives his life upon the divine principles that spring from the character of God. His life with God has been surrounded with the lovingkindness of God; he has absorbed this spirit, and thus, this trait of goodness comes out in his treatment of others. His interpersonal relationships are coated with the kindness and gentleness with which God has treated him.

A PROMISE (15:5b)

5bHe who does these things will never be shaken.

Verse 5b. A final word, a brief consolation, is given about the one who pleases God. He is consistent in his faithfulness and will not be affected by the changing winds of life. He will not lose his hold on God, and God will not lose His hold on him. He will stand firm no matter what comes. The promise is this: **He who does these things will never be shaken.** He will dwell with God, making his home in God. Trials will come, but they will not shake him or make him fall. He must live in a world that has gone astray from God's will, but God is his rock of protection and his source of life.

APPLICATION

In God's Presence

We have seen one of life's most significant answers in this psalm. The question has been asked of God, "What kind of person do You invite into Your fellowship? Whom do You allow to live with You?" God has given His response in ten beautiful qualities. No one can misunderstand His reply.

All of us would be in full agreement with the description that has been given. Thomas Jefferson said that Psalm 15 gives the earmarks of a "True Gentleman."[1] Most of us would say that these characteristics go beyond being a "gentleman." We, like the psalmist, would contend that the person who fits this description—the one who is sincere of heart, who lives with in-

---

[1]Henry H. Halley, *Halley's Bible Handbook*, 24th ed. (Grand Rapids, Mich.: Zondervan, 1965), 253.

tegrity and righteousness, who encourages the righteous, who restrains his or her tongue, who is dependable as a friend, who keeps promises, who does an honest day's work for an honest day's pay, who seeks no more than a fair use of money, who never takes a bribe, and who always tells the truth—is a godly person.

Such a person walks with God, is able to worship God acceptably, is at home with God, and stands approved by God in this world and in the world to come.

At Home with God

The first verse of this psalm speaks of "abiding" and "dwelling" with God. These two words suggest being permanent guests in the presence of God.

Life with God begins when we approach Him. From the perspective of the New Testament, we understand that we can only come to God through Jesus (Jn. 14:6). His gospel must be obeyed so that our sins can be washed away in His blood. It is obvious that we must come to God before we can dwell with Him.

Further, *we cannot live with God unless we daily walk with Him.* We must do more than just enter His house. Many people have walked into His house as a visitor only to stay for a brief visit and then leave.

Then, *with the passing of time, we become at home with God.* Life with God has developed into a permanent lifestyle; it has become natural to us. We know God intimately, and He knows us. We have become His children in practice.

Entering His house is a choice; being at home with Him comes from living with Him over a period of time, with the "at-homeness" growing out of going His way, going His speed, and enjoying the journey of life with Him.

Dwelling with God has to be the most encouraging image one can contemplate. It means that wherever we are, we are at home, for our home is not a location on earth but a life in God. A woman once said, "Since my home is in God, anywhere I am, I am at home."

Abiding in God means the highest and most complete rest. Only the person who *nests* in God will truly find *rest* in Him.

God's peace is found in the hearts of the permanent dwellers in God's house, not in the visitors who pass through for only a brief stay.

How Does Your Biography Look?

If God were writing your biography, could He describe you with the résumé given in this psalm?

> He walks uprightly.
> He works righteousness.
> He speaks truth in his heart.
> He does not slander.
> He does not do evil to others.
> He does not take up a reproach against a neighbor.
> He despises the reprobate.
> He honors God's people.
> He keeps his promises.
> He does not put his money out for interest.
> He will not accept a bribe to wrong the innocent.

Transparency Before God

In this psalm we have been looking into spiritual transparency. We have seen a clear answer to what genuine people are like.

They are people who *walk uprightly*. Sincerely honest before God, their hearts are pure and undefiled. Their walk—lifestyle—springs up from their integrity.

They are people who *work righteousness*. One aspect of sincerity is doing what is right in deeds. Consequently, their lives are filled with the actions and works of uprightness.

They are people who *speak truth in their hearts*. They are honest with themselves, God, and others. What goes on in their hearts shows up in the other areas of their lives. Their lips do not say the opposite of what is in their hearts.

PSALM 15

The Life of the Righteous

How do the righteous live? Observe the general, positive traits of their lives.

They walk with integrity. They live blameless lives before God. They are perfect in the sense that they are without legitimate accusation. Though they are not perfect in sinless perfection, their hearts are dedicated to sincerely doing the will of God.

They work righteousness. This phrase is probably another way of saying that they walk in integrity. However, there may be a slight difference: They "do" righteousness. They keep their hearts and lives the way a righteous person would.

They speak truth in their hearts. They tell themselves the truth about themselves, God, and others. Someone has said, "Look at what you say to yourself about God, and you will see the true picture of your spirituality." The man who wrote this psalm speaks truth to himself.

They honor those who fear the Lord. Not only do they fear God, but they encourage others to fear Him. When they find people who fear God, they congratulate them and inspire them to continue. They approve of righteous living by the example they set before others and the words of commendation they give to others.

They despise the reprobate. They abhor evil—whether it be abstract evil or personified evil. When they see it, they reprove it and seek to eliminate it. If they can do nothing about it, they carry a firm protest against it in their hearts.

They swear to their own hurt and do not change. Promise-keeping is part of their spiritual commitment. When they give their word, they will keep it—even if that commitment costs them dearly.

The main theme that runs through these traits is the leadership of God in their lives. They have come to God, and they are sincerely living in God. To be in the presence of God means that they have taken into their lives the attributes of God Himself.

The Refusals of the Righteous

Righteous living is positive to be sure, but the positive descriptions guarantee negative ones.

They do not slander with their tongues. Righteousness shows up in their words. Devoted hearts will not allow them to assassinate others with vicious talk.

They do not do evil to their neighbors. The godly will guard the reputations of their friends, and they will not stoop to degrade their neighbors with hurtful words. They will shield their neighbors and friends from all evil.

They do not take up a reproach against their friends. There is something especially telling about people who would besmirch the reputation of those who are near to them. All slander is evil, but it is worse to slander a friend.

They do not put out their money at interest. War has been declared against taking advantage of someone who is in need. Making money with money is not evil within itself, but the Lord condemns making money at the expense of a neighbor's desperation.

They do not take a bribe against the innocent. If the righteous are in public office, they should be public servants who cannot be bribed or swayed from an honest judgment.

Once again, it is noticeable that all of these negative traits grow out of the overarching trait of integrity. Walking with moral honor precludes slandering a friend or neighbor, taking advantage of someone in need, or taking a bribe.

Who Can Be God's Guest?

Derek Kidner has suggested an outline for this psalm under the title, "A Portrait of the One Who Can Be God's Guest."

His Character: True. God's guest is a genuine person, and this blamelessness is reflected in his innermost being, words, deeds, and worship.

His Words: Restrained. This person does not use the tongue for evil purposes, especially to cut down a friend or brother.

His Allegiance: Clear-cut. This person's faithfulness to God is obvious through his deeds.

His Dealings: Honorable. God's guest keeps a promise when it is easy to do so and also when it is difficult.[2]

---

[2]Derek Kidner, *Psalms 1—72*, Tyndale Old Testament Commentaries (Downers Grove, Ill.: InterVarsity Press, 1973), 82.

Psalm 16
God: The Supreme Good

The Superscription: A Mikhtam of David. The ancient heading given to this psalm refers to the psalm as **a Mikhtam [מִכְתָּם] of** ["by," "for," or "to"] **David** (לְדָוִד, *l^edawid*). Five other psalms have this designation (56—60). The term "mikhtam," a word that has been brought over from Hebrew into English in a transliterated form, is unclear. Some scholars have tried to trace it to a root meaning "gold" and have argued that the word says that this is a "golden" psalm. Others believe that it means a poem of epigrammatic character. Still others believe it is some kind of musical term.

The New Testament confirms that this psalm of confidence in God is a prophecy of the Messiah's relationship to God in His life and in His resurrection from the dead (Acts 2:25–28, 31; 13:35). Furthermore, Peter testifies to the Davidic authorship of the psalm with his clear statement in Acts 2:25.

The writer sings of how good God has been and is to him. As he does so, he says the greatest blessing that he has received from the Lord is the Lord Himself, the Giver instead of His gifts. His anthem of praise describes the good life he has with God, the joys he has known, and the pleasures that he anticipates in the days to come. In a deeper sense, as substantiated by the New Testament's interpretation of the psalm, it gives a prophetic picture of the walk that the Messiah would have with God.

The psalm perhaps should be divided into only two parts: verses 1 through 7 and verses 8 through 11. However, for the sake of convenience, we will divide it into five parts: seeing God as his refuge (vv. 1–4); acknowledging the saints and the horror of worshiping other gods (vv. 3, 4); thinking of God as his portion (vv. 5, 6); praising the Lord for His blessings (vv. 7–10); and finding full satisfaction in God (v. 11).

"GOD IS MY REFUGE" (16:1, 2)

¹**Preserve me, O God, for I take refuge in You.**
²**I said to the** LORD**, "You are my Lord;**
I have no good besides You."

Verse 1. David begins his praise of God with a declaration of the faith that is at the core of his being. His life is safe only because it is surrounded by God's protective hand. In this confident faith he prays, **Preserve me, O God.** His word is the one for "keep" or "secure" (שָׁמַר, *shamar*) that indicates that he wants God to hold him in His care.

He has made a singular response to the grace of God: **For I take refuge in You.** God has been his invincible shelter in the past, and he is asking Him to put His almighty arms around him as he goes into the future. No conceivable place could rival the haven of safekeeping that he believes he can experience in God.

Verse 2. God is not only his refuge but also his Lord. He tells us that he says **to the** LORD**, "You are my Lord."** He uses two Hebrew words that are translated "Lord." The first is Yahweh (יהוה, *YHWH*), the tetragrammaton, which is usually indicated in a translation with small capital letters (for example, LORD). Yahweh is the personal name for God. Hebrew scribes did not pronounce it for fear of taking the Lord's name in vain. While reading out loud, they substituted "Lord" (אֲדֹנָי, *ᵃdonai*) for the divine name. We do not know for sure how to pronounce it because the vowel pointings have not been preserved; consequently, we usually see it written by only its consonants.

The second word is אֲדֹנָי (*ᵃdonai*), which is printed in the majority of translations with the first letter as a capital and the remaining letters in lower case. *'Adonai* means "Master, Ruler, or Lord." David is saying, "My soul says to Yahweh, 'You are my Master, my Ruler, my Lord.'"

He says, **"I have no good besides You."** This phrase is difficult for translation, as is indicated by the different renderings that have been given to it. The sentence literally says, "My good is not above you" (טוֹבָתִי בַּל־עָלֶיךָ, *tobathi bal-'aleka*). The KJV has translated it, "My goodness extendeth not to thee." The ASV has, "I have no good beyond thee," while the NRSV has, "I have no good apart from you." The NASB and Moffatt translations have: "I have no good besides You."

All things considered, the best interpretation of this phrase seems to be that he is saying that God is greater than anything and everything of true worth in his life, above every type of genuine prosperity and happiness (see Ps. 73:25). He sees God as the supreme good that anyone can receive. The life of faith that he knows is the highest life because it brings him into a blessed walk with God.

SAINTS AND OTHER GODS (16:3, 4)

³**As for the saints who are in the earth,**
They are the majestic ones in whom is all my delight.
⁴**The sorrows of those who have bartered for another god**
  will be multiplied;
I shall not pour out their drink offerings of blood,
Nor will I take their names upon my lips.

Verse 3. David delights not only in God but also in those who belong to Him. With the phrase, **As for the saints who are in the earth**, he turns to rejoicing in God's people. The Hebrew phrase, "as for the saints," could be translated "to the saints." If it is so translated, the meaning is that the goodness of God rebounds from the one who experiences it to the saints of God. The benefits that one who loves God receives will radiate out to the surrounding community of believers.

He further describes these saints with the beautiful phrase, **They are the majestic ones in whom is all my delight.** Is David speaking from his viewpoint or God's? If he is speaking of his view, then he is rejoicing in God's family. He is a servant in God's house, and he rejoices in all the other servants God has in that house. If it is from God's view, then we see here the attitude that

God has toward His people. Whether seen from David's viewpoint or God's, saints are the honored ones, the excellent ones.

Verse 4. The psalmist could not imagine worshiping a lifeless idol of stone or wood. **The sorrows of those who have bartered for another god will be multiplied.** The word "god" is not in the original text. The NASB has assumed that "god" is meant because of the flow of the context. It must mean that idolatry increases sorrow instead of diminishing it. Anyone, he declares, who leaves God and lusts after another god will find endless trouble, grief, and sorrow.

He resolves that he will never offer the sacrifices that idolators offer. With deep pathos, he says, **I shall not pour out their drink offerings of blood.** The reference to offering blood is also a difficult Hebrew phrase. Drink offerings of actual blood are not mentioned elsewhere in the Scriptures unless they are alluded to in Acts 15:20. His statement must either mean that he will never participate in their drink offerings of blood or that he will not engage metaphorically in their drink offerings because he sees them as detestable to God as drink offerings of blood (Is. 66:3).

It is abhorrent to him to think of deviating from the worship of God. He refuses even to talk about the pagan deities. He vows not even to **take their names upon** [his] **lips.** He will not allow his tongue to be soiled by mentioning them. They are nonentities and do not deserve the time it takes to say their names (see Deut. 12:3). In the writer's day, taking a god's name on one's lips could refer to worshiping that god. Thus this phrase possibly means more than just the mere utterance of the god's name in a conversation.

"THE LORD IS MY PORTION" (16:5, 6)

⁵The LORD is the portion of my inheritance and my cup;
You support my lot.
⁶The lines have fallen to me in pleasant places;
Indeed, my heritage is beautiful to me.

Verse 5. God is David's "portion." When the Promised Land was divided among Israel, it was measured out by line and then assigned by lot. David says that **the LORD is the portion of my inheritance**. He sees what has been marked out and given to him as the choicest possession. His gift is God, the greatest gift anyone can receive.

God is his "portion"—his allotment, his possession, his "inheritance." As the people of each tribe of Israel were given a place in the new land to call their own (Josh. 13:7; 14:2), they rejoiced in thanksgiving over the fertile fields they had received. The psalmist is different. He is thankful for God Himself—for the Being who gives—more than for the blessings given, more for the hand than for the bounties in the hand. Moffatt's translation of this sentence is especially vivid: "Thou art what I obtain from life, O thou Eternal, thou thyself art my share."[1] God Himself, more than all His endowments, is the reward of those who love Him.

He says that God supports his **lot**. In other words, God makes what has been assigned or awarded to him secure. He sees to it that he has this special, "beautiful-beyond-description" privilege of walking with God.

Mixing another figure into his praise, David says that God is his **cup**—his food and water, his life, his source of sustenance. God is all he needs to satisfy his desire for possessions, life, and his purpose for living.

Verse 6. He says that these **lines have fallen to [him] in pleasant places**. The use of the word "lines" shows that he is still rejoicing in his allocation, in that which has been parceled out to him, the boundary lines of his possession. He further says as a parallel thought, **Indeed, my heritage is beautiful to me.** His inheritance is the Lord; what he has received is of unspeakable worth to him.

A background to these thoughts is the manner in which God dealt with the Levites. God was the inheritance they actually received; no land was given to them. Because of their continual work in relation to the worship at the tabernacle and because of

---

[1]James Moffatt, *A New Translation of the Bible* (New York: Harper & Brothers Publishers, 1954), 612.

the constant spiritual leadership they provided Israel, God was their possession. They were granted the high honor of being with God daily in their worship and work, and this assignment was seen as the highest position and pleasure (Num. 18:20; Deut. 10:9). The psalmist would argue that the Levites, in their unique fellowship with God, had been favored above all other tribes.

"I WILL BLESS THE LORD" (16:7–10)

> ⁷I will bless the LORD who has counseled me;
> Indeed, my mind instructs me in the night.
> ⁸I have set the LORD continually before me;
> Because He is at my right hand, I will not be shaken.
> ⁹Therefore my heart is glad and my glory rejoices;
> My flesh also will dwell securely.
> ¹⁰For You will not abandon my soul to Sheol;
> Nor will You allow Your Holy One to undergo decay.

Verse 7. God has been his Teacher and Instructor, and thus he says, **I will bless the LORD who has counseled me**. He has taught the psalmist to love and follow Him. Treasuring that guidance, he praises and blesses God for providing it.

He says, **Indeed, my mind instructs me in the night.** In the quiet hours of the night, while awake upon his bed, David had allowed his mind to admonish him concerning the value of his relationship with God and his need to guard that relationship. The KJV has "reins" instead of "mind." The term "reins" is the older word for "the emotions, feelings, and the conscience." The actual Hebrew word is the one for "kidneys" (כִּלְיָה, *kilyah*), a word that was used for the seat of the emotions, thoughts, and will. We use the physical heart; they used the kidneys.

Verse 8. God is David's constant companion. He can say, **I have set the LORD continually before me**. He had chosen to be constantly in His presence. This decision was made by a resolve to obey the Lord and to meditate upon His fellowship and blessings. He would seek to behold His face and meditate upon His love and life throughout his future days. God **is at [his] right hand**—He is near him. Because of the fact of God's proximity, he will not be afraid. The Lord is a defender, a warrior, a champion who stands on his right side in the important place of honor and in a place of readiness to assist him. Because of the Lord's companionship and faithfulness he can say with confidence, **I will not be shaken.** The Lord's presence will sustain him, and he will not be disturbed, defeated, or overcome.

Verse 9. His relationship with God brings music to his soul. **Therefore my heart is glad and my glory rejoices.** Numerous benefits come from fellowship with God, chief of which are joy, confidence, and peace. In a typical synonymous parallelism, the writer speaks of his "heart" as "glad" and his "glory" (or soul) as rejoicing. The second phrase has essentially the same meaning as the first phrase.

He further says, **My flesh also will dwell securely.** David sees God as watching over those who trust Him in this life and in the life to come. His flesh will not have to worry about its destruction or deterioration.

Verse 10. In this spirit of trust, he speaks with confidence about the future: **For You will not abandon my soul to Sheol; nor will You allow Your Holy One to undergo decay.** Perhaps as David writes these words he is only thinking of the glorious life he has with God—the undisturbed peace he has in this life and the assurance that God will provide an even greater walk with Him in the life to come.

Albertus Pieters observed that the one tenable argument for a future life is *the belief* that a person in fellowship with God will not be abandoned by Him in death. He wrote of David in this psalm: "He looked beyond the fact of physical death and was confident that even in death God would not abandon him, or leave him to the power of the grave."[2]

Even if David is thinking this way when he writes this passage, the Holy Spirit has much more in mind. As Peter pointedly declares on the Day of Pentecost and as Paul faithfully preaches in a Jewish synagogue at Antioch of Pisidia, these words that David writes are a prediction of the resurrection of Christ

---

[2]Albertus Pieters, *Psalms in Human Experience* (New York: Half Moon Press, 1942), 46–47.

(Acts 2:31; 13:35). We can be confident of this interpretation. The New Testament explanation of it settles it for us.

David may be writing an expression of trust in God for the indefinite future, but the Holy Spirit is uttering through him a prophetic portrayal of the greatest event of all time: Jesus' bursting forth from the dead. The Christ will not be left in the grave (or Sheol). He will not remain dead, nor will His body stay in the grave long enough to undergo decay. The deeper meaning of this psalm is realized by the unbroken fellowship Jesus has with God and His release from death's grip in that tomb outside of Jerusalem.

SATISFACTION IN GOD (16:11)

> ¹¹**You will make known to me the path of life;**
> **In Your presence is fullness of joy;**
> **In Your right hand there are pleasures forever.**

Verse 11. God is the writer's source of satisfaction. He sees God not just as the One who leads to life; he sees Him *as* life to those who put their faith in Him, for in His **presence is** [the fullness of life and the] **fullness of joy**. Whether in this life or in the life to come, endless delight belongs to the one who walks with God. The path of oneness with God leads through this earthly life into the abundant life in eternity.

Therefore, he says, **In Your right hand there are pleasures forever.** The joys of the Lord come from who He is (His "presence") and from what He gives (His "right hand"). The presence and provisions, the fellowship and blessings He bestows are completely satisfying to the soul. The thrills of this world fade; the joys of the Lord are continuous and grow sweeter and sweeter with the passing of time.

APPLICATION

The Highest Good

David writes of his life with God in picturesque and moving language. He sees His relationship with God as the *summa bonum*, the supreme good of this life, the absolute good that towers above any other good. For him, nothing can compare to the life he has with God in quality or enjoyment.

Though he understands it dimly, he confidently believes that what he has experienced here in his earthly journey with God will continue to be his experience in a far more wonderful sphere beyond the grave. His words have meaning both for his day and for a distant day—for the Old Testament period and, through prophecy, for the beginning of the Christian Age in our Lord's life, death, and resurrection. He may not have known it, but he was prophesying concerning a glorious new era of time that would be brought in by the coming of the Messiah.

For us, this psalm—in the imagery of Old Testament life and in the fulfillment depicted by the life of our Lord Jesus Christ—pictures walking with God in terms of unbounded joy and limitless pleasures. As one experiences this walk with God, even death loses its dreadful power. Thus, to be linked with the eternal God in such unending fellowship is human life at its highest and best.

Making God Our Refuge

Thinking of God as a refuge is a tremendously comforting thought to those hounded by life. He is almighty and can wipe out any enemy with one word. However, the big question is this: How does He become our refuge? How do we enter into the circle of His protection?

A decision has to be made. Recognizing who God is, we choose Him to be our spiritual shelter. In the Christian Age, we make this choice by obeying the gospel of His Son (2 Thess. 1:7–9). In doing so, we crown Jesus as our Lord and God as our Father. Jesus is the way to God, the haven from all trials.

We must put ourselves under God's care. One can acknowledge God as the great rock of strength and not allow Him to give that strength to us. One can even be His child and not live in His peace. There is peace *with* God and there is the peace *of* God—the first type is legal peace, and the second type is practical peace. We can only have this personal, practical peace if we lay our problems at His feet.

One must trust God to do what He has promised. One can bring his troubles to God and then worry as to whether or not God will do His part. Once the deposit is made we have to trust the bank to care for our money. Once we spread out our difficulties before God, we must put our hope in His faithfulness.

God is willing and able to be our shelter. He is the highest type of protection there is; however, whether or not He is our refuge will depend upon our response to His invitation.

We are to live in His refuge in sunshine as well as in storm. The writer resolves that he will trust God to watch over him. God has sought us, but we also must seek Him. We must come under His protective hand and stay there.

What Is Most Meaningful?

We have come to the top of the mountain. God has brought us to the most meaningful plateau in life.

In Him is the richest *relationship*. To the Israelite, the greatest thing that could ever happen to anyone is for that person to have the privilege of knowing God. The Old Testament followers of God did not know much about eternity; and consequently, they sang more about their walk with God, about the blessing of being with God, than about heaven.

Through God are the real *provisions* of life. Although some do not see His hand supplying our needs, He gives us all that we have. He is the author of all our riches, whether they are spiritual or physical blessings. Our most meaningful assets are the spiritual ones.

With God we have true *security*. God is the refuge and preserver of our lives and souls. He holds us in His hand and protects us according to His will.

Thus, with God we have everything; without Him we have nothing of value.

What Does God Look Like?

Here are seven descriptions of God. When they are brought together, they form a composite picture that is one of the most beautiful in the entire Book of Psalms.

He is our refuge (v. 1). He is our keeper, protector, and shield.

His invisible hand surrounds the believer.

He is our Lord (vv. 2–4). He is our Master, our Supreme Overseer, our Guide, and our King.

He is our portion (vv. 5, 6). Of the many gifts we have received, the greatest one that has been allotted to us is the Lord. Instead of land, we get the Lord; instead of money, we get the Master; instead of stocks we get the sovereign God. The child of God covets this relationship above all others.

He is our counselor (v. 7). The essential guidance and leadership that we require come from Him.

He is our companion (vv. 8, 9). It is never necessary to be without Him. He stands beside us, available for all situations and trials that descend upon us.

He is our security (v. 10). He watches out for us, sustaining us and encircling us with His love. If God is not present, even the safest place on earth is a haunt of horror.

He is our true satisfaction (v. 11). We find no greater joy in anything or anyone else. A little child misquoted Psalm 23 but stated the view of this psalm when he said, "The Lord is my shepherd, and He is all I want!"

In these words the psalmist has described what God is to him. Now let us ask, What is God to us?

Substance and Sustenance

God is the supreme good: There is no good greater than He. In verses 5 and 6 God is described as being everything to the writer by means of two figures.

God is his substance. Drawing from the dividing up of the land of Caanan for Israel, he says that God is his portion. Measuring lines were used to sectionize the land, and lots were cast for the determination of who received what. He says that he has received the best portion, for the allocation has given him a pleasant place. He has received God.

God is his sustenance. He changes the figure and refers to God as his cup. God is his life, his food, and his drink. God has not only given him life, but God sustains his life.

When you think about it, God is all we really have and should be all we really want. We have been given God's lovingkindness, and we are under the care of His omnipotent grace. God is our all in all. He is our possession and our provisions, our portion and our peace.

The Joys of the Lord

The one who trusts in God has a supreme spiritual happiness and an inexpressible joy.

They come from the presence of the Lord. Just being with the Lord brings untold pleasures. Joy is found in the fellowship with the right people, but the greatest happiness comes from a continued companionship with God.

They come from the provisions of the Lord. As we behold what God has done for us and is continually doing in our lives, we rejoice with thanksgiving. We do not need to ask for more blessings; we only need to ask for the wisdom to use what we have been given.

They come from the promises of the Lord. As we look at what we are experiencing, we are made to rejoice even more in what has been promised for the future. We know that God will be faithful to us. The bounties we enjoy now are a prophecy of what is to come. His promises are never empty; together they make up our living hope.

The order of these sources is important. We enjoy first the Giver, second the gifts, and finally the promises of more gifts to come.

God's People—in Heaven and on Earth

How should we picture God's people? They seem to be described from two viewpoints—from God's and from ours.

They are referred to as saints. The phrase means "the holy ones." Although they are not perfect, they are dedicated to God; through His forgiveness and constant cleansing, they are set apart for His service.

They are also referred to as the majestic ones. From heaven's viewpoint, they are special and glorious. God rejoices over them even as we rejoice over our children.

On earth they are the ones in whom God's people delight. The writer says that he delights in them. This is the natural attitude family members should have toward each other.

To be in the family of a wonderful Father means that the love we have for our Father will flow out to each member of the family. We belong to each other because we are bound to Him.

Other Gods?

Devotion to God brings with it a definite, exclusive, non-tolerate attitude toward other gods. The writer makes an affirmation about what he will do regarding pagan gods.

He recognizes what they are—nonentities. Consequently, anyone who turns to them will find that his sorrows are increased. They bring no comfort, no assistance, and no hope.

He will not worship them. He will not do anything to lend credence to their existence. The thought of offering any kind of worship to them is detestable to him.

He will not in any way acknowledge them. He will not even mention their names. Probably this expression means that he will not have any responsible relationship of any kind with them.

Here then is a pattern to follow regarding the gods of this world: Recognize what they are in truth, refuse to worship them, and put them out of your mind, off your tongue, and out of your relationships. Let us have no intentional connection with them.

Satisfaction in God

The writer finds complete satisfaction in God. With him, God is not just his salvation, but He is also his sustenance, his being, his life-support.

God is his path to life. Real life is only found in Him. He gives biological life to each baby, but he gives spiritual life to each believer.

God is the fullness of joy. Only as we rest in God, the refuge and the source of life, do we find deep satisfaction that bubbles forth in continual rejoicing.

In God he finds pleasures forevermore. God does not bring a temporary high or a momentary excitement. Sometimes as we live in God we go to the mountaintop, but our continual dwelling in God results in perpetual pleasure. His presence, love, and invitation to be a part of His overarching eternal purpose bring us pleasures that will never end. We experience them now—even as we live in this world of sin, sorrow, and pain—and we anticipate them in all the ages to come.

Old Testament Prophecy

Fundamentally, three types of prophecy are seen in the Old Testament. *First, we behold with wonder the "name prophecy."* A specific place or name is foretold by the Holy Spirit. Two samples would be 1 Kings 13:1–4, where Josiah was called by name many years before he lived, and Micah 5:2, where Bethlehem was identified by name as the place of the Messiah's birth.

Second, we often see the "dual prophecy." Like our text, there was a message for the day when the prophecy was given, and that message becomes in a deeper sense a message for a distant day. David wrote of his belief that God would take care of him even beyond the grave but was unaware that his words prophesied the resurrection of Jesus. The statement had meaning for him, but it also had a far greater meaning for the future. Only the Holy Spirit could plan such a prophecy.

Third, there is the "typical prophecy." Usually, these prophecies must be identified for us by an inspired writer. For example, Hosea 11:1 says, "Out of Egypt have I called my son." This reference is obviously to God calling Israel out of Egypt, but, according to Matthew, the event is a typical prophecy of God calling the Christ out of Egypt when he was only a baby (Mt. 2:15). The typical prophecies are the hardest to observe and to interpret. It is best to let an inspired man explain them to us.

Most of us are used to thinking of prophecy as only a prediction of some great biblical event, but biblical prophecy is far more complex. Sometimes it is easily seen; sometimes it has a dual function, providing meaning not only for the day of the prophet but also for a day of the future; and sometimes it comes in the form of a type and an antitype.

Psalm 17
A Prayer for Protection

The Superscription: A Prayer of David. This psalm is called by its heading **a Prayer** (תְּפִלָּה, *tᵉpillah*), and it is the first psalm in the Book of Psalms to be so entitled. Only four other psalms are designated as prayers by their ancient titles (86; 90; 102; 142). Furthermore, only three of these five are spoken of as prayers **of** ["by," "for," or "to"] **David** (לְדָוִד, *lᵉdawid*) (17; 86; 142).

The content of this psalm indicates that its writer is in imminent danger. Although his exact circumstances cannot be determined, he is clearly surrounded by conflict and turmoil.

A possible setting to this prayer is David's flight from Saul in the wilderness, for his words intimate that one enemy in particular is a prime source of danger to him (see 1 Sam. 18—27). Running for his life, he finds himself all but hemmed in by his enemy. Instead of leading his nation, Saul, the king of Israel, has dedicated himself to capturing and destroying David. Experiencing the fury of Saul's determination, David finds himself in the thickest struggle.

As he prays, he knows that warlike men, determined to kill him, are nearby. Perhaps he can hear them as they walk about, planning their methods of attack and watching for an opportunity to capture him. Most likely, David is not far from the murderous grasp of the enemy as he writes this psalm. If this setting is not the background of the psalm, such a setting provides a good illustration of the kind of circumstance that is envisioned by the writer.

From beginning to end, the psalm is a petition to God, having as its chief characteristic supplication. His prayer is a plea for protection, a request for refuge. Expressing a lament, he brings his precarious predicament to God in prayer. He asks God to hear him on three grounds: because of his integrity, because of His grace, and because of the future he wants to have with Him.

"HEAR MY PRAYER" (17:1–5)

> ¹Hear a just cause, O LORD, give heed to my cry;
> Give ear to my prayer, which is not from deceitful lips.
> ²Let my judgment come forth from Your presence;
> Let Your eyes look with equity.
> ³You have tried my heart;
> You have visited me by night;
> You have tested me and You find nothing;
> I have purposed that my mouth will not transgress.
> ⁴As for the deeds of men, by the word of Your lips
> I have kept from the paths of the violent.
> ⁵My steps have held fast to Your paths.
> My feet have not slipped.

Verse 1. The writer appeals to God to help him because of his integrity. He cries, **Hear a just cause, O LORD**. Literally, the Hebrew text reads "Hear, O Lord, righteousness" (שִׁמְעָה יהוה צֶדֶק, *shim'ah YHWH tsedeq*). He believes that he deserves vindication and justice because of the righteous nature of his cause.

He is fervent in his prayer as is indicated by the intense words and phrases he uses: **hear**, **give heed to my cry**, and **give ear to my prayer**. The word for "cry" (רִנָּת, *rinnath*) suggests a shrill, piercing type of cry; it can be a cry of pain or a high-pitched shout of joy. Here it is a desperate, emotional supplication for help.

His prayer does not come **from deceitful lips**. He contends that he is uttering a sincere prayer to a righteous Judge. He is genuine and free from hypocrisy. Thus, in his petition, he reminds us that a good conscience is the soil of true prayer.

Verse 2. He pleads for God to render a **judgment** regarding his case. He trusts that God—unlike Saul, whose judgment has been distorted by hate—will look upon him **with equity**, or impartial consideration.

Verse 3. Rising to another level in his prayer, he says, **You have tried my heart**. Believing that God has examined or proved his heart, has investigated the secret recesses of his soul, and has found in him no evil purposes, he can ask God to respond to his request.

He says that God has **visited him by night** in order to judge him. The word "night" suggests that God has looked into his private life and found nothing amiss. In the quietness of the evening, when one is alone with God and one can see himself without pretense or excuses, God conducts His examination.

He urges God to search his heart again, for he is confident that God's scrutiny of him will not surface any thought, word, or deed that is rebellious to His will. The testing for which he pleads is the type done to metal as that metal is refined into a product of greater purity.

He says, **I have purposed that my mouth will not transgress.** He wants to state openly to God that he has been a man who has decided to be righteous and has, to a reasonable degree, carried out that commitment.

Verse 4. Concerning deeds and actions, he says, **I have kept from the paths of the violent.** He is emphatic. The Hebrew reads, "As for me" or "I myself." As a man among men, as a warrior among warriors, he has been free from mistreating others.

Verse 5. He further says, **My steps have held fast to Your paths. My feet have not slipped.** He has walked in the paths of righteousness, not allowing his feet to stumble in it or slip from it. Driven by a resolute purpose of being faithful to God, he has stayed with God's guidance.

The writer's supplication to God is so solidly based upon his righteousness that he appears to be arrogant or self-righteous. One must note, however, that the innocence he professes is in regard to his present dilemma. His plea parallels Job's when Job contended that his calamities had not come upon him because of sin (Job 27:5; 31:6). Neither David nor Job claims sinlessness, but each insists that his current trouble has not been brought about by his sins. Like Job, David believes that when God looks at his heart, He will find that his assertions are true and that he is seeking to conform to His will. David's first basis for his prayer, then, is not sinlessness, but blamelessness.

"SHOW YOUR LOVINGKINDNESS" (17:6–12)

⁶I have called upon You, for You will answer me, O God;
Incline Your ear to me, hear my speech.
⁷Wondrously show Your lovingkindness,
O Savior of those who take refuge at Your right hand
From those who rise up against them.
⁸Keep me as the apple of the eye;
Hide me in the shadow of Your wings
⁹From the wicked who despoil me,
My deadly enemies who surround me.
¹⁰They have closed their unfeeling heart,
With their mouth they speak proudly.
¹¹They have now surrounded us in our steps;
They set their eyes to cast us down to the ground.
¹²He is like a lion that is eager to tear,
And as a young lion lurking in hiding places.

Verse 6. With an obvious fervency in his prayer, he says, **I have called upon You, for You will answer me, O God**. His prayer is bathed in the confidence that God will hear him. He says, **Incline Your ear to me, hear my speech.** This line is synonymous with the previous line. As he beseeches God, it is as if he is commanding God. Like a little boy turning his father's head his way so that his father will hear every word he is saying, David begs God to turn His ear toward him.

Verse 7. Another ground for the writer's prayer is the grace of God. He asks God to **wondrously show [His] lovingkindness**. He wants God to answer him according to His covenant loyalty. *Chesed* (חֶסֶד) is the characteristic term for the covenant love of God. This term is translated in different ways: "mercy," "steadfast love," "unfailing love," and "lovingkindness." Its meaning comes close to that of the New Testament word "grace." He knows that God always hears the cries of those who trust Him because of His kind and merciful heart.

God has a heart of compassion for the mistreated ones who trust in Him. He is always looking out in tender care for them. Thus he says, **O Savior of those who take refuge at Your right hand from those who rise up against them.** God is the "Savior" or deliverer of those of His family who are in trouble. The one who puts his obedient faith in God has made God his refuge. It is as if he actually lives near God, even at his "right hand," and is in the presence of God's great hand of power which is always available to assist him in his time of need.

As a sinner, David knows that he should not base his prayer solely on his innocence. Extolling God's goodness, he asks Him to respond to his need out of His infinite lovingkindness. God acts in behalf of man, not because of who man is or what man has done, but because of who He is.

Verse 8. He asks God to see him, His righteous one, as **the apple of the eye.** The "apple," or pupil, of the eye (אִישׁוֹן, *'ishon*) is the most vulnerable and precious part of the eye, the part of the eye that all of us guard with utmost care, knowing that any injury to it could result in loss of sight or in serious impairment of vision. With this metaphor, David asks God to look at him with the eager attention and concern one gives the pupils of his eyes (see Deut. 32:10; Prov. 7:2; Zech. 2:8).

Using another figure, he asks God to **hide** [him under] **the shadow of** [His] **wings**, a figure that probably comes from the way a mother bird protects her little ones under her wings (Ruth 2:12; Ps. 36:7; 57:1; 61:4; Mt. 23:37). He desires God to hover over him with His divine protection.

Verse 9. Enemies are after the writer. He is feeling the hot breath of their savage pursuit. He calls them **the wicked who despoil me**, for they want to destroy him. To say it another way, he refers to them as his **deadly enemies who surround** him. The phrase literally means "my enemies in soul." They have a deep-seated desire to defeat him. Their resolve for him runs deep within their spirits. It is as if a violent flood is rising on each side of him.

Verse 10. He says his enemies are oppressing him and have encircled him; they are after him, and nothing can dissuade them. They have shut their hearts against him, and he calls their hearts **closed** and **unfeeling**. This phrase in the Hebrew reads, "They have closed their fat [חֵלֶב, *cheleb*]." Obesity is sometimes used to illustrate a rebellious spirit in the Old Testament (Deut. 32:15; Ps. 73:7; Jer. 5:28). They are totally against him. In their wickedness, in their fat hearts, they are set upon capturing him and killing him. Arrogantly or **proudly**, they speak against him. From their viewpoint they have already fought with him and defeated him. The battle is over and the outcome settled.

Verse 11. With a determined look, they have set their hearts to take him out. **They set their eyes to cast us down to the ground**. The MT has "cast me down" instead of "cast us down." The NASB has used the marginal (Qere) rendering which used the plural "us." Although this verse is difficult, in light of the context (such as vv. 6 and 8), it seems best to stay with the singular pronoun as used in the MT.

Enemies are pursuing the writer. Their total devotion is given over to finding him and removing him. Nothing but his annihilation will satisfy them.

Verse 12. One enemy, perhaps Saul, is of special concern to David. **He is like a lion that is eager to tear, and as young lion lurking in hiding places.** The first lion may be a picture of a lion whose basic nature is to destroy. He kills for the sheer enjoyment of it. The second lion is the younger one who kills to capture his prey or food by violence. He lies in wait and pounces upon it. The two words may be part of a parallelism. Both figures suggest the viciousness and violence of his enemy.

"ARISE, O LORD" (17:13–15)

[13]Arise, O LORD, confront him, bring him low;
Deliver my soul from the wicked with Your sword,
[14]From men with Your hand, O LORD,
From men of the world, whose portion is in this life,
And whose belly You fill with Your treasure;
They are satisfied with children,

PSALM 17

And leave their abundance to their babes.
¹⁵As for me, I shall behold Your face in righteousness;
I will be satisfied with Your likeness when I awake.

Verse 13. He needs a divine defense because of what he faces; so he prays, **Arise, O LORD, confront him, bring him low.** Similar expressions are found in 3:7; 7:6; and 9:19. He wants God to stand between the advancing enemy and him. His request is that the enemy be made to bow in subjection to God, to be disappointed in their evil undertaking, and to be thrown down from their arrogant perch. He knows that God has His ways of fighting for His people, so he prays that God will **deliver** [his] **soul from the wicked with** [His] **sword.**

Verse 14. Those seeking David's life are **men of the world, whose portion is in this life.** They are evil men who have centered their goals in the things of the earth. God has blessed them by filling their bellies with good things or with His **treasure,** but they never look to God in gratitude. He says that **they are satisfied with children, and leave their abundance to their babes.** As materialists, they gather and accumulate only to leave their possessions to the children God has given them. They live in this world, are satisfied with it, and never see anything outside of it.

Verse 15. David vows that he will be different from these men: **As for me, I shall behold Your face in righteousness.** The highest aspiration for the Israelite was to behold the "face" of God. "Beholding Your face" may be just a figurative phrase for being in God's special presence. He wants to be with God—now and forever. Further he says, **I will be satisfied with Your likeness when I awake.** Should God rescue him, he would continue serving Him in this life with the longing of awakening in His "likeness" in the next life.

A belief in dwelling with God in eternity is seen in the Old Testament, but it is not the brilliant, bright, life-sustaining faith in the hereafter that is pictured in the New Testament. The trust that is expressed in the Old Testament is more of a confidence in the relationship with God that has been enjoyed. Since God has met his needs in this life, he believes that God will meet his future needs in eternity. Walking with God, making Him one's refuge, and trusting Him in life and in death is to the Old Testament believer the highest good, the greatest life. He knows little about what is beyond the grave, but he believes that God will guide him through death and into a higher life on the other side. Faith to the writer is trusting God for all his needs, both present and future.

APPLICATION

Praying in Trouble

From his nightmare of terror, David prays for protection. He knows what to do when he is in trouble. He knows he must bring his peril to God. His supplication contains four ideas that are symbolized by four words: "hear" (v. 1), "heed" (v. 5), "hide" (v. 7), and "hinder" (v. 13). These words constitute an outline for praying when in trouble.

He asks God to hear his prayer. "I am in trouble, but I am calling upon You to help me. Listen to my prayer" is his request.

He wants God to heed his innocence. "They are accusing me of wrong, but I am free from such guilt. Search me, O God," he pleads.

He beseeches God to hide him in His love and strength. He wants God to be his refuge and hiding place.

He prays that God might hinder the enemy. He yearns for God to rise up and stand before the enemy and prevent them from doing any harm to him.

When we are in trouble, we should remember the order of the petitions of this prayer.

The Foundations of Prayer

The writer's supplication rests upon the three foundation stones for genuine prayer.

A life dedicated to God. Both the Old and New Testaments confirm that God listens to the prayers of the righteous.

A plea for God's grace. We want God to respond to us according to His mercy, not according to our mistakes.

A resolve to live faithfully in the future. David plans not only to live for God here but to also be with Him in eternity, rejoicing over His goodness.

Upon these grounds, prayer to God can always be freely made.

What the Saint Receives

The people of this world may rejoice in their providential gifts and be content to receive these blessings and pass them on to their children, but the believer in God will enjoy God's blessings in this life and far more. He will bask now in God's acceptance, righteousness, justification, and fellowship while he entertains the anticipation of living in His presence in the other world.

Serious Praying

Verse 1 focuses on an intense prayer. When we call upon God during a time of great need, how do we pray?

There is fervency. The psalmist's prayer is a piercing cry to God. The seriousness reflects his dependence upon God and his trust in Him.

There is a righteous cause for which prayer is made. He knows that he has done nothing wrong, and he is asking for God's vindication. This prayer might be called "A Prayer for Righteousness."

There is integrity of heart. He asks God to look at his lips and see if they have been soiled with deceit. Any divine examination will only confirm the sincere life he is living.

When we ask God to hear us during times of need, our prayers usually will have these three characteristics. God appreciates and approves earnestness, a righteous cause, and integrity in His children.

The Man of the Psalm

Let us make a careful note of the man who is praying this psalm. What kind of man is he?

He is an honest man. No deceit has been on his lips. He has sought to be transparent before God.

He is a man of purpose. He has resolved that he will not transgress with his lips. His mouth has been a fountain of truth, not error.

He is a man of peace. He has not been cruel or violent to others. He is guided by God in his relationships with other people.

He is a man who walks with God. He knows where to go with his problems. He has not allowed his steps to slip from the paths of God's will.

The Assurance God Gives

The writer of this psalm has a faith in God that is expressed in daily trust in Him.

He has assurance in God's response to his prayers. He knows that God will hear him. He says, "I have called upon You, for You will answer me, O God."

He has trust in the lovingkindness of God. He believes that God has such a spirit and has manifested it countless times toward those who call upon Him.

He has belief in God's power. He is confident that God can overcome any of his enemies if He so desires. In life he is literally surrounded by enemies, but his heart leaps with joy because of the realization that God can deliver him.

Do we have this kind of confidence in God?

True Comfort and Strength

Three figures are used to show the strength and comfort that God provides for those who trust in Him.

Those who walk with God find a refuge *at His right hand.* This location is the place of the surest safety. God's right hand stands for His great power. The believer stands next to His might and protection.

The true believer is *the apple of God's eye.* The apple of the eye is the pupil of the eye. Think of how we respect and care for this part of the eye. Other passages as well suggest that this is how God views his children (Deut. 32:10; Mt. 10:30).

The faithful ones are hidden in *the shadow of God's wings.* The figure here must be an allusion to the protection given the little chicks by their mother. She hovers over them, using all the power she has to shield them from harm. Other passages also

PSALM 17

express God's protection (Is. 49:2; 51:16; Hos. 14:7).

God's follower rests in the comfort and protection of God. If God is almighty, and if we are under His power, why should we be afraid?

The Terrifying Enemy

How is the enemy of the writer pictured? Perhaps this portrayal that is given can remind us of the devil himself, the foe of every believer.

The enemy had this writer surrounded. It seems everywhere we look, we see our enemy the devil. He is everywhere, seeking to overthrow us.

The psalmist says that *the enemy was bent on his destruction.* This attitude is clearly the attitude of the devil toward us. He does not want just to wound us; he wants to destroy us.

He says that *their hearts were set or determined.* Their hearts were hardened with rebellion. Nothing would turn them back. The devil is not going to change. He will not be converted. He will have only one thing continually on his mind—our demise!

The writer says that *they were speaking proudly of their victory.* The devil pretends that he has already won the battle. He is celebrating our damnation in advance.

David says that *they were like lions because they are violent and vicious.* The older lions tear a prey for the fun of it. The younger lions prowl in search for food. Both the young and the old accomplish their purposes by destroying their prey. The devil is pictured by Peter as a roaring lion walking about seeking whom he may destroy (1 Pet. 5:8).

What a vicious foe we have! It would be easy to be discouraged if we did not believe that He who is in us is stronger than he who is in the world.

The Noblest Desires

What do the children of God really want?

They seek *to walk with God in this life.* To be in His presence, to adore Him, to live beside Him, and to know His fellowship are their highest goals. Nothing else comes close to this desire.

They want *to behold God's face in righteousness.* We would like to behold His face in righteousness in this world by living close to Him, and we look forward to a greater, closer beholding of His face in eternity.

We have walked with Him by faith here; therefore, the strongest anticipation in our hearts is the actual moment when we will behold His face and the face of Jesus in the hereafter. A mother during pregnancy thinks about the baby and lives for the baby. Her greatest desire is to behold his face.

They want *to awake in God's likeness.* We have admired God's attributes and traits, and we have partaken of His lovingkindness endless times. Our supreme joy would be to awake in His likeness on the other side.

These aspirations cultivate and constrain our hearts.

A Heart Examination

The writer predicates his prayer upon the righteousness of his heart. He says that his heart has been examined and found innocent.

It was a divine examination. He says that God has done it, and he wants God to do it again. Human examinations fail because of prejudice and inaccuracies, but God's judgment of our hearts is perfect.

It was an honest examination. He has sought to look at every motive and every action that has grown out of his thinking. He asks God to do it at night when he will be alone and can think clearly about God's will.

It was a continual examination. He asks God to examine his heart anew even as he has asked Him to examined it before.

The heart, the source of our thinking and living, must be continually scrutinized by God to insure purity and true righteousness.

PSALM 18
A SONG OF THANKSGIVING

The Superscription: For the choir director. A Psalm of David the servant of the LORD, who spoke to the LORD the words of this song in the day that the LORD delivered him from the hand of all his enemies and from the hand of Saul. And he said,

Uniquely, this psalm has an extended title that is more of an introductory paragraph. According to the title, directions are given to **the choir director** (לַמְנַצֵּחַ, *lamnatstseach*). Furthermore, the piece is identified as being **of** ["by," "for," or "to"] **David** [לְדָוִד, *lᵉdawid*] **the servant of the LORD** (לְעֶבֶד יהוה, *lᵉʿebed YHWH*), a phrase which is used also in Psalm 36. Except for two or three variations, the rest of the title is the same as the beginning words of 2 Samuel 22. It is used here as a brief description of the psalm.

On the basis of the title's connection to 2 Samuel 22:1 and the psalm's content, we can say the psalm was possibly written after David had been delivered from Saul and was finally placed on the throne of Israel. His struggles in fleeing from Saul were behind him. At last he was free from running; and being fully aware that God had brought him to the throne of Israel, he burst forth in praise of God for the prosperity He had given to him.

The longest psalm in Book I of Psalms and practically identical to the psalm of praise in 2 Samuel 22, this psalm recounts how David gave God the credit for his successes. It is almost a continuous stream of praise for what God had done in David's life. In light of verse 50, it should be called a royal (or king-related) psalm of thanksgiving.

As free-flowing praise, it is without much organization or outline. One thought leads to another, weaving back and forth from addressing God to giving joyous descriptions of His power, mercy, and lovingkindness.

From this psalm we receive implicational instruction on the importance of praising God for our blessings.

"I LOVE YOU" (18:1–3)

¹"I love You, O LORD, my strength."
²The LORD is my rock and my fortress and my deliverer,
My God, my rock, in whom I take refuge;
My shield and the horn of my salvation, my stronghold.
³I call upon the LORD, who is worthy to be praised,
And I am saved from my enemies.

Verse 1. The Hebrew text puts **And he said** as this psalm's first words. However, the NASB makes these words the last three words of the superscription and uses them to indicate that the psalm is what David is saying about God.

David begins with a strong declaration of his love for God. **"I love You, O LORD, my strength."** His affection for God is expressed with a word that appears only here in the Scriptures in the qal (the imperfect active) form. In the intensive form, it is used consistently to picture God's compassion for His people; but here, in this form, the writer uses it to mean something like "to love fervently" (רָחַם, *racham*). David has this deep love for God because He has been his "strength" in times of great trial. He has known a long history of deliverances with God, and his love has grown into an intimate love fashioned and nurtured by His compassion and care. David's zealous affection for God must be openly expressed. This touching statement about his love for God is not included in 2 Samuel 22.

Verse 2. He piles metaphor on top of metaphor as he refers to **God** as his **rock, fortress, deliverer, refuge, shield, horn of my salvation**, and **stronghold**. Such designations as "my fortress," "my shield," and "my stronghold" (or high tower) are drawn from the military terminology of the day. God is to him a "fortress" for safety, a "shield" for protection, and a "stronghold" for a refuge.

Inspired by the geographical landscape, he uses another figure, a rocky shelter. God to him is an impregnable "rock." Two different rocks are used to express this idea of invincibility and endurance: the crag (סֶלַע, *sela'*) in verse 2a and a cliff (צוּר, *tsur*) or giant rock in verse 2b. One can see strength and certainty in these terms. Those who put their trust in God will find Him to be as firm in His faithfulness as a mighty rock.

The "horn of salvation" may also be a military term. God is David's refuge in defense and his "horn" (קֶרֶן, *qeren*) in offense. The horn of an animal represents strength and is often used in the Scriptures to portray influential and powerful rulers.

In connection with each metaphor, David attaches the possessive pronoun "my," denoting his personal connection with the One he praises. The figures employed could be applied to the relationship Israel has sustained with God, but the writer is not thinking about the nation at this point in his praise. He is contemplating his own daily walk with God. To him, God is an intimate and lifesaving helper.

Clearly, David is reliving the events of his past, the times when he saw the strong arm of the Lord coming to his defense in rocky, mountainous regions as he was fleeing from Saul. He knows that he has been the object of God's grace.

Verse 3. He says, **I call upon the Lord, who is worthy to be praised**. The Lord is extolled in almost every phrase of this psalm; however, sometimes the praise given Him is secondary, a parenthetical insertion, as we see here. God has answered his call, and he says, **I am saved from my enemies.** God in His grace and lovingkindness has delivered him.

"I CRIED TO MY GOD" (18:4–6)

⁴The cords of death encompassed me,
And the torrents of ungodliness terrified me.
⁵The cords of Sheol surrounded me;
The snares of death confronted me.
⁶In my distress I called upon the Lord,
And cried to my God for help;
He heard my voice out of His temple,

And my cry for help before Him came into His ears.

Verse 4. David can remember tragic times when he was at death's door, when **the cords of death** encircled him. The parallel passage, 2 Samuel 22:5, says, "For the waves of death encompassed me." At these times, the grave seemed to be closing in on him. **The torrents of ungodliness** rushed at him with a terrifying power. The Hebrew word for "ungodliness" (בְּלִיַּעַל, *bᵉliyya'al*) is the word that is often used with "sons of" to suggest men of worthlessness and destruction (1 Sam. 2:12; 1 Kings 21:10; 2 Cor. 6:15). The forces of evil swept over David like the rushing waters of a violent storm.

Verse 5. The cords of Sheol (שְׁאוֹל, *shᵉ'ol*; "the grave") moved around him to tie him up and bring him down to death; "Sheol" and death were like cables or ropes coming toward him to wrap themselves around him and pull him down to the dark confines of the grave. From his perspective, to use another figure, **the snares of death** confronted him and threatened to take him. Death is pictured as a great hunter who was hiding with nets and snares to capture him.

Verse 6. What did David do in such times of great **distress**? He **cried to** [his] **God for help**. How did God respond? In harmony with His faithfulness, God **heard** [his] **voice out of His temple**. His "temple," a word which also means "palace" (הֵיכָל, *heykal*), must be the heavenly one, since no temple had been constructed in David's time in Jerusalem. Even though God was enthroned in His temple looking after the affairs of the universe, He opened His ears to His servant's cries for assistance. "To hear" means to "come to the aid of" in the way that has been requested. From His trusting follower, a prayer **for help** [went up] **before Him** [and] **came into His ears**, and God heard him. David's praise rises from a heart that has seen the Lord's mighty hand numerous times.

ANSWERING WITH POWER (18:7–15)

⁷**Then the earth shook and quaked;**
And the foundations of the mountains were trembling

And were shaken, because He was angry.
⁸Smoke went up out of His nostrils,
And fire from His mouth devoured;
Coals were kindled by it.
⁹He bowed the heavens also, and came down
With thick darkness under His feet.
¹⁰He rode upon a cherub and flew;
And He sped upon the wings of the wind.
¹¹He made darkness His hiding place, His canopy around Him,
Darkness of waters, thick clouds of the skies.
¹²From the brightness before Him passed His thick clouds,
Hailstones and coals of fire.
¹³The Lord also thundered in the heavens,
And the Most High uttered His voice,
Hailstones and coals of fire.
¹⁴He sent out His arrows, and scattered them,
And lightning flashes in abundance, and routed them.
¹⁵Then the channels of water appeared,
And the foundations of the world were laid bare
At Your rebuke, O Lord,
At the blast of the breath of Your nostrils.

God's intervention is described with hyperbole. David uses violent forces of nature—earthquakes and storms, fire and water—to picture God's might and wrath.

The most beautiful scene given in the Old Testament is that of God's coming down to be among His people. His appearance among them was symbolized by the shining cloud (the *shekinah*) by day and the fiery cloud by night (Ex. 19:16–18). If the Israelites ever doubted God's presence among them, all they had to do was pull back the flaps of their tents and look at the cloud or fire. All doubt would immediately dissipate.

Verse 7. The second greatest picture of the Old Testament is God's deliverance of His people. Such an act is described here in the grandest and most elegant language. David says, **The earth shook and quaked** as God came to the aid of His people. Nothing could stand in His way. **The foundations of the mountains**

were trembling and were shaken, because He was angry. The strongest objects that man sees around him, such as the "mountains," trembled when God came in hot wrath against the enemies.

Verse 8. God is pictured as a great warhorse running swiftly into battle. Before Him, no one could stand. **Smoke went up out of His nostrils, and fire from His mouth devoured.** So fierce was He that **coals were kindled by** the breath of His mouth. It was as if "fire" poured forth from "His mouth" and "devoured" everything in its path.

Verse 9. All of nature moved at His command. **He bowed the heavens also, and came down with thick darkness under His feet.** He used clouds as His chariots as He came down to fight the battles of His people.

The convulsions of the earth and sky, the trembling mountains, and the violent storms were so far-reaching in their extent, so global in their impact, that such language seems inappropriate for describing God's meeting the needs of one person. David employs these figures of speech to convey how great God is, how strong His actions are, how important he (or any righteous person) is to God, and how grateful he should be to God for all that He has done.

God can come to our assistance wherever we may be. No mountain can hide us from His benevolent view; no forest can remove us from His watchful care; no force can shield us from the protection of His great power.

Verse 10. God was carried through the heavens by the highest of His messengers: the cherub. **He rode upon a cherub and flew.** A cherub ("cherubim" is the plural) is a type of angelic being usually seen in the Scriptures in connection with God's throne and sovereignty (see Ps. 80:1; 99:1; Ezek. 1:4–20). It may be that the clouds and the winds are being spoken of figuratively as the cherubim that carry the Lord (see Ps. 68:4, 33; 104:3; Is. 19:1).

He sped upon the wings of the wind. He soared with the swirling air and descended to avenge the enemies of those who trust Him.

Verse 11. The righteous saw God's might, but the unbelievers were shielded from it. **He made darkness His hiding place, His canopy around Him, darkness of waters, thick clouds of the skies.** He manifested Himself to the world, but He also concealed Himself. He was at once a revelation and a mystery. He was hidden from the unbelieving and mightily revealed to those who trusted in Him. Behind the dark clouds and the fierce winds of nature was the strong hand of God. "Darkness of waters and clouds of the skies," says the Hebrew in the last phrase of this verse. Perhaps the phrase means that it was as if God were surrounded by a great thunderstorm.

Verse 12. In the Old Testament writings, God is often pictured as using natural phenomena in order to confound the enemy in the thick of battle. For example, we may think of Barak and Sisera (Judg. 4:15; 5:20, 21). **From the brightness before Him passed His thick clouds, hailstones and coals of fire.** From His shining presence came billows of judgment and hailstones and perhaps lightning that hit like coals of fire. This image could be a figurative representation of God's power, or it could be an image of God going before Israel and fighting for them.

Verse 13. God had only to speak, and the whole world of nature would go forth to obey Him. The thunder is depicted as the voice of God (Ps. 29:3; 104:7). **The Lord also thundered in the heavens, and the Most High uttered His voice, hailstones and coals of fire.** He is the "Most High" (עֶלְיוֹן, *'elyon*) God because He is above all things, beyond both man and the universe.

Verse 14. When God came in defense of His people, it was as if He were sending out hundreds of arrows to pummel the enemy. **He sent out His arrows, and scattered them, and lightning flashes in abundance, and routed them.** The arrows that He sent can be compared to the "flashes" of "lightning" that streaked across the sky. No enemy could defend against such artillery. Whoever fights against God will be "routed."

Verse 15. At the great flood in Genesis 6, God gave the command and **the channels of water appeared.** The streams came as His means of destruction. He affected the whole earth, for **the foundations of the world were laid bare at [His] rebuke.** When God comes in judgment, nothing in the world—not even the world itself—can prevent it. The writer says, "**O Lord, at**

the blast of the breath of Your nostrils Your judgment comes upon the wicked." With only one breath, He can blow away any opposition that comes before Him.

"HE DELIVERED ME" (18:16–19)

¹⁶He sent from on high, He took me;
He drew me out of many waters.
¹⁷He delivered me from my strong enemy,
And from those who hated me, for they were too mighty for me.
¹⁸They confronted me in the day of my calamity,
But the LORD was my stay.
¹⁹He brought me forth also into a broad place;
He rescued me, because He delighted in me.

Verse 16. Being more specific, the psalmist focuses on the deliverances that he has experienced. He says, **He sent from on high, He took me.** From His high throne, God came to his rescue. He **drew** [him out] **of many waters.** This word (מָשָׁה, *mashah*), outside of this verse and 2 Samuel 22:17, is used only one other time in the Old Testament, appearing in connection with the drawing out of baby Moses from the Nile in Exodus 2. David's trouble is described as a flood swirling around him. He was ready to go under, never to rise again; however, God reached down and drew him out of this difficulty.

Verse 17. God **delivered** [him] **from** [his] **strong enemy,** protecting him from **those who hated** him. The enemy was too strong and numerous to handle with his own power. They had targeted his destruction, but God confounded them.

Verse 18. The writer knows that the enemy was too much for him. Wise is the man who recognizes that the problems of life are too big for him and that he must have divine help. **The day of** [his] **calamity** was the day that his enemy came against him; but God was his **stay** (מִשְׁעָן, *mish'an*), the One who supported him, his anchor.

Verse 19. God brought David to **a broad place,** that is, to an expanse free from snares, traps, and ambushes, free from the vile and vicious. Such mercy was shown to David, the Lord's servant **because He delighted in** him. Those who trust in God are people who bring God great pleasure and joy. He loves them and acts in their behalf.

"FOR MY RIGHTEOUSNESS" (18:20–24)

²⁰**The Lord has rewarded me according to my righteousness;**
According to the cleanness of my hands He has recompensed me.
²¹For I have kept the ways of the Lord,
And have not wickedly departed from my God.
²²For all His ordinances were before me,
And I did not put away His statutes from me.
²³I was also blameless with Him,
And I kept myself from my iniquity.
²⁴Therefore the Lord has recompensed me according to my righteousness,
According to the cleanness of my hands in His eyes.

Verse 20. David knows why the Lord has been generous toward him. God walks with and works for the righteous. David can see that **the Lord has rewarded** [him] **according to** [his] **righteousness**.

A divine response was given to his pleas in times of need for two reasons: because of God's lovingkindness and because of his life of "righteousness." Though imperfect, David has remained blameless before God. He can say with sincere honesty, **According to the cleanness of my hands He has recompensed me.** God has found him to be a man of integrity in the matter of doing His will. The phrase "filthy hands" is used to indicate deeds contrary to God's law (Ps. 24:4; 26:6).

Verse 21. David's righteousness should not be seen as perfection but as faithfulness in doing God's will, as the sincere desire and effort to do what is right. He has been upright—not sinless, but committed to obedience to God.

In humility, he can claim, **For I have kept the ways of the**

LORD, **and have not wickedly departed from my God.** To depart "wickedly" from God would be to turn aside deliberately from His commandments and to pursue the evil passions of one's heart.

Verse 22. He further says, **For all His ordinances were before me, and I did not put away His statutes from me.** He has kept God's commandments before him by thinking of them and obeying them. He has not engaged in willful and persistent rebellion.

Verse 23. He affirms still further, **I was also blameless with Him, and I kept myself from my iniquity.** He has remained free from the willful transgression of God's law. He may be referring to a special sin, one to which he was especially vulnerable, a sin against which he constantly had to be on his guard.

Verse 24. Why has the Lord come to his aid? Why has the Lord blessed him? He says, **The LORD has recompensed me according to my righteousness.** God has seen that David has not engaged in violence and that his **hands** [are clean] **in His eyes.** "Clean hands" in Hebrew idiom, as we have seen, refers to the deeds and actions of righteous character.

GOD'S FAIRNESS (18:25–29)

> ²⁵With the kind You show Yourself kind;
> With the blameless You show Yourself blameless;
> ²⁶With the pure You show Yourself pure,
> And with the crooked You show Yourself astute.
> ²⁷For You save an afflicted people,
> But haughty eyes You abase.
> ²⁸For You light my lamp;
> The LORD my God illumines my darkness.
> ²⁹For by You I can run upon a troop;
> And by my God I can leap over a wall.

Verses 25, 26. David has seen the wonderful equity of the Lord. From his experience with God, he has concluded: **With the kind You show Yourself kind; with the blameless You show**

PSALM 18

Yourself blameless; with the pure You show Yourself pure, and with the crooked You show Yourself astute. As a general rule, God acts toward people in harmony with the way they act toward Him. This truth gives insight into how God morally governs the world—in the sense of judgment for sin and grace for obedience. For example, if a person is "kind," that is, gracious or generous toward God, God will be loving toward that person. If someone is upright or "blameless," God will respond to that person in a similar fashion. The "pure" in heart are allowed to see God in a special way (Mt. 5:8; 1 Jn. 3:2, 3).

The converse is also true. The "crooked" will never understand God, and they will find that God always frustrates their plans, bringing them into judgment. There is a sense in which God troubles them, but there is also a sense in which their own perversity troubles them. God cannot be perverse or "crooked" in terms of His character, but He does permit people to be harassed by the evil they have chosen.

Verse 27. God will **save an afflicted**, downtrodden, righteous **people, but haughty eyes** He abases or brings down. The humble man will be received by the Lord; the haughty man, the one who lifts himself up in his own estimation, will always be brought low by the Lord.

Verse 28. God is a "light" to David, who says, **For You light my lamp.** God gives him life and a radiating influence for good. The "lamp" of Israel suggests that David has given righteous leadership to his people, but he is quick to confess that God has given him such ability and position. He acknowledges, **The LORD my God illumines my darkness.** God has arranged for David to see in the dark by guiding him through confusion, befuddlement, and ignorance.

Verse 29. The Lord has always supplied strength for David and will continue supplying strength. He says, **For by You I can run upon a troop; and by my God I can leap over a wall.** God has brought light into his darkness and has prepared him to face any foe, regardless of how strong that foe may be. God is the source of his energy and knowledge. He gives him strength that no man has in himself.

Running upon "a troop" may refer to overcoming a garrison of foes through God's power, or it may envision coming against "a troop" as he discharges the duties the Lord has given him. Either way, the Lord provides the overcoming power. David has no reason to be afraid.

The leaping over "a wall" may refer to surmounting obstacles or climbing the walls of protection that surround a city under siege. Nothing is too big or too strong to prevent the victory God gives. Whether "running upon a troop" or leaping "over a wall," he can say that his agility and ability come from the Lord, for as a trusting servant he lives in the power of his God.

FOR HIS STRENGTH (18:30–36)

> ³⁰**As for God, His way is blameless;**
> **The word of the** Lord **is tried;**
> **He is a shield to all who take refuge in Him.**
> ³¹**For who is God, but the** Lord**?**
> **And who is a rock, except our God,**
> ³²**The God who girds me with strength**
> **And makes my way blameless?**
> ³³**He makes my feet like hinds' feet,**
> **And sets me upon my high places.**
> ³⁴**He trains my hands for battle,**
> **So that my arms can bend a bow of bronze.**
> ³⁵**You have also given me the shield of Your salvation,**
> **And Your right hand upholds me;**
> **And Your gentleness makes me great.**
> ³⁶**You enlarge my steps under me,**
> **And my feet have not slipped.**

Verse 30. Three observations come to David's mind: **As for God, His way is blameless; the word of the** Lord **is tried; He is a shield to all who take refuge in Him.** He testifies from his experience with God that His works are "blameless" and effective. Second, never has God broken a promise to him. The word of the Lord has been tested, tried, and refined in fire and proven to be pure. Furthermore, he has found that God protects, as a "shield" protects a soldier, all those who trust in Him. Therefore, since God is the one and only God, the true God of lovingkindness, absolute confidence can be placed in Him.

Verse 31. In light of these facts, a wonderful conclusion must be reached: **For who is God but the LORD?** The writer uses "Eloah" (אֱלוֹהַּ, *eloah*) for "God," the singular form of Elohim, and Yahweh, the covenant name for "LORD" (יהוה, *YHWH*). There is no rock of refuge except the true God. Indeed, **Who is a rock, except our God?** There is only one God, the One who is the true strength for anyone who trusts in Him.

Verse 32. David's journey has taught him that the only answer to these questions is Yahweh, for He is **the God who girds [him] with strength and makes [his] way blameless.** God, the great God of Israel, is the only One who can guide people through the perils of life and make them come before Him as innocent servants. God encircles David as with a garment of His mighty power. In addition, He leads him so that he may walk in the way of truth. The Hebrew word for "blameless" is תָּמִים (*thamim*); translated "perfect" in the KJV, it is a word that means "without legitimate accusation."

Verse 33. He sets forth his conclusions about how God has been with him by using figurative expressions of gratitude. He says, **He makes my feet like hinds' feet, and sets me upon my high places.** The hart (the male) and the hind (the female), red deer common to the area, were swift and sure-footed. When pursued by the hunter, they would climb up the rocky crags without missing a step. The Israelites prized the qualities of agility and endurance because of their usefulness in hunting, war, and travel.

God has given David firm and effective footing among his enemies. He has placed him in "high places," out of the reach of those seeking to destroy him. He has made him to walk without slipping or falling, even in their midst.

Verse 34. God has further assisted David by training his **hands for battle.** He has prepared him to face any opposition. The NASB says that his **arms** [could] **bend** [or break] **a bow of bronze** when he had to confront foes. The Hebrew sentence is difficult to translate, and various translations of it have been given. Bows were not made of bronze. They were made of wood and could be broken.

If he is referring to strengthened arrows, like bronze-tipped arrows, his figure is accenting what the bow does. If this is the case, the power of the bow is enhanced because the arrows can penetrate their targets more effectively, and his arms are made to be more deadly in battle.

If he is referring to the bow itself, he is alluding figuratively to the amazing strength of the bow. It cannot be broken and is much stronger than any ordinary bow. "A bow of bronze" would be a bow that was unbreakable and the epitome of power. He would be empowered to bend it and use its deadly force.

If the sentence is stressing his strength alone in terms of being able to break "a bow of bronze," then he is affirming that God has given him superhuman strength.

Verse 35. The saving love of God is acknowledged by David. He says, **You have also given me the shield of Your salvation.** God's powerful hand has acted as an encircling protection for him. He does not need to worry because God, the invincible God, is his shield. **Your right hand upholds me.** God's strong hand sustains him and makes him stand straight. He has behind him the omnipotence of God. He adds, **Your gentleness makes me great.** In humiliation, God comes down to the level of the writer and exalts him. The fact that God would attend to his needs shows God's "gentleness," His condescension. God has made David great by giving him victories, putting him on the throne, and giving him the respect of the nation.

Verse 36. God has given him room to move. **You enlarge my steps under me.** He has not been cramped by having to live in a small place. Because of God's grace and help, he is able to take sure-footed steps. **My feet have not slipped.** God has prevented him from making tragic mistakes.

FOR HIS VICTORIES (18:37–48)

³⁷I pursued my enemies and overtook them,
And I did not turn back until they were consumed.
³⁸I shattered them, so that they were not able to rise;
They fell under my feet.

PSALM 18

³⁹For You have girded me with strength for battle;
You have subdued under me those who rose up against me.
⁴⁰You have also made my enemies turn their backs to me,
And I destroyed those who hated me.
⁴¹They cried for help, but there was none to save,
Even to the Lord, but He did not answer them.
⁴²Then I beat them fine as the dust before the wind;
I emptied them out as the mire of the streets.
⁴³You have delivered me from the contentions of the people;
You have placed me as head of the nations;
A people whom I have not known serve me.
⁴⁴As soon as they hear, they obey me;
Foreigners submit to me.
⁴⁵Foreigners fade away,
And come trembling out of their fortresses.
⁴⁶The Lord lives, and blessed be my rock;
And exalted be the God of my salvation,
⁴⁷The God who executes vengeance for me,
And subdues peoples under me.
⁴⁸He delivers me from my enemies;
Surely You lift me above those who rise up against me;
You rescue me from the violent man.

Verse 37. As the writer becomes even more specific about his victories, he remembers, **I pursued my enemies and overtook them.** These enemies were unequivocally routed. His claim is this: **I did not turn back until they were consumed.** God did not permit the battle to end until David had brought about a decisive victory.

Verse 38. His victory was so complete that he can say, **I shattered them, so that they were not able to rise.** The defeated enemy lay before him. **They fell under my feet.** Crumpled on the ground, they had been humiliated and rendered powerless by the might of his army.

Verse 39. What God has done provides the basis for David's expression of praise. **For You have girded me with strength for battle.** God has supplied the strength and given the victory. The writer says, **You have subdued under me those who rose up against me.** God has brought his enemies under his power, leaving them in total subjection. "I have recalled all this to say that You did it, and I want to extol Your name for it," David is saying.

Verse 40. He continues, **You have also made my enemies turn their backs to me.** Probably, the image is that of the enemy suffering complete defeat with a few survivors fleeing. He can affirm, **I destroyed those who hated me.** His opposition, the ones who wanted to see him eliminated for personal and national reasons, were removed.

Verse 41. So final was the victory that the enemy **cried for help, but there was none to save.** In the heat of the battle, they had no one to turn to but their gods; but those lifeless gods could not help them. In their desperation they cried to the Lord for help. At their wits' end, they raised their voices **even to the LORD, but He did not answer them.** No answer came from the Lord because the Lord only responds to those who trust in Him.

Verse 42. So decisive and so thorough were the victories that it could be said that the enemy was literally pulverized. With graphic figurative language, he says, **I beat them fine as the dust before the wind.** The enemy was pounded down until they were nothing but dust. **I emptied them out as the mire of the streets.** Their army became so broken up that they were like dirt that was trampled or (as perhaps the figure includes) garbage that would be thrown away.

Verse 43. In addition to all this, God has not only delivered David from his enemies, but He has also exalted him by making him king over the nation of Israel. Indeed, he can pray, **You have delivered me from the contentions of the people.** The divided nation has come together and crowned him king over them. For seven and a half years, he has ruled over only one nation, Judah; now the other tribes have come under his leadership (2 Sam. 5:1–5). He says, **You have placed me as head of the nations.** It is God who has made him king, even though the people placed the crown on his head. In addition, God has given him honor beyond Israel. **A people whom I have not known serve me**, he says. As king, he is privileged to see other nations come and recognize his authority.

Verse 44. God has made him a respected leader among the nations. Therefore, **as soon as they hear** [of his might], **they obey** him. They observe the strength of his nation and want to be united with it. Other nations behold the greatness of his throne, and with gratefulness David says, **Foreigners submit to me.** The nations around him yield to his leadership and power.

Verse 45. Impressed by his great strength, the **foreigners fade away, and come trembling out of their fortresses.** They lay down their arms and refuse to fight against him. Some of the enemies leave, fading from his field of foes. Others melt because of broken spirits. Their hearts, exhausted from thinking of ways to overcome him, give up. Knowing that they cannot win, they readily bow to his sovereignty.

Verse 46. Recalling all that God has given causes David to say in praise, **The LORD lives, and blessed be my rock**. These words are written to extol God, who is the One behind all his successes. David prays, **Exalted be the God of my salvation**, because He is the One who has done it.

Verse 47. What does God do for David? He is **the God who executes vengeance**, the One who wins the battles and annihilates the foes. He is the One who **subdues peoples** and puts them under David. God brings subjugation to his foes but exaltation to him.

Verse 48. For emphasis, he says, **He delivers me from my enemies**. Then he prays, **Surely You lift me above those who rise up against me**. God gives him victory over the enemy. He says, **You rescue me from the violent man.** Evil, vicious men seek his life, but God enables him to overcome them.

As he reflects on God's care for him, David says that he has never lost a battle. When he was in aggressive pursuit of his enemies, he was able to overtake and destroy them. God acted as his Captain in battle, going before him and defeating the opposing armies. Humiliated, they turned their backs and fled. The victories recounted were so complete that it was as if his adversaries had been pounded into dust, blown away by the wind, or smashed into the streets like mud or trash.

God avenged David from the cruel injustices of Saul (see

1 Sam. 24:12), and He brought him to the throne of the greatest nation, the nation God had chosen as His own. God brought David through the internal divisions of the people that disturbed the early years of his reign and made him ruler over a united Israel. He not only became the respected leader of Israel, but he also became the admiration of nations throughout the Near Eastern world.

God raised David to a place of international eminence. Foreign nations were subject to him. When they heard of his power, some immediately submitted to him. Others tried to stand against him but faded from opposing him like a flower without water before the sun. They soon came out of their strongholds and laid down their armor before their conqueror.

Having emerged from these experiences, David knows from whom he has received his power and popularity, and he knows what he should do about it. He is aware that God not only rules him but also rules the world, controlling even the destinies of the nations of the earth. In the heart of David, all glory belongs to God—and he promises to give Him that glory by singing praises to His name.

"I WILL SING PRAISES" (18:49, 50)

> ⁴⁹Therefore I will give thanks to You among the nations, O Lord,
> And I will sing praises to Your name.
> ⁵⁰He gives great deliverance to His king,
> And shows lovingkindness to His anointed,
> To David and his descendants forever.

Verse 49. This psalm has moved through forty-eight verses of praise to a climatic **therefore**. Because of God's deliverances, His righteous nature, His almighty works, and the victories He has given, David sings God's praises. In the first part of his "therefore," he declares, **I will give thanks to You among the nations, O Lord**. He does not confine his extolling of God's goodness to the nation of Israel; he chooses to broadcast it wherever he goes. "O Lord, **I will sing praises to Your name**," he says.

The implication may be that he hopes that the nations, upon hearing his praise of God, will join him in praising Him.

This verse is quoted by Paul in Romans 15:8–12 as the first of four prophecies to show that Christ came for the Gentiles as well as the Jews. Perhaps David thinks that he is simply giving God praise in the words of a psalm. His words, however, through the direction of the Holy Spirit, also contain a prophecy of the Messiah's praise of God and foretell Jesus' bringing the Gentile worshipers into the family of God.

Verse 50. As an addendum to his "therefore," he says, **He gives great deliverance to His king, and shows lovingkindness to His anointed, to David and his descendants forever.** God has made him king through His "lovingkindness," and David knows that God will continue that lovingkindness toward his descendants. "Anointed" refers to the chosen earthly king who was brought into office by the pouring of oil on his head. "David" identifies himself as this king.

APPLICATION

Giving Thanks

This psalm should cause all believers to reflect upon how God has delivered them. It should inspire them to break forth in praise and thanksgiving for a God who continually covers them with His lovingkindness. Thinking brings thankfulness, and thankfulness brings praise.

Let us, like David, recall the times when God has given us His grace and power; then let us praise Him with voices of adoration and gratefulness.

Why Should We Give Thanks?

This hymn of gratitude, this psalm of praise, inspires us to give thanks for what God has done for us.

For His deliverance (vv. 1–19). The writer acknowledged this wondrous fact, and so should we. God has rescued us in various ways from trials and difficulties.

For His acceptance (vv. 20–29). By His grace we have been received into His fellowship. His love has overcome all our sins.

For His strength (vv. 30–36). Frail human beings ought to give thanks for the almighty power of the Lord. God can, has, and will see us through all situations.

For His victories (vv. 37–48). Think of the victories that we have enjoyed. They are really too numerous to count. All we can do is group them together and praise God for them.

We should not be surprised that this psalm, the longest in Book I, is a hymn of praise and thanksgiving. Who would wonder at its length? We could continuously praise God for what He has done for us.

The Attributes of God

When we stop and think about it, we can use metaphors similar to those used in this psalm in describing how God has been as gracious and merciful to us.

He is our "rock." Firm in His faithfulness, God has been and is the one certainty on which we can depend.

He is our "fortress." When hounded by the enemy, we have been able to retreat into God as our fortress. Our foe has never been capable of breaking into our refuge.

To say it another way, *He is our "stronghold."* He has been as the high tower, the unreachable pavilion, to which we have retreated from the enemy that would destroy us.

He is our "deliverer." In all kinds of difficulties God has come to our aid and rescued us.

He is our "refuge." When storms have raged around us, God has protected us.

He is our "shield." God has protected us from the fiery darts of the wicked one.

He is our "horn of salvation." A horned wild animal was to be feared. God has been our strong offensive power acting in our behalf.

The numerous episodes of grace that we have experienced have built in us an appreciation and an abiding love for our God, causing us to praise Him openly and freely.

God, Our Defense

In figurative language, we can say that God utilizes the forces of nature as He takes care of His own. God is like fire, hailstones, wind, smoke, earthquakes, darkness, floods of water, clouds, thunder, and lightning. These figures illustrate the mighty characteristics of God that we see when He defends His people.

We see *His strength*. His force is almighty, and nothing is stronger than His hand.

We see *His endurance*. He comes to stay until the battle is won. Mountains tremble before Him.

Likewise, we see *His irresistibility*. The world of nature, the mountains, the heavens, and the seas in all their might cannot prevent Him from doing His will.

When God comes down in judgment on sin and sinners, or when He comes in defense of His people, nothing—not even the powers of the natural world—can prevent Him from accomplishing His task.

"Through Many Dangers, Toils, and Snares"

David is singing about the triumphs that God has brought to him. His use of different expressions to describe the dangers from which God has rescued him reminds us of the dangers from which God has rescued us.

From enemies. Some of these are seen, and some of them are unseen. Some of them intend to harm us; some harm us unintentionally. God has protected us from both.

From sin. Sin is an enemy that is worse than any physical enemy. It can approach us with deceptive cunning and take us over before we are fully aware of it.

From ourselves. We can be our own worst enemies. As we look back, we can easily see how God has rescued us from the ridiculous mistakes we have made.

From vicious circumstances. Along the way, we have found ourselves thrust into difficult predicaments that require wisdom and determination to overcome. Were it not for God's grace, adverse environments could have swallowed us a long time ago.

God's Perfection

One view of God that is highlighted in the Scriptures is His perfection. He makes no mistakes, has no character flaws, and never needs to apologize.

Jesus said that *God is perfect* (Mt. 5:45–48). His love is perfect toward all people. He sends the rain upon the just and the unjust. He makes the sun to rise upon the evil and the good.

In light of God's perfection, we would expect to see other similar characterizations of Him in the Scriptures.

His works are perfect (Deut. 32:4). "His work is perfect, for all His ways are just; a God of faithfulness and without injustice, righteous and upright is He."

His words are perfect (Ps. 19:7). "The law of the Lord is perfect, restoring the soul." His word is complete, unerring, and perfectly suited to our needs. He does not tell us everything we may want to know, but He has told us what we need to know.

His ways are perfect (Ps. 18:30). His ways are blameless. We cannot bring an honest accusation against what He has done. He has never erred in judgment, miscalculated, or forgotten.

If we stand with Him, we are winners who cannot lose; if we stand apart from Him, we are losers who cannot win.

A Humble Confidence

Can the children of God have confidence before God? This psalm says that they can. Isaiah 64:6 says that all our righteousness is "like a filthy garment" before God, but the writer of this psalm says that "according to the cleanness of my hands He has recompensed me" (Ps. 18:20).

Confidence comes from the knowledge of God's lovingkindness. We know that God sees our trusting hearts and responds to us in grace. He is love, and He acts in love toward those who believe and obey Him.

Confidence comes from our obedience to His will. No, we will not obey Him perfectly, but He is pleased when we faithfully apply His will. We want to think the way He does, and we seek to honor His will at all times.

Confidence comes from a righteous prayer life. The psalmist has walked with God. He has seen the deliverances of the Lord. It is natural for him to have confidence in God because of the thrilling history he has experienced with Him.

Isaiah wrote of a time of great sinfulness—even among God's

people. He used hyperbole to show their lack of loyalty. Even their religious activities were filthy rags because their lives did not match their confession. Here, the psalmist speaks of his genuine attempt to walk with God in obedience. He is sincere and faithful, and God has given him confidence before Him.

Do we have confidence in God?

The Justice of Life

We sometimes complain, "Life is not fair!" Indeed, there are times when it seems that way. When we see a child born crippled or a young mother whose life is cut short by cancer, we accuse life of being unfair. However, there is another side to the coin: the justice of life.

The psalmist says, "With the kind You show Yourself kind; with the blameless You show Yourself blameless; with the pure You show Yourself pure, and with the crooked You show Yourself astute" (vv. 25, 26). As we think about this justice, let us especially notice four truths.

God works through His sovereign choices. He chose Abraham, Jacob, and Joseph. Why did He select these men? His choice was not based upon their goodness, for they were sinners like the rest of us. He made these selections in His infinite wisdom. He is God, and He has the right to choose as He sees best. His ways are above our ways.

God treats us the way we treat Him. There is a sense in which this is true. God acknowledges those who honor Him and His word by crowning them with His grace and help.

God works in harmony with His natural and spiritual laws. When people are careless and reckless, they may have to pay for it. God has ordained that people cannot and will not win with sin. "Whatever a man sows, this he will reap" (Gal. 6:7).

God respects our free moral choice. He has given us freedom to choose and allows us to suffer the consequences of our choices. He has given us minds with which to think and reason. He leads us with His instructions. When we ignore His teachings, we suffer the consequences of such rebellion.

These truths converge to create a justice to life. In summary, we receive out of life what we put into it.

How Do We Read It?

How should the Bible be read? Do we read it as history, poetry, or God's revelation? Do we read it because of our devotion, to be more informed, or out of curiosity?

It is good to read it with *a lively, but accurate, imagination.* These passages are of divine origin, and they convey an actual relationship with God. It is helpful, therefore, that we try to visualize the setting and circumstances of the piece of Scripture we are reading. This approach will "put us in" these scenes that are taking place. It will keep us from seeing the Scriptures as dry and dusty or as archives of the ancient past.

It should be read with *personal application.* Ask yourself as you read, "How should I apply this passage to myself? Do I understand that this is the way God treats me?"

Let us read it with *the attitude of praise.* God is speaking to us in these passages. He shows us who He is and how He interrelates with His people. How can we read these great passages and not pause to thank Him for who He is and what He does?

The Scriptures should be read with *obvious reverence.* The book in our hands is God's book, not man's. He has provided it for us. We will never be closer to God's heart than when we are reading and digesting the teachings of His divine record. He has recorded His thinking for us to meditate upon, trust in, and practice. God does His work in and through the Word He has given. The Holy Spirit works through it to accomplish God's divine purposes.

As we read this psalm, let us picture in our minds how God has fought our battles and given us the victory, praise Him for who He is and what He does for His people, and realize that God has provided this Word for us so that we can see His heart.

Psalm 19
A Mirror of God's Magnificence

The Superscription: For the choir director. A Psalm of David. The title gives instructions **for the choir director** (לַמְנַצֵּחַ, *lamnatstseach*) and calls this composition **a Psalm** [מִזְמוֹר, *mizmor*] **of** ["by," "for," or "to"] **David** (לְדָוִד, *lᵉdawid*).

As one of the most popular of all the psalms, every line of this psalm is familiar to the student of the Bible in the twenty-first century. C. S. Lewis said of Psalm 19, "I take this to be the greatest poem in the Psalter and one of the greatest lyrics in the world."[1]

The golden thread running through it is the glory of God. The psalm can easily be divided into three parts: the glory of God as reflected by His world (vv. 1–6), the glory of God as revealed by His Word (vv. 7–11), and the glory of God as received by His servant (vv. 12–14). W. Graham Scroggie has alliteratively pointed out, "Contemplate therefore either the Skies, or the Scriptures, or the Soul, and you are face to face with God. In the Skies is revealed His Glory; in the Scriptures, His Greatness; and in the Soul, His Grace."[2]

Nothing can be more wonderful to the believer in God than receiving and radiating the majesty of His being. Through the lens of this psalm, we behold anew the reflected splendor of God.

---

[1] C. S. Lewis, *Reflections on the Psalms* (New York: Charles Scribner's Sons, 1950), 63.

[2] W. Graham Scroggie, *The Psalms* (Old Tappan, N.J.: Fleming H. Revell Co., 1973), 123.

THE SKY: HIS GLORY ANNOUNCED
(19:1-6)

> ¹The heavens are telling of the glory of God;
> And their expanse is declaring the work of His hands.
> ²Day to day pours forth speech,
> And night to night reveals knowledge.
> ³There is no speech, nor are there words;
> Their voice is not heard.
> ⁴Their line has gone out through all the earth,
> And their utterances to the end of the world.
> In them He has placed a tent for the sun,
> ⁵Which is as a bridegroom coming out of his chamber;
> It rejoices as a strong man to run his course.
> ⁶Its rising is from one end of the heavens,
> And its circuit to the other end of them;
> And there is nothing hidden from its heat.

Verse 1. The writer begins by observing that **the heavens are telling of the glory of God; and their expanse is declaring the work of His hands.** God's magnificence is made known by the starry sky, His natural revelation. The verbs translated "are telling," "is declaring," and "pours forth," two participles and one imperfect verb, suggest a continuous proclamation. "The heavens [tell of His] glory," and the "expanse" (רָקִיעַ, *raqia'*), the awesome distances of space, tells of "the work of His hands."

From his earliest days, David had studied the heavenly bodies and thought upon the obvious lessons they teach. Perhaps this psalm was written as the sun sent its orange streaks across the eastern sky. Having looked in wonder at the stars before dawn, he is now captivated by the beauty of the rising sun.

In the first part of the psalm (vv. 1–6), God is referred to one time with the name El (אֵל, *'el*), the powerful One, while in the latter part of the psalm (vv. 7–14), He is referred to seven times as Yahweh (יהוה, *YHWH*), the covenant-keeping God.

The sermon spoken by the silent witnesses of the night cannot reveal God's will for human beings or tell what God is planning to do for His creation at the cross, but they can bring the observers to their knees in reverence and awe at the power of God's fingers and the artistry of His mind.

Verse 2. This message is being proclaimed nonstop by the heavens: **Day to day pours forth speech.** Continuously, it gushes out or "pours forth" (נָבַע, *nabaʻ*) for all to hear. Furthermore, the sermon does not stop with the sunset, for **night to night reveals knowledge** of God's existence and nature. "Speech" and "knowledge" go out from the light of the starry hosts, the moon, and the sun; from the firmament or expanse with its bigness, depth, and space; from the days with their light, warmth, rain, sunshine, and regularity; and from the nights with their stillness, solemnity, and various shades.

Verse 3. The fact is, **there is no speech, nor are there words** [in which] **their voice is not heard.** No person of the earth, regardless of the language that he or she speaks, is deprived of this presentation. It skips across all linguistic and geographical barriers. Therefore, regardless of their language, culture, or education, all people can see it and understand it.

Verse 4. These divine announcements are made to those who will look up and see them. **Their line has gone out through all the earth, and their utterances to the end of the world.** "Utterances" and "line" are parallel. In the place of "line" in the MT, the LXX has "sound." The point is that the voice of this testimony goes throughout the earth, being heard in all its spaces and places, and will continue to do so as long as the heavens and the earth stand. In Romans 10:18, Paul adapted these words and used them to describe the gospel's coverage of all the world.

These missionaries go into every land and will never step aside from their duty of telling about God's glory until they are called out of existence by the hand that made them.

In them He has placed a tent for the sun. One predominant and conspicuous harbinger of praise is especially brilliant with testimony. The Egyptian civilizations worshiped the sun as the power behind all other powers, but this psalm declares that God is the power holding up the sun.

In a sense, God has made a "tent" for it in the heavenly expanse. "Tent" may be synonymous with "night," referring to where the sun goes at evening.

Verse 5. The sun is as a bridegroom coming out of his chamber. Coming up each morning and moving across the sky in a mysterious manner, it is like a bridegroom coming out of his house handsomely arrayed, radiating youthful happiness, and setting out to claim his bride. To change the figure, the rising sun **rejoices as a strong man** [who is about to] **run his course.** In its appearance, the sun is like a valiant young man—prepared, confident, eager, determined, and ready to run in a race or go to battle to prove his strength.

Verse 6. The sun, like the stars, brings its message to every gazing eye. **Its rising is from one end of the heavens, and its circuit to the other end of them.** It obediently runs its God-given track, spreading its influence across the planet. **There is nothing hidden from its heat.** Its healing is felt by people from one end of the globe to the other. If anyone, anywhere, should miss the lesson that the sun teaches, it is not because he has not been blessed by its rays or been under the spell of its warmth.

Who could miss the truth of God's nature as preached by the heavens? God speaks to every person throughout the day and night, through every hour and minute, telling them who He is and what He has done. He has left Himself the witness of the heavens (Acts 14:17).

THE SCRIPTURES: HIS GLORY ANNOUNCED MORE FULLY (19:7–11)

⁷The law of the Lord is perfect, restoring the soul;
The testimony of the Lord is sure, making wise the simple.
⁸The precepts of the Lord are right, rejoicing the heart;
The commandment of the Lord is pure, enlightening the eyes.
⁹The fear of the Lord is clean, enduring forever;
The judgments of the Lord are true; they are righteous altogether.
¹⁰They are more desirable than gold, yes, than much fine gold;

> Sweeter also than honey and the drippings of the honeycomb.
> ¹¹Moreover, by them Your servant is warned;
> In keeping them there is great reward.

Verse 7. God's glory is seen more fully in the Scriptures— in His more specific and inspired revelation. If the glory declared by His world is resplendent with His greatness and wisdom, the glory declared by His Word is even more aflame with His eternal plans, love, and grace.

In this half of the psalm, the writer begins to speak directly with the Lord. In his prayer, six synonyms are used to describe His written revelation, the Torah (תּוֹרָה, *torah*): "the law," "the testimony," "the precepts," "the commandment," "the fear of the LORD," and "the judgments of the LORD." Each expression presents a different shade of meaning for one supreme idea: The God of glory has revealed His grace to us in the Scriptures.

What kind of law is the law of the Lord? A multifaceted answer is given. **The law of the LORD is perfect, restoring the soul.** His written message has qualities that show His wisdom, compassion, and perfection. As the Lord's perfect law—complete and flawless—the Scriptures provide the means by which the soul is saved, sanctified, and guided (1 Pet. 1:23; Jn. 17:17; 2 Tim. 3:16, 17). The law puts the soul in its proper relationship with God.

The testimony of the LORD is sure, making wise the simple. The revelation that makes known the existence of God's will and our duty is "the testimony of the LORD." As such, His revelation is "sure" or reliable, bringing wisdom and understanding to "the simple" (פֶּתִי, *pethi*), to those who are uneducated and ignorant but teachable and open to God's truth.

Verse 8. Further, **the precepts of the LORD are right, rejoicing the heart**. These divine obligations are for us to fulfill; they are not arbitrary burdens placed upon us by a tyrannical God. They were formed because of His love for us, and they speak to the deep aspirations of our hearts. Obedience to them results in a clean conscience, a peaceful inner self, a purpose in living, and a happy, contrite spirit.

The commandment of the LORD is pure, enlightening the eyes. Because of its binding nature, His Word has the character of directives. These commandments are "pure," that is, without any pollution from falsehood or inaccuracy. They bring knowledge and understanding to the one who reads and follows them. The entrance of His Word into the heart dispels impurity from the life and darkness from the mind.

Verse 9. The fear of the LORD is clean, enduring forever. His Word implants respect in the minds of those who receive it. Consequently, "the fear of the LORD" is used as a synonym for the "law of the LORD," for His law creates and engenders this attitude in us. This "fear" is wholesome reverence and moral respect.

The judgments of the LORD are true; they are righteous altogether. God's Word contains His decisions, His ordinances, and His decrees; thus they are His "judgments." Coming from the righteous God who is the Judge of all the earth, His edicts can be trusted to be "true" and thoroughly "righteous."

Verse 10. How precious is His Word? **They are more desirable than gold, yes, than much fine gold; sweeter also than honey and the drippings of the honeycomb.** Knowing what God's Word is, from whom it came, the binding character of its contents, and the changing and saving power it has, one can only value it as treasure to be coveted. Indeed, it is a gift from God more precious than the finest "gold" and sweeter to the hungry soul than pure "honey." In David's day, one of the most desired metals was "gold," and the sweetest delicacy was "honey." In this symbolism, God's Word is pictured as superseding all other precious objects.

Verse 11. What else does the Word do? **Moreover, by them Your servant is warned; in keeping them there is great reward.** The servant of God is "warned" by His Word about what is displeasing to God, and he is informed about the rewards that await those who keep it. The Word is a thunderclap and a ray of sunshine, a rebuke and an encouragement.

More wonderful than the declaration of God's glory through the sky is His revelation in the Scriptures. The sun gives heat, but God's Word gives light and understanding; the sun gives physical life, but the commandments of God give spiritual life.

A SERVANT: HIS GLORY APPLIED
(19:12, 13)

> [12] Who can discern his errors?
> Acquit me of hidden faults.
> [13] Also keep back Your servant from presumptuous sins;
> Let them not rule over me;
> Then I will be blameless,
> And I shall be acquitted of great transgression.

Verse 12. Thinking of God's natural and specific revelations will cause any person to praise God and engage in personal inventory regarding his life.

Who can discern his errors? A rhetorical question is asked by the psalmist: "Who can fully judge one's own life?" The answer is self-evident. No one. The Word of God, as an impartial judge, fulfills this responsibility.

Acquit me of hidden faults, the writer pleads. As he examines his heart, he is compelled to make a penitent plea: "Cleanse me from secret sins." Note that the word "faults" does not appear in the Hebrew. The writer is concerned about innermost mistakes he has made without thinking, sins he has committed unknowingly. The law of Moses spoke of sins unwittingly committed (Num. 15:27–36). The eye can see the sins of the life but not of the heart. God can and does see the spirit, and He should be asked to cleanse it. As we study and meditate upon God's law, we are made more conscious of our sins and are motivated by that law to be penitent of known and unknown sins.

Verse 13. His companion request is **Also keep back Your servant from presumptuous sins**. This is the sin most feared by a faithful servant: the sin of highhanded rebellion. "Don't let me be ruled by pride and deliberate violations against Your law" is his solemn prayer. **Let them not rule over me**, he further asks. God's servant needs restraints as well as constraints. When we take lightly this type of sin, we put ourselves in a position in which we can be dominated by it.

Then I will be blameless, and I shall be acquitted of great transgression, he believes. Guided by God's Word, David will not be a slave to any sin. He will be cleansed from the unintentional sin and restrained from the rebellious sin. He will be blameless, without willful fault before God, and thus cannot be accused of having deliberate sin in his life.

A CLOSING PRAYER (19:14)

¹⁴**Let the words of my mouth and the meditation of my heart
Be acceptable in Your sight,
O LORD, my rock and my Redeemer.**

Verse 14. A final prayer is prayed, **Let the words of my mouth and the meditation of my heart be acceptable in Your sight.** In other words, "I want my words and thoughts always to be an acceptable sacrifice to You."

God is addressed with the designation, **O LORD, my rock and my Redeemer.** He is appealing to God as his refuge, or "rock," and his "Redeemer," or Savior. The word "redeemer" (גאל, *go'el*) is actually the word for kinsman redeemer, the one who looks after the needy relatives within a family.

The psalmist is not asking that God approve of his life as it is, but he asks that the cutting edge of God's Word would make him the sweet-smelling offering he desires to be. He wants God to look at his heart and his lips, the core of his being, and make him fit for worship.

This kind of request should be at the center of the heart of every child of God. As true worshipers come before God, they want their lives and worship to be received as a wonderful fragrance at His throne.

APPLICATION

God's Glory Reflected

We have seen God's glory as it is echoed through the sky, the Scriptures, and a servant. In essence we have found that nature, the Scriptures, and man are three chapters of one story, three views of one grand theme: the majesty of God.

God created the world and man, inspired His written revelation, and invited man to serve Him. He has expressed His wisdom and power in the created world, declared His mind in the Scriptures, and worked to fulfill His will in man—all of which combine to proclaim His transcending glory.

If Evolution, Then What?

If the world of nature has just evolved, if the Scriptures are only a sophisticated guess at what the truth is, and if Jesus is merely an invention of the imagination, then what the psalmist wrote is nothing but error written as poetry and sung as music. However, no person who is reasoning accurately would claim that such is the case. Our intelligence, our consciences, and our ability to reason join to voice our agreement with what the psalmist said. We know he wrote the truth.

The Stars' Sermon

The starry sky preaches a convincing sermon that all hear with their eyes, a sermon that extols the greatness and grandeur of God.

The heavenly hosts of the night sky carry on a conversation with us every time we look up—twenty-four hours a day, 365 days a year. Preoccupied minds can ignore them some of the time but not all of the time.

It is a silent sermon. The moon and the stars do no vocal ranting or raving; they convey a muted testimony to the reality and magnitude of God. It is quietly and profoundly given. Any mind that can think and any eyes that can see will be challenged by it.

It is a universal sermon. The message goes forth throughout the whole earth. Wherever the moon and the stars shine, the message is preached.

It is a glorious sermon. Those who behold the heavens recognize its greatness. No one would ever miss the point. If our minds can comprehend, then we leave in breathless wonder because of the spell it has cast over us. We have seen the glory of God, and we can never be the same.

It is a continual sermon. It is preached day after day and night after night. We may stop listening, but it does not stop preaching. The sermon is ever before us, reminding and rebuking us.

Everything in the inanimate world preaches the glory of God.

Learning Without a Bible

Hugo McCord delivered a lecture at Harding University several years ago on the theme "What We Can Learn About God Without a Bible." It was a very touching and informative presentation. Let us think through several of the truths that he gave.

God is all-powerful. Numerous psalms make this point (19; 57; 108; 113; 146—150). As we gaze into the night sky we are lost in its magnitude. His great might far exceeds our comprehension.

God loves beautiful things. Yes, we can think of tornados, hurricanes, and floods; but our minds quickly return to the realization that the world is really a lovely place. Looking at a child, a mountain peak, a stream, a newborn kitten, or the smile of a mother or a sweetheart erases all doubt from our minds.

God is good to His creation. He has provided the exact habitat that we need. Before us and around us are the essentials and beyond for the sustenance and happiness of the human race.

God is faithful. We can count on the seasons coming and going, water boiling over fire, and our growing up and growing old. There is a continuity that forms the basis to life.

God is the author of order and design. Everything around us fits together as part of a great blueprint. Read through Genesis 1 and 2, and notice the overarching plan for the creation.

The Ministry of the Scriptures

The writer reminds us of what the Scriptures do for us. Let us remember, too, that this writer had only a limited amount of the Scriptures. Having the Old and New Testaments, we should be able to rejoice even more fully in God's Word.

The Scriptures teach us. While the natural revelation shows God's glory, the specific revelation, the Bible, tells us in greater detail about God and give us the way of salvation as well.

They search us. They examine our hearts each time we study them. They will probe even the thoughts and intents of our hearts, searching and removing the wrong motivations, desires, and ambitions (Heb. 4:12).

They cleanse us. They point the way to God's grace and love. We do not have to wonder about what to do when we make mistakes, for we have the Word of God, the law of the Lord, reminding us and guiding us.

They sustain us. They restrain and constrain us in the way of righteousness. Mortal man must have divine guidance for his life. He needs both a correcting rod and a sustaining staff.

How grateful we ought to be for the testimony of the Lord! It brings before us the way of righteousness and peace.

In light of these facts we must ask ourselves, "Will we allow the Scriptures to search us and cleanse us so that His glory may shine through us?"

The Marvel of the Scriptures

One of the most beautiful descriptions of the Scriptures is found in this psalm.

The Scriptures are perfect. God has designed them to accomplish a special purpose, and they achieve that purpose perfectly.

They are righteous. They do not create criminals; they make godly people. All His judgments are righteous and without flaw.

They are precious. More precious are the Scriptures than the finest gold. They are more valuable than all things of the world.

They are delightful. They are more tasteful than honey, the sweetest delight the writer could contemplate.

They are compassionate. They were given to us, not to condemn us, but to save us. Their purpose is to warn and guide us into the paths of great reward.

They are eternal. "The fear of the Lord is clean, enduring forever" (v. 9). Everything around us is passing away, "but the one who does the will of God abides forever" (1 Jn. 2:17).

No wonder the writer sings of the beauties of the Lord's Word; how could he do anything but rejoice over them because they are perfect, righteous, precious, delightful, compassionate, and eternal?

The Sun and God's Glory
The sun can show us the splendor of God's work.

It is handsomely adorned. It is like a bridegroom coming out to receive his bride. Only a few people would not see that beauty.

It is the picture of strength. It rises early, as a young man who is eager and determined to run a race or to go to battle.

It is an illustration of faithfulness. Everyday, in a well-planned circuit, it moves across the sky in its daily routine.

It conveys impartiality. It gives healing to the whole earth. Everyone benefits from its healing rays. We may ignore it and never acknowledge it, but it bathes us in its medicinal rays anyway (Mt. 5:45).

How can anyone study the sun and not realize that its glow and light speak to us of the glory of God?

God's Servant and Sin
When the servant of the Lord thinks of the law of the Lord, he thinks of his sins and mistakes (vv. 11–13).

He wants God to root out *the hidden, secret sins of his heart.* He does not wish to offend God even unintentionally, for he is aware that only the pure in heart will see God.

He is especially concerned about *any presumptuous sins.* These are the sins of arrogant rebellion. He shudders at the thought of coming close to committing this type of sin.

The long and short of his thinking is that he would like *to be blameless before God.* He wants a heart and life against which one could not bring an actual accusation.

All of this can only be accomplished by living in the Word of God. His law not only instructs us, but it also redeems us from ourselves.

The Big Sin
There is one sin that this writer fears above all—the sin of rebellion. Call it presumptuous sin or deliberate sin—it is the worst kind, the one before which every child of God stands in horror.

It is terrible because it is deliberate. The servant who commits it has knowingly done so. He is well aware of God's will, but he goes on doing what he knows is wrong.

It is terrible because it bars one from God. The fellowship of God is destroyed by rebellion. When one is living in conscious opposition to God's will, God removes His Spirit from him and allows him to be dominated by sin.

It is terrible because this sin truly breaks the heart of God. One simply cannot hurt God more than when he deliberately and defiantly rebels against His will.

It is terrible because it is the most selfish of sins. It puts our wills before the fellowship and wisdom of God. We are saying, "I do not care about what You say, and I do not care about our relationship; I am going to do what I choose to do."

Every child of God should tremble at the thought of defying the Father's will. Rebellion destroys everything that the Father has built in us.

The Worshiper's Wish

The one who worships God has only one real aspiration and ambition. It can be viewed from three viewpoints.

May what I say be pleasing to God. The words that I use in my worship of God are carefully chosen, just as we carefully choose the words we use to encourage our loved ones. We would like to use the best choice of words and the truest and most beautiful thoughts as we praise Him.

May what I think be pleasing to God. We want the highest thoughts, and we want the purest and most holy hearts as we worship. God not only hears our words, but he also sees the thoughts and meditations behind the words.

May my worship be pleasing to God. We worship God to please Him. It is our desire for our worship to come to Him as a sweet-smelling sacrifice. Our worship will be acceptable only if we have the right hearts and lips involved in it.

These wishes are present in us because of who God is. He is our rock, our stronghold; and He is our Redeemer. We have no deliverer like our God.

Our one wish should be that the thoughts of our hearts and the words that we speak will be acceptable to God as we come before Him to praise Him.

Psalm 20

Before the Battle

The Superscription: For the choir director. A Psalm of David. The ancient title labels this piece **a Psalm** (מִזְמוֹר, *mizmor*) and identifies it as being **of** ["by," "for," or "to"] **David** (לְדָוִד, *lᵉdawid*). This guidance is given **for the choir director** (לַמְנַצֵּחַ, *lamnatstseach*).

This psalm and the one that follows it are prayers for the king. Thus we call them royal psalms. Apparently, this one was written by David to be prayed or sung on behalf of the king as he prepared to depart with his army for battle. It may have been revised later by an inspired hand, making it address more completely the new circumstances that had arisen (see comments on vv. 2 and 3).

These two psalms are companions in the sense that this psalm is a prayer for success in battle, while the next is a praise of thanksgiving for the victory the king has received. This psalm looks forward, and the next psalm looks backward; this psalm asks for God's help, and the next one rejoices over the help God had given.

In the world in which David lived, the king was God's representative to the people and the people's representative to God. His success in battle would bring glory to God and security to the national life of his people. Bringing the king before God in prayer was a recognized responsibility of every citizen. The occasion of this psalm reminds us of Paul's injunction to Christians in 1 Timothy 2:1, 2:

> First of all, then, I urge that entreaties and prayers,

petitions and thanksgivings, be made on behalf of all men, for kings and all who are in authority, in order that we may lead a tranquil and quiet life in all godliness and dignity.

Perhaps this psalm pictures that emotional time when David and his army are preparing to leave for battle. The warriors have assembled with their swords, bows and arrows, spears, and shields in place. Fearful forebodings and visions of triumph are intermingling in their hearts. Solemn goodbyes and expressions of Godspeed are being exchanged. Israel knows that the solidarity of the kingdom and the lives of the king and his soldiers are at stake. In this day, the king will lead his army to battle. Before leaving, the king gathers his leading men together and begins the process of offering the appropriate sacrifices (see 1 Sam. 7:9), after which he prays to God. He commits his cause to his God, calling upon Him to give the outcome that He sees fit (see 1 Sam. 7:5, 6). Perhaps while the sacrifices are offered, the people pray or sing this psalm.

In their prayers, what requests are made? What petitions are voiced?

"BE WITH OUR KING" (20:1–3)

> ¹May the LORD answer you in the day of trouble!
> May the name of the God of Jacob set you securely on high!
> ²May He send you help from the sanctuary
> And support you from Zion!
> ³May He remember all your meal offerings
> And find your burnt offering acceptable! Selah.

Verse 1. Their prayer begins with the request for God to be with their king. Such a petition is made because, in truth, they know that God's presence means victory. A series of imperfect verbs are used. They say, **May the LORD answer you in the day of trouble!** Although the words in the beginning of this psalm are actually addressed to the king, they clearly represent what the people are saying to God about him.

The immediate "trouble," the reason for the prayer, is the ensuing military campaign. The requested outcome is a triumph that would honor God, the king, and the nation.

The other part of the first petition, and a parallel to it, is, **May the name of the God of Jacob set you securely on high!** Special emphasis is given to the "name of the God of Jacob" because the name itself is equated with God and suggests His attributes and personality. He is the God who has long been the Leader and Protector of Israel.

"God of Jacob" is synonymous with "God of Israel," but the choice of this name echoes Jacob's description of God: "God, who answered me in the day of my distress" (Gen. 35:3; see also Hos. 12:4, 5). Their request is really, "May the power and wisdom of God which have so often been manifested in behalf of His people be your protection and guidance today."

Verse 2. The God of Israel, the true God, is petitioned to strengthen the king. **May He send you help from the sanctuary and support you from Zion!** The reference to the "sanctuary," literally "holy (place)" (קֹדֶשׁ, *qodesh*), of "Zion" implies that the psalm was written after the ark of the covenant was moved to Jerusalem. The word "Zion" is used figuratively for Jerusalem. The temple actually stood on Mount Moriah according to 2 Chronicles 3:1. The people pray for the king's help to come from God, who resides at the "sanctuary" in the great city called "Zion." Jerusalem was the location of the earthly symbol of God's presence, the tabernacle and later the temple. This prayer, therefore, is for the God of Israel, the One whom they worship, to watch over the king as he faces the enemy. If "sanctuary" and "Zion" refer to Solomon's temple, then an adaptation has been made of the original psalm by some inspired person to make the psalm current with the prevailing circumstances.

Verse 3. This appeal to God is made on the basis of the king's righteous conduct: **May He remember all your meal offerings and find your burnt offering acceptable! Selah.** God is asked to remember the sacrifices and offerings the king has made in the past that confirm his devotion to God and demonstrate his dependence and reliance on Him. Perhaps He is implored to think of the sacrifices offered just before the king departed for other battles. A righteous king made the appropriate offerings as his people called upon God to be with him as he defended His people.

The word "remember" does not imply that God might have forgotten. It conveys the idea of recalling the sacrifices of a faithful servant, and, as a result of that recalling, granting the promised assistance to a servant who has tried to carry out His will.

The king stands naturally in need of two blessings in order for success to attend his battle plans: He requires the security and protection of God, and he must have the endowment of God's power. Therefore, these two petitions are made for the king. The king's subjects ask God to set their king "securely on high," far away from the reach of danger. They ask that the "God of Jacob" come to his aid and give him the strength necessary for victory.

Made popular by this psalm, this petition to God has been uttered for numerous armies going out to engage in wars. Use of it probably has given rise to the cliché-like prayer "Go with God."

"ANSWER HIS PRAYERS" (20:4, 5)

⁴May He grant you your heart's desire
And fulfill all your counsel!
⁵We will sing for joy over your victory,
And in the name of our God we will set up our banners.
May the LORD fulfill all your petitions.

Verse 4. After praying for God's protection of their king, a petition is made about the king's prayers: **May He grant you your heart's desire and fulfill all your counsel!** The people are led by the psalm to pray that the king's own prayers would be answered and that his personal plans for their nation would be fulfilled.

They hope before God that all the king's "desire[s]" and "counsel[s]" would become realities. The underlying assumption is that the king does not have the selfish ambitions of a tyrant but possesses the aspirations of glorifying God and preserving His people. In other words, their prayer is that both his innermost wishes and ambitions would be in accord with the will of God and would be the kind that God could and would grant.

Verse 5. The supplication for God to answer the king's petitions in verse 5 could be a one-line summary of the entire prayer.

Should God give them victory, they promise to praise Him for it. **We will sing for joy over your victory, and in the name of our God we will set up our banners.** They vow to the king (and God) that they will rejoice over the victory by giving God all the glory. The true King and Savior of Israel was God, and this military venture was undertaken to bring honor to Him. Upon conquering their enemies by the hand of God, the Israelite army would wave their banners in the air and thank Him for granting their king (and his people) a triumphant outcome.

As a summary to their prayer, they say, **May the LORD fulfill all your petitions.** Once again they petition God, using an expression that implies that the king's petitions are righteous and worthy of a divine answer.

Whoever goes out to fight for God is richly endowed if he has his people praying for him, as this psalm depicts. As he approaches the field of battle, the people are in the posture of prayer asking that the king's petitions be answered by the God of all grace.

"MAY HE GO FORTH IN FAITH"
(20:6–9)

⁶Now I know that the LORD saves His anointed;
He will answer him from His holy heaven
With the saving strength of His right hand.
⁷Some boast in chariots and some in horses,
But we will boast in the name of the LORD, our God.
⁸They have bowed down and fallen,
But we have risen and stood upright.
⁹Save, O LORD;
May the King answer us in the day we call.

Verse 6. The request made for the king is expressed in words that envision the outcome from the beginning. **Now I know that the LORD saves His anointed.** The psalm changes to first person singular. The king himself or the king representing the people replies to the expressions of faith that have been given.

Although this reply is the response of the king and the people to the prayer, it conveys the faith God expects them to have toward their petitions. In boldness and confidence, they express their trust that God will respond from heaven and deliver their king. **He will answer him from His holy heaven with the saving strength of His right hand.**

After praying, it is time to trust God for the victory. An assurance that God will take care of His own is evident in the remaining part of the psalm. In the heart of the faithful one, the battle is over and the victory has been won. God's positive answer to their prayer is viewed as present fact. He has already granted from His divine abode, His "holy heaven," the success needed. This prayer begins with petitions and ends with praise; it begins with concern and ends with confidence.

A reference is made to the "right hand" of God, a figure that assumes that because of continual use the right hand is usually stronger than the left one. This figure symbolizes God's greatest strength. The people are expressing belief that God will come to their aid with His strongest power.

Verse 7. In what then should a nation place its trust? **Some boast in chariots and some in horses, but we will boast in the name of the LORD, our God.** In the Hebrew the verb has to be added in the first part of this sentence. The text literally says, "These in chariots and these in horses, but we in the name of Yahweh our God place our remembrance." A contrast is drawn between what "they" do and what "we" do. Basing their decision on the context, the translators of the NASB have added a strong verb "boast" and translated זָכַר (*zakar*, a word often rendered "remember") also "boast," to make the sentence read, "They boast in chariots and horses . . . but we boast in the name of Yahweh." Perhaps the contrast structure of the sentence justifies using intensive verbs.

The psalm is saying that the people of faith are confident

that God will defend His chosen (anointed) king. He will come from His throne on high to give deliverance. The king will not win with physical might, horses, or chariots; he will succeed by the might of God's own hand. The pagans trust in numbers, armor, and human strength; God's army trusts in Him and glories in His name.

Verse 8. With the eyes of faith, they see the defeat of the enemy. **They have bowed down and fallen, but we have risen and stood upright.** In confiding trust in God's leadership, they must be singing of victory as if it has already been given. The enemy have already "fallen," and the righteous have "risen" and are standing "upright" in the presence of triumph. Those who put their faith in man are always vanquished, while the righteous always conquer. The righteous may sometimes lose a battle, but they always win the war. God is their Warrior-Leader, and He will not and cannot fail.

Verse 9. The prayer closes with a final expression of dependence upon God: **Save, O Lord; may the King answer us in the day we call.** The conquest, God's people know, must come from the "Lord." They address God as their true "King," the supreme power behind the earthly king. As they pray for their king, they evoke the blessings and watch-care of the absolute Monarch—God Almighty—who can see the end from the beginning and control the outcome before the battle begins. In keeping with the spirit of this psalm, someone has said, "The battle is always won the day before in the closet of prayer."

APPLICATION

The Biggest Concern
What does a righteous king who is going into battle actually need? A bigger army? Favorable weather? Brilliant strategy? This psalm says he must have God, the answer to his prayers, and faith.

We can see through the eyes of faith a young man, still in his teens, going out to face Goliath of Gath in 1 Samuel 17. What did that confrontation require? Saul first said that David could use *better judgment* and change his mind (v. 33). He later said that David should have his *armor* (v. 38). Others (including his own brothers) said that he *ought to go home* (vv. 28–30).

David said that he would *go with God* into the valley and remove the reproach from the army of God (v. 36). David, the teenager, needed God; and he was wise enough to know it. As he walked out to face the Philistine representative, the righteous could have prayed for him in the vein of this psalm: "Lord, as this young man faces the enemy, be with Him. Answer his prayers, and may he walk up before the giant believing that You will give the victory!"

As one confronts a wicked foe, he should pray in a way similar to this psalm; and others should pray for him as well. God's presence, righteous prayers, and faith are the true keys to victory.

The Major Prayer

What is the highest prayer that we can pray for our leaders? What petitions tower above all others? We can pray . . .

That their prayers will be answered. They should be praying for deliverance from evil and enemies, and we can pray that their prayers will be heard.

That they will lead in the name of God. Leaders should go with God and lead God's people in the paths of righteousness. Even as they go to battle, they should be going to accomplish God's will. So, they do not go in their own names but in the name of God.

That God will see them as righteous. We can pray that God will see their faithful service and righteous living and bless them because of their walk with Him.

These traits are assumed of the king for which this psalm was written.

The Greatest Needs

All servants of the Lord have three paramount needs. They are in a vicious world and move daily at cross purposes with the devil.

They need the security of the Lord. They want God to defend them by placing them on high, far away from the enemies' arrows.

They need power. Our human strength is too weak; our only hope is to receive divine strength. Our mission is too great for human energy alone.

They need to be positive in faith. They have the right faith, and now they must believe this faith. If they do, they can rejoice in victory before it ever occurs.

This psalm promises protection and power for the servants who go forth in the name of the Lord; it also pictures the king and people rejoicing in victory before the battle is even fought.

The Righteous Man and God

To say it simply, the righteous man wants God to hear his prayers.

He wants God to listen to his prayers. He knows God will, but consciously voicing his petitions gives him great comfort. When he calls, he believes that God will hear him!

He wants God to remember his devotion. He knows that God never forgets, but it encourages him to remember that God will remember all his attempts at worshiping Him. God is aware of his deepest desires to do His will.

We might say, "If God knows all these things, why does the psalmist bother to pray about them?" This prayer/psalm shows us the routine of a life of faith. The writer's requests are a way of reminding himself of what he believes. His communion with God strengthens his trust and love of God. He honors God by reminding Him of what He has promised to His people.

Holy Assumptions

Faith makes assumptions based upon the evidence God has given. This prayer could not be prayed unless God's promises are seen as if they have already been fulfilled.

Assume that the desires of the one for whom the prayer is made are holy. The prayer is that the desires of the king will be answered. This petition presupposes that his desires are right, proper, and in accordance with God's will.

Assume that the plans of the one for whom the prayer is made are righteous. The prayer is that the counsel of the king will meet with success. This petition grants that the king has planned wisely and faithfully. It is assumed that his counsel or directions are true to the purposes of God.

Winston Churchill said, "The best way to create a virtue in someone is to attribute it to them." There is a time to rebuke and correct, but there is also a time to ascribe faithful ambitions and actions to the person for whom we are praying.

The Anticipation of Faith

There is a certain anticipation of faith that believers know. How is this the case?

Anticipate by faith the outcome. Read carefully verse 5. The king was going to battle, but the people were singing of victory. We do the same. Listen to us singing, "I'll reach the land of corn and wine" and "in the sweet by and by." We are not there yet and may have quite awhile to wait, but we are voicing our expectation of what we know is to come.

Prepare for celebration. The people said, "We will go ahead and get our banners ready for your return." When the king returned, he was greeted by a victory celebration. Before he left, they said, "As you go to battle, we will go ahead and set up the victory celebration." Faith sees the outcome from the outset, the ending from the beginning.

Rejoice in God even now. Yes, he rejoiced over the victory as if it were a present fact. Some say, "I am going to wait until I can touch it before I rejoice in it!" That is one view, but it is not the view of this psalm. The people were saying, "We trust in God and will honor Him by treating His promises as present facts."

This psalm views this kind of action not as presumptuous, wild-eyed faith, but as trusting faith, a faith acting upon God's promises. Presumptuous faith assumes that God will do something He has not promised; a trusting faith believes that God will do what He has said. Furthermore, read verse 6 and look at the use of "I know." This verse shows us the "I know" of faith. Paul said, "I know whom I have believed." There is a certainty that grows out of the evidence upon which our faith rests (2 Tim. 1:12). There is a sense in which every believer can say, "I know."

Should We Boast?

We do boast, but we must be careful to glory only in the Lord.

We boast in God. This psalm says, "Some boast in chariots and some in horses, but we will boast in the name of the Lord, our God" (v. 7). We do not exalt human strength—such as armies, artillery, or flesh. The believer said, "In God we have boasted all day long, and we will give thanks to Your name forever" (Ps. 44:8). We do not boast in riches (Ps. 49:6) or in time (Jas. 4:15, 16), for we may not have either for very long (Prov. 27:1). We do not rejoice in our proven skills, past successes, or physical strength.

We boast in the cross of Christ (Gal. 6:14). Yes, in God's salvation we glory. We do not brag about our good works as if that were the source of our salvation (Eph. 2:9). The great price of redemption was fully paid by the sacrificial death of our Savior.

All the things in which we are tempted to glory are too frail to merit our trust. They are powerless, temporary, and fleeting. God and His salvation comprise the only reason for true rejoicing and praise. We lift up our voices in praise to God because of who He is and what He has done.

PSALM 21
PRAISING GOD FOR THE VICTORY

The Superscription: For the choir director. A Psalm of David. The title says this composition is **a Psalm** [מִזְמוֹר, *mizmor*] **of** ["by," "for," or "to"] **David** (לְדָוִד, *lᵉdawid*). It is addressed to **the choir director** (לַמְנַצֵּחַ, *lamnatstseach*). The time and place for its writing are unknown to us.

A reading of this psalm reveals that it is akin in structure and content to the preceding psalm. Both weave back and forth from the first person to the third, both have the setting of a victory of the Lord, and both refer to the anointed king.

Is this psalm a prayer that asks for success as did the previous one, or is it a psalm that is rejoicing in a triumph that has been given? When a comparison is made between 20:4 and 21:1, 2, it appears that this psalm celebrates a victory that has been given. Thus the two psalms are companions in that one is a petition and the other seems to be an expression of joy over an answer given. Apparently Psalm 20 was a prayer to be prayed for the king as he and his army were going off to war, while this one is an anthem of praise to be sung about the victory God had given the king in the battle.

Much of our praying consists of asking God for His protection, prosperity, pardon, and provisions, instead of giving thanks for what He has already done. We are long on petition and short on praise, often spending quality time asking for blessings while we spend little time thanking Him for the bounties we are enjoying. Written from a heart overflowing with appreciation for the gifts of God, this piece is clearly a royal, thanksgiving psalm.

A military battle is likely the backdrop for the psalm. The

dust from the field of battle has settled. Bloodstained swords, broken spears, and battered shields are scattered across the plain, giving a silent testimony to the major struggle that has occurred. A beaten army has moved back with its wounded and dead to the city from which it came. The triumphant army, the army of Israel led by the king himself, has returned to Jerusalem to report how God has given a decisive victory to His people.

The psalm shows the reaction of the king, the army, and the people to this victory. They gather to accept the conquest God has provided. The jubilation of the city is more of a worship service than a celebration of success. They have joined together to praise the One who granted them the triumph, expressing their rejoicing by praying or singing this thanksgiving psalm.

PRAYERS ANSWERED (21:1, 2)

¹**O Lord, in Your strength the king will be glad,**
And in Your salvation how greatly he will rejoice!
²**You have given him his heart's desire,**
And You have not withheld the request of his lips. Selah.

Verse 1. Adoration is given to God for His answering their prayers. Their hymn of thanksgiving begins with **O Lord, in Your strength the king will be glad**. The king is filled with joy because of what God has done for him and his nation.

The people are led by the psalm to say further, **In Your salvation how greatly he will rejoice!** After making supplication to God, they have sent their king to war on the wings of prayer. With God fighting for them, they have been victorious. God has provided their nation with the leadership and strength needed, so they are engaging in a celebration of the triumph with God in their midst.

Verse 2. The people asked in Psalm 20 that the king's aspiration be honored, and God has fulfilled them. They say, **You have given him his heart's desire**. To say it another way, **You have not withheld the request of his lips**. The king has planned and dreamed properly for his nation and himself, and God has accepted those ambitions, the silent prayers, and answered them.

PSALM 21

Selah is used probably to emphasize that this thought is worthy of prolonged meditation. By God's hand, their men of war had routed the enemy, and they are giving the credit to God. Their king has trusted in Yahweh instead of horses and chariots. The success has come from heaven, not the skill and valor of the king and his men. Therefore, the king is rejoicing over God's might that has been demonstrated in their behalf and the salvation (or victory) He has provided.

BLESSINGS WERE SENT (21:3–6)

³**For You meet him with the blessings of good things;**
You set a crown of fine gold on his head.
⁴**He asked life of You,**
You gave it to him,
Length of days forever and ever.
⁵**His glory is great through Your salvation,**
Splendor and majesty You place upon him.
⁶**For You make him most blessed forever;**
You make him joyful with gladness in Your presence.

Verse 3. They are thanking God for His graciousness to them. He has not only given what they have asked, but He has given to them in a rich and superbly generous way.

They say, **For You meet him with the blessings of good things.** The KJV uses the word "prevent" in the older sense of "going before," and the NASB has "meet." The word is קָדַם (*qadam*), meaning to anticipate, to go before, to be in front of. The thought is that God goes before His people to lay out a multitude of choice bounties. When they arrive, God's provisions are waiting on them.

They say to God, **You set a crown of fine gold on his head.** The gift of supremacy that God gave fittingly reconfirmed the sovereignty of their king. The golden "crown" (עֲטָרָה, *ᵃtarah*) refers not to his original physical coronation, but to a spiritual and practical identification. The crown was sometimes a wreath made of flowers or leaves; sometimes, if the occasion were special enough, it was made of gold. It was given as a gift to a valued personality or for the celebration of a rare and wonderful event. The symbolism suggests that by handing the king this enemy nation, God was saying, "I crown you as My king. You are serving Me and My people, and I am giving you this victory as evidence that I have accepted you anew as My king."

Verse 4. They say, **He asked life of You, You gave it to him, length of days forever and ever.** The king asked God to save his life, but God did much more—He gave him a long life. "Length of days" (אֹרֶךְ יָמִים, *'orek yamim*) means a long life, but the appendage "forever and ever" (עוֹלָם וָעֶד, *'olam wa'ed*) adds emphasis. God had answered them generously, going way beyond what they had asked or thought.

Verse 5. Furthermore, they can say, **His glory is great through Your salvation, splendor and majesty You place upon him.** He has not only delivered the king from harm in the battle, but He has also given him a permanent and enduring family, popularity, and prosperity. He has bestowed upon him "glory" and "majesty." God did what He characteristically does: He gave more than that which was asked of Him. Solomon asked for wisdom, and God said, "Behold, I have given you a wise and discerning heart. . . . I have also given you what you have not asked, both riches and honor . . ." (1 Kings 3:12, 13).

On a higher level, these words may go well beyond David's life and apply to the coming of the Messiah and the spiritual kingdom that He would set up (Acts 2:30). David may or may not have known about any future prediction that his words might contain. His words initially applied to his situation, but the Holy Spirit must have had something much bigger in mind.

Verse 6. The favors God granted have not just been physical, but they have also been spiritual and emotional. The people say, **For You make him most blessed forever; You make him joyful with gladness in Your presence.** The bestowing of these blessings upon the king and the people brought happiness in the superlative degree. The king knows that God's presence has enabled him and sustained him. Being in God's presence has brought him unspeakable joy. No sweetness of earth can replace the presence of the Lord.

PSALM 21

TRUSTING IN THE LORD
(21:7–12)

⁷For the king trusts in the LORD,
And through the lovingkindness of the Most High he will not be shaken.
⁸Your hand will find out all your enemies;
Your right hand will find out those who hate you.
⁹You will make them as a fiery oven in the time of your anger;
The LORD will swallow them up in His wrath,
And fire will devour them.
¹⁰Their offspring You will destroy from the earth,
And their descendants from among the sons of men.
¹¹Though they intended evil against You
And devised a plot,
They will not succeed.
¹²For You will make them turn their back;
You will aim with Your bowstrings at their faces.

Verse 7. The people turn to giving thanks for God's trustworthiness. His dependability is the foundation of their confidence.

The day has gone well with the king, and the reason is obvious: **For the king trusts in the LORD**. The king's part is that of believing in God. Because he has looked to God and followed Him, he has been the recipient of good things from His hand. He has experienced the glorious truth that God blesses those who trust Him.

The lovingkindness of God has been and will be the mainstay of the king. **And through the lovingkindness of the Most High he will not be shaken.** The king finds his strength in God's grace. God's part is steadfast loyalty to those who love Him. It is a foregone conclusion that God will always be generous to the righteous. He is continually a God of grace, and He never steps out of character. The king, therefore, is held steady by God's "lovingkindness." He is motivated to stay with God by the realization that God will never forsake him.

Verse 8. Therefore a prediction can be made on the basis of the relationship that God sustains with the king and His people: **Your hand will find out all your enemies; Your right hand will find out those who hate you.** God searches and discovers those who are opposed to the king. He is God's representative on earth, and anyone who opposes him stands as an affront to God. He will use His great might, His "right hand," to destroy those who are set against him.

What God has been to the nation in their time of crisis, they know He will continue to be in any circumstance that may arise. The victory that He has given is a down payment on the victories that are to come. Consequently, they rejoice even now over their defeating all of the enemies of the future who may approach them.

Verse 9. The figurative expressions that follow show how completely God deals with those who oppose His people. **You will make them as a fiery oven in the time of your anger.** No enemy is too powerful for God to destroy, too cunning for God to find, or too elusive for God to catch. The opposers of God will be consumed like chaff in a "fiery" furnace. The word for "oven" (תַּנּוּר, *thannur*) is normally used in the Scriptures for a cooking oven, but here it is used metaphorically as the confinement of God's anger.

Also, God's wrath is like a swelling, leaping fire that engulfs, covers up, and sweeps away. He will **swallow them up in His wrath, and fire will devour them.** Fire provides the appropriate imagery for God's consuming judgment. His anger as a raging, devouring fire reduces to ashes anything in its path. No destruction is as complete as the destruction brought on by fire.

Verse 10. The demise of the enemies of God is so complete that even their descendants will be removed from the earth. **Their offspring You will destroy from the earth, and their descendants from among the sons of men.** To the people of the Old Testament times, having no offspring would be the worst disaster conceivable. The enemies of God were headed toward the worst possible tragedy—for them and for their families.

Verse 11. No evil devised against God will ever succeed. **Though they intended evil against You and devised a plot,**

they will not succeed. The pernicious plans of the wicked seem to prosper at times, but they eventually and ultimately fail.

Verse 12. God fights the battles of His people. **For You will make them turn their back.** God is deadly in war—saving the righteous and annihilating the sinner. No enemy is too great for Him. **You will aim with Your bowstrings at their faces.** As the evil men march forward to execute their sinister intentions, the Lord pulls His bow in their faces, and they are forced to retreat. When God aims His bow, He does not miss. His arrows strike the opposing army in the face, one of the most vulnerable places for an arrow to strike. The figure portrays an army experiencing defeat and retreating to safety. However, the figure contains no safety to which the wicked can retreat. They are swallowed up by the fury of God.

All of these figures and parallelisms are used to declare one truth. The Lord foils the work and lives of those who oppose Him. With the teachings of the New Testament, we see beyond the figurative expressions to the ultimate judgment of the wicked in an eternal judgment. Whoever fights against God is destined to lose.

BETWEEN THE VICTORIES (21:13)

> ¹³Be exalted, O Lord, in Your strength;
> We will sing and praise Your power.

Verse 13. When recounting what God has done for us, we move quickly from a description to a beautiful ascription. May God be exalted above all the people of the earth, and may all human beings come to acknowledge Him as the true God. With these words the psalm ends: **Be exalted, O Lord, in Your strength; we will sing and praise Your power.** May what He does with His great "strength" cause people to extol His name. All should come to know of the Lord's might. As for us, we will "sing and praise" His great "power" forever. We have learned the truth about God, and we will tell it to ourselves and others in our continual praises.

APPLICATION

Praise Be to God!

This psalm begins and ends with the praise of God. The first and last verses use the phrase "in Your strength," extolling the mighty hand of God. Just so, each event in our lives should be hedged in with the adoration of God, with an awareness of God's manifestation of His strength. With each demonstration of the Lord's power comes a new and wonderful reason to praise Him.

Let us pray and praise Him as we go to war. Obstacles confront us, and we must face them. As an army marching out to do battle with the enemy, we go in the name of Lord. We will be saved by His strength, and we will lay the trophies of victory at His feet.

Let us give thanks for what the Lord has done after every victory. We must say with David, "Thank You for answering our prayers, for being so gracious to us, and for Your trustworthiness."

As we receive favors from God, let us ask for one more gift: the gift of a thankful heart.

The God of Abundance

How does God answer His children's prayers? Two words come to mind: "abundantly" and "generously."

He grants our requests. The king and the people petitioned God, and He heard their desires. On the basis of this psalm alone, we can say that He is a prayer-answering God.

He gives us more than we ask. The king and people asked for life, and God gave him a long life. They asked for victory, and God gave a great victory. God will grant what we ask and then some.

He fills our hearts with gladness. God did not reluctantly answer their prayers; He did it with the enjoyment of a father responding to the requests of his son. As we see His generosity, we are filled with joy.

He condescends to dwell with us. He not only gives us His provisions, but more importantly He gives us His presence. Our experience is that we find His fellowship to be greater than all His gifts.

When God answers our prayers, our rejoicing quickly turns

to praise, for we have seen how graciously, lavishly, and lovingly He has responded to us.

The God of Three Tenses

The God who is praised in this psalm is the God who has been, is, and will be.

He is the God of the past. We have a history with God. We have prayed, and He has answered. We cannot forget what God did for us yesterday.

He is the God of the present. He walks with us now. Jesus was to be Immanuel or "God with us." God is transcendent but He is never far away. Christ walked among the candlesticks in Revelation 1. He was with His followers down in the furnace of affliction. If His children must walk in the fires of trial, He will walk in those fires with them.

He is the God of tomorrow. He holds our future in His hand. When we get to the tomorrows that lie ahead, we will find that God has already been there and cleared away debris to make smooth the road we must travel. Jesus had John the Immerser leveling the hills and filling in the valleys for Him; and we have Jesus and the almighty God going before us, defending us and getting tomorrow ready for us.

God sees and meets all our needs—those that arise from the past, the difficulties of the present, and the ones that glare at us from the high perch of the future. He has made provisions to heal our past, He walks with us now, and He guarantees a beautiful tomorrow.

When God Destroys

God opposes evil. He blows it away through the gospel and through His righteous providence. The future of evil is bleak because God stands against it.

Its destruction is certain. No enemy of truth and righteousness can avoid a collision with Him.

Its destruction will be complete. The victory will be glorious, not meager and minimum. There will be no survivors. All evil will be found, rooted out, and brought into the blinding light of God's righteousness.

Its destruction will be in harmony with His justice and integrity. The war between God and evil is a "just" war; it must be fought and it must be won. God's hatred of evil is right and in harmony with His love.

The line is clearly drawn: Whoever stands with God wins; whoever stands on the side of evil will suffer the same fate as evil.

In Between the Victories

This psalm rejoices in a victory that God has given. The final verse emphasizes a constancy about the believer's life. How does the believer live during victories and especially when he is waiting on victories?

We will exalt Him by telling of His wondrous love and grace. We can do it by sitting down and rejoicing over a gift that He has given, and we can do it by living an ordinary, commonplace day with the radiance of divine appreciation characterizing us. We can also do it by anticipating with faith His blessings of tomorrow. Whether sitting, working, or looking ahead, we will be glorifying God.

We will sing of His grace and power. What He has done for us will be constantly on our lips and in our hearts. Who can forget His grace? Who can cease to be amazed at His power?

We will rest in His provisions. We know that there will be other battles, but we will not worry about them. The God who has delivered us in the past will deliver us in the future.

There is a continuity about praising God. We praise Him when He has given a great victory. We can praise Him even when we have experienced a defeat because we know that He wants us to learn valuable lessons that we could not learn any other way. Even when we do not know what to do, we can praise God because we know He will lead us out of the confusion.

What Do You Say to Yourself?

When we return from the field of battle savoring a decisive victory, we are prone to congratulate ourselves, saying, "You did a great job!" This psalm was written to remind the king and his people that God is the only Champion. The words of the psalm guide the king and the people into proper thinking about what has occurred.

In one of the parables that Jesus told, a rich man is pictured as reasoning "with himself" (Lk. 12:17). What this man said to himself brought about his downfall. He listened to the wrong preacher, taking to heart the wrong message.

Ask yourself, "What am I saying to myself about God?" This psalm reminded the king and the people to speak faithfully about God to themselves.

What we say to ourselves is the true measure of our spirituality. If someone could look into my heart and observe what I am saying to myself about God and spiritual concerns, my true spiritual qualities would become known. I can mislead others with my actions, but my thoughts present the true picture of what I am.

What we say to ourselves is the mainspring of life. It is the source, the origin, of all words and actions. The conversations that we carry on with ourselves form the fountainhead of the living that we do. No person rises above the thinking that he does deep within his soul.

What we say to ourselves is that part of us that is of greatest interest to God. It seems that God weighs our intent more than He does our actions (1 Sam. 16:7). First and foremost, we worship and serve God with our minds, by our innermost thoughts and aspirations about Him.

Let us allow the psalms to teach us how to think about God. Sometimes we read a psalm and exclaim, "That's exactly what I was thinking!" Sometimes we read them and moan, "That's exactly what I should have been thinking!"

The God Who Goes Before

God has always been the God who has gone before us. Think of the little flower girls who go before the bride, throwing out flowers to decorate her path. God has been to us like those little princesses decorating the pathway of the bride with beautiful things, but in a far greater sense. He has gone before us tossing out His grace, precious gifts, and numerous other favors.

He has gone before us in this life. When we came into this world, we found that God had already been here and had prepared everything for us. He had good parents waiting on us, and if He did not, He had prepared other ways of caring for us. He had a world waiting that would sustain us, people who would love us, and opportunities that would invite us to grow.

He has gone before us in the spiritual realm. He has been planning for us through three biblical ages. He brought Christ into the world, He created the church for us, and He had the everlasting gospel waiting for us to be our means of salvation. All spiritual blessings were available for us when we made the decision to put Jesus on in baptism (Gal. 3:27).

On the basis of what He has done in the past, we can trust that He has gone before us in eternity. Jesus said, "I go to prepare a place for you" (Jn. 14:3). When we step over to life's other side, we will find that God is waiting on us with far greater blessings than we have seen in this life. Paul said that to depart and be with Christ is far better than to remain here (Phil. 1:23).

God went before ancient Israel and fought the battles and gave the victories, and we have found Him to be the God who goes before us as well. As we make our way through the wilderness of this world, it helps us to remember that God has preceded us, removing the tangled vines and the wild beasts of the future, charting the map for our journey so that we will not make a wrong turn. Let us follow His leadership, and all will be well—in life, in the church, and in eternity.

Psalm 22
Overwhelmed but Trusting in God

The Superscription: For the choir director; upon Aijeleth Hashshahar. A Psalm of David. The title says that this piece is **a Psalm** [מִזְמוֹר, *mizmor*] **of** ["by," "for," or "to"] **David** (לְדָוִד, *lᵉdawid*). We have no reason to doubt that David wrote the original psalm, although we cannot determine the circumstance in David's life to which the psalm refers. Obviously, he was in the throes of some great danger and distress too terrible for common words to describe. He piled description on top of description in a highly figurative and emotional wording as he made his pitiful situation known to his God.

The title adds the Hebrew terms עַל־אַיֶּלֶת הַשַּׁחַר (*'al 'ayyeleth hashshachar*) to the ascription of the authorship. The meaning of these words is obscure, but they may mean "upon 'The Hind of the Morning,'" which may be the name of a melody by which the song was to be sung.

This well-known lament psalm is the most quoted psalm in the New Testament. A sampling of its use would be as follows: verse 1 is appropriated by Jesus on the cross (Mt. 27:46; Mk. 15:34); verse 18 seems to be in the background of Matthew 27:35, Mark 15:24, Luke 23:34, and John 19:23; and verse 22 is applied to Jesus in Hebrews 2:12. Because of these prophetic indications, the psalm has been referred to as "A Passion Psalm," one that pictures the rejection and pain of Jesus as He died for our sins. In this vein, it has long been recognized as one of the great "messianic" psalms.

As one begins reading it, however, his first impression is that David is writing in figurative language about a siege of persecution he is undergoing—perhaps as he flees from the attacks of Saul. Because of the intensely personal character of the psalm, one does not immediately notice the detailed prediction of the sufferings of Christ. The writer presents his deathly struggle in prayer to God in the first person. This fact has led to two questions: "How are we to interpret this psalm?" and "Is the psalm presenting the writer's experience, the Lord's, or both?"

The best explanation of this interpretative difficulty seems to be the view that the psalm has its roots in David's own trial of fire, but its language reaches beyond his experiences to the sufferings of Christ. While David may have understood that he was writing in exaggerated, poetic language about a bitter experience, he was in fact—by the guidance of the Holy Spirit—portraying the actual sufferings of Jesus in pictorial prophecy. His sufferings typify the far greater sufferings that the Christ would know. The account of the writer's sufferings is recorded by the Holy Spirit in such a way that the descriptions foreshadow in detail many of the circumstances of the crucifixion of our Lord.

The psalm is clearly divided into two parts: verses 1 through 21, and then 22 through 31. The first part is a lament, and the second part is thanksgiving and praise.

"MY GOD, MY GOD" (22:1–5)

¹My God, my God, why have You forsaken me?
Far from my deliverance are the words of my groaning.
²O my God, I cry by day, but You do not answer;
And by night, but I have no rest.
³Yet You are holy,
O You who are enthroned upon the praises of Israel.
⁴In You our fathers trusted;
They trusted and You delivered them.
⁵To You they cried out and were delivered;
In You they trusted and were not disappointed.

Verse 1. The opening scene of this psalm is that of a believing soul all alone in the midst of a terrible crisis. It begins with a heart-rending cry: **My God, my God, why have You forsaken**

me? The intensity of his prayer is seen in his use of "my God" three times in two verses. No one is responding to his pleas for help, not even God. **Far from my deliverance are the words of my groaning,** he laments. This afflicted one is in such pain that his prayers are expressed in groans, and he has not seen immediate help coming to him. "Deliverance," he moans, is "far from [me]."

The words of this first line are immortalized by our Lord as He experienced the darkness of separation from God when He became "sin on our behalf " (2 Cor. 5:21). "Eli" (ἠλί) in Matthew is the Greek transliterated Hebrew word אֵלִי which means "my God" (Mt. 27:46), while "Eloi" (ἐλωϊ) in Mark is the Aramaic variant of that expression (Mk. 15:34).

Verse 2. He has been praying about his persecution—even beseeching God unceasingly: **O my God, I cry by day, but You do not answer; and by night, but I have no rest.** His appeals to God were continual, "day" and "night." Heaven has been strangely silent to his endless calls. Such praying has brought him to a state of exhaustion.

Verse 3. The description of the loneliness that he feels is followed by a recounting of the faithfulness of Yahweh to Israel in the past. He says, **Yet You are holy, O You who are enthroned upon the praises of Israel.** He knows that God is "holy," pure, free from defilement, and without evil. God would never be unfaithful to any of His people. He has been and is "enthroned upon the praises of Israel." His people's praises for His mighty acts in the past rise up to Him. They are like a huge cloud, a cloud that is received by God, who allows it to surround His throne as acceptable worship. It is as if His throne is lifted up by that cloud. "Surely, the Lord wants the same type of praise now," the psalmist implies.

Verses 4, 5. The writer's case is different from that of his forefathers. **In You our fathers trusted; they trusted and You delivered them.** God had come to the assistance of his forefathers, but, his implication is, He has not come to his. David argues, **To You they cried out and were delivered; in You they trusted and were not disappointed.** His ancestors had looked to God in their time of need, and God had come to their rescue.

However, in his desperate situation, he finds that he is not being heard by God as his forebears had been.

HIS SITUATION (22:6–10)

⁶But I am a worm and not a man,
A reproach of men and despised by the people.
⁷All who see me sneer at me;
They separate with the lip, they wag the head, saying,
⁸"Commit yourself to the LORD; let Him deliver him;
Let Him rescue him, because He delights in him."
⁹Yet You are He who brought me forth from the womb;
You made me trust when upon my mother's breasts.
¹⁰Upon You I was cast from birth;
You have been my God from my mother's womb.

Verse 6. Because of the horrible circumstance he is in, he sees himself as despised and forsaken. **But I am a worm and not a man, a reproach of men and despised by the people.** He feels he is seen as less than human, regarded as a mere "worm." Defenseless and worthless, he is the object of the worst words that could be uttered and the most insulting gestures of ridicule that could be made.

Verse 7. Part of his trial is the way others look at him. **All who see me sneer at me; they separate with the lip, they wag the head.** As people pass him, they make scornful facial expressions at him and motion suggestively with their heads, jeering and humiliating him. All of this adds to his affliction. Some reject him and indicate their rejection by their silent body language; others perhaps visibly and vocally announce their astonishment at his terrible plight.

Verse 8. They are saying to him, **"Commit yourself to the LORD; let Him deliver him; let Him rescue him, because He delights in him."** The RSV adds "cause," picturing them saying to him, "Commit your cause to the LORD." The Hebrew just has "Roll upon the LORD" (גֹּל אֶל־יהוה, *gol 'el YHWH*). Those who see him say, "If you really think that God is pleased with your life, ask Him to deliver you from the danger you are in. He will, if

He is pleased with you." Their implication is that God has brought this disaster upon him because he had displeased Him. Similar words to these—maybe a fulfillment to these words—are used in Matthew 27:43 to describe the taunts of the crowd as Jesus hangs suspended upon the cross.

Verse 9. God has been the Lord of his life from birth. **Yet You are He who brought me forth from the womb; You made me trust when upon my mother's breasts.** As he prays, he reminds God that he has believed in Him and served Him from his infancy. Yahweh had been his God from the day of his birth. With exaggerated emphasis, he says that he has always trusted in God, even from the time of his birth.

Verse 10. His point is that he has leaned upon God from the very beginning of his life, and he is leaning upon God now. **Upon You I was cast from birth; You have been my God from my mother's womb.** The exaggerated argument that he makes is a strong one: "You have protected me from the earliest days of my life. Will You not be with me now?"

ENEMIES SURROUNDED HIM
(22:11–16)

¹¹**Be not far from me, for trouble is near;**
For there is none to help.
¹²**Many bulls have surrounded me;**
Strong bulls of Bashan have encircled me.
¹³**They open wide their mouth at me,**
As a ravening and a roaring lion.
¹⁴**I am poured out like water,**
And all my bones are out of joint;
My heart is like wax;
It is melted within me.
¹⁵**My strength is dried up like a potsherd,**
And my tongue cleaves to my jaws;
And You lay me in the dust of death.
¹⁶**For dogs have surrounded me;**
A band of evildoers has encompassed me;

They pierced my hands and my feet.

Verse 11. He looks to God as the only One who can help him. **Be not far from me, for trouble is near; for there is none to help.** He says he has no one else to come to his aid. If his God does not assist him, then there could be no hand of mercy at all for him.

Verse 12. He compares his enemies to horned bulls that charge at him with the intention of goring him. He says, **Many bulls have surrounded me; strong bulls of Bashan have encircled me.** These bulls from Bashan were the strongest of bulls due to Bashan being a region of rich pasture lands that produced the highest quality of cattle.

Verse 13. Changing the figure, he says that his enemies are coming at him with their mouths open, like lions approaching their prey. **They open wide their mouth at me, as a ravening and a roaring lion.** His foes were ferocious and were coming in for the kill.

Verse 14. He asks God to look at him and behold his terrible predicament. **I am poured out like water, and all my bones are out of joint.** He has no strength; he is like water poured out, like water on the ground or like an empty bowl. He is like a skeleton with its bones out of joint. His whole body was in disarray. **My heart is like wax; it is melted within me.** He has no "heart"; it has dissolved as "wax" does before a fire.

Verse 15. His energy is gone. He cannot reason because he is sick with pain. **My strength is dried up like a potsherd, and my tongue cleaves to my jaws.** His tongue seems to be sticking to the top of his mouth, and he cannot talk. **You lay me in the dust of death.** God has allowed him, he says, to be thrown into the dust of death or thrown down at the door of death.

Verse 16. Encircling him are his enemies, like a band of wild, snapping dogs who are encouraging the coming of his death by biting his hands and feet. **For dogs have surrounded me.** Furthermore, he says, **A band of evildoers has encompassed me.** His enemies can be compared to a group or congregation (עֵדָה, *'edah*) of vicious "evildoers" standing around him, coming closer and closer to him. They are after his blood.

PSALM 22

So dangerous are they that he says, **They pierced my hands and my feet.** He is punctured by their teeth. The word "pierced" has been supplied by the translators. This phrase has no verb. The sentence actually says, "Like lions, my hands and my feet." Some translations, such as the KJV, ASV, NASB, and RSV, have concluded that the word for "lions" should be translated with the verb "pierced." In fact, this particular translation goes all the way back to the Syriac and the Vulgate translations. They arrived at this translation no doubt because the text is obviously pointing to a torturing of his hands and feet.

In prophecy, a far higher truth is likely pictured: the actual crucifixion of Jesus that involved the piercing of the hands and feet of Jesus.

HIS PHYSICAL CONDITION
(22:17–21)

¹⁷I can count all my bones.
They look, they stare at me;
¹⁸They divide my garments among them,
And for my clothing they cast lots.
¹⁹But You, O LORD, be not far off;
O You my help, hasten to my assistance.
²⁰Deliver my soul from the sword,
My only life from the power of the dog.
²¹Save me from the lion's mouth;
From the horns of the wild oxen You answer me.

Verse 17. He bewails, **I can count all my bones.** In his sufferings, he has been reduced to a skeleton, and he can even number his bones. **They look, they stare at me.** So pathetic is he that people come by and gaze profanely at his physical condition.

Verse 18. These enemies of his are waiting for his death so that they could divide up his clothes among them. **They divide my garments among them, and for my clothing they cast lots.** No doubt this passage is a type prophecy whose fulfillment is found in all four Gospels in the scene of the soldiers' rolling dice for the seamless robe of Jesus (Mt. 27:35; Mk. 15:24; Lk. 23:34; Jn. 19:24).

Verse 19. His prayer continues and becomes more and more intense. **But You, O Lord, be not far off; O You my help, hasten to my assistance.** After depicting his awful physical and emotional condition, he calls upon God again to remove his enemies and his grief.

Verse 20. He asks God to save him from death. **Deliver my soul from the sword, my only life from the power of the dog.** He likens himself to an "only" child of God, someone very precious to God. He is going under to the dogs around him, and he begs that he be delivered from them.

Verse 21. Switching metaphors, he uses a lion's mouth and the horns of the wild oxen as figures for death. **Save me from the lion's mouth; from the horns of the wild oxen You answer me.** He pictures his enemies as lions, as wild oxen with sharp horns. "Save me," he says, "from this life-threatening situation."

Through this portrayal the psalmist gives of himself, we can almost see his tormented body and hear his cries for God to listen. To this point, God has not seen fit to answer him. The writer knows that he should continue to pray and describe his misery to God.

"I WILL PRAISE HIM" (22:22–26)

²²I will tell of Your name to my brethren;
In the midst of the assembly I will praise You.
²³You who fear the Lord, praise Him;
All you descendants of Jacob, glorify Him,
And stand in awe of Him, all you descendants of Israel.
²⁴For He has not despised nor abhorred the affliction of
    the afflicted;
Nor has He hidden His face from him;
But when he cried to Him for help, He heard.
²⁵From You comes my praise in the great assembly;
I shall pay my vows before those who fear Him.
²⁶The afflicted will eat and be satisfied;
Those who seek Him will praise the Lord.

PSALM 22

Let your heart live forever!

A marked change comes at this point in the psalm. The writer seems to have decided to praise God *as if* an answer had already been given to him. He knows that God will answer in His own way and at the appropriate time. The response of the writer must be the anticipation of a trusting heart.

Verse 22. He mentions a resolve he has made: **I will tell of Your name to my brethren; in the midst of the assembly I will praise You.** The writer of the Book of Hebrews in 2:12 borrows the phrases "I will tell of Your name to my brethren; in the midst of the assembly ["congregation"; KJV, NIV] I will praise You," putting these words in the mouth of Jesus. The "congregation" is the Old Testament term for what the New Testament calls the church (or assembly). In other words, he leads his fellow Israelites to praise and glorify God because he knows that God is always moved by the pain of the afflicted and hears the cries of His people.

Verse 23. All those who fear the Lord are called upon to praise Him. **You who fear the LORD, praise Him; all you descendants of Jacob, glorify Him, and stand in awe of Him, all you descendants of Israel.** All the nation of Israel is to glorify Him and stand in reverence before Him. He is worthy to be praised for His goodness toward Israel.

Verse 24. God is gracious toward the troubled who trust in Him. **For He has not despised nor abhorred the affliction of the afflicted; nor has He hidden His face from him; but when he cried to Him for help, He heard.** It may appear that he hides His face from them and does not assist them, but in truth He loves them and answers their cries for help when the time is right.

Verse 25. God is the source of his praise. **From You comes my praise in the great assembly; I shall pay my vows before those who fear Him.** He offers thanks to Him and fulfills the vows that he has made (Lev. 3). Vows were usually made during a time of great trial (Jon. 2:9).

Verse 26. The afflicted will eat and be satisfied; those who seek Him will praise the LORD. Let your heart live forever! He invites the meek to join him in his sacrificial meal and rejoice with him over God's goodness. At that meal, he encourages the dispirited to take heart and praise God. His wish for them is "May you be quickened by the thought of God who defends His people."

We have here a picture of one trusting in God while in the dark pit of suffering. He has not received an answer to his prayers, but he believes it will be given because he knows that God is full of lovingkindness and grace. He trusts God so completely that he praises Him for answering his prayers in advance. He knows that God will do what is right—in His own time and within the confines of His holy will. God is absolutely faithful, and one will never need to question His actions.

TRUSTING HIM (22:27–31)

> ²⁷All the ends of the earth will remember and turn to the LORD,
> And all the families of the nations will worship before You.
> ²⁸For the kingdom is the LORD's
> And He rules over the nations.
> ²⁹All the prosperous of the earth will eat and worship,
> All those who go down to the dust will bow before Him,
> Even he who cannot keep his soul alive.
> ³⁰Posterity will serve Him;
> It will be told of the Lord to the coming generation.
> ³¹They will come and will declare His righteousness
> To a people who will be born, that He has performed it.

Verse 27. As God has been compassionate in the past, the writer believes that He will act similarly in the future. **All the ends of the earth will remember and turn to the LORD, and all the families of the nations will worship before You.** In these words he speaks of God, the future of mankind, and the world. He believes that God will act graciously toward all people in the days ahead.

Verse 28. With a view to the future, he says, **For the king-**

dom is the Lord's and He rules over the nations. The earth is the Lord's. It is His domain. A time is anticipated when all will acknowledge God's authority. They will see that He is the true King of the earth and is in charge of all nations, whether they know it now or not. Perhaps these lines refer to the coming of Christianity, as the Word goes out from Jerusalem to all nations (see Acts 2); or perhaps his words telescope into the ultimate judgment when all will confess Him as the true God.

Verse 29. All the prosperous of the earth will eat and worship, all those who go down to the dust will bow before Him, even he who cannot keep his soul alive. Even the wealthy will find their strength in the worship of God. Those who have come to the portal of death will receive new hope because of God and will be revived. God will continue to be the source of strength to those who are in trouble or in need.

Verse 30. Posterity will serve Him; it will be told of the Lord to the coming generation. A small number of people will serve the rest; the multitudes will be blessed by a few. God will always have His faithful who inspire others to worship Him. The good works of God will be told from one "generation" to the next as the story of God's love is passed on.

Verse 31. They will come and will declare His righteousness to a people who will be born, that He has performed it. The psalmist believes that the praise which he has started will be taken up by Israel and from them by the whole world in the ages to come.

He trusts in God completely and views the future in light of how God has treated His people in the past. Those who are in God's hands—whether an individual, a nation, or the world—are in safe hands, for His hands are hands that will bring glorious events to pass.

On a higher level, the Holy Spirit foresees through prophecy, through the psalmist's description of the future praise of God, a time when even the Gentiles would praise and trust God. This prophetic depiction includes the death, burial, and resurrection of Jesus, as well as the going out of the gospel into all the world in the Christian Age.

APPLICATION

Overcoming When Overwhelmed

How does the psalmist overcome when he is overwhelmed? In the middle of his agony, he prays earnestly to his God. Even though he has not been heard, he continues to pray. He takes heart in his praying and resolves to praise God, knowing that, at some point and in the way of God's choosing, He will come to his rescue. In his praise he anticipates what will happen in the future. Regardless of how dark the moment is, he believes that God will do wondrous deeds for him, for Israel, and for the world.

In his faith in God for the present and for the future, he demonstrates the response we ought to make in any crisis. We should pray about it, praising God for who He is, for what He does, and for what He will do for His people. We should trust Him to do wonderful things today and tomorrow. "When we cannot see what He is doing with the physical eye, we can watch for His gracious providence with the eye of faith."

When We Pray

Whenever we suffer intolerably from the torment of enemies or distress of any kind, the first response this psalm teaches us to make is to pray. When we pray, we should remember that our prayers may not be immediately answered. For that matter, some prayers may never be answered the way we thought they would be.

One of the most difficult lessons to learn in the school of Christ is that of praying even when we do not see God responding to our prayers. This psalm says that we should talk to God about the fact that no answer to our prayers has come.

When Prayers Are Not Heard

As we survey the Old and New Testaments, we are struck with the truth that God does not always answer our prayers. He did not answer every prayer that the sinless Son of God prayed, so why should we expect Him to answer all of ours? What should we do when our prayers are not heard?

PSALM 22

As is indicated by the first few verses of this psalm, *we must remember to praise God*. The writer experienced great agony. He prayed for deliverance from his trial, but he received no answer from heaven. He did not give up on God, but rather he praised God for all that He had done for him. When one is in the valley of despair and his prayer is not heard, the next step is to praise God. Any time—even in the midst of an indescribable ordeal—is an appropriate time to give glory and thanks to God.

When He does not answer our prayers, *let us remember God's faithfulness*. We can look back at what God has done in the past and see His loyalty to His people. We have no reason to question His trustworthiness. This writer remembered that God had been faithful to the fathers when they had trusted in Him. This backward look helped him to conclude that God treats all believers the same way. He will care for us the way He cared for Abraham.

It would be absolutely contrary to His nature to fail to keep His word or to betray a promise He has made to us. His silence cannot be explained by saying that God has forsaken His own. When He does not answer our prayers, some sin somewhere, some aspect of His plan, or some connection with our growth has prevented Him from doing so.

When He does not answer our prayers, *let us remember that God is holy*. He is pure and free from evil, and He will not mistreat anyone—certainly not His children. If saying yes to our prayers would go against His righteous nature or His holy will, He will say no to them.

Therefore, *let us remember to trust God*. When we are in the crucible of misery, let us trust Him to work out our predicament according to His will. He has a plan that is far greater than ours. In the case of Jesus, He could not say yes to His supplications and say yes to our salvation at the same time. If God should say no to us, let us recognize that He is working out a higher and better plan for us and the world.

When God says no to our prayers, it is not a time to plunge into disbelief and disown Him; it is not a time to say that God does not care or that He is not interested in our frustrations. It is a time to praise Him, reflect on His faithfulness, and trust Him.

The Struggles to Which We Are Heirs

We see a picture in this psalm of terrible ordeals. While the trials mentioned are far more severe than many of us will ever know, they remind us of the troubles common to the human race.

Enemies who seek our harm. All of us have at least a few enemies—some we know about and some we do not know about. What do we do about them?

Friends who forsake us. At times we are jilted by those we hold dear. We are surprised and amazed by their actions. Sometimes these experiences are more cutting and hurtful to us than what our enemies are attempting to do to us.

Physical pain that devastates us. All of us must face this calamity. The body wears out or is injured. We live in it, and its failures and pains affect us. When our bodies are sick or crippled, we have a hard time controlling our emotions.

The approach of death that terrorizes us. We are all under the sentence of death. Unless the Lord comes, our earthly lives will end with physical death. We can put it out of our minds, but the reality eventually must be faced.

What should we do about these problems that are not far from any of us? The answer is: We should look to God by bringing our deplorable difficulties before Him in prayer, implore Him to come to our aid, trust Him, praise Him, and rely on His faithfulness. We can do other things about these ills that prey on us, but our entry point in dealing with them is that of bringing them to God.

When to Remember

What will we think about when God is silent to our groans and cries? Make the following resolves with me.

I will remember that He cares for the afflicted. Even though I cannot see Him answering my prayers right now, I know that His heart goes out to those who are hurting. He will always do what is right and appropriate for those who are in trouble.

I will remember that He is a God of lovingkindness. He has never mistreated anyone and never will. He will always answer us according to His mercy and not according to our sins. He will keep the covenant He has made with us.

I will remember that His answer may be far greater than that for which I asked. David perhaps did not know it, but his sufferings prefigured the sufferings of the Christ. Think of the millions who have read Psalm 22 and have been directed to the Christ. When Jesus prayed for the passing of "the cup" in the garden, He did not want to avoid doing God's will as is indicated by His "nevertheless." He knew that God's will—regardless of what it might cost—was best. God said no to the passing of "the cup," but He said yes to the doing of His will, which resulted in salvation for millions.

I will praise Him for always doing what is right. Even though it breaks His heart to refrain from removing my pain, He will do so in order that He may do what is right. He will strengthen me to endure the trial that I face as He lifts up holiness and truth. I will praise Him for this and teach those around me to praise Him for the same reason.

Someone has said, "God answers all prayers. To some He says yes; to others He says no; and to still others He says later." Together with Abraham we can say, "Shall not the Judge of all the earth deal justly?" (Gen. 18:25).

Remembering God's Future

All of us think about the future. We wonder what will take place tomorrow. This psalm (especially vv. 27–31) helps us. What is the truth about the days ahead?

Tomorrow, there will be people who will praise God. He is great and almighty, and every generation will have those who will recognize, honor, and serve Him.

Tomorrow, God will be in charge. He is the eternal God, and when tomorrow gets here, He will already be in it. He will still be controlling the nations. His providence will be at work; His gospel will still be redeeming mankind from sin.

Tomorrow, people from all walks of life will be blessed by God. The rich will benefit from serving Him, and those who have come down to pain and death will be strengthened by Him. People will cling to His name as they pass from this life to the next.

Tomorrow, God's name and goodness will be proclaimed from one generation to another. His works are so wonderful that the news of them will be passed to the next generation. Our children will serve Him. They will proclaim His works even as we have.

Tomorrow, there will always be a remnant that will serve God. No generation will be without those who love and adore Him. God will always have His faithful ones who trust in Him.

Why should we worry about the future? Let us do all the good we can, praise Him with all our being, and commit the future to the eternal God to whom one day is as a thousand years and a thousand years are as one day.

Proper Living for Others

We are part of the human family and have certain responsibilities toward those around us. We are reminded of the big ones in this psalm (vv. 22–24).

With my life, I should set the example before my family of praising God. Every person should give thanks for God's blessings. I must lead others by my example in fulfilling this great responsibility. My life should show forth His praise.

With my lips, I will teach my family to praise Him. It is not enough to set the appropriate example; I must also vocally instruct them to be forthright in their standing in awe before Him and in their glorifying Him. My lips should instruct others to revere Him.

With my love, I will tell of His lovingkindness to all. He is the great God of love, and the world—especially my brethren—must be reminded of it. He does not forget the afflicted, nor does He turn His face from those who call upon Him. My love should reflect His wonderful love.

I am His servant, and my life, lips, and love should invite and encourage others to honor God and to praise Him with awe.

What Have We Been to Jesus?

With its prophetic picture of the sufferings of Jesus as He died for our sins, this psalm reminds us of our sins and the need for the crucifixion.

PSALM 22

To have been the cup
His lips touched and blessed,
To have been the bread
Which He broke;
To have been the cloth
He held as He served,
Or water He poured
As He spoke;

To have been the road
He walked on the Way,
To have been His print
In the sand;
To have been the door
That opened the tomb,
But I was a nail
In His hand.[1]

Sue Fife, "Remorse," *Christianity Today* (1 April 1966), 17. (Emphasis added.) Used by permission, *Christianity Today*, 1966.

Psalm 23

Satisfied with God

The Superscription: A Psalm of David. The title says that this song of assurance is **a Psalm** [מִזְמוֹר, *mizmor*] **of** ["by," "for," or "to"] **David** (לְדָוִד, *lᵉdawid*). No indications are given concerning the time or circumstance of writing.

Because of its popularity and sweet spirit, this psalm has been called "The Pearl of the Psalms." It is a beautiful song of confidence, trust, and satisfaction in Yahweh. The writer does not begin with a lament describing a problem he is facing or with asking God for an immediate answer to his prayer; he begins and ends by extolling God's goodness to him. A string of touching phrases stretches from the first mention of God to the last, as His care and grace are recounted with grateful appreciation.

The relationship with God is described as an intensely personal one. The entire psalm is about one man and his life with God. Seventeen times in six verses the writer refers to himself, and thirteen times he refers to the Lord. This personal testimony makes it truly the "He/me" or the "I/Lord" psalm.

The reader learns that true peace is rooted in an unwavering fellowship with God. This psalm's words bring serenity to God's servant, whether he reads it at the highest pinnacle of spiritual growth or in the lowest moment of despair.

Two figures are used in the psalm to convey this special walk with God: a shepherd and a host. Another figure, a guide for a traveler, may have been intended in verses 3 and 4. God is pictured under these two (possibly three) images as sustainer, guide, teacher, companion, protector, encourager, and host. Beginning with an affirmation of satisfaction in God, the psalm continues with descriptive phrases of the writer's relationship with God and ends with an expression of confidence, affirming that God will encircle him with His gracious goodness in the future as He has in the past.

THE FAITHFUL SHEPHERD (23:1–4)

¹The LORD is my shepherd,
I shall not want.
²He makes me lie down in green pastures;
He leads me beside quiet waters.
³He restores my soul;
He guides me in the paths of righteousness
For His name's sake.
⁴Even though I walk through the valley of the shadow of death,
I fear no evil, for You are with me;
Your rod and Your staff, they comfort me.

Verse 1. The first line of this psalm is the greatest of all expressions of contentment: **The LORD is my shepherd**.

These five words constitute the NASB's translation of two words in the Hebrew text יהוה רֹעִי (*YHWH ro'i*). The metaphor pictures the sustaining relationship a shepherd has with his sheep. Under this pastoral motif, the believer and his God are portrayed—the trusting follower is the sheep, and God is his faithful shepherd, the One who provides for him, guides him, and restores him.

I shall not want. The word "want" (חָסֵר, *chaser*) is from a Hebrew word that really means "lacking." The idea is more like "I will not lack for anything," meaning that the true believer in God will find fulfillment in God. We might wonder how a man can no longer "want" for anything, but this psalm answers this question by reminding us that God is our sufficiency. The remaining part of the passage elaborates upon the answer.

David writes about sheep with the authority of one who has

been a shepherd and has lived with sheep. He knows the traits of a good shepherd; he knows the weaknesses of sheep. His experience as a shepherd gives him the practical knowledge to describe God's love for him in an illustrative analogy.

Verse 2. After feeding and eating sufficiently, the psalm says, **He makes me lie down in green pastures**. An obvious responsibility of the shepherd is to make sure that his sheep have tender grass for grazing. He therefore leads them to luscious feeding areas. Thus, when they have eaten their fill, they lie down in the leftover grass completely satisfied.

In this relationship, the child of God shall not want for sustenance, for the essentials of spiritual life and growth are always supplied.

Sheep not only require food but also relaxation. Hence, we are further told, **He leads me beside quiet waters.** "Quiet waters" (מֵי מְנֻחוֹת, *mey m^enuchoth*) are "waters of rest." Sheep appreciate the quiet pool, away from noise and activity, away from a life of hurry and worry. The thoughtful shepherd sees that his sheep are properly fed and given quiet times beside a body of water to drink and rest.

The believer will not want for refreshment, relaxation, or rest. God does not keep His servants in a frenzy or in a whirlwind of concern. He satisfies the appetite of the soul and provides repose of the spirit through the assurance of salvation and love.

Verse 3. He restores my soul. The literal translation of this phrase is "He causes life to return to me" or "He returns my soul to me" (נַפְשִׁי יְשׁוֹבֵב, *napshi y^eshobeb*). In addition to the sheep's need for food, water, and rest, the alert shepherd takes to heart their disposition. When they are dispirited, weary, anxious, or downcast, he comforts them.

God gives His children reassurance when they are uncertain, revival when they are worn out from discouragement, and spirit when they are disheartened by the world.

He guides me in the paths of righteousness. Here the psalmist may be switching to another figure—the figure of a guide leading a traveler—or he may be continuing his shepherd figure and thinking in terms of the leadership a shepherd gives his sheep. With either figure, the thought of guidance remains the same.

The follower of God will not want for direction and guidance. His God not only provides sustenance for him, but He also gives him truth.

For His name's sake. For the honor of His name, God leads His own in "paths of righteousness," in the right paths that bring peace and spiritual prosperity. He never misleads or betrays His own. He cannot misguide because His inherent righteousness would forbid it.

Verse 4. God's people do not lack companionship even in the toughest times. **Even though I walk through the valley of the shadow of death, I fear no evil, for You are with me.** When the terrain is hilly and dangerous for clumsy sheep, the shepherd walks near to steer them past dangerous places, through the narrow and slippery paths. During these times of potential harm, the shepherd no longer leads his sheep but moves alongside of them with his rod and staff to give the assistance and encouragement that only he can give.

A noticeable change to second person is observed in this line: "For You are with me." It is as if the writer moves from commentary into prayer.

"The shadow of death" (צַלְמָוֶת, *tsalmaweth*) is one word in the Hebrew and probably should not be limited to the experience of death. The phrase really should be seen as including not only the idea of death, but also any horrid, lonely event similar to it. The writer apparently is thinking of the big valleys of life, the ones which cause us to cringe in fear when we think of them.

Your rod and Your staff, they comfort me. The shepherd is ready for any eventuality. His "rod" (שֵׁבֶט, *shebet*) is for defense and his "staff" (מִשְׁעֶנֶת, *mish'eneth*) for offense; one is a weapon, while the other is an instrument of service. In his belt he keeps his rod, with which he could handle any harmful intruder; in his hand he holds his staff, which he uses for correction and guidance. In the company of this shepherd, the sheep have no fear.

The fears that the gloomy happenings of life infuse into our hearts are chased away by God's presence. He alone can see us through death or any experience similar to it. Other guides can walk with us to the door of death, but then they must discontinue their journey with us leaving us to face death alone. Our Lord always walks ahead of us when we need His guidance and beside us when we need His companionship.

THE GRACIOUS HOST (23:5, 6)

⁵You prepare a table before me in the presence of my enemies;
You have anointed my head with oil;
My cup overflows.
⁶Surely goodness and lovingkindness will follow me all the days of my life,
And I will dwell in the house of the LORD forever.

Verse 5. In the midst of a hostile world the child of God is fully protected. The writer perhaps moves from the shepherd and sheep motif to the figure of a host and guests.

The psalm says, **You prepare a table before me in the presence of my enemies**. The scene he relates is that of a well-set table (literally a feast) for guests. Evil forces form a circle that surrounds the table, but they are powerless to disturb the occasion. If he is continuing the shepherd/sheep analogy, he is referring to removing dangerous grasses from their feeding areas and warding off any violent animals searching for prey. If he has switched to a host and guests, then we are being told that all possible foes have been dealt with, and these enemies can do nothing but gaze at the feast. God provides His people a banquet of blessings, even though the table of good things is in the middle of potentially harmful circumstances.

When three Hebrews—Shadrach, Meshach, and Abednego—had to walk into a fiery furnace, they saw God's powerful hand in the presence of their enemies (Dan. 3:13–30). In that situation God produced an immortal event that has provided continual encouragement to faithful followers of God. The perpetrators of the evil could only watch in amazement.

You have anointed my head with oil. The trusting servant shall not want for encouragement and acceptance. The oil spoken of here is not the oil used in anointing a king or a priest as he was ushered into office; this oil is the perfumed oil used for hospitality and for expressing favor and happiness. This oil is the same type that Mary poured on the head of Jesus (Jn. 11:2). Anointing the head in this way expresses the highest joy and honor by the host.

At the end of the day, a shepherd also provides healing oil for any cuts or bruises on the sheep. He gives tender, personal care to each of his sheep.

My cup overflows. God is not a stingy host. He never gives sparingly. Those who know His fellowship say that the cup He pours is always filled to the brim, declaring in satisfied appreciation, "What more could we want?"

Our Lord instills within us worth, overflowing peace, and confidence as He conveys that He enjoys fellowship with us. We are His chosen ones, His peculiar people, His prized possessions.

Verse 6. In summary, God's children will not need anything in this life or in the life to come. Indeed, the children of God can say, **Surely goodness and lovingkindness will follow me all the days of my life.** The righteous should know that what they have experienced with God will continue in all of their tomorrows. The thrilling past is a forecast of a beautiful future.

The first word of this sentence could be translated "only" (אַךְ, 'ak). The point is, only "covenant love" (חֶסֶד, chesed), grace, and "goodness" (טוֹב, tob) will "follow" (יִרְדְּפוּ, yird^{e}pu) the righteous man or will pursue him wherever he goes. Through His providence, God pours goodness and mercy upon him. The writer knows that he has received nothing but grace and generosity from God. His future is unknown to him, but he knows the One who leads him into and through it.

And I will dwell in the house of the LORD forever. The idea of abiding "in the house of the LORD" is the thought of continual fellowship with God, the owner of the house. The word "forever" (לְאֹרֶךְ יָמִים, l^{e}orek yamim) is translated from two words which literally mean "to length of days." Perhaps this phrase should be understood to refer to all the days that may be ahead—those known and unknown to us. The psalmist has walked with God in the past, and he has made the commitment to dwell with God all his days. He will forever be satisfied with God.

APPLICATION

"I Shall Not Want"
Several years ago I heard a radio sermon that emphasized that the first line of this psalm is really the theme of the psalm. I was impressed with that emphasis; in my subsequent study of Psalm 23, I have become more convinced that the first line could indeed be thought of as its theme.

Notice how this idea goes throughout the psalm. I shall not want for sustenance (v. 2a), refreshment (vv. 2b, 3a), direction (v. 3b), companionship (v. 4), protection (v. 5a), or acceptance (v. 5b). I shall not want for anything in this life or in the life to come (v. 6). Because I am walking with God, my constant companions will be goodness and mercy in this life and in the next. Indeed, in light of this psalm, I can announce for all to hear: I shall never be in want!

You and God
The psalm is about a personal relationship with God. We may know facts about God, but the big question is, "Do we know God?"

Living with God means submitting to Him. One cannot actually know God without obeying Him. Sheep follow the shepherd. They honor him and live by His directions.

Living with God means walking with Him. One cannot know God unless he lives in the conscious fellowship of God. We go God's direction, walk His speed, and desire the things He desires.

Living with God means enjoying Him. Praying to Him, doing His will, and worshiping Him are not burdens. Does one find the fellowship of his dearest friend to be a hardship?

Do we really know God?

"Lord" and "Shepherd"
"The Lord is my shepherd" is a two-word affirmation in

Hebrew with the verb implied. Nevertheless, what a mighty declaration this statement is!

Deity is included. "Yahweh" is the first word. The statement affirms that Yahweh is the main thought. The only true God, the almighty One of Israel, is the One with whom we have a relationship.

Present time is included. The sentence does not speak in the past but in the present tense. It affirms what is going on right now. Future overtones are found in the sentence, but the emphasis is on this moment.

Personal possession is included. "My" indicates the possessive part of the sentence. The writer is proclaiming his current relationship with God, the one that he has at the time of the writing. He belongs to God, and God belongs with him.

Divine care is included. The word "shepherd" says it all. God is a shepherd to him—He looks after him, provides for him, encourages him, and sustains him.

The foundations of the Christian faith are expressed in these two words. When one understands what a shepherd does for his sheep, he can see what God does for those who trust in Him.

Spiritually Content

"I shall not want" are words that suggest total contentment. The satisfaction is spiritual, deep-seated, and abiding. How can we have it?

We come to God. The unique relationship of this psalm must be entered. From the perspective of the New Testament, we understand that this life with God is entered by conversion to Christ. Jesus said, "No one comes to the Father but through Me" (Jn. 14:6). We believe in Him, repent of sins, confess Him, and are baptized into Him. Jesus is the way to God and the way through whom we live with God.

We walk with God. Life with God is continual and perpetual. We have to begin it and then "walk" it. We are conscious that we live daily in the presence of God.

We partake of His provisions. God has a storehouse of blessings for our use—for our sustenance, our enjoyment, and our protection. The question is, "Do we utilize His riches?"

Only when we come to God, walk with Him, and partake of His bounties do we find the contentment in God that is reflected by the opening words of this psalm.

If we are not content with God, it is not because He has not given to us; it is because we have not been willing to receive.

Righteous Thinking

One of the great benefits of the psalms is that they teach us to think as godly people should think. Righteous living springs from righteous thinking. Look at the "then," "thus," and the "therefore" of it.

"Then"—my thinking is the source of my life. Solomon wrote, "For as he thinks within himself, so is he" (Prov. 23:7). In other words, we will never rise higher than our thoughts. We are not what we think we are, but what we think, we are.

"Thus"—the transforming process must begin with the renewing of the mind (Rom. 12:2). When we change the way we think, we change the way we live. Conversion is not just a physical change; it is spiritual, mental, and internal—from the inside out, not from the outside in. My lifestyle changes because my mind has been transformed. The mind is renewed and reconstructed by the Spirit of God. Conversion is an event in time, but transformation is a process over time.

"Therefore"—being a Christian means adopting and living by the mind of Christ (Phil. 2:5). We receive His mind when we choose to live by His teachings, to love the way He loved, and to adopt the values that He saw.

This psalm begins with, "The LORD is my shepherd, I shall not want." The question is, "Is this the way I think?" If not, then this satisfaction can be mine only if I choose the path of righteous thinking. I must obey His will and become one of His sheep, but conversion alone is insufficient. My mindset must be daily transformed so that the truth of my conversion becomes the way I think. My mind must be continually renewed by absorbing the mind of Christ.

Why Worry?

As is the case with sheep, children of God can be upset, disturbed, and bewildered by all that is going on in the world. Fraught with cares, they come to the Good Shepherd to find the peace that no one else can give.

When worried about life. They do not have to worry about life because they walk with the Author of life.

Believers in God receive the fullest care from God. Their spiritual hunger is satisfied with God. The restlessness and poverty of the world are gone; a spiritual "having-fully-eaten" contentment is theirs.

When disappointed in themselves. They may be frustrated by their failures, but the Good Shepherd is gracious and forgiving. He puts life back into them.

When discouraged by the world. They may be disheartened by the persecution and the wickedness of the world around them. The Good Shepherd gives heart. Walking with God, the One who made the world and owns it, they know that in the end all wrongs will be made right.

The basic meaning of "I shall not want" is "What do I lack?" We may not have anything, and yet, we have everything. We may be paupers when it comes to possessions, but we are kings when it comes to provisions. Whoever walks with God can say with Paul, "The world is mine!" (See 1 Cor. 3:21, 22.)

Companionship in the Dark Times

Think about the words "Even though I walk through the valley of the shadow of death, I fear no evil, for You are with me" (v. 4).

One young man followed me to the car after an evangelistic service. He said to me, "I am a Christian, but I am afraid of dying. What can I do?"

A Christian who was a highly-educated college professor learned that she had an incurable disease. As she lingered, more dead than alive, she told visitors, "I've spent my life learning how to live, and I'm afraid I do not know how to die."

How does this psalm address this fear? *Divine companionship.* The writer says that he will not fear the dark times of life because he has God, the Good Shepherd, walking with him. He has the omnipotence of God on his side.

An oft-told story helps to illustrate this truth. A farmer had a faithful dog who went with him everywhere. They were seldom apart. Their friendship was uncanny. Once when the farmer had gone to a neighbor's house, the dog waited patiently outside the door for the return of his master. Finally, the dog began to scratch lightly on the door to indicate that he wanted to be with his master. The dog had not been in that house before. He knew nothing of what was in that house or anything about who lived there. He wanted to be inside because his master was there. He wanted to be wherever his master was. The dog was not afraid to go anywhere—whether it was in the darkest night or into the vast unknown—as long as he was with his master.

We do not know what death is like, but we know who will walk with us in it and through it. Jesus even said that the angels will meet us at death's door and accompany us to the other side (Lk. 16:22). Perhaps the first words we will hear when we enter the exit called death are, "Don't be afraid. I will be with you. Just walk close by My side."

The Deep Needs

This psalm is about the big needs that all of us have. It speaks so deeply to us because it addresses our deepest longings.

We need provisions for living. Our God gives us spiritual food and spiritual rest. "Green grass" and "quiet waters" minister to the inner person. We are able to grow because of the abundant supplies He gives.

We need pardon for sin. God restores our wayward souls. He strengthens us when we are weak, disciplines us when we sin, and forgives us when we repent. He treats us as a father does his children.

We need His presence for comfort. He is God, and we are humans. We were made for God. Our lives can be summed up in the words "walking with God." The greatest blessing of life is knowing that God is with us (1 Jn. 4:4).

We need protection from evil. All around us are vicious foes; with only half an opportunity they can destroy us. The devil is stronger than we are, but greater is He who is in us than he who is in the world. He prepares a table of good things in the presence of our enemies, so that all they can do is watch us enjoy God's bounty.

We need peace regarding tomorrow. The unseen future will have trials of its own. We could easily worry about it. We need Someone to guide us who sees the future as clearly as He sees today. We need Someone who can go before us and clear away any problems that we are going to meet. We have been privileged to know God, and this knowledge gives us confidence that only goodness and mercy will surround us and that we will dwell in His house forever.

We have God's provisions, pardon, presence, protection, and peace. What more could anyone want?

"I Will Dwell in the House of the Lord"

"I will dwell in the house of the Lord forever" brings this psalm to an end. One could say that there are three ideas within this phrase.

There is a resolve. The writer is saying, "I have found satisfaction in God, and with Him I shall forever stay. With Him I plan to live the 'length of my days.'" Here is the resolve, the determination, the core dedication of his life.

There is an implied promise. "God has been good to me here. I can believe that He will be even more gracious to me over there," the writer is implying. As people look at what God has done for them in this world, they see implied in His grace a foretaste of the wonderful things to come. A veiled promise is hidden in the Lord's goodness.

There is a privilege. "What an honor it will be to dwell in the house of the Lord forever," he observes. "I have known His wonderful fellowship, and I know that living in His house days without end, will be the greatest of all privileges."

We could use these words as a summary of our prospects for the future. When asked, "What is your future going to be like?" we can answer, "I will dwell in the house of the Lord forever."

Reading the Psalm

Don Shackelford tells of a preacher who read this psalm three times, giving emphasis to different parts of it each time. The first time he read it, he stressed *the Lord,* saying with a strong voice in the course of his reading "Lord," "He," "His," and "Your." The second time he read it emphasizing *the sheep,* accenting "I," "me," and "my." The third time he read it emphasizing *the provisions* the Good Shepherd gives to His sheep, such as "makes me lie down in green pastures," "restores my soul," etc. This would be a good exercise. Do it, and rejoice in the goodness of God!

Psalm 24
Celebrating the Presence of God

The Superscription: A Psalm of David. Only two items of description are given in the title to this song. It is called **a Psalm** [מִזְמוֹר, *mizmor*] **of** ["by," "for," or "to"] **David** (לְדָוִד, *lᵉdawid*). The LXX includes in its heading the words τῆς μιᾶς σαββάτων (*tēs mias sabbatōn*, "the first of the Sabbath or week"), perhaps suggesting that this psalm was to be read on the first day of the week to commemorate the creation of the earth.

It is possible that this psalm was written for the occasion of the bringing of the ark of the covenant from Obed-edom's house in Kiriath-jearim on the western border of Benjamin to Mount Zion (2 Sam. 6:12–19; 1 Chron. 13). No other event in David's reign fits the psalm and harmonizes with the progression seen within its strophes quite as well as does this momentous event. If this is not the case, the reverence and wonder of that scene provides a good illustrative setting for the psalm.

The ark was a symbol of the presence of God, and its arrival in Jerusalem was one of the greatest occurrences in David's life and in the national life of Israel. Perhaps this psalm was sung as a part of the celebration when the ark was brought into the tent that David had prepared for it on Mount Zion.

Such a view of the psalm would not preclude the Holy Spirit's intending a wider future use for it. In fact, its place in the Book of Psalms may even suggest a purpose for it that reaches beyond the event for which it may have been originally written.

A major theme of the psalm is the character required of the worshiper of God, taking us back to Psalm 15 and forward to

Psalm 100. It identifies the worshiper who will be accepted by God and (by implication) the worshiper who will be rejected by Him. The last three verses may picture a veiled prophecy of Jesus returning to the throne of God after His earthly ministry, although no clear New Testament confirmation is found for this view.

"THE EARTH IS THE LORD'S" (24:1, 2)

¹**The earth is the LORD's, and all it contains,**
The world, and those who dwell in it.
²**For He has founded it upon the seas**
And established it upon the rivers.

Verse 1. The psalm begins by proclaiming the sovereignty of the Lord. The location of the ark in Jerusalem should not lead anyone to believe that the great God of Israel could be contained in a chest, held within a city, or confined within the borders of a nation. He created all things and reigns as Lord over all the earth.

Therefore, the writer declares at the outset the fact of God's extensive rulership. **The earth is the LORD's, and all it contains**. The entire earth, not just Palestine, belongs to God. "LORD's" (לַיהוָה, *lᵉYHWH*) is emphatic—meaning that absolutely no one owns the world but God. James Burton Coffman wrote,

> No man possesses the earth, or any portion of it, except in a very limited and accommodative sense. The title deeds which men treasure are merely the written permission of the societies in which they live, conveying the right of use for the brief period of their earthly lives. The cattle upon a thousand hills are God's possession, not men's. All of the earth and everything in it belong to God.[1]

The second part of the parallelism reads, **The world, and**

---

[1] James Burton Coffman and Thelma B. Coffman, *Commentary on Psalms 1—72* (Abilene, Tex.: ACU Press, 1992), 1:181.

those who dwell in it. He owns the physical world and everything in it, including the inhabitants, every living creature, and all its physical substance. He is the one Supreme Processor of all created beings and things.

Verse 2. What is the rationale for such an inclusive declaration of ownership? **For He has founded it upon the seas and established it upon the rivers.** God owns all because He has made all. By right of creation He is the unrivaled Lord of everything. He separated the water in the beginning and caused the dry land to appear (Gen. 1:9). At His command, land emerged from water. In this way the habitable earth was "founded" upon seas and "established" upon "rivers." The term "rivers" (נְהָרוֹת, $n^e haroth$) may refer to the swift currents of the seas or to the streams and rivers that resulted from the creating of the land.

WHO MAY WORSHIP? (24:3, 4)

> ³**Who may ascend into the hill of the LORD?**
> **And who may stand in His holy place?**
> ⁴**He who has clean hands and a pure heart,**
> **Who has not lifted up his soul to falsehood**
> **And has not sworn deceitfully.**

Verse 3. After affirming the universal kingship of God, the psalmist moves to the question of who can come to Him in worship. **Who may ascend into the hill of the LORD? And who may stand in His holy place?** What kind of fellowship does this almighty God permit? What kind of worship does He accept?

The place of reference, "the hill of the LORD," is Zion, the earthly residence of the presence of God. David's question, then, is, "Who may go up to the tent where the ark is and remain to lead the people in worship?" Implied in this question is another question: "Who are the worshipers in whom the Lord delights?" The psalm answers the second part by telling how a person can come into the presence of God.

The directive in verse 3 says that those who come must come in godliness. Stress is placed upon purity, and the answer is divided into two mandates: outward and inward requirements.

Verse 4. On the outward side of the question, the psalmist says that the worshiper should have "clean hands" and has not "sworn deceitfully." **He who has clean hands and a pure heart, who has not lifted up his soul to falsehood and has not sworn deceitfully.** "Clean hands" are hands that are free from violence or other acts of sin (Is. 1:15–17; see 1 Tim. 2:8). The hands are unsoiled in the sense of being morally pure, blameless in action. The hands do not act separately from the heart and the mind, but they are singled out for the purpose of placing emphasis upon the deeds of the worshiper.

His lips have not been used to swear *in order to* deceive. Speaking falsely is especially abhorrent to the God of all righteousness. The true worshiper is to be honest in mind and word.

On the inward side of the question, it is said that the worshiper is to have "a pure heart" and a truthful soul. The "hands" stand for what a person does; the "heart" stands for what a person is. Out of the impure heart come evil thoughts; out of the pure heart come righteous thoughts, beliefs, and designs (Mt. 15:19). God looks at the motives as well as at the actions of the worshiper.

To "lift up his soul to" means "to set his heart or mind toward" (see Ps. 25:1). The righteous worshiper does not desire or put his heart upon deceit; he abhors evil and loves good. The NASB uses the word "falsehood" in this verse, but the KJV has "vanity." The term is broader than simple falsehood in speech (שָׁוְא, *shawe'*) and may even include some relationship to false gods (Ps. 31:6). God does not want a person who yearns for the false and vain to bring offerings of worship to Him.

THE BLESSED WORSHIPER (24:5, 6)

⁵**He shall receive a blessing from the Lord**
And righteousness from the God of his salvation.
⁶**This is the generation of those who seek Him,**
Who seek Your face—even Jacob. Selah.

Verse 5. The psalm at this point turns to the gratuities that the worshiper will receive. Beautiful rewards come to those who seek to worship God sincerely and properly. **He shall receive a blessing from the L**ORD. The psalmist in particular says that the true worshiper will receive an extraordinary gift from God, one which includes God's presence and promises. He will have the privilege of enjoying God's gracious fellowship and His generous treatment.

He shall be granted **righteousness from the God of his salvation.** The one who does what is right will obtain "righteousness from . . . God"; the one who is faithful to God will receive the promises that have been made to the faithful.

Verse 6. The description of the character of the true worshiper dovetails into a picture of a generation of people who have genuine devotion to the Lord and who earnestly aspire to do His will. The writer says, **This is the generation of those who seek Him, who seek Your face—even Jacob.** There are those who desire to be righteous before God—in heart, hand, and tongue. They are pursuing the "face" (the fellowship presence) of the God of "Jacob."

Selah is included to ask the reader to pause and think about the significance of the statement that has been made and to provide a division in thought. What has been said is of supreme importance.

REVERENCE AND GLORY (24:7–10)

> [7]Lift up your heads, O gates,
> And be lifted up, O ancient doors,
> That the King of glory may come in!
> [8]Who is the King of glory?
> The LORD strong and mighty,
> The LORD mighty in battle.
> [9]Lift up your heads, O gates,
> And lift them up, O ancient doors,
> That the King of glory may come in!
> [10]Who is this King of glory?
> The LORD of hosts,

He is the King of glory. Selah.

With exalted progression, this section of the psalm presents the reverence and the glory that is due the God of heaven, the Warrior King of Israel. These words are not just pageantry; they are a depiction of the awesome being of God, the great God of Israel. He is the King, the almighty One, the Lord of Hosts, the Lord of all places and all people. His worship is to be entered with the full recognition that is due the great Sovereign of the universe.

After a pause, indicated by "Selah," a call is given for the top of the gates (the lintels) to be lifted up so that the great King of Israel can enter. These gates are called "ancient doors" or "everlasting" gates because of their antiquity and their connection with the everlasting God.

Verse 7. Those who approach the Lord to worship Him are to be characterized by respect and awe. This truth is presented indirectly through a figurative description of the glorious moment that the ark is brought into the tent that had been erected for it.

Perhaps this part of the psalm was sung as the ark reached the hill of Zion to summon the gatekeepers to open the gates for its entrance. Since the sacred chest symbolized God's pledge of His presence among the people, this passage represents God as actually entering the gates as a great King.

The Old Testament portrays God as dwelling between the cherubim on the mercy seat in the holiest place of the tabernacle. It pictures the Shechinah (the cloud by day and fiery pillar by night) resting above the tabernacle (Ex. 40:38). The ark was built by Bezalel for Moses in the wilderness of Sinai (Ex. 37:1–9). It was called the ark of the covenant because it symbolized God's special relationship in love and covenant loyalty to Israel and to David and all the kings of Israel (Ps. 132:8).

As the ark approaches, the call goes out, **Lift up your heads, O gates, and be lifted up, O ancient doors, that the King of glory may come in!** Approaching the tent where the ark is to be placed, a reverential request is made that the doors or gates be opened wide. These gates and doors are personified and are

PSALM 24

asked to arise to attention because the greatest of all personalities will be entering through them. The ark represents the Lord, the King of glory. He is to be admitted with all the glory and sacred honor that belongs to Him.

Verse 8. For poetic emphasis, a question is asked of those approaching with the ark, **Who is the King of glory?** The answer is given, **The LORD strong and mighty, the LORD mighty in battle.** God is described as the Warrior God of Israel. He is a glorious King, a King of splendor and majesty. He is Yahweh, the strong and mighty One—eternal in word, almighty in acts, and invincible in battle.

Verse 9. Another call comes, **Lift up your heads, O gates, and lift them up, O ancient doors, that the King of glory may come in!** Once again, we see the request for the gates to be lifted up for the ark to make its way in.

Verse 10. In response, the same refrain-like question is asked, **Who is this King of glory?** The repetition is poetical and perhaps is arranged for antiphonal singing. **The LORD of hosts, He is the King of glory.** In this second answer the Lord is described as "the LORD of hosts" (צְבָאוֹת, $ts^eba'oth$), the God who not only acts as the Captain of the armies of Israel, the God who leads His heavenly warriors in behalf of those who trust in Him, but as the sovereign Ruler of the universe. This occurrence is the first time that the Lord is referred to as "Yahweh of Hosts" in the Book of Psalms. It pictures God as the great military Leader of Israel.

When the gates are thrown open, the ark is brought in and set in its place in the midst of the Holy of Holies in the tabernacle. The procession ends with the symbolized presence of God appropriately placed on Mount Zion.

This latter part of the psalm may typify the coming of Jesus—upon His return from His earthly mission—into God's presence in heaven. However, there is no indication that the inspired writers of the New Testament interpreted the psalm in this way.

APPLICATION

The Sovereignty of God
The first line of this psalm affirms the Lord's sovereignty in three ways—once by implication and twice by express statement.

He created everything. He separated the dry land from the water and founded the earth upon the seas and established it upon the rivers. He structured the earth according to His wisdom and according to the needs of mankind.

He dwells everywhere. The thrust of the first line is to announce that God fills His universe. As the ark of the covenant is brought up to Jerusalem or to some similar place, one is not to suppose that God only dwells in the location of the ark. He is everywhere, keeping watch over everyone and everything.

He owns everyone. He is Creator of all and Lord of all. He claims the world and everything in it as His own—even the people.

No one has the proper view of himself or of God unless he sees God as everywhere, Creator of all things, and owner of all people and things.

What Belongs to God?
The principle of stewardship begins with the clear understanding of "who owns what." Someone has said, "If we want to know what we own, all we have to do is to ask ourselves two questions: 'What do I have that money cannot buy?' and 'What do I have that death cannot destroy?'"

This psalm states that God owns everything: the world, the contents of it, and the people who live in it.

This truth is abundantly obvious to us when we think about it. We do not have any trouble seeing the rationale for it.

He owns everything by right of creation. He made everything from nothing. Since He is the Creator, He is Lord of His creation.

He owns everything by right of control. He sustains His world. He provides the water, the oxygen, and the sunlight. He keeps our earth suspended in space on nothing, spinning like a top in midair. The world and the people in it could not exist for one minute without His almighty, supportive hand.

He owns everything by right of redemption. He paid the ultimate price to redeem His world from the grasp of sin. We belong to God in a triple sense: through His creation, through His control, and through His cleansing.

Our time in heaven will not be spent bragging about what we did or what we owned while on earth. As Charles Coil said in one of his gospel meetings, "We will not sit in groups singing, 'O what especially good fellows we are.' We will spend our time extolling the goodness of God and singing 'Amazing grace . . . that saved a wretch like me!'"

The Requirements of Worship

The first part of the answer to the question in verse 3, "Who may ascend into the hill of the LORD? And who may stand in His holy place?" is "Those who come with godliness." Stress is placed upon purity, and the answer may be divided into three parts: outward requirements, inward requirements, and relational requirements.

The outward requirement is that we come with clean hands. This expression is a poetic depiction of righteous actions. The hand stands for deeds. It is figurative because the hand cannot do anything without direction from the head.

The inward requirement is that we come with a pure heart. This godly heart had not lifted up itself to falsehood and had not sworn deceitfully. God wants integrity above all things. An honest heart can be taught and will respond to teaching. A dishonest heart cannot bring acceptable worship before God.

The relationship requirement is that we come with a faithful tongue. The true worshiper does not lie to others or swear falsely to others. His word is his bond. Those who know him need no other surety than his word.

The preacher must prepare for a sermon, and the worshipers must prepare for worship. The preparation by the worshipers is made by washing the hands of filthy deeds, cleansing the hearts of evil, and removing deceit from the tongue.

Coming Before Him

We are to approach Him with reverence and purity of life—

reverence because God is our Creator and Redeemer, and purity because of His holy nature.

It has been said that one becomes like the God he worships. In light of this psalm, it can also be said that God requires us to become like Him if we desire to worship Him. He is God and not mortal. He is transcendently high above us, and yet He is gracious, approachable, and accessible. He is not on our level, but He invites us to walk with Him. He loves all people (2 Pet. 3:9) and entreats all people to come to Him, but He receives only those who come to Him on His terms. His worship is to be in harmony with His character. He is holy, and holiness is the characteristic of admission into His presence.

The worship of Yahweh is the greatest, single privilege that human beings ever know—and one of the supreme duties, from which no human being is excused. Proper worship requires that we come as cleansed people with the appropriate offerings, fulfilling with joy the adoration of the Great King.

The Rewards of Worship

We come to worship because we wish to give God the honor and praise due Him. No one, however, does what is right without receiving benefits for it. What do sincere worshipers receive?

They receive God's blessing. Their Father bestows upon them favors that are in harmony with His will, grace, and wisdom. No one can praise God and not be made better by it.

They receive God's righteousness. They become like the One they worship. They are cleansed, molded, and made more usable through worship.

They receive God's approval. Their fleshing out the will of God brings the applause of heaven. To know that we have brought gladness to God's heart is one of life's greatest rewards.

We do not go to worship dominated by the question, "What will I get out of this?" However, faithful worshipers, as a kind of serendipity, are bathed in the glory of the God they praise.

People in Worship

The writer of this psalm speaks of his generation as containing people who seek the Lord. He implies that those with him have certain spiritual traits and determinations.

They recognize Him as Creator and Lord. They know that there is no other God but Yahweh. Having accepted this truth, they rejoice in it.

They seek the Lord. They are driven by the ambition to know God and to live in His presence. To behold His face is their greatest delight.

They aspire to incarnate His will. The attributes of those who are welcome at the holy hill have been given. The implication is that these worshipers who are being mentioned exhibit these traits and are gladly received by Him.

They want to keep on worshiping Him. They are seeking to rejoice before Him over His goodness, grace, and greatness. They plan to engage in this worship as long as they have breath. They do not see the worship of His name as a burden or a hardship. Always careful to make time for these opportunities, they enter into them with reverence and joy.

Are we a part of this generation of people who seek the Lord?

On the Other Side?

Have you asked yourself, "When Jesus ascended, what happened on the other side of the clouds?" Remember Acts 1:9–11? What was it like when, beyond the wondering gaze of the apostles, with unimaginable speed, without being susceptible to gravity or to the cold space, Jesus went beyond the separating earthly and heavenly spheres and entered triumphantly into the presence of God?

Verses 7 through 10 have been thought of as a veiled prophecy concerning Jesus' entrance into heaven. Thinking about this event brings to mind profound truths.

His entrance into heaven was a time of eternal completion. God's great, overarching plan of salvation had been finally put in place for all mankind. The sacrificial atonement had been offered and crowned with the Resurrection and Ascension, making salvation available to all people until the end of the age.

His entrance into heaven was a time of unsurpassed heavenly joy. If the angels rejoice over one sinner who repents (Lk. 15:6, 7), how they would have rejoiced over the possibility of millions being saved through the blood of Christ! We can envision no celebration equal to this one.

His entrance into heaven was a time of unparalleled honor and glory. Jesus had come back to take His seat at the right hand of God and to reign as King of kings and Lord of lords. He will now act as the head of the church or the King of the eternal kingdom that had been set up. Paul said, ". . . God highly exalted Him, and bestowed on Him the name which is above every name . . ." (Phil. 2:9).

In His providence, God has allowed us to live during the Christian Age, in which we can see the glory of the things that Jesus provided through the cross. The time of restoration is now here, and we have been honored to be a part of it.

"Who Is This King of Glory?"
This question is asked twice in verses 7 through 10. The answer is scattered throughout the Scriptures.

He is the Creator of all things. Without him nothing was made that had been made (Gen. 1:1). In Him all things consist. He brought everything into existence, and with His hand of power He sustains all existing things.

He is the Good Shepherd over those who trust in Him. He provides for them—giving the sustenance they need and the rest they require (Ps. 23:1). He provides for them in the midst of an evil and vicious world.

He is a Mighty Warrior for His people. He goes before them into every battle they must fight (Ps. 18:7–15). They are delivered by His strong hand from every foe who would harm them.

He is the Lord Almighty for whom nothing is too hard. He can deliver us from every trial, and He can strengthen us for every victory (Ps. 121:5–8). He stands above time with all power, guiding unerringly by love, watching over His own.

To stand in the presence of this glorious One is the greatest experience that a human being can know. He is the great and mighty, glorious and transcendent Lord. May all creatures of the earth bow down and acknowledge Him as the true God!

What Is God Like?

Willem A. VanGemeren has pointed to the three pictures of God in this psalm: He is the Creator-God, the Holy God, and the Warrior King.[2]

The Creator-God. He has made everything, and thus all things—animals, people, and matter—come under His domain.

The Holy God. One who seeks to enter His assembly of worship must be prepared to do so. A sanctified life is required.

The Warrior King. God is the great Leader of His people. He is strong, mighty, and arrayed in power. He is not coming to fight against His people but to fight for them.

When we add to these truths the truth that this God comes to dwell among us and even in our hearts, we fall on our knees in grateful worship!

---

[2] Willem A. VanGemeren, "Psalms," in *The Expositor's Bible Commentary*, ed. Frank E. Gaebelein (Grand Rapids, Mich.: Zondervan Publishing House, 1991), 5:219.

PSALM 25

PIETY PORTRAYED

The Superscription: A Psalm of David. This psalm's title simply has **of** ["by," "for," or "to"] **David** (לְדָוִד, *lᵉdawid*). The NASB adds **a Psalm** to the title and puts it in italics to show that the two words are not part of the superscription. This simple phrase "of David" serves as the only title of Psalms 25—28, 35, 37, 103, 138, and 144. Since no other clues about the psalm are given by its title or by its contents, we have no way of determining where or when it was written.

With its alphabetical arrangement, this psalm is regarded as one of the nine acrostic psalms in the Book of Psalms (9; 10; 25; 34; 37; 111; 112; 119; 145). This rigid way of organizing a psalm follows the pattern of the first verse or line beginning with the first letter of the Hebrew alphabet, the second verse or line beginning with the next letter, and so on through the alphabet, until all twenty-two letters have been successively used in the verses or lines. Occasionally we use this style of writing in English. It is a literary structure that lends itself especially to memorization (and maybe even visualization).

The alphabetical psalm is not usually noticeable in the English translations of the Bible. Because of this, more recent versions add a footnote that alerts us to this special acrostic design to the psalm.

Inspired writers did not always carry through with the complete alphabetical form; sometimes they deviated slightly from the pattern. This psalm, for example, does not follow a perfect acrostic pattern. The letters ב (*Beth*), ו (*Vav*), and ק (*Qoph*) are missing from the list of letters used at the first of the line; furthermore, two verses begin with ר (*Resh*), and two verses begin with פ (*Pe*). For some reason, by design or as a result of ancient transcription or translation, the psalm does not complete the alphabetical arrangement.

The acrostic psalms are generally thought of as wisdom or teaching psalms. They were not written to be sung but to be learned, although this psalm may be an exception to that rule.

Made up of two prayers, between which are reflections and praises about piety and godliness, the psalm is only loosely organized. However, what it lacks in systematic order, it makes up for in beauty. It contains some of the most admired, spiritual thoughts in the Book of Psalms.

TRUSTING IN GOD (25:1–3)

¹**To You, O Lord, I lift up my soul.**
²**O my God, in You I trust,**
Do not let me be ashamed;
Do not let my enemies exult over me.
³**Indeed, none of those who wait for You will be ashamed;**
Those who deal treacherously without cause will be ashamed.

Verse 1. The acrostic letter is א (*Aleph*).

The psalm begins with a yearning for God's help: **To You, O Lord, I lift up my soul.** The previous psalm declared that God does not want to be worshiped by someone who lifts "up his soul to falsehood [vanity]" (24:4), that is, by a person who longs for that which is empty, meaningless, and idolatrous. This writer turns the phrase around and says that he is lifting "up [his] soul" to God. His mind, innermost feelings, and desires are toward God. He is looking to God as a hungry man looks to one who can supply his food. He has been and is focusing his entire being on God.

The dedication he has to God is not something he has just decided upon in a flash of commitment; his affections and interests have been permanently set on God. God has been, is, and will be the center of his life.

Verse 2. The acrostic letter ב (*Beth*) is missing, suggesting that this line is not part of the organizational design of the psalm.

He further says, **O my God, in You I trust.** He has put his faith completely in God, putting down his entire weight of confidence and hope upon what God says and does.

Do not let me be ashamed. He prays for God to answer his request so that he might not be disappointed or embarrassed. **Do not let my enemies exult over me.** His petition is that God might deliver him from his enemies. If God does not hear his plea, his enemies will gloat, "exult," and rejoice over his humiliation. Their delight at his downfall will reflect on God because he had taken refuge in Him. With appropriate respect, he is reminding God of His promise of protection.

Verse 3. The acrostic letter is ג (*Gimel*).

As he thinks about the faithfulness of God, he realizes that God never forsakes those who trust in Him; so, he says, **Indeed, none of those who wait for You will be ashamed.** Anyone who waits on the Lord will not be forgotten. One waits on God when he comes to God as a faithful follower of His will, prays for a blessing, and then goes on his way with the confident anticipation that God will respond to his prayer according to His wisdom and grace. No one who waits on God in this fashion will be unheard, unassisted, or frustrated in his hope.

The converse of this statement is also true: **Those who deal treacherously without cause will be ashamed.** The person who will be "ashamed" or humiliated is the one who faithlessly ("treacherously") walks away from God. The disloyal will find failure at the end of the roads they have taken.

SEEKING GOD'S WAY (25:4, 5)

⁴**Make me know Your ways, O Lord;**
Teach me Your paths.
⁵**Lead me in Your truth and teach me,**
For You are the God of my salvation;
For You I wait all the day.

Verse 4. The acrostic letter is ד (*Daleth*).

He continues to pray, **Make me know Your ways, O LORD; teach me Your paths.** The person of piety seeks God's way and continually realigns his life with His will. He wants to know the Lord's ways, but he knows that he must be taught them.

Verse 5. The acrostic letter is ה (*He*).

He desires God to lead him. **Lead me in Your truth and teach me, for You are the God of my salvation; for You I wait all the day.** His prayer for salvation *from* his enemies is followed with a prayer for God to guide him *to* safety. "From" is not enough; we have to come around to the "to." The life that Yahweh wants for His people is the lifestyle that the psalmist is seeking to know and receive. They are to live by what God sees as true. God is his only source of rescue, the "God of [his] salvation"; and he will "wait" on God continually, confidently believing that God will hear his prayer and reveal His will.

ACKNOWLEDGING SIN (25:6, 7)

⁶Remember, O LORD, Your compassion and Your lovingkindnesses,
For they have been from of old.
⁷Do not remember the sins of my youth or my transgressions;
According to Your lovingkindness remember me,
For Your goodness' sake, O LORD.

Verse 6. The acrostic letter is ז (*Zayin*).

The letter ו (*Vav*) is skipped. **Remember, O LORD, Your compassion and Your lovingkindnesses, for they have been from of old.** God is asked to remember His nature and history, that He is a God of lovingkindness, and that He has shown grace ("compassion") to His people in the past. The psalmist clings to the unchangeable character of God. A merciful God of yesterday is a prophecy of what God will be today and tomorrow.

Verse 7. The acrostic letter is ח (*Heth*).

Do not remember the sins of my youth or my transgressions. The psalmist wants God to view him with His covenant loyalty (lovingkindness) and compassion because he has sinned throughout his past. The word "sins" (חַטֹּאות, *chatto'wth*) is a term that means to miss the mark or to lose one's way; while "transgressions" (פְּשָׁעַי, *p^esha'ay*) means literally "rebellions" and may suggest the deliberate offenses of later years. The "sins" of youth are the thoughtless, careless instances of missing the mark, sinning in ignorance, or sinning without thinking, without considering the consequences. The sins of later years are transgressions, rebellious moments when one consciously turns away from God's will. As he meditates upon the goodness of God, all of these previous sins and transgressions loom before him, interrupting His fellowship with God.

According to Your lovingkindness remember me. The writer makes a dual request, one negative and one positive, "Do not remember" and "remember me." Both petitions involve the lovingkindness of God. He wants forgiveness, and he wants God's personal attention.

For Your goodness' sake, O LORD. The basis of his appeal is the grace and mercy of God. His forgiveness, if given, will bring glory to God; it will reflect how God treats His own. "I ask not for 'my sake only,' but for 'Your goodness' sake,'" he argues.

Sin has disrupted his life with God and gone against the covenant he has made with Him. Therefore, he beseeches God to blot out his sin.

PRAISING GOD (25:8–11)

⁸Good and upright is the LORD;
Therefore He instructs sinners in the way.
⁹He leads the humble in justice,
And He teaches the humble His way.
¹⁰All the paths of the LORD are lovingkindness and truth
To those who keep His covenant and His testimonies.
¹¹For Your name's sake, O LORD,
Pardon my iniquity, for it is great.

Verse 8. The acrostic letter is ט (*Teth*).
The psalmist turns now from petitioning God to praising

Him. Thinking of God's goodness—how He responds to those who need Him—causes him to extol God's name.

He says, **Good and upright is the LORD**. God, he declares, is "good," kind, tender, merciful, and gracious; He is "upright," righteous, just, and never deviates from the path of truth. **Therefore He instructs sinners in the way.** Because of these attributes, God wants "sinners" to know the righteous paths and to come into them. His goodness goes out to sinners, but His uprightness will not allow Him to save them in their sins. He will instruct them about the right way.

Verse 9. The acrostic letter is י (*Yodh*).

He leads the humble in justice, and He teaches the humble His way. Teachable sinners will be led in His way. Those who yield to His will soon find that walking in God's instruction brings grace and truth. They will have the joy of God's forgiveness and the guidance of His Word.

Verse 10. The acrostic letter is כ (*Kaph*).

All the paths of the LORD are lovingkindness and truth to those who keep His covenant and His testimonies. Two characteristics of God come to mind: His "lovingkindness" or covenant love and His "truth." His response to those who trust in Him will always be prompted, characterized, and blessed by these two attributes.

Verse 11. The acrostic letter is ל (*Lamedh*).

The psalmist's praise of God motivates him to return to petitioning God. He asks, **For Your name's sake, O LORD, pardon my iniquity, for it is great.** As the writer thinks of the surpassing love of God, he remembers his sins again and asks God to pardon him. He makes this request because the character of God is so gracious and because his own iniquity is great. Therefore, He asks God to think of His honor as He considers his request.

REVERENCING GOD (25:12–15)

¹²**Who is the man who fears the LORD?**
He will instruct him in the way he should choose.
¹³**His soul will abide in prosperity,**
And his descendants will inherit the land.

>¹⁴The secret of the Lord is for those who fear Him,
> And He will make them know His covenant.
> ¹⁵My eyes are continually toward the Lord,
> For He will pluck my feet out of the net.

Verse 12. The acrostic letter is מ (*Mem*).

Who is the man who fears the Lord? The writer delineates the benefits that God gives to those who fear, or revere, Him. They are four in number. The first one is instruction. **He will instruct him in the way he should choose.** God will help him to know the truth, providentially assisting him to see the path he should follow.

Verse 13. The acrostic letter is נ (*Nun*).

The second blessing is personal prosperity. **His soul will abide in prosperity,** in the good favors of God. "Soul" probably designates the individual being. The word "prosperity" is a translation of the Hebrew word "in good" (בְּטוֹב, *b*ᵉ*tob*). In other words, he will enjoy grace and goodness of all kinds during his days upon the earth.

The third one is posterity. **His descendants will inherit the land.** He will be granted meaningful offspring. Sons and daughters will have the hand of the Lord upon them. Under the influence of the man who fears the Lord, his children will, through the spirit of godliness, see the goodness of God.

Verse 14. The acrostic letter is ס (*Samekh*).

The fourth blessing is a deep and personal walk with God. **The secret of the Lord is for those who fear Him.** The word "secret" comes from "secret counsel" and suggests the intimate communication of close friends. Moses saw some aspects of God that those who were not as close to God did not get to see (as did Paul, Peter, and John). The man who fears the Lord will enjoy a covenant relationship with Him. This relationship means a special, revealing friendship with God.

He will make them know His covenant. The covenant is not merely a conditional contract offering rewards in return for obedience. It is a privileged and close relationship with God.

Verse 15. The acrostic letter is ע (*Ayin*).

My eyes are continually toward the Lord, for He will pluck

my feet out of the net. The eyes (heart) of the pious person are continually upon the Lord. His habitual state of mind is being indicated. His life is absorbed with thinking of God, praying to Him, seeking His will, and longing for His fellowship.

The writer's mind is calmed by the realization that God cares for him as He cares for all those who love Him. His enemies will not be able to entrap him, for God will bring his feet out of their snares. He has not been caught by their devices yet, and he believes that God will prevent them from overtaking him in the future.

HOPING IN GOD (25:16–22)

> ¹⁶Turn to me and be gracious to me,
> For I am lonely and afflicted.
> ¹⁷The troubles of my heart are enlarged;
> Bring me out of my distresses.
> ¹⁸Look upon my affliction and my trouble,
> And forgive all my sins.
> ¹⁹Look upon my enemies, for they are many,
> And they hate me with violent hatred.
> ²⁰Guard my soul and deliver me;
> Do not let me be ashamed, for I take refuge in You.
> ²¹Let integrity and uprightness preserve me,
> For I wait for You.
> ²²Redeem Israel, O God,
> Out of all his troubles.

Verse 16. The acrostic letter is פ (*Pe*).

The writer turns once more to petition, looking to God as his only hope. **Turn to me and be gracious to me, for I am lonely and afflicted.** He calls upon God to look upon him and to cover him with His grace. He says that he is without friends; he is desolate and alone, afflicted and hurting. He needs God as his refuge and strength.

Verse 17. The acrostic letter is צ (*Tsadhe*).

The heaviness of his heart becomes greater as he thinks about his sins. **The troubles of my heart are enlarged.** Perhaps his troubles have been brought about in some way by his sins. He asks for God to deliver him from his troubles. **Bring me out of my distresses**, he says.

Verse 18. The acrostic letter is ר (*Resh*). This verse skips ק (*Qoph*).

Look upon my affliction and my trouble, and forgive all my sins. Special concern for his sins is seen throughout the psalm. He brings these sins before God three times (vv. 7, 11, 18). The heart of the psalm is his two-part petition: "Forgive me of my sins, and deliver me from the enemies around me."

Verse 19. The acrostic letter is ר (*Resh*), a repeat of the previous letter.

Look upon my enemies, for they are many, and they hate me with violent hatred. Many enemies no doubt are near him, moving toward him, and probably seeking to kill him. He asks God to rescue him.

Verse 20. The acrostic letter is ש (*Shin*).

Guard my soul and deliver me; do not let me be ashamed, for I take refuge in You. If they succeed in destroying him, his refuge in God would get the blame, for he has put his future in God's hands.

Verse 21. The acrostic letter is ת (*Tav*).

Let integrity and uprightness preserve me, for I wait for You. In other words, "May it be that my unwavering devotion to You and my upright life before people will be reasons enough for You to grant my petitions." He wants integrity and uprightness to watch over him and "preserve" him. For the third time, he says that he is leaving his situation up to God. He will "wait" on God (vv. 3, 5, 21).

Verse 22. The acrostic letter is פ (*Pe*). This letter is used a second time. Nineteen letters of the Hebrew alphabet have been used thus far. With *Pe* and *Resh* used twice and one line not included in the acrostic scheme, the total number of lines comes to twenty-two, the number of the letters in the Hebrew alphabet.

The concluding petition is **Redeem Israel, O God, out of all his troubles.** Thus the psalm closes with a prayer for the entire nation. This request could be a type of afterthought for it seems to be introducing a new thought in the final line. Could it be that this portion was added by a later inspired hand to adapt the song to a new situation? Does the writer, in addition to his personal requests, think of God's nation and beseech Him to deliver His nation in harmony with His lovingkindness from trouble and turmoil?

APPLICATION

A Pious Person

This psalm is full of the fragrance of trusting in God, progressing from prayer to praise to prayer again. The golden threads binding the psalm together are the descriptions of the man who puts his faith in the Lord and the Lord in whom man has placed his faith. These loosely connected reflections are aligned under the two major headings of piety and trust.

Let us review the psalm, looking specifically for the qualities that a pious person should possess.

The pious man trusts in God. He looks to God to deliver and save him.

He seeks God's way. He yearns for God to teach and guide him. He knows that God's way is infallible and that his own way is sure to fail.

He acknowledges his sin. Aware of his sinfulness, he humbly confesses his sins and pleads for God's forgiveness.

He praises God. He recognizes that God has been good to him, and he remembers that God has always answered him with lovingkindness and forgiveness.

He reverences God. He sees the transcendence of God, the One who towers above him more so than the universe towers beyond his grasp and understanding.

He hopes in God. He sees God as his only real future. He does not worry; he prays.

In summary, a pious person is a soul who is focused on God and whose life is ordered by God's will.

Trusting in God

What does it mean to trust in God? Look at the descriptions

of trust given in verses 1 and 2 of this psalm.

Trusting in God means lifting up our souls to God. Lifting up our souls to God means putting our affections, love, and aspirations upon God. In other words, God becomes the heart of our being.

Trusting in God means looking to God for our success. We have given all to God, and we will depend upon Him for the outcomes of our lives. In light of what He chooses, we will either be ashamed or crowned with victory on Judgment Day. We know that the latter will be true because of the commitment we have made to Him.

Trusting in God means waiting for God. We know that God will act at the appropriate time. We are aware that He is acting even now. Although we may not see His hand at work, we know His gracious hand of providence moves behind the scenes.

> The future beckons and I bow.
>   My God removes the care!
> Behold, He goes before me now,
>   And will my way prepare.[1]

The Believer and God's Will

Those who believe in God are never far away from God's will, for it is more precious to them than fine gold.

They yearn to know it. They seek it earnestly on their own, and they are grateful to anyone who can teach them a deeper understanding of it.

They meditate on it day and night (see Ps. 1:2). They think about God's will, pray over it, and dive into it as deeply as they can. They know that "you do not go deep and find God, but you find God and then go deep."

They want to walk in it. One aged lady said that she read the Bible every day. When asked why, she replied, "I am checking to see if there is a command in it that I have not obeyed."

Believers do not worship the Word of God; they worship

---

[1]W. E. Brightwell, "The Providence of God," *Songs of the Church*, comp. and ed. Alton H. Howard (West Monroe, La.: Howard Publishing Co., 1977).

the God of the Word. They see God as their salvation and His will as guidance for walking with Him. If God is "set above all things" in their hearts, then the will of God will be more precious to them than all the world.

Thinking of Our Sin

The closer we get to God, the more we think about our sin. God's holiness highlights our mistakes like spots on a white cloth. This psalm tells us what to think about when we remember our sinfulness.

Think of God's nature. He is full of love. He has always treated His children with compassion because of who He is.

Think of God's integrity. He has a faithfulness to His covenant that stands above our sin. He has a grace that reaches all of our transgressions. We want mercy, not justice; we want God's lovingkindness, not His severity. Inasmuch as He has forgiven our sins, He will remember them against us no more. Remember this truth!

Think of God's reputation. He is known for His goodness, and He does not change. He will respond today the same way that He responded yesterday.

We all have spiritual flashbacks when we remember what miserable failures we have been. The thought of our sin humiliates us and puts the fear of judgment into our hearts. However, when we focus upon God's nature, integrity, and reputation, our fears are relieved.

God Is Good

The goodness of God implies certain other truths. How does His goodness show itself?

It is seen in His instruction of sinners. He loves every sinner. He therefore seeks to bring each one into His way.

It is seen in His leading the humble justly and faithfully. He comes down to those who are in need and treats them graciously. He is the great King of the universe, but He condescends to lead the humble in the right way.

It is seen in His manifestation of lovingkindness. He is always faithful in keeping His promises. His covenant loyalty is clearly seen in all of His actions. Grace is part of His eternal nature.

It is seen in His standing with the truth. He never lies or promotes falsehood. He never has and never will lead anyone to honor error.

It is seen in His willingness to forgive. When anyone fulfills the requirements and cries out for God's grace, He grants it in abundance. He covers all sins with the blood of Jesus.

Yes, God is so good. His goodness is expressed in dozens of ways. Our spiritual lives have their origin and continuance in His goodness.

What to Expect from God

Most of us would say, "I'd rather know a few things for certain than a thousand things that aren't so." This psalm brings before us two truths on which we can always rely.

God will respond with lovingkindness to the pleas of those who come to Him. It is the way the Lord always takes. As surely as the sun, moon, and stars exist, God will respond to those who come to Him with grace and covenant loyalty.

He will stand on the side of truth. His integrity will not be sacrificed or compromised. All real truth springs from Him, and He will never ask us to live by falsehood and error.

These two certainties bring two blessings to us. First, they give us peace. They enable us to relax in God. Second, they make us into the kind of people we ought to be. If it is true that we will become like the God we worship, then it follows that we will be people of compassion and truth, lovingkindness and holiness.

The Man Who Fears the Lord

The person who fears God is commended in the psalm. This man, the psalm says, will be abundantly blessed.

He will be blessed with guidance. He will receive the instructions of God because he is eager to listen to God. God will guide him in the way that He has chosen because the man who fears the Lord understands who God is and follows His guidance.

He will be granted prosperity. Even though the Old Testament emphasizes physical prosperity more than the New Testament, the point is that God will grant him success even as he did Job after he faced his trials (Job 42:10–17). Today, in New Testament Christianity, the prosperity we receive is more spiritual, such as the abundant life (Jn. 10:10).

He will be given numerous descendants. Once again, this part of the promise is more of a physical promise. In Old Testament times a choice lineage was prized above all other blessings. Today, the man who fears the Lord will have kindred spirits who follow in his train, providing him with the joy of having a spiritual lineage.

He will know the secrets of the Lord. He will have the privilege of walking closely with the Lord and seeing His glory as no one else sees it. God does not have favorites, but He does have intimates who see His majesty in a way that others do not. These people will see His covenant loyalty as they experience the joy of being a part of that covenant. However, only those who fear Him can enter into the deep things of God.

He will be protected by the Lord. The Lord will snatch his feet out of the net. He will shield him from those who want to harm him. He will be kept alive to do what God wants him to do as long as God wants him to do it.

If all of this is true of the man who fears the Lord, there is only one appropriate resolve for us to make: We must keep our eyes turned to the Lord. Nothing must be allowed to obscure our view of Him. To look toward God is to depend upon Him, watch for His leadership, and look for His blessings. He is our God, and we should submit to Him and walk beside Him.

Walking with God

In these verses we see the beauty of fellowship with God. What is this walk like?

It means entering His covenant. One cannot enter into a relationship with God without becoming part of His covenant.

It means coming to know God Himself. God's covenant is more than a contract. It is a relationship within a contract that is personal and intimate. The supreme goal of the covenant is that of God's becoming our heavenly Father and His allowing us to become His children.

It means coming into the sphere of the blessings of God. Special blessings are showered upon those who are in the circle of His friendship. He looks after His own in a particular way even though He sends the rain on the just and the unjust.

No greater walk is known than that of walking with God.

True Hope

One of our most meaningful words is "hope." It glows like a diamond in the darkness of despair. The person who has no hope is a person to be pitied; the person with hope has strength that others do not have. This psalm holds out true hope to those who yearn for it.

One can have the hope of forgiveness. The writer cries out for God's forgiveness, implying that God can and will forgive the penitent.

One can have the hope of protection. Perhaps the problem the writer faces is that of vicious enemies who seek his life. He seeks the strength of an almighty hand. He believes that God can and will help him.

One can have the hope of answered prayer. This psalm is filled with prayer. We should live in a continual, prayerful relationship with God, and we must not forget that God hears the trusting heart that calls upon Him in an hour of great distress. Such praying is not evidence of a crisis religion, but it is a religion that prepares us for any crisis.

One can have the hope of companionship. The writer describes himself as lonely and afflicted. He asks for deliverance, but more than that, he pleads for companionship with God. Wonder of wonders, God extends His fellowship to those who believe in Him!

One can have hope for his nation. He prays for Israel, asking God to deliver them out of their troubles. The only hope for any nation is God.

In this psalm is hope, shining brightly and more gloriously than ever before. It is a hope for all the problems that we have. The bottom line is that all true hope is found in God.

Standing in the Safety of the Lord

Everyone wants to be in the hand of the Lord's protection. However, it is obvious that He is not a refuge for saint and sinner alike. How then is His guardianship secured?

Through integrity. We have to be honest with God. He does not bestow His blessing of care upon the cheating and treacherous person.

Through obedience. We must sincerely seek to do His will. Perfection is not demanded, but obedience is. We are His servants, and we live to do His will.

Through trust. We must trust Him to do for us what is best. Faithful servants put themselves in the hand of God and go on their way, knowing that God will do what is best for them.

God is faithful. He knows those who are His, and He watches over them with unfailing care.

Looking Unto God

This psalm begins with the phrase "To You." The image of looking to God is found throughout the psalm. It is important to notice the different shades of meaning connected with this thought.

Spectators look "on"—from seats in the grandstands. That is, they only observe and watch what is before them. They are detached and removed from what they are viewing. Their looking is impersonal and can even be indifferent. They watch for enjoyment; there is no real involvement.

Students look "at"—from their seats behind their desks. Their looking grows out of a desire to learn. It is academic and factual. They would like to know everything they can about what they are watching. However, there is a broad expanse between the students and what they study. Their lives are separated from what they consider; their goals may well be fulfilled when knowledge has been gathered.

Servants look "unto"—from their posture of need. They are dependent upon the One to whom they look. Their eyes look with an appeal and a prayer. With their eyes and hearts, they are asking for support and sustenance. They are somewhat like a pet dog who sits beneath his master's table and looks with pleading eyes at his hand for his sustenance. It is a matter of life and death with him, for he lives his life out of his master's hand.

This psalm is about a man who looks to God as His own servant would look to him. He has experienced the lovingkindness of God before, and now, as one who is in desperate need, he calls upon the God of his salvation. He looks to His gracious hand with love and humility for the deliverance that only He can give.

PSALM 26
LIVING WITH INTEGRITY

The Superscription: A Psalm of David. Containing only one bit of information, the ancient title simply says **of** ["by," "for," or "to"] **David** (לְדָוִד, *lᵉdawid*). The NASB adds **a Psalm**, but the two words are not part of the Hebrew title. The NASB uses italics to show that the two words have been supplied by the translators.

This touching and popular psalm emphasizes the topic of integrity in an inclusio format. It begins with this quality—"I have walked in my integrity"—and ends with it—"I shall walk in my integrity." The writer has chosen spiritual genuineness to be his way of life.

In light of its content, we might call this piece "A Psalm of Innocence." Bewilderment had descended upon the psalmist because he had been accused of being a hypocrite. He adamantly recoiled at the insinuations and earnestly besought God to judge him and make known his blamelessness. He lists the evidence that confirms his righteousness and thus proves that he should not be grouped with evildoers.

Because of this psalm's exposition of this crucial theme, it has become a thorough illustration of honesty and how it is demonstrated in the life and worship of the devout believer. No psalm addresses this topic of integrity quite the way this psalm does. As defined in this context by A. F. Kirkpatrick, integrity is "sincerity of purpose and single-heartedness of devotion" to God.[1] H. C. Leupold said that it is "conduct from which no

---

[1] A. F. Kirkpatrick, *The Book of Psalms*, The Cambridge Bible for Schools and Colleges (Cambridge: University Press, 1901), 1:137.

essential element is missing."² Whether we call it "serving God sincerely" or "consistent godly living," the basic thought of the attribute is that the motives of the heart and the actions of the life should match the professed spiritual commitment. Genuineness is not sinlessness but devoted sincerity, not flawlessness but faithfulness. Integrity has to do with more than a person's reputation; it concerns following what he or she knows to be true and right.

"EXAMINE ME, O LORD" (26:1–3)

¹**Vindicate me, O LORD, for I have walked in my integrity,**
And I have trusted in the LORD without wavering.
²**Examine me, O LORD, and try me;**
Test my mind and my heart.
³**For Your lovingkindness is before my eyes,**
And I have walked in Your truth.

Verse 1. The writer begins with a plea for God to search his heart and confirm his genuineness. He uses a word that has been translated "integrity," "blameless life," or "a life without reproach" (תם, *thom*). The adjective form of this word is used as God describes Job in the prologue of that book (Job 1:1).

So sure is the writer of his devoted heart that he calls upon God to be his witness: **Vindicate me, O LORD, for I have walked in my integrity.** He wants God to look into his character and divinely re-enforce his own self-evaluation. He believes his undivided commitment to God will stand even the scrutiny of God's searching eyes.

He further says, **I have trusted in the LORD without wavering.** He declares to God that he has not deviated from trusting in Him. He has been constant and immovable in his faith in the Almighty. Neither the circumstances around him nor the people who have opposed him have been able to pry him away from his life in God.

---

²H. C. Leupold, *Exposition of the Psalms* (Columbus, Ohio: The Wartburg Press, 1959; reprint, Grand Rapids, Mich.: Baker Book House, 1969), 230.

PSALM 26

Verse 2. His cry for a divine examination becomes more intense as the prayer proceeds: **Examine me, O LORD, and try me; test my mind and my heart.** In verses 1 and 2, he uses four strong words in his request: "vindicate" (שָׁפַט, *shapat*), "examine" (בָּחַן, *bachan*), "try" (נָסָה, *nasah*), and "test" (צָרַף, *tsarap*). "Vindicate" ("judge"; KJV) means to look over and weigh. "Examine" suggests a refiner who assays his metal before purchasing it. "Try" indicates his plea to be put in circumstances that would put his faith into action. "Test" illustrates placing him like gold in a smelter to get rid of the dross that might be present.

The "mind" and the "heart" refer figuratively to his whole inner being—his feelings, thoughts, conscience, and will. He asks God to look within him and judge the spirituality of his heart.

He seeks the most complete test possible, and he is thoroughly convinced of his trustworthiness. He believes he has walked in unswerving obedience.

Verse 3. The psalmist identifies the twofold thrust of his life as God's covenant loyalty and truth. He says, **For Your lovingkindness is before my eyes, and I have walked in Your truth.** The Lord's grace ("lovingkindness") has been constantly before him, and he has committed himself to doing God's will. Realizing who the Lord is and knowing his own commitment to keep God's "truth," he believes that a divine inspection will validate his integrity.

These words may appear as almost arrogant and self-righteous; however, they should be seen as a sincere, righteous man's desire for God to vindicate him from the unjust accusations that have been made against him. He does not claim perfection, but he does claim faithfulness as a diligent servant of God. He believes that he is free from false goodness. He loves God and finds his hope in Him. In the words of W. O. E. Oesterley:

> For a man to recognize, in a spirit of true humility, that he is striving to live according to the will of God, need not generate spiritual pride, but should be a source of sanctified joy. While, on the one hand, to confess sin is a supreme duty of man, the recognition of his virtues, when rightly envisaged, is, on the other hand,

to acknowledge the action of divine grace.[3]

True integrity demands that one's practice match his profession.

A RIGHTEOUS REFUSAL (26:4, 5)

**⁴I do not sit with deceitful men,
Nor will I go with pretenders.
⁵I hate the assembly of evildoers,
And I will not sit with the wicked.**

Verse 4. The writer moves from his life before God to his life with others. He affirms, **I do not sit with deceitful men, nor will I go with pretenders.** He has been careful about his conduct, making sure that he did not engage in deliberate and prolonged friendship with "deceitful" and hypocritical men. He has not relished or desired their company. "Vain persons" is used in the KJV translation. "Vain" (שָׁוְא, *shawᵉ*) is the opposite of reality, truthfulness, and right living. The word "dissemblers," used in older translations (for example, the KJV, ASV, and RSV), is an old word for "hypocrites," the people who hide from the public what they are in their hearts.

Verse 5. Revealing his heart, he declares, **I hate the assembly of evildoers.** He despises the gatherings of men for evil and sinful scheming. He has maintained a settled practice: **I will not sit with the wicked.** Whether they have come together to sin or to lead others into sin, he has resolved to avoid that type of assembly.

He knows that people cannot claim to be righteous if they walk in fellowship with evildoers and encourage them in their wicked works.

---

[3]W. O. E. Oesterley, *The Psalms: Translated with Text-Critical and Exegetical Notes* (London: S.P.C.K., 1939), 194.

PSALM 26

LOVING WORSHIP (26:6–10)

⁶I shall wash my hands in innocence,
And I will go about Your altar, O LORD,
⁷That I may proclaim with the voice of thanksgiving
And declare all Your wonders.
⁸O LORD, I love the habitation of Your house
And the place where Your glory dwells.
⁹Do not take my soul away along with sinners,
Nor my life with men of bloodshed,
¹⁰In whose hands is a wicked scheme,
And whose right hand is full of bribes.

Verse 6. On the positive side, he says, **I shall wash my hands in innocence, and I will go about Your altar, O LORD.** Having maintained a blameless life, he can come before God with hands unstained by evil. Washing the hands was a figurative way of declaring one's innocence (Ex. 30:17–21; Deut. 21:6, 7). Pilate washed his hands to proclaim that he was free from any involvement in the sentencing of Jesus, but he was not really innocent (Mt. 27:24). This writer *is* innocent. He can wash his hands in true innocence and approach the altar for the sacrifice with a sincere heart.

Verse 7. What are his reasons for coming before God in worship? He says that he makes that journey **that [he] may proclaim with the voice of thanksgiving and declare all [God's] wonders.** The purpose of his worship is to express joyful gratitude for the wonderful works of God. Having abstained from iniquity, he can happily and freely appear at God's sanctuary to offer sacrifices and give thanks and praise to God for His grace, leadership, and salvation. His would not be a superficial offering; his would be genuine worship springing from a thoughtful, godly, and appreciative heart.

Verse 8. He further says, **O LORD, I love the habitation of Your house and the place where Your glory dwells.** His affections are set upon the fellowship and worship of God. He finds his utmost pleasure in going to the tabernacle where God's "glory" resides. The major attraction in worship was not the place, the people, or the stimulation, but the presence of God. He wants to be where God is, to be in the shadow of His radiance.

Verse 9. His plea is this: **Do not take my soul away along with sinners, nor my life with men of bloodshed.** Since his heart is pure and his hands free from the stain of overt sin, and since he loves the presence of God, it is natural for him to withdraw from the judgment due those who practice evil. He pleads for God not to group him with sinners and violent men, men of "bloods" (דָּמִים, *damim*) as the Hebrew says, who are always carrying out wicked designs.

Verse 10. He thinks of those who do not walk in integrity, and he does not want to be classed with them or taken away with them. "Do not put me with those **in whose hands is a wicked scheme, and whose right hand is full of bribes**," he pleads. These must have been people of significant influence in the community. He does not want to be linked with men who accept bribes, pervert justice, or deceive the innocent. Their lifestyle is not his. He has no affinity in heart or action with them. Integrity of spirit affects not only our worship of God, but also the friends we keep.

WITH THE FUTURE (26:11, 12)

> ¹¹But as for me, I shall walk in my integrity;
> Redeem me, and be gracious to me.
> ¹²My foot stands on a level place;
> In the congregations I shall bless the LORD.

Verse 11. He forecasts his future with a godly resolve: **But as for me, I shall walk in my integrity.** He will continue to live the way he has been living. Integrity has been his course of conduct, and it will continue to be so. He has set his heart and determined his route.

Upon the basis of his resolve, he petitions the Lord, **Redeem me, and be gracious to me.** Out of his integrity has grown his confidence in God. If one has walked with God in truth, he will believe that God can be and desires to be "gracious" toward him. In addition, he knows that God is dependable and trustworthy and that he can trust Him to care for him tomorrow as He has in the past. His faith in God has emerged from his genuine life with God.

Verse 12. Because of his life, convictions, and God's faithfulness, he is sure of his footing: **My foot stands on a level place**. His feet are planted where they cannot slip. They are free from tripping or stumbling. Difficulties will have to be faced, but he believes that God will keep him safe.

For his safety and salvation, he will praise God in the great assembly: **In the congregations I shall bless the LORD**. The Hebrew word for "congregations" (מַקְהֵלִים, *maqhelim*) is plural. The NIV interpreted it as "the great assembly." The writer is announcing his resolve. He is committing his future to the praising of God. In faith he will be thanking God in the gatherings of the righteous for what He has done and for the kindness He will give him throughout the days ahead.

APPLICATION

What Is Integrity?

Integrity is not perfection, but righteous consistency. It is not sinlessness, but a day-in-day-out dedication to doing God's will. We call it a transparent life, one that can be judged by God and mankind and found blameless.

How did David describe the integrity of his life? He said that his heart was right and that uprightness had manifested itself in the right kind of life with God—such as shunning evil men, worshiping God genuinely, and anticipating His blessings in the future.

We must say, then, that integrity will be clearly seen in several important areas of life. It will express itself in key relationships, all of which are mentioned in the psalm.

First, it will appear in our relationship with God. A person is not truly honest unless he is first honest with God. The psalmist said that he was faithful in his walk in the truth.

Second, it will be seen in our worship. Our integrity with God will manifest itself in the worship that we bring Him. The righteous one comes into the place of worship with a life that passes divine inspection. He does not cheat or cut corners. His word is good, and his heart is clean.

Third, it will be evident in the associations we choose. Uprightness of heart will be observable in our relationships with the people of the world. We will neither join nor encourage the vain, deceitful, or evil people around us.

Fourth, it will affect our view of the future. Transparency of heart will show itself in our trust in God to keep His promises.

Integrity will run through our lives like our blood, affecting all phases of our living. When we can say, "He is an honest person," we ought to mean that the whole person has been affected and infected with right thinking and right living.

Integrity and Mercy

David coupled his integrity with God's mercy. He did not base his request to God solely upon his blamelessness; he knew he must have God's grace. He would continue to lead an honest life and seek God's deliverance, but he would do so by focusing on God's mercy and His truth. Further, he resolved to praise God for what He had done and what He would do.

The Side Effects of Integrity

The life of integrity brings two desirable spinoff gifts: God's peace and God's provisions. When accused of evil, blameless people realize that they are innocent before God. Having walked in integrity before God, they can rest assured that God will be with them and watch over them, guarding their hearts with His peace and surrounding their lives with His supplies.

Passing the Inspection

When we bring our integrity before God and let Him go over it, will it hold up?

Can it be examined? When God looks it over like a refiner assaying his metal before purchasing it, will it be worth anything to God?

Can it be tried? When God puts us in circumstances which try our faith, will it pass the trial?

Can it be tested? When God places it in a smelter like one would gold to get rid of the dross that might be present, will anything be left?

Can it be vindicated? When God looks over it and weighs it, will it remain intact?

These are just figurative ways of referring to God examining our hearts for the dross and impurities. Can we bring our feelings, thoughts, and will before Him for examination and reproof? Do we dare ask God to look within us and see the kind of hearts we have, even as this psalmist did?

One-Track Living

Living righteously is really not complicated. Through the lens of this psalm, we see that the godly approach to life can be boiled down to two traits.

First, there is integrity. We must be thoroughly honest, beginning with God. We cannot be perfect, but we can be honest.

Second, there is trust in God. Beyond integrity, we put our trust in God and never waver in that trust. When we do not understand and cannot add up everything on our computers, we can trust God.

These two traits cover all situations, obligations, and genuine aspirations.

The Power of the Proper Focus

David said that he kept his eyes on the lovingkindness of God and walked in His truth (v. 3). Remember this statement, for perhaps no better approach to life can be stated in so few words.

One man said, "Before I became a Christian, I was an evil man. I hurt others with my life and influence. Now that I am a Christian, it is hard for me to forget what I have done. I know that God has forgiven me, but my past haunts me. What should I do?" He was told to read verse 3 and let it guide him.

Keeping our eyes on God's lovingkindness and living according to His truth *will give us the right perspective.* The reality is that God is love, and the eternal salvation He grants us will be based on His grace. The prodigal son learned this lesson when he came home (Lk. 15:20, 21). No sinner can earn his way into the fellowship of God. However, God's grace does not eliminate the need to walk in His truth. Living in it opens our lives to receive His grace.

Keeping this focus, therefore, *will give us peace*. We cannot have serenity of soul unless we know that we have been forgiven and that we walk in the light of God's will. One good way to remind ourselves of the grace of God is to keep our eyes on His nature—on His attribute of love. God loves us as no human being can.

Keeping this focus *will also give us hope*. We will have a realistic expectation because of the gracious Spirit of our God. He does not change, so we know what He is going to do tomorrow because of who He is today. He is not capricious, vacillating, or changing into different personalities from day to day.

What is our focus? We can summarize it with two emphases: keeping our eyes on His lovingkindness and keeping our feet in His path of truth.

The Company We Keep

Integrity insists that we reveal who we are by the fellowship we extend and the fellowship we refuse. Someone has said, "Tell me with whom you associate, and I will tell you who you are." Water seeks its own level.

The person of truth does not fellowship *the deceitful people*. These are vain people who seek lies, tell them, and live by them. They are the opposite of genuine people. The honest person has no interest in the hypocritical, the two-faced, or the gossipers. He does not agree with them and, consequently, will not "fit in" with them.

The person of truth does not fellowship *evildoers*, neither by encouraging wickedness nor by knowingly abiding in the company of those who do. This person will not give credence and approval to the wicked assembly by his word or presence.

Integrity goes deeper than just words. It affects every aspect of our lives. One cannot be honest in merely a word or two; integrity is a lifestyle.

Coming to Worship

How should we come before God in worship?

With innocent hands. The writer of this psalm said that he had washed his hands in innocence before he came. He was righteous before God. All wrongs had been dealt with, and his heart was genuine before God. He did not want God to see him as being among those who do evil. He did not belong to that crowd and had worked hard to shun them.

With a grateful heart. He said he had come to give "thanksgiving" to God. His heart was filled with gratitude, and he wanted to declare all of His wonders in his worship.

With genuine love. He said he loved to worship. It was not a burden to him. He wanted to come where God's glory was and worship.

A true heart recognizes truth and true reality. If we are genuine in thinking and living, we will see God for who He is and will seek to have the appropriate relationship with Him. We will not come to worship as spectators but as eager participants.

What Really Matters?

As is seen in this psalm, the platform of life can be nailed down easily.

We need redemption. We have all sinned. It does not necessarily take a Bible verse to bring us to the awareness that we have sinned and fallen short of God's glory. All we have to do is think about how we have lived and what we have said, and we will see our sinfulness.

We need grace. Only God's grace can provide the redemption that we must have. We cannot earn it; we cannot buy it or be awarded it for good works. Our deliverance from sin's guilt and grave will be through mercy, not merit.

We need integrity. Without it, we will not take the proper steps to deal with our desperate situations. Integrity gravitates to the truth of God's will. A blind man cannot see; a dishonest man cannot understand because he will not open his mind to the truth.

Integrity brings us to God, and God through His wonderful grace brings us to an eternal redemption. When we have integrity, grace, and redemption, we have a solid place to stand. If we can say, "Your lovingkindness is before our eyes, and we are walking in Your truth," then we are living upon the only enduring foundation of life.

Viewing Ourselves

We should be able to have a wholesome spiritual respect concerning ourselves. In this regard, Psalm 26 is an example to us. How did this righteous man see himself?

He saw himself as dependent on God's grace. He said the lovingkindness of God was ever before his eyes. He knew that he had to have God's mercy.

He saw himself as honest before God. He asked God to look at his heart and test it. He knew that he was walking in integrity. He did not brag about it, but he was confident of his walk in faith.

He saw himself as engaged in righteous living. He loved the worship of God and refused to be counted with the wicked and the hypocrites. He asked God to see him as he really was.

He was committed. His heart was set, and he believed that he would not waver from his trust in God. He was not boasting; he was relating where he stood and where he planned to stand.

No one desires to be a Pharisee; neither does one desire to be a spiritual dwarf, unsure and half-convinced. On one side there is arrogance; on the other side there is no confidence. However, in the middle of these two, we will find a trustworthy confidence in our spirituality. John wrote, "These things I have written to you . . . so that you may know that you have eternal life" (1 Jn. 5:13).

At the Place of Worship

God chose to dwell with Israel. He made His presence known at the tabernacle and later in the temple. David said that he loved to go to the habitation of God. What happens when we go to worship God?

We come into God's presence. Yes, God is present everywhere, but we especially experience His divine presence when we become a part of the worship assembly.

We behold His glory. Yes, His glory is seen all around us, but there is a unique beholding of His glory when we worship Him. Where God's special presence is, there is His glory.

We have the privilege of doing something for God. We cannot bring Him anything, for He needs nothing. We really cannot do anything for Him, for He is self-sufficient. The only thing we can do for Him is extol His greatness with our lips and serve mankind in His name.

The one who loves God will surely love to worship Him. Where there is no consciousness of God, there can be no real worship of Him. Where there is an awareness of God, there will surely be praise of Him, reverence of Him, and a sense of His glory.

The Importance of Integrity

Integrity is one of the foundation stones of life.

Without it, we cannot have an authentic relationship with God. It is true that we are saved by grace through faith (Eph. 2:8), but the reception of that grace requires a faith-based honesty with God. Will we seek His will and apply it to ourselves? Will we walk in the light of His Word?

Without it, we cannot have the proper relationship with other people. Deeper than any likes and dislikes, any personal prejudices or base desires, an all-consuming ambition should be to treat people right.

Without it, we cannot have the proper attitude toward things or the world. Paul said, in effect, "We should use the world, but we should not use it fully" (1 Cor. 7:31). Our business here is not to fulfill every fancy; we are here to do the will of God. Integrity is required to fulfill such a mission in a world like ours.

Look at this list: God, others, and things. What is left? If integrity affects all three of these, then it is the most basic trait. Surely the major question of life has to be "Am I an honest person?"

Psalm 27

An Antidote for Fear

The Superscription: A Psalm of David. The ancient title just says **of** ["by," "for," or "to"] **David** (לְדָוִד, *lᵉdawid*). The NASB has added **a Psalm** to the superscription but has placed it in italics. We do not know when the psalm was written. There does not seem to be any reason to disagree with the authorship ascription.

The two themes of this psalm are faith and fear. It swings from faith to fear and then back again to faith. The psalmist is afraid of the enemies who are converging upon him and asks God to deliver him from them. The antidote for his fear is God. He cannot keep terrifying thoughts out of his mind; but when they threaten to dominate his thinking, he confronts them with his energetic trust in God. The demons of fear are chased away by the angels of faith.

The first half of the psalm expresses faith in God (vv. 1–6). In the second half, fear over enemies emerges and becomes prevalent; but faith takes over, with the psalm ending on the high note of trust in God's salvation (vv. 7–14). The contrast in emphasis between the two halves is so pronounced that it seems as though two different psalms, one stressing faith and the other highlighting fear, have been brought together to compose the psalm. Since no justifiable reason can be given as to why two different psalms might be united this way, it is more reasonable to believe that the Holy Spirit gave us this psalm to remind us of the wide mood changes experienced by the believer in God who is beset by perilous circumstances.

Perhaps it was penned during a low time in David's life.

For example, it may have been composed when David fled from Absalom. Imagine David's conflicting emotions at such a time. At one moment, he would be thinking of God's tender treatment of him in the past and his hopes for the future. The next moment, he might plunge into the realization of the tragic predicament he was in—a father/king being hunted down by his son. In that kind of circumstance, one could write a psalm that goes from one extreme mood to another in a few verses. The horror the writer experienced weighed so heavily on his mind that he moved quickly from exulting confidence to a plaintive call for help and then back again to confidence.

The psalm begins and ends with faith in God. Between the first verse and the last one, the writer utters urgent pleas for assistance; but he ends the psalm expressing his determination to wait in faith on the Lord.

HE IS OUR DEFENSE (27:1–3)

>¹**The Lord is my light and my salvation;**
>**Whom shall I fear?**
>**The Lord is the defense of my life;**
>**Whom shall I dread?**
>²**When evildoers came upon me to devour my flesh,**
>**My adversaries and my enemies, they stumbled and fell.**
>³**Though a host encamp against me,**
>**My heart will not fear;**
>**Though war arise against me,**
>**In spite of this I shall be confident.**

Verse 1. The writer recognizes God as both his spiritual and physical defense against his enemies. In the end, this view of God will win over his fears.

He begins his composition with a tremendously encouraging picture of God. He says, **The Lord is my light and my salvation**. In this crisis, he remembers that God is his "light" (understanding) and his "salvation" (deliverance). This reference to God as "light" is the only time in the Old Testament that God is specifically referred to as "light"; however, the Old Testament often alludes to God under this figure. The New Testament also has one specific reference to God's being "light," plus many allusions to Him as such. (See, for example, Ps. 4:6; Is. 10:17; Mic. 7:8; 1 Jn. 1:5.) As "light," God removed the darkness of ignorance, sin, and death from the writer's life.

In addition to being "light," God is his "salvation." He would be his source of deliverance from all the violent circumstances in which he might find himself. Thus he can say, **The LORD is the defense of my life**. His God has been, is, and will be the "defense" (מָעוֹז, *ma'oz*) or stronghold of his soul and body.

Upon the basis of God's being "light," "salvation," and his stronghold, he can confidently affirm to himself, **Whom shall I dread?** God brings hope and encouragement. He replaces the gloom of doubts with the glory of His presence. Since God, the almighty One, is his salvation, he has no reason to tremble before anyone. God will fight his battles, defend him against all enemies, and sustain him in all the precarious situations that might arise.

Verse 2. Looking back on his walk with God, he remembers, **When evildoers came upon me to devour my flesh, my adversaries and my enemies, they stumbled and fell**. His life had not been free from serious difficulties. Evil ones had come after him to eat ("to devour") his "flesh." His enemies had been like wild beasts who pounce on their prey, rip it up, and consume it. However, their assaults had failed. God had been his Savior. These victories had not come to David from his own abilities or military forces. The Lord had dealt with his foes, causing everyone of them to stumble and fall.

Verse 3. Faith will give a person confidence to face even a multitude of enemies. He exults, **Though a host encamp against me, my heart will not fear**. He sees God as the One who shielded him and protected him from the surrounding violent forces. The Lord went before him, doing for him what he could not do for himself. Thus, in faith, he says, **Though war arise against me, in spite of this I shall be confident**. The conquests he had enjoyed gave him confidence to believe that though a whole war broke out against him and enemy soldiers encircled him, God would fight for him and keep him secure. Does not God do the same for every Christian today? Did not Paul say that in Christ we are more than conquerors (Rom. 8:37)?

HE IS OUR STRENGTH (27:4–6)

⁴One thing I have asked from the Lord, that I shall seek:
That I may dwell in the house of the Lord all the days of my life,
To behold the beauty of the Lord
And to meditate in His temple.
⁵For in the day of trouble He will conceal me in His tabernacle;
In the secret place of His tent He will hide me;
He will lift me up on a rock.
⁶And now my head will be lifted up above my enemies around me,
And I will offer in His tent sacrifices with shouts of joy;
I will sing, yes, I will sing praises to the Lord.

Verse 4. The writer expresses his greatest desire: **One thing I have asked from the Lord, that I shall seek: that I may dwell in the house of the Lord all the days of my life**. More than anything else, he wants to be in God's presence and "dwell in [His] house." Is this our chief yearning? The "house" which he seeks is not a physical one, but a figurative "house," one that is synonymous with God's presence. Where God is, he wants to be.

Dwelling with God will give him special privileges. For example, he will have opportunity **to behold the beauty of the Lord and to meditate in His temple**. He will have the joy of beholding God's glory continuously. He will be able to gaze upon His kindness and goodness without interruption. Proximity means privilege in this case. He will be able to inquire in His temple and to come to know His will more perfectly. His greatest ambitions are to look upon God's presence, actions, and love and to grow in an understanding of His mind. No nobler aspiration can be entertained by any person.

Verse 5. He says, **For in the day of trouble He will conceal**

me in His tabernacle. He is not naive about life. He knows that he will never be exempt from trials. If he does not find them, they will find him. However, God will help in his days "of trouble." What will He do? He will hide him within His presence. He says, "He will conceal me in His tabernacle"; **in the secret place of His tent He will hide me**. Furthermore, He will shield him with His strength. David says, **He will lift me up on a rock.**

Three metaphors are used to describe God's protection: a "tabernacle," "a tent," and "a rock." God will put him in a house, sheltering him from the earthly concerns that distract him. He will take him into a "secret place" in His tabernacle for security, hiding him in His presence. He will set him high upon a "rock" so that he will be far from the arrows and slingshots of the enemy. These are figures and should not be taken literally. The thought behind all three is that God will place him in the hollow of His hand and prevent harm from coming to him by protecting him with His presence and strength.

Living with God will wonderfully prepare him for trials in the future. Walking in God's fellowship will keep him conscious of who God is and reinforce his realization that no servant of His will be forsaken by Him. God prepares us to handle difficulties by giving us levelheadedness and by granting us His strength.

Verse 6. His conclusion from such lofty thinking is this: **And now my head will be lifted up above my enemies around me**. Carried away with the consciousness that God will provide for him in times of danger, he praises God for lifting up his head in victory over his enemies while they were debased by defeat. In faith, he is singing thanks and praise in advance of these actual victories. What will he do when victory comes? His resolve is this: **I will offer in His tent sacrifices with shouts of joy; I will sing, yes, I will sing praises to the LORD**. He believes that these triumphs will be given, and he envisions going to the tabernacle and making thank offerings with "shouts of joy" for the victories God will give him. When we think of what God has done for us and what He has promised to do for us, noble resolves naturally well up within our hearts.

PSALM 27

HEAR MY CRY (27:7–10)

⁷Hear, O Lord, when I cry with my voice,
And be gracious to me and answer me.
⁸When You said, "Seek My face," my heart said to You,
"Your face, O Lord, I shall seek."
⁹Do not hide Your face from me,
Do not turn Your servant away in anger;
You have been my help;
Do not abandon me nor forsake me, O God of my salvation!
¹⁰For my father and my mother have forsaken me,
But the Lord will take me up.

Verse 7. Beginning with this verse, the mood changes. Perhaps the psalmist turns his mind back to the problems staring at him. His eyes move from the clouds above to the conflict at hand below. He cries out in prayer, **Hear, O Lord, when I cry with my voice, and be gracious to me and answer me.** As a terrorizing vision comes over him, he passionately petitions God to come to his support. He has not forgotten the faith he has just sung about. He is putting that faith into practice in a unfriendly world by asking God to place His protective arms around him. He prepared himself for this prayer by thinking of who God is and what God has done for him. In earnest entreaty, he begs his God to come to his defense against his foes.

Verse 8. As a needy servant, he is not coming to God in prayer unbidden. God has asked him, as He has asked all of His children, to seek His "face." The "face" of God symbolizes special fellowship and favors with Him. God does not have favorites, but He does have intimates. He has invited each of us to be one of them.

So he says, **When You said, "Seek My face," my heart said to You, "Your face, O Lord, I shall seek."** The Hebrew is unusual here. Is David reminding himself of what God has said, or is God actually speaking and inviting him to seek Him? The former is probably the better translation. It is hard to know, but either way the thought is basically the same. He has accepted God's invitation to pray and begins a fervent prayer.

Verse 9. He prays, **Do not hide Your face from me, do not turn Your servant away in anger; You have been my help; do not abandon me nor forsake me, O God of my salvation!** His phrases in these verses—"I cry"; "answer me"; "do not hide Your face from me"; "do not turn Your servant away in anger"—emphasize the intensity of his supplication and the depth of his need. Every emergency demands urgency. He is in real trouble and asks for immediate assistance, pleading with God to hear him and respond in mercy. He knows that the response he seeks of God, if given, will be an act of grace, not of merit.

Verse 10. He further says, **For my father and my mother have forsaken me, but the LORD will take me up.** He likens himself to the most extreme case of abandonment that an Israelite could imagine: a child being forsaken by his parents. He felt as if he has been discarded by everyone, for even his dearest loved ones have turned against him.

Faith sings in the night; it sees a rainbow in the storm; it sees one like the Son of Man in the furnace of fire. Even though a blanket of loneliness is upon him, he believes that God will care for him more completely than the dearest people he has known in this life. When all others have failed him, he is confident that God will be with him.

Although he has voiced intermittently two ideas in this section of the psalm—the concepts of refuge in God and strength from God—we have especially seen in the first part the internal strengthening that results from fellowship with God. His consolation is this: God will shield him from the outside and strengthen him on the inside when trouble splashes over him. This comfort belongs to every child of God.

HE IS OUR GUIDE (27:11–14)

[11]**Teach me Your way, O LORD,
And lead me in a level path
Because of my foes.
[12]Do not deliver me over to the desire of my adversaries,
For false witnesses have risen against me,
And such as breathe out violence.**

PSALM 27

¹³**I would have despaired unless I had believed that I would see the goodness of the** LORD
In the land of the living.
¹⁴**Wait for the** LORD;
Be strong and let your heart take courage;
Yes, wait for the LORD.

Verse 11. Faith also answers our fears through the guidance God gives. David prays, **Teach me Your way, O** LORD, **and lead me in a level path because of my foes.** As is true of every distressed servant of God, he wants to know God's "way." He desires that God lead him to a "level" place. Walking on a path that winds through hilly terrain or slippery rocks is difficult. The psalmist wants God to place him on a level path that will be easy to follow. He wants the Lord's way to be plainly indicated to him so that it can be easily seen and obeyed. He did not want to be hemmed in by his enemies; he wants to stand on the solid footing of God's path when he faces them.

Verse 12. A special plea is made for his protection: **Do not deliver me over to the desire of my adversaries, for false witnesses have risen against me, and such as breathe out violence.** Should the Lord hand him over to his enemies, he will be destroyed in the blink of an eye. Slanderous men are speaking against him. Violent men are trying to catch him. With every breath, they are seeking his harm. This adversity will be enough to overcome him.

Verse 13. His circumstances are so desperate that were it not for the goodness of the Lord, he would have already given up. He confesses, **I would have despaired unless I had believed that I would see the goodness of the** LORD **in the land of the living.** His hope in the Lord sustains him. He believes that he will see God's kindness. God will come to his rescue, and through His "goodness," will keep him in "the land of the living."

Verse 14. Therefore, the most important resolve he can make is to **wait for the** LORD. He reminds everyone in a situation like his to **be strong and let your heart take courage**. He will wait for the Lord. Through his faith in God, he rebukes his own misgivings and resolves to wait for God's goodness. Someone has said, "Do not let yourself talk to you; you talk to yourself." That is what David is doing. He vows to be strong in heart and not give in to his doubts. He believes that God will extend His grace to him. Between his present conflict and the future deliverances, he chooses to be patient until God sees fit to give him the victory. He recommends this approach to anyone else who is facing any kind of trial.

APPLICATION

God Is Our Answer

This psalm puts before us the question "How does faith in God win over fear?" It says that God is the answer to fear by being our defense, our strength, and our guide.

Often, our Father delivers us *from* the fiery furnace. He does not let the devil's cohorts put us in it. At times we need a shield, a defense. Our enemies can destroy us if they can reach us. When we are in this volatile circumstance, God surrounds us with His almighty arms and prevents enemies from touching us.

At other times, He does not deliver us *from* the fiery furnace, but He delivers us *in* it. God shows us where to stand in the fiery furnace so we will not be burned. Consequently, in the midst of trials, we must be strong in God's strength so that we can withstand their heat. God did not protect David *from* facing Goliath. He sent him down *to* the giant, but He *enabled* David to overcome him. Sometimes God chooses to strengthen us to overcome the trials we face.

God delivered David in both of these ways, and He does both for us. Through these avenues, God is David's answer to fear.

Fear is always close to faith. At one moment we can be exulting in God's care, and the next we can be pleading for God to deliver us from an evil force. We must encourage our faith, not our doubts, and walk by faith, not by fear.

Our Great God

The first verse of this psalm describes how one who trusts in God should view Him.

God is our light. His truth brings us out of the darkness of ignorance and into the glorious sunlight of what is genuine and reliable. Nothing consoles like the truth. He will provide the guidance life requires.

God is our salvation. When we are immersed in awful difficulties that are brought about by life and even by enemies, God delivers us with His strong hand.

God is our defense. God puts His trusting servant on a high rock away from the danger that pursues him. He loves him and protects him as a mother and a father attempt to guard and watch over their children.

Should we not praise God right now for being our light, salvation, and defense?

"In Spite of This I Shall Be Confident"

If people are realistic about life, what will they anticipate? What should they expect to find along the way as they journey through this world?

It is reasonable to believe that life with God is the highest type of life anyone can live. After all, He made and controls this little earth, watches over all the people in it, and keeps running the entire universe. If He is the God the Bible says He is, the God of amazing love and forgiveness, then walking with Him would have to be the greatest of all experiences.

It is realistic to believe that hardships of some kind will come. David, with all his honors, popularity, leadership abilities, and mighty army, had tragedy in his home and enemies around him with which he had to deal. If life is smooth for someone, then that person is living the exception and not the rule.

It is sensible to believe that God cares for His children. If an earthly father and mother would give their lives for their children, how much more would God love, defend, and bless His children? He is infinitely greater than any parent the world has ever known.

It is appropriate to believe that God will see His trusting children through the trials of this life. He will do so according to His own wisdom and His detailed plan for the world. A little boy may not understand why he must go to the dentist, but his parents do. Later, when the child is much older and wiser, he will understand the kind and gracious plan of his parents. We may not always see the design of God's plan, but we can be sure that it is supported by the kind intentions of a gracious Father.

It is, therefore, the way of wisdom to choose to face each trial that comes with an unwavering faith in His kind providence. He is not only a God of love, but He is also a God of truth. He has never betrayed anyone, and He will not in any circumstance turn His back on us. All of His servants have made mistakes—witness the lives of Moses, David, and Peter—but He did not abandon them. Parents are the last ones to give up on their children. We will give up on ourselves before God does.

Faith is not a blind leap into the dark; it must have evidence undergirding it and creating it. However, the evidence is abundant, for we have a Bible full of it. Therefore, the most sensible approach to life with its turns and troubles, its difficulties and downfalls, is the road of faith and trust in a gracious, loving, truthful God. When devastating difficulties come, let us say, "In spite of this I will be confident."

What Shall We Seek?

One index to our character is to ask, "What is our chief ambition? What do we really want? What is our highest goal?"

In verse 4, David said that he had one great aspiration. This one, overarching desire had three attractive aspects to it. As we consider them, let us see if our main yearning matches his.

He wanted to dwell with God. He sought to be where God is, to walk with God, to be His companion, and to be a member of His family. He did not want to be a visitor in God's house; he wanted to "dwell" in it as one who belonged.

He wanted to behold God's beauty. His glory dazzles the child of God. Anyone who has received even a glimpse of God's beauty would like to see more of it. David wanted to behold it and allow it to flood his life with its purity and love. Nothing to him could be greater than to be surrounded by God's magnificence.

He wanted to know God's truth. He aspired to know the thinking of God. He wanted to do things God's way. Reaching this goal would necessitate a learning experience, requiring meditation, studying, thinking, and time.

What is our deepest longing? Has not David expressed it in this one verse?

"In the Day of Trouble"

What does God do for His children when they are in the pit of difficulty? We might compare His response to the response that is made by loving parents when their child is in trouble. Look carefully at verse 5.

He will give us His presence. The parents want to be with their child during his or her time of need. God loves us, and He wants to surround us with His presence.

His love goes out to us. God has not abandoned us, but His heart of love goes out to us and covers us with its warmth and strength.

He will give us deliverance from our trials if that deliverance is best for us and in harmony with His plan. God will not lift a tree out of the way of a car that has gone out of control. That would not be part of His plan. We must live our lives within God's natural laws.

He will give us spiritual victories over our difficulties in accord with His will. Someone has said, "If God answered every prayer that everyone prays, no one would ever die." Even though God does not give us a physical victory from every trial, He can and will give us a spiritual one if we will let Him. Sometimes we may not understand the victory until years later. Like Jacob, we can wrestle with it until a blessing is given. We may not get well, but through the trial we become more like Christ.

We can rejoice over the goodness of the Lord even in a time of difficulty. Regardless of what happens, if we ask Him, God will give us His presence, His love, and spiritual success.

Saying "Thank You" to God

When God goes before us and routes the enemy that is attacking us, how do we say "Thank You"? Verse 6 provides a good, clear answer.

We should offer Him the sacrifices of joy. These sacrifices are not so much physical sacrifices as they are moments of rejoicing before the Lord. God welcomes our joy as any parent would. His heart is gladdened by the joy we experience over the victory He has given.

We should praise Him. We should sing about His wonders and good things. Praise should be the dominate note in our songs. The best way to say "Thank You" is in words—the words of worship. We cannot repay God, but we can tell Him how grateful we are for what He has done for us.

We can live a life of gratitude. If we should use our newfound life to do evil, we have insulted God's gift and grace. We demonstrate gratitude by the way we live out His Word.

When Praying for Help

When trouble comes and you ask God to come to your aid, what should be your next step? In the last part of this psalm (vv. 12, 13), the writer is in the throes of trouble and recommends to us what to do after we have asked for help.

Believe that you will see the goodness of the Lord in the land of the living. After you have prayed, it is time to trust in the goodness of God. You will see it at the appropriate time. Just tell yourself, "I will see the faithfulness of God in the time of His choosing.

Wait on the Lord. Waiting is hard, but necessary. God never gets in a hurry, but He is never late. You cannot throw an egg over in the barnyard and expect it to crow tomorrow. God will be faithful, but He is on a schedule that is in accord with His will and in our best interest.

Be strong in His truth. Talk to your heart and encourage it to be valiant in its stand on God's truth. Much of life is spent standing on the promises of God. The best plea anyone can make is to echo the promises God has made. He will not fail us; He will not forget what He has said to us.

Often God does not respond to our prayers immediately after we have prayed. Some of our prayers will be answered on earth after we are in heaven. It is our duty and privilege to pray; then we are to see to it that we trust in God's faithfulness, wait on Him, and remain strong in His truth.

PSALM 27

Looking Up from the Pit

In verses 7 through 10 we see a godly man praying from the pit of despair. If you have not been in such a swamp, you probably will be in one at some time in the future. The sky will be black, and you will be encircled by the angry clouds of tragedy. How do you pray at such a time?

Seek God's face. Pray for His fellowship and favor. In your time of trouble you will want to be close to God. Nothing will take His place. A clap of thunder will drive us to the safe, secure place of our Father's side.

Express your feelings to God. Tell Him how you feel. An emergency is not a time for pious platitudes. God will welcome your deep feelings, even your broken sentences of distress. You can be assured that He wants His children to bring their fears and tears to Him. What parent would not!

Abandon yourself to God. Put yourself in God's hands. Let Him have total charge of the outcome of the situation. He expects us to use our heads and be guided by His words, but we must let Him be in charge of the results.

Plead the promises of God. Probably the best prayer to pray in this situation is a prayer that echoes the promises God has made. The writer said, "You have told us to seek Your face, and I am doing it! I want to be with You."

We cannot impress God with our words, but we do touch His heart by our sincere wishes and worship. A boy in the backyard, playing intently in the sandbox, loves his mother but may not be thinking of his tremendous need for her. However, if he falls and cuts a knee, he will run to his mother for encouragement. The mother is not insulted by his coming in this way—she is complimented and opens her arms and suffers with him. On a far higher level, you can be confident that God will open His arms of protection and love and receive His trusting child during the dark night of trouble.

One mother was asked, "Which of your children do you love the best?" She answered, "The one who is sick until he or she gets well, and the one who's away until he or she gets back." God has a special love for His child who is in the pit of despair. When in the pit, look up in prayer!

PSALM 28

PRAYING IN A CRISIS

The Superscription: A Psalm of David. Once again the title only says **of** ["by," "for," or "to"] **David** (לְדָוִד, *lᵉdawid*), although the NASB adds **a Psalm**. We do not know when the psalm was written or the circumstances in which it was written. We will assume this statement of authorship can be trusted.

This psalm is properly called a lament psalm. The writer is praying to God out of great distress. In typical lament format, the psalm contains an invocation, a plea for help, a complaint, a petition that the wicked receive their due, a hymn of praise, and an expression of confidence in God's response. It does not contain a confession of sin.

Of the seven typical traits usually found in the lament psalm, confession of sin is the only one that this psalm does not contain. We do not expect to find all seven elements in every lament psalm. These types of psalms vary in their structure. Their chief characteristic is that they are prayers rising up from souls in severe pain who are asking God to do something about their situations. They seek divine intervention in crises.

We do not know the exact nature of the trouble that prompted this prayer. The text indicates that the writer is especially disturbed by the wickedness around him. He does not want to be connected with these evil men in any way. He certainly does not want to be a part of their judgment.

PSALM 28

"TO YOU, O LORD, I CALL" (28:1, 2)

¹To You, O Lord, I call;
My rock, do not be deaf to me,
For if You are silent to me,
I will become like those who go down to the pit.
²Hear the voice of my supplications when I cry to You for help,
When I lift up my hands toward Your holy sanctuary.

Verse 1. The psalm begins with an emphatic declaration concerning the intent of the prayer: **To You, O Lord, I call**. The writer is calling to God from his dungeon of despair. He is asking for His hand of mercy to be placed upon his tragic circumstance.

Desperate, he goes to the only One who can assist him, his God. He pleads, **My rock, do not be deaf to me**. God is his "rock," a metaphor that stands for power, durability, and firmness. The One to whom he prays is his invincible security.

He beseeches God to give him an immediate response. Prayers had ascended from him in the past, but it is as if God has been deaf to him. The Hebrew literally says, "Do not be silent or deaf from me." In other words, "Do not turn away from me like someone who cannot hear." He asks God to break His silence and answer him.

He says, **For if You are silent to me, I will become like those who go down to the pit.** He is aware that if God does not hear him, he will go down to the grave. He uses a word that is translated "the pit" (בּוֹר, *bor*) in the NASB, a word that means a "hole" or "cistern." It is used here as a figurative reference to death or Sheol. Earnestness and intensity characterize his plea. He is sure that without God he will die! He sees himself as solely dependent upon God.

Verse 2. With great pathos, he prays, **Hear the voice of my supplications when I cry to You for help**. His word "supplications" (תַּחֲנוּן, *thach^{a}nun*) is a word that includes within it the idea of crying for mercy. The word "cry" (שׁוּע, *shawa'*) is a stronger word than the word "call" (קָרָא, *qara'*) in verse 1. He is making an urgent "cry" for merciful assistance.

The parallel thought to the previous line is **when I lift up my hands toward Your holy sanctuary.** Is He referring to heaven, the place of God's throne, or the Most Holy Place of the tabernacle? Perhaps the latter. The Most Holy Place was that part of the tent closely associated with the presence of God. In it stood the ark of the covenant, protected symbolically by the cherubim. If the writer is referring to heaven, his thought remains essentially the same. He automatically turns toward the dwelling place of God and prays with uplifted hands.

The posture of lifting up the "hands" in prayer has several connotations. Here it symbolizes the lifting up of the heart in earnest entreaty (see Lam. 3:41), implying that the life behind the hands requires immediate attention from God. In Psalm 63:4 the "hands" indicate a reaching up for God and His fellowship. In Exodus 17:9–13, they express the interceding nature of Moses' prayer for the army that was fighting in the valley below. The symbolism was that the power for victory came from God. In 1 Timothy 2:8, they convey innocence and purity (see 1 Kings 8:22, 54; Lam. 2:19). The raising of hands toward heaven in this psalm portrays the action of calling upon God for help.

An invocation is a natural way to begin a supplication that asks God to take care of His own.

"DO NOT PLACE ME WITH THE WICKED" (28:3–5)

> ³**Do not drag me away with the wicked**
> **And with those who work iniquity,**
> **Who speak peace with their neighbors,**
> **While evil is in their hearts.**
> ⁴**Requite them according to their work and according to the evil of their practices;**
> **Requite them according to the deeds of their hands;**
> **Repay them their recompense.**
> ⁵**Because they do not regard the works of the LORD**
> **Nor the deeds of His hands,**
> **He will tear them down and not build them up.**

Verse 3. His prayer to God has at the center of it the wicked people that he sees around him. He asks, **Do not drag me away with the wicked and with those who work iniquity.** He does not want to be linked with them, to receive what they will justly receive, or to be a part of the disgrace they had earned. He envisions the wicked in the near future being carried away for judgment. He believes that he may be grouped with these wicked people somehow, and he cannot bear that thought. The figure he uses suggests the picture of prisoners being "dragged away" (מָשַׁךְ, *mashak*) to punishment. When the day of reckoning comes, he wants to be far removed from them.

He says the evil ones are those **who speak peace with their neighbors, while evil is in their hearts.** The KJV has the word "mischief" instead of "evil." W. T. Purkiser wrote,

> The term "mischief" was a much stronger word in 1611 when the KJV was translated. It is far too weak now to describe the unmitigated *evil* intended by the original Hebrew. With sense of justice outraged, the Psalmist prays that those wicked persons may be given in judicial sentence what their works deserve.[1] (Emphasis added.)

These people are hypocritical. Their lips speak good things, but "evil," in its worst form, is in their hearts. They smile and express good will with their words while inwardly they plan the destruction of those to whom they speak.

Verse 4. He asks God to judge them, to give them a sentence that is in harmony with their deeds. He says, **Requite them according to their work and according to the evil of their practices.** He wants judgment to come to them in proportion to the evil that they commit. His concern for retribution does not arise from a sinister sense of pleasure in seeing someone "get what he deserves." His prayer is the protest of a healthy conscience to a holy God. He asks God to repay **them according to the deeds**

---

[1] W. T. Purkiser, "Psalms," in *Beacon Bible Commentary*, vol. 3, *Job Through Song of Solomon*, ed. A. F. Harper, W. M. Greathouse, Ralph Earle, and W. T. Purkiser (Kansas City, Mo.: Beacon Hill Press, 1967), 207.

of their hands and to give them the **recompense** that is appropriate for them. The wicked are given opportunities to do right. Instead of accepting that responsibility, they disregard the opportunities and disdain them. They laugh in the face of privilege, blatantly choosing evil instead of good.

Verse 5. He asks God to judge them **because they do not regard the works of the Lord nor the deeds of His hands.** They reject and deny the works or creation of the Lord and "the deeds" or providential workings of His hands. He says that God will **tear them down** [or overthrow them] **and not build them up.** They despise the Lord, ignore His works, and shun His love. They live for themselves and for their own selfish pursuits. He knows that God must call the wicked into account, for in their evil activities they work against God and His purposes.

Perhaps the wicked are near David in some way, and he prays that he may be distinguished from them. He does not want to be a part of their works, and he definitely does not want to be a part of the judgment coming to them. His prayer is that God's righteous judgment may fall on the wickedness in the world and those who are synonymous with it.

God has asked His children to come to Him with their requests or petitions. A truth that we see frequently in the Psalms is that prayer is talking over with God what one thinks is important or what one sees as crucial to life. Such a discussion often focuses on the devil's army and what it is doing to God's work and world.

"BLESSED BE THE LORD" (28:6–8)

⁶**Blessed be the Lord,**
Because He has heard the voice of my supplication.
⁷**The Lord is my strength and my shield;**
My heart trusts in Him, and I am helped;
Therefore my heart exults,
And with my song I shall thank Him.
⁸**The Lord is their strength,**
And He is a saving defense to His anointed.

Verse 6. He further prays, **Blessed be the LORD, because He has heard the voice of my supplication.** These words may have been added sometime later after the writing of the first part of the psalm, or it could be that they are words of thanksgiving for what the writer knew that God would do. The psalmist may have been thanking God in advance for His response. Maybe his words just constitute a prayer of thanksgiving for what God has done in the past.

No longer does he feel threatened or hopeless. He is overjoyed and jubilant. He knows his confidence in God is properly placed, and he will not be brought to shame. He is resting in God's strength and in a victory that has been or will be provided.

"Blessed" (בָּרַךְ, *barak*) carries the meaning of "glory, praise, and adoration of." As used here, the word is the beginning of a brief doxology, a bursting out in praise of God.

Verse 7. He happily says, **The LORD is my strength and my shield.** He describes God as offense and defense, as his "strength" and "shield," his leader and protector. God has guarded him inside and out, placing a wall around him and putting spiritual fortitude within him. He says, **My heart trusts in Him, and I am helped.** He has put his faith in God, and God has not disappointed him. Therefore, God has filled his heart with joy. He says, **Therefore my heart exults, and with my song I shall thank Him.** Growing out of his joy will be songs of praises to God. Experience mandates that God must be put at the center of his singing.

Verse 8. Further, he prays, **The LORD is their strength, and He is a saving defense to His anointed.** Broadening his praise, he asserts that God is the "strength" of those who trust Him. He would be the stronghold of salvation to His "anointed" (מָשִׁיחַ, *mashiach*), the king. This reference to the king is not necessarily a prophetic reference to King Jesus. It is to the earthly king who has been chosen by God and, consequently, is protected by God.

The writer has reason to thank God, and so do we. Every prayer should include jubilant thanksgiving.

"SAVE YOUR PEOPLE" (28:9)

⁹Save Your people and bless Your inheritance;
Be their shepherd also, and carry them forever.

Verse 9. In harmony with what any righteous king should do, this worshiper prays earnestly for his nation. He asks, **Save Your people and bless Your inheritance.** He petitions God to deliver them from any kind of oppression or disaster and to preserve His "inheritance." He regards Israel—and so did God—as a cherished heritage.

God's possession requires God's watch-care, so the writer prays for it: **Be their shepherd also, and carry them forever.** David does not see himself as the supreme king; he sees himself as a representative of God, the true Sovereign. The word for "carry" (נָשָׂא, naśa') means literally to "bear up," as if to take a child in His arms and carry it. He is praying that God may care for his nation as a father cares for his child.

God is asked to "save," "bless," "shepherd," and "carry" Israel. They need deliverance from oppression (saving), prosperity (blessing), guidance and watchful care (shepherding), and sustenance (carrying). In one sentence, he includes all of the major needs of his nation.

A righteous heart will pray for others as this writer does.

APPLICATION

How Does One Pray?

In this psalm David used different types of prayer as he implored God to help him.

Using this psalm as an outline, how should we pray? David addressed God by invoking His blessings upon his life and expressed to God specifically what he wanted God to do for him. He gave thanks to God for all that He had done for His people in the past and asked God to meet his needs and the needs of those around him.

This prayer of David was prayed before Jesus came into the

world. As practical as the form is, from the perspective of the New Testament, we know that the prayer would be incomplete for us. In His model prayer, Jesus taught us to ask God to forgive our sins (Mt. 6:12). He also taught us to pray in His name or by His authority (Jn. 16:23). Other passages of the New Testament teach us to give thanks for the vicarious sacrifice of Jesus. When these items are added to the outline we have seen in this psalm, a helpful pattern for prayer develops that the Christian can follow.

The Types of Prayer

Prayer can be made in many different forms and types. Several kinds of prayer are mentioned in this psalm.

First, we see an invocational prayer, an invoking of God's assistance, one of the most natural ways to begin a prayer.

Next, David petitioned God. He articulated what he believed he must have from God. This is the "asking part" of prayer, the time when the petitioner gets down to specifics.

A big portion of prayer should be thanksgiving for what God has done. We see this truth illustrated by the latter part of the psalm.

Then, the psalm closed with intercession, with David's prayer for others. Any righteous person wants to bring others before God in prayer.

All of these types of prayer are mentioned in the New Testament and are thus enjoined upon Christians. With these different types in mind, it is easy for us to "pray without ceasing" (1 Thess. 5:17).

Prayer: Approaching Our Father

To David, prayer was a natural, daily activity, not an uncomfortable conversation with a God whom he did not know. Part of fellowship with God is communication with Him. It would be odd indeed if two friends could not talk to each other. How sad it is when a child is a stranger to his father! Prayer is nothing more than children conversing with or petitioning their Father.

Because of who God is and what He has done, we can approach Him with invocation, supplication, thanksgiving, and intercession as David did.

Praying in a Crisis

How does David pray when he is in the throes of difficulty?

He prays with faith. There seems to be no question about his belief in God. He has not heard from God in a while, but he still believes that God is good and will care for him. He lets God know what he is doing: "I am calling upon You."

He prays with perseverance. Apparently, his prayers had not been heard, for heaven had been silent. At least, his specific petition had not been answered. However, he does not stop praying. There is a continuance about his praying.

He prays with intensity. One sees a fervency to his praying. He pleads, cries, and appeals to God with uplifted hands. God is his only hope, and he brings his need before Him in frank petition.

These characteristics seen in David should be traits in all of God's sincere people. Sometimes God answers our specific requests immediately; sometimes He delays His answer for our good; sometimes He says no to our requests because saying yes would hurt us or affect His great plan.

Regardless of His answer to our specific requests, He always responds to our praying with love, grace, and strength. In one sense, we can say that something is going to happen as a result of our praying that would not have happened had we not prayed.

The Order of Blessing

God has an order to all things. With Him, nothing just happens. He either makes it happen according His design, or He permits it to happen according to the devil's design.

What is His order for righteousness and righteous living?

First, comes trust. We put our faith in God. He gives us the evidence or the basis for faith, and we accept it and trust in Him. His first goal for each of us is to bring us to trust in Him. He works toward this relationship continually.

Next comes God's help. He comes to the aid of those who trust

Him in a special way. He regards the prayers of the wicked as an abomination. They are not His children, and they are not His responsibility.

Then comes joy. We exult in God. The hand of God in our lives brings joy. Nothing brings peace and happiness like knowing that we are in His fellowship and that He is watching over us.

Last comes praise. Those who have been redeemed by the Lord break forth in praise. Thanksgiving is the natural result of salvation. The person who knows God and has been blessed of God finds it easy to worship Him.

Consider carefully the order: trust, help, joy, and praise. Sometimes out of His gracious heart God steps in and rescues those who have become careless and cold. Sometimes He shows His love in various ways for those who have rebelled against Him to get their attention and win their hearts back to Him. These times are exceptions that He chooses in His infinite wisdom, but the normal order of the Christian's walk is asking, receiving, exulting, and praising.

Believing in God

When one realizes what God actually means to the believer, he wonders how anyone could ever live without Him.

He is our sustenance. In other words, He is our life. In Him, we not only live, breathe, and have our being; but also in Him, we have our spiritual life—our salvation and spiritual growth. Without Him, we would be living dead people—alive physically but dead in trespasses and sins. With Him, we are dead living people—dead to sin and evil but alive to God and His provisions.

He is our strength. He sustains us daily. He provides the internal strength we need to meet the challenges that confront us. How do we do what we do? The answer is—God!

He is our security. He protects us when we are not even aware of it. His protection is more spiritual than physical; but behind the unknown, He shields us from physical dangers in ways beyond our understanding. The psalms teach us to believe that God protects us when we are doing His will.

The totality of life can be covered with three words: "sustenance," "strength," and "security." What else is there? If God provides for us in these ways, we can trust Him to provide for us on a much higher level in eternity. If He does it in life, will He not do it in the great beyond? With God, we have everything; without Him, we have nothing.

Wickedness Pictured

This psalm has at its center the wicked people who are near the writer. Perhaps they are the reason for his fervent request at the beginning of the psalm. They may have been threatening his life or planning some other scheme against him.

Consider his description of them.

They are evil. Their lives are devoted to wickedness rather than righteousness. They have chosen a way of destruction rather than a way of peace.

They are hypocritical. They are two-faced, as we say. In conversation they say one thing to their neighbors, and in their hearts they aspire to wickedness. Their lips and hearts are going in different directions.

They are irreverent. They do not acknowledge God, observe His works, or give thanks for His blessings. They have shunned His love and thus live as though God is not.

These characteristics serve as signposts that indicate the nature of a person. Do we love evil more than good? Are we hypocritical in our thinking? Do we ignore God?

The Judgment of Sin

The one who casts his lot with sin will find himself walking down a difficult road, for the way of the transgressor is hard (Prov. 13:15). Life will be a bed of rocks for him—and judgment and eternity will be worse!

David pleads with God that he not be put in with the sinners around him. He does not want to be one of them, and he certainly does not want to receive their punishment.

It would be good if all sane and sensible people would ask, "How will the sinner be judged?"

He is judged by his sins. His sins make life difficult for him.

Our sins find us out in life as well as in eternity (Num. 32:23). Sin never helps or heals; it always hurts. "Can a man take fire into his bosom and his clothes not be burned?" (Prov. 6:27).

He is judged for his sins. Indeed, at the end of the way, he will be judged for his sins. He will stand before the judgment seat of Christ and receive for what he has done in his body (2 Cor. 5:10). Every sinner is on a collision course with the God of righteousness.

He is judged with his sins. There will come a time when he becomes one with his sins. Consequently, he will receive the punishment that his sins do. Before that time, he will experience a time of grace, when he can repent. However, if repentance is not manifested, the day will come when the sinner and his sin will merge.

This thought helps us to understand the imprecatory psalms that call down curses upon the ungodly. These psalms picture the sinner and his sin as united into one force that stands opposed to God. A day of accounting always comes for those who devote themselves to sin and do not turn to God.

Two great forces exist in the world: the force of righteousness and the force of sin. We must choose the side with which we will align ourselves. This decision affects the kind of lives we live and the nature of the judgment that will be given at the end. David made his choice. Have we made ours?

The Bottom Line of Concern

Let us ask, "What is the basic help that we must have?"

We need His deliverance. We require saving from our sin, ourselves, and this world. In spite of our efforts, we cannot rescue ourselves.

We need prosperity. We need the spiritual prosperity that only God can give. Growth in spirituality originates with God.

We need shepherding. We cannot lead ourselves; we require an almighty hand to direct us. On our own, we will wind up lost or in a ditch.

We need carrying. Sometimes God just has to reach down, pick us up, and carry us as a father does his child.

God was asked to "save," "bless," "shepherd," and "carry

Israel." In these words, we see a clear depiction of what we need individually as well as what we need as a nation. We are totally dependent upon God. The question is "Do we see what God means to us?"

The Righteous and the Wicked

Here is an important relationship question: What kind of association will I have with wickedness and the wicked? Every person confronts this question. This writer had made his decision about it.

We may be around the wicked, but we cannot be a part of them. The flow of life may throw us near them, but we must not become one of them. Since our aspirations and love are different from theirs, we are not one of them and they are not like us.

We acknowledge the wickedness of sin and have judged it in our hearts. Our view of sin has been to renounce it and to live in a relationship with the Lord. His mind has become ours. We hate what He hates. A judgment awaits all who give themselves to sin, and we do not want to be a part of it.

We will gladly use our abilities to help anyone who is willing to leave sin and enter the proper relationship with God. Our task could be labeled "Mission Rescue." We will be dedicated to pointing out the horror of evil, and we will continually search for ways of delivering the perishing.

There is an unfairness to life. Poor people are often mistreated. When such happens, we are moved deeply about it. There is also a justice to life. The righteous recognize it, approve of it, and shun it. The wicked inevitably will be brought into judgment. Because of the nature of God, this judgment of sin has to be.

Nevertheless

In the garden Jesus said, "Nevertheless, not what I will, but what You will" (Mk. 14:36; NKJV). You might say that the salvation of the world hinged on the word "nevertheless." Had Jesus not uttered it, the cross would not have been a reality. He knew that many would reject the way of salvation that He was securing by His sacrificial death, but He chose to die for us anyway.

He knew that the way of the cross was going to be painful and the worst experience imaginable, but He chose that route anyway. He knew that if He chose the will of God, His wishes could not be granted; but He elected to do the will of God anyway.

There is a "nevertheless" for each of us as is indicated by this psalm. Our "nevertheless" will not be as clear and dramatic as was our Savior's; however, it still exists. Let us consider our own personal "nevertheless" from the viewpoint of the resolves that a righteous person must make. At some time along the way, he or she must say:

> God cannot say yes to all my prayers—nevertheless, I will continue to pray and trust Him for the proper answers to my prayers.

> Doing God's will may not always be easy—nevertheless, I will choose to do it.

> I may not always see God's hand at work in my life—nevertheless, I will continue to trust Him to provide for me as He sees fit.

> I may not be applauded and sometimes may be hated for doing God's will—nevertheless, I will choose to do it.

> Doing the will of God may be very expensive in terms of likes and dislikes that must be given up—nevertheless, I will choose to do it.

As we view the cross from the vantage point of our salvation, we can easily see that God's will was best and had a lofty purpose, a holy goal that could not be achieved any other way. When we are in the crucible of suffering, we may not see how doing His will is helping us or is even best for us; however, years from now, as we look back on a life lived in the will of God, we will see that doing His will was the best choice.

Living in Community

The community concept of living is evident in many of the psalms. The Israelite knew full well that no one lives alone. God wants a village. This psalm has three traces of how the ancient believer in God viewed himself in connection with others.

There was a dependent fellowship. The Israelite saw himself in fellowship with God. He looked to God as his shield, defense, strength, deliverer; and he even saw himself at times being carried by Him. He saw his walk with God as the highest life he could attain.

There was an interdependent fellowship. The Israelite saw himself as part of a family, a clan, a tribe, and a nation. He had a responsibility toward the community, and each member of the community had a responsibility toward him. Together, they reared their children, cared for their needs, buried their dead, and married their young.

There was a despised fellowship. The evil man did not belong to their community. He was an outcast, an unwelcome guest. As David showed, he did not want to walk with him, listen to him, or work with him. He certainly did not want the judgment that was coming to him. He even prayed that the evil man be removed from their midst.

God did not create us to live alone. Some decisions and some parts of our journey have a loneliness to them; but, in the main, God wants us to live in a family and as part of a spiritual body. This is "the belonging" that God intended in the families and communities of the Israelite nation.

PSALM 29
GOD AND THE STORM

The Superscription: A Psalm of David. The title simply refers to this composition as **a Psalm** [מִזְמוֹר, *mizmor*] **of** ["by," "for," or "to"] **David** (לְדָוִד, *ledawid*). We do not know when or where it was written.

A beautiful hymn of praise, this nature psalm has as its central theme the greatness and grandeur of God that is being displayed in a rainstorm. Adoration is given to God because His magnificent, hidden power is reflected in a tempest of nature.

The LXX adds a note at the end of the superscription reading "final day of [Feast of] Tabernacles" (Gk.: ἐξοδίου σκηνῆς, *exodiou skenēs*). The indication apparently means that this psalm was used by the Hebrews on the last day of the Feast of Tabernacles, a major feast in the fall that came at the end of the dry season. Perhaps the psalm reminded them that a storm—like the one it pictures—would bring needed rain and relief from the dry spell they had been experiencing. To them, a thunderstorm was the herald of God's tender care for another season.

Some scholars have argued that this psalm is an adaptation of a Canaanite hymn that was in use at the time of its writing; however, no hymn of this kind has been found. Determining the background of a psalm is a difficult, if not an impossible, task. It could be that the writer used existing imagery and language and adapted it to lead the reader to see Yahweh as the true and living God, the only Ruler over nature and mankind. The fact that these psalms were inspired of God through the Holy Spirit means that the Holy Spirit used the thoughts and wording that would convey the message that He wanted taught.

The body of the psalm is a description of a storm that is described as having originated over the Mediterranean Sea in the north, coming inland to the Lebanon mountain range, and then sweeping southward across Palestine. It elicited the awe of the writer, not as a phenomenon of the physical world, but as a chorus of praise, a sermon in song, to the God who made it. The psalm has been appropriately called "The Song of a Thunderstorm" because of the sevenfold reference to the voice of God.[1]

In this hymn of praise, we see the spiritual view we should have of the marvels of nature around us. God's name (יהוה, YHWH) is used eighteen times in these eleven verses. David and the Israelites show us how to see God in the rain, the rivers, the rushing winds, and even in trembling rocks. A. F. Kirkpatrick has observed:

> The devout Israelite's view of Nature was profoundly religious. He did not contemplate its wonder and beauty and variety simply for their own sake. All spoke to him of God's power and glory and beneficence, or supplied him with emblems and figures for the delineation of God's attributes and working. Thus the thunder was to him the Voice of God, and all the terrible phenomena of the storm were an expression of the majesty of the Eternal Sovereign of the Universe.[2]

The major purpose of the psalm is to proclaim God's supremacy in the heavens and the earth. All things, even the minute raindrop and the snowflake, are under His command.

---

[1] Leslie S. M'Caw, "The Psalms," *The New Bible Commentary*, ed. Francis Davidson (Grand Rapids, Mich.: Wm. B. Eerdmans Publishing Co., 1956), 432.

[2] A. F. Kirkpatrick, *The Book of Psalms*, The Cambridge Bible for Schools and Colleges (Cambridge: University Press, 1901), 1:47.

PSALM 29

"GIVE GOD GLORY" (29:1, 2)

¹**Ascribe to the Lord, O sons of the mighty,
Ascribe to the Lord glory and strength.
²Ascribe to the Lord the glory due to His name;
Worship the Lord in holy array.**

Verse 1. The psalm begins with an invitation to worship the true God of the universe because of the glory that belongs to Him: **Ascribe to the Lord, O sons of the mighty, ascribe to the Lord glory and strength.**

Who are the "sons of the mighty" (בְּנֵי אֵלִים, *bᵉney 'elim*)? Are they holy angels before the throne of God? Is this designation intended as a figurative reference to the noblemen of the earth? A similar call to worship God is used in Psalm 96:7 as humanity at large is urged to praise Him. However, this ascription has a uniqueness about it. The word translated "mighty" can also be translated "God." It is a plural, masculine noun. If the phrase should be translated "sons of God," then the heavenly host must be intended. A similar phrase in other passages denotes heavenly beings or angels (Gen. 6:2; Job 1:6; 2:1; 38:7; Ps. 82:6; 89:6). Perhaps this is a call for heaven and earth to join together in giving praise to God.

Verse 2. The appeal continues, **Ascribe to the Lord the glory due to His name; worship the Lord in holy array.** Three times, this prelude employs the word "ascribe," the imperative form of יָהַב (*yahab*), meaning "give," or "attribute."

The radiance that is to be given to God is "glory" that already belongs to Him—not anything that we can add to Him. Neither we nor angels can contribute to God any splendor that He does not already possess; we can only recognize who He is and tell Him and others what we have seen. The writer urges the "sons of God" to see and proclaim His magnificence and power.

The ones addressed are to behold how high and lifted up the Lord is and extol Him. God has defended Israel and has been the nation's strength. Thus "the glory [of] His name" has been seen in His works and His words in behalf of Israel. The same God who has been Israel's defense is broadcasting His powerful hand and supreme majesty in the violent storm. The glory that goes with His "name" is to be voiced in song or in words of praise.

While we may be in doubt about who these "mighty" ones are, we know what they are to do. They are to acknowledge God's attributes, give Him the praise that is due His name, and worship Him in holy array or attire.

The phrase regarding their coming to worship Him is usually translated "in holy attire" (בְּהַדְרַת־קֹדֶשׁ, *bᵉhadrath qodesh*), although the NIV translated it "in the splendor of his holiness." There is no "his" in the Hebrew, and the phrase likely describes the worshipers and not God.

The "mighty" ones are to worship and adore God because of who He is. They are to come before Him dressed for the awesome occasion, but their attire is not the external clothing of extravagance and ornamentation. Charm, costly robes, a fair complexion, and gleaming jewels are not required. This service demands the beautiful apparel of holiness.

The worship service that is being called together is to feature praise to God for His magnificent greatness, a dazzling majesty that was displayed in the raging winds. Thus these words point us beyond God's strength to His great splendor. He is worthy of all the praise that humans or angels can give Him. All honor belongs to His name. Everyone on earth and in heaven should observe God for who He is and give Him the worship that He alone should receive.

GOD IN THE STORM
(29:3–9)

> ³The voice of the LORD is upon the waters;
> The God of glory thunders,
> The LORD is over many waters.
> ⁴The voice of the LORD is powerful,
> The voice of the LORD is majestic.
> ⁵The voice of the LORD breaks the cedars;
> Yes, the LORD breaks in pieces the cedars of Lebanon.

⁶He makes Lebanon skip like a calf,
And Sirion like a young wild ox.
⁷The voice of the LORD hews out flames of fire.
⁸The voice of the LORD shakes the wilderness;
The LORD shakes the wilderness of Kadesh.
⁹The voice of the LORD makes the deer to calve
And strips the forests bare;
And in His temple everything says, "Glory!"

Verse 3. For those who have an eye to see it, the wonder of God can be seen all around us: in the darkened sky, the sea, the towering mountains, and even the placid meadows. In this case, the psalmist sees God's unmatched power in the thunder, lightning, and rain that were racing across the landscape.

The description of the violent weather is the heart of the psalm; it is one of the most sublime pictures of a thunderstorm found anywhere in the Scriptures. In verses 3 and 4, the storm is approaching. In verses 5 through 7, the storm descends in its fury. In verses 8 and 9, it trails away in the distance, leaving with us its profound impressions about God.

The writer sees the beginning of the tumult: **The voice of the LORD is upon the waters; the God of glory thunders, the LORD is over many waters.** The storm begins over (what must have been) the western Mediterranean Sea with claps of thunder. From a distance, one can see the building of the clouds. Although the sea is strong and destructive, the psalmist knows that God is stronger than the sea. The peals of the thunder are "upon" the sea or "over" it, illustrating to David the sovereignty of God. He is "over" all things, even the world of nature.

Verse 4. The sound of thunder echoes throughout the sky: **The voice of the LORD is powerful, the voice of the LORD is majestic.** The thunder figuratively depicts the voice of God and is referred to seven times as such (vv. 3, 4, 5, 7–9) in connection with the storm. His voice is said to be "upon the waters" (v. 3), "powerful" (v. 4), and "majestic" (v. 4). It "breaks the cedars" (v. 5), "hews out flames of fire" (v. 7), "shakes the wilderness" (v. 8), "makes the deer to calve" (v. 9), and "strips the forests bare" (v. 9). God was providentially behind the peals as their

Creator and Sustainer. The writer called them God's voice.

Verse 5. The swirling winds and rain begin to move across the land: **The voice of the LORD breaks the cedars; yes, the LORD breaks in pieces the cedars of Lebanon.** "The voice of the LORD" becomes the Lord Himself, acting through the various characteristics of the storm. These stormy winds break the "cedars of Lebanon," the strongest and most stately trees of that region.

Verse 6. The land shakes and trembles under the spell of nature's rage: **He makes Lebanon skip like a calf, and Sirion like a young wild ox.** The mountain range of Lebanon, the prime range of Syria, is figuratively pictured as skipping like a calf frolicking in the field. Perhaps the trees are swaying so that it appears that the whole range is trembling. Sirion, an older name for Mount Hermon in northern Palestine, shakes during the violence like a wild ox leaping about.

These figures mean that the towering mountains, rising up ten thousand feet above sea level, are pummeled by the winds and rain. Since Lebanon was in the north of Palestine and the movement of the storm is apparently toward the south, the entire length of Palestine seems to be swept over by water, wind, and fury.

Verse 7. Having told of the mighty force crossing the land, the writer now describes the tumult in the sky: **The voice of the LORD hews out flames of fire.** Streaks of lightning light up the sky. These fireworks of nature are brought about by "the voice of the LORD."

Verse 8. The trees wave back and forth and break in the midst of the turbulence: **The voice of the LORD shakes the wilderness; the LORD shakes the wilderness of Kadesh.** Wooded areas are blown about, as if trembling before nature. "The wilderness of Kadesh" is mentioned. Perhaps this is ancient Kadesh, located in the northern part of Palestine between Aleppo in the north and Damascus in the south. If this is not the case, then it could mean Kadesh Barnea in the southern extremity of Canaan. It may be that a figurative reference is being given by this term to any wilderness-like region whose trees would be tortured by the storm. Kadesh, whether actual or figurative, was reeling from the storm. Its trees were beaten violently by the winds.

Verse 9. The voice of the LORD makes the deer to calve. Some translations (such as the NRSV and NIV) render this phrase "causes the oaks to whirl." The word of the text is the word for "deer" or "does" (אַיָּלוֹת, *'ayyaloth*). For the phrase to be translated with "oaks," the text has to be emended and the word "oaks" put in the place of "deer." The translations that have done so have argued that the word "deer" does not fit the context and thus should be changed to "oaks." Other scholars working from the MT contend that fear generated by the storm caused the deer to give birth to their young prematurely.

And strips the forests bare. Nature's fury is unleased on the mountains—and the trees, leaves, branches, and dead bark are stripped away by the furious wind. All things, especially the trees, feel the devastating lashes of the gales.

As the writer turns toward heaven in his thoughts, he says, **And in His temple everything says, "Glory!"** In heaven, observing the raging wind and rain, the angelic beings say with reverential awe, "Glory!" The manifestations of the powerful winds and pouring water fill them with the wonder and greatness of God's almighty power. They express their worship of God in one great, tremendously important, summary word: "Glory!"

In the storm, the writer sees the greatness of God. He notices that God is stronger than the crash of the thunderbolt, the fire of the lightning, and the shaking power of the wind. Our Lord is bigger than the mountains, the seas, and the heavens. He commands the floods, the trees, and the raging rivers. The Creator is above all that He has created.

GOD, THE GREAT KING
(29:10, 11)

[10]The LORD sat as King at the flood;
Yes, the LORD sits as King forever.
[11]The LORD will give strength to His people;
The LORD will bless His people with peace.

This violent, raging event conveys God's goodness to the

writer. The psalm ends with a reminder of what this tempest should say to God's people.

Verse 10. The Lord of heaven is in control of the flood and is over all of nature. **The LORD sat as King at the flood; yes, the LORD sits as King forever.** He rules throughout the earth and history. The flood mentioned is the great flood of Noah's day (see Gen. 6—9). The word for "flood" (מַבּוּל, *mabbul*) is used only one other place in the Old Testament: in Genesis concerning the judgment flood that came. God's decision to bring the great flood reflects His transcendence and rulership of the whole earth.

This aspect of God's world that the penman has just seen reminds him of the kingship of God, that He rules over all people and is the One to whom all will give an account. In the great flood, He destroyed the wicked and saved the righteous; in the angry blast at hand, He blesses His people according to His will.

Verse 11. The final thought that grows out of what has crossed the land is a word of consolation: **The LORD will give strength to His people.** Nature has taught the viewer to sing about God's goodness. A destructive wind of this kind may strike terror in the hearts of God's people; but according to the Holy Spirit, it should instill faith in us, not fear. The power seen in the thunderbolt, the wind, and the flashes of lightning are just representations of God's power—a power that He uses for (not against) His people.

The LORD will bless His people with peace. He loves His people and bestows "peace" (שָׁלוֹם, *shalom*) upon them. The word "peace" connotes completeness and wholeness. Windswept plains and flooded regions may cause us to think of God as angry and violent, harsh and forbidding. He is righteous to be sure and never excuses sin, but central to His being is lovingkindness. The billowy blast is to remind us of the strength that He wants to use for us, not of the terror of judgment that His strength will bring to the wicked.

APPLICATION

Nature Talking About God

No storm comes and goes unnoticed. Rushing across the

land, it gets everyone's attention. Even the most unobservant see and hear it. Why do not all people discern in violent weather what the psalmist did?

Without a Bible, we can conclude from a thunderstorm, as did David, that God is *almighty, glorious,* and *gracious.* His power is evident. His glory shines in every blast of wind, and His goodness is behind it all. The falling rain may inconvenience us, but we soon observe its watering of the land. The earth responds to the moisture to give us food, making every raindrop a drop of kindness from God. No one, from David's viewpoint, should ever go through a storm without seeing God's glory, greatness, and goodness.

Each time we hear and see a storm, may the thunder and lightning sing to us of God, who made us, loves us, and wills for us to have peace.

Giving Glory to God

God is all-glorious whether we choose Him to be so or not. By our actions or our lips, by our accomplishments and achievements, we cannot add one glimmer of glory to His character. He is self-sufficient. How then do we give glory to God?

We observe who God is. We have not treated God right until we have studied Him and recognized who He actually is. We meditate through the Scriptures and observe the world of nature around us—and we come to know God.

We behold His glory. We cannot tell of His glory until we see it. Sometimes we look but we do not see, we study but do not behold. We may know the facts about God and not know God. We can absorb information about God without declaring His glory.

We proclaim His glory. We reflect it in our lives; we tell others about it with our lips; and we give God thanks for revealing it to us in all the ways that He does.

All the created things of the earth give glory to God naturally by doing what they were created to do. A star just shines down on us and preaches God's glory. It has no voice with which to speak, so it makes known His splendor by what it does. Of all God's creation, only people have to discipline themselves to give glory to God. They have to study God, behold His grandeur; then they must proclaim the glory they have seen.

The Right Thing to Do
There is one thing that is always the right thing to do. What is it? It is outlined for us in the first two verses of this psalm.

Acknowledge God's glory and strength. We can recognize God's glory and strength, tell God we see them, and proclaim them to others.

Give God the praise that is due His name. He is worthy of praise, for in Him we live, move, have our being, and have the glorious salvation. He deserves all the worship we can give Him.

Worship Him in holy attire. We bring Him our praise and worship robed in the garments of righteousness. His worship requires special adorning—the blood-washed suit of salvation.

When we give this kind of worship to God, we are having a joint worship service with the entire heavenly host. Heaven and earth unite for that moment of praise. We have been taught to pray by our Savior "Your will be done on earth as it is in heaven" (Mt. 6:10). When we praise God appropriately, this brief petition in the prayer that Jesus taught us is fulfilled, for we are doing what heaven is doing.

What to Say About God
Three truths should always be declared about God. Two are mentioned in the first two verses in a kind of call to worship, and the third one is mentioned in the concluding verse.

First, we are to declare His glory. There is a glory about God that transcends all the faint signs of glory that can be mustered by this earth. He is so much higher than mankind that we cannot even begin to comprehend Him. All we can do is to look in His direction and cry, "Glory!"

Second, we are to make known His strength. Sometimes we see His power in a clap of thunder and are reminded of the great events of the Bible, such as the great flood (Gen. 6—9), which show us His strength. We cannot even think about Him without becoming lost in the wonder of an almighty Power who holds the universe in His hand and at the same time condescends to dwell in the hearts of those who follow Him.

Third, we are to preach His grace. Whoever does not tell of His grace has failed to see His righteousness. He will either be a consuming fire or compassionate Father to each of us, a Judge or Savior. All of us must understand that it takes His infinite grace to save any one of us.

Praising God ought to be the easiest thing in the world to do. He is glorious, powerful, and gracious. These traits are beyond our ability to grasp. They are infinite and perfect in their quality.

Seeing God in the Gales

We have seen God's glory in a violent thunderstorm. The scene included the black clouds, crashing winds, and falling rain! As we look at this fury of nature from a spiritual viewpoint, what do we see?

We see God's voice in a clap of thunder. He controls the world of nature, and it is as if we hear His voice in the thunderbolt. The noise of that thunder reverberates throughout the region, disturbing the animals and the inhabitants. It is so with His voice! When God speaks, all the earth responds to His voice, consciously or unconsciously.

We see His strong hand in the shattering of trees. The strength of His power is reflected in the wind that breaks the strongest of trees. We knew that He was and is all-powerful, but the irresistible force of nature tells us about it all over again.

We see His fingers in the flashes of lightning. The forked fire crossing the night sky appears to be sparks flowing from His fingertips. One touch of His hand blisters a mountainside. He raises one finger, and the world trembles.

We see His smile in the watering of the earth. As the cycles of nature replenish the earth, God's consideration falls upon the land, animals, and humans. Without His rain, the world would die.

God is everywhere, but oftentimes we fail to see Him. More than twenty-twenty vision is required to see Him. The eyes of faith are needed. One unbeliever had on his desk a sign that read, "God is nowhere." A little boy looked at it, put in a space in his mind, and said, "Your sign says, 'God is now here.'" To those who have eyes to see, God is here and everywhere. He is in the events of nature, in every living thing, and in the races of people around us. See Him and praise His glory and strength.

"Glory!"

Someone has said, "When I get to heaven, I have about five questions I want to ask God!" Responding to such a remark, someone else has said, "When you get there, you will be so overwhelmed by what you see that you will forget your questions, and all you will be able to do is praise Him."

Indeed, when we stand before His throne, perhaps we will be so immersed in His greatness that all we can do is utter, "Glory! Glory! Glory!" If the angelic beings looked at a raging wind, the storm of God, and cried, "Glory!" will we be able to do more when we see the God of the storm?

A Significant "If"

If the angels and David saw God's greatness and glory in a thunderstorm and cried, "Glory!" then a significant "if" surfaces. We live in the Christian Age and have been able to behold far greater marvels, wonders, and glorious things from God than what David saw in a storm.

If they saw God's glory in a violent rain cloud, *should we not see it in the Scriptures?* We hold in our hands the completed revelation, Genesis to Revelation. We have been blessed to feed upon it daily, and we know of its supernaturalness and the breath of its coverage of God's eternal purpose. Has it caused us to shout, "Glory!" unto Him?

If they saw God's glory in a tempest sweeping across Palestine, *should we not see it in the Savior, Jesus Christ?* David perhaps only saw the Messiah as a faint figure of the future. The Messiah has come, and we know Him to be the second member of the Godhead. Matthew, Mark, Luke, and John have paraded before us the earthly life that He lived, His agonizing death, His glorious resurrection, and the creation of His church. Have these amazing truths caused us to cry, "Glory!" to God?

If they saw His glory in rain and rushing wind, *should we not see it in the great salvation God has given?* We are the recipients of the great salvation that He spent two long ages bringing into existence. The full salvation is here for anyone, for "whosoever will," to receive. We have received it, and our sins have been forgotten and will not be remembered against us anymore. We know far more about heaven than David ever knew. Have these wondrous blessings caused us to cry, "Glory!" to Him?

If we have not seen God's grandeur in the Scriptures, in the Son, and in the salvation, then we have the worst case of blindness the world has ever known.

The Storm and God's Grace

The psalm does not end on the note of terror but on the high note of faith.

The God of the storm gives His people protection. His power as seen in the outbursts of nature protects His people. The power behind the storm is the very power that He uses to watch over us and fulfill His promises to us.

The God of the storm gives His people peace. The hands that hurl thunderbolts across the sky also pour down blessings, protection, victory, and peace. He looks after our total being—spirits, minds, and bodies.

The God of the storm gives His people guidance. His voice behind the clap of thunder is the voice that speaks hope and words of truth to His people. His breath that causes the winds to blow also inspired through His Spirit the divine revelation of truth.

As with David before Goliath, God has given us five smooth stones with which to slay the giants before us. The stones are these: God is, God has, God can, God does, and God will.

The power behind the storm is the power of our heavenly Father who loves us and gave His Son to die for us. It is easy to see God as we contemplate the starry sky on a calm evening, but this psalm reminds us that we should also see Him in a fierce storm that leaves the hillside in disarray. Ask yourself, "In a storm, do I see only gusts of wind, or do I see God's grace? Do I see just the dark clouds and the thunder, or do I see the showers of blessings and the tenderness of God?"

Psalm 30
When a Disaster Has Passed

The Superscription: A Psalm; a Song at the Dedication of the House. A Psalm of David. This age-old heading says that this is **a Psalm** [מִזְמוֹר, *mizmor*] **of** ["by," "for," or "to"] **David** (לְדָוִד, *l^edawid*) and that it was written as **a Song** [of] **the Dedication of the House** (שִׁיר־חֲנֻכַּת הַבַּיִת, *shir ch^anukkath habayith*). The second appearance of "psalm," as is indicated by the italics, is an addition by the NASB translators. The "house" alluded to is hard to identify. Perhaps this designation simply tells how the psalm was later used, making this part of the title more of a subscription than a superscription.

Judging from the superscription and the content, this thanksgiving song springs from a tragic page from the writer's life. He has just emerged from a near-fatal incident. As he rejoices over God's preservation of his life and as he reflects on the lessons he has learned from the bitter episode, he writes this psalm of thanksgiving.

Joseph A. Alexander proposed that this psalm was written directly after God had lifted a plague from Israel (2 Sam. 24; 1 Chron. 21) and had spared the lives of David and many Israelites. Because of David's presumption in numbering the people, God gave David three punishments from which to choose: three years of famine, three months of defeat by enemies in battle, or three days of pestilence. David had put himself in the hands of God, pleading that he not be allowed to fall into the hands of man (2 Sam. 24:14). What happened? God sent the pestilence. Seventy thousand Israelites died because of it. As the destroying angel moved toward Jerusalem, David built an altar on the floor of Ornan and offered burnt offerings and peace offerings to God. At that point, the death angel sheathed his sword and turned away.

As one compares this psalm with 1 Chronicles 21, he is impressed with the fact that this event seems to fit the background of the psalm. Although Alexander's suggestion is reasonable and may be true, we cannot prove it conclusively.[1]

A good possibility as to the later use of the psalm is that it was used at the various, special services that celebrated a new beginning of some kind. When an occasion gave the nation a new life, a new resolve, or a kind of revival, this psalm provided the language to express the attitude of the nation toward that resurgence of life. It would be read or sung at those juncture times.

The psalm speaks of what should happen after a person has been granted a reprieve from death, the ultimate calamity.

"YOU HAVE LIFTED ME UP" (30:1–3)

¹**I will extol You, O LORD, for You have lifted me up,
And have not let my enemies rejoice over me.**
²**O LORD my God,
I cried to You for help, and You healed me.**
³**O LORD, You have brought up my soul from Sheol;
You have kept me alive, that I would not go down to the pit.**

Verse 1. Praise is the first note sounded in the psalm. The writer says, **I will extol You, O LORD, for You have lifted me up, and have not let my enemies rejoice over me.** When God in His great grace moves our feet back from the slippery edge of the grave to the solid path of life, extolling His name is the natural reaction to His kindness. Since God "lifted" David up from some awful fate, David is lifting up God or "extolling" (רום, *rum*) Him by his thanksgiving. A great suffering had brought him down to the narrow slit of twilight that hovers between this life

---

[1] Joseph A. Alexander, *Commentary on Psalms* (Grand Rapids, Mich.: Kregel Publication, 1991), 137.

and the next. As he neared the brink and was about to slide over to the other side, God's mercy was extended to him, and he was rescued.

The phrase "You have lifted me up" is from the Hebrew word דָּלָה (*dalah*) that means "to draw up out of." As a bucket is lowered into a well for the purpose of bringing up water, God reached down and raised him out of the pit of death. God's pulling him to safety causes him to see anew God's amazing love for him.

Had he not been saved, his enemies would have rejoiced over his demise. They would have danced about, saying, "What a happy day! We will not have to deal with him anymore. His God could not save him, and we are free from him!"

Verse 2. In his great crisis, he turned to the Lord for help: **O Lord my God, I cried to You for help, and You healed me.** His prayer or prayers were offered for deliverance, and God answered them. He refers to this rescue as a "healing" (רָפָא, *rapa'*). Could this be an indication that his distress was some sickness?

Verse 3. He compares his victory to being pulled up from death, as he says, **O Lord, You have brought up my soul from Sheol.** The death-peril from which he was freed must have been one of his most tragic experiences. He says that his soul was brought up from the grave, "from Sheol" (שְׁאוֹל, *sheʿol*). To say it plainly, God "kept [him] alive." He says, **You have kept me alive, that I would not go down to the pit** (בּוֹר, *bor*). In the midst of his awful trial, he cried to God, asking Him to spare his life, and God heard his prayer. Had it not been for the hand of God, he would have gone down to "the pit," a figurative synonym for death or the grave.

LEAD OTHERS TO PRAISE HIM (30:4, 5)

⁴**Sing praise to the Lord, you His godly ones,
And give thanks to His holy name.
⁵For His anger is but for a moment,
His favor is for a lifetime;
Weeping may last for the night,
But a shout of joy comes in the morning.**

Our immediate counter reply to any rescue by God's gracious hand, the life-threatening ones and even the smaller ones, should be to praise Him with heartfelt gratitude.

Verse 4. The writer not only wants to praise God, but he wants to lead others in exulting in Him. He says, **Sing praise to the LORD, you His godly ones, and give thanks to His holy name.** The grace he received is just one manifestation of God's universal love for mankind. Those who are "godly," the "ones" who take on the character of the lovingkindness of God (חָסִיד, *chasid*), are urged to join him in giving thanks to God's "holy name," according to the NASB. This is an interpretive translation. The Hebrew word that is used is "memory," not "name." They are to sing to God's "holy remembrance" (לְזֵכֶר קָדְשׁוֹ, *lᵉzeker qadsho*). He wants a chorus to praise God for what He has done.

Verse 5. Understanding his ordeal to have been discipline from God, he observes, **For His anger is but for a moment, His favor is for a lifetime.** The Hebrew for this first phrase literally says "a moment in His anger" (רֶגַע בְּאַפּוֹ, *rega' bᵉapo*). The verb has to be supplied by the translator. Should the phrase be translated, "For his anger endureth but a moment," as the KJV translated it?

Peter C. Craigie proposed that the Hebrew word for "moment" be translated "death."[2] In other words, "In His anger is death." His translation is based upon paralleling the Hebrew word translated "moment" with the word "lifetime" in the following line, but such a translation must rest upon redefining the Hebrew word that is consistently translated "moment," "instant," or something similar. The best translation appears to be, "In His anger a moment."

For additional insight into divine discipline, Hebrews 12:4–11 may be read with this section. The psalmist's affliction had come upon him as a rebuke from the Lord, but the discipline had been for a brief period, as symbolized by the word "night." The pain of life is periodic, but God's goodness spans one's entire lifetime. Rainstorms make up only a small part of the year;

---

[2]Peter C. Craigie, *Psalms 1—50*, Word Biblical Commentary, vol. 19 (Waco, Tex.: Word Books, 1983), 250.

life has much more health than sickness; our days are filled with more laughter than tears. When one is penitent and submissive to God's chastisement, the bitter tears and remorse pass quickly and are soon forgotten in the light of God's forgiveness.

To say it another way, **Weeping may last for the night, but a shout of joy comes in the morning.** Implied is the psalmist's belief that this tragic experience had come because he had not been as faithful to God as he should have been. The "weeping" represents the time of discipline and the correction that God had sent. It had become an emotional, deeply-felt period of rebuke. When the time of reproof passed and resulted in repentance, the "shout of joy" came from a grateful soul who had learned that God cared enough for him to correct him and give him a new life.

Weeping is temporary, but joy comes "in the morning" to fill our hearts with permanent happiness. God's long-term mercy and grace far outweigh any short-term wrath or discipline that He may have to give.

"HEAR ME, O LORD" (30:6–10)

⁶Now as for me, I said in my prosperity,
"I will never be moved."
⁷O LORD, by Your favor You have made my mountain to stand strong;
You hid Your face, I was dismayed.
⁸To You, O LORD, I called,
And to the Lord I made supplication:
⁹ "What profit is there in my blood, if I go down to the pit?
Will the dust praise You? Will it declare Your faithfulness?
¹⁰Hear, O LORD, and be gracious to me;
O LORD, be my helper."

The writer acknowledges his redemption from God with humility. He knows that pride can bring another rebuke from Him.

Verse 6. In reflection, he writes, **Now as for me, I said in my prosperity, "I will never be moved."** God had allowed him to descend into suffering because he had become prideful and vain regarding his prosperity. He had said to himself, "I will never be moved." Since everything was going well with him, he had started to feel self-sufficient and to view his prosperity, not God, as his security.

Verses 7, 8. Looking back, he can see how the Lord had led him out of his heady vanity. He remembers, **O Lord, by Your favor You have made my mountain to stand strong.** The Lord had so prospered him that he could say that God had made him into a "mountain"—strong, firm, and immovable.

Then, as a rebuke, God turned from him. **You hid Your face, I was dismayed.** To deflate his haughty spirit, God permitted a tragedy to descend upon him. Immediately, he pleaded with God to remove it; but God, as it were, "hid [His] face" from him, ignoring his prayers for a time. His soul turned sick with sorrow. He examined the way he had lived, repented, and approached God by seeking forgiveness and deliverance from death. Over a period of time, he continued to pray, asking for mercy and waiting for God's answer.

Verse 9. The plea he made is a common one in the psalms (see 6:5; 88:10, 11). He reasoned, **"What profit is there in my blood, if I go down to the pit? Will the dust praise You? Will it declare Your faithfulness?"** He embodied within his supplication a question that he phrased in three ways: "How would my death benefit Your cause?"; "I would not be able to praise You from the dust or the grave, would I?"; "If I died, I could not tell others how faithful You have been to me, could I?"

These questions are rhetorical, implying an immediate negative answer. A similar appeal was made to God by Hezekiah in Isaiah 38:18, 19. His point was that death would interrupt his praise of God and his proclamation of His truth and would profit neither of them. If God let him die, He would have one less person singing His praises in this world.

Verse 10. He asked God to come to his help: **"Hear, O Lord, and be gracious to me; O Lord, be my helper."** God, the only One who could help him, heard his prayers and raised him up. He accepted God's gift of grace humbly and joyfully, having learned valuable lessons from his journey to death's door.

Times of hardship and pain come to every person. When God brings us through them, we should accept such grace in gratitude by faithfully and selflessly doing His will.

"I WILL GIVE THANKS" (30:11, 12)

> ¹¹You have turned for me my mourning into dancing;
> You have loosed my sackcloth and girded me with gladness,
> ¹²That my soul may sing praise to You and not be silent.
> O LORD my God, I will give thanks to You forever.

Verse 11. As he draws important conclusions from what has happened to him, he says, **You have turned for me my mourning into dancing.** God heard his prayer and prolonged his life, and he is thankful. The gratitude of his heart is made known in expressions of gladness.

As he looks back at how God answered his supplications, he can see how God dramatically redirected his life. He compares the change to God's transforming his "mourning into dancing," his tears into laughter. Happiness was expressed in his day by dancing about in exuberance. He says that he has gone from being bent over with grief to leaping about with joy.

He says, **You have loosed my sackcloth and girded me with gladness.** "Sackcloth" was worn during a time of mourning and of penitence as an outward indication of the sadness of the heart. Generally, it was dark in color, made of goat's hair, and worn next to the skin. It was without much shape, perhaps looking like a sack, with holes for the head and arms.

God had re-clothed the writer—giving him the garments of "gladness" for the sackcloth of sadness. God had removed his sackcloth and dressed him with the robes of sunshine, tearing away his garment of grief and wrapping him in heavenly joy.

Verse 12. One of the reasons for his salvation is so that he may rejoice in God, and he acknowledges this truth by saying, **That my soul may sing praise to You and not be silent.** The Hebrew text has the word "glory" (כָּבוֹד, *kabod*) that is translated by the NASB and NRSV as "soul." The NIV translates it "heart."

He has learned well the lesson of his trial. God has raised him up that he may praise Him, not so that he may just live for his own pursuits. Thus a promise is made: **O LORD my God, I will give thanks to You forever.** From that moment forward, David promises to give thanks to God. His new full-time employment will be that of praising and thanking God for what He has done.

APPLICATION

A Believer's Biography

Out of gratitude for the redemption that God had given David, he praised Him in humility and thankfulness. So should it be with all who have received life from the hand of God. As we study this psalm, let us ask a question that permeates it: "How should I respond to God's redemption?"

The biography of each person's life should read: death, life, humility, praising God, teaching others to praise God, and lifelong thankfulness to God. In other words, all of us should be able to see ourselves in Psalm 30.

An Attitude of Gratitude

David had been brought out of a great calamity that he likened to death. All of us have faced grave circumstances—physical illnesses, automobile accidents, etc. What should be our reaction to God's preservation?

Let us give God the credit for our salvation. David realized that he did not do it, although he might have had a hand in the victory. God often uses us in His work. However, David was wise enough to recognize that God was really the great Deliverer in this case.

Let us praise Him for what He has done. One of the basic responses we can make to God's goodness is to praise Him for His grace and to share the same type of goodness with others.

Let us plant in our minds that God is good. We have seen God's grace, and now let us resolve that we will never forget it. He has answered us according to His love, and we must remember that God will cover us with His love before He brings judgment.

Let us lead others in praising God. It is true that God should not be praised alone. All have been blessed by Him, and all should give thanks to Him. We should provoke one another to love and good works (Heb. 10:24), but we should also provoke one another to the praise of the Lord.

David had been through a trying experience, but he had come out on the other side of it more conscious of God's goodness. God, at times, allows us to experience trouble so that we may see more clearly His strong arm, our failures, and His infinite grace.

Discerning the Discipline of God

David saw his trip to death's door as a rebuke from God. Maybe his trouble had come as a result of poor judgment on his part, or maybe it had come because of sin he had committed.

His experience causes us to ask, "How should we look at God's discipline?"

We should see it as an act of love. If God did not care, He would not chastise us. A father loves, and therefore he corrects. If God did not correct us, He would not have the tough love an earthly father must have for his children.

We should see it as temporary. It is a momentary unpleasantness that gets our attention and teaches us a valuable lesson. His anger lasts only a moment, but His love covers our lives.

We should see it as needful. God does not allow the unnecessary. He does not waste time or energy. He gives us what we need when we need it. We accept correction in athletics, in child-rearing, and in other areas of life. Why then do we not accept it in spiritual training?

David advised that we look at the result of the discipline we receive. We may weep at the time of it, but we will shout for joy the next day. We may find God's discipline to be inconvenient for our agenda; but as we mature spiritually, we are glad it was given.

When God Corrects Us

When God corrects us, three visitors come: audible weeping, shouts of joy, and the Father's love.

Weeping comes first and spends the evening hours with us. It is an unwelcome guest, but a necessary one. Our hearts break because of our sins. We engage in spiritual inventory and search our souls.

Then, when we repent and rededicate ourselves to God's way, joy comes and continues with us as a cherished guest. We rejoice that we have been brought back to the way of righteousness.

Emerging from difficulties and repentance is the recognition of the Father's love. We learn from experience a fact that is clearly stated in the Scriptures, "Whom the Lord loves He disciplines" (Heb. 12:6). Any earthly father who loves his children will give them the necessary reproof so that they may mature in character.

Discipline is only a temporary detour from the main road of Christian living, but the lessons that it brings are permanent. The character of righteousness is formed in us, and that trait is more valuable to us than any inconvenience or pain that the formation may have caused us. Yes, in connection with this fatherly correction, "weeping may last for the night, but a shout of joy comes in the morning."

The Path to Humility

We see in this psalm a journey—from pride to humility. How was it made? David outlined it for us.

We see success. At the pinnacle of achievement, he had become filled with pride. He had gloried in his victories, his army, his wealth, and his position.

We see the discipline of disappointment. David was wise enough to observe God's hand behind his pain. God had entered his life to teach him a valuable lesson.

We see introspection and spiritual inventory. He examined his heart before God. He weighed his actions and his motivations. Spiritual renewal is preceded by honest examination.

We see humility, as David called upon God to grant His tender mercy. David saw what he had done in the midst of his great need. Furthermore, he could see his feet slipping down into the pit. Death loomed before him.

We see a soul receiving the precious gift of deliverance from God. A loving hand reached out to him and pulled him from the well of death. David took that hand and recognized it as the gracious hand of God.

We see a thankful servant of God. David resolved that he would give thanks to God and lead others to rejoice in Him as well. He had been redeemed by God, and he recognized that now he would belong to God.

Just about any believer can relate that he has taken a similar painful journey—from pride to humility, from the hill of "I did it" down to the narrow road of "Praise God for saving me!" God has brought us to the level ground of grateful, righteous living, and on this plain is the place where we should stay forever.

True Gratitude

What can we do for God? We cannot bring Him food, for He never gets hungry. We cannot give Him money because He already owns it all. We cannot fight battles for Him, for He can speak a word and wipe away the strongest enemy from before Him.

Nevertheless, we see in many of these psalms one obvious gift that we can give Him—we can be grateful for His numerous deliverances.

We can respond to His great acts of mercy with gratitude. David did. He saw that God had extended his life, and he quickly voiced the appreciation that a child of God should have. He gave God the thanksgiving of his soul.

We can lead others to give thanks to Him. David urged the godly ones to praise Him. He said, "I will not only praise You, but I will lead others in giving praise to You." The whole world has the obligation of giving thanks to God, and we can help those around us to do it.

We can have a permanent gratitude that shows up in our daily walk with Him. David did. He said, "I will praise You from now on." Thanksgiving is not a day, but a daily attitude. The Christian takes seriously Paul's injunction, "In everything give thanks" (1 Thess. 5:18).

One man prayed, "Lord, You have given us so many blessings. We ask for only one more gift: Give us grateful hearts."

The Short-Term and the Long-Term

Life can be divided into short-term and long-term segments. It is instructive to consider these divisions.

Correction is short-term, and grace is long-term. Discipline is often required; but as a general rule (if we learn from it), it is only momentary in length. His grace overarches our lives, surrounding us continually with His kindness. His love for us is behind everything He does for us.

Unpleasantness is short-term, and happiness in the Lord is long-term. When reproof is given, our hearts break. We are disappointed at our failure. We grieve over our sin. However, when we realize that God has corrected us in love and we have been brought back to faithful living, we have the joy of salvation and the happiness of knowing that we are walking in His truth.

Shame and embarrassment are short-term, and forgiveness is long-term. Following on the heels of sin is the blush of embarrassment and the troubling pangs of conscience. We are miserable and descend into the valley of despair, but God's hand raises us up through our repentance and our acceptance of His forgiveness. When we are back on the narrow road of godly living, we realize that His forgiveness is forever. Because those sins have been taken away, He will never need to forgive them again.

The sweat and stress of our labors are short-term, and the eternal rest that awaits us is long-term. Life here is a brief moment when compared to eternity. We enter into a rest now as we find our home in God, but we have an even greater rest coming, the rest of eternal life.

The long-term picture must overshadow our short-term view. A detour is sometimes necessary, but it is on the main road that life is lived. When a rebuke is given, we must look to the continual, eternal grace of God as our encouragement and motivation, quickly deal with our sin, and climb back on the main road. When we become discouraged and are almost at the point of being weary in well-doing, we must remember the long-term, our eternal rest where we will know pleasures forever.

Psalm 31
"Into Your Hand I Commit My Spirit"

The Superscription: For the choir director. A Psalm of David.
The heading in the Hebrew Bible says that this piece is **a Psalm** [מִזְמוֹר, *mizmor*] **of** ["by," "for," or "to"] **David** (לְדָוִד, *lᵉdawid*) and that the superscription was written **for the choir director** (לַמְנַצֵּחַ, *lamnatstseach*) of music. Perhaps it was written during those awful days when David was fleeing for his life from Saul.

With its plaintive and emotional content, this psalm has been appropriately labeled a psalm of lament. Interlaced with the praise of God and the depiction of intense struggles, it sounds like the pitiful cries and the agonizing loneliness found in Jeremiah when he was beaten down by persecution and hopelessness. R. E. O. White has noted the following comparison between this psalm and Jeremiah's writings:

> One phrase [in Ps. 31], "terror on every side" (v. 13), occurs five times in Jeremiah; verses 7–18 read like a commentary on Jeremiah 20:7–13; verse 12 recalls Jeremiah's parable of the potter; verse 6 reflects Jeremiah 8:19 and 10:8.[1]

Since a close parallel exists between this psalm and passages in Jeremiah, it is reasonable to believe that the prophet read the psalm and used it. In addition, Jonah seems to have quoted from

---

[1] R. E. O. White, *A Christian Handbook to the Psalms* (Grand Rapids, Mich.: Wm. B. Eerdmans Publishing Co., 1984), 59.

it (compare v. 22 with Jon. 2:4) as he prayed from the stomach of the great fish. Our Lord used a line from verse 5 as He was dying on the cross (Lk. 23:46). These words have been useful because they describe so well the trusting heart in the midst of life's torrential sorrows and calamities.

We cannot tell which days of trauma in David's life prompted him to pen this psalm. The text indicates that at the time of writing the author was wrestling with persecution, fatigue, slander, and maybe physical illness—a host of troubles that had caused him indescribable anguish. Having been knocked down by life, he looked up to God. Throughout the psalm, an alternating movement occurs between despair and dependence upon God.

The psalm puts into expression some of the deep-felt questions and fears of affliction and woe that are common in life. Tears, smiles, and blood are universal. "The last place to look for originality," said Alexander MacLaren, is among the sorrows of man. The needs of the human heart are uniform.[2]

For us, the psalm answers the question "What can you do when you are worn out, beaten, and broken by the battles of life?"

COMMITMENT TO GOD (31:1–5)

¹**In You, O LORD, I have taken refuge;**
Let me never be ashamed;
In Your righteousness deliver me.
²**Incline Your ear to me, rescue me quickly;**
Be to me a rock of strength,
A stronghold to save me.
³**For You are my rock and my fortress;**
For Your name's sake You will lead me and guide me.
⁴**You will pull me out of the net which they have secretly laid for me,**
For You are my strength.
⁵**Into Your hand I commit my spirit;**

---

[2]Alexander MacLaren, *The Psalms*, The Expositor's Bible (New York: A. C. Armstrong and Son, 1904), 1:291.

You have ransomed me, O LORD, God of truth.

Verse 1. The writer begins with a beautiful declaration of trust in God. Emphatically, he says, **In You, O LORD, I have taken refuge; let me never be ashamed; in Your righteousness deliver me.** The idea of "refuge" is that of trusting or putting one's hope in God. The believer sees God as the only One to whom he can commit his life and spirit. David's undergirding belief is that whoever surrenders to God's protection will not be disappointed, embarrassed, or humiliated, for God will be faithful to him. God, the righteous One, never fails His own.

Verse 2. Moving from praise to petition, he asks God for guidance on what to do and how to live, as well as for deliverance from those who are trying to capture him: **Incline Your ear to me, rescue me quickly; be to me a rock of strength, a stronghold to save me.** He asks God to "incline [His] ear" or listen to his prayer. Urgency is expressed as he asks God to come "quickly" to his aid. He believes that he needs immediate help.

He and God are inseparable. God is his "refuge," "rock," "fortress," "guide," and "strength." These are metaphors that convey God's great ability to shelter and lead His people. Without his God, neither he nor Israel has life or any kind of hope.

Verse 3. What reasons are given for making such a request as this? He says, **For You are my rock and my fortress; for Your name's sake You will lead me and guide me.** His rationale for these petitions consists of two truths about God: God's strength and reputation. He is a "rock" to His people, and He will act because of His "name's sake." God has made promises to His people, and the righteousness behind His name requires that He keep those promises.

Verse 4. His prayer becomes even more specific as he says, **You will pull me out of the net which they have secretly laid for me, for You are my strength.** He wants God to demonstrate His righteousness by judging the wrong done against him and by delivering him from evil men who seek his life. He uses the figure of hunters setting a trap (a net) for an animal or a bird. His enemies are putting together schemes for his capture and death. He describes them as hunters seeking to entrap him.

Verse 5. As difficulties swirl around him, he places his life in God's hands for His protection and guidance. Calmness comes with surrender, resignation, and trust. He says, **Into Your hand I commit my spirit; You have ransomed me, O LORD, God of truth.** A memorable line in this part of the psalm is this phrase "Into Your hand I commit my spirit," the words used by Jesus in His dying moments on the cross (Lk. 23:46). With these words, David entrusts his life and future to God. If David lives, it will be because God chooses for him to live. These words were appropriate for Jesus to use as He committed His spirit to God in His death.

He knows that God can be trusted, because He is ever the "God of truth" and is, therefore, absolutely reliable and faithful. He will guard with integrity any deposit that is put into His hands.

"TRUST IN THE LORD" (31:6–8)

⁶I hate those who regard vain idols,
But I trust in the LORD.
⁷I will rejoice and be glad in Your lovingkindness,
Because You have seen my affliction;
You have known the troubles of my soul,
⁸And You have not given me over into the hand of the enemy;
You have set my feet in a large place.

From his broken condition, David resolves to rejoice in God's faithfulness and lovingkindness.

Verse 6. He draws a contrast between the true God and idols. He says, **I hate those who regard vain idols, but I trust in the LORD.** Anyone who loves God and trusts Him will abhor "idols" and the horrible act of worshiping them. The Hebrew expression for "vain idols" (הַבְלֵי־שָׁוְא, *habley shaw^e*) is really "vanities of vain." The phrase means "absolutely meaningless." The false god is a nonentity, a figment of the imagination of the pagans who worship it. Whoever worships an idol is worshiping a lie. The writer has decided to put his "trust" in God, not in a senseless, speechless, powerless piece of rock or wood.

Verse 7. His focus will be upon God's wonderful attributes. He resolves, **I will rejoice and be glad in Your lovingkindness, because You have seen my affliction; You have known the troubles of my soul.** He is concentrating upon God's covenant loyalty (His "lovingkindness") to His people. He knows that God has seen his distress and will not allow the enemy to triumph over him. God is always faithful in observing the "troubles" that confuse and upset His people.

Verse 8. He knows that God will be faithful to him. **And You have not given me over into the hand of the enemy; You have set my feet in a large place.** His God, he believes, has confined or corralled his enemies, limiting their movement, and has put his feet in a wide open place where he can move freely unafraid.

"BE GRACIOUS TO ME" (31:9–13)

⁹Be gracious to me, O Lord, for I am in distress;
My eye is wasted away from grief, my soul and my body also.
¹⁰For my life is spent with sorrow
And my years with sighing;
My strength has failed because of my iniquity,
And my body has wasted away.
¹¹Because of all my adversaries, I have become a reproach,
Especially to my neighbors,
And an object of dread to my acquaintances;
Those who see me in the street flee from me.
¹²I am forgotten as a dead man, out of mind;
I am like a broken vessel.
¹³For I have heard the slander of many,
Terror is on every side;
While they took counsel together against me,
They schemed to take away my life.

Verse 9. He pleads, **Be gracious to me, O Lord.** As one who is in need of God's grace, he begins to describe his physical and mental condition: **I am in distress; my eye is wasted away from grief, my soul and my body also.** Longing for God to understand his condition, David gives Him a personal tour through his plight. "Look with grace at my pain and perils," he says with the greatest emotion and feeling.

Verse 10. His description employs exaggerated emphasis in order to show the depth of his distress: **For my life is spent with sorrow and my years with sighing; my strength has failed because of my iniquity, and my body has wasted away.** His life has been the converging place of physical illness, bereavement, betrayal, and natural disaster; and his body and spirit are showing the telling effects of it all. His eyes are red from the flood of tears. His soul and body are filled with grief. Since he has been in this condition for some time, his life has been consumed by it. Anguish has sapped his physical strength. He admits that some of the pain has come because of sin. The total impact of his woes has thrust him into deep despair, and he is worn out from it.

Verse 11. In addition to his physical stresses, he is hounded by enemies who seek his life. He says, **Because of all my adversaries, I have become a reproach, especially to my neighbors, and an object of dread to my acquaintances; those who see me in the street flee from me.** The enemies who are trying to kill him have hurt him not only by demoralizing his spirit, but also by destroying his reputation among his friends and acquaintances. The betrayal of love ones may wound him more deeply than the threatened arrows of his enemies.

Verse 12. He has become a nobody, even as a deceased person does. **I am forgotten as a dead man, out of mind.** A man lives, dies, and is forgotten. He believes that he is as forgotten "as a dead man," even though he is still alive. **I am like a broken vessel.** He is like a cracked piece of pottery which is of no use and has been discarded.

Verse 13. He pictures himself surrounded by vicious men who are putting together rancorous schemes. **For I have heard the slander of many, terror is on every side; while they took counsel together against me, they schemed to take away my life.** The circle of horror is made up of attempts on his life, cutting remarks about him, and aggressive meetings to harm him.

He says, ". . . terror is on every side," which is a phrase Jeremiah used as an apt description of his situation (Jer. 6:25; 20:10; 46:5; 49:29; Lam. 2:22). It must be that this psalm had been around a long time, for Jeremiah and Jonah were influenced by it.

A RIGHTEOUS RESOLVE (31:14–18)

> ¹⁴But as for me, I trust in You, O LORD,
> I say, "You are my God."
> ¹⁵My times are in Your hand;
> Deliver me from the hand of my enemies and from those who persecute me.
> ¹⁶Make Your face to shine upon Your servant;
> Save me in Your lovingkindness.
> ¹⁷Let me not be put to shame, O LORD, for I call upon You;
> Let the wicked be put to shame, let them be silent in Sheol.
> ¹⁸Let the lying lips be mute,
> Which speak arrogantly against the righteous
> With pride and contempt.

Verse 14. Coming back to the attitude of trust, he makes a promise, **But as for me, I trust in You, O LORD, I say, "You are my God."** His only solution to his dilemma is to "trust" in his God. The ideas of intimacy, endearment, and faith are included in his expression "my God." All his hope is placed in God. He is close to God, and he knows that God is close to him.

Verse 15. He has resolved to yield to the sovereign control of God. He acknowledges, **My times are in Your hand.** With this phrase, he relinquishes to God his whole life, whether it be made up of adversity, prosperity, or the status quo. His future will be under God's oversight. He asks God to deliver him, but he is turning the "how" and "when" over to God.

He beseeches God, **Deliver me from the hand of my enemies and from those who persecute me.** To put it simply, he is saying, "I do not know how You will choose to deliver me from my enemies, but I know that I can put myself in Your hands and You will deliver me."

Verse 16. Above all, he wants fellowship with God. He prays, **Make Your face to shine upon Your servant.** This phrase is one of the most beautiful phrases in the Old Testament. It was first used in connection with Moses (Num. 6:25); and it suggests the brightness of God's fellowship, grace, and presence.

Save me in Your lovingkindness, he prays. He knows that he is safe under God's unfailing love. The safest place on earth to be is within God's gracious care.

Verse 17. Once again, he asks that God deal with his enemies: **Let me not be put to shame, O LORD, for I call upon You; let the wicked be put to shame, let them be silent in Sheol.** He has been God's worshiper and prays to Him continually. As His servant, he is subject to His protection. "The wicked should be dumbfounded, confused, and judged, not me," he says.

This portion of the psalm turns into an imprecatory petition, a request that God destroy the wicked who are opposing him. He asks that they be put to silence by being sent into "Sheol." He has combined in his mind the enemy with their sins, and his prayer calls upon God to judge them. This type of prayer will be prayed often in the Psalms.

Verse 18. He continues the imprecatory part of his prayer by saying, **Let the lying lips be mute, which speak arrogantly against the righteous with pride and contempt.** "Let the lies of my enemies be stopped, and may they be unable to utter anything else against You or me. May they become as silent as dead men," he says. The enemies about whom he prays oppose God and His ways. As the Caananites in the past had been opposed to what God was doing and had to be judged and taken out of the way, even so these enemies fall under God's condemnation.

REMEMBER WHAT GOD HAS DONE
(31:19–22)

¹⁹How great is Your goodness,
Which You have stored up for those who fear You,
Which You have wrought for those who take refuge in You,
Before the sons of men!

²⁰**You hide them in the secret place of Your presence from the conspiracies of man;
You keep them secretly in a shelter from the strife of tongues.
²¹Blessed be the LORD,
For He has made marvelous His lovingkindness to me in a besieged city.
²² As for me, I said in my alarm,
"I am cut off from before Your eyes";
Nevertheless You heard the voice of my supplications
When I cried to You.**

Verse 19. Having prayed for his enemies' downfall, he now turns to the praise of God. He says, **How great is Your goodness!** Finding renewed spiritual energy, David looks back at what God has done. He knows that what God has been, He will continue to be. When overwhelmed by suffering, we should recall how God has defended us in the past and view that as a prophecy of what He will do in the future.

God's "goodness" is displayed in His righteous acts of love, grace, and kindness in the lives of those who serve Him. His goodness is abundant and strong.

This wonderful divine goodness is not poured out indiscriminately, but as he says, **You have stored** [it] **up for those who fear You.** Furthermore, he says, **You have wrought** [it] **for those who take refuge in You.** Those who have feared (reverenced) God receive untold gifts from Him. He has always been faithful to His own. It is as if God has an inexhaustible storehouse filled with His bounties, and He continually gives from it to those who love Him.

These special gifts have been sent out to His faithful ones **before the sons of men.** He has made known His partiality to those who trust in Him for any bystander to see. The story of the Old Testament is replete with illustrations of this truth.

Verse 20. He now hugs to his heart one of the great assurances of believers in God. What does God do with his faithful children? He says, **You hide them in the secret place of Your presence from the conspiracies of man; You keep them secretly**

in a shelter from the strife of tongues. God conceals His loved ones in His glorious "presence," far away from the reach of the filthy fingers, mean minds, and the haughty hands of the wicked. Anyone who resides in the covert of God's presence is safe from all harm. When we are hidden away in God, the foul tongues and slanderous lips of perverted people cannot hurt us. We are shielded by God Himself, being protected by His very presence.

Verse 21. Such thoughts cause him to burst into the praise of God: **Blessed be the Lord, for He has made marvelous His lovingkindness to me in a besieged city.** He remembers how God has come to his rescue when he was inside a city that was being besieged by an alien army. God manifested amazing grace and mercy toward David and delivered him.

Verse 22. At low times in his life, David wondered and prayed, **As for me, I said in my alarm, "I am cut off from before Your eyes."** He thought that all was lost, that he could not escape. In his despair he believed that he was separated from God's strength. Then he remembered God's faithfulness: **Nevertheless You heard the voice of my supplications when I cried to You.** David prayed in the past, and God answered him by giving him the success he sought. The thought of this rescue brings renewed hope to David. Even though God has not yet helped him out of his current difficulty, he believes that He will. As He has done before, so will He do again.

When trouble descends like a flood and we pray but no answer is forthcoming, let us remember how God has treated His people in the past. We should continue to pray to our heavenly Father and remember that in His time He will answer us.

WAIT ON GOD (31:23, 24)

²³**O love the Lord, all you His godly ones!**
The Lord preserves the faithful
And fully recompenses the proud doer.
²⁴**Be strong and let your heart take courage,**
All you who hope in the Lord.

Verse 23. Having considered all this, he now begins to exhort the faithful ones: **O love the LORD, all you His godly ones!** Looking beyond himself, he thinks of others in similar straits and urges two attitudes upon them. First, he says, "[Continue to] love the LORD." Regardless of life's circumstances, persevere in trusting God. The truth is, **The LORD preserves the faithful and fully recompenses the proud doer.** He says that we must remember that God is faithful to bless the faithful ones and to judge the haughty ones.

Verse 24. His second admonition is, **Be strong and let your heart take courage, all you who hope in the LORD.** The faithful should "be strong [in faith and in] courage." "Waiting on God" (a concept introduced in Ps. 27:14) means that we know He has a purpose behind our suffering, and if we will wait for Him we will eventually see the blessing of God. If we patiently wait for Him, He will fulfill what He has in mind for us. After all, He did not come to the rescue of Jesus when He died on the cross. Had He taken His Son down from the cross, the world would have had no hope. Through the perspective of the New Testament, we can see His design behind the cross.

The broken heart must not give up, but must wait on God. He will resolve our difficulties and wipe away our tears when He deems it best for His holy purposes and for us.

This psalm sings of trust in God when our present and future are obscured by the dark clouds of suffering and the enmity of evil people. It shows that, through faith, we can handle hardship by trusting God to keep the precious deposit made to Him.

APPLICATION

Walking in the Dark

David did not know the answers to his difficulties, but he knew where to go to get those answers. In this psalm he shows us the way to walk before God when we are in the dark.

The route to victory that he took involved four steps: committing oneself to God, trusting in God, remembering what God has done in the past, and choosing to wait on God. It was the appropriate way for him; it will work for us.

The Great and Wonderful God

Who is God? How shall we describe Him? Verses 6 through 8 give us a brief, exhilarating picture of Him. Let these words be one more basis for worshiping and adoring Him.

He is the true God. He who worships God is in the truth. Those who bow down before idols are bowing down before nonexistent beings. Idols are hopeless vanities, empty and meaningless. God is the only true God.

He is the God of grace. Contemplating what He is like instills joy in those who worship Him. His great attributes, such as lovingkindness and mercy, fill us with appreciation and love for Him. Who can think about His grace and not praise Him?

He is the God of compassion. He sees the troubles of our souls and delivers us. Sometimes He goes before us and removes the difficulties that beset us. Sometimes He comes to us and delivers us from a crisis that encircles us. Sometimes He comes behind us and helps us deal with the problems we have created for ourselves.

He is the God of strength. No enemy is too strong for Him. He rescues us from all dangers and puts us in a wide open place where we are free from worry. We are not cramped or hemmed in, but through His grace we live in freedom from all harm.

In summary, we see God as embodying truth, love, compassion, and power. He not only loves His people, but He leads them and gives them life.

Giving One's Life to God

David faced swirling problems of all kinds—disappointment, enemies who sought his death, confusion, and pain. He was in the valley of despair. When one is in his situation, what can he do?

This psalm shows that David gave his life to God in four steps. He placed himself on the island of God's lovingkindness and omnipotence.

He affirmed his confidence in God. He reminded himself of who God is, what He had done for him, and the traits of His character. He saw God as His only hope, and he turned to Him as his refuge, stronghold, and defense.

He submitted his circumstances and changes to God's sovereign control. "My times," he said, "are in His hands." He was turning over his whole life to God. Wherever God might lead him, he was ready to go; and whatever might be involved in such a journey, he was ready to do. His future would be in God's hands; he would allow God to do with him whatever He desired.

He surrendered himself to God's lovingkindness. "Make Your face to shine upon Your servant," was his prayer. Above all else he wanted God's favor. His desire was to live in His grace.

He prayed that God would remove his enemies. He had been God's servant, and he was under His protection. He asked God to take care of those who threatened him and sought to destroy him. Let us remember Matthew 6:33, "But seek first His kingdom and His righteousness, and all these things will be added to you."

Unable to change his condition, David committed himself to God. He trusted God for the outcome of his life. He knew all would be well with him if God was in charge.

Trusting in the Lord

One big question that all of us would do well to ask is this: "What does it mean to trust in the Lord?" Let us notice the answer to this question that is given in verses 1 through 5.

It means putting all our confidence in Him. We see Him as our rock, our stronghold, our fortress, our strength. There is no one else who can grant true salvation to us.

It means calling upon Him for deliverance. Prayer is the avenue God has chosen for us to use to make known our needs to Him. God knows our dilemma before we ask, but He has willed that His children come to Him with their requests. Such asking is good for the children and unites them in a daily walk with God.

It means committing our lives to Him. The ultimate trust is to put ourselves in the hands of God. We trust Him to deal with our situations as He sees fit. We know that God is a God of truth and will do what is best for us. Desiring Him to fulfill His will in us, whatever that will is, we yield to His control.

PSALM 31

"Trusting God" is sometimes a tall order. However, when we think of who God is, how He has always treated us, His absolute integrity, and His lovingkindness for all His children, we know that He is worthy of our trust. We further know that those who trust in Him will never be put to shame.

Thinking with the Psalms

Perhaps one of the great values of the psalms for the Christian is the assistance they give in teaching us to think correctly about God. True, we cannot pray some portions of them, such as those parts that are uniquely directed toward the Old Testament circumstance; but most of them describe the deep thoughts we have concerning God's dealing with His people.

A good illustration of this truth is seen in our Lord's use of the psalms in His thinking and praying. He used the words of verse 5 of this psalm to present His spirit to God at His death (Lk. 23:46). Further, He used the words of Psalm 22:1 to express His thoughts to God when He was at the pinnacle of His sufferings for our sins.

We have only seven recorded sayings of Jesus from the cross. Three of the seven are prayers; and two of the prayers are made up of expressions to God that are taken from the Psalms.

Jesus was the all-wise Son of God. He knew all the words and thoughts that one could think and say, but He chose to use words and thoughts from the Psalms to express Himself in prayer during the most critical times of His life.

The Psalms especially help us in our praying as we walk through the crucible of suffering. Most were written in the valley of sorrow and pain; they reflect the believer's exercise of faith in the midst of hardship and trial. Consequently, most of them relate to God in prayer the deep longings of the human heart when besieged by the arrows of disappointment, pain, loneliness, and forsakenness.

Let us study carefully the Psalms, and let us allow them to assist us in our praying.

"Into Your Hand I Commit My Spirit"

This phrase appears in verse 5 of this psalm as an expression of surrender to God's will. It can have a general application to life.

For times of trial. Apparently, this phrase was a prayer/commitment during a period of great distress. The writer used it to say to God, "I do not know what Your will is for my life. My future, as far as I can tell is uncertain, but I am committing my circumstances, difficulties, and the days ahead to You. I believe You can direct me through all of this." It can be a prayer for the confused servant.

For times of labor. We do not always know what the future holds for the work we are doing. James said that we must be careful to say "if God wills" when we plan (Jas. 4:15). The Bible is clear about what God wants us to do (Mk. 16:15, 16). God achieves His purposes in and through the spiritual labor of His people. We must use the best judgment we have, put our finest efforts into what we have concluded should be done, and then commit it all—judgment and efforts—into God's hands to bless and control as He sees best. It is a prayer for the committed servant.

In the hour of death. Our Savior used this phrase in His dying breath to hand over His spirit to God. He knew what the future held for Him; but in a moment of great submission to His Father's will, He submitted His spirit into His Father's control. For us, the time when this phrase is especially relevant is when we are getting ready to embark to the eternal shore. That particular journey is unknown to us, and we need to put ourselves in the hand of Someone who knows the way. It is a prayer of completion for the servant who has come to the end of the way.

This phrase will always be precious to us because our Savior used it in prayer during the last moment of His life; however, it should also mean much to us because of the guidance it contains concerning what to do in times of trial and intensive spiritual labors. These words teach us that our lives, longings, and labors should be placed in God's hands for safekeeping.

The Ground of Our Hope

On what basis can we say that God is our rock? One powerful answer is given in this psalm.

PSALM 31

The first basis is God's unchangeableness. He has defended His people in the past, and what He was yesterday He will be today and tomorrow. He does not change. We can look back to God's actions in the Old Testament toward all those who trusted in Him and say, "That is how God will deal with me today."

The second basis is God's lovingkindness. It is His nature to love His people. We can plead for His grace, and He will grant it to the penitent person. His covenant loyalty requires Him to be gracious to those who love Him and walk in His precepts.

The third basis is God's integrity. He never lies. He will faithfully do what He said He would do. His righteous character guarantees His trustworthiness. We can rest our lives and eternity upon the fact that God will always tell the truth.

Our faith grows out of evidence, and the evidence we have comes in the form of divine testimony. In other words, the divine record of God's unchangeableness, lovingkindness, and integrity provides the evidence for our working faith in God. This kind of faith will sustain us regardless of the nature of the trial.

In His Presence

In verses 19 and 20, the writer's praise of God emphasized the presence of God. He found that in God's presence is the fullness of joy. How was this the case?

Because in His presence *we are in His fellowship.* Nothing surpasses in value the joy of His presence. Walking with God is the highest blessing we have.

Because in His presence *we are surrounded by His goodness.* He says that the goodness of God has been stored up for those who fear Him. God makes it obvious to all that He has given His grace to those who have taken refuge in Him. From our viewpoint, He has proclaimed it in the cross, the Scriptures, and the church; from the viewpoint of the psalmist, He has made it known by His deliverances from harm.

Because in His presence *we are in His protection.* The writer says that in His presence he is hidden from all the intrigues, the gossip, and the evil of men. He is kept safe from the devil, the world, and sin. One would have to overthrow God in order to destroy His servant because His servant is hidden in God.

Perhaps we should remember that we have only one need—to be in the presence of God. With the shadow of His presence over us, living beneath His wings, we will have no fear and no further ambitions.

The God of Love

Verses 21 and 22 comprise a short doxology that extols God's loving nature. His praise of God's love was initiated by his remembering that God had poured out His love upon him when he was within a besieged city. Contemplate the great love with which He has loved us.

He loves us in word. Over and over again in eloquent and picturesque language, God tells of the love that He has for us. Every book of the Bible in some form declares His love for us.

He loves us in deed. His love does not end with words—He has and does demonstrate it in the highest and most positive ways. His deliverances, His meeting our needs, and His providing for our salvation speak of His affection for us.

He loves us in faithfulness. His love is continuous and unrelenting. In a world of uncertainty, one certainty that we will always have is God's amazing love. The writer reached a time when he thought he was cut off from God, but shortly thereafter God answered his prayer. We must never conclude that God has forsaken us.

The believer spends much of his life rejoicing in the love God has for him. He remembers it, lives in it, and looks forward to it.

What Should the Godly Do?

During difficult times, what should the righteous do? What should be the pattern of their lives? Verses 23 and 24 give a clear, concise answer.

Love the Lord. Put your affections and aspirations upon God. Love Him with your emotions and will. Walk with Him and intellectually pursue His will.

Trust in His faithfulness. Do not let anyone or any circumstance persuade you that God will not keep His promises. Trials may cloud our vision, but remind yourself that behind a frowning providence is the sunshine of His glorious face.

Be of good courage. March forward in His strength. He will defend His people. He will go before them into battle.

Job was beset by financial calamities and physical afflictions, but he remembered God. He saw past what his friends were saying, past his agonizing trials, past the discouragement of his wife, to the faithful hand of God. We too must look past all the difficulties that may come and see the faithfulness of God.

Living by Faith

The psalms remind us of what it means to walk by faith. Scattered throughout them, popping up in the daily grind of the life of the writer, we have seen the dimensions of true biblical faith.

Faith means abandonment to God. Those who trust in God give themselves fully to God. They have placed themselves under His care and shepherding.

Faith means yielding to the sovereignty of God. Those who trust in God submit to the decisions He makes about their lives and the future of His work and world. We cannot always see the reasons behind His decisions, but we know that they are benevolent and in keeping with a gracious Providence.

Faith means loving God. Those who trust God respond to His love with love. Faith sees the lovingkindness of God and loves Him in return. There can be no devotion without emotion; however, devotion is not just emotion. True devotion has within it the integrity of our intellects and the purest of our emotions.

Faith means living in the strength of God. Those who trust in God look to Him for their salvation and daily life. The victories they enjoy have come from His hands. They know that they have "lived, moved, and had their physical and spiritual being" in Him (see Acts 17:28).

Faith means abiding in the Word of God. Those who trust in God obey His Word. Their commitment is to do His will on earth. They are not perfect, but they love His will and give themselves to following it completely.

We are saved by a faith that works (Jas. 2:24). It is a faith that lives, loves, and labors in the strength of the Lord. It looks to Him in daily living and for eternity. He who lives by this type of faith will one day see the outcome of it—the salvation of the soul.

The Troubles of the Soul

In verse 7 the writer affirms that God has known the troubles of his soul. This statement reminds us of what God does about the struggles we confront.

Remember that *He sees them.* Yes, He knows all things, and He observes the hardships of His children. Earthly parents carefully watch over their children, and our heavenly Father gives His attention to anything that troubles us.

We know that *He sympathizes with us.* His heart goes out to us. As we stand at the side of a grave, He weeps with us. As we suffer in the hospital, He sends to us His heavenly flowers if we will only see them and receive them.

We can say, on the basis of this Scripture, that *He delivers us according to His righteousness and lovingkindness.* He rescues His children when it is best for them and His will. No wise, earthly parent would choose to deliver his or her child from every conflict or disturbance that comes along. However, we can trust Him to care for us and to deliver us from the furnace of affliction in which we must walk.

Jesus gravitated to those who needed Him the most. His compassion reflected the loving nature of our Father. In any trial, therefore, we can rest assured that we have the sympathy, strength, and succor of God the Father.

PSALM 32

THE FRUIT OF REPENTANCE

The Superscription: A Psalm of David. A Maskil. The two words **a Psalm** do not appear in the Hebrew text. The expression **of** ["by," "for," or "to"] **David** (לְדָוִד, *l^edawid*) means, as is confirmed by Romans 4:6–8, that David wrote this psalm. It is counted as the second of the seven penitential psalms. These popular psalms contain heartfelt expressions of repentance over sins committed (6; 32; 38; 51; 102; 130; 143). Beyond the emphasis on confession of sin and forgiveness, the psalm also has the characteristics of thanksgiving and instruction.

The psalm's title further refers to it as **a Maskil** (מַשְׂכִּיל). This is the first time this term has been used in superscriptions, but it is later used with twelve other psalms (42; 44; 45; 52—55; 74; 78; 88; 89; 142). The designation may mean "teaching, instruction, or guidance," and thus may convey that it was written to be a didactic psalm.

Because of its assurance of God's forgiveness for the penitent believer, this "account of repentance" has been a favorite of Bible believers over the centuries. Before his death, Augustine, who believed that the beginning of knowledge is to know oneself to be a sinner, asked that this psalm be written on the wall next to his bed so that he might read it and be comforted by it in his sickness.[1] Apparently, during his last days, he used this psalm to remind himself of God's mercy toward those who turn to God from sin.

In the psalm David writes about how he himself has received God's grace after acknowledging his sin. The background of the

---

[1] A. F. Kirkpatrick, *The Book of Psalms*, The Cambridge Bible for Schools and Colleges (Cambridge: University Press, 1901), 1:161–62.

psalm must have been the forgiveness that God granted David after his sin with Bathsheba. This sin had resulted in lying, having Uriah killed, and concealing his sins for almost a year (2 Sam. 11; 12). Nathan's stinging rebuke sent the fire of conviction into David's heart, and he responded with deep sorrow and repentance. God removed David's guilt, but the sword of violence followed his house as a consequence of his sins (2 Sam. 12:9–14).

Psalm 51, a moving plea for pardon that was written shortly after Nathan called David to repentance, must have been written before this psalm. Sometime later, this psalm was written, as David looked back at what had happened and how God had responded to him. Perhaps he wrote it for the instruction and encouragement of others, desiring that they might learn from his experience.

The heart of this saga of turning back to God is the truth that repentance is necessary to receive forgiveness and the blessings associated with forgiveness.

BLESSED ARE THE FORGIVEN
(32:1, 2)

¹**How blessed is he whose transgression is forgiven,
Whose sin is covered!**
²**How blessed is the man to whom the LORD does not impute iniquity,
And in whose spirit there is no deceit!**

Verse 1. God had responded to David's repentance with His gracious forgiveness. With proper appreciation, he says, **How blessed is he whose transgression is forgiven, whose sin is covered!** Before telling of his conversion, he announces the result of it—forgiveness. So beautiful is this picture of the remission of guilt that Paul used it to depict what Christ does for us through His cross in the Christian Age (Rom. 4:7, 8).

The word "blessed" (אַשְׁרֵי, 'ashrey), a plural word in Hebrew, speaks of the complete happiness of the one who has received

PSALM 32

God's cleansing grace. Because of this fact, the word could be translated with the more picturesque word, "happinesses." The word is an interjection declaring that one receives multifaceted benefits with God's pardon.

The word for "covered" means more than that of draping a spread of some kind over sins and hiding them from view. It carries the thought of removing them totally. They are covered in the sense of their being completely rubbed out.

Verse 2. Repeating the thought in different words, David says, **How blessed is the man to whom the LORD does not impute iniquity!** To emphasize God's absolute redemption, he uses the word "blessed" twice, three synonyms for "sin," and three descriptions of "forgiveness."

Whether David's mistake is seen as a "transgression," "sin," or "iniquity," God's mercy forgave it and removed it. "Transgression" (פֶּשַׁע, pesha‘) is an act of rebellion or disloyalty; "sin" (חֲטָאָה, chªta’ah) is the act of missing the mark; and "iniquity" (עָוֹן, ‘awon) is a crooked or wrong act. These three words overlap in this setting and are probably not intended to be precise definitions of the different types of sin. They are used to show that the totality of his sin had been dealt with by the Lord. He had sinned against God's law, the immutable rule of right, and the purity required of the soul. His condition had required God's lovingkindness, and he had received it.

God had "forgiven" his transgression, had "covered" his sin, and had not "impute[d]" his iniquity. His sins—whether against God or man, intentional or inadvertent, sins of omission or commission—had been taken away. "Forgiveness" (נָשָׂא, nasa’) means to send away; "covered" (כְּסוּי, kªsuy) implies that God hides it; and "does not impute" (חָשַׁב, chashab) suggests that God does not count it or consider it against the repentant one. These words unite to express the eternal removal of anything that was charged against the psalmist.

Such salvation is granted to those **in whose spirit there is no deceit**. One must bring to God a "spirit" free from guile, deceit, or hypocrisy. Frankly and honestly, he had poured out his confession and contrite heart before God. He had been sorry for his sin because he had hurt God, others, and himself. His genuine repentance had opened up his life to God's cleansing.

God's washing the soul clean from all guilt is one of the most beautiful and meaningful blessings one can receive. The genuinely penitent person would rather have God's grace than anything else.

These verses show that a joy stemmed from the blotting out of transgressions in Old Testament times. Consequently, how much more is there the joy of redemption in the Christian Age, the age that has followed the death of Jesus through which full and complete forgiveness has been provided!

THE RESULT OF SILENCE (32:3, 4)

³**When I kept silent about my sin, my body wasted away Through my groaning all day long.**
⁴**For day and night Your hand was heavy upon me; My vitality was drained away as with the fever heat of summer. Selah.**

Verse 3. When David had lived as an impenitent person, an indescribable misery gripped him. He relates his pain: **When I kept silent about my sin, my body wasted away through my groaning all day long.** Nothing can disturb one's tranquility like trying to conceal sin or refusing to repent of sin. During the time that David had tried to hide his sin, he had become more and more beaten down by his sin. His whole body had seemed to rebuke him because of his transgressions. In figurative exaggeration, he describes his body as wasting away or falling apart from the heavy strain of the load of his guilt.

Instead of confessing his sin, he had been "groaning" (שְׁאָגָה, *sheʾagah*) or roaring "all day long." He must have complained about the severity of his pain, with his complaints surfacing as a continual moaning over his plight and situation. Instead of fixing the problem, he had roared about it with the whines of distress.

Verse 4. He asserts, **For day and night Your hand was heavy upon me.** The torment of his guilt had revealed itself in both mental and bodily agony. "Day and night" he had been burdened with grief. The NASB translates the second part of this verse, a difficult Hebrew sentence, **My vitality was drained away as with the fever heat of summer.** The idea is that the moisture of his body had dried up as water does in a drought. His body had deteriorated, and his spirit had been immersed in torment and sorrow. He says that God's "hand was heavy upon" him. God used this pain to turn his mind toward godly sorrow. Remorse, a hurting conscience, and the inability to sleep were built-in rebukes from God. They seemed to point divine fingers at him and say, "You have sinned, and you need to repent!"

The word **Selah** must conclude the thought and is an indication that the reader should spend some time thinking about this truth.

CONFESSION AND REPENTANCE
(32:5)

⁵I acknowledged my sin to You,
And my iniquity I did not hide;
I said, "I will confess my transgressions to the LORD";
And You forgave the guilt of my sin. Selah.

Verse 5. A major turning point in the psalm appears in this verse with David telling of his confession of sin: **I acknowledged my sin to You, and my iniquity I did not hide.** Through the preaching of Nathan, a convicting conscience, and the unspeakable torture that he had suffered, he resolved to turn to God with tearful and resolute repentance (see 2 Sam. 12:13). He made up his mind to confess his sin to God. His decision is embodied in ten words in English and five in the Hebrew. **I said, "I will confess my transgressions to the LORD."** Thus the repentance of his heart was expressed in a straightforward acknowledgment to God.

"Acknowledging sin" and "not hiding iniquity" comprise a synonymous parallelism. Sin is not dealt with until it is confessed without any deceit or dishonesty before God.

The results of such a confession are not surprising in light of the lovingkindness of God. David says, **You forgave the guilt of my sin.** God, in keeping with His character, sent away his horrible guilt. His prayer was heard, and God forgave him.

These were Old Testament times, and this man had fallen out of a covenant relationship with God. His return to God is pictured in terms of confession and repentance. It would be inappropriate to conclude that this is the way a non-Christian comes to Christ in the Christian Age (see Mt. 28:19, 20; Acts 2:38).

Once again it must be that **Selah** is used to motivate the reader to pause and think deeply about this thought.

A RECOMMENDATION (32:6, 7)

> ⁶**Therefore, let everyone who is godly pray to You in a time when You may be found;**
> **Surely in a flood of great waters they will not reach him.**
> ⁷**You are my hiding place; You preserve me from trouble;**
> **You surround me with songs of deliverance. Selah.**

Verse 6. Upon the basis of what had happened to David, a recommendation is given to others. He advises, **Therefore, let everyone who is godly pray to You in a time when You may be found.** He urges everyone to learn from his mistakes and from his forgiveness. Those with genuine hearts can pray to God for the same deliverance he received. God will be gracious to them as He was with him. Those who are right with God can ask Him to be their constant companion. He is confident that those who need forgiveness will find it; those who need shelter will receive it. If one in such need of forgiveness lingers and does not repent, the time will come when it will be too late. The Hebrew has "a time of finding only," indicating a restricted time of opportunity.

Surely in a flood of great waters they will not reach him. One hidden in God will not be affected or "reach[ed]" by the flood of calamity. However, one needs to prepare for the great trials in advance. If he waits to decide about this until he is surrounded by "a flood of great waters," he will not be able to come to Him.

Verse 7. This truth about God's willingness to pardon sin reminds David of what God is to all penitent souls: **You are my hiding place.** When we come to God, He will protect, shield, and deliver us. Only God can conceal us from the disasters of life. To the righteous, He will be a "hiding place." This means that God will **preserve** [the godly man] **from trouble** and trials of all kinds. He encircles him with His love and strength when difficulties come. David further affirms, **You surround me with songs of deliverance.** The security found in Him will be so complete that the redeemed will continuously sing and shout in joy about the redemption God has given. The word for "songs" (רָנֵּי, *ranney*) can mean a shout or cry of excitement. The melody of triumph will be in their hearts and on their lips daily.

The person who repents not only has forgiveness from God, but he also has peace and security with God.

Again, **Selah** is apparently used to ask the worshiper to pause and consider this truth.

"LISTEN TO MY INSTRUCTION" (32:8, 9)

⁸I will instruct you and teach you in the way which you should go;
I will counsel you with My eye upon you.
⁹Do not be as the horse or as the mule which have no understanding,
Whose trappings include bit and bridle to hold them in check,
Otherwise they will not come near to you.

Verse 8. The text changes to a new spokesman: God speaks and tells how He will guide the forgiven one into the paths of righteousness. He says, **I will instruct you and teach you in the way which you should go.** David is being assured that he will be guided into righteous living. God says, **I will counsel you with My eye upon you.** God will keep His watchful "eye" upon him and give him "counsel" or the direction he needs. He offers to assist David in his life struggles in three ways: He will "instruct" him, that is, give him understanding, "teach" him, and "counsel" or advise him. These words overlap as they convey the complete guidance that God will give.

Forgiveness and faith must lead to obedience and righteousness. God and David will walk together, and David will have the advantage of God's wisdom, love, and leadership. He will benefit immensely from his fellowship with God. David will need to remain open and receptive to God's guidance for this relationship to remain intact.

A result of repentance, then, is fellowship with God. This fact is alluded to in the final verses, but it is addressed specifically in verses 8 and 9. No one but the penitent can have genuine and continued companionship with God.

Verse 9. Because of the relationship God now sustains with David, the importance of David's obedience is accented with a vivid illustration: **Do not be as the horse or as the mule which have no understanding, whose trappings include bit and bridle to hold them in check, otherwise they will not come near to you.** Two beasts of burden are used for comparison. They cannot consider carefully what they need to do. They are dependent upon outside forces, such as bits and bridles, to guide them, curb them, and hold them in check. To bring horses or mules to our assistance, we put harnesses on them and compel them with our commands.

God's directive is cast in the plural: "You [plural] be not." His initial description to what He was going to do was phrased in the singular: "I will instruct you [singular] and teach you [singular]." It must be that His guidance was meant for a larger hearing than just David. Perhaps He intended for David to receive it and in turn pass it on to others.

Do we have to be made to follow God? If so, we are like horses or mules. Our obedience and conformity to righteousness should be freely given, not constrained by discipline. We should not have to be made to yield to God's will. If we do not obey Him freely, choosing to submit to His will out of love, we may have to be brought back to obedience by discipline and judgment.

PSALM 32

PENITENCE BRINGS JOY (32:10, 11)

¹⁰Many are the sorrows of the wicked,
But he who trusts in the LORD, lovingkindness shall surround him.
¹¹Be glad in the LORD and rejoice, you righteous ones;
And shout for joy, all you who are upright in heart.

Verse 10. A summary conclusion can now be stated: **Many are the sorrows of the wicked, but he who trusts in the LORD, lovingkindness shall surround him.** Sorrows will follow the wicked as morning follows the night. The two are inseparable. The converse is also true: God's lovingkindness, His gracious providential care, will surround the righteous. Just as surely as one trusts in God, he will know His mercies.

Verse 11. Because of what God has done for us, it is appropriate for us to exhort one another to be joyous; and David does. He admonishes, **Be glad in the LORD and rejoice, you righteous ones; and shout for joy, all you who are upright in heart.** A reward of repentance is joy. It is a consequence that flows from the good things that have been received from the Lord's hand. Therefore, the psalm ends with a plea for the righteous to rejoice. The invitation is deeper than the charge to put a smile on one's face; it is an exhortation to have a deep appreciation for what God has done. The godly are bountifully blessed by God, and their rejoicing should be an overflow from the consciousness of the spiritual treasures filling their lives.

APPLICATION

The Benefits of Repentance
After reading this psalm, we understand the benefits of repentance. Granted by a gracious God to the penitent person are the gifts of forgiveness—complete and full; peace—thorough and enduring; fellowship with God—daily and uninterrupted; and joy—deep and flowing out of a heart at rest in God's assurances.

Rededication to the Lord

We would call the change experienced and explained by David a "conversion" or "rededication." After knowing God and walking with Him, David had sinned grievously. Therefore, he did not tell of his initial coming to God in this psalm, but he recounted how he *came back* to God after falling away.

Upon returning, he received a new life, a life re-created by God's grace. God received him back into His fellowship and began anew to shower him with His mercies.

In light of what is to be gained by repentance, why would anyone try to hide his sins? The most sensible response to guilt is to do quickly what David eventually did about his sins.

In the Christian Age

Under the Christian dispensation, one must obey the gospel of Christ to be forgiven. He believes in Christ, repents of his sins, confesses Jesus as the Christ, and is baptized for the forgiveness of his sins (Acts 2:36–38). An erring or unfaithful Christian comes back to the Lord by repentance, confession, and prayer (Acts 8:12–24).

Will you try to cover your sins, or will you allow Jesus to cover them for all time and eternity through His blood?

True Forgiveness

Let us look at forgiveness anew. What is it? What is the meaning of it?

It is divine. Forgiveness is granted by the Lord. Others can forgive us of any injuries done to them, but that is only an earthly forgiveness that is partial and frail. God is the One who has truly been sinned against. It is His will that is violated and His love that is shunned. He alone can fully forgive.

It is complete and full. When God forgives, sins are totally put away. He does not forgive half of our sins and leave the other half credited against us. Every sin is dealt with in mercy.

It is eternal. He has no time limit on His forgiveness. When He forgives, He forgives forever.

Let us respond to His forgiveness in two ways: First, with rejoicing. Let us sing and be happy over it. Second, with revealing. Let us tell others about the way into His forgiveness.

What God Does with Sin

What happens when God deals with our sins? What does He do with them?

First, He forgives them. This word carries the idea of "sending away" our sins. He removes them "as far as the east is from the west."

Second, He covers them. This word is not about whitewashing our sins. It suggests completely covering them where they do not exist and will never exist again.

Third, He does not impute them to us. God keeps a record of our lives, noting every sin or mistake. However, when He forgives us, those sins are removed and will never be a part of our record again. Our sin is no longer counted against us.

No wonder David begins this psalm with an expression of happiness. God had dealt with his sin, and nothing could make him happier. When one is overwhelmed with guilt, he has only one ambition—to be forgiven, to be done with his sin forever!

God and Pardon

Forgiveness is granted through repentance. This truth points us to God's relationship to our pardon. What does forgiveness tell us about God?

He is able to pardon us. He does what is necessary to pardon us. If it means sending His Son to the cross to pay the price for our sins, He will do it. He is righteous and full of love. When we come to Him in faith, penitence, and obedience, He works it out to pardon us.

He is willing to pardon us. Motivating God's forgiveness is His willingness to forgive us. It would be the greatest of all tragedies if God were able to forgive but were unwilling to do so. He does not wait for the sinner to come to Him, but, as in the case with Adam (Gen. 3:9), He goes to the sinner and makes known His desire to welcome him back.

He will guide after He has pardoned us. He does not stop with forgiveness. After pardon come the precepts; after the cleansing come the commands. He does not just pardon so that we may be forgiven; He pardons us so that we may live with Him. He saves us so that we may enjoy His fellowship in righteous living and service. After David told of his forgiveness and peace, God spoke and told how He would guide, counsel, and teach him.

Those who have come to know God's forgiveness find it easy to praise Him. Most of our spiritual songs lift up His holy name because of the great salvation He has given. Great grace displays the great heart of God!

Having the Right Heart

The heart of the matter is the matter of the heart. David said that the condition of forgiveness is having toward God a spirit that is free from deceit (v. 2). This thought should suggest a broad characteristic of repentance to us.

It means being honest with God, being open with Him, and being sincere with Him. We are not trying to hide anything from Him. We say, "God, I want to bring every aspect of my life to You. I do not want to conceal any part of it."

We freely acknowledge our wrong to Him. It is a thorough confession that does not leave out anything.

We want to see our sins as He does. Our hearts are eager to be done with every wrong that we have committed.

One is not really penitent until he brings his sins to God in an honest, open, sincere confession in the spirit of having turned from his sins. No one will be perfect after such a confession, but God looks upon the heart. He asks that we come clean with our sin in His appointed way, and then forgiveness will be ours.

The Effects of Guilt

Especially in verses 3 and 4, we see the terrible effects of sin. It is as if those consequences spread throughout the whole personality.

The mental effect. The mind is stressed with guilt. Confusion and disappointment prevail.

The physical effect. The state of the mind affects the state of the body. It is as if the body is worn out. It is as exhausted as it would be from working in the summer's heat.

The social effect. The state of our minds and bodies makes us unfit friends, unwelcome company to others.

The spiritual effect. The main effect of sin is the destruction it brings to our relationship with God. Sin separates us from God, erecting a barrier between God and us that only the blood of Jesus can break down.

God uses these terrible effects to bring us to repentance.

What We Can Do with Our Sin

All of us are sinners (Rom. 3:23). Deep within, we know that we have sinned. What can we do with our sin?

We can deny it. We can look squarely into the face of our sinfulness and tell ourselves that we are not sinners. However, denial never erases the fact of sin; it only complicates its existence.

We can ignore our sin. We can look the other way and pretend that our sin is unimportant. We can fill our hands with activities and our minds with pleasure and other pursuits, thinking that our sin problem will go away.

We can hide it. We can attempt to conceal it by blaming others, sweeping it under the rug and removing it from our view. However, if such is done, we will only learn the hard way about the testimony of Solomon: "He who conceals his transgressions will not prosper" (Prov. 28:13).

We can confess it. We can acknowledge it to God and let Him cover it with His grace. This approach is the only real approach to sin.

We must decide about what we will do with our sin. Usually, if the conscience is still sensitive, if we deny it, ignore it, or hide it, we will be miserable. If we confess it and make it right with God, we will find the peace we are seeking.

The Path to Peace with God

True peace can only be received from God, but how do you receive it?

Open your heart to God. Come before Him with an honest heart that is free from all deceit, sham, and make-believe.

Repent of your sin. Turn from the evil of your life. If you do not forsake your sin, you cannot be forgiven.

Acknowledge your sin. Confess your sin to God, seeing it as God sees it. Bring it out in the open before Him, and renounce it.

Accept God's forgiveness. God will freely grant forgiveness, but you must accept His gift. You can afflict yourself with the burden of sin even though it has in reality been taken away.

The Roots of Joy

What is the source of our joy? From what does it spring?

Joy springs from the blessings of God. David had descended into the throes of misery and despair because of his sin. However, when he received the gifts of forgiveness and peace, he could rejoice once again.

Joy springs from a righteous life. Sin steals our joy; righteous living restores it. When we know that our sins are forgiven and we are walking in the counsel of our God, we have a refreshment and delight that can come from no other source.

Joy springs from walking with God. In His presence are joys forevermore. As we walk with Him, the sunlight of His love surrounds us. His presence brings peace and an awareness of His protection. From these blessings that flow from our personal fellowship with Him comes a joy inexpressible and full of glory.

Joy is not something we grasp as if we were pursuing an ambition. It is a consequence of holiness. To the righteous, David could say, "Be glad in the Lord and rejoice, you righteous ones, and shout for joy, all you who are upright in heart." We live out God's will, and joy comes to us as the fruit of it. Sin is the joy robber; God is the joy giver.

Psalm 33
Let Us Praise Him!

The Superscription: None.

Like Psalms 1, 2, and 10 in Book I, this psalm is an orphan psalm, having no superscription in the Hebrew text. The LXX says that David wrote it (τῷ Δαυιδ, *tō Dauid*). Ten Hebrew manuscripts of the Old Testament unite this psalm with the previous one. Perhaps no superscription is found in the Hebrew Bible for this psalm because Psalms 32 and 33 were regarded as one and the title above Psalm 32 stands as the title for both.

Likely this psalm was composed to celebrate Israel's victory over a strong enemy, but the date and the reason for its writing are unknown. As a hymn of praise, it stresses what God has done and is doing with Israel and the nations of the earth. Psalm 32 ends with an exhortation to be glad in the Lord, and this psalm begins with a continuation of that exhortation.

The body of the psalm answers the major question of why we should give praise to God. In arrangement, it begins with a call to worship Him (vv. 1–3), proceeds to give four reasons why He should be worshiped (vv. 4–21), and then ends with a benediction (v. 22).

"RIGHTEOUS ONES, PRAISE THE LORD"
(33:1–3)

¹Sing for joy in the Lord, O you righteous ones;
Praise is becoming to the upright.
²Give thanks to the Lord with the lyre;

Sing praises to Him with a harp of ten strings.
³Sing to Him a new song;
Play skillfully with a shout of joy.

Verse 1. Emphasizing the same note with which the previous psalm ended, this psalm opens with a call to worship: **Sing for joy in the LORD, O you righteous ones.** The admonition to worship God is addressed to the "righteous" (צַדִּיקִים, *tsaddiqim*) and the "upright" (יְשָׁרִים, *yᵉsharim*). He accepts worship from those who are pure in heart and righteous in life—those who are blameless, not faultless, before Him.

Praise is becoming to the upright. The righteous will find it appropriate ("becoming") to praise God. They see it not only as their duty but also as their honor to praise Him. They know that they are His creation, the result of His redemption, and have been adopted by grace into His family.

Verse 2. How was worship to be given to Him in the context of the Old Testament? The psalm says, **Give thanks to the LORD with the lyre; sing praises to Him with a harp of ten strings.** Four terms are used to describe the gratitude the righteous are to give: "sing," "praise," "give thanks," and "a shout of joy." Praise can be given to God as needs are voiced to Him, as seen in the latter part of this psalm; but most often praise springs from joy because of our gratitude for what God has done for His people.

Verse 3. Because of God's kind benefits, a new song comes from their lips. **Sing to Him a new song; play skillfully with a shout of joy.** The Israelites were to sing "a new song" about the recently bestowed mercies of God, a song that was old in form but new in content. Each recent act of grace was acknowledged in grateful appreciation.

Two instruments are named as accompaniments to these expressions of gratitude: the "lyre" or psaltery (כִּנּוֹר, *kinnor*) and the "harp" (נֶבֶל, *nebel*). The "lyre," one of the oldest musical instruments known (see Gen. 4:21, where the KJV calls it a harp), was used by the Egyptians as well as the Israelites. David was skilled at playing it (1 Sam. 16:23).

The "harp" is first mentioned in the Old Testament in

1 Samuel 10:5, where the ASV and KJV call it a psaltery. It must be that its basic difference from the lyre is the arrangement and number of strings. Both are stringed instruments and are very similar. Other instruments were used in connection with the worship of the Old Testament Era, but only two are referred to in this psalm.

The fact that instrumental music was urged upon Israelite worshipers by this psalm does not mean that these instruments, or instruments in general, should be used in the worship that Christians offer to God in the Christian Age. Numerous methods of worship used in Judaism have been omitted from the worship of the New Testament church by Jesus Christ, the Founder of the church. Worship in the Old Testament included animal sacrifices, burning sacred incense, sprinkling blood upon an altar, dancing before God, the observance of the Sabbath, and ceremonial feasts such as the Day of Atonement, the Passover, the Feast of Weeks, and the Feast of Tabernacles. However, Christ brought to us a new and living way superior to the Old Testament, excluding by command and divinely directed examples all the items mentioned above and many more from the worship of the New Testament church. The Christian follows the New Testament for his prescription on how to worship God in an acceptable manner today.

Even though instrumental music is not included in the New Testament church, we are instructed by the New Testament Scriptures to praise Him, give thanks to Him, and rejoice in Him (Eph. 5:19; Col. 3:16). This psalm can remind the Christian of the worship that we are to give to God, even though the Old Testament method of worshiping with instrumental music is not enjoined upon Christians.

BECAUSE OF HIS CHARACTER
(33:4, 5)

⁴For the word of the LORD is upright,
And all His work is done in faithfulness.
⁵He loves righteousness and justice;

The earth is full of the lovingkindness of the LORD.

The heart of this psalm is the answer to the question "Why should worship be given to God?" When a question of this kind is asked, countless answers come up, four of which are given by this psalm.

Verse 4. Four moral attributes are delineated in verses 4 and 5 as bases for the adoration of God. His integrity—as expressed in His words and deeds—is the first mentioned. **For the word of the LORD is upright, and all His work is done in faithfulness.** God should be worshiped because of who He is. His character sets Him apart, making us understand that He is God, not man. His Word is always true. "Upright" means "without deception" and "the opposite of false." God's faithfulness prevents Him from having any false actions or words. He does all His work out of the absoluteness of His "faithfulness."

Verse 5. What God loves is stressed next: **He loves righteousness and justice; the earth is full of the lovingkindness of the LORD.** Following the mention of His integrity, His holiness is described with the attributes of "righteousness and justice." God loves these traits in His people and exhibits them in His own personality. As God works out His will in the world, He facilitates its growth through the perfect principle of righteous judgment. Further, His "lovingkindness" is listed. His actions are governed by His covenant loyalty to His people.

These attributes—faithfulness, righteousness, justice, and lovingkindness—in their completeness comprise the character of God's being.

Furthermore, as a result of His providence, all "the earth" is full of God's grace. Everywhere we look, we are constrained to behold His merciful activities.

Thus, God's goodness elicits from us devoted praise of Him.

BECAUSE OF HIS CREATIVE POWER
(33:6–9)

⁶**By the word of the LORD the heavens were made,
And by the breath of His mouth all their host.**

⁷He gathers the waters of the sea together as a heap;
He lays up the deeps in storehouses.
⁸Let all the earth fear the LORD;
Let all the inhabitants of the world stand in awe of Him.
⁹For He spoke, and it was done;
He commanded, and it stood fast.

Verse 6. We are also to worship God because of His creative power. **By the word of the LORD the heavens were made, and by the breath of His mouth all their host.** The fact that He brought everything into existence should inspire us to engage in thankfulness and adoration. He spoke, and the heavens above appeared. One breath from His mouth formed all the stars, solar systems, and galaxies.

Verse 7. A brief command from Him configured the earth into its proper form. **He gathers the waters of the sea together as a heap; He lays up the deeps in storehouses.** The Genesis 1 picture is given of God's creative activity at the beginning of time. He gathered the "waters" into one place and made dry land come into being. He "heap[ed]" (נֵד, *ned*) them up the way He did the waters at the Red Sea, as if placing them in treasuries or "storehouses" (אוֹצָר, *'otsar*) in the deep. He gave vast depths to the seas as He stacked them up in various places.

Verse 8. His creative might should cause us to recognize His greatness and sing freely His praises. Indeed, **Let all the earth fear the LORD; let all the inhabitants of the world stand in awe of Him.** All the people of the earth should stand before God in awe. His mighty word and hand of power should humble us. Who can deny this truth? Look at hurricanes, flash floods, droughts, and the vast oceans; and see how His divine strength supersedes man's like the universe over a speck of dust. Mankind possesses a power, but it comes from the source of all power—God.

Verse 9. All creation attests to the divine strength of His word. **For He spoke, and it was done; He commanded, and it stood fast.** God spoke, and the heavens came into being. Genesis 1 portrays God uttering a command that instantly fashioned into existence a part of the universe; He spoke again and another part obeyed His command by appearing. His brief instruction gave all things reality and gave life. The act of creation required only a word from God, an order from His mouth. The Latin expression is *dictum factum,* meaning "said done." We often say, "No sooner said than done." His directives, encoded with His divine energy, were given; and the animate beings and the inanimate things obeyed. No person or thing could resist His words. Even "nothing" yielded entities and mature life when ordered to do so. Oh, the power of God's voice!

BECAUSE OF HIS WORK IN THE WORLD
(33:10–17)

¹⁰**The LORD nullifies the counsel of the nations;**
He frustrates the plans of the peoples.
¹¹**The counsel of the LORD stands forever,**
The plans of His heart from generation to generation.
¹²**Blessed is the nation whose God is the LORD,**
The people whom He has chosen for His own inheritance.
¹³**The LORD looks from heaven;**
He sees all the sons of men;
¹⁴**From His dwelling place He looks out**
On all the inhabitants of the earth,
¹⁵**He who fashions the hearts of them all,**
He who understands all their works.
¹⁶**The king is not saved by a mighty army;**
A warrior is not delivered by great strength.
¹⁷**A horse is a false hope for victory;**
Nor does it deliver anyone by its great strength.

Verse 10. Still another reason to praise God is His control over the world and His work in it. He raises up nations, and puts them down. **The LORD nullifies the counsel of the nations; He frustrates the plans of the peoples.** He turns the best laid plans of men into cobwebs of the past. No nation is totally in charge of its own destiny. No person, group, or nation can overrule His purposes.

PSALM 33

Verse 11. The guidance of the Lord endures and sustains. **The counsel of the LORD stands forever, the plans of His heart from generation to generation.** Nothing that happens upon the earth is accidental. The world has an order and a flow that come from God. Overarching the whims of people is the gracious determination of God to bless the godly and accomplish His holy purposes through them. Above the proposals of people are set the plans of God. What one chooses to do can retard God's will, but his choices cannot totally foil it. God seeks salvation for everyone; but if only a few choose His way and are saved, God's purposes have not been destroyed. He will work out His eternal design regardless of what people do, say, or think.

Verse 12. The reasons for praising God coalesce into a pronouncement of blessing upon Israel, God's chosen nation. **Blessed is the nation whose God is the LORD, the people whom He has chosen for His own inheritance.** "The nation whose God is the LORD"—that is, Israel—would be especially blessed and honored. This nation had been chosen by God as the people through whom He would work out His purposes. Thus the Israelites received special status in God's sight. The righteous ones in Israel would be the recipients of sustenance, security, and salvation.

Verse 13. The Lord can care for His own because He knows everything that occurs on earth. **The LORD looks from heaven; He sees all the sons of men.** The Lord on high observes the world He has made, carefully watching over it with sustaining care. His gaze is all-inclusive: He sees "all" the sons of men (v. 13); He considers "all" the inhabitants of the earth (v. 14); He has fashioned "all" hearts (v. 15); He understands "all" works.

Verse 14. Continually, the Lord from His throne observes and monitors. **From His dwelling place He looks out on all the inhabitants of the earth.** No one, righteous person or rebel, is outside His oversight. He sees all and knows all.

Verse 15. God not only knows what happens on earth, but He is also fully aware of how it happens and why it happens. The Creator intimately understands His creation. He is the One **who fashions the hearts of them all, He who understands all their works.** He made their bodies and minds, and He notes all that they do. Everyone is accountable to Him. As the Maker of all things, He is the ultimate and final Judge of all the earth.

Verse 16. A man looks at military strategies and plans for his comfort and confidence; his hopes center in what he can do. However, the wise understand that **the king is not saved by a mighty army; a warrior is not delivered by great strength.** The rulers of the earth may value the might of soldiers and the muscle of standing battalions, but behind earthly authority is God's authority. The "strength" of an "army," "a warrior," and horses cannot save. God is the absolute Ruler who gives energy to the nations and decides on their positions of influence.

Verse 17. Physical power is a broken reed, unable to hold up any weight. **A horse is a false hope for victory; nor does it deliver anyone by its great strength.** Fleshly strength, like a warhorse, is a lie, a "false hope" (שֶׁקֶר, *sheqer*), if one is looking to it for success. The word for "victory" comes from the Hebrew word that means "salvation" (תְּשׁוּעָה, *th^eshu'ah*). People depend upon other people for deliverance and wisdom, but the strongest efforts of mankind melt like snowflakes before a rising sun if God is against them. The righteous remember that God rules over human affairs. God should be praised for what He does on earth with nations and people.

BECAUSE OF HIS CARE FOR HIS OWN
(33:18–21)

¹⁸**Behold, the eye of the LORD is on those who fear Him,
On those who hope for His lovingkindness,
¹⁹To deliver their soul from death
And to keep them alive in famine.
²⁰Our soul waits for the LORD;
He is our help and our shield.
²¹For our heart rejoices in Him,
Because we trust in His holy name.**

Verse 18. Another reason to bow down before God and worship Him is the care He gives His own. God has a special concern for those who trust in Him. Here, then, is an eternally important observation: **Behold, the eye of the Lord is on those who fear Him, on those who hope for His lovingkindness.** The righteous man can rest assured that God has a watchful "eye" and preserving hand upon him. "The eye of the Lord" is a figurative way of referring to His favor and goodness. God's face and eyes turning toward the righteous is synonymous in thought to the kindnesses and bounties of God being extended to them.

Verse 19. God's protection has spiritual and physical dimensions. He will watch over the righteous **to deliver their soul from death and to keep them alive in famine.** Those who revere God and reach out for His grace will be providentially protected as they face enemies and the ravages of natural disaster.

Verse 20. The believers therefore put their trust in Him. They have made a commitment to Him. They can say, **Our** [souls wait] **for the Lord; He is our help and our shield.** Because of His protective care, His servants resolve to wait for Him. They look to Him as their guide and "shield."

Verse 21. The proper trust in God brings a permanent joy in God. **For our heart rejoices in Him, because we trust in His holy name.** When we understand who He is and what He does for His children, our hearts will overflow with joy because He is our God.

A BENEDICTION
(33:22)

²²**Let Your lovingkindness, O Lord, be upon us,**
According as we have hoped in You.

Verse 22. A brief prayer or benediction ends the psalm: **Let Your lovingkindness, O Lord, be upon us, according as we have hoped in You.** We can put our trust in Him, knowing that He will do for us what He has promised. Our real need is God's "lovingkindness." However, the gift of His grace will be in proportion to the trust and hope we have in Him. Those who put their faith in God can expect full deliverance from God. He has never failed and will never fail those who trust in Him. Praise God for His love for His people!

APPLICATION

The Naturalness of Praise
When we think of who God is, the character He possesses, His creative power, His control over the world, and His care for His own, we cannot help but praise Him. We should be constrained by these facts to come before Him continually with adoring worship.

The Refreshing Acts of God
Regardless of the age or circumstances in which we live, we will experience acts of love from God. We will see His greatness anew, His providence encircling us, and His grace daily saving us. In every new situation and day, He is extending His mercy toward us. Thus we can sing a brand new song to Him each time we come to Him (Lam. 3:22).

Praising God
The Christian should be adept in praising God. Such an activity is normal with him. From verses 1 through 3 of this psalm we can draw important lessons about praising the Lord.

We see that praise is an expression of gratitude. Praise is an overflow and outflow of thanksgiving. We celebrate thanksgiving in America, but many families do not know whom to thank. The Christian does.

We see that praise should emerge from joy. The happiness God has given us should express itself in praise. Worship should be a joyous occasion, with worshipers gathering to sing with happy hearts.

These verses make clear that praise should be given by righteous people. The call to worship is given to God's blameless people. God is a righteous God, and He wants His righteous ones to worship Him (see Is. 6:4, 5).

We learn that praise is a recurring theme. We sing a new song each time we come together because we have new reasons to praise our God. In 1 John 2:7, John said that he was writing about the old commandment to love one another that had become new. It was old in age but new in quality. Jesus had made it new because He had shown us how to exhibit it. So it is with praise. God's recent mercy gives us a reason to add new songs of praise to our worship. We may sing an old song, but we sing it in a new way or with new meaning.

One call that Christians hear regularly is the call to worship. It comes through our joys, our righteous lives, the recurring mercies of God, and the gratitude of our hearts for all that God has done. Let us hear these calls and eagerly respond to them.

"Tell Me About Your God"

Suppose someone asked you, "Tell me about your God. What is He like?" What would you say? If you used this psalm as your guide, here is what you would say:

He created all things. He is the Originator of all things and all people.

His word is upright. He tells the truth, and no word of His has ever failed or fallen to the ground.

His deeds are faithful. He acts out of covenant loyalty by keeping His covenant and standing by His people.

He loves righteousness. The core of His being is righteousness. He is righteous, and He loves those who are righteous.

He fills the earth with His lovingkindness. As we look around us, we are reminded that all lovingkindness flows from Him. His first response to all people is the response of grace.

He is to be praised because He is almighty, His word is upright, His deeds are faithful, He loves righteousness, and He is filling the earth with lovingkindness. Any inquiring person who understands these attributes of God will be constrained to turn to Him and give Him the praise of which He is worthy.

The Word of the Lord

One's words represent his personality, power, and being. Therefore, when we think of God's Word, we think of His mind, His innermost being, His personality, and His strength.

His words create. He spoke, and the heavens appeared; He

spoke again, and the waters gathered together in the form of seas. He drew the waters together and put a border around them, as if He had put them in a bottle.

His words sustain. He speaks, and His sustaining force enters the world. He upholds the world continually. Hence, He holds together, as in the palm of His hand, all created life and inanimate things.

His words save. These great attributes of His Word suggest to the believer how God's words are words of salvation. If He can create and sustain, He can save us from any peril. He has only to speak the word.

No one is more protected and more free from harm than the one surrounded by the promises of God. How comforting it is to remember that He sent Jesus, the Word, into the world as the expression of His being, to provide eternal salvation for all who come to Him in obedient faith!

Transformed by His Nature

This psalm was written to inspire the praise of God. It is a call to worship, containing an invitation to worship, a list of the attributes of God that engender worship, and a benediction. Notice how this psalm leads us into worship.

His creative power should produce awe. To contemplate the words "He spoke, and it was done" should cause us to be lost in the wonder of God's great power.

His sustaining power should create dependence. Nothing stays in place except through His continued superintendence, and no life continues except through His supply of energy and support. Knowing this should cause us to say, "In Him, we live, move, have our being, and have our spiritual life" (Acts 17:28).

His lovingkindness should generate thanksgiving. Thinking of His grace, His mercy, and His love should inspire us to sing His praise each day. Everywhere we look, we see His sustaining strength and His fresh lovingkindnesses.

We will become like the way we think. Thinking of God and praising Him changes us into His likeness. God is our guiding star in character development and in learning to think as a person ought to think.

The Sovereign God

In verses 10 through 12 we see the sovereignty of our God. He is not only life to us but also Lord over us. His decisions are final, and His actions are incontestible.

He lifts up. He raises up the nations that He wants. He controls not only individuals but also races of people. In His great providence He increases the power of nations and decreases the power of others.

He puts down. He destroys and eliminates as He sees fit. He brought down the great Roman Empire in His own way and at the time He chose. By changing the trade routes, He destroyed Edom, who lived high up in the rocky cliffs (see Obad. 3). He overcame Egypt through rearing the boy Moses in Pharaoh's palace (Ex. 2:10).

His plans are eternal. He keeps all His actions within the confines of His eternal purposes. Our plans are fleeting; but God's plans stretch from eternity past to eternity future. Nothing that we do will destroy God's eternal will.

His people endure forever. Those who put their faith in Him become His people, and they will be blessed eternally. God takes those who have chosen Him and makes them into His nation. His promises undergird us, and His almighty hand shields us.

Nothing should be more encouraging than thinking of the sovereignty of God. He has no rival in time or in eternity. No one can fathom His might or absorb His wisdom. Obviously, the safest place anyone can ever be is in the shadow of His wing.

What God Beholds

God holds the universe in the palm of His hand. He created it, and He controls it. He is omnipotent and omniscient. Think of what God sees on earth from His glorious throne.

He sees all people. No one slides past His notice or is ever lost in the crowd. He can know everything about everyone without even straining His eyes. He sees every move and hears every heartbeat.

He observes every work or deed that is done. Our works are before Him. He analyzes them from top to bottom, beholding their value and their worthlessness. He sees our efforts before they even come into existence.

He understands the motives that we have. He made our hearts; He knows how they work. He considers why we do what we do, beholding us from the inside out, seeing our hearts as clearly as He sees our actions.

He knows how weak our efforts are. When we lean on futile efforts, when we try to win with an army, warriors, or horses, we reveal our stupidity. Our greatest accumulation of strength is but sawdust in the wind before Him. The mightiest army we could bring together would be seen by Him as nothing more than a little boy attacking the tallest mountain with a toy gun.

He knows all things; we know only a little. He has all power; we have only a thimbleful of strength. He is God, and we are His children. These traits of God should elicit praise from any thinking person.

The Lord and His People

This psalm ends with a benediction, an expression that calls for God's blessings to be upon the reader or worshiper. This final word answers an important question for us: What does the Lord do for His people?

He watches over them. He keeps His searching eyes on every move they make. Anyone who doubts this truth just needs to casually survey biblical history.

He protects them. He delivers their souls or lives from death by being their help and shield.

He sustains them. He gives them life at all times by permitting His children to live in Him. They do not have to fear famine or any other perils because He gives them strength and deliverance, life and joy, even in the midst of tragedy.

He extends lovingkindness to them. His grace is evident in His forgiveness and in the opportunities He supplies for spiritual growth.

He guarantees their future. He fulfills their hopes for tomorrow, whether in time or in eternity.

How blessed the obedient believer in God is!

PSALM 33

Glorying in God's Grace

In this hymn of praise, a special picture of God's grace is given. His lovingkindness is conveyed to us from four different viewpoints.

We see His grace in His Word. In verses 4 through 9 the Word of the Lord is described. His commands are filled with creative power and bring order out of chaos. His Word has created this world for our enjoyment; it has brought into existence His great scheme of redemption for our spiritual welfare.

We see His grace in His plan. His gracious plan is depicted in verses 10 through 12. He will not allow any disobedient nation to destroy His purposes. His guidance and counsel stand forever. He overrules the actions of mankind to accomplish His eternal design.

We see His grace in His eyes. In verses 13 through 19 a description of the Lord's eyes is given. He watches over the sons of men and never misses a single move that they make. He observes His people so that He may bless and guide them. He will not allow any need they have to escape His notice.

We see His grace in His might. In verses 16 through 19 the Lord's great power is extolled. He uses His might in behalf of those who trust in Him. He delivers them from death and famine and the other dragons of this world.

Grace flows from every part of God for those who put their faith in Him. His Word describes it; His plan provides it; His eyes manifest it; and His strength implements it. His grace brought us into His salvation, and His grace sustains us in His salvation as we walk with Him.

Psalm 34
"The Lord Has Been Mindful of Me"

The Superscription: A Psalm of David when he feigned madness before Abimelech, who drove him away and he departed. According to the heading, this is a psalm **of** ["by," "for," or "to"] **David** (לְדָוִד, *lᵉdawid*). **A Psalm** does not appear in the Hebrew text although the NASB includes it. The heading also indicates that this piece was composed sometime after David feigned madness before Abimelech.

One question regarding this superscription is that it refers to the king of Gath as Abimelech, while 1 Samuel 21:10 calls him Achish. The king may have been known by two names, with perhaps Abimelech being a dynastic name.

This event could have been the background of the psalm, or it could be one illustration of how the Lord delivered David on various occasions.

Obviously, this beautiful psalm was composed by a writer who wanted to give thanks to God for the special help he had received from Him. It contains two types of literature, an individual thanksgiving section and a teaching part.

The thoughts are cast in an acrostic pattern, with each couplet starting with a different letter of the alphabet, much like Psalm 25. The entire Hebrew alphabet is used except ו (*Vav*). An extra פ (*Pe*) was added at the end to replace the missing *Vav* and complete the number of twenty-two letters.

With Saul on his trail, David fled to Gath in Philistia, thinking the Philistines would not recognize him. He hoped to find asylum among them for a brief time and escape the sword of Saul. Being immediately identified by the Philistines, he had to improvise. He began to act as an insane man, scribbling on the doors of the gate and making spittle run down his beard. Convinced of David's insanity, the king drove him away from Gath, wanting nothing to do with him. David's life was saved by his impersonation, and he fled to another place for safety from Saul, the jealous king. According to the title, David later thought of this event of deliverance and wrote this psalm to express his gratefulness for God's protection. If this event in David's life is not the background of the psalm, it does provide a graphic representation of the type of circumstance the psalm is depicting.

The theme of the psalm is the comforting truth that God looks after those who trust in Him and fear Him. The writer praises God and urges others to join him in thanking God because of how He cares for His people.

BLESSING THE LORD (34:1–3)

¹**I will bless the LORD at all times;**
His praise shall continually be in my mouth.
²**My soul will make its boast in the LORD;**
The humble will hear it and rejoice.
³**O magnify the LORD with me,**
And let us exalt His name together.

Verse 1. The acrostic letter is א (*Aleph*).

The psalm begins with the writer announcing his intention to praise God continuously. He resolves, **I will bless the LORD at all times; His praise shall continually be in my mouth.** "To bless" (בָּרַךְ, *barak*) in respect to God means to worship Him, to praise Him, and to thank Him. God blesses us by what He gives us; we bless God by what we think about Him, say to Him, and by the service to others that we render in His name. These words suggest the basic elements of praising God. We are to bless Him with our lips and hearts, praise Him continuously, and praise Him with joy and gratitude of the soul.

Verse 2. The acrostic letter is ב (*Beth*).

He further says, **My soul will make its boast in the LORD; the humble will hear it and rejoice.** The word for "boast" is a form of the word for "praise" (הָלַל, *halal*). He will "boast" in the Lord by rejoicing and glorying in Him. He will not congratulate himself on anything that he has accomplished or possessed; however, he will remind himself that his most valuable asset is that he has chosen the Lord as his God.

This testimony is good news to "the humble," to those who are beaten down by circumstances or foes. They will hear what God does for the writer and rejoice because they know that He will do the same for them. God will be the refuge of anyone who seeks Him!

Verse 3. The acrostic letter is ג (*Gimel*).

He calls upon others to join him in magnifying the Lord. **O magnify the Lord with me, and let us exalt His name together.** "Magnify" is from a word that means "to make great" (גָּדַל, *gadal*). We cannot make God any greater by what we say or do, but we can tell others how great He is, amplifying Him in their eyes by teaching and instruction. The main purpose of such worship is not to make us feel good, but to acknowledge together who God is and how He has bestowed His love upon us.

HE ANSWERS OUR PRAYERS (34:4–7)

⁴I sought the Lord, and He answered me,
And delivered me from all my fears.
⁵They looked to Him and were radiant,
And their faces will never be ashamed.
⁶This poor man cried, and the Lord heard him
And saved him out of all his troubles.
⁷The angel of the Lord encamps around those who fear Him,
And rescues them.

Verse 4. The acrostic letter is ד (*Daleth*).

The psalmist worships God faithfully and urges others to join him, but this is not sufficient for him. He has other reasons for wanting to express his gratitude to God. He says, **I sought the Lord, and He answered me, and delivered me from all my**

fears. As he thinks of what God has done for him, he remembers anew that God has answered his prayers.

The psalmist is talking about his own experiences. His words are not a sermon, but more of a testimony. Surrounded by many terrors, he fled to God for refuge through his prayers, and God brought him through his dark nights. He removed all his fears.

Verse 5. The acrostic letter is ה (*He*).

His past history with God reminds him of how God treats all others who trust in Him. He says of believers in God, **They looked to Him and were radiant, and their faces will never be ashamed.** Because of the assistance they receive from Him, those who look to God are made "radiant" (נָהַר, *nahar*) with the afterglow of His presence and the joy of victory. Isaiah used this word "radiant," the only other time it is used in the Old Testament, in connection with the Lord rising up in behalf of His people. He said, "Then you shall see and be radiant" (Is. 60:5). God's trusting ones are never disappointed. When they emerge triumphant from a death-like struggle, their faces shine with the happiness of conquest. They look to their God who has rescued them, and their thoughts of Him fill their hearts with gladness. They are set aglow with love and appreciation for God, knowing they will never be defeated in Him.

Verse 6. The acrostic letter is ז (*Zayin*). The letter *Vav* is skipped.

David remembers his plight and his dire need: **This poor man cried, and the LORD heard him and saved him out of all his troubles.** As a poor fugitive without a home or money, he had gone to God with his petition—and God had heard him. He had nothing to offer God except his heart; but God, the great King of the earth, accepted what he had given and fought for him.

Verse 7. The acrostic letter is ח (*Heth*).

God has helped him in a never-to-be-forgotten way. Figuratively portrayed, the Lord's army surrounds him to protect and fight for him: **The angel of the LORD encamps around those who fear Him, and rescues them.** The Lord has put an invincible wall around him so that he cannot be harmed by the forces of this world. He has been preserved in this way because he has feared the Lord. "Fear" as used here refers to the different aspects of the Christian's relationship with God. It refers to the basic godly respect that should be present in one's daily life with Him.

HE MEETS ALL OUR NEEDS (34:8–10)

⁸O taste and see that the LORD is good;
How blessed is the man who takes refuge in Him!
⁹O fear the LORD, you His saints;
For to those who fear Him there is no want.
¹⁰The young lions do lack and suffer hunger;
But they who seek the LORD shall not be in want of any good thing.

Verse 8. The acrostic letter is ט (*Teth*).

An appeal is made for anyone interested to experience the goodness of God and see if He is not the highest and best of all refuges. He says, **O taste and see that the LORD is good**. As he thinks of another reason for his gratitude, David says that God has supplied his needs and will meet the needs of those who come and put their trust in Him.

Anyone who doubts this sweeping affirmation ought to trust in the Lord and find out for themselves. He urges, "O taste and see!" The original word "taste" (טָעַם, *ta'am*) carries the idea of discerning, perceiving, judging. His statement is like the expression "The proof of the pudding is in the eating." One must *try* it to understand the truth. God is not a fairy tale. He is real, and He delivers on His promises. **How blessed is the man who takes refuge in Him!** Anyone who comes to God for refuge will find Him to be a refuge that is authentic and almighty.

Verse 9. The acrostic letter is י (*Yodh*).

Nothing can compare to the security that God gives. Appropriately, an exhortation is given to all saints: **O fear the LORD, you His saints; for to those who fear Him there is no want.** He pleads for all true saints, those who are set apart for God, to "fear" the Lord and follow Him in reverence and love. He can testify that all of their legitimate human and spiritual needs will be met by Him. They will experience "no want," no deficiency, no poverty. A similar word is used in Psalm 23:1: "I shall not want."

Verse 10. The acrostic letter is כ (*Kaph*).

The righteous one's situation with God is compared to the needs of the young lions: **The young lions do lack and suffer hunger; but they who seek the L**ORD **shall not be in want of any good thing.** Those who are self-sufficient and proud, like lions of the forest, may become destitute and needy; but that will never be the case with God's people. Those who seek Him shall never be without anything that is truly necessary.

"LET ME TEACH YOU" (34:11–14)

> ¹¹**Come, you children, listen to me;**
> **I will teach you the fear of the L**ORD**.**
> ¹²**Who is the man who desires life**
> **And loves length of days that he may see good?**
> ¹³**Keep your tongue from evil**
> **And your lips from speaking deceit.**
> ¹⁴**Depart from evil and do good;**
> **Seek peace and pursue it.**

Verse 11. The acrostic letter is ל (*Lamedh*).

The writer now becomes a teacher, explaining what it means to fear the Lord: **Come, you children, listen to me; I will teach you the fear of the L**ORD**.** "Let me tell you what it means to respect God properly and live for Him obediently," he says.

Verse 12. The acrostic letter is מ (*Mem*).

"Let us take one of the dominate desires that each person has and use it as an illustration," he proposes. **Who is the man who desires life and loves length of days that he may see good?** He posits a rhetorical question to which a positive answer is expected. In order to live long on the earth and have a good life, he argues, three traits must grow out of our submission to God.

Verse 13. The acrostic letter is נ (*Nun*).

First, he says, it is essential to **keep** [the] **tongue from evil**

and [the] lips from speaking deceit. Purity of language is mandatory. The tongue must be free from "evil," and the lips must be free from "deceit"—such as insincerity, hypocrisy, or guile.

Verse 14. The acrostic letter is ס (*Samekh*).

Turning to the other side of the question, the positive side, one is required to practice good. **Depart from evil and do good.** In addition, we are not to violate the laws of God or the demands of our consciences since our consciences operate by what we understand God's Word to teach. We should do God's will from the heart, fulfilling our duties and exhibiting the virtue of goodness.

Furthermore, one should **seek peace and pursue it.** We should do more than just appreciate peace; we must follow it diligently. The word "peace" is שָׁלוֹם (*shalom*), which means completeness, wholeness, soundness in all parts. Conflicts, personal wars, quarrels, and any kind of disturbances are shunned by the follower of God.

This type of life, the writer declares, has rewards in this world as well as in the world to come. God approves of this manner of living and will crown it with His favor and blessings. Peter used this description of the fear of the Lord to tell the suffering Christians to whom he wrote how to live during their time of peril (1 Pet. 3:10–12).

HE PROTECTS US (34:15–22)

> [15]The eyes of the LORD are toward the righteous
> And His ears are open to their cry.
> [16]The face of the LORD is against evildoers,
> To cut off the memory of them from the earth.
> [17]The righteous cry, and the LORD hears
> And delivers them out of all their troubles.
> [18]The LORD is near to the brokenhearted
> And saves those who are crushed in spirit.
> [19]Many are the afflictions of the righteous,
> But the LORD delivers him out of them all.
> [20]He keeps all his bones,
> Not one of them is broken.

PSALM 34

²¹Evil shall slay the wicked,
And those who hate the righteous will be condemned.
²²The LORD redeems the soul of His servants,
And none of those who take refuge in Him will be condemned.

Verse 15. The acrostic letter is ע (*Ayin*).

The Lord ceaselessly watches over His people. **The eyes of the LORD are toward the righteous and His ears are open to their cry.** The phrase "eyes of the LORD" represents His concern and care, His observant tenderness, and His eagerness to help. "His ears are open" means that He stands ready to respond to the prayers the righteous pray.

Verse 16. The acrostic letter is פ (*Pe*).

Although it overlaps with other thoughts already mentioned, his next reason for thanking God is that God protects His people. Just as the Lord faces the righteous to assist them, He turns from the wicked and judges them. **The face of the LORD is against evildoers, to cut off the memory of them from the earth.** A constant theme used in the Psalms is that the righteous man has fellowship with God and the wicked man is rejected by Him. God cannot do what He would for us unless we do what we should for Him. The wicked man is not part of God's plan and will eventually pass into oblivion as he is "cut off [from] the memory of [the people of] the earth."

God gives to the godly man His gracious providence and His attentive ear when he prays; however, He sets Himself against evil. He judges evil because of what it does to mankind and because of His displeasure with it. He is opposed to it and will eventually bring an end to it. By the choice of our relationship with good and evil, we determine God's attitude toward us.

Verse 17. The acrostic letter is צ (*Tsadhe*).

The troubled righteous man will see the Lord come to his rescue. **The righteous cry, and the LORD hears and delivers them out of all their troubles.** The Lord is tenderhearted, and He will reach out His hand of mercy to the righteous poor. The Hebrew has simply "They cry" (צָעֲק, *tsa'aq*), instead of "the righteous cry" as the NASB has. An assumption has been made by the NASB translators that righteous people are being discussed, but they put the words "the righteous" in italics to show that these two words are not part of the Hebrew text.

Verse 18. The acrostic letter is ק (*Qoph*).

There is a special affinity that God has for the godly man who is pushed down and persecuted. Indeed, **the LORD is near to the brokenhearted and saves those who are crushed in spirit.** The Lord especially sympathizes with the "crushed in spirit" (נִשְׁבְּרֵי־לֵב, *nishbᵉrey leb*), the brokenhearted. Righteous living does not mean that we will never face any conflicts or trials. In fact, doing what is right may bring persecution that otherwise we would not have had. However, the righteous have God's promise that He will be with them in their time of need.

Verse 19. The acrostic letter is ר (*Resh*).

Trouble multiplied by troubles may come to the righteous. We could say, **Many are the afflictions of the righteous.** However, we can also say, **But the LORD delivers him out of them all.** Being righteous means that we will have God with us in times of difficulty to defend and deliver us. "Many afflictions" may pommel and pelt the righteous man; but none of these can surprise God or go beyond His power to handle. He can and will guide the righteous man out of any struggle.

Verse 20. The acrostic letter is שׁ (*Shin*).

With figurative language, he declares the completeness of the Lord's protection of His own. **He keeps all his bones, not one of them is broken.** The physical frame is composed of skeleton bones; and when they are in place, the man, so to speak, is together. This expression is a poetic way of saying that God keeps the whole man together.

Verse 21. The acrostic letter is ת (*Tav*).

Evil will eventually destroy the evil man. **Evil shall slay the wicked, and those who hate the righteous will be condemned.** The evil man will in time be overcome by his sins. Evil has within it the seeds of destruction; it is a time bomb just waiting to explode. Those who permit evil to reign in their lives will—in the fullness of time—self-destruct. Evil opposes righteousness; therefore, those who "hate the righteous" oppose God and the righteous life. They stand "condemned" because of the evil that they have chosen.

Verse 22. The acrostic letter is פ (*Pe*).

The converse of the Lord's condemning the wicked is also true: **The LORD redeems the soul of His servants, and none of those who take refuge in Him will be condemned.** Someone has said, "I would rather be delivered from a thousand trials than have only one and be overcome by it!" The righteous man should not worry, for he is safe in God. Far from being condemned by the Lord, God will be his place of safety, his "refuge." Whether he faces ten thousand trials or just one, he will be the overcomer, not the one who is overcome. God will not forget us, overlook the size of the foe, or fail us when we need Him. If we have taken refuge in Him, we need not fear.

APPLICATION

Why Praise Him?

David knew that he should praise God, and our knowledge of God should also convince us to lift up our hearts in praise to Him. He had seen God answer his prayers and had witnessed His constant protection. The generous bounties from God put a continual song of praise in his heart and on his lips.

However, above all the concerns of life, David valued his relationship with God. He would boast of his walk with God, not in his own personal achievements, in God's grace, not in his human goodness. God would be at the center of his thinking, not just in intermittent thoughts as he went about the business of living. The crux of life, for David, was being in God and having God in him!

The How of Praise

This psalm begins with an exhortation to praise the Lord, and includes in the exhortation a description of how the praising of God should be done.

The writer first says that praise should be *a continuous activity for the believer*. It is to be done at all times and in all places—in times of gladness and in times of sadness. David says that he would bless the Lord at all times.

Second, he says that praise *should spring from a grateful heart.* He boasts in the Lord by being thankful for what the Lord has done for him and by glorying in the Lord's great grace and strength.

Third, he says that he was going *to lead others to praise the Lord.* It is not enough to praise God ourselves; we must exhort others to recognize who God is and what He has done. "O magnify the LORD with me," he says to others (v. 3).

Praising God is a delightful and necessary song in our hearts that finds continued expression through our lips—because it brings pleasure to God, it allows us to express our faithfulness to Him, and it inspires others to trust in Him.

The Lord and His Own

God's heart and love go out to His people. In verses 4 through 7, God is pictured as acting in behalf of His own.

He hears their prayers. The writer remembers his past and recalls that when he was in the throes of trouble, God heard his cry for deliverance. The Lord rescued him from all his fears or terrifying circumstances.

He fills them with joy. Those who have looked to God for their help and strength have received what they need and consequently are filled with joy. The writer says that they are radiant. Their faces glow with the joy of His presence and with the happiness emerging from the realization of His help and the confidence that He will never disappoint them.

He puts His arms of protection around them. Those who trust in God live their lives within the center of God's mighty power. The angel of the Lord, the symbol of the Lord's strength, encamps around them. Encircled by the Lord's might, why should they fear? No foe can break through that shield.

God loves His people as a father loves his children. His kindness is lavished upon those who fear Him by His answering their prayers, filling them with joy, and surrounding them with His protection. Let us rejoice in what God does for His own.

Tasting the Goodness

The word "taste" is used in this context for experiencing first-hand the grace and kindness of God (v. 8). The idea is "Come and see, and you will find that the Lord is good."

Consequently, the question for us would have to be: "How do we taste the goodness of the Lord?" Verses 8 through 10 lay out the God-ordained way of partaking of His goodness.

We do so by taking refuge in Him. The writer says, "How blessed is the man who takes refuge in Him" (v. 8). One comes to God by putting his trust in Him and setting out to do His will. As he lives this type of life, he immediately finds that the Lord is an unparalleled refuge for him. No fortress of earth can compare to His protection.

We taste His goodness by fearing Him in our daily walk. "Fear" is not terror, but respect and wholesome reverence. The writer says that the one who so lives can say with Psalm 23, "I shall not want."

We do it by seeking Him. "Seeking God" means pursuing the right relationship with Him. God provides for those who make Him their passion.

The young lions, as strong as they are, often face a lack of food and other deficiencies; but such is not the case with the one who trusts in God. The true believer in God will never want for any good thing.

The Secret to a Good Life

The writer takes the role of a teacher and says that he will teach us about "the fear of the Lord" or a life of obedience to Him. So he asks, "Who wants to live a good life?" Obviously, the majority of people would say, "I do!" The writer says, "Let me tell you how to get it."

You must keep your tongue from evil. The mouth is not meant for saying evil things. It is intended to be an avenue of truth, not deceit. A good life can only come to one who guards his lips.

You must depart from evil. A person's life is to be dedicated to goodness, not wickedness. Evil brings heartbreak and misery; goodness brings life.

You must do good. A good life has goodness at its center, and it is aggressive about doing good.

You must seek peace. This word "peace" means complete wholeness. The good person is vigilant about maintaining peace with God and others. He chases after it. He will be a peacemaker, not a peacebreaker; a joymonger, not a warmonger.

The good life is not elusive and beyond our grasp. It grows out from a righteous tongue, a righteous life, a life of doing good, and an energetic pursuit of peace.

The Face of the Lord

How arresting is the phrase "the face of the Lord" (v. 16)! Of course, we are not to think of the Lord as having a face like ours—two eyes, a nose, and a mouth. This language is accommodative and pictures God in human terms.

These verses point us to what "the face of the Lord" means by giving us a figurative look at God's character. What is God like?

His face is turned toward the righteous. He loves the righteous, and His favor is extended to them.

His face is turned against evil. God is offended by evil. He has rebuked it and will one day judge it.

It is turned especially toward the poor. His heart goes to the mistreated person. The righteous poor man will be heard by the Lord, for there is a sense in which He is always near the brokenhearted. He sends His great power and mercy to the ones who need them the most.

Comfort for the Afflicted

How shall we think of afflictions? In what way should the righteous person look at them? An answer is given in verses 19 through 22.

First, we need to remember that afflictions will come. A life that is free from them is the exception, not the rule. Just because one is righteous does not mean that he will be excused from trials of all kinds; in fact, we may have affliction because we are righteous.

The comforting news is that the Lord is stronger than our afflictions. He is able to deliver His people out of any kind of difficulty that may arise. He is greater and stronger than anything that the devil can throw at us.

Furthermore, it is good to remember that evil will destroy the wicked. The wicked man will self-destruct. Evil will slay him. It is as if evil is a vicious person who will attack and destroy the person who befriends him.

The best news of all is that the Lord will be a refuge for the righteous in any kind of storm. At all times He is the invincible fortress, a haven from the storms of trial and suffering. He is our rock and can withstand the worst that may come. The Lord will not allow any of our bones to be broken. He will keep us from all harm.

Praise God! We have His approval, and He can protect us from whatever difficulty may come. We have His strength and His salvation.

"No Good Thing Will He Withhold"

The amazing promise of verse 10 is one of the most sweeping promises of the entire Bible. Coupled with a condition, it is given as an encouragement to God's faithful children, not to the unbeliever or the disobedient person.

God gave us this promise to cherish, and it is appropriate to ask, "Is this promise always true? How shall we understand it or interpret it?" Perhaps the best way to grasp it is to look at the life of Jesus. He is the perfect illustration of how God carries out His loving care for His people.

In light of how God cared for Jesus, we can say that this promise is a promise about responsible care. God will not satisfy our vain greed, but He will meet our true needs. He has never allowed any child of His to experience the loss of the actual help that is needed. No "truly good thing" will be withheld from them.

Further, we can see that it is a promise that is more about spiritual sustenance than physical security. Jesus received God's gracious benefits, but He never lived in a palace. His needs were always met, but He never had an abundance of money. From the viewpoint of the world, He lived without luxury and conveniences; but from the observation of heaven, He was blessed with the gold of God.

Through Jesus, we see that it is a promise that God will keep within the confines of His eternal purposes. He will not throw away His plan for all people in order to satisfy the wants or wishes of one person. We do not do this type of thing in a family, and He does not do it in His. He has to consider the needs of His other children as He ministers to ours.

Jesus was crucified for our sins, but God supplied the strength for Him at His chosen hour. God has allowed some of His people to be offered as sacrifices on the martyr's altar, but behind the dim unknown He sustained them. He provided for their real needs during their darkest hours. Through their examples, He provided for His other children by giving them inspiration and courage to be faithful until the end. Neither the martyr nor the others who needed the example were deprived of what they needed the most.

Jesus illustrated that this promise would be carried out in the midst of afflictions. In verse 19 the warning is given that the righteous will face many "afflictions." In other words, the promise does not preclude difficulties. The promise is that God will sustain the righteous in, or will deliver the righteous from, the afflictions that will come.

Behind this wonderful promise is trust in our heavenly Father's wisdom and knowledge. He will faithfully keep it according to His wisdom and our best interests.

PSALM 35
EVIL RETURNED FOR GOOD

The Superscription: A Psalm of David. The ancient title simply says that this psalm is **of** ["by," "for," or "to"] **David** (לְדָוִד, *l^edawid*). The two words **a Psalm** are not in the Hebrew text even though the NASB includes them.

We will assume the ascription is referring to authorship, labeling this psalm as being written by David. Although we do not know the exact time or place of its writing, when we survey David's life, we are reminded of two periods during which it could well have been written: when he was fleeing from Saul or when he was dealing with the mutiny led by Absalom.

A lament prayer, this psalm expresses tremendous feeling and an impassioned plea for immediate help. Although it has been interpreted as a national psalm that asks God to deliver the nation from its foes, the text is best understood as being written by a godly man who was ruthlessly mistreated by people around him, even people who had been the recipients of his kindness.

The psalm provides the language and emotions with which anyone who has been betrayed, mocked, plotted against, maligned, or threatened by friends and enemies can identify. The writer is experiencing what happens when one's goodness has been ignored and those benefiting from it have turned against him and are heartlessly seeking to harm him.

It is composed of three natural divisions, each of which contains a complaint and ends with an expression of praise (vv. 1–10, 11–18, 19–28). The three parts could be describing three different groups of enemies—those who seek his life, those who are false witnesses, and those who have no reason for hating him but would delight in his downfall; or they could be depicting one set of enemies in three different ways. The latter must be the case.

An expression of praise ends each section. These three phrases are among the most beautiful words in the Book of Psalms, reminding us that dark days can force us to think deeply about the greatness and love of God.

A DIVINE SOLUTION (35:1–8)

¹Contend, O LORD, with those who contend with me;
Fight against those who fight against me.
²Take hold of buckler and shield
And rise up for my help.
³Draw also the spear and the battle-axe to meet those who pursue me;
Say to my soul, "I am your salvation."
⁴Let those be ashamed and dishonored who seek my life;
Let those be turned back and humiliated who devise evil against me.
⁵Let them be like chaff before the wind,
With the angel of the LORD driving them on.
⁶Let their way be dark and slippery,
With the angel of the LORD pursuing them.
⁷For without cause they hid their net for me;
Without cause they dug a pit for my soul.
⁸Let destruction come upon him unawares,
And let the net which he hid catch himself;
Into that very destruction let him fall.

Verse 1. The writer is facing a severe, heart-rending experience, one that has been brought on by the people around him. Wanting God to resolve his problem, he prays, **Contend, O LORD, with those who contend with me**. He pleads for God to come to his defense, to take his side against his foes. Certainly, God is more adept at handling such intense cases than we are. We get emotionally caught up in the personal pain and the spirit of revenge, and our thinking becomes confused.

Fight against those who fight against me, he petitions. As he asks God to handle this aggravation for him, he uses two metaphors—a military image, asking God to go before him in battle, and a legal figure, soliciting God to be his counselor and prosecutor. "Contend" (רִיב, *rib*) could also be translated "plead," "argue," or "strive," as a lawyer would do.

Verse 2. Thinking of God as his divine Warrior, he further says, **Take hold of buckler and shield and rise up for my help.** Military imagery is used as he urges God to secure weapons from His heavenly armory for the battle that must be fought. He asks for defensive equipment: a small "shield" (מָגֵן, *magen*) and also a "buckler" (צִנָּה, *tsinnah*), a large shield, almost body length.

Verse 3. As he continues with "battlefield" terminology, he pleads, **Draw also the spear and the battle-axe to meet those who pursue me.** The Hebrew of the last part of this sentence could be translated "stop the way against them" (סְגֹר לִקְרַאת רֹדְפָי, *sᵉgor liqra'th rodpay*). The NASB has interpreted the phrase to mean that another weapon, like the battle-axe, should be brought out for use. This specific weapon is not found in the text, and consequently, was read into the phrase by the translators. He is praying for God to utilize offensive equipment, such as the "spear" (and, by implication, something like the battle-axe), and attack his pursuers.

Further, he asks God to speak to him and promise deliverance. He says to God, **Say to my soul, "I am your salvation."** Above all, he wants God to tell him that He will be his Redeemer. His deep desire is for God to say, "I am your God, and I will keep My promise to protect those who have a covenant relationship with Me."

Verse 4. Imprecatorily, he pleads for God to humiliate those who would hurt him: **Let those be ashamed and dishonored who seek my life.** Because of his innocence, he asks that those who are after him become confused, embarrassed, and frustrated in their attempts to destroy him. He further says, **Let those be turned back and humiliated who devise evil against me.** His request would be tantamount to asking for God's judgment to fall upon them. Remarkably, this verse is almost identical with Psalms 40:14 and 70:2, and the superscriptions of all three psalms ascribe them to David in some way.

Verse 5. His prayer is a curse-like prayer, the kind often uttered against those who opposed God and God's people in Old Testament times. The writer wants God to take the enemies away from him, and he wants God to judge them and destroy their opposition to His cause.

Specifically, he asks God to drive away his enemies by His angel. **Let them be like chaff before the wind, with the angel of the LORD driving them on.** "Chaff" is made of the husks of grain that are separated from the grain during the winnowing process. The chaff was regarded as worthless and usually burned. "The angel of the LORD" is referred to in the Book of Psalms only here and in the previous psalm (34:7). The prayer here is for the angel of the Lord to defeat the wicked, but in the previous psalm "the angel" was to protect or defend the godly. This angel suggests the presence of the Lord although the angel is always distinguished from the Lord Himself.

Verse 6. He further prays, **Let their way be dark and slippery, with the angel of the LORD pursuing them.** "May their road be rough and difficult," he says. He wants them to have a hard time walking and running as they flee from the angel of the Lord.

Seven curses are mentioned in his prayer: "Let those be ashamed and dishonored"; "Let those be turned back"; "Let those be . . . humiliated"; "Let them be like chaff before the wind, with the angel of the LORD driving them on"; "Let their way be dark and slippery, with the angel of the LORD pursuing them"; "Let destruction come upon him unawares"; and "Let the net which he hid catch himself." In summary, he is asking God to prevent them from succeeding in their intended evil upon him and to frustrate any of their plans that may oppose God's will.

Verse 7. Intermingled with these requests is David's affirmation of innocence. He says, **For without cause they hid their net for me; without cause they dug a pit for my soul.** His foes had no "cause" to come against him the way they had. Using the figure of hunters setting traps for wild game, he says they regard him as a menace to society, an evil man, who should be captured and removed from the earth.

Verse 8. Dropping from the plural to the singular, he asks that God see to it that the evil man face destruction: **Let destruction come upon him unawares**. If his prayer is answered, the evil person will be caught to his astonishment in the net that he has set for the writer. He prays, **Let the net which he hid catch himself; into that very destruction let him fall.** Through the metaphor of hunters and the hunted, he prays that the destruction the evil man had planned for him would fall on his own head, that he would fall in his own traps.

A PRAYER FOR DELIVERANCE (35:9, 10)

⁹**And my soul shall rejoice in the Lord;**
It shall exult in His salvation.
¹⁰**All my bones will say, "Lord, who is like You,**
Who delivers the afflicted from him who is too strong for him,
And the afflicted and the needy from him who robs him?"

Verse 9. The first division of the psalm (vv. 1–10) closes with this expression of praise in verses 9 and 10. He promises, **And my soul shall rejoice in the Lord; it shall exult in His salvation.** He trusts in God to help him. He knows that God will come to his assistance; when He does, he will greatly rejoice over the Lord's kindness and His deliverance.

Verse 10. Anticipating God's intervention, he vows to give Him glory and praise with his whole being. **All my bones will say, "Lord, who is like You, who delivers the afflicted from him who is too strong for him, and the afflicted and the needy from him who robs him?"** With poetic exaggeration, perhaps drawn from the song Moses sang after the Exodus (Ex. 15:11), he says, "With every bone of my body, I will give thanks to You." His whole body will proclaim, "There is no other god than Yahweh. He is the true God. He will rescue those who call upon Him and look out for those who are mistreated." He will especially tell of how the Lord has delivered the "needy" and the "afflicted." God has a special sympathy for those who have been abused and those trodden down by life and others.

"EVEN FRIENDS ARE AGAINST ME"
(35:11–16)

> ¹¹Malicious witnesses rise up;
> They ask me of things that I do not know.
> ¹²They repay me evil for good,
> To the bereavement of my soul.
> ¹³But as for me, when they were sick, my clothing was sackcloth;
> I humbled my soul with fasting,
> And my prayer kept returning to my bosom.
> ¹⁴I went about as though it were my friend or brother;
> I bowed down mourning, as one who sorrows for a mother.
> ¹⁵But at my stumbling they rejoiced and gathered themselves together;
> The smiters whom I did not know gathered together against me,
> They slandered me without ceasing.
> ¹⁶Like godless jesters at a feast,
> They gnashed at me with their teeth.

Verse 11. After the interlude of praise, the writer returns to describing his desperate situation. He pleads, **Malicious witnesses rise up**. Slanderous accusations are being made against him. "Malicious [ruthless, violent, or false] witnesses," he says, have spoken and are speaking against him. Perhaps some who have been his friends have told Saul that he is trying to take over the throne or is attempting to assassinate him. He says, **They ask me of things that I do not know.** They accuse him of things about which the writer knows nothing.

Verse 12. He is not talking about close friends, but about people whom he has treated as friends by praying for them out of deep concern for their welfare. He says, **They repay me evil for good, to the bereavement of my soul.** He is being injured by the very ones to whom he has been gracious in the past. His prayers for them have not been answered, but he has done what he could.

Verse 13. He has manifested compassion toward these people when they were in trouble. He argues, **But as for me, when they were sick, my clothing was sackcloth.** He has donned garments of mourning on their behalf. In addition, he says, **I humbled my soul with fasting, and my prayer kept returning to my bosom.** He has given time to fasting and praying for them. However, these people for whom he has prayed have become his worst enemies. The result of his praying is seen in his words, "My prayers kept returning to my bosom." His prayers for them have to some extent blessed him, but they have not brought change and life to the ones for whom he has prayed.

Verse 14. His concern for them has been clearly evident. He says, **I went about as though it were my friend or brother.** When they have been sick, he has not only mourned, fasted, and prayed for them; but he has also acted as a brother and friend to them. He says, **I bowed down mourning, as one who sorrows for a mother.** He has taken them to heart with the same earnestness and sympathy as one would his own "mother" when she becomes ill. His conduct and spirit have expressed deep concern, and yet they are now seeking to harm him.

Verse 15. The ones who have been the object of his prayers receive the news of his adversity with gladness. He says, **But at my stumbling they rejoiced and gathered themselves together.** When life became to him like that of "stumbling" down a path, like a harsh journey, they rejoiced at the hardships he was having. The word "stumbling" is used figuratively for the tragedies attending his life. They "gathered themselves together" to watch his struggle with trouble, as spectators gathering for a sporting event.

Not only are they rejoicing over his problem, but they have also joined with mean men who are always trying to hurt others and who have turned against him even though they do not know him. He says, **The smiters whom I did not know gathered together against me, they slandered me without ceasing.** The Hebrew word rendered as "smiters" (נֵכִים, *nekim*) is difficult. It has been translated "cripples," "slanderers," and "ruffians." The point is that these people are adding to his pain by shredding his reputation with their slander. Their baseless criticism is continual and derogatory. What they are doing overwhelms him with sorrow. These destructive people are not known to him. They have joined with those who know him to participate in the vicious statements about him.

Verse 16. They went about their gossiping with a type of godless glee. **Like godless jesters at a feast, they gnashed at me with their teeth.** Engaging in this wickedness is fun to them; it is like going to a festive occasion. They are mockers, impious brutes, silly, profane men. They tear his reputation into pieces and relish every minute of it. "Gnashed at me" is a metaphor suggesting a violent type of criticism, comparable to a lion chewing up his prey.

"COME TO MY AID NOW" (35:17, 18)

> ¹⁷**Lord, how long will You look on?**
> **Rescue my soul from their ravages,**
> **My only life from the lions.**
> ¹⁸**I will give You thanks in the great congregation;**
> **I will praise You among a mighty throng.**

Verse 17. At the end of this second section (vv. 11–18) of the psalm, another vow of praise is made. He prays, **Lord, how long will You look on?** He urges God to hurry to his assistance. He pleads, as many righteous people have, for God to bring his grief to an end. Job asked "Why?" but this psalmist asks "When?" His request is, **Rescue my soul from their ravages, my only life from the lions.** He says that his soul needs to be plucked from the destruction around him, and he needs protection from the lions. The word "lions" is figurative for "strong ones," standing for a powerful army of men from whom there does not seem to be any deliverance.

Verse 18. He promises that he will express gratitude and praise for the rescue that God may see fit to provide: **I will give You thanks in the great congregation.** In advance, he vows that he will praise Him in the "congregation" (בְּקָהָל רָב, *b̵qahal rob*), the great assembly, for the victory He will give. Synonymously, he says, **I will praise You among a mighty throng.** He will tell the large gatherings of God's people what God has done for him, refusing to keep His mercy a secret.

"ACT IN RIGHTEOUSNESS FOR ME"
(35:19–26)

> [19]Do not let those who are wrongfully my enemies rejoice over me;
> Nor let those who hate me without cause wink maliciously.
> [20]For they do not speak peace,
> But they devise deceitful words against those who are quiet in the land.
> [21]They opened their mouth wide against me;
> They said, "Aha, aha, our eyes have seen it!"
> [22]You have seen it, O LORD, do not keep silent;
> O Lord, do not be far from me.
> [23]Stir up Yourself, and awake to my right
> And to my cause, my God and my Lord.
> [24]Judge me, O LORD my God, according to Your righteousness,
> And do not let them rejoice over me.
> [25]Do not let them say in their heart,
> "Aha, our desire!"
> Do not let them say, "We have swallowed him up!"
> [26]Let those be ashamed and humiliated altogether who rejoice at my distress;
> Let those be clothed with shame and dishonor who magnify themselves over me.

Verse 19. He begins his third section by continuing to ask God to rescue him from those who were unjustly condemning him. **Do not let those who are wrongfully my enemies rejoice over me.** His petition is that his enemies, those who have no reason to hate him, will not be able to triumph over him and rejoice in his demise. He says, **Nor let those who hate me without cause wink maliciously.** He does not want them to look at each other, nodding and winking, as if to say, "We did it! We destroyed him!" or as if to say, "See, we knew that this wicked man would come to this end!"

Verse 20. One of the reasons he is praying this prayer is because of the dishonesty and deceit that have given rise to his trial. **For they do not speak peace, but they devise deceitful words against those who are quiet in the land.** These people, he observes, will not rest until more evil is done. He is content to live in quietness away from Saul and his court, but his enemies will not allow him to do so. They wickedly put together additional devious plans for those who are trying to live peaceful lives. They do not promote peace; they create disruption.

Verse 21. He wants a solution to his dilemma that is in harmony with God's righteousness. In a great surrender to evil, these people have **opened their mouth wide against** him to say horrible things about him. One thing in particular that they were saying is the aspersion, **"Aha, aha, our eyes have seen it!"** With sinister laughter, they arrogantly are saying, "We knew it! We could have told you that this would happen to him!" David pleas, "God, do not let my enemies gloat over me, bragging, 'He fell as we thought he would. We predicted it! We could have told you that this was going to happen to him!'"

Verse 22. He prays, **You have seen it, O Lord, do not keep silent.** Justice and righteousness must triumph. He says, **O Lord, do not be far from me.** He wants God to fulfill His promises and bring upon his enemies the curses of the covenant. God's nearness means God's protection.

Verse 23. In familiar language, he urges God to act: **Stir up Yourself.** As if God is a sleeping giant, he asks Him to arise and fight in his behalf: **Awake to my right and to my cause, my God and my Lord.** He wants God to judge his cause, declare it to be free from evil, and to judge those who are attacking him. In short, he wants God to come to his side and fight for him.

Verse 24. He prays for God to examine him and his enemies according to His righteousness: **Judge me, O Lord my God, according to Your righteousness.** With him, everything has to line up with God's righteous judgment. Truth is his standard of evaluation. God is asked to analyze the writer and his foes with the measuring line of His Word.

Verse 25. He does not want his enemies to rejoice over his tragedy. Thus, he pleads, **Do not let them say in their heart, "Aha, our desire!" Do not let them say, "We have swallowed him up!"** The wicked continue to scheme and deceive, with vocal predictions of his coming demise. If given the opportunity, they will even contend that they have brought him down. In contrast to what they would say they have seen, he knows that God has seen his innocence.

Verse 26. Returning to an imprecatory petition, he says, **Let those be ashamed and humiliated altogether who rejoice at my distress.** He prays for God's response to be a decisive victory in behalf of righteousness. **Let those be clothed with shame and dishonor who magnify themselves over me.** To "be clothed" is to be overwhelmed with shame, dishonor, and disgrace.

A SOLUTION OVER WHICH ALL CAN REJOICE (35:27, 28)

²⁷**Let them shout for joy and rejoice, who favor my vindication;**
And let them say continually, "The LORD **be magnified,**
Who delights in the prosperity of His servant."
²⁸**And my tongue shall declare Your righteousness**
And Your praise all day long.

Verse 27. He wants a resolution to his dilemma about which good people can rejoice. When that solution is given, he will tell others about His righteousness and salvation; and he will lead them in praising God. He says of God's people, **Let them shout for joy and rejoice, who favor my vindication**. He wants those who see his vindication to say, "The Lord has delivered him. He should be praised, for He did not forsake His servant during his time of need." Furthermore, he says, **Let them say continu-**

ally, **"The LORD be magnified, who delights in the prosperity of His servant."** An outcome in violation of truth, righteousness, and God's name would not satisfy him. He desires that his case be dealt with in such a way that the answer and outcome will bring glory to God.

Verse 28. To end the psalm, a special commitment is made by the writer. **My tongue shall declare Your righteousness and Your praise all day long.** He promises to praise God continually for delivering him. He will express his gratitude freely and without interruption.

APPLICATION

The Worst Hurt

One of the worst kinds of pain can be the wounds inflicted by people we think are our friends. They have received our love, time, and encouragement; but when the days are stormy and we ask for their support, they desert us and join forces with those who oppose us.

Honoring God is easy when encouraging friends surround us, we have good health, and no problems glare at us. In such congenial times, we can pray the prettiest prayers and sing the loveliest songs. However, the true test of faith comes when friends have turned into enemies, our bodies ache with pain, and we have problems that we must solve immediately. What kind of prayers do we pray when we have to pray alone?

This psalm suggests that in the blackest of nights we can ask God to fight our battles for us. The psalm further says that He will give victories according to His righteousness. His great deeds will elicit praise from our hearts and the hearts of all those who see them.

Bringing Betrayal to God

How does one handle the sickness of heart that comes when he has been attacked by friends as well as enemies? How does he pray about it?

The writer is an example for us. He wanted a special kind of help: a solution that God would give, a solution that would be in harmony with God's righteousness, a solution for which he could praise God, a solution in which all righteous people could rejoice.

Asking God to Be God

God is God, and we are sinful human beings. We cannot do for ourselves what God alone can do for us. We must let God be God to us. Man cannot make God into his image, but he can make himself through God's Word into His image.

When trouble comes, what will God do for us?

He will be our legal representative. He will be prosecutor and defender. Consequently, it is best to let God handle our case. He knows how to present it, prosecute it, and judge it.

He will be our military army. He will fight for us when necessary. He will go before us, route the enemy, and win our battles. We do not have the strength, wisdom, or equipment to oppose the enemy that we must face.

He will be our spiritual Redeemer. Whatever happens to us, we want a spiritual victory, and only God can give it to us. We want God to say to us through our surrender to His will and through the teachings of His Word, "I am the God of your salvation."

According to Paul the apostle, "If God is for us, who is against us?" (Rom. 8:31). Abraham Lincoln said, "With God we cannot fail; without Him we cannot succeed."

Praying for Our Enemies

How do we pray for our enemies in this Christian Age?

We must pray that we may see who is the real enemy. Behind all the evil people and evil ways is the devil and his scheme to condemn. Our fight is not with people but with the Prince of Darkness.

We should pray that our enemies may be converted. Perhaps this request is the meaning of Jesus' prayer from the cross (Lk. 24:43). He knew that God could not forgive while they were in rebellion against Him. His prayer was answered in part in Acts 2.

We need to pray that they may not hurt God's cause. His work is the most important work on earth. It is appropriate that we entreat God that this work not be hindered.

We must pray that they may not prevent us from serving God. Sometimes enemies can put us into situations in which our service is affected. We can focus on the enemies so much that we lose sight of our work.

Our ultimate prayer should be that we may have a spiritual victory over them. Enemies can cause our attitudes to sour or our spirits to become discouraged.

Few Christians will journey through this world without running into enemies who would like to bring about their destruction. Christ leads us into having the proper frame of mind toward them.

The Elements of Praise

It is always appropriate to praise God. In times of happiness and in times of difficulty, we can offer up the adoration of our hearts to the Lord.

Let us rejoice in the Lord. Who can look at God and not break forth in praise? When one realizes who He is and what He is like, all of the troubles and trials of life pale. Someone has said, "When I get to heaven, I will spend the first ten thousand years lost in the wonder of His goodness."

Let us exult in His deliverance. His salvation is the great salvation of which the prophets spoke and which our Lord fulfilled. It is the heart of the Bible. If one cannot praise God for it, he simply does not understand it or has not tasted of its sweetness.

Let us rejoice in His strength. He holds the universe in the palm of His hand. He commands the seas, and He sustains the earth. Nothing is too hard for Him. He has all power. No problem is too big or too little for Him.

Let us rejoice in His compassions. His offer of salvation reflects His great love, and anyone who wishes may be saved by His grace. His mercy reaches out to all men, it will lift the vilest sinner all the way to heaven, and it is extended so continually that we have to bring out the word "longsuffering" to describe it. Underneath His overarching compassion and love are His daily mercies that are "new every morning."

Every person on earth at all times and in all places has numerous reasons for praising God. It is never out of place to lift our hearts and voices to God as we extol His name.

An Imprecatory Prayer

Much of this psalm would be considered an imprecatory prayer. The word "imprecation" comes from a Latin word (*imprecārī*) that means "to curse." Notice especially verses 5 through 8. These are strong petitions and appear un-Christlike to us, but W. O. E. Oesterley has pointed out an important truth about this type of prayer:

> In spite of grievous wrong suffered by the psalmist, he nowhere expresses the intention, or even the wish, of taking personal revenge upon his enemies and traducers; that he should desire their punishment is natural enough; but this is left wholly in the hands of the Almighty; we recall Rom. 12:19: "Vengeance is mine, saith the Lord, I will repay," cp. Deut. 32:35. This wholehearted placing of his cause in the care of the all-knowing God witnesses to a true sincerity of religious belief.[1]

Robert Alden also made the following observation concerning the imprecatory nature of David's praying:

> Perhaps one explanation is found in the nature of the hatred mentioned here. It is holy hatred. David viewed these enemies not so much as his own personal foes, but as adversaries of God and of God's nation, and of God's plan. The king so identified himself with the kingdom of God on earth that any opposition to it was opposition to God. The enemies were not under God's covenant. They were not believers. They were not concerned with the progress of Israel. Therefore, they must be cursed.[2]

---

[1] W. O. E. Oesterley, *The Psalms: Translated with Text-Critical and Exegetical Notes* (London: S.P.C.K., 1939), 218–19.
[2] Robert Alden, *Psalms: Songs of Devotion* (Chicago: Moody Press, 1974), 1:86.

The difference between the time of the writing of this psalm and the Christian Age is that Christ taught His followers to pray for their enemies' salvation (see Lk. 23:34; Mt. 5:44). Furthermore, Christians can understand that even evil plans can result in the spreading of the gospel (Phil. 1:12). God can also be glorified in those who are praying regardless of the circumstances and time (Phil. 1:29). Certainly also, we need to understand that vengeance belongs to God (Rom. 12:19).

David knew of God's promise to bless those who blessed God's people and to curse those who cursed them (Gen. 12:3). His prayer was asking God to fulfill that promise. In the Old Testament setting, God was preserving a nation for the foundation of the New Testament Era and the establishment of His Messiah and His kingdom, the church. The implementation of this divine plan required judging and defeating the enemies of God's people, which God did at times. In light of these truths regarding the Old Testament period, the imprecatory prayer was appropriate for the writer to pray, although Christians should exercise great discernment in praying such a prayer now.

When we are in a situation similar to the psalmist's, we can do what he did in the sense of asking God to provide the solution. Praying in this way, we can ask Him to act according to what His will is now.

The Gall of Gossip

The writer calls some of the ones around him "malicious witnesses," and he later said of them, "They devise deceitful words against those who are quiet in the land" (vv. 11, 20). These people were gossipers of the worst kind.

The difficulty he faced reminds us of the sin of gossiping. Let us, therefore, ask, "What harm does gossip do? Why is it wrong?"

It hurts God. The writer was God's servant, and any cruel word uttered against him would affect God's cause. Our Father in heaven is always hurt deeply when His children on earth bite and devour one another. We are to encourage one another in the truth, not make it hard for each other to walk in the truth.

It hurts the gossiper. The one who engages in gossip lowers himself to the level of an evil person. Our words reveal our attitude and mindset.

It hurts the one gossiped about. The gossiper is not physically killing another person; but by using words as a knife, the gossiper is cutting up another's reputation or good name. We do not have to have a good name, but it sure helps at times! One word well spoken at the right time can make a world of difference.

We do not know a lot about the writer's enemies; but one thing is certain, they were malicious in speech. David had been gracious to them; and in return for his kindness, they cut up his life, reputation, and good name with their vile tongues. He prayed earnestly that he might be delivered from the enemies, and so should we.

Praying for Others

As David described the way he had treated those around him who were in trouble, he gives us a picture of how a genuine believer should respond to others who are in need.

First, he saw their need. He paid attention to others. When they were in trouble, he noticed it. Observing others is an important part of godly living.

Second, he sympathized with them. It is one thing to see; it is another thing to do something about what we see. He said that when he saw their difficulty, he went immediately into action. The godly man acts in behalf of others.

Third, he fasted and prayed. He said that he put on sackcloth, humbled his soul with fasting, and prayed for them, treating people to whom he was not very close as if they were his friend or brother. He said that he took to heart their pain as he would do if the person were his mother. He engaged in meaningful identification. Maybe he even asked himself, "What would I do about this situation if the person or persons in question were my brother or mother?"

Christianity in a sense is a "one another's religion." Jesus said that love is the badge of discipleship, and we are to even love our enemies (Jn. 13:35; Mt. 5:44). Paul said to "give preference to one another in honor" (Rom. 12:10). Peter said, "Love the brotherhood" (1 Pet. 2:17). What kind of attitude have we had toward others? What kind of action have we taken toward others who are in trouble?

Remembering God's Deeds

All of us can look around and see the wonderful things that God has done for us. For example, He has forgiven us, given us eternal promises, and provided the church for us. Praising God for His blessings should be a natural reaction for each of us. David said, "My tongue shall declare Your righteousness and Your praise all day long" (v. 28).

Let us thank Him for what He has done. It can be done in worship—in the observance of the Lord's Supper, in prayer, in song, in our giving, and in our listening to the Word being proclaimed.

We should also declare what God has done. We can declare it in prayer, in our daily thinking about God, and we may even want to write it down. Obviously, we can declare what He has done is in our daily conversations.

Then, let us lead others to praise Him for what He has done. David said that he would find his place in the assembly and would praise God there. He would relish the opportunity to join with others in worshiping his great Benefactor. He wanted others to see how God had blessed him.

The Christian is a trophy to God's grace. We are what we are through His mercy. Everything we have comes from God. Any hope we have for the future rests squarely on what God has done for us. Charles Hodge has said, "Let us tell others what God has done before we tell them what they should do."

God and Forgiveness

Arthur G. Clarke has rightly observed: "To return evil for good is demon-like; to return evil for evil is man-like; to return good for evil is God-like."[3]

---

[3]Arthur G. Clarke, *Analytical Studies in the Psalms* (Kilmarnock, England: John Ritchie, 1949), 99.

PSALM 36
GOOD OR EVIL: WHICH?

The Superscription: For the choir director. A Psalm of David the servant of the LORD. Like fifty-four other psalms, this psalm was written **for** [or "to"] **the choir director** (לַמְנַצֵּחַ, *lamnatstseach*); like seventy-two others, its title claims it is **of** ["by," "for," or "to"] **David** (לְדָוִד, *lᵉdawid*); and like one other (18), it refers to David as **the servant of the LORD** (לְעֶבֶד־יהוה, *lᵉebed YHWH*). The two words **a Psalm** are not part of the Hebrew text even though the NASB includes them. The time and place of its composition are unknown.

Uniquely, this psalm contains three types of literature—the lament, the wisdom, and the hymnic genres. Each section is so different that it has been argued that three pieces have been brought together to compose the psalm. Such an inference is unnecessary if we see the psalm as a blending of three styles in order to accomplish the writer's special purpose.

We will regard the psalm as primarily a wisdom psalm. As a unit of thought, it draws a contrast between wickedness and godliness, resulting in a clear choice—the way of godliness. Life's choices can be narrowed to two options: God or evil. Wisdom suggests that one should weigh the advantages and disadvantages of the options so that an intelligent decision can be made—one that will not be regretted.

The psalmist presents characteristics of the alternatives and then announces his commitment in a prayer.

THE CHOICE OF SIN
(36:1–4)

¹Transgression speaks to the ungodly within his heart;
There is no fear of God before his eyes.
²For it flatters him in his own eyes
Concerning the discovery of his iniquity and the hatred of it.
³The words of his mouth are wickedness and deceit;
He has ceased to be wise and to do good.
⁴He plans wickedness upon his bed;
He sets himself on a path that is not good;
He does not despise evil.

The early part of the psalm (vv. 1–4) is a section of wisdom literature which portrays the character of the godless man who has made evil his deliberate choice. Because of his decision, he has become so entrenched with evil that he has become dominated by it.

Verse 1. The beginning words, **Transgression speaks to the ungodly within his heart**, are unusual and pose a translation problem. The NIV has given an interpretive rendition: "An oracle is within my heart concerning the sinfulness of the wicked." Several ancient versions (LXX, Vulgate, and Syriac) treated the noun "oracle" as a verb, translating it "say" or "speak." In addition, they regarded the noun "transgression" as a participial form of the verb "transgress," all of which resulted in the translation "The rebel speaks wickedly deep in his heart." The word נְאֻם (n^e'um) that has been translated by the NIV as "oracle" and "say" by ancient versions may also be translated as "utterance"; and if the phrase "within his heart" is the correct rendering of לְבִּי בְּקֶרֶב (b^eqereb libi), then the translation should be something like "An utterance of transgression belongs to the wicked, within his heart." In fact, Mitchell Dahood[1] has translated it "Perversity inspires the wicked man within his heart."

---

[1]Mitchell Dahood, *Psalms I (1—50)*, The Anchor Bible, vol. 16 (Garden City, N.Y.: Doubleday & Co., 1965), 217.

This personification of sin would be a *hapax legomena,* the only time that this phrasing is used in the Old Testament. The description is apparently picturing a man's sins as speaking to him, delivering an oracle to him deep within his spirit, deceiving and corrupting him, and leading him downward into the destruction of his soul. "Transgression" or rebellion within the evil man's heart whispers to his soul the allurements, habits, actions, and invitations of sin. The man is told such falsehoods as:

"There is no use to fear God."
"There is no danger in disobeying God."
"Your sins will not be discovered by God."
"God does not care about your sins."
"It is not such a tragic thing to sin."
"Sinning continually is the best way to live."

Having listened to these seductive influences, the man has developed no concern for the "fear" (or terror) of God (see Prov. 1:7). He has turned from God, and **there is no fear of God before his eyes.** Paul used this phrase in his description of the sinful world in Romans 3:18. It pictures a man who has reached a point where he has a total disregard for God. He does not "fear" Him, dread Him, or even think of Him. He has completely pushed God out of his mind.

Verse 2. The sin within his heart flatters him: **For it flatters him in his own eyes concerning the discovery of his iniquity and the hatred of it.** Evil says, "You have made the right choice. How wise you are! You have chosen to walk in wickedness and not to hate it. You are to be commended." Sin is deceptive, and it applauds the one who embraces it.

Verse 3. Having been deceived, his mouth is devoted to the service of evil. **The words of his mouth are wickedness and deceit**, says the writer. Because the wicked man's heart is controlled by evil, his tongue becomes the instrument of wickedness. The words that flow from his lips are deceitful troublemakers that wound and mislead. The verdict is this: **He has ceased to be wise and to do good.** At one time, he exercised good sense and did good; but those days have passed. He now devotes his energies to sin. Transgression has become his master.

Verse 4. The man so characterized has become settled in his decision to live in sin. His way of life is no longer accidental; it is now habitual: **He plans wickedness upon his bed.** Before sleeping, he lies awake, plotting and devising evil. Day and night, while walking and while lying down, wickedness is in his mind, emanating from his thinking. He is wholly given to it.

The man has been living in wickedness for some time and has become so corrupted that his conscience is dead. His noble impulses have been put to silence. By deliberate choice **he sets himself on a path that is not good.** He has had opportunities to see the value of doing good, but he has chosen the way of evil instead. Hence, with all restraints cast aside, he races into a wasted life and into God's judgment. He should be loving good and hating evil; but now, because of his twisted set of values, it can be said that **he does not despise evil.** He has developed an appreciation for it and has joined with it. Hardened by his life of sin, he has become one with evil and has entered into the worst of all marriages, a wedlock with iniquity.

THE CHOICE OF GOD (36:5–9)

⁵Your lovingkindness, O Lord, extends to the heavens,
Your faithfulness reaches to the skies.
⁶Your righteousness is like the mountains of God;
Your judgments are like a great deep.
O Lord, You preserve man and beast.
⁷How precious is Your lovingkindness, O God!
And the children of men take refuge in the shadow of Your
  wings.
⁸They drink their fill of the abundance of Your house;
And You give them to drink of the river of Your delights.
⁹For with You is the fountain of life;
In Your light we see light.

Verse 5. The writer begins his description of godliness where it must begin: by referencing the character of God. His depiction of God covers five verses. Four literary brush strokes are needed to make it. He speaks of God's lovingkindness, faithfulness, righteousness, and justice. In prayer, he praises God's covenant loyalty, **Your lovingkindness, O LORD, extends to the heavens.** With the expression "extends to the heavens," he shows its measureless character.

In addition, he describes God's loyalty: **Your faithfulness reaches to the skies.** His faithfulness is also limitless in its integrity and reliability.

These two attributes of God—lovingkindness and faithfulness—bring before the reader the assurance that God will keep all the promises He has made to those who trust in Him. They tell us that all of God's actions toward us are full of grace, comfort, and truth.

Verse 6. Drawing from the world of nature to construct his comparison, the writer extols the dimensions of God's righteousness: **Your righteousness is like the mountains of God.** Such holiness as His rises above all holiness known to man. He is absolutely pure, never swerving from the purity of His character by compromise or error. His "righteousness" is like a mighty mountain, immovable and eternally unchangeable.

His justice is like valleys of the ocean: **Your judgments are like a great deep.** They are unfathomable and inexhaustible.

His providence covers all of His living creation: **O, LORD, You preserve man and beast.** It is God who keeps alive all people and all other living creatures. With His caring nature, God is considerate of people and beasts.

The great entities of nature—the heavens, the sky, the mountains, and the ocean depths—as illustrations of the attributes of God, accent their greatness, grandeur, and uniqueness.

Verse 7. The writer in prayer ponders the value and scope of this lovingkindness of God. He says, **How precious is Your lovingkindness, O God!** His love for each person is priceless and rises above and beyond all the riches of the world in value. Since His love goes out to everyone, it can be said that **the children of men take refuge in the shadow of** [God's] **wings.** Any person—regardless of color, culture, or social standing—may come to Him for salvation and hope.

Verse 8. Those who come to God find complete satisfaction through the rich provisions that He supplies them. **They drink their fill of the abundance of Your house,** he says. Those who live at God's house may partake of the endless provisions of that dwelling place. As a storehouse, it is filled with all the bounties any houseguest could ever need. Its resources are more than adequate.

He says in praise, **And You give them to drink of the river of Your delights.** It is as if God is a gardener and a river is in His garden, like in Eden, that is filled with divine blessings. It flows out to anyone who comes to God, and he may drink continually of the special goodness of God found in this river. Unlimited access to this healing stream is given to all residents in God's house.

Verse 9. God is described as a fountain: **For with You is the fountain of life.** Those who drink of the fountain of life will have perpetual life. God is the source of life and whoever partakes of Him has real life in this world and eternal life in the world to come.

Likewise, God is described as light that begets light: **In Your light we see light.** Those who come to Him will have light, for they will be able to truly see. Those who do not come to Him live in continual darkness. As the sun provides light for our physical eyes, God provides light for our spiritual eyes. "Light" means life and understanding. God, true light, becomes our source of light.

"CONTINUE YOUR LOVINGKINDNESS"
(36:10–12)

¹⁰O continue Your lovingkindness to those who know You,
And Your righteousness to the upright in heart.
¹¹Let not the foot of pride come upon me,
And let not the hand of the wicked drive me away.
¹²There the doers of iniquity have fallen;
They have been thrust down and cannot rise.

PSALM 36

Verse 10. The psalmist declares his choice between sin and godliness. How could he (or anyone else) choose any life but the life of God? He says, **O continue Your lovingkindness to those who know You, and Your righteousness to the upright in heart.** The psalm ends with a prayer. He cannot think about the perfect attributes of God without bowing his head and asking Him to continue loving His people as He has in the past. The writer's choice is understood and praised by all who know anything about God.

The decision to serve God is so obviously sensible and superior to any other choice that he does not take time to tell about it; he just puts his choice into practice. So overwhelming is the God-ward side of the contrast that he has made that he does not ask, "Which choice will you make?" He takes for granted that everyone will see the glory of God and will make the same choice he has made.

Verse 11. His final petition is this: **Let not the foot of pride come upon me.** He asks that he might be delivered from the wicked man's oppression and be spared from having a proud victor's foot placed on his neck as one who has been vanquished. Further he prays, **And let not the hand of the wicked drive me away.** He does not want "the hand of the wicked" man to be permitted to drive him from God, truth, and righteousness. He desires, as all righteous people should, to be free from the wicked man's fellowship, fruits, and influence.

Verse 12. To think of the end of the wicked makes the psalmist shudder. He can say in faith that their destruction is sure. It is as if they have already fallen. He says, **There the doers of iniquity have fallen; they have been thrust down and cannot rise.** He can see their end, and he wants no part of it. The evil man will be thrown "down," never to rise again. Evil cannot go on forever; it cannot coexist with God. At the time God chooses, sin will be judged. However, the godly will live by God's unfailing love and righteousness and will know an abundant life with Him.

APPLICATION

Which Side?
God and godliness comprise the alternative to the sinful life. The psalmist's declaration is that the first option—choosing sin—leads only to more pain, deception, violence, and selfishness. The second option—choosing God—leads to exquisite fellowship, pleasures untold, an enduring life, and helpfulness toward all people.

If one is disappointed in his choice of sin, he can turn to the only other choice he has, the choice of godliness. The psalmist wanted to live on God's side, far removed from the end of the wicked. The teaching of this psalm is that only the foolish will turn from God's lovingkindness to the life of sin.

The Progression of Sin
Note the progression that has occurred in the life of the sinner. Although he received teaching, at one time demonstrated wisdom, and did good deeds, he decided *to join the ranks of the wicked.* For a while he was miserable, but *he became more and more one of them.* At some point, *he abandoned himself to this way of life.* His decision was not a one-moment-in-time decision, but a slow-moving involvement until he became immersed in evil. Alexander Pope described poetically the process:

> Vice is a monster of so frightful mien,
> As to be hated needs but to be seen;
> Yet seen too oft, familiar with her face,
> We first endure, then pity, then embrace.[2]

Having made this decision, he now is *a disciple of sin from head to heel.* He lives for sin, defends it, and preaches it.

The Nature of Evil
Verses 1 through 4 of this psalm comprise a piece of wisdom literature that instructs concerning wickedness. It reminds us of

---

[2]Alexander Pope, *Essay on Man*, II. v. 1–4.

PSALM 36

some of the wisdom passages in Proverbs.

The psalm begins by presenting evil as a kind of oracle in our hearts. What does this sinister prophet say?

Naturally, evil seeks to guide one into its paths. As part of our hearts, it takes over the leadership of our lives. We are dominated by it. Deep within us, it whispers its message of direction and devilment.

It is a flatterer. When one has second thoughts about his choice, evil reassures him by telling him that he has made the best choice. It declares that it takes one of the smartest people to make this decision. It reinforces and strengthens the horrible choice that has been made.

It will even speak through one's lips. Before one knows it, he is declaring its message with the deceitful words that stream from his heart through his mouth. The citadel of the soul has been captured and is now used as the headquarters of wickedness. He has become the instrument of evil.

We understand the rationale behind giving our minds, bodies, and futures to that which is noble, right, and true; but evil asks us to give up everything for that which is hurtful, destructive, and humiliating. The ones taken in by evil have been duped. The only way evil can get one to make such a sacrifice is for the person to be hoodwinked from the inside into believing he has chosen the best way, when in reality he has chosen the worst.

The Man Evil Made

What kind of man does evil make?

One who makes bad choices. He has had the opportunity to choose the right, but he has chosen the wrong. He has not only made the choice to pursue evil, but he has stayed with the choice, refusing to repent. His thinking has become dominated by evil.

One who has no fear of God. The word "fear" is more like dread. The thought of God does not cause him to stop and think about where he is going and what he is doing. He sees himself as accountable to no one, not even to the One who made him.

One who is foolish. He has turned from wisdom to foolishness. Perhaps there was a time when he embraced wisdom, but now he is on the path that is trodden only by fools.

One who loves evil and hates good. He no longer despises evil. He has gotten used to it and perhaps has grown to love it. His value system has been turned upside down.

One who has the wrong aspirations in his heart. Instead of lying awake planning for the good of mankind, he lies awake planning evil. In the quietness of the night, he plots his next day's agenda of wickedness.

Attitudes Toward God

All that *is* can be divided into two classes: that which is God and that which is not God. To say it another way, there is God, and there is what God has created. God is the self-existent One, and all else depends on Him for its life and sustenance.

This psalm presents four attitudes concerning God. Two are clearly stated, and two are implied.

First, we see those who have no fear of God in their hearts. They have completely discarded the thought of God. Having become hardened in their lifestyle and thinking, they have lost all dread of God. No more tragic condition can be conceived than this one.

Second, implied in these verses is the pushing of God out of the mind. The man in the psalm has already done the unthinkable—he has eliminated God from his thinking. However, he had to go through a process of demise in order to reach this stage. Many people of the earth are still in this process. The thought of God does not leave them without a struggle. Before they can remove God from their minds, they must choose to do so. In fact, they have to make such a choice over and over until their hearts have hardened to the thought of God.

Third, there is the group that is indifferent concerning God. They are not opposed to Him. They may even have kind thoughts about Him when they think of Him, but they have not surrendered to Him. They may be reachable, but at this point they have not been reached.

Fourth, we see the person who seeks to keep God before his heart and in his heart. In the latter part of the psalm, this truth is illustrated. Walking with God is viewed as the highest ambition of life. God's lovingkindness, greatness, and power are extolled.

The writer says that he is lost without God and recognizes that he is ignorant without His guidance.

All of humanity can be placed in one of these four classifications. Each person has one of these attitudes: seeking God, being indifferent about God, trying to get rid of God, or living totally without God.

Thinking of God

One can easily get lost in the wonder of contemplating God. Involving our minds in this contemplation is life's greatest occupation and privilege. A tea cup cannot contain or comprehend the ocean; nor can a person even begin to understand God. However, meditating on Him lifts us and ennobles us.

He is inexhaustible in His lovingkindness and faithfulness. His lovingkindness extends to the heavens; His faithfulness reaches to the skies. He loves everyone and lives to save us from our sins and pull us into His fellowship.

He is unchangeable in His righteousness. Just as His mountains do not move, He does not waver in His justice and truth.

He is unsearchable in His judgments. They are like the great depths of the oceans. They are beyond our abilities to attain, but they provide the standards that guide us and challenge us to reach up to the likeness of God.

Even though He is righteous, holy, and just, He is gracious, welcoming, and hospitable. Anyone who chooses may rest under the shadow of His wings. He will bring those who trust in Him into His great house for sustenance, delight, and life.

The Greatness of God's Grace

Some of the most beautiful expressions concerning God's lovingkindness and faithfulness are found in this psalm. His lovingkindness "extends to the heavens"; His faithfulness "reaches to the skies" (v. 5). These expressions cause us to recognize the incomprehensible nature of salvation.

It is too good to miss. How can anyone ignore who God is and what He has done? Just think: The God who has created all things has extended His tender mercies and kindness to frail, sinful people like us. One of the greatest truths is that God loves us.

It is too great to grasp. In our living of it and in our lifetime of study, we will never be able to fully absorb its meaning. Perhaps in eternity our greatest occupation will be that of comprehending it more and more with greater and purified minds.

It is too grand to fail. Those who enter this covenant relationship with God have entered into God's eternal purpose. His great salvation is greater in its design and creation than the creation of the universe itself. Angels were breathless over it, and people of all the ages have stood amazed at it.

Too great to grasp; too good to miss; too grand to fail! This description is true of salvation because it is true of God. He is too great to grasp. Who can understand Him? He is too good to miss. Who can envision greater love and grace? He is too grand to fail us. His faithfulness and truth abide forever.

In the Shadow of God's Wings

We come again to the expression of taking "refuge in the shadow of [His] wings" (v. 7). Perhaps it comes to us from the figure of a mother chicken hovering over her little ones, using her life to protect them. Those who trust in God have come under His shelter, His protection.

Think of the implications of this phrase, and rejoice in God's goodness to us.

It implies that God is approachable. We need help, and we can come to Him for it. We are as much in need of protection as are little chickens. Such a realization rebukes our pride and imparts humility to our hearts.

It implies God's strength. He is the great I Am. He is our rock, our fortress. No one would think of taking refuge under the paper-thin wings of man. The wise turn to God, the almighty One.

It implies God's compassion. Why would God take time for us? There is only one answer: He has eternal love for us. He is like a mother to us.

What is God to us? He is either a refuge or a judge, wings of shelter or arms of judgment.

The Satisfactions of God

Four images are used to convey the extravagant blessings God gives to those who love Him.

First, *God is pictured as a host,* providing for His guests an abundant feast along with their fellowship with Him. His guests are completely satisfied. His goodness and provisions are ever available to those who live with Him.

Second, *God is seen as a keeper of a garden* in which those who come to Him are given unlimited access to a river that flows with endless pleasures. They have the opportunity to drink of the river of delights.

Third, *God is portrayed as a fountain of life.* Those who come and drink of Him have perpetual life. He is their source of eternal life.

Fourth, *God is described as light.* Those who come will have light and will be able to truly see. As a flashlight provides light for our physical eyes, God provides light for our spiritual eyes. The words "light" and "life" speak of the fullness of salvation and understanding in the presence of God.

What an array of significant terms: "house," "river," "fountain," and "light." Together they suggest that the Lord, the source of all wisdom and love, will grant His children all their needs.

These beautiful scenes remind us of the Garden of Eden where man enjoyed a perfect paradise. The point is, the experience of Eden may be experienced again in a righteous fellowship with God.

The Wrong Question

When someone asks, "Do you believe in life after death?" they have asked the wrong question. What should be asked is "Do you believe in the faithfulness of God?" God has clearly told us what He will do about all the tomorrows of those who trust in Him. Thus only one question needs to be asked, "Will God keep His promises?" If the answer to that question is "Yes!" then there is a glorious life beyond the grave!

PSALM 37
DO NOT FRET ABOUT THE WICKED

The Superscription: A Psalm of David. The title simply has **of** ["by," "for," or "to"] **David** (לְדָוִד, *lᵉdawid*), although the NASB and other translations add **a Psalm**. However, they normally indicate by the use of italics that the two words are their addition and are not part of the superscription.

The writer of this psalm arranged through the Spirit what he wanted to say in the acrostic format, a pattern that we have seen in Psalms 9, 10, 25, and 34. Every other verse (or every fourth line in the Hebrew text) begins with a different letter of the Hebrew alphabet. For example, verse 1 begins with the first letter, verse 3 (since there are two lines per verse) begins with the second, and so on.

However, the psalm does not perfectly follow the acrostic pattern, as is true of some of the other alphabetical psalms. Irregularities appear in verses 7, 14, 20, 25, 28, 34, and 39. In verses 7, 20, and 34, a letter is used to begin a single verse or three lines. In verses 14, 25, and 39, a letter begins two verses made up of five lines instead of four. In verse 28, the acrostic letter is placed at the beginning, it seems, of the second line.

Deviations from the rigid acrostic pattern are seen in other places in the Psalms. They may be part of the writer's intentions, or they may result from the translation and preservation of the text. Such an arrangement has nothing to do with the meaning or accuracy of the psalm; it simply relates to how the message was originally presented by the writer or a minor translation problem. Perhaps the writer used this alphabetic technique to enable the reader to memorize the psalm more easily.

This composition is one of the four psalms in the Book of Psalms that discuss in detail the disturbing problem of the power, greed, and prosperity of the wicked. The other three are Psalms 10, 49, and 73. The body of the psalm is a lesson addressed to the godly man; it is not a prayer to God, as is the case with many of the psalms. The writer assumes the role of a teacher, instructing the reader on how to react to the success of the wicked. The psalm contains a clear affirmation that God will keep His promises to sustain the righteous in all types of trying circumstances and He will fulfill His prediction that He will remove the wicked from the land.

Possessing a similarity to Proverbs, it is classified as a wisdom or teaching psalm. Verse 1 is almost identical to Proverbs 24:19; verse 16 compares to Proverbs 15:16 and 16:8. Throughout the psalm are proverb-like sayings that appear nowhere else in the Scriptures (for example, see vv. 21, 25, and 35).

The core truth of the psalm is the safety and blessing of those who trust in God and the eventual judgment of the ungodly. The reader is asked to look at the big picture, the working out of God's plan over time. The psalmist wrote this piece late in his life (see v. 25). Some of his sayings are deductions that he has drawn from observation. For example, he argues that God's people should not "fret" when an evil man succeeds, but that they should maintain a righteous attitude toward his prosperity.

Since the psalm is written somewhat like Proverbs, outlining it is difficult. We will approach it by grouping the verses into paragraphs of reasonable lengths.

"TRUST IN THE LORD" (37:1–6)

¹**Do not fret because of evildoers,**
Be not envious toward wrongdoers.
²**For they will wither quickly like the grass**
And fade like the green herb.
³**Trust in the LORD and do good;**
Dwell in the land and cultivate faithfulness.
⁴**Delight yourself in the LORD;**

And He will give you the desires of your heart.
⁵Commit your way to the LORD,
Trust also in Him, and He will do it.
⁶He will bring forth your righteousness as the light
And your judgment as the noonday.

Verse 1. After the superscription, the acrostic letter for the first four lines is א (*Aleph*).

The psalm begins with a practical exhortation to the righteous: **Do not fret because of evildoers, be not envious toward wrongdoers.** The godly are not to "fret" (חָרָה, *charah*) or become "agitated, heated, or stirred up" about the prosperity that has come to those who are morally corrupt. The righteous are also urged, "Be not envious toward wrongdoers." It is easy to give way to envy when we see the wicked prospering; however, when we remember that their situation is not as it appears, the temptation to be jealous subsides.

Verse 2. The injunction not to fret is followed by a convincing reason as to why the lifestyle or condition of the wicked should not be coveted. The psalmist says, **For they will wither quickly like the grass and fade like the green herb.** The lives of the wicked should not be sought because one day, when God sees fit, they will get their just reward. As the "grass" withers, as the "herb" fades, even so the wicked will come to their time of judgment and will pass away. The grass in the Middle East can spring up and flourish for a brief time and then suddenly wither and die in the hot, dry wind. Therefore, the vegetation around the writer is short-lived and provides a good illustration of the prosperity of the evil man.

Verse 3. The acrostic letter is ב (*Beth*).

Instead of looking with eager eyes toward the prospering wicked man, the righteous are admonished with four imperatives: "Trust in the Lord"; "Do good"; "Dwell in the land"; and "Cultivate faithfulness." **Trust in the LORD and do good.** The faith that is enjoined is a tough faith, a faith that submits to God's will as it waits for Him to resolve the dilemma that has arisen. The righteous are told to trust in God's plan and do His work. They are also told to **dwell in the land and cultivate faithful-**

ness. They are to believe in God's trustworthiness and to build this view of God into their hearts and into their relationships with others, making it the cornerstone of their living. "Cultivate" could also be translated "feed."

Verse 4. The righteous are to find their joy in the Lord. **Delight yourself in the Lord**, the psalmist says. They are to lose themselves in a wondrous, happy contemplation of God, rejoicing in His love, His goodness, and His will. As ones who are joyously united with God in this way, they are assured that He will hear their prayers. **He will give you the desires of your heart**, the writer asserts. The deep, true longings of their hearts will be granted. This promise assumes that the heart of the believer is committed to God and will naturally be seeking the things of God as the next verse indicates.

Verse 5. The acrostic letter is ג *(Gimel)*.

God, in harmony with His nature, will honor the goodness of those who are righteous. They are instructed, **Commit your way to the Lord, trust also in Him, and He will do it.** God, the object of their love and devotion, will be faithful to reward the faith and obedience of righteous people.

Verse 6. Thus vindication will come for the mistreated righteous. **He will bring forth your righteousness as the light and your judgment as the noonday.** Their good decisions and faithful living will one day come to "light" and will become as visible as the "noonday" sun. Their genuine lives will be recognized, and their good deeds will be properly remembered. Regardless of the way the wicked fare today, the righteous will one day be exonerated. Their righteousness will be brought out of the shadows, and its true beauty will be seen.

"REST IN THE LORD" (37:7–11)

⁷**Rest in the Lord and wait patiently for Him;**
Do not fret because of him who prospers in his way,
Because of the man who carries out wicked schemes.
⁸**Cease from anger and forsake wrath;**
Do not fret; it leads only to evildoing.
⁹**For evildoers will be cut off,**

> But those who wait for the LORD, they will inherit the land.
> ¹⁰Yet a little while and the wicked man will be no more;
> And you will look carefully for his place and he will not be there.
> ¹¹But the humble will inherit the land
> And will delight themselves in abundant prosperity.

Verse 7. The acrostic letter is ד (*Daleth*).

Another admonition is given to the righteous man: **Rest in the LORD and wait patiently for Him.** To "rest" or "wait" is to trust in His Word and in the integrity of His promises. Here we see the more difficult side of faith, that of submitting to His will when the circumstances and people around us urge us to do otherwise. God cannot always remove our enemies or adversities as quickly as we would like. He has to think of our spiritual growth, the free will He has given to mankind, and other contingent values. The one who waits on God, however, rests in the assurance that God will care for him in harmony with His will and in full keeping with His love and grace.

Further, he says to the godly man, **Do not fret because of him who prospers in his way, because of the man who carries out wicked schemes.** Those who have faith in God believe that He will deliver what He has promised for the righteous at the appropriate time.

Trusting in the Lord means active obedience to Him. It means reliance on the Lord, fully expecting Him to justify the righteous, as He has promised.

Verse 8. The acrostic letter is ה (*He*).

Further exhortations are given: **Cease from anger and forsake wrath.** The righteous man is not to become "angry" (אַף, *'ap*) or resentful at the seeming advancements of the wicked. Specifically, the writer says, **Do not fret.** "Fretting" is becoming agitated and "heated up." It means to "burn."

Why is fretting forbidden? The reason is that **it leads only to evildoing.** Being distraught over what the wicked are accomplishing can lead to doubting God's providence and may cause us to give up and conclude that the wicked are right. The godly must leave to God the punishment and retribution of the wicked.

God will deliver what He has promised for the righteous at the time of His choosing. Trusting God means making a full commitment to the Lord, rolling any anger, resentment, and jealousy on Him, and delighting in His way (see 1 Pet. 5:7). God expects His children to put themselves under His fatherly care and allow Him to handle concerns that are beyond their control.

Verse 9. What will be the destiny of the wicked? Their future is predetermined in the wisdom of God: **For evildoers will be cut off**. The primary truth presented so far is that those who trust in the Lord will eventually be rewarded by Him, while the wicked will face their destiny and, in God's time and way, cease to be. The wicked will be removed from the land, **but those who wait for the LORD ... will inherit the land**. God gave the land of Canaan to His people, and He removed it from the Canaanites. Those who trusted in the Lord received; those who lived for wickedness were cut off.

Verse 10. The acrostic letter is ו (*Vav*).

God will deal with the wicked man when He deems best. **Yet a little while and the wicked man will be no more**. A day is with the Lord as a thousand years and a thousand years as a day, but timing is important to God. He does not judge too early, and He does not hand out His verdict too late. His judgment upon the evil man will be decisive and final. The accounting will be thorough and will cover the totality of life. The evil person will answer for every deed, and his sentence will be irrevocable. A time is coming when we **will look carefully for his place and he will not be there**. The wicked man has no future. In God's ultimate plan, he will pass away. It will be as if he had never existed.

Verse 11. The future of the godly man is attractive and enduring, for **the humble will inherit the land and will delight themselves in abundant prosperity**. In other words, the humble, the meek, the obedient ones, will receive the fulfillment of God's promises. Perhaps Jesus drew His beatitude (Mt. 5:5) from the theology of this psalm. The word "prosperity" is a translation of the word שָׁלוֹם (*shalom*), the word for "peace."

Old Testament theology centers more on physical prosperity than does New Testament teaching. During the time the psalmist wrote, God was preserving a nation to be a vehicle for the bringing the Messiah into the world. His reassurance to the reader that God would prolong his life and cut off the evil man's life surely should be understood in light of these physical promises made to the nation of Israel. However, an application of this truth can be made to Christians in the sense that God will faithfully keep His promises to us and will one day bring the wicked into a final reckoning.

THE SUCCESS OF THE WICKED IS TEMPORARY (37:12-15)

¹²**The wicked plots against the righteous
And gnashes at him with his teeth.**
¹³**The Lord laughs at him,
For He sees his day is coming.**
¹⁴**The wicked have drawn the sword and bent their bow
To cast down the afflicted and the needy,
To slay those who are upright in conduct.**
¹⁵**Their sword will enter their own heart,
And their bows will be broken.**

Verse 12. The acrostic letter is ז (*Zayin*).

The wicked man may be the enemy of the righteous man. Sometimes **the wicked plots against the righteous and gnashes at him with his teeth.** The evil man often takes advantage of the good man and schemes against the innocent by making plans to cheat him or rob him. His plans are sometimes vicious, as if they had the teeth of lions in them.

Verse 13. However, the Day of Judgment for the wicked man is as sure as God's integrity. **The Lord laughs at him, for He sees his day is coming.** His frail plans will pass away like thread burning in a fire. The idea that anyone could win against God is so incredulous as to be a humorous matter with God. The truth is that the prosperity of the wicked man will be short-lived. His days will rapidly come to an end. This fact, which has already been mentioned, is more fully discussed in verses 16 through

22. God is on the side of the righteous, and He has already foreordained the demise of the wicked.

Verse 14. The acrostic letter is ח (*Heth*).

Enemy nations come against God's people, God's righteous ones, but they become the victims, not the victors. **The wicked have drawn the sword and bent their bow to cast down the afflicted and the needy, to slay those who are upright in conduct.** What the wicked propose to do will fail miserably.

These affirmations about the destruction of the wicked and victory of the righteous are directed to the godly people of Israel and are grounded in the promises that God made to Abraham in Genesis 12:1–3. God repeatedly affirmed that Abraham would be given descendants and land. Over time, God, in His overruling providence, fulfilled each of these promises.

Another application, a secondary one, is to the righteous in general. God will defend and protect them. He will confound the wicked in their attempts to harm them. The righteous may lose some battles for the strengthening of their faith, but they will always win the war.

Verse 15. The final end of the wicked is figuratively pictured: **Their sword will enter their own heart, and their bows will be broken.** They will be destroyed by their wickedness. Their implements of war will be broken, and they will find out in the end that their might is not strong enough to save them.

THE RIGHTEOUS MAN'S REWARD
(37:16–22)

¹⁶**Better is the little of the righteous**
Than the abundance of many wicked.
¹⁷**For the arms of the wicked will be broken,**
But the LORD sustains the righteous.
¹⁸**The LORD knows the days of the blameless,**
And their inheritance will be forever.
¹⁹**They will not be ashamed in the time of evil,**
And in the days of famine they will have abundance.
²⁰**But the wicked will perish;**

>   And the enemies of the LORD will be like the glory of the pastures,
>   They vanish—like smoke they vanish away.
>   ²¹The wicked borrows and does not pay back,
>   But the righteous is gracious and gives.
>   ²²For those blessed by Him will inherit the land,
>   But those cursed by Him will be cut off.

Verse 16. The acrostic letter is ט (*Teth*).

An encouraging comparison between the godly and the wicked is now drawn: **Better is the little of the righteous than the abundance of many wicked.** In the end the righteous are far better off than the wicked, even though the wicked may have more in the way of material goods.

God has not promised that the righteous will always live in palaces and eat each meal at a banquet table. The writer gives balance to his statement by saying that a little with righteousness is better than much with wickedness.

Verse 17. God will cause the wicked to go down in defeat. **For the arms of the wicked will be broken, but the LORD sustains the righteous.** The God of Israel is against the wicked. In His own way, God will see that the wicked fall and never rise again. The defeat may not come immediately, but it will inevitably come. He will hold up or preserve the righteous while He brings about the collapse of the wicked.

Verse 18. The acrostic letter is י (*Yodh*).

God's eyes of tender care are always upon the righteous. **The LORD knows the days of the blameless, and their inheritance will be forever.** He will never overlook the life of the sincerely obedient person. He loves him and will bless and save him. The word for "knows" is יָדַע (*yada*), meaning "to know intimately." He knows, in the sense of "caring for," the righteous. If it seems that a good man is forgotten, it will only be for a brief period. Ultimately, God will give him an "enduring inheritance."

Verse 19. God will see that the righteous are never disappointed. The psalmist says, **They will not be ashamed in the time of evil, and in the days of famine they will have abundance.** The righteous will be providentially protected, and their needs will be met even in times of crisis. In the days of famine and of war, the good will have the kind hand of God hovering over them. Even when surrounded by trouble, they will be in the fortress of God.

Verse 20. The acrostic letter is כ (*Kaph*).

The writer says, **But the wicked will perish**. Only one destiny awaits the wicked—destruction. They have set out to eliminate others, but they themselves will be eliminated. **The enemies of the LORD will be like the glory of the pastures**. The wicked are condemned to a brief existence, as flowers of the field bloom for a few days and then die and are forgotten. **They vanish—like smoke they vanish away**. They are like "smoke" that is seen for a moment and then forever passes from sight. "Vanish" (כָּלָה, *kalah*), meaning "to come to an end," is used twice for emphasis, stressing the certainty of the fact.

Verse 21. The acrostic letter is ל (*Lamedh*).

A further contrast can be made between the resources of the wicked and those of the righteous. **The wicked borrows and does not pay back, but the righteous is gracious and gives.** The life of the godly is much different from that of the wicked. The evil person mistreats others, while the righteous person is gracious toward all people. The wicked man hoards and lives only for himself. He does not pay back what he has borrowed. "Pay back" (שָׁלֵם, *shalem*) comes from a word that means "to complete or put back in place," a word that is related to the word "peace." The wicked man does not care about others except as they might serve him. The godly man gives; the evil man takes. The wicked man exacts high interest from others, but the righteous one extends love and concern. Thus the godly life has intrinsic value. Wickedness is rebellion against God and brings harm and injury into the world.

Verse 22. The righteous will be blessed of God. **For those blessed by Him will inherit the land, but those cursed by Him will be cut off.** The wicked will become destitute, and the righteous will have enough to share with others.

Only one thing matters in life: "Am I blessed of God?" If one is blessed by Him, he will live the good life; if one is not blessed by Him, he will be cut off.

The facts are these: The upright will endure, and the wicked will be destroyed. The ungodly must face their destiny of death through God's judgment. Though the verdict may tarry, it will surely come.

The righteous will inherit the land because they are the ones to whom God has made His promises. The wicked may be given time to repent, and God may try the faith of the righteous; but His promises, from the least to the greatest, will be kept.

THE RIGHTEOUS LIFE (37:23–26)

> ²³The steps of a man are established by the LORD,
> And He delights in his way.
> ²⁴When he falls, he will not be hurled headlong,
> Because the LORD is the One who holds his hand.
> ²⁵I have been young and now I am old,
> Yet I have not seen the righteous forsaken
> Or his descendants begging bread.
> ²⁶All day long he is gracious and lends,
> And his descendants are a blessing.

Verse 23. The acrostic letter is מ (*Mem*).

The good man walks in the ways of God, for **the steps of a man are established by the LORD, and He delights in his way.** He not only walks in God's truth, but he "delights" or finds his happiness in this way of life. His "steps" (all parts of his life) are strengthened by God, who helps him to stand even in times of severe adversity. The good man knows that God looks upon him with favor; and this realization brings him inner joy, pleasure, and peace.

Verse 24. The life of the good man will face its difficulties. **When he falls, he will not be hurled headlong, because the LORD is the One who holds his hand.** He may "fall," make a mistake, or be persecuted; but God will keep him from ruin.

The righteous life has merits of its own that outweigh the selfish pursuits and ambitions of sinners. The wicked man is always one step from disaster as he awaits God's judgment; the good man is sustained by Him even in tragedy and death.

Verse 25. The acrostic letter is ‫נ‬ (*Nun*).

An observation from the summit of the years is given by the writer: **I have been young and now I am old, yet I have not seen the righteous forsaken or his descendants begging bread.** The writer has studied life, making special note of it over time. He has not seen "the righteous" man destitute or his descendants "begging" for help. God has always taken care of those who trust in Him. He has always acted at the appropriate time.

Some may ask, "How about the man Job? Didn't God let him experience deprivation?" Yes, for a period of time He did, but God was in charge of the whole affair. He was giving Job a place of signal honor as He allowed him to show the world how faith can sustain a man in the greatest of affliction. At the appropriate time, God came to his rescue and blessed him more than he had ever been blessed. Even though in a world like ours trials must be faced, the righteous always come out on top through the favor of God.

Verse 26. Blessings emanate from the righteous man even to his descendants. **All day long he is gracious and lends, and his descendants are a blessing.** He will be blessed, and those around him will benefit from the blessings he has received. He is "gracious" in that he shares what he has with others. Those who know him are made better by this relationship.

God's commitment to the righteous is to vindicate them and to see that they inherit the land. This truth implies certain conclusions, and these conclusions are given in the next few verses.

HOW THEN SHALL WE LIVE?
(37:27–34)

^{27}Depart from evil and do good,
So you will abide forever.
^{28}For the LORD loves justice
And does not forsake His godly ones;
They are preserved forever,
But the descendants of the wicked will be cut off.
^{29}The righteous will inherit the land

And dwell in it forever.
³⁰The mouth of the righteous utters wisdom,
And his tongue speaks justice.
³¹The law of his God is in his heart;
His steps do not slip.
³²The wicked spies upon the righteous
And seeks to kill him.
³³The Lord will not leave him in his hand
Or let him be condemned when he is judged.
³⁴Wait for the Lord and keep His way,
And He will exalt you to inherit the land;
When the wicked are cut off, you will see it.

Verse 27. The acrostic letter is ס (*Samekh*).

Because of God's faithfulness, the righteous man is given a practical exhortation. **Depart from evil and do good, so you will abide forever.** Since God will faithfully care for those who trust in Him, let us make sure that we "depart from evil" and cleave to the "good." God will be reliable, so let us walk in His Word. We should not be blinded or misled by what we see around us. We walk by faith, not by sight (2 Cor. 5:7). Therefore, our lips should be dedicated to speaking what is true; God's Word should fill our hearts.

Verse 28. The acrostic letter ע (*Ayin*) may appear in the second line of this verse.

God's promises grow out of His integrity. **For the Lord loves justice and does not forsake His godly ones.** He will always stand with righteousness and truth. He will not fail on any promises He has made to them. **They are preserved forever, but the descendants of the wicked will be cut off.** The integrity of God will bless the righteous but condemn the wicked.

Verse 29. Only the righteous have a right to claim the good things of the Lord. **The righteous will inherit the land and dwell in it forever.** God will sustain the righteous man and fulfill all the promises He has made to him.

Verse 30. The acrostic letter is פ (*Pe*).

From head to toe, the righteous man is affected by the Word of the Lord. **The mouth of the righteous utters wisdom, and**

his tongue speaks justice. The righteous man is not perfect in his actions, but his heart belongs to the Lord. His mind, guided by the Lord, speaks words of wisdom to those who will listen.

Verse 31. God's law is precious to him. **The law of his God is in his heart; his steps do not slip.** Since he has God on his heart, he conforms to God's will. Precautions are taken by the righteous man so that he does not slip into sin or fail to fulfill His Word. Sin does not ensnare him because he has hidden God's Word in his heart.

The promise to the Israelites is clear. If they stay away from evil, exhibit good, and love God, they will see His benefits. If we incorporate into our lives what God loves, He will favor us with His special care.

Verse 32. The acrostic letter is צ (*Tsadhe*).

The righteous often have to deal with the wicked. **The wicked spies upon the righteous and seeks to kill him.** The arena of life is a place of conflicts and not always a place of peace. The wicked try to trip up the righteous. They hate the righteous because their righteousness is a rebuke to their evil (Heb. 11:7). As the good man does God's will and loves what God loves, he interferes with the plans of the wicked. Recoiling to this, the wicked man attacks the righteous man in various ways, perhaps even seeking to take away his life.

Verse 33. The righteous man does not have to face the wicked man alone, for **the LORD will not leave him in his hand or let him be condemned when he is judged.** God interposes with His providence in one way or another, refusing to allow the righteous man to be condemned when he is falsely judged. He will not leave the righteous in the hand or power of the wicked. These are general promises and should not be understood as universal or absolute (see Gen. 4:8; Acts 12:2).

Verse 34. The acrostic letter is ק (*Qoph*).

Sometimes the righteous man must trustingly give God time to act in His own way. Hence, this injunction is given: **Wait for the LORD and keep His way, and He will exalt you to inherit the land.** In general, God does not allow the wicked to do what they wish with the righteous. When He chooses not to rescue His people, He strengthens them to fulfill His purposes in the fires of persecution. **When the wicked are cut off, you will see it.** The Lord's judgment of the wicked is sure, and the righteous will see it.

COMMIT YOURSELF TO THE LORD
(37:35–40)

³⁵I have seen a wicked, violent man
Spreading himself like a luxuriant tree in its native soil.
³⁶Then he passed away, and lo, he was no more;
I sought for him, but he could not be found.
³⁷Mark the blameless man, and behold the upright;
For the man of peace will have a posterity.
³⁸But transgressors will be altogether destroyed;
The posterity of the wicked will be cut off.
³⁹But the salvation of the righteous is from the LORD;
He is their strength in time of trouble.
⁴⁰The LORD helps them and delivers them;
He delivers them from the wicked and saves them,
Because they take refuge in Him.

Verse 35. The acrostic letter is ר (*Resh*).

The psalmist returns to what he has seen. **I have seen a wicked, violent man spreading himself like a luxuriant tree in its native soil.** He has beheld the wicked man strutting in pride about his deeds, thinking of himself as being safe from all harm. He is like a tree of great strength in the strongest soil. The tree of the wicked, though thought to be mighty and enduring, will fall.

Verse 36. As the writer watched, the ungodly man was suddenly brought down, never to be heard from again. **Then he passed away, and lo, he was no more; I sought for him, but he could not be found.** He has seen the fulfillment of God's Word.

Verse 37. The acrostic letter is ש (*Shin*).

He says, "Look at the blameless man. See how God has blessed him." **Mark the blameless man, and behold the upright; for the man of peace will have a posterity.** If you look, you will see the perfect, blameless man being blessed. The writer's conclusion from his study of life is that the wicked man always meets his due and the righteous man always wins. God's people have total peace and families who enjoy the fruit of their faithfulness.

Verse 38. Transgressors will come to the judgment they deserve. **But transgressors will be altogether destroyed; the posterity of the wicked will be cut off.** They will be ultimately defeated. Their influence and children will be brought to an end.

Verse 39. The acrostic letter is ת (*Tav*).

God watches over the righteous and sees that they are delivered and honored. **But the salvation of the righteous is from the Lord; He is their strength in time of trouble.** They receive good things in this life and a wonderful future because God makes sure that they receive the best of His riches.

Verse 40. He is the strength behind the righteous. **The Lord helps them, and delivers them.** He is their salvation and refuge in the time of storm. **He delivers them from the wicked, and saves them, because they take refuge in Him.** Because they trust in Him and come to Him for salvation, the Lord extends His hand of grace to the righteous. God will deliver them from the schemes of the wicked and strengthen them for any trial.

APPLICATION

God's Word to the Righteous

God has not promised a utopia for the righteous, but He has made several wonderful and precious promises to them. Some are mentioned in this psalm. All who trust in Him will be blessed; the wicked will be cut off; the righteous life is the best life; and those who commit their lives to Him will be delivered in the day of trouble.

The Purpose of Suffering

We are not told all the reasons for the sufferings that may come to us, as is so elaborately illustrated in the Book of Job. However, God's grace provides us with the spiritual resources—

both external and internal—to withstand anything that the devil and his wicked helpers can set before us. The life of the godly individual is characterized by three traits: (1) He puts his hope in the Lord, not in people or possessions. (2) He shows his loyalty to God by obeying His Word. (3) He has faith in God's righteousness. He accepts by faith that God will one day deal with the wicked person.

The School of Life
This world is a proving ground, not our eternal destination. If we are faithful throughout the school of life, God will walk with us in the graduation line and give each one of us a diploma, the crown of life. School comes first—and then graduation!

Viewing the Wicked
Let us approach this psalm with these questions: "How should the righteous respond to the good fortune of the wicked? What is the proper attitude to have toward them?"

Regardless of what we see, we must trust in God (vv. 1–11). The first and foremost attitude the godly person should have is that of trusting in God regardless of what may be happening around him. God has not forgotten His people. We may need to "wait" on the Lord as He works out His eternal purpose.

The success of the wicked is temporary (vv. 12–22). We often say, "God does not settle all His accounts at the end of the month." Sometimes the day of reckoning is in the distant future. God's judgments are sure, accurate, and often slow; but they are inevitable.

The righteous life is the highest quality of life to live (vv. 23–34). All things considered, the righteous life has the most benefits. The wicked life hurts the one who lives it and others. It will eventually self-destruct. The righteous life is a blessing in this world, it is a blessing to those nearby, and it will be rewarded in the world to come.

Let us commit ourselves to the Lord (vv. 35–40). We will not be called to judge the wicked—God will call them into account. We are to remember what God's judgment is, but we will not be the ones before whom the wicked will stand. Our main responsibility here is to commit our ways to God. He will provide for us, protect us, and do the judging that is necessary at the appropriate time.

Fret Not!

John Wesley said, "Fretting is as bad as swearing." His statement is worth thinking about, for in swearing people take lightly the name of God, and in fretting they take lightly the promises of God.

When Evil Surrounds You

At times you will find yourself seemingly hedged in by evil. Everywhere you look, you see it. What should you do about it? This psalm gives three answers.

Focus on God. Do what you can to prevent evil, but commit your ways to God. Trust in Him and delight in Him. He will judge evil in His own time.

Focus on the future. Remember that evil has no future; it will be removed from the earth. The wicked man will fade like grass in the sunlight.

Focus on doing good. Busy yourself with God's work on earth. He will give you safer pasture and fill your hands with good things if you trust Him.

Do Not Be Tripped Up!

The wise man carefully watches his attitude toward the ungodly. It is easy to become affected by their prosperity. The wicked may be rewarded by men. They may receive power and prestige because of their wickedness or in spite of it. What should godly people do about them?

Do not fret over them. Do not become "steamed up" over them. Do not let them irritate you.

Do not be envious of them. Do not long for what they have. In reality, they only have what is fading away.

Do not join them. Stay focused on God. Keep things in the right perspective.

Viewing the prosperity of the wicked can cause us to be filled with negative emotions that can harm us. Anger, resentment, and jealousy can short circuit our faith in God's goodness and justice, affecting our attitude toward life in general and toward the value of godly living.

Daily Life with God

How do we walk with God?

We walk with God by trusting in Him. Faith in God means that we believe that He will keep His promises and that we should keep His Word.

We walk with God by committing our ways to Him. We are to abandon our lives to Him and roll on Him the care of our lives, our future, and the outcomes of our service in His vineyard.

Walking with Him means delighting in Him. We enjoy God. He becomes the object of our love and hope. He is our best friend.

God knows that we are His children, and so He asks us to put ourselves completely under His fatherly care. Our part consists of trusting in Him, committing ourselves to Him, and delighting in Him. His part involves caring for every part of our lives.

Having Faith in God

Instead of allowing self-pity and hatred to dominate him, the godly man trusts in the Lord. He possesses the faith that God honors. He will be given the true desires of his heart.

Faith has a tough element to it. He believes in the Lord and waits for Him to resolve a difficult situation. He knows that God will act in His own time. He will not be motivated to give up his trust. He walks by his trust in God, not by his sight.

Faith rejoices in the promises before they are even kept. He knows that God will do what He said that He would do. God's Word is so sure that one can rejoice in the fulfillment of it even before the promise comes to pass. He rejoices in the Lord—in who He is, what He has said, and what He is going to do.

Faith will engage in active obedience. He commits his ways to the Lord and goes about doing God's work while waiting for God to handle his problems. He does not have to worry about God acting; the righteous man knows that He will act in the right time.

This kind of trust is rewarded. God will bring forth our righteousness as the light and our judgment as the noonday. His people will enjoy the promises that have been made. Difficulties may have to be dealt with, enemies may have to be confronted, but God will vindicate righteous people at the right time.

What God Does for the Believer

This psalm pictures what God is to those who trust in Him.

He is our salvation. He has delivered us from the perils of life. For Christians, He has brought Christ into the world to deliver us from our sin and has given us eternal life.

He is our refuge. He protects in times of trouble. Sometimes we are led out of the pathway of harm; and sometimes we are sustained in the midst of its circumstance.

He is our sustenance. He is our spiritual life. We have no will or spirituality without Him.

He not only has saved us, but He works in our lives to keep us saved. He watches over us with His tender care as the best of fathers watches over his children.

The Confidence of a Living Faith

The psalms are about a living faith, a faith that acts and trusts. We see in them the testimony that a faith that does not work is dead (Jas. 2:24–26).

Notice these actions of the vibrant faith of the godly person:

A living faith knows that God is good. God watches over His children to bless them and enjoys having them in His fellowship. He never acts to hurt His children.

A living faith knows that God will act against evil. The ungodly will eventually answer to God. Sometimes the wheels of judgment must turn slowly because of many aspects to His will, but they do turn. They will come to the judgment God has decreed.

A living faith knows that God will keep His promises. The righteous may have to wait on God because the time is not right for Him to act. The one who trusts in God believes that He will do what He said He would do.

A living faith knows that God watches over His own. The meek will inherit the land. They will receive the end of their faith. God will make sure that His people have the protection they need.

True faith grows out of the evidence God has given, and it accepts that evidence and reveals itself in a joyous confidence in the loving God. Faith has to be living, or it means nothing.

Waiting on God

This psalm refers to waiting on God in three verses (vv. 7, 9, 34). We know that God is never slow, never forgets, and is never disorganized. "Waiting" on Him has to do with a faithful, fruitful walk with Him. Waiting is a necessity in light of the nature of our relationship with Him. He is almighty and loving, and we are weak and shortsighted.

Consider what it means to wait on God.

It means submissive obedience. We are told, "Wait for the LORD, and keep His way" (v. 34). God cannot always respond immediately to our situation or prayers because of the broad designs of His eternal purpose. While we wait for the fullness of time to come, we obediently do His will, looking to Him with trusting obedience.

It means eager, longing expectancy. The ones who wait know that God will keep His promises. Waiting rests upon His reliability. Verse 9 says that those who wait for the Lord will inherit the land. The faithful anticipate with expectancy, knowing that they will see the fulfillment of His Word.

It means confidence that God, at the right time, will do the right thing. The writer urges the reader who is wondering when God will deal with the wicked to "rest in the Lord and wait patiently for Him." Do not fret. He will act! We can relax with complete assurance in that fact. He will act in perfect agreement with His will and with perfect love for His children.

Those who wait on the Lord will never be put to shame or be disappointed. He has His own timetable, to be sure, one that takes in His whole creation, His whole scheme of redemption, and His whole development of each child of His. The fact that He responds perfectly to every need and every problem requires time and wisdom; and on this basis, the child of God "waits."

PSALM 37

The Knowledge of the Lord

We know that the Lord "knows" all things. He does not have to be informed about anything. Nothing escapes His all-seeing eyes. This psalm speaks of two truths God especially knows. Highlighting what God knows is a way of calling special attention to how He cares for His own.

He knows the days of the blameless (v. 18). He watches carefully the days of the righteous. He will give special care so that they will have their inheritance. In other words, if there is any one thing to which God gives His utmost attention, it is the fulfillment of His promises to the righteous.

He knows the time of the judgment of the wicked (v. 13). This knowledge of the Lord emphasizes the certainty of His righteousness. As surely as there was a flood, a cross, and an inspired book called the Bible, God will judge sin.

His life and love are directed toward blessing the righteous; but His wrath and anger are aimed toward bringing the wicked into judgment. We see here His goodness and severity.

Who Are the Righteous?

How does this psalm describes the righteous?

They are obedient to God. They keep the Lord's way (v. 34). They love God and treasure what He has commanded and promised. His Word is hidden in their hearts and fleshed out in their lives.

They patiently trust in God. They wait on Him (v. 7) and trust that He will keep His promises. When He does not step in and correct the ills of the day, they trust that in time He will. They believe that He will be faithful to them in the time of His choosing.

They are gracious like God. They are generous and give (v. 21). They share with others and serve others. They want to live so that others may be blessed of God as they have been.

They are the recipients of God's blessings. They know that the righteous will inherit the land (v. 29). God has promised them His blessings, and they know that those blessings will be given. They know that God has chosen to limit the abundance of His blessings to those who trust in Him.

They do not fear, even in the day of adversity. They know that in the day of famine they will have abundance (v. 19), trusting God to sustain them in whatever trial they may have. Nothing is too great for God to overcome, and nothing is too small for Him to care about.

They may stumble, but God will sustain them. When they stumble, they will not fall headlong (v. 24). Tough times come; but they do not give up, and they will not go under. They look to God to hold them and to establish them in difficult places.

They believe that they will never be abandoned by God. They have never seen the righteous begging bread (v. 25). They are people who are confident that God will never turn His back on His people. They believe that God is the only trustworthy being there is. They rest all their hopes, dreams, and even their lives on God's integrity.

What Are the Wicked Like?

What does this psalm say the wicked are like?

They are given to hoarding things for themselves. They live for themselves. They sacrifice others for their own interests.

They are temporary. They appear for a while and then they pass away. They have no future or life.

They sometimes hate the godly. The righteous get in their way of doing what they want to do. The wicked may cheat, rob, or even kill the godly.

They are slated for destruction. Their destiny is clear. They will be destroyed. It is only a matter of time.

They sometimes prosper, but their prosperity will be short-lived. Their advances and successes are only mirages; they are like smoke that appears for a little while and then disappears forever.

The psalm forces us to decide a major issue. It asks the grave question: Will we be numbered among the righteous or the wicked?

Psalm 38

"Grace Greater Than My Sin"

The Superscription: A Psalm of David, for a memorial. The title says that this composition is **a Psalm** [מִזְמוֹר, *mizmor*] **of** ["by," "for, " or "to"] **David** (לְדָוִד, *lᵉdawid*). It further says that it is **for a memorial** or **of** ["by," "for," or "to"] **remembrance"** (לְהַזְכִּיר, *lᵉhazkir*), as does the title for Psalm 70. Thus the superscription suggests that the psalm was either written or was later used to bring a person's or a nation's extreme plight to God's remembrance or to bring God's kindnesses to the remembrance of a person or a nation.

In this individual lament, listed as one of the seven penitential psalms (6; 32; 38; 51; 102; 130; 143), the writer brings before God a stricken conscience and a broken body, as he asks for forgiveness and healing. The psalm contains a graphic description of human distress that was caused by iniquity.

Although the time of writing is difficult to determine, the psalm may be referring to the torturous time that followed David's sins involving Bathsheba and Uriah (2 Sam. 11). Franz Delitzsch[1] has argued that a chronological development can be seen in Psalms 6, 38, 51, and 32 regarding David's fall and restoration. At this point in time, David first acknowledged to God his agony of soul and body, how he was wasting away mentally and physically because of what he had done (6; 38). Later, after being rebuked by Nathan, he penitently called upon God to pardon him for his sin (51). Finally, after receiving forgiveness,

---

[1]Franz Delitzsch, *A Commentary on the Book of Psalms*, trans. David Eaton and James E. Duguid (New York: Funk and Wagnalls, 1883), 235.

David looked back over what had happened to him and how God, in response to his repentance, had graciously removed his sin and saved his life (32).

The writer was experiencing four types of pain. To begin with, a bodily illness was wracking his frame with deterioration and suffering (vv. 3–10). Furthermore, he was enduring alienation, for his friends were deserting him (v. 11). Still further, persecution from his enemies added to his grief and created for him an even more agonizing circumstance (vv. 12, 16, 19). Finally, weighing heavily upon his mind was the guilt of sin and sorrow for breaking God's law (v. 18). He believed that much of what he was experiencing was chastisement from God because of his sins. He did not reveal to us what sin or sins he had committed.

The body of the psalm is a description of his humiliated condition, with only a brief proposed resolution of his difficulties in the final verses. Even though he was overwhelmed, he knew that God was his true hope. Therefore, he was clinging tenaciously to Him (vv. 1, 9, 15, 21, 22).

"REBUKE ME NOT" (38:1)

¹**O LORD, rebuke me not in Your wrath,**
And chasten me not in Your burning anger.

Verse 1. In words almost identical to Psalm 6:1, the writer approaches God and acknowledges that he sees his suffering as chastisement from Him. He prays, **O LORD, rebuke me not in Your wrath, and chasten me not in Your burning anger.** He implies that he has sinned and that his sin has produced much, if not all, of his pain. In providential discipline, God has permitted the mental and physical agony that he is experiencing to serve as a rod of correction to bring him back to the path of righteousness.

Two words are used to describe God's discipline: "wrath" (קֶצֶף, *qetsep*) and "anger" (חֵמָה, *chemah*). He pictures God's chastisement as emanating from His righteous "anger" and divine "wrath." Having taken note of what God is doing and having accepted the instruction, he asks God to temper His discipline of his sinfulness with mercy.

He pleads for God to give him relief from the affliction he has brought upon himself. "I have thought about the cause of my pain and have concluded that it is Your discipline for my waywardness. I acknowledge the judgment You have given and now ask You to lighten it or even remove it," he prays.

"YOUR HAND HAS PRESSED DOWN ON ME" (38:2–8)

²For Your arrows have sunk deep into me,
And Your hand has pressed down on me.
³There is no soundness in my flesh because of Your indignation;
There is no health in my bones because of my sin.
⁴For my iniquities are gone over my head;
As a heavy burden they weigh too much for me.
⁵My wounds grow foul and fester
Because of my folly.
⁶I am bent over and greatly bowed down;
I go mourning all day long.
⁷For my loins are filled with burning,
And there is no soundness in my flesh.
⁸I am benumbed and badly crushed;
I groan because of the agitation of my heart.

Verse 2. Using emotional, poetic language, he describes the depths of his pain. **For Your arrows have sunk deep into me, and Your hand has pressed down on me.** In His divine indignation, God has shot "arrows" of pain into his soul, piercing and punishing his innermost being (see also Job 6:4; 16:12, 13; Lam. 3:12, 13). His hurt is the deepest kind. God's almighty "hand" is pressing down upon him, squeezing him and holding him fast, making him face the aftermath and guilt of his sin. The verb נָחֲתָה (*nacheth*) is used twice and is translated "sunk deep" in the first line and "pressed down" in the second line. Perhaps

God is doing this "pressing" through the natural consequences that have emerged from the highhanded sinning. Thus God's discipline must have been administered to him over a period of time.

Verse 3. All of his being has been affected by his transgression. In hyperbolic exaggeration he says, **There is no soundness in my flesh because of Your indignation.** If one were to look for a place on his body that was not hurting, diseased, corrupted, or wounded, he says that he would not find it. His body is one solid disaster area, one big unsightly bruise. **There is no health in my bones because of my sin.** His bones ache with pain. "Bones" suggest the internal and complete nature of his hurting. The Hebrew says that there is no peace (שָׁלוֹם, *shalom*) in his bones. He is tortured spiritually, emotionally, and physically. He calls his departure from God "sin" (חַטָּאת, *chatta'th*) (v. 3), "iniquity" (עָוֹן, *'awon*) (v. 4), and "folly" (אִוֶּלֶת, *'iwweleth*) (v. 5).

Verse 4. He is weighed down with the heavy weight of guilt. **For my iniquities are gone over my head; as a heavy burden they weigh too much for me.** He is not excusing himself or trying to deny his guilt, but he is emphasizing the enormous weight of the consequences of his sins. The burden of his sin's guilt and aftereffects have swept over him like a flood, overwhelming him. Completely immersed, as if by a leaden blanket too heavy to lift, his sins are draped over him, pressing him down so that he is unable to move. He has become immobilized by a biting conscience and tormenting remorse. The burden is too heavy for him.

Verse 5. As he has wrestled with the consequences of his sin, he has not improved his condition. It seems to have grown worse. **My wounds grow foul and fester because of my folly.** With poetic license, he portrays his body as having cuts and bruises from stripes that sin has inflicted. These wounds are growing increasingly worse, becoming infected and giving forth a repulsive odor. From his current vantage point, he is constrained to characterize his sin as "folly," as silliness of the worst kind.

Verse 6. His struggle and pain have taken away his life and worn him out. His ordeal of suffering has made an old man out of him. **I am bent over and greatly bowed down; I go mourning all day long.** Sin has robbed him of the joy of life. He envisions himself as an aged man whose back is "bent" low. Because of his sorrows, his days have been filled with moaning. It is as if he is going about wailing, dressed in funeral garb.

Verse 7. His anguish has resulted from physical, mental, and spiritual suffering. **For my loins are filled with burning, and there is no soundness in my flesh.** Within the internal parts of his body, it is as if a fever is raging like a fire.

Verse 8. His life has been devastated, as though crushed by some great force. **I am benumbed and badly crushed; I groan because of the agitation of my heart.** His flesh and his bones, the whole framework of his being, are inflamed and saturated with pain. He is experiencing the chill of approaching death. All parts of his personality have been touched.

The most wrenching of all of his pain is his sickness of heart. He is experiencing deep depression and despair in his soul. His thoughts, speech, and emotions come out in the form of groans. Absorbed with his sin, he cannot communicate normally with others. His sufferings are the groaning and heaviness of his heart stemming from the awareness of his wickedness.

"MY DESIRE IS BEFORE YOU" (38:9–14)

⁹Lord, all my desire is before You;
And my sighing is not hidden from You.
¹⁰My heart throbs, my strength fails me;
And the light of my eyes, even that has gone from me.
¹¹My loved ones and my friends stand aloof from my
　　plague;
And my kinsmen stand afar off.
¹²Those who seek my life lay snares for me;
And those who seek to injure me have threatened destruction,
And they devise treachery all day long.
¹³But I, like a deaf man, do not hear;
And I am like a mute man who does not open his mouth.
¹⁴Yes, I am like a man who does not hear,

And in whose mouth are no arguments.

Verse 9. He looks to God as his only hope of recovery. **Lord, all my desire is before You; and my sighing is not hidden from You.** He places his desire for wholeness before the Lord, believing confidently that God sees his great longing and is aware of his intense godly sorrow over what he has done. He believes that God knows how earnestly he yearns to be right with Him once again. He turns his eyes toward God, believing that He will understand his cries of pain, remembering that the Lord hears even the groans of His people (Ex. 2:25).

Verse 10. Exhausted, physically and mentally, he says that he is drained by the trauma of it all. **My heart throbs, my strength fails me; and the light of my eyes, even that has gone from me.** He has been left spent, panting, half-blind, and helpless. The "light of [his] eyes" is gone. It is as if he has died, and his eyes can no longer see. They stare into open spaces as if fixed in place by death.

Verse 11. Amazingly so, those around him are unsympathetic to his condition. He says, **My loved ones and my friends stand aloof from my plague; and my kinsmen stand afar off.** When he needs his loved ones the most, they have turned away from him. His friends have deserted him, thinking that he has been smitten of God and that he could possibly infect them. Even cherished relatives keep their distance from him.

Men do not and cannot understand, but God does, can, and will. Apparently, the writer has not attempted to explain his situation to others; he has brought his desperate predicament only to God in prayer.

Verse 12. His sin has provided an occasion for his enemies to try to destroy him. **Those who seek my life lay snares for me**, he says. You can just hear them: "Have you heard that David is sick? This is a good time to strike him. While he has his mind on his illness, let us put together a plan to overcome him." Maybe they had already set in motion criticism of him that would in time do its deadly work. In addition, his friends were shunning him because they regarded him as being under God's judgment.

He can surmise the evil designs of his foes: **Those who seek** to injure me have threatened destruction, and they devise treachery all day long. Aware of his incapability, they are rejoicing over his humiliation and are working to use it to accomplish their godless schemes.

Verse 13. When it comes to defending what he has done, he has chosen to be meek and speechless, vulnerable and defenseless. He will not respond to his enemies with a counterattack. Concerning those who want to harm him, he will be **like a deaf man** [who does] **not hear; and** [he will be] **like a mute man who does not open his mouth.** He has not reached a point that he cannot hear and cannot speak to others. Instead, he has chosen to turn a deaf ear to his critics and a mute mouth toward their baseless arguments. His case will be presented to God but not to his enemies.

Verse 14. Consequently, his enemies will be answered with silence. **Yes, I am like a man who does not hear, and in whose mouth are no arguments.** Had he decided to rebut what they are saying, what would he say about his situation? He is in this disastrous turmoil because of his sin. He cannot plead integrity. He cannot say that he has been misunderstood. He has no plausible arguments with which to defend his actions and decisions. He cannot exonerate himself with any explanations or alibis. What can a guilty man say? He is deaf and dumb before the evidence.

"I HOPE IN YOU" (38:15–20)

¹⁵For I hope in You, O Lord;
You will answer, O Lord my God.
¹⁶For I said, "May they not rejoice over me,
Who, when my foot slips, would magnify themselves against me."
¹⁷For I am ready to fall,
And my sorrow is continually before me.
¹⁸For I confess my iniquity;
I am full of anxiety because of my sin.
¹⁹But my enemies are vigorous and strong,
And many are those who hate me wrongfully.

²⁰**And those who repay evil for good,**
They oppose me, because I follow what is good.

Verse 15. Even though he is depressed by his sickness and sin, he has kept his belief in God. **For I hope in You, O LORD; You will answer, O Lord my God,** he prays. He knows that his only redemption is in God. The only hope that continues when all other hope is gone is the "hope" one has in God. No situation is hopeless unless one turns from God. The writer believes that God through His lovingkindness will come to his aid.

Verse 16. Aware that his enemies are waiting to capitalize on his sin, he mentions his feelings to God in prayer. **For I said, "May they not rejoice over me, who, when my foot slips, would magnify themselves against me."** They are waiting for an opportunity to celebrate his downfall. Heavy on his heart is the fear that his sin might rebound to the injury of God's cause. The Hebrew has "make themselves great against me" (עָלַי הִגְדִּילוּ, *'alay higdilu*). Utilizing this tragedy in his life, they would be able to "make great" their opposition against him.

Verse 17. He has used up all of his energy dealing with his remorse and opposition: **For I am ready to fall, and my sorrow is continually before me.** Having come to the end of his strength, he anticipates that the end is near if God does not graciously intervene.

Verse 18. In penitence, he acknowledges his sin, seeking restoration to God. **For I confess my iniquity; I am full of anxiety because of my sin.** He aspires to have a righteous heart before God. He has kept himself from making the greatest mistake—that of not returning to God. Bedraggled, broken, and battered, he lifts his eyes to heaven believing that God never gives up on a repentant sinner.

Verse 19. Confident that there are many who are against him, he trembles at their strength and number. **But my enemies are vigorous and strong, and many are those who hate me wrongfully.** His foes hate him "wrongfully" or falsely (שֶׁקֶר, *sheqer*), having no valid basis for their hatred. Some may have had no reason at all to hate him; some of them hated him for the wrong reasons. The bases of their hatred are groundless.

PSALM 38

Verse 20. Even those who should be helping him have turned against him. **And those who repay evil for good, they oppose me, because I follow what is good.** Of all things, some even hate him for his commitment to doing good. He has been good to some of them, but they have renounced him and are standing with his enemies. In his loneliness, he finds himself without self-respect, without friends, and worst of all, without a righteous relationship with God.

"DO NOT FORSAKE ME" (38:21, 22)

²¹Do not forsake me, O Lord;
O my God, do not be far from me!
²²Make haste to help me,
O Lord, my salvation!

Verse 21. Having led up to this focal point, he makes his main request. He has given his confession and expressed his penitence; he comes to his appeal, the brightest part of the psalm. He pleads, **Do not forsake me, O Lord; O my God, do not be far from me!** "O Lord" and "O my God" suggest his tender appreciation of God. Understanding God's gracious nature, he does not hesitate to ask Him to intervene in his behalf.

God does not hear us because of our beautiful, well-chosen words; He listens, as all fathers do, because of our integrity of heart and sincerity of soul. The writer has spent almost the entirety of the psalm establishing his contrition of heart. Now, in a simple sentence, he makes his full petition and begs for God to come near to him. If God remains aloof and far removed, he knows that he has no hope.

Verse 22. Because of dire necessity, he wants God to act quickly in his behalf. **Make haste to help me, O Lord, my salvation!** His prayer is not specific. "Help! Come to my rescue!" is really the basic content of it. He leaves the "how" up to God. He asks the God of salvation to save him!

As a person who is in God's covenant, he would be the equivalent of a child of God in the Christian Age. Indeed, he has sinned horribly. His life has become a disaster. Gripping his body and spirit is the chastisement of God. Learning from His discipline, he repents, confesses his sin to God, and prays for God's salvation. The non-Christian cannot come to God by this type of penitent prayer (Acts 2:36–40); he must first become a child of God. One cannot live the life of God until first he enters it. However, for the wayward child of God, the approach this writer takes—repentance, confession, and prayer—is the golden road back to God (see Acts 8:20–22).

APPLICATION

Faith's Answer for Your Problems

David was guilt-ridden and joyless under the heavy hand of chastisement and discipline. On top of his sin and accusing conscience was his physical condition; his body was groaning with sickness and fever. When he needed his friends the most, they had turned away from him. When he could have done without enemies, they were present and intensifying their assault upon him. The world would say that he was beyond hope, but his faith in God had another answer—it taught him to take his burdens to God, who would answer him in lovingkindness.

The Journey to God's Grace

When we become a meeting place of affliction and pain because of deliberate mistakes we have made, what should we do? The answer is given in this psalm.

Acknowledge with gratitude the chastisement of God (v. 1). David started where anyone must start in such a situation: with an acceptance of correction. A parent spanks a child as a means of guidance; God through His great providence permits, directs, and allows the discipline of His children. Discipline is a reclaiming process, a refiner's fire. When we are on the receiving end of the rod of correction, let us acknowledge what has happened to us and receive the lesson of our Father's discipline.

Describe the pain we are undergoing to God (vv. 2–8). David detailed his pain and problems to God. Talking over our troubles with our heavenly Father is good for us. He related all the struggles he was having—those within and without.

Bring all the problems we have to God (vv. 9–12). All he could do was bring all to God—the whole tangled mess. He must lay everything before the gracious eyes of God.

Ask God to supply His grace and wisdom to our predicament (vv. 21, 22). This request should be the main object of our prayers. We must never, regardless of how bad the situation, lose our faith in God. He is full of lovingkindness and will come to our help.

The Basic Element—Integrity

The underlying fabric of the writer's hope was his honesty with God. Put into identifiable steps, his integrity included accepting in penitence and confession what had happened to him as a chastisement from God, describing to God in detail the problems he had, maintaining his hope in God throughout the grim night, and asking God to help him. Flowing out of each step was complete openness to the will of God.

Any child of God in a situation like David's should pray with penitence and purpose, approaching prayer with an openhearted surrender to the will of God. What else can one do?

Hoping in God

How do we articulate hope in God? Do we do it with words or with actions? This psalm teaches us to put boots on our hope.

Hope is expressed in repentance and confession to God. David could not undo the evil he had done, but he could be penitent. He could also ask God to help him straighten out his life.

Hope is expressed in one's seeking to maintain God's integrity. David did not want his enemies to use his fall to hurt God's cause. This desire would be a fruit of repentance.

Hope is expressed in our asking God to be gracious toward us. The lovingkindness and mercy of God guarantees that He will hear His penitent child, regardless of what he has done.

Hope in God involves God's cleansing, God's cause, and God's compassion. God will come to anyone's defense who will put his trust in Him, repent of his sins as God has directed, value God's work and plan, and recognize the place of God's grace in his salvation.

At the End of Strength
What do you do when you have come to the end of your strength? Where do you turn when you have no place to turn?

Remember that He does care. God has not given up on you. He loves you far more than any parent ever loved his child. He will respond to the penitent's prayer with grace and love.

Explain to Him your agony. You need to tell your troubles to someone. God is always ready to listen. You can mention to Him all the horrible details.

Plead for His grace. The writer had come to the place where nothing could save him but God's love. He saw this truth vividly. All of us have come to that place—whether we realize it or not. We must admit that if God does not respond to our sin problem, we are doomed. He is our only hope.

Follow His plan for receiving forgiveness. He has told us what to do to receive His pardon. We must walk to God by obeying the plan He has given (Acts 2:38; 8:22).

Let Him help you repair the broken pieces. After the child is spanked and expresses penitence, there is hugging and joining together in assessing the damage and repairing what can be reclaimed. God responds to us in the same way.

God's grace is remedial, not unaccountable and irresponsible. Grace demands changes and calls for restitution and spiritual introspection. "God loves us as we are, but He loves us too much to leave us as we are."

God's Discipline in the School of Righteousness
What kind of discipline does God provide for His children? If we add to this psalm Hebrews 12 in the New Testament, we will have a thorough discourse on it. Let us think about His chastisement.

It is for our good. It must never be seen as sinister or vengeful. It is administered out of love. We require it for our spiritual development.

It can sometimes be very painful. It was for David. He thought he was going to die. However, the discipline turned him around. Had he not experienced it, he would have been lost. Serious disease requires major surgery.

It can and often is administered through natural laws. Oftentimes God disciplines us by our sins themselves. God has told us that sin will hurt us, but sometimes we forget or ignore what God has said. A child is warned that fire burns. If he forgets or ignores this truth, the child will have to learn it the hard way. His mistake can bring great suffering, but it can teach him a tremendously important lesson.

God will assist us in bearing it. This fact is good news. A woman said, "What good is forgiveness if I have to bear the consequences of my sin?" She was told, "When you are forgiven, you have God on your side helping you bear the consequences!"

How thankful we should be for the discipline of the Lord! Even though it comes into our lives wearing the garments of pain and rebuke, it is a veiled blessing to us, one that we cannot do without.

Identifying God's Discipline

How do we determine whether or not what is happening is the discipline of God?

Spiritually analyze what happens. Perhaps the best approach is to ask when something unpleasant comes into life, "Can I learn from this?" If you can, then simply say: "Yes, I can see where I have sinned. I have an unpleasant situation because of my sin. I must learn from this and not make this mistake again!"

Review what has happened. Hindsight is always better than foresight. It is easier to see how God has worked in our lives by looking through the rearview mirror than through the windshield. Do I see where God has corrected me?

Be obedient to God, and expect Him to work in our lives. We must resolve to serve the Lord faithfully and realize that He will help us grow. When instruction or guidance comes—whether through a friend or some teaching circumstance—that makes clearer what God has obviously said in His Word. We can thank God for the pruning He has given our lives.

Every good gift comes from God. Even the gifts that change us, correct us, and improve us come from the gracious hand of our loving God.

How Sin Hurts Us

Sin can devastate our lives.

It affects us spiritually. The writer was suffering great anguish of heart because his relationship with God had been impaired. In penitence and confession he cried out to God for forgiveness.

It hurts us physically. He described his body as a solid sore. There was no soundness at all in it. It had become the body of an old man. Almost overnight, sin can wear us down and wear us out.

It harms us emotionally. He was so emotionally drained that he could not think. He went about groaning and mourning. Sin robs us of our minds.

It has social repercussions. Friends stood aloof from him because of what he had done and what sin had done to him. Enemies were seeking to cash in on his weakness. Sin brings out those who would like to gather up the spoils of a broken life.

In the previous psalm we saw that the righteous life had a precious quality to it that made it the highest life anyone could live, even though he has little in the way of earthly goods. In this psalm we see how the wicked life is surrounded with many sorrows and has nothing to commend it.

God Hears

God told Moses that He had heard the groans of His people in Egypt (Ex. 2:25). The pain-wracked writer of this psalm said that he believed that God saw and heard his sighing (v. 9). Give this truth more thought.

Do you realize that God is moved and touched by your groaning? This fact reminds us of the sympathy, tenderness, and compassion of God's heart. He is moved by our pain. He feels with us when we hurt. Even moans of pain that result from the agony inflicted by sin are heard by Him. He does not sanctify our sin, but He reaches out His hand for our forgiveness and restoration.

PSALM 39
GOD AND THE MEANING OF LIFE

The Superscription: For the choir director, for Jeduthun. A Psalm of David. The title of this psalm calls it **a Psalm** [מִזְמוֹר, *mizmor*] of ["by," "for," or "to"] **David** (לְדָוִד, *ledawid*) and says that instruction is provided **for the choir director** (לַמְנַצֵּחַ, *lamnatstseach*).

Furthermore, the title says that it is **for** ["by," "of" or "to"] **Jeduthun** (לִידִיתוּן, *liydithun*). This musician's name, Jeduthun, also appears in the titles before Psalms 62 and 77, although in these two psalms it is rendered עַל־יְדוּתוּן (*'al yeduthun*). The *'al* before the name, perhaps meaning "upon," may have something to do with the tune; whereas the *li* before the name, perhaps meaning "for," may indicate that it was written for Jeduthun's use. It could be that the use of *li* and *'al* were just two different ways of saying the same thing, such as identifying the purpose of the song. Thus the phrase "of David" may indicate authorship, while "for Jeduthun" may refer to the purpose for which the song was written.

Jeduthun, along with Heman and Asaph, is mentioned in the Old Testament as one of the directors of the temple music (1 Chron. 16:41; 25:1). He may be the man referred to as Ethan in 1 Chronicles 15:17.

Centering on the perplexities of life, this individual lament is possibly a sequel to Psalm 38. The riddles of life are not confronted by the writer with a philosophical discussion; they are dealt with in connection with his personal experience with a life-threatening illness or chastisement for his sin. The exact time or occasion of the writing is unknown.

The writer looks back on a time when he was troubled by three issues: the fleeting nature of life, the prosperity of the wicked, and the seeming purposelessness of human life. Perhaps he was languishing in poor health and believed that he was nearing the end of his earthly journey. He faced these tough mental struggles with his faith in God. By experiencing the discipline of God, he came to see the true meaning of life.

AN ATTEMPT AT SILENCE (39:1–3)

¹I said, "I will guard my ways
That I may not sin with my tongue;
I will guard my mouth as with a muzzle
While the wicked are in my presence."
²I was mute and silent,
I refrained even from good,
And my sorrow grew worse.
³My heart was hot within me,
While I was musing the fire burned;
Then I spoke with my tongue:

Verse 1. The writer tells how he made a resolve deep within his soul. **I said, "I will guard my ways that I may not sin with my tongue."** He made the commitment to watch carefully his behavior and speech; especially he desired to be cautious about what he would say about God. He said, **"I will guard my mouth as with a muzzle while the wicked are in my presence."** For a while at least, he wanted to put a "muzzle" (מַחְסוֹם, *machsom*) on his mouth. In his bewilderment over what to do and say about his troubles, he resolved to weigh every word that he said for fear that his enemies might misunderstand him or twist his words. They might charge him with believing and reporting a critical view of God's goodness. Thus, concerned that they might construe what he said as an indication that he was dissatisfied with God, he vowed to be silent.

Verse 2. His determination was so strong that he went into silence and inactivity for a period of time. He says, **I was mute and silent, I refrained even from good, and my sorrow grew worse.** He completely shut down his communications with others. He even refused to speak about good things, but his course of action did not help him. His troubles grew worse.

Following carefully what the writer says, we are able to see his resolution (v. 1), his fulfillment of that resolution (v. 2), and the effect that the fulfillment of his resolution had on him (vv. 3, 4).

Verse 3. In spite of his determination to be silent, there arose within him a compulsion to speak: **My heart was hot within me, while I was musing the fire burned; then I spoke with my tongue.** Apparently, while his mouth was "muzzled," he did not even break his silence to speak of good things that needed to be voiced. However, this silence did not bring him the satisfaction he sought. It intensified his sorrow and sparked an inner drive to speak; it fanned a flame of desire to be heard. His condition reminds us of Jeremiah, who had to speak because of the fire that burned within his bones (Jer. 20:9).

SEEING THE TRANSIENCE OF LIFE
(39:4–6)

⁴"LORD, make me to know my end
And what is the extent of my days;
Let me know how transient I am.
⁵Behold, You have made my days as handbreadths,
And my lifetime as nothing in Your sight;
Surely every man at his best is a mere breath." Selah.
⁶"Surely every man walks about as a phantom;
Surely they make an uproar for nothing;
He amasses riches and does not know who will gather them."

Verse 4. Prompted by a determined motivation within his heart, he was compelled to speak. Wisely, he addressed God in prayer as he requested an understanding of the nature of life, **"LORD, make me to know my end and what is the extent of my days; let me know how transient I am."** His prayer to God included three expressions that convey life's brevity: "know my end," "the extent of my days," and "how transient I am." To "know my end" (קִצִּי, *qitstsi*) means that one is aware that death is quickly coming. "The extent of my days" (מִדַּת יָמַי, *middath yamay*) comes from a phrase that appears only here in the Old Testament. It stresses the brief span, the short measure, of one's life. The term "transient" (חָדֵל, *chadel*), the nonpermanent nature of life, sums up the two previous expressions.

The writer was carrying within his soul a perplexing question that all of us ask: "What is the meaning of my life?" Perhaps what he saw around him gave energy to his doubts, adding other questions, such as, "Should I pursue money as I see the wicked doing? Where am I headed? How much time do I have? What does it all mean?" He wanted God's guidance to help him plan his days carefully and to assist him toward a better understanding of the purpose of life in general.

His concern about the meaning of life is brought into sharper focus by a personal trial of suffering he was undergoing because of his sin. This pain forced him to weigh thoughtfully the temporary character of life.

Verse 5. Although he addressed his big question to God, he began to answer it himself. It seems that as he framed the question, the solution came to his mind. He said, **"Behold, You have made my days as handbreadths."** He observed that God regarded his life as a few "handbreadths," as several of the smallest units of measure brought together. Apparently, this unit, the handbreath, is described as "four fingers in thickness" in Jeremiah 52:21, which means that it constituted about three inches in length. Perhaps he had been thinking of his life as long and enduring, as five miles long, but now he realized that in God's sight it was only a few inches in duration. Reality set in.

He further concluded that his **lifetime [was] as nothing in [God's] sight.** From one viewpoint, from the perspective of the eternal God to whom a day is as a thousand years and a thousand years as a day, a person's life is "as nothing." The worthlessness of life is not in view; it is duration of life compared to the eternalness of God that is being considered. Even if one lives seventy years on this earth, his life is only a fleeting moment on the never-ending scale of vast eternity.

Using another figure, he said, **"Surely every man at his best is a mere breath."** A person's life is as transitory as a single "breath." We breathe without even thinking about it, and then that breath is gone forever. Life passes as quickly as does a puff of smoke disappearing into the air.

Selah probably indicates that the reader should ponder this truth. "You had better consider how quickly life passes," he is saying.

Verse 6. His recognition of the frailty of life led him to acknowledge that he must not expect any permanence in this world. He said, **"Surely every man walks about as a phantom."** The word from which "phantom" (צֶלֶם, *tselem*) is translated can also be rendered "image." It is a word like "shadow" or "likeness," and it is the same word used in Genesis 1:26 which describes the creation of man in the "likeness" of God. People—even the rich—move through life rapidly as if only a shadow.

The person who focuses on riches and possessions becomes disturbed and overwrought about something that is temporary and frail. The writer concluded, **"Surely they make an uproar for nothing; he amasses riches and does not know who will gather them."** The rich people will leave everything behind when they make their departure from the earth. They do not know who will enjoy their wealth when they die, for they cannot be sure of who will be the recipients of their lifelong accumulations. Often the rich man does not even get to enjoy the wealth he has accumulated. By the time he has stored up treasures, he dies.

As the psalmist grasped the momentary character of living in this world, he gained a clearer view of life's hardships. The value and purpose for which we yearn must rise above the brevity of life. Riches and earthly pleasures end with this life; something more durable than these must give life meaning.

RECOGNIZING TRUE HOPE
(39:7–11)

⁷"And now, Lord, for what do I wait?
My hope is in You.
⁸Deliver me from all my transgressions;

Make me not the reproach of the foolish.
⁹I have become mute,
I do not open my mouth,
Because it is You who have done it.
¹⁰Remove Your plague from me;
Because of the opposition of Your hand I am perishing.
¹¹With reproofs You chasten a man for iniquity;
You consume as a moth what is precious to him;
Surely every man is a mere breath." Selah.

Verse 7. What is the answer to this puzzle at the heart of our existence? In light of these observations that have been made, a fundamental question must be raised: **"And now, Lord, for what do I wait? My hope is in You."** It became obvious to the psalmist that the purpose of life is not wealth, success, victory, freedom from persecution, or other temporary achievements. For the answer to this thorny question, one must return to the basic truth about life: Enduring hope comes from God Himself. Thus the writer acknowledged, "My hope is in You."

Verse 8. The realization that God is at the center of life caused the psalmist to forget temporal concerns and focus on his sins. He cried, **"Deliver me from all my transgressions."** If life soon vanishes, if God is the core of our meaning and existence in the world, then our sins must be properly handled. Otherwise, they will interfere with the purposes God has for us here. The writer, a follower of God, recognized that he must repent and confess his sins and thus properly deal with them: **"Make me not the reproach of the foolish."** If He did not do so, even a foolish person would be able to see that the writer is not following what he believes.

Verse 9. The psalmist was profoundly impressed by what he had learned: **"I have become mute, I do not open my mouth, because it is You who have done it."** He became silent again, but this time his silence was due to his belief that God had brought him new insight and understanding. He realized that the sufferings that motivated him to consider anew the brevity of life had been used by God.

Verse 10. The meaning of life brought him back to his guilt and God's chastisement. He pleaded, **"Remove Your plague from me; because of the opposition of Your hand I am perishing."** He said that he had received a "plague" ("hostility," "stroke") from God. This word "plague" (נֶגַע, *naga'*) is probably a figurative reference to some kind of divine chastisement that he had received.

Verse 11. He appealed to God for mercy: **"With reproofs You chasten a man for iniquity."** He believed that he had learned from God's discipline. His rebuke had been severe; he had been beaten by God's rod of indignation. He prayed for its removal with the confidence that he had received the intended benefits from it.

People of this world often allow worldly desires to fill their hearts, and possessions become precious to them. However, they often find that God steps in to **consume as a moth what is precious to** [them]. God uses His hand of correction to remove inordinate dreams, even as a "moth" devours a beautiful garment. He slips into our hearts with His reproof and destroys these secret ambitions that are contrary to His will and good sense. Their destruction may be a trying time for the person being disciplined, but the divine discipline restores him to the only permanent foundation for his brief earthly existence—God. Thus the writer closes this section of the psalm with the refrain **"Surely every man is a mere breath,"** the same phrase with which he started his contemplation of the meaning of life in verse 5.

"MAKE MY LAST DAYS HAPPY"
(39:12, 13)

> ¹²"Hear my prayer, O LORD, and give ear to my cry;
> Do not be silent at my tears;
> For I am a stranger with You,
> A sojourner like all my fathers.
> ¹³Turn Your gaze away from me, that I may smile again
> Before I depart and am no more."

From the point where he started, the psalmist has traveled a great spiritual distance. In this learning process, he has become penitent, tearful, and understanding.

Verse 12. He closes his song with a prayer, **"Hear my prayer, O LORD, and give ear to my cry."** He is earnest and desirous of a sympathetic response to his request. **"Do not be silent at my tears; for I am a stranger with You, a sojourner like all my fathers,"** he says. Because of its momentary nature, life cannot be related merely to what we see around us. Our lives need more permanence, as the psalmist has learned.

He wants God to see his "tears." It would bother him greatly if his God ignored them, were "silent" about them, or were unresponsive to them.

The psalmist is fully aware that he is a guest in this world—a transient "sojourner" whose home is with God. An alien lived in Israel by permission. He received protection and certain privileges from its citizens, but he never had full legal status (see Deut. 24:17–22), with all the rights of citizenship. David, as an Israelite and a king, has been at home in Israel. However, he comes to a new understanding of this world. His experience has washed his eyes so that he can see more clearly; he no longer sees himself as an owner. He is a pilgrim, a passerby, finding his strength and future only in God.

Verse 13. His final request contains a strange tone: **"Turn Your gaze away from me."** Normally one would pray for God to turn His face toward him, but this petition is unusual in that it asks God to turn His face away. It is the hand of discipline about which the psalmist writes. He is asking that it be removed from him. He wants God to change His "gaze" of anger and correction, so that he can live and die in peace with God.

His great desire is **that** [he] **may smile again, before** [he departs and is] **no more.** Before leaving this world, he wants to strengthen his fellowship with God; he wants to live according to the true meaning of life. The only thing that will please him is for God to give him a happy walk with Him during his final days.

PSALM 39

APPLICATION

Moving to Meaning

Let us follow the writer's journey and learn, as he did, what God intends for us to do while we are on the earth.

There is a question. All of us wrestle with the question, "What is the meaning of life?" Our question may come even more forcefully to us when we are sick or have grown older and see the end of our days coming to meet us. We may try to dodge the question, but the question stands before us demanding an answer. We have to work hard to avoid it.

There is an observation about the nature of life. This solemn question that comes should motivate us to see the true nature of life—to see it as temporary, as short-lived, as a breath. We consider how life moves by so quickly and is gone. All are affected by the frailty of life. We acknowledge that nothing we gain—such as riches, possessions, or even friends—can be enjoyed very long in this world.

There is a need to come to God. Such a journey as this should bring us to our knees in prayer as we affirm that our only hope is in God. We acknowledge our sins, and we ask God to bring us into His fellowship that we may enjoy and use wisely whatever time we have here.

Every human should make such a journey. His good sense and human wisdom should direct him down this road and to the conclusion that the psalmist has reached.

Looking Again at Life

The Scriptures and our own observations tell us that we are hedged in by our mortality on one side and the eternal God on the other. God says to us, "Sooner than you think, you will come to meet Me, leaving all material possessions behind. You will come to Me as a spiritual being, stripped of the transitory body. Prepare for this journey by putting your hope and trust in Me now."

The psalmist had to walk through the valley of sorrow to understand what life is intended to be. When his walk ended, he was weary with pain and tired from thinking about his questions, but he knew what God wanted of him. If we learn from his journey, perhaps God will spare us from a similar journey through the land of correction.

The Puzzle of Life

What do you do when you are confused about the meaning of life?

A good way to begin is to go back in your mind to the basic truths about life. Remember that life is brief and will quickly come to an end. Soon we will leave this earth and leave all our possessions behind. Then let the fact of life's fleeting nature motivate you to concentrate upon what is really important.

Bring your confusion to God and renew your commitment to following His truth. When you do not know where to turn, approach God in prayer and ask for His wisdom. Ask Him to help you unravel the tangled strings of confusion and focus on what really matters.

In the midst of all this, maintain a right relationship with God. If sin is in your life, confess it and ask God to cleanse you. Nothing will replace being right with God. Do what God has asked you to do to receive His forgiveness.

We may never know the answers to all of life's puzzles. Job was not given all the answers that he wanted. However, it is clear how we should live, even when we must live with many of our questions unanswered.

When to Be Silent

Sometimes "silence is golden." The writer of this psalm had decided that it was best for him not to speak; however, he discovered that he could not keep silent. Something was boiling within him, and he had to talk to God about it.

This fact brings to mind a good question: "When should we not speak?"

When you might be misunderstood, it is best to keep quiet. If you are in a situation that is fraught with possibilities of being misinterpreted, the way of wisdom is not to speak. It is better to say one word with clarity than a thousand without meaning or with confusion.

PSALM 39

When you do not know what to say, it is best to remain silent. If you are not clear on what to say, if you are not sure what a Christian should say, then it would be appropriate not to speak. We would like to always speak the truth. If we cannot, we should be silent or talk about a topic we understand.

If you might be arguing against God, it is essential not to say anything. If your talking might be interpreted as an angry outburst against God, then it would be best to spend time thinking the matter through before talking about it. Reverence should characterize us at all times. God is always right, and His treatment of us is always in our best interests.

Let us watch our words and make sure that our speech is always seasoned with salt.

Another Look at Life

Let us take another look at life. Perhaps such a look will give us the proper perspective on what should be done with our days.

As we view life from the viewpoint of time—our lives here are brief and fleeting. The writer says that life is like a handbreadth. That is, it is short—it is like the width of the hand, one of the smallest units of measurement in the ancient world. So we are reminded that even the longest life is only a small span of time when compared to eternity. From any viewpoint, we have to say that we will not be here very long.

As we view life from the viewpoint of significance—we know that our contribution is small. We could be compared to a breath. After all, how significant is one breath? We breathe it, and it is gone. It does make a small contribution to keeping us alive, but not much more can be said about it. How long will we be remembered after we are gone?

As we view it from the viewpoint of permanence—we are pilgrims. We are guests here—briefly stopping while on a very important journey. We are only passing through as we continue to life on the other side. This world cannot be viewed as our home. Everything that we have is borrowed. We have only our hearts, our souls, and nothing else.

When we view life as it really is, we are brought down to

size and made to humble ourselves before God. Life cannot be lived properly until life is seen through the lens of truth.

When You Have to Speak

The writer said that there came a time when he had to speak. He had tried to be silent but just could not remain quiet. A fire was burning within him to speak, and he had to put his emotions into words.

Perhaps we would be better off if we did what he did before he spoke.

Observe, think, and weigh before you speak. The writer looked at life and considered the nature of life before he prayed.

Reach some essential conclusions before you speak. He had concluded that life is really temporary and no one is going to remain here. Thus he was driven to the realization that true hope is only possible in God.

Speak in prayer first. When the writer did speak, he went to God in prayer. Someone has said, "Talk to God before you talk to man." The psalmist was laying his life before the Lord. He asked for cleansing and a life of fellowship with God.

What Is Life?

The writer was longing to know the basic meaning of life. As he pursued an answer to his question about life, he began with a conclusion concerning the brevity of life. The figures he used are most revealing and insightful.

It is like a handbreadth. Life is short and can be compared to one of the smallest units of measurement.

It is like nothing. When compared to God's life, life is nothing, for God is the eternal God. Life is like a bubble that will soon break. Life's span is only a moment on God's calendar.

It is like a breath. Life is frail. It is visible and then passes away. One cannot build on it, for it is fleeting and transitory.

It is like an image. Life is almost like an illusion. We are not quite reality. Apparently, the true reality of humanity is that of being in God's presence.

We all long for certainty and stability. These cannot be found in life because it is so frail and changing. Our conclusion must be the conclusion of the writer: God is our only hope.

The Time of Life

Both the Old Testament and the New Testament tell us that life is a brief journey. A favorite Christian song is "This World Is Not My Home." No doubt its popularity stems from the fact that it gives the true picture of our lives.

Since life is a pilgrimage and quickly passes, we should see it as a special time.

It is a time of decision. One cannot come to God without making a determined decision to do so. Therefore, nothing else should interfere with our making this all-important commitment.

It is a time of salvation. The nature of life makes this world a place for preparation.

It is a time of maturing. We are to be growing in our relationship with the Lord. The trials only assist us in becoming more godlike. They serve as whetstones to sharpen our spirituality.

Even though life is brief and passes by as quickly as does a breath, properly lived, it can be a prelude to entering the eternal glory of God.

"Surely"

The Hebrew word that is translated "surely" or something similar is found three times in verses 5 and 6. Consider the emphasis that is given by the use of this word.

The "surely" of frailty. The writer says, "Surely everyone stands as a mere breath." The phrase he uses suggests briefness, shortness, and frailty.

The "surely" of reality. He says, "Everyone goes about like a shadow." Some translations have "phantom" or "image." True reality is being with God; life without Him is only a likeness to life.

The "surely" of purpose. He says, "Surely for nothing they are in turmoil. . . ." Those who spend their time amassing things will eventually find that they have lived for a worthless purpose.

The Highest Request

The writer said, "Turn Your gaze away from me, that I may smile again before I depart and am no more." Look closely at his petition.

He asked that God relieve him of the chastisement for his sin. He wanted a purer relationship with God. He was sorry about his sin and wanted to put the discipline God had given him behind him. He asked God to turn His gaze, His look of rebuke, away from him. Should we not seek this kind of life, one that is free from the rebuke of God?

He asked that he might be happy in his relationship with God once again. He knew that when all was well with his walk with God, he would be filled with contentment and peace. The greatest joy comes when one has a covenant fellowship with God. Should we not ask God to give us a meaningful, happy, authentic life with Him?

He wanted to live out his final days with this dear, precious walk with God. He knew that a time was coming when he would be no more. The writer was probably an aged man who could see his days on the calendar of life. He did not want to have a shipwreck while coming into the final harbor. Should we not request that God see that the rest of our lives be taken up with a wonderful relationship with Him?

The final prayer of this psalm could well be the highest prayer we can pray.

Life as an Illusion

We have seen in this psalm that our stay here can be characterized with the figures of "handbreadths," a "breath," and an "image." Thus a very important question arises: "Can life be an illusion to us?" Yes, it can be.

If we see life in this world as permanent, then our view of it is an illusion. Just a glance around us will prove that all of us are just passing through. The person who ignores this truth refuses to acknowledge a truth that is vital to him.

If we view life as a time to possess and amass earthly materials, then we are deceived about life. The person who approaches life with the aim to buy, accumulate, and store earthly possessions will recognize at death that he has labored in vain. The greatest and wealthiest have gathered only to leave everything behind. We are promised that there will be no exceptions.

If we picture life as a time of living without God, then our view of life is illusional. One must look beyond the briefness and transitory nature of life to something eternal in order to be happy and filled with an enduring purpose. The writer found that true hope can only be found in God.

Let us not twist a wonderful reality into an illusion. If our view of it is legitimate and based on the facts, then life can be good and meaningful, a time of walking with God and a time of preparing ourselves to be with Him in eternity.

PSALM 40

THE EVER-PRESENT GOD

The Superscription: For the choir director. A Psalm of David. The title labels this composition **of** ["by," "for," or "to"] **David** (לְדָוִד, *lᵉdawid*), identifying it as **a Psalm** (מִזְמוֹר, *mizmor*). It further says that these instructions are to be understood as directed to **the choir director** (לַמְנַצֵּחַ, *lamnatstseach*).

The reader of this psalm is presented with two pictures of God—which together comprise a third picture of Him. The first portrait says that He is the God who has acted in the past; in the second He is the God who helps with any existing trial. United, they depict a God who is ever-present to defend, deliver, and sustain His people.

Uniquely, verses 13 through 17 of this psalm in a somewhat modified form comprise Psalm 70, a fact that raises several compositional questions. Both Psalms 40 and 70 are ascribed to David by their titles and give instructions to the chief musician. Did the writer later take part of this psalm and convert it into Psalm 70? Did a later inspired writer lift from Psalm 40 wording that was especially applicable to his own situation and form Psalm 70? Did David incorporate in Psalm 40 a portion of a psalm that he had written earlier? The best guess seems to be that later David or another writer appropriated a paragraph from this psalm and made it into Psalm 70 for a special purpose.

Another uniqueness of this psalm is that verses 6 through 8 are applied, at least in part, to Jesus in Hebrews 10:5–9. In that sense, this psalm may be identified as a messianic psalm.

Because its emphasis and tone vary, the psalm can also be

classified either as a thanksgiving psalm or a lament psalm. Generally, it is considered a lament psalm because of the strong call for divine assistance in its last few verses.

The psalm can be divided into two sections, a part that considers the past (vv. 1–10) and another part that looks at the present (vv. 11–17). The emphasis of the first part is praise; the second stresses petition. The first section is thanksgiving for the victories given by the Lord, and the second is a request for the Lord to deliver the writer from some calamity he is enduring.

Overall, the psalm teaches that God is the God of the past and of the present. He has delivered the writer from a pit of persecution before; and now, He is being asked again to come to the writer's aid and rescue him from his current distress. The main thrust of the psalm is to show how God has assisted His people in the past and continues to be their great arm of strength. Let us rejoice with this writer over the truth that God is our ever-present help, a constant Redeemer for His people.

"GOD HEARD MY PRAYER" (40:1–3)

¹**I waited patiently for the Lord;**
And He inclined to me and heard my cry.
²**He brought me up out of the pit of destruction, out of the miry clay,**
And He set my feet upon a rock making my footsteps firm.
³**He put a new song in my mouth, a song of praise to our God;**
Many will see and fear
And will trust in the Lord.

Verse 1. The writer begins by praising God for what He has done for him. As he looks back on his life, he sees God. The history of his life has been the story of God's hand upon him.

When troubles came, he prayed for help and then "waited" on the Lord to answer him. He says, **I waited patiently for the Lord.** His phrase is something like "I waited and waited." Persistently he prayed with confident faith that God would answer him, and at the appropriate time God did answer.

He says, **He inclined to me and heard my cry.** As if bending low to hear better, where He might take in every part of his request, God "inclined" to him and answered his supplication.

Verse 2. God's response to his prayer was a major rescue, for he says, **He brought me up out of the pit of destruction, out of the miry clay.** It was as though the writer had been thrown into a deep "pit" whose bottom was made of miry clay—a figure that reminds us of the cistern into which Jeremiah was thrown (Jer. 38:6). The writer is referring to a sickness that almost took his life, a deadly encounter with enemies, or some comparable crisis. From the depths of trouble, he called to God for salvation and then waited for God to come to his aid.

In time, God lifted him out and placed his feet upon a solid "rock." **He set my feet upon a rock making my footsteps firm.** Placing his "feet upon a rock" is a figurative expression for complete reclamation from the danger he was in. God made his "footsteps firm" in the sense that He delivered him from his difficulties and put him on the level ground of the robust life.

Verse 3. In light of what God has done, how altogether appropriate it is for him to rejoice in God! Thus he says, **He put a new song in my mouth, a song of praise to our God.** As a result of the salvation God has given, he can sing a fresh, new song of praise. His expressions of thankfulness for the gracious deed of the Lord will redound to the glory of His name in numerous ways. **Many will see and fear and will trust in the LORD.** For one thing, the writer will make sure that others hear about what the Lord has done for him. Perhaps when others are told about the marvelous kindness of the Lord, they will look to Him with the same reverence and trust the writer now has.

HOW WONDERFUL TO TRUST IN THE LORD! (40:4, 5)

⁴How blessed is the man who has made the LORD his trust,
And has not turned to the proud, nor to those who lapse into falsehood.
⁵Many, O LORD my God, are the wonders which You have done,

PSALM 40

And Your thoughts toward us;
There is none to compare with You.
If I would declare and speak of them,
They would be too numerous to count.

Verse 4. From a joyous heart, he must pronounce a blessing upon the person who trusts in the Lord. He says, **How blessed is the man who has made the LORD his trust.** His good news is that anyone can have the assistance he has received if he will walk with God in faith, living in a genuine, obedient relationship with Him and waiting on His promises.

The man who trusts in the Lord **has not turned to the proud, nor to those who lapse into falsehood** for his strength. To be surrounded by the Lord's goodness in the way he has in mind, one must put his confidence in the Lord's wisdom and strength—not in "the proud" who boast in their physical power or in the unfaithful, who have gone into "falsehood," having committed themselves to lies. Trusting in God is the opposite of leaning on humanism, the intelligence and muscle of mankind, and false philosophies about God and life. Only those who turn to God will be recipients of His mercies.

Verse 5. The writer's praise of God moves from a specific event to a general litany of events that reflect the "wonders" of God. He says, **Many, O LORD my God, are the wonders which You have done, and Your thoughts toward us.** These great, generous acts of God are the expressions of His continual grace toward His people. They convey how He thinks toward His chosen ones. Anyone who trusts in God comes under His protection and is the recipient of His loving care and provisions.

In praise, he says, **There is none to compare with You.** "There is none to compare with [God]" because there is no other God besides Him. Furthermore, He is incomparable in the sense that His goodness far exceeds anything we can imagine. The psalmist cannot begin to name God's great acts toward him. He says, **If I would declare and speak of them, they would be too numerous to count.** God has been so merciful in acting in behalf of His people that it would be an inconceivable task to try to enumerate them.

GOD HAS HEARD MY PRAYER
(40:6–10)

⁶Sacrifice and meal offering You have not desired;
My ears You have opened;
Burnt offering and sin offering You have not required.
⁷Then I said, "Behold, I come;
In the scroll of the book it is written of me.
⁸I delight to do Your will, O my God;
Your Law is within my heart."
⁹I have proclaimed glad tidings of righteousness in the great congregation;
Behold, I will not restrain my lips,
O LORD, You know.
¹⁰I have not hidden Your righteousness within my heart;
I have spoken of Your faithfulness and Your salvation;
I have not concealed Your lovingkindness and Your truth from the great congregation.

Verse 6. Thanksgiving involves more than the lips; it requires being obedient to God from the heart. The writer says, **Sacrifice and meal offering You have not desired**. His expression "sacrifice and meal offering You have not desired" does not mean that he is not obligated to offer the sacrifices commanded by the law of Moses. His phrase may be thought of as a synecdoche, a part standing for the whole. The description of sincerely worshiping God stands for the total response that one is to make to God. For the writer, sincere obedience includes everything that the law requires. However, he recognizes that God does not want sacrifices without sincerity, ritual without righteousness, or the actions without the heart.

God has taught him obedience: **My ears You have opened**. God has dealt with his "ears." He has consecrated them. They are now committed to hearing and obeying God's will. A life of obedience begins with listening to the mind of God revealed in His will.

The phrase **burnt offering and sin offering you have not required** gives double emphasis to the necessity for the heart to be involved in the service of God.

Verse 7. Obedience is paramount to the servant of God. **Then I said, "Behold, I come; in the scroll of the book it is written of me."** When God's servant is aware of God's requirements, he will obey them completely. His commitment to the Lord includes following whatever is prescribed for him in the Word or the "scroll" of God.

Verses 8, 9. The servant of God does not find submission a burden. **"I delight to do Your will, O my God; Your Law is within my heart."** God's man will be obedient to Him and will rejoice in the privilege of carrying out His will. Fulfilling God's law will be his chief ambition.

In Hebrews 10:5–7, the words of verses 7 and 8 of this psalm in the LXX are used to picture Christ's obedience to the will of God. The writer perhaps sees them as the response the godly man should make to God's wonderful grace, but in a deeper sense they foreshadow the life Jesus would live and the obedience He would render in His earthly life.

Verse 10. True religion expresses itself; so the psalmist says, **I have not hidden Your righteousness within my heart**. He shares his gladness over the goodness of God with "the great congregation," the assembly of God's people. He has proclaimed it to them and will continue proclaiming it to them. **I have spoken of Your faithfulness and Your salvation**. It is natural for us to tell others about what our Father has done that fills our hearts with joy.

He will speak of the righteousness of God—how He loves His people and keeps His promises to them. He says, **I have not concealed Your lovingkindness and Your truth from the great congregation**. Truth of this magnitude cannot be kept inside one's heart; it must be shared. God can see his heart; consequently, He knows what he has done and will do to proclaim God's truth.

THE GOD OF THE PRESENT (40:11, 12)

¹¹**You, O LORD, will not withhold Your compassion from me;**

Your lovingkindness and Your truth will continually preserve me.
¹²For evils beyond number have surrounded me;
My iniquities have overtaken me, so that I am not able to see;
They are more numerous than the hairs of my head,
And my heart has failed me.

Verse 11. God is not just the God of the past. A God who has only acted in the past would be merely ancient history to us. He would be interesting but irrelevant. The writer's predicament calls for more than past records; he wants a current victory. He wants to write about what God is to His people in the present. God is the ever-present One, the eternal One, the One above time, the great I AM. He stands ready to answer the prayers of His people now and will be eager to hear the groans of their hurting hearts tomorrow.

Because of his condition, the writer returns from joyous thanksgiving to a cry for immediate help: **You, O LORD, will not withhold Your compassion from me.** He knows enough about God to know that He will not "withhold His compassion" (His tender sympathy) from those who trust in Him. **Your lovingkindness and Your truth will continually preserve me.** He knows his situation will require God's "lovingkindness" (His covenant loyalty) and His "truth" to keep him from sinking. He wants the mercies that God has always lavished upon His people to be generously supplied to him. Furthermore, he needs God to guide him with His eternal truth and be his ever-present source of preservation.

Verse 12. He sees two problems that will necessitate God's guidance and grace. First, he sees evil around him. **For evils beyond number have surrounded me.** The exact nature of these "evils" is not delineated. Second, he sees evil within him. He expresses a deep consciousness of sin and that awareness is devastating to him. Seeing his own sin clearly and realizing the multitudes of them, he confesses that they have a numbing and blinding effect. **My iniquities have overtaken me, so that I am not able to see.** His sins have caused him to lose the right view of things. He cannot even begin to count them. **They are more numerous than the hairs of my head,** he said. Trying to list his sins would be as useless as trying to number the hairs of his head. He feels so overcome by the sense of guilt that his spirit within him begins to lose its zest and zeal for living. He says, **My heart has failed me.** With his courage gone and his strength sapped, his case becomes an emergency. He asks the Lord to come quickly to his side.

AN APPEAL TO THE LORD (40:13–17)

¹³**Be pleased, O Lord, to deliver me;**
Make haste, O Lord, to help me.
¹⁴**Let those be ashamed and humiliated together**
Who seek my life to destroy it;
Let those be turned back and dishonored
Who delight in my hurt.
¹⁵**Let those be appalled because of their shame**
Who say to me, "Aha, aha!"
¹⁶**Let all who seek You rejoice and be glad in You;**
Let those who love Your salvation say continually,
"The Lord be magnified!"
¹⁷**Since I am afflicted and needy,**
Let the Lord be mindful of me.
You are my help and my deliverer;
Do not delay, O my God.

Verse 13. He prays for God to come quickly to his aid. A signal of distress is sent up. **Be pleased, O Lord, to deliver me; make haste, O Lord, to help me.** He asks for God to rescue him if He is "pleased" to do so. God's will must be done. Even personal disaster could not make him put his own will before God's.

Verse 14. With an imprecatory petition, he says, **Let those be ashamed and humiliated together who seek my life to destroy it; let those be turned back and dishonored who delight in my hurt.** He asks that embarrassment and disgrace fall upon his enemies so that they will cease their evil intentions and works. These foes are probably national enemies who hated

David, Israel, and God. They ridicule God's people with words of contempt. He prays that they might in turn receive the same treatment.

Verse 15. In derision they are laughing at his trouble; so he prays, **Let those be appalled because of their shame who say to me, "Aha, aha!"** They have said, "Look at him and his men. He is supposed to be strong and have a powerful God, but look at how weak he is!" He prays that God will powerfully change their plans so that they will recognize God and praise Him.

Verse 16. He includes the righteous in his prayer, **Let all who seek You rejoice and be glad in You.** He has praised God for past and present deliverances. He now urges everyone who has been brought to safety by God to be glad and sing aloud about it. **Let those who love Your salvation say continually, "The LORD be magnified!"** God's people everywhere are invited to join with him in making known what God has done for them.

Verse 17. His prayer ends with a personal petition. **Since I am afflicted and needy, let the Lord be mindful of me.** Describing himself as "afflicted and needy," he asks God to look at his condition and think about him. "Be mindful of me," he says. He knows that God's heart is especially touched when the innocent are mistreated.

He reminds God that he honors Him in his heart as the true God and views Him as his source of life. **You are my help and my deliverer; do not delay, O my God.** His final petition therefore is "Come to my aid quickly, for You are my only hope." He is in a desperate circumstance, and he humbly casts himself and his people upon the Lord's mercy. He does not want to presume upon his relationship with God by telling God what to do. He is willing to wait patiently for Him to come bringing whatever support He chooses to bring.

APPLICATION

God, Our Help

Our God, the God of David, is ever-present—He has helped us in the past, He is our present help, and He will be our future help. God will walk with His people through any crisis. Therefore, the worship of God should include our praise for His assistance in the past and petitions for Him to stand by us in our current difficulties.

Is God Really My God?

This psalm compels us to ask ourselves, "What do I believe? Is God really the true God to me? What is my relationship with Him? Is His existence just a fact, or is He a divine Being who has been my companion in the past and is my coworker and mighty God today?" The center of true religion is to obey God, out of a realization of who He is, what He has done, is doing, and will do for us.

Waiting on the Lord

Of necessity, "waiting" will have to be a characteristic of a true relationship with the Lord. We saw this concept in Psalms 37—39; and now we see the results of it in 40. The writer says that he prayed, and then he waited. At long last, God answered his prayers.

How does the godly man wait?

He waits in obedience. While we wait, we obey. We go on doing the commands of the Lord. Waiting does not mean "sitting down," but it means "settling in" to doing what God has said.

He waits in faith. The believing heart knows that God will respond to any requests made of Him. His answer is going to be within the boundaries of our faith, our needs, and His will.

He waits in confidence. Faith produces assurance. We may not see God's answer for a long time, but trust in the Lord has given us the expectation that He will faithfully do what He said He would do. He may even answer some of our prayers after we are dead.

Waiting is an expression of faith. We walk by faith, not by sight (2 Cor. 5:7). The Christian life is a spiritual walk with God, who is absolutely faithful to His children. We do not mind waiting on God because the anticipation of how and when God is going to answer our prayers adds a beautiful dimension to our life with Him.

Teaching Others

Three ways of teaching others surface in verse 3. One is expressed, and two are implied.

We teach by what we are. The writer mentioned that his praising God and reflecting on what He had done for him inspired others to see, fear God, and trust in Him. They were convinced by what they saw more than by what was said to them.

We teach by what we do. Those who know us will see us praying, reading God's Word, and giving thanks for what God has done for us. They will be influenced by what they observe us do.

We teach by what we say. The implication is that one is to tell others who God is and what He does for His own. The child of God always has a message for others. He cannot be silent about it. If he fails to share it with others, he simply has not been walking with God.

We probably can say that a natural teaching of others about God takes place in our circle of influence. The people around us learn about God from what they see in us, by what we are doing, and through what we are continually saying about God.

The Great "I Am"

God lives in the eternal now, but there is a sense in which He is the God of the past, present, and future. He has worked, does work, and will work.

The past is full of His wonders. Surveying the past is very encouraging to the child of God because such a survey reminds us of all that God has done for us. We usually see more looking back on our days than we ever saw when we lived them.

The present is full of His thoughts and actions. God is active now—thinking gracious thoughts toward us and working His will in our lives. He works in plain sight and behind the scenes to achieve His divine purposes in concert with mankind's free moral agency. If the curtain were pulled back and we were allowed to see what God does for us, we would be overwhelmed.

The future is full of His plans. As we squint our eyes and look at what is coming, we can only characterize it with one word—God. He will bless us tomorrow, save us tomorrow, mature us tomorrow, and introduce us to heaven tomorrow. Think of all His plans that are yet to be fulfilled.

No human being can say that he or she is not surrounded by God—God is in our past, our present, and our future. We have lived, moved, and breathed through Him, and we will do so today and throughout all the future that awaits us.

What God Has Done

If one does not remember, he will not praise God. Looking back on His kind deeds will remind us of His goodness and will put a song of praise on our lips.

Re-read the history book of your life, and see what God has done for you!

He has heard our prayers. Surely everyone who trusts in the Lord can glance back over the years and see where God has answered his or her prayers. We have prayed, and God has bent low and heard our feeble petitions.

He has rescued us from destruction. As we scan the pages of the past, we can see where God has lifted us out of the miry pit of destruction. Perhaps we were slipping over the brink into the hellish pit of sin and God lifted us out, rescuing us from the greedy fingers of the devil. Maybe we were going down to the door of death through a sickness or an accident and God pulled us back and gave us new life. Innumerable times we have been at the mercy of God.

He has put our feet on solid ground. We can see that God has given us firm footing so that we can serve Him once again. He has put us on a level place so that we can do His will and fulfill His plan.

He has given us a new song. His grace to us and His great acts of kindness should put a new song in our hearts and on our lips. Are we singing it? If we do not have a happy song of deliverance to sing, we simply have not walked with God or have not looked carefully at the past.

Do what the psalmist did. Stop and look back at what God has done for you. His hand of grace has been upon your life, and seeing it will set your soul to singing of His wonderful love and enduring mercy.

Considering the Works of God

As we look back over the actions of God toward His people, we are able to reach some important conclusions about God's grace.

First, we can say that He has blessed all who trust in Him. There are no exceptions. He has never forsaken any of His children. He has never broken a covenant or violated a promise.

Second, we observe that His deeds are not only kind but also gracious. Kind deeds are generous deeds, but *gracious* deeds are undeserved deeds. He has loved His people when they did not deserve loving. He has always given them what they have needed, not what they have deserved.

Third, we can see that He is full of gracious thoughts toward His people. His wonderful actions were spawned by wonderful thoughts. Sometimes we say to one another, "What are you thinking?" We know that the one to whom we are speaking might be thinking a wrong thought about us. How comforting it is to realize that God is always thinking good, noble, and gracious thoughts about His people!

Fourth, we have seen that His deeds of grace are continuous and innumerable. There have been so many of them that we could not count them if we really tried. Everywhere we look we see the hand of God. He has surrounded those who trust in Him with gifts of His love.

How great our God is! His power transcends our feeble ability to comprehend, but so does His grace. His wonders are inconceivable, innumerable, and impartial.

The Servant of God

How shall we picture God's servant? It is doubtful that a better description of servanthood could be found than in verses 6 through 10 of this psalm.

What are the characteristics of God's faithful servant?

He serves from the heart. He sees beyond just the ritual of offering sacrifices to the sincere heart that is needed for the sacrifices to be acceptable.

He is obedient. He wants to obey all of God's commandments. The scroll of God's Word is for him. His life is dedicated to keeping it. Consider the picture of Jesus portrayed here.

He finds serving God a delight. God's commandments are not a burden but a joy. God's laws are written on his heart. He has allowed God's will to mold his thinking. God's will has become his.

He shares God's lovingkindness with others. He cannot help but speak of God's goodness in the congregation of God's people. He speaks often of God's faithfulness and salvation to those around him and to those he meets.

Here then are the major areas of servanthood: heart service, obedience, delighting in God's will, and sharing God's goodness with others. Are we God's servants?

The Living Hope

A time had come when the writer saw God as his only hope. He had been overrun by a flood of troubles, and he cried out for God to rescue him. What did he want God to do for him? Look at verses 11 and 12.

He wanted God to forgive him. He was in need of the compassion and lovingkindness of God. Sins had piled up and made a leaden blanket over him. His sins had found him out and had captured him. They were more numerous than the hairs of his head.

He asked for deliverance from the evils that surrounded him. Life had become too big for him. His circumstance required an almighty hand to shield him from all that threatened him.

He sought God's guidance. He needed truth, not fiction, and an everlasting way, not a temporary respite. In his state only compassion and truth could save him. He could not see clearly, and he pleaded for God's truth so that he might have the proper vision.

He besought God to restore his life. He had lost the heart to live. His spirit was gone. Blinded by his sin and with all his energy gone, he had become a walking mannequin. He needed God to remake him and put a new soul, one that was revived and rekindled, in his body.

Have we not been in a similar situation?

How Shall We Pray?

Although it is inappropriate for the Christian to pray for a curse to fall upon his enemies, this prayer in verses 13 through 17 in other ways influences our praying to God.

It suggests that we are to pray reverently. "Be pleased" indicates respect for God's will.

God's servants pray humbly. He does not tell God what to do but simply lays before Him his condition and asks that God tend to it as He sees best. He prays for God in His own wisdom to handle his situation.

Here is an example for praying specifically. A specific request is made about his enemies and his condition.

We are instructed to pray thankfully. Our prayers should rise from hearts that are full of joy and gratitude for what God has done.

Joy is to characterize us as we pray. The trusting person is glad in God. He prays with happiness in his heart about who God is and over the wonderful relationship he has with God.

In other words, in this psalm we are taught to come before God with reverence, thankfulness, joy, and humility, and place before our God the specific requests that we have.

Psalm 41
Hope in the Midst of Suffering

The Superscription: For the choir director. A Psalm of David. With this psalm the first of the five divisions of the Book of Psalms ends. The superscription calls this piece **a Psalm** (מִזְמוֹר, *mizmor*), and it is addressed, with seventeen others in Book I, to **the choir director** (לַמְנַצֵּחַ, *lamnatstseach*). Perhaps the psalm was written for use during times of suffering from illness or times of extreme pressure from difficult circumstances. The title's ascription has **of** ["by," "for," or "to"] **David** (לְדָוִד, *lᵉdawid*) as is the case with every other psalm in Book I except 1, 2, 10, and 33.

Even though this psalm has a strong lament character, it rises to a high note of gratitude for the gifts that have been bestowed and could well be classified as a thanksgiving song. The writer is either presently suffering from a life-threatening sickness or is reflecting on a time when he was suffering.

The penman writes about a circumstance in which he faced a double hardship: a time when he was wrestling with an illness and when he was being afflicted by enemies and a turncoat friend, both of whom were poised and ready to rejoice over his death. However, in spite of his troubles, he looks to God with thanksgiving and a confident faith.

The heart of the psalm is the section that is made up of verses 4 through 10. These verses comprise a prayer/lament, written in the form of an inclusio appeal—that is, a petition that is hedged in by the plea "be gracious to me."

Through the words of this psalm we see the royal road to triumph over the problems that may beset us. We are shown that the godly person is blessed even though he may be in pain, almost friendless, and hounded by insensitive and senseless foes.

CONSIDER THE HELPLESS
(41:1-3)

¹**How blessed is he who considers the helpless;**
The LORD will deliver him in a day of trouble.
²**The LORD will protect him and keep him alive,**
And he shall be called blessed upon the earth;
And do not give him over to the desire of his enemies.
³**The LORD will sustain him upon his sickbed;**
In his illness, You restore him to health.

Verse 1. Like Psalm 1, this last psalm in Book I begins with a beatitude. **How blessed is he who considers the helpless.** The first psalm declares that the godly man will be blessed because of his character; this psalm affirms that the godly man will be blessed because of his compassion for "the helpless," the poor, or the weak.

If the two appearances of the word "blessed" in Psalm 32:1, 2 are counted as the same, then seven beatitudes are mentioned in Book I of Psalms (1:1; 2:12; 32:1, 2; 33:12; 34:8; 40:4; 41:1). Combining all of these, we learn that true happiness comes from walking in righteousness, finding refuge in God, enjoying forgiveness, being a nation under God, trusting in the Lord, and considering the weak.

The happinesses or blessednesses (אַשְׁרֵי, 'ashrey) announced in this verse come to the one who "considers," remembers, or wisely understands "the helpless," the ones beaten down by circumstances or made destitute by the unkind turns of life. Actually, the Hebrew does not contain the word "considers"; it uses a word that means "prudently understands" (שָׂכַל, śakal). This blessed one is a person who possesses a sympathy that manifests itself in loving concern and astute consideration instead of harsh judgment, and extends a heart and hand of tender assistance to those who have fallen upon hard times. This beatitude is the Old Testament counterpart to our Lord's "Blessed are the merciful" (Mt. 5:7a).

PSALM 41

How will the merciful man be blessed? Six characteristics of his prosperity are given. First, the writer says, God will deliver him. **The LORD will deliver him in a day of trouble.** The compassionate man will receive grace upon grace. God will grant mercy to him during his trying times. Through God's providence, He will be able to sail through the rough waters that flood his life.

Verse 2. Since he has had pity on others, God will have pity on him. **The LORD will protect him and keep him alive, and he shall be called blessed upon the earth.** He will enjoy preservation of health and extension of life. God says that he will live and live well. Those who know him will see his goodness and will applaud it.

God will encircle him with His hands and prevent the vicious forces around him from harming him. [The Lord will] **not give him over to the desire of his enemies.** He will not permit him to fall into the cunning and evil plans of his enemies.

Verse 3. When sickness comes, God will turn his sickbed into a bed of radiant health and restore him to life. **The LORD will sustain him upon his sickbed; in his illness, You restore him to health.** Instead of fluffing up his bed to make it more comfortable for his time of sickness, God will turn it into a mattress of flourishing life.

The benefits promised to the tenderhearted, sympathetic person are basically in the form of physical blessings. Among the highest goals of the people in the Old Testament times were the aspirations of living a long life, having a large family, and enjoying a good life. The one who considers the poor, he says, will be granted the cherished desires that every Israelite held in his or her heart.

The writer himself is in need. His tormenting illness has been made even more unbearable by the hostility of enemies and former friends. Nevertheless, he declares that the first trait that godly people must exhibit is a compassionate, understanding heart. The sufferer must not think only of what he is going through; he must be generous in his spirit toward those who need assistance. Concern for others has been an emphasis in his life, and he resolves that this emphasis will continue.

"BE GRACIOUS TO ME" (41:4)

⁴As for me, I said, "O LORD, be gracious to me;
Heal my soul, for I have sinned against You."

Verse 4. Turning now to his own life that is confounded by sickness, he begins his actual prayer/lament with a request for mercy, **As for me, I said, "O LORD, be gracious to me."** His use of "I" indicates that he is emphatic: "Now, Lord, I want to ask for myself, not humanity in general," he is saying. He goes from "them" to "me."

In particular, he pleads, **"Heal my soul, for I have sinned against You."** A man's greatest problem is sin. He always needs forgiveness. Unless a person's guilt is removed, no other healing can mean much. David may be referring to a specific sin that he has committed and is suffering from, or he may be referring to his sinfulness in general, a realization that would naturally come to his mind as he contemplates his life-threatening illness or as a result of his praying this type of prayer.

Since iniquity is a crime against God, a sinner must go to Him for forgiveness. Because of His lovingkindness, He is always gracious to the servant who comes penitently to Him.

He asks for complete "heal[ing]" (רָפָא, *rapa'*). He is reminded that a person cannot be whole without God's mercy. One can have a sound body, with every member in working order, and still not be complete. If he is incomplete spiritually, he is deformed before God. "Soul" (נֶפֶשׁ, *nepesh*) encompasses the entire person—personality, body, and spirit. The truly handicapped are those who are deficient spiritually. The writer wants completeness. He pleads for the grace of God to bring him into a wholeness of health.

CLAIMING GOD'S HELP
(41:5–11)

⁵My enemies speak evil against me, "When will he die, and his name perish?"

⁶**And when he comes to see me, he speaks falsehood;**
His heart gathers wickedness to itself;
When he goes outside, he tells it.
⁷**All who hate me whisper together against me;**
Against me they devise my hurt, saying,
⁸**"A wicked thing is poured out upon him,**
That when he lies down, he will not rise up again."
⁹**Even my close friend in whom I trusted,**
Who ate my bread,
Has lifted up his heel against me.
¹⁰**But You, O LORD, be gracious to me and raise me up,**
That I may repay them.
¹¹**By this I know that You are pleased with me,**
Because my enemy does not shout in triumph over me.

Verse 5. Living in a pool of enmity, he is surrounded by destructive enemies. He says, **My enemies speak evil against me, "When will he die, and his name perish?"** The Hebrew is literally, "My enemies speak evil to me." Their words were coated with the acid of hatred, like poison-tipped arrows. They expressed the opposite of sympathy toward his sickness and pain. God has been and is gracious to him, but his enemies are resentful to him. These evil ones are so set against him that they are wishing for his death. The spirit of murder is in their hearts. They want him gone from the earth.

Verse 6. He pictures a single enemy coming to see him and telling lies while with him. **And when he comes to see me, he speaks falsehood.** His visitor does not come to encourage a man who is struggling with some kind of sickness; he comes to mislead. While in his presence on seemingly an errand of mercy, the enemy plans for his destruction. He says, **His heart gathers wickedness to itself; when he goes outside, he tells it.** After gathering up what he could about him, he left his bedside to spread slander about him or to harm him in other ways. Anything that he had seen in his sickroom, he twisted into misrepresentations about him.

Verse 7. A more comprehensive statement or grouping of his troubles is seen in the word "all": **All who hate me whisper**

together against me. Apparently, a judgment of his adversaries is that his illness is a punishment from God. He adds, **Against me they devise my hurt.** They are hurting him by spreading gossip about him and by leading others to believe that his sickness is a direct result of his sin.

Verse 8. He repeats what they are saying, **"A wicked thing is poured out upon him, that when he lies down, he will not rise up again."** This quoted remark reveals the malicious slander they were spreading. They say that "a wicked thing" or "a thing of Belial" (דְּבַר־בְּלִיַּעַל, *dᵉbar bᵉliyya'al*), has been "poured out upon him." Their prediction is that he will not get well. "God is removing him from the earth," they are saying. In gossipy whispers they tell one another about his imminent death. They happily plan his funeral—even before he dies.

Verse 9. Among these enemies is a friend, a man who has eaten at his table. This friend's unfaithfulness to him must have hurt him the most. He laments, **Even my close friend in whom I trusted, who ate my bread, has lifted up his heel against me.** The Hebrew refers to him as a "man of my peace" (אִישׁ שְׁלוֹמִי, *'ish shᵉlomi*). Is David speaking of Ahithophel, his trusted counselor (2 Sam. 15:12) and close friend, who defected and joined Absalom's rebellion? Possibly. If not, he is referring to someone like him.

He is saying, "He has lifted a great heel against me" (עָלַי עָקֵב הִגְדִּיל, *higdil 'alay 'aqeb*). It seems that he is comparing him to a horse that kicks at its owner. Later Jesus referred to this verse as being fulfilled in His betrayal by Judas (Jn. 13:18). Echoes are also seen in Matthew 26:23, Mark 14:18, and Luke 22:21. What this friend did to David was a type of what Judas would do to Jesus.

Verse 10. The psalmist prays that God may raise him up from his illness and restore him to his place of leadership. He requests, **But You, O Lord, be gracious to me and raise me up, that I may repay them.** His petition is that their prophecies concerning his death will not come true, but that he will live to repay them. If the background of this psalm is the insurrection of Absalom, David could have been thinking of administering justice to those who were seeking to overthrow the kingdom.

Verse 11. The deliverance that God gives him will be an indication of God's approval upon his life. **By this I know that You are pleased with me, because my enemy does not shout in triumph over me.** He believes that if he regains his health and can resume his leading of the nation, that this healing will be the bestowal of the favor of God, a granting of the gift of grace. Such a rescue would prove that God did not want his enemy to win over him.

CONFORM TO GOD'S WILL (41:12)

¹²As for me, You uphold me in my integrity,
And You set me in Your presence forever.

Verse 12. He wants to be open, honest, and penitent before God: **As for me, You uphold me in my integrity, and You set me in Your presence forever.** He is not sinless, but he has a dedicated heart and intends to be loyal to God by walking obediently with Him. He believes that the Lord will be true to every promise He has made to him. Therefore, he can speak boldly about being forgiven and enjoying God's "presence forever."

How will he have this standing with God? God has seen his "integrity" and honored it. To the loyal heart, He promises to show Himself loyal (see Ps. 18:25). God has welcomed him into the warmth of His fellowship because he has allowed no sham, hypocrisy, or deception to form a wedge between them.

To continue in this state for the duration of his life and beyond is his greatest ambition. By nature, the highest expectation of the faithful is the abiding presence of God.

THE DOXOLOGY FOR BOOK I (41:13)

¹³Blessed be the LORD, the God of Israel,
From everlasting to everlasting.
Amen and Amen.

Each of the five books of the Psalms closes with a doxology (41:13; 72:18, 19; 89:52; 106:48; 150). Psalm 150 functions as a doxology for the entire Book of Psalms. The expression of praise which closes this first book is verse 13. Perhaps this verse was added by the final inspired editor, or perhaps this psalm was placed at the end of Book I because it already had this doxology as its concluding thought.

Verse 13. Blessed be the LORD, the God of Israel. The word "blessed" is used in two ways in this psalm: as an expression of congratulation (v. 1) and as an expression of adoration (בָּרַךְ, *barak*). In verse 1, it is used as a pronouncement of blessing upon the compassionate man. In this verse, it is used as an ascription of praise to God.

He recognizes God as "the God of Israel," the eternal God who has chosen Israel as His people and has promised to fulfill His covenant with them. God is equally praiseworthy today, because He is God, the One who sent Jesus and formed the new covenant of grace.

Let us praise Him **from everlasting to everlasting.** The adoration that He deserves should be given to Him forever, from eternity past to eternity future, continually and without end, by all people and for all time.

To this doxology, the writer responds with a twofold agreement: **Amen and Amen** (אָמֵן וְאָמֵן, *'amen wᵉ'amen*). Perhaps the congregation is to give this response to the reading of the psalm.

"Amen" is an affirmation of approval that means "May it be so." Derived from a Hebrew word that means "true" or "faithful," it is sometimes translated into English from the Greek New Testament word ἀμήν (*amēn*) as "truly" or "verily." Most of the time the word is not translated from the Hebrew or the Greek but appears as a transliteration or anglicized form, rendered "amen." The repetition of the word suggests intensity or emphasis. The idea of its double use is "May this be especially so!"

APPLICATION

Oneness with God

David's circumstances were doubly bad. He was recovering

from an illness that had brought him to the brink of death. Instead of growing in popularity, he was declining. In fact, many were wishing that he would die. Surrounded by such problems, where could he turn? Reflected in this psalm is the answer: His victory was in God, not in man or in circumstances.

His first step toward victory was *to have tender sympathy for and prudent understanding of the poor.* He wanted to have the same type of consideration for the needy as God.

Furthermore, he chose *to acknowledge his sins and determined to lead a blameless life before God.* He wanted to be clean and honest with his God.

His third step was *to pray.* He pleaded for God's help as he struggled with circumstances that were too big for him.

In addition to all this, he resolved *to remain conformed to God's will,* to continue a transparent and blameless life before Him.

He teaches us that the route to radiant hope is lined with compassion for the poor, confession of sin, claims to the promises of God, and conformity to God's will. A person may not have the best of health, the friends he wants, or a peaceful environment; but he can still find fulfillment regarding life's deepest longing if he has true oneness with God.

Considering the Poor

The first part of this psalm is one of the most beautiful descriptions of how God looks upon those who wisely respond to the poor. How does God bless the one who shows sympathy, tenderness, and benevolent understanding for the poor?

He delivers him in the day of trouble. God watches over him because he has looked out for those who are in need.

He protects him and keeps him alive. God saves him when his life is threatened. When evil men are against him, God puts a wall around him.

He gives him a good name. He sees to it that he has the popularity he needs. God gives him a respected and admired name.

He keeps him from the desire of his enemies. Enemies of truth want to rid the world of the righteous, but God sees them and protects the good man from them.

He restores him to health when sickness comes. When he faces his day of sickness, the Lord raises him up.

For the Old Testament day, these promises were more physical than spiritual, but today they come to us as more spiritual than physical.

God and the Poor

What do we learn about God and the poor from this psalm?

God is touched by the poor. Throughout the Old Testament, His concern for the poor is made known. We would expect such kindness from our God. He has poured out His mercy on us, so why would He not show special generosity for those who are down and out?

God's true people will be concerned about the poor. They take on the characteristics of God. They absorb His lovingkindness into their personalities and attitudes. They learn to look at the poor the way God does.

God blesses those who show compassion on the poor. "How blessed is he who considers the helpless" (v. 1). God will not allow those who have carried out His will to go unblessed.

When Sin Is Present

Perhaps David is asking for forgiveness because he sinned in some special way and is suffering for it, and he wants to deal with the barrier affecting his relationship with God.

In his appeal to God, we see an admirable attitude toward sin and its relation to God.

Repentance of our sins is always appropriate. Actually, repentance is expressed in the confession that is coming up. True believers will be working to eliminate all types of sin from their lives. Repentance should be a continual effort, a never-ending ambition.

Confession of sin is made to God. If the one seeking forgiveness is a child of God, he comes to God in prayer (Acts 8:22 and Jas. 5:16) and seeks it. As one in the covenant, he has been given by God's grace the approach of prayer. The non-Christian finds forgiveness when he becomes a Christian (Acts 2:38).

Out of penitence and confession, God is asked to heal the soul. Spiritual cleansing should precede requests for physical healing.

Our prayer is based upon His grace. Sin can only be forgiven by God's lovingkindness. Salvation cannot be earned or merited.

Analyzing Sin

What is our relationship with sin?

Sin is a crime against God. Our sin is against God because He is the author of all moral law. It is His will that we have violated.

Only God can forgive sin. Because our sin is ultimately against God, only He can forgive it. He has asked us to clear up our mistakes with one another, but His plan runs vertically first, from man to God, and then horizontally, from man to man.

One is not fully whole until he is forgiven. One can be robust physically but terribly crippled spiritually—if he has not been forgiven by the Lord. No real wholeness exists unless spiritual health is included in it.

During Times of Trial

The writer finds himself in a terrible strait. He is surrounded by enemies—men who are hateful and conniving. They would send him death wishes if they could. They come to see him under the guise of expressing sympathy, but in reality, they gather up bullets for their gossip gun. Some of these foes are telling others that he has been cursed by the Lord because of his sin. "His sickness came from the devil," they say. At least one who opposes him is a person who has been a friend but now is kicking against him like a horse.

It would be hard to envision a more depressing situation. The writer could easily give in to his fears and disappointments, but he does not. He knows what to do. He brings his situation to God.

He knows God will hear him. He prays in the wonderful expectation of receiving an answer from God, an answer that is in harmony with His will and the writer's need.

He knows God will sustain him. He is confident that God will sustain him in his trial. With energy in short supply, he believes that God will give him whatever he needs for his life with God.

He knows God will deliver him. Yes, he talks to God in trusting prayer as if the deliverance he needs has already come. God, to him, is the greatest of all certainties. As surely as he has put his trust in God, as surely as he has prayed for God to rescue him, he can consider his situation met.

Why should we fret when God has already met all our needs through Christ. He is not the "God of the almost" but the "God of the altogether."

The Sure Way to Happiness

In this early part of the Book of Psalms—the first book—the word "blessed" appears eight times (1:1; 2:12; 32:1, 2; 33:12; 34:8; 40:4; 41:1). When these passages are traced out, we see the pathway to true happiness.

Happiness comes from being a righteous person (1:1). This beatitude is presented in a negative statement—by affirming what the righteous person does not do. He does not walk, stand, or sit with the wicked. It reminds us of our Lord's words: "Blessed are the pure in heart" (Mt. 5:8) and "Blessed are those who hunger and thirst for righteousness, for they shall be satisfied" (Mt. 5:6).

Happiness is found in finding refuge in God (2:12; 34:8). This beatitude highlights the man who allows God to be his shield. He comes to God and asks Him to be his fortress, defense, and stronghold. Perhaps this promise is similar to our Lord's beatitudes: "Blessed are the poor in spirit, for theirs is the kingdom of heaven" (Mt. 5:3), and "Blessed are those who have been persecuted for the sake of righteousness" (Mt. 5:10).

Happiness is enjoying forgiveness (32:1, 2). The word "blessed" is used twice in these two verses, but forgiveness is emphasized in each case. There is simply no peace without forgiveness. One might say that this beatitude is about making peace with God and with others—somewhat like, "Blessed are the peacemakers, for they shall be called sons of God" (Mt. 5:9).

Happiness is being a nation under God (33:12). No nation can find true prosperity, peace, and success unless it lives and rules under God's leadership. This beatitude would be the only one of the seven that admonishes a community. This felicitation hints at another beatitude: "Blessed are the gentle, for they shall inherit the earth" (Mt. 5:5).

Happiness is trusting in the Lord (40:4). Life can be miserable unless one is living by faith in God. He who puts his confidence in anything in this world is headed for a tragic disappointment. God gives us stability, and through His stability we find peace.

Happiness is considering the weak (41:1, 2). One cannot find the peace of God unless he is treating others right. This beatitude has to do with a heart of compassion. It a blessing that is in line with our Lord's beatitude: "Blessed are the merciful, for they shall receive mercy" (Mt. 5:7).

When these beatitudes are combined, we have a beautiful picture of how a godly person is to live. Having this lifestyle not only brings a life of harmony with God's will, but it also guides one into the good life of prosperity, peace, and happiness.

BOOK II
PSALMS 42—72

Psalm 42 begins the second book of Psalms, a collection containing thirty-one psalms (42—72).

Two general characteristics of these psalms are immediately apparent. In the first book (1—41), David is the only author who seems to be named in the superscriptions; in this book, only eighteen psalms out of the thirty-one are superscriptionally attributed to him. In addition, this group of psalms has been referred to as the "Elohistic Psalms" because the name Elohim is the name most often used for God in them. Elohim (אֱלֹהִים) is used 198 times, while Yahweh (יהוה) is used 32 times.

Some illustrations in this group of psalms are taken from the Book of Exodus and this characteristic has given rise to referring to Book II as the "Exodus Book."

Concerning the designations appearing in the superscriptions, seven psalms in Book II (42; 44—49) are said to be "of the sons of Korah"; one (50) is designated "of Asaph"; eighteen psalms (51—65; 68—70) are said to be "of David"; one is an anonymous psalm (71); and one has "of Solomon" (72).

A total of eleven psalms contain references in their titles to the "sons of Korah" (42; 44—49; 84; 85; 87; 88). Because the majority of these psalms are located in Book II, the book has also been referred to as the "Korahite Book."

The priest Korah was a descendant of Levi. He is mentioned in Numbers 16 as leading a rebellion against Moses, but God judged and destroyed him, along with the men who stood with him. His descendants, known simply as the "sons of Korah," are often mentioned as temple servants (1 Chron. 9:19; 26:1, 19).

In 2 Chronicles 20:19 they are spoken of as singers, and in 1 Chronicles 9:19 they are described as keepers of the thresholds. Heman, one of the Korahites (1 Chron. 6:33–38), was chosen to be a leader of the three great choirs organized by David for the temple (1 Chron. 15:17; 16:41, 42; 25:1, 4, 5).

The Korahite psalms were hymns, songs, prayers, and expressions of wisdom used by the sons of Korah in connection with the worship of the temple. In addition to other similarities, each of these psalms makes some reference to the temple and its worship. Psalm 43 is considered to belong to this group, but no title is attached to it. This psalm has not been included in the count listed above. This psalm may have been joined to Psalm 42 at one time. Thus, if Psalm 43 is included, the actual number of the psalms of the "sons of Korah" totals twelve.

A group of twelve psalms are designated "of Asaph": one in Book II (50) and eleven in Book III (73—83). We know very little about this man. Perhaps he was the author of these psalms; perhaps they were written under his direction as he led the music program at the Jerusalem sanctuary (1 Chron. 15:19); or maybe the title just refers to a certain style of writing used in the psalm.

Eighteen psalms (51—65; 68—70) in Book II are said to be "of David." Book I may contain the first collection of his psalms, and the ones found in this book may come from the additional ones that he wrote that were added later as the editor(s) brought together the final form of the Book of Psalms.

One psalm in Book II contains no superscription (71), and it falls into the group called "orphan psalms."

One psalm has "of Solomon" (72). The phrase may indicate that this psalm was a prayer composed by Solomon to be used by the people in their intercession to God on behalf of their king.

Psalm 42
Thirsting for God

The Superscription: For the choir director. A Maskil of the sons of Korah. The superscription addresses **the choir director** (לַמְנַצֵּחַ, *lamnatstseach*) and identifies the psalm as **a Maskil** (מַשְׂכִּיל), which probably means that it was written for "instructional" purposes.

Like ten others in the Book of Psalms, the title contains the reference of ["by," "for," or "to"] **the sons of Korah** (לִבְנֵי־קֹרַח, *libney qorach*) (42; 44—49; 84; 85; 87; 88). These psalms must have been hymns or songs written or used by the Korahites in connection with the temple.

This psalm and the next one are closely connected. At some time, the two probably comprised one song. They emphasize the same theme, have the same spirit, use similar language, and share the same refrain: "Why are you in despair, O my soul?" (42:5a, 11a; 43:5a). Furthermore, every psalm in Book II has a title except Psalm 43. Could it be that it does not have a title because this psalm and 43 were one psalm when the titles were assigned?

Even though considerable evidence exists that these two were once a single psalm, the majority of the Hebrew manuscripts and the ancient versions of the Scriptures present them as two psalms. For this reason, let us study them as separate but companion psalms.

In these eleven verses the writer expressed his love for the temple and the worship of God. For some reason or in some way he was isolated from the temple and was unable to participate in its services, feasts, and festivals. In addition, he was surrounded by people who taunted him regarding his God. These circumstances combined to make him lonely and homesick for God. He yearned for an opportunity to worship Him in the magnificent temple in Jerusalem.

The thought pattern of the psalm weaves back and forth from lament to hope. The writer was experiencing the ups and downs of a discouraging, disappointing separation from the object of his affections.

Sometimes the difficulties that plague us rush forcefully into our minds, producing fears and doubts, taking us into a downward spin. When they fill our minds, we have to chase them away with the assurance that God has not forsaken us. The pain that we endure in these valleys and how to handle it are described in this psalm and the next.

THIRSTY FOR GOD (42:1–4)

¹**As the deer pants for the water brooks,**
So my soul pants for You, O God.
²**My soul thirsts for God, for the living God;**
When shall I come and appear before God?
³**My tears have been my food day and night,**
While they say to me all day long, "Where is your God?"
⁴**These things I remember and I pour out my soul within**
    me.
For I used to go along with the throng and lead them in
    procession to the house of God,
With the voice of joy and thanksgiving, a multitude keeping festival.

Verse 1. In vivid language, and with unforgettable metaphors, the writer begins with a lament over his deepest emotional and spiritual longing. He says, "Just **as the deer pants for the water brooks,** so I yearn for God." His depression arises from the fact that he cannot worship at the temple as he once did. He is possessed by an unusual craving: He is thirsty for God. He compares himself to a "deer" (אַיָּל, *'ayyal*) crying for rivers of water, during the heat of the day, perhaps during a time of drought. He pictures for the reader a suffering animal, perhaps a stag, with its tongue hanging out of its mouth, and its strength all but gone. It is walking about as if it is in prayer to God for water.

The original word that is translated "pants" in the NASB (עָרַג, 'arag) appears only here and in Joel 1:20, where it refers to the beasts of the field "weeping" before God in the midst of a famine. The word means "to look for, long for, or intensely desire." The way a thirsty deer roams about searching for life-giving brooks or streams typifies the writer's eagerness to be in the special presence of God. He says, "Like a deer 'pleading' for water is the way my soul seeks after You, O God."

Verse 2. The writer bares before us the deep desire of his heart. **My soul thirsts for God, for the living God**, he says. The almighty One for whom he yearns is not a senseless idol, but "the living," active, and true God. He says his "soul" (נֶפֶשׁ, nepesh) thirsts for God; his innermost being craves God.

In particular, the writer seeks to appear before God in worship at one of the feasts or times of sacrifice at the temple. He asks, **When shall I come and appear before God?** Living in isolation, he cannot experience God's presence in the place that God has ordained for worship. "Appear before God" is an expression used to refer to the annual visits to the temple that are mentioned in Exodus 23:17. This "joy of His presence" has been taken from him by the circumstances he is in, and he wants these meaningful opportunities back.

Verse 3. So deep is his grief over missing this privilege of special worship that tears have become his food. His words, **My tears have been my food day and night**, express his continual sorrow at being away from the temple. Weeping is as much a part of his life as his daily bread. Perhaps sometimes he weeps instead of eating. His mourning is "day and night," a perpetual heaviness of heart. The burden incessantly presses down upon his mind.

The jeers of those around him intensifies his loneliness for God. **While they say to me all day long, "Where is your God?"** One tormenting question that people frequently ask him is, "Where is your God?" They mean, "If your God cares for you so much, why has He allowed you to be taken from your people and the temple? Why has He not come to your rescue, giving you the help you need?" The writer, far removed from Jerusalem, must have been among people who neither acknowledged God nor sympathized with his aspiration to worship His God.

Verse 4. A conversation is going on within him. He says to himself, **These things I remember and I pour out my soul within me.** As he reflects, he remembers how it was in the past, conjuring up memories that were deeply moving to him. His "soul" is poured out like water "within" him. These terms suggest highly emotional thinking.

He recalls what he used to do. **I used to go along with the throng and lead them in procession to the house of God**, he says. His mind races back to when he could freely attend the worship services at the temple. Pictures of past events crowd into his soul, bringing the greatest spiritual impact. He can see himself once again with unhindered access to the house of God. He is going with **a multitude** [for the purpose of] **keeping** [a] **festival** in Jerusalem. He had gone often, and he had even at times led groups of people to the temple for worship. These were the happiest episodes of his life, and he went **with the voice of joy and thanksgiving.** Journeys to the temple were characterized with gratefulness. Considered his fondest memory treasures, they are now providing the subject matter for his spiritual contemplation.

"WHY ARE YOU IN DESPAIR, O MY SOUL?"
(42:5–8)

⁵Why are you in despair, O my soul?
And why have you become disturbed within me?
Hope in God, for I shall again praise Him
For the help of His presence.
⁶O my God, my soul is in despair within me;
Therefore I remember You from the land of the Jordan
And the peaks of Hermon, from Mount Mizar.
⁷Deep calls to deep at the sound of Your waterfalls;

All Your breakers and Your waves have rolled over me.
⁸The LORD will command His lovingkindness in the daytime;
And His song will be with me in the night,
A prayer to the God of my life.

Verse 5. He bolsters his heart by asking himself a question from a new perspective: **Why are you in despair, O my soul? And why have you become disturbed within me?** His soul is roaring (הָמָה, *hamah*) within him. Remembering the joy of worshiping at the temple has immersed his soul in sadness and revived in him a hungering to return to the temple; however, thinking about the past has also prompted him to reach a new conclusion. He will set his mind on God, for he believes that he will praise Him again. He says to his soul, **Hope in God, for I shall again praise Him for the help of His presence.** The opportunity, he believes, will come again for him to thank God for His goodness and grace. He will once more praise Him for "the help of His presence." The word "help" comes from a plural word for salvation (יְשׁוּעוֹת, *yᵉshu'oth*), suggesting the multiplicity of or the majesty of the blessings that have come from the Lord. "His presence" is a translation of the Hebrew wording "His face" (פָּנָיו, *panayw*). The gifts have come from His presence or before His face. "Hoping in God" has inspired him to trust in God's providence.

Verse 6. He cannot go to the temple to worship Him, so he will remember God where he is. With great resolve, he affirms, **O my God, my soul is in despair within me; therefore I remember You from the land of the Jordan and the peaks of Hermon, from Mount Mizar.** Under his present handicap, he will think of the Lord from "the land of the Jordan," from "the peaks of Hermon," and "from Mount Mizar." The mention of these places suggests that he is in the neighborhood of Dan or the place that became Caesarea Philippi in the New Testament period, where the Jordan River descends from the foot of Hermon. "Hermon" is plural and either denotes the Hermon mountain range in general or refers to the three peaks into which Mount Hermon culminates. "Mizar," meaning "little," was probably some small hill near him which is unknown to us.

Verse 7. The thoughts of God elicit from deep within him a spiritual response that can be likened to nothing else. **Deep calls to deep at the sound of Your waterfalls.** Anguish rushes over him like waves of the sea. Sorrow is following sorrow, like billow after billow in the ocean. **All your breakers and Your waves have rolled over me.** Moffatt rendered this phrase, "Flood follows flood, as thy cataracts thunder, thy breakers and billows are surging over me."[1] Floods of misery have come trooping over him, submerging and drenching him in depression.

Verse 8. In the midst of his despondency, he makes a resolution: He will reach up to God, his rock and strength. He says, **The LORD will command His lovingkindness in the daytime.** The word "LORD" is "Yahweh" (יהוה, *YHWH*), a name that appears only once in this psalm. "Daytime" figuratively portrays times that are free from trials. He pictures a "daytime" coming when he will be able to worship once again at Jerusalem.

God's "lovingkindness" is the source of his support. He knows God to be full of mercy; thus he realizes that God will manifest His grace to him in the future. He says, **His song will be with me in the night.** Because of God's "lovingkindness" during "the daytime," he will be able to sing "in the night," in the difficult times. Because of God's multitude of mercies, he will survive loneliness and persecution. He believes that the Lord in His lovingkindness will provide times ahead in which he can fulfill his dreams.

God will make it possible for him to praise Him even when the circumstances are not favorable. The song that will be with him "in the night" will be a prayer of gratitude. Nothing can keep him from offering to God a song of praise, not even the darkest of circumstances. He will not allow affliction to destroy his relationship with God. In the midst of pain, he will go to Him even more earnestly and implore Him for assistance. He refers to God as the **God of** [his] **life**. God has given him "life," and he knows that He will continue to sustain his life.

---

[1]James Moffatt, *A New Translation of the Bible* (New York: Harper & Brothers Publishers, 1954), 632.

PSALM 42

"WHY HAVE YOU FORGOTTEN ME?"
(42:9–11)

⁹I will say to God my rock, "Why have You forgotten me?
Why do I go mourning because of the oppression of the enemy?"
¹⁰As a shattering of my bones, my adversaries revile me,
While they say to me all day long, "Where is your God?"
¹¹Why are you in despair, O my soul?
And why have you become disturbed within me?
Hope in God, for I shall yet praise Him,
The help of my countenance and my God.

Verse 9. Great sorrow surfaces again, which gives rise to a new resolve. **I will say to God my rock, "Why have You forgotten me?"** His question means, "Why does God not remove my difficulties from me?" He further asks, **"Why do I go mourning because of the oppression of the enemy?"** "Why does He permit me to be in exile from the temple so long? Why does He allow me to be in a situation that causes me to be depressed by what I see and hear from those around me?" he moans.

Verse 10. When his foes reproach him, he is moved so deeply that it seems as if he is being crushed to death on the inside. **As a shattering of my bones, my adversaries revile me, while they say to me all day long, "Where is your God?"** It is as if his "bones" are broken into pieces by this burden of his grief. Hostile people argue that if he is truly a friend of God, his God would not leave him in this condition. He has heard a barrage of painful comments day by day. Their words are like fiery arrows that are sent into his heart, and they are about to kill him.

Verse 11. Again he questions his own heart in the deepest part of his being. **Why are you in despair, O my soul? And why have you become disturbed within me?** He realizes, as we all must, that the solution to his grief is to focus on his faith, and this will bolster his sagging and despondent spirit. He encourages himself by remembering what he believes. He says to himself, **Hope in God, for I shall yet praise Him, the help of my**

countenance and my God. Hope in God will provide for him the strength that he needs.

If what we believe does not *secure us in adversity*, it is not worthy to *sing about in prosperity*. He asks himself, "Why are you in despair? Why have you allowed this to disturb you so?" He is telling himself that he will trust God to bring him to the divine place of worship again. He believes that when God brings him into His presence in the future, he will be able to praise Him as he has in the past. He chooses to put his confidence in God. When the soul is worn down by disappointment, God revives it with an invitation to hope in Him.

The writer mentions the fellowship of God as his help and stay as he exhorts himself to trust in God. The glad assurance that he will be permitted to praise God in the future inspires him. He regards God as "the help" or salvation of his "countenance," the deliverance before his face. Through the recognition of God's presence and grace, his "countenance" has brightened from its saddened appearance brought on by his afflictions. He does not say, as so many do, "I will serve God in the future when I get past these troubles." He is choosing God to be His God in his present situation, even though he lives in undesirable surroundings and depressing discouragement.

APPLICATION

The Message for Us

What is the message for us in this psalm?

We are taught *that we must always look up to God.* The psalm pictures the emotional roller coaster that we sometimes ride when batted about by the forces around us that are opposed to God and His people. We may be submerged in the boisterous waves, but we must lift up our heads above the waters and look up to God. With every wave that engulfs us, we must remind ourselves that God is our hope. As again and again the waves come, we say to ourselves, "I am hoping in God." Each time we go under, we swim to the top with faith that God will see us through these trials—and faithfully, according to His own timing and methods, He does.

The second message is that *no one goes to heaven in a straight line.* Smooth seas will come, but periods of storm and persecution will also come. Living for God on a vacation spot where all is ideal will most likely not be true for any follower of God.

In fact, this psalm tells us *that trials may be our normal fair.* Jesus did not live in a secluded palace, shielded from the evil designs of men. In the midst of the sinister ordeal of temptation, He kept telling Himself, as does the psalmist, "God is My hope. Why should I be cast down, for God is with Me?" In the storm, the believer must look beyond adversity and see the hope that he has in God.

> Judge not the Lord by feeble sense,
> But trust Him for His grace;
> Behind a frowning providence,
> He hides a smiling face.[2]

Panting for God

The psalmist pictures himself with the metaphor of a deer panting for water. With tongue hanging out, the deer is roaming the land searching for water perhaps in the midst of a drought. He says that this is the kind of thirst he has for God. The figure is graphic and insightful.

We see a deep longing. The deer yearns for water. He knows that he must have it.

We see a desperate searching. Every moment he is looking for water. The search consumes him. He can think of nothing else.

We see a fervent persevering. He stays with the search until water is found. It is his one, conscious pursuit. If he does not find it, he will search for it until he falls lifelessly to the ground.

Perhaps all of these elements of the deer's search for water are included in what the writer has in mind regarding his search for God. He longs to be in God's presence. He searches for that opportunity. It is his one holy ambition.

---

[2]William Cowper, "God Moves in a Mysterious Way," *Songs of the Church*, comp. and ed. Alton H. Howard (West Monroe, La.: Howard Publishing Co., 1977).

Eager for God

The writer is longing to go to Jerusalem and engage in worship at the temple at one of the special prescribed times of worship. He is far removed from the temple and is unable to go, and being in such a situation breaks his spirit. He compares his yearning for God to *a deer craving water* (v. 1).

Other figures are used in the Scriptures to express this great longing for God. Consider three more.

Later in the Book of Psalms, we see this desire for God pictured as being *like a man craving water* (Ps. 63:1). You can see a man in the desert. His lips are cracked and his tongue is swollen. His whole body cries out for water. Unless he finds water he will die. Does our desire for God come anywhere near such a picture? Is our yearning for God just a temporary and fleeting ambition, or, does it possess us totally?

Our thirst for God is seen as being *like parched land crying out for water* (Ps. 143:6). The land is dry and cracked. The vegetation is dead, and the trees are brown. The dirt has grown hard and barren. Only one thing can give it life: water. Is your heart like that dry, dead land without water? Do you see God as the only source that can give life to your inner being?

You will remember that Jesus described our appetite for God and righteousness as being *like a man craving water and food* (Mt. 5:6). A man cannot live without them; a life-pursuit is being mentioned. Jesus pronounced a blessing upon the person who has such a desire. He sees the things of heaven as more important to him than food and water.

These figures help us to see the intensity and fervency of the writers of the Psalms for a relationship and a walk with God. They could not imagine being without Him. They longed for Him above all other concerns of life. May it be so with us!

An Appetite for God

Here is a passionate appetite for God. It behooves all of us to ask, "How is my appetite for Him?" Look at the writer's quest for God.

He yearned for God deeply. It moved him to tears. It was as if he would die without God. Is this true of us?

He yearned for God continually. It was a night and day longing. It did not go away. It did not subside with the passing of time.

He yearned for God with resolve. He was determined to do something about his need to worship. He was not going to just talk about it; he was going to act.

Do we yearn for God deeply, continually, and with resolve?

The Source of Strength

Three cardinal tenets of belief in God are singled out as sources of encouragement to the downcast soul: hope, God's lovingkindness, and God's presence.

Hope in God. Regardless of a person's circumstances, he can always hope in God. No storm, trial, or dark night can hide God's gleam of hope if we will look for it.

God's lovingkindness. Even though we have made mistakes, God will forgive. He will never turn away the penitent soul. God will believe in you long after you have given up on yourself.

God's presence. Wherever we might be, we can always be in God's presence. There is no place that He is not.

The darkest night cannot take from us these wonderful truths: We can hope in God, we can be forgiven, and we can be in God's glorious presence.

Hoping in God

The writer strengthens himself by telling himself to put his hope in God. What does it mean to hope in God?

Hope is believing that God is going to act. The one who is hoping in God knows by faith that God will do what He said He was going to do. Hope looks beyond our present circumstances and stands on the promises of God.

Hope springs from the stability of God's integrity. True hope cannot be based on anything but the truthfulness of God. Hope rests upon this unchangeable fact that God cannot lie.

Hope is expectant anticipation. Hope is Bible-based waiting. It expects through the authority of God's revelation that His promises will come to pass.

Hope grows out of and lives in harmony with faith. We are expectant, and we trust in God's goodness to fulfill His promises in His own time and in His own way. Faith accepts and acts upon what God has said.

When one is discouraged, he can help himself greatly by telling himself to "hope in God." This wonderful admonition reminds us to anticipate the future that God has promised with genuine faith.

Actual Worship

Through his mournful craving, the psalmist illustrates that people who are indifferent about worshiping God do not really know what worship is.

One who has personally experienced the holy communion with God that takes place in worshiping Him will not be flippant about any opportunity to engage in that worship, whether it be in private devotions or in public praise. The one who has a spiritual appetite, whose soul hungers for God, can only be satisfied by worshiping the God he loves. The deep longing of his soul compels him to pour out his praise and adoration to God.

We gain a different perspective on worship when the privilege of gathering to worship has been taken away. As the writer looks back, he remembers how happy were the occasions when he could worship God.

When Should We Worship?

Worship is the believer's life. His life is lived around it, and he devotes his energies to it. He loves God and seeks to worship and praise Him.

It is a superfluous question, but nonetheless let us ask it, "When should we worship?"

At God's appointed times. God has always given us guidelines and commands regarding His worship. In the Mosaical Age He specified times that His people were to come together for worship. The Christian Age has similar specifications. We are to be dedicated to these times. They should be times of wonder, beauty, and the highest significance to every believer. These times should be at the top of everyone's list of values.

When you have the opportunity. In addition to the designated times, we must make private time for worship. We may need to worship alone, but worship is a must. We always find a time and place to eat, whether we are with the family or not. Such should be the case with our commitment to worshiping God.

When circumstances are not conducive to worship. There will be times when we will be in circumstances that make it hard for us to worship, but we must find a way regardless of the situation. The writer found himself far removed from the temple. He yearned to be nearer, but his aspirations could not be fulfilled. He had to go with what he had and worship where he was. Often this will be the case with us.

The worship of our God should be one of the highest moments of our lives. We should never allow it to be a burden. It is a time of special fellowship with our Father, a time of thanksgiving and rejoicing. No believer should allow these times to slip from him.

Talking Yourself out of Discouragement

The writer asks himself, as all of us at times should, "Why are you cast down, O my soul?" He talks to himself and encourages himself with what he believes. We should often ask ourselves, "Do we really believe our beliefs?" We could even ask ourselves, "Do my beliefs hold me up, or do I hold them up?"

If you faithfully trust in God, you can talk yourself out of discouragement. When you are downcast, ask yourself these questions:

"Am I not walking with God?" Why should we doubt our relationship with God? Have we not become His children, and are we not living for Him? If we are honest in our relationship with God, then we know that we are doing His will.

"Will God not keep His promises?" Why should I be discouraged? Do I not know that God is faithful? He will keep every promise He has made to me. I must get my mind off my circumstances and place it on God's integrity. I must look at His promises, not at my problems. The circumstances around me may deny the truth of God's faithfulness, but God is greater than any of my circumstances. He cannot lie to me or to anyone else.

"Is God not good?" His basic nature is goodness. Do I not believe that God will always seek my best interest? Will He not look out for me? He will be with me, and He will use whatever situation I am in to increase my faith and maturity in Him. He encircles His children with His constant love and care. I have no reason to doubt His goodness even when I am in the worst of conditions.

When we stop and think about what we believe, we will conclude that we have no reason to be discouraged, regardless of how dark the night is that surrounds us. We can look at our trials and say, "My soul, remember that I am walking with God, that He will always keep His promises, and that He is continually seeking my growth and maturity. You have no reason at all to be downcast!"

If you are discouraged, talk yourself out of it by resolving to believe your beliefs!

Psalm 43
"Bring Me to Your Temple"

Superscription: None.
Every psalm in Book II has a title except this psalm. Perhaps this is the case because at the time these ancient titles were being added to the psalms, 42 and 43 comprised one psalm. Since the majority of the Hebrew manuscripts and the ancient versions of the Scriptures present the two as separate psalms, we will view them as distinct also.

The fact that this psalm is similar to Psalm 42 in content, language, and style may indicate that the two psalms were composed by the same writer and for the same reason. They have basically the same theme, make the same requests of God, and use the same refrain: "Why are you in despair, O my soul?" (42:5a, 11a; 43:5a).

The psalm is made up of three short, passionate petitions. The writer is being severely afflicted by the adversaries of God and His people. They are scorning him and making sport of his faith. They ridicule him by saying that his God has forgotten him, and this taunt has brought him the most misery. Coupled with the pain inflicted by his foes is his sorrow over being separated from God's chosen place of worship. He prays fervently, therefore, that he might worship God in Jerusalem once again.

To "feel with" the writer, picture yourself in a foreign land, among people who do not believe in God, who scoff at you because you cling to your faith in Him. Within you is an intense struggle about worshiping God at His appointed place and in His appointed way. When these woes are combined and poured into the life of the psalmist, they produce a heart that is burdened with painful emotions like sorrow, disappointment, loneliness, misunderstanding, and a sense of separation from God.

When a person is in this type of emotional matrix, what are his real needs? How should he pray? Let us see.

"VINDICATE ME" (43:1, 2)

¹Vindicate me, O God, and plead my case against an ungodly nation;
O deliver me from the deceitful and unjust man!
²For You are the God of my strength; why have You rejected me?
Why do I go mourning because of the oppression of the enemy?

Verse 1. The psalmist, wanting confirmation that he is in the right, prays, **Vindicate me, O God, and plead my case against an ungodly nation.** Believing that he is walking in the faith, he wants God to defend his cause. He knows that he is not guilty of the charges his enemies are making against him, and he wants his integrity to be made known.

Using the imagery of a heavenly court, picturing God as both his defense counsel and his Judge, he asks that his "case" against the ungodly be upheld. Those around him are contending against him with sinister lies, saying his faith is baseless and useless. The "ungodly nation" around him, unfaithful Jews or pagan Gentiles, is hurling the most hurtful insults at him. He knows that their accusations are untrue. He has confidence that every promise of God is trustworthy. However, he wants his faithful relationship with God vindicated and made public.

He further prays, **O deliver me from the deceitful and unjust man!** Any genuinely righteous man will desire that his name be cleared of false accusations. He will be concerned when others' remarks reflect upon his faith and upon his God. We are not surprised, then, that the psalmist's first request is that he be exonerated.

Attacked without mercy, he thinks, "Enough is enough!" The men around him are "deceitful" and do not care about the truth.

They are "unjust" men who have no sense of fairness or rightness. Collectively, they are an inhuman nation, given over to the mistreatment of others and dishonesty. They are not his kind of people, and the writer wants to be removed from them. He prays that God will deliver him from these wicked men.

Verse 2. He says, **For You are the God of my strength; why have You rejected me?** God is his stronghold, refuge, and strength; but what is happening to him seems to contradict what he believes about God. If God is a great source of strength to him, why is he in so much trouble? Has God forgotten His promise to protect and care for him? It seems that God has cast him off, thrown him away like some repulsive object. In the previous psalm, he asked why God had "forgotten" him (Ps. 42:9), but here he uses the word "rejected" (זנח, *zanach*).

Out of heaviness of heart, he asks, **Why do I go mourning because of the oppression of the enemy?** He respectfully asks God why he has to go about filled with the anguish he is experiencing at the hands of wicked people.

His prayer is a kind of dialogue with God. Like Job, he inquires of God regarding his predicament (see Job 7:20, 21; 10:2). He has been beaten down by his circumstances, and his cry for help to God takes the form of questions about why this tragedy has happened to him. He has not plunged into doubt, but he is perplexed about what he has seen and felt. His bewilderment surfaces throughout his prayer.

"GUIDE ME" (43:3–5)

³O send out Your light and Your truth, let them lead me;
Let them bring me to Your holy hill
And to Your dwelling places.
⁴Then I will go to the altar of God,
To God my exceeding joy;
And upon the lyre I shall praise You, O God, my God.
⁵Why are you in despair, O my soul?
And why are you disturbed within me?
Hope in God, for I shall again praise Him,
The help of my countenance and my God.

Verse 3. He appeals to God to lead him saying, **O send out Your light and Your truth, let them lead me.** Clouded by the confusion in his heart and the loud jeers of the wicked, he asks God for guidance on how to face his trials. He yearns to be clear-headed about what God wants him to do.

He pleads for two angels of mercy to be sent to him: "light" and "truth." He wants God to provide a special manifestation of His face and will as an expression of His guidance. Personifying "light" and "truth," he thinks of them as kind helpers who can lead him out of the difficulty he is in. He knows that God has them, and he wants them to be in his life more fully. "Light" must refer to the glory of God's countenance, the sunshine of His presence, the brilliance of His favor. Shrouded in the darkness of persecution, the writer prays for the "light" of God's face to shine upon him so that he might be more conscious of His presence and His way.

"Truth" would refer to God's reliability and faithfulness. He wants to know and be directed by God's unerring will.

He says, **Let them bring me to Your holy hill and to Your dwelling places.** One of his innermost longings is to be granted the pleasure of returning to Jerusalem so that he can worship God in the divinely chosen place. The "holy hill" he mentions is Zion, where the temple is located. "Your dwelling places" (מִשְׁכַּן, *mishkan*) refers to the Holy Place, the Holy of Holies, and the ark of the covenant, the symbolic dwelling places of God.

Verse 4. He envisions a time of wonderful worship at the temple. He says, **Then I will go to the altar of God, to God my exceeding joy; and upon the lyre I shall praise You, O God, my God.**

These petitions imply that the author is exiled from Jerusalem for some reason and eagerly seeking to return in order to worship God as he has in the past. If this part of his prayer is granted, his request to be brought to Jerusalem, he will go immediately to the temple and offer the appropriate sacrifices required by God. He refers to God as "the God, the joy of [his] joy" (גִּילִי שִׂמְחַת אֶל־אֵל, *'el 'el śimchath gili*), an expression exhibiting the gladness he has in God. He will unite with others in giving God the worship He desires and deserves. Walking with

God, worshiping God, and telling others about God will bring him what he considers his highest happiness.

Verse 5. Encouraged by the thought of God's answering His prayers and granting him the privilege of worshiping in Jerusalem again, he strengthens his heart by asking a question he has asked three times before (Ps. 42:5, 6, 11): **Why are you in despair, O my soul? And why are you disturbed within me?** He comes to the same answer that he reached earlier, and he tells himself to do the most important thing he can do: "Hope in God."

He believes that God will hear his prayer. He says, **For I shall again praise Him.** Indeed, he says, "I will praise **the help of my countenance and my God.**" He believes he will be privileged to go to Jerusalem and worship the One who gives life and light to his "countenance" or face. He speaks of God as the salvation of his face (יְשׁוּעֹת פָּנַי, *yᵉshu'oth panay*).

His deep desire is to go to Jerusalem once again. He longs to worship there as he has in past days. He ends his psalm on the high note of faith, with the radiant belief that God will provide him with the opportunity that he seeks. He can have such confidence in God because he knows that God is faithful to provide for those who put their trust in Him. He looks at his request as if the request has already been granted.

A postscript: We are not informed in this psalm whether or not the writer ever returned to Jerusalem. We can rest assured that God answered his prayer in harmony with His will and in harmony with the writer's need and faith.

APPLICATION

What's It All About?

This brief psalm shows the prayer of someone in the turmoil of despair and criticism. His problem was twofold: His faith was besieged, and he was unable to worship God as he desired. How did he handle his dilemma? He brought his situation to God.

He prayed for vindication. He wanted everyone to know that he was right in his faith. Since he had been unjustly accused, he wanted God to make known to all that he had been righteous.

He prayed for deliverance. He wanted to escape the snares of the wicked. He believed that being caught in the traps of the evil people around him would reflect upon the reputation of his God. He could not stand this thought.

He prayed for guidance. He wanted to be led by God and have the confirmation that He was in God's will. This could only happen if truth and light became his companions.

What other solution is there? When one is falsely accused, when one is surrounded by evil, what can he do? Should he not pray for vindication, deliverance, and guidance?

Prayer and Faith

With his prayer concluded, he went back to the refrain that appeared twice in the previous psalm (Ps. 42:5, 11): "Why are you in despair, O my soul?" (v. 5a). Praying focuses our minds on what we believe about God. One *will not* pray unless he believes in God; one *cannot* pray without articulating his beliefs about God. Putting our trust in God into action drives away our fears and causes us to relax in the confidence we have in God.

After You Pray

The writer ended this psalm by talking to himself. In the early part of the psalm he was conversing with God; at the end of it he was having a dialogue with himself. He was saying, "If you believe what you've been saying in your prayer, why are you downcast? Quit complaining. Live the way you believe." We should not talk to ourselves when we pray (Lk. 18:10–12); but we should talk to ourselves after we pray and tell ourselves that we will think the way we have prayed.

When in trouble, pray that you are right with God, that you will stay right with Him, and that you will see His righteousness regardless of your circumstances. After praying, tell yourself to believe and live the faith that motivated you to pray that prayer.

How Do We See God?

Note how the writer of this psalm sees God, and ask yourself, "How do I see God?"

"*O God, my God.*" Do you have a personal relationship with Him? Do you just know facts about God? When you think of God, do you see only a system of religion, or do you see God as your personal, heavenly Father? Have you made a commitment to walk with Him and love Him?

"*O God, my exceeding joy.*" Do you find your great joy in God? Is He the gladness of your heart? Do you run to be with Him?

"*O God, my strength.*" Do you find your power for living in God? When overwhelmed, do you first call out for His strength?

"*O God, my Vindicator.*" Do you place before God your situations for Him to judge and analyze? Is He your first and foremost critic?

"*O God, my Guide.*" Do you long for His truth and light? Is God the One who teaches you the way to live?

The big issue of life is this, "Is God truly God to us?" This is a personal matter. The writer has given his answer to this question. What answer will we give to it?

God Leading Us

The writer asked God to lead him. He said, "O send out Your light and Your truth, let them lead me" (v. 3a). He found himself in a difficult strait, and he needed God's guidance.

His request raises the question "How does God lead us?" Two ways are evident in this passage.

He leads us by His person. We can look at God's love, work, and aspirations and see how we are to live. One big part of our Savior's mission was to show us the Father (Jn. 14:9). He has revealed the Father clearly to us so that we can imitate Him. We want to be like Him. He leads us with His example. When in doubt on what to do, just do what God would do.

He leads us by His precepts. He has given us His Word to shape our thinking and point out the path for our footsteps. His will in our hands allows us to think God's thoughts after Him.

When struggles come, cry out for God's guidance—His light and His truth. He answers those who ask for guidance with the light of His Person (as reflected through Jesus) and the truth of His Word (as given in the Scriptures).

PSALM 44

IN THE ABSENCE OF MIGHTY WORKS

The Superscription: For the choir director. A Maskil of the sons of Korah. The title gives guidance to **the choir director** (לַמְנַצֵּחַ, *lamnatstseach*). Further, it says the composition is **a Maskil** [מַשְׂכִּיל] **of the sons of Korah** (לִבְנֵי־קֹרַח, *libney qorach*). Thus, according to this heading, the psalm was used by the temple singers. As a "maskil" psalm, this piece perhaps was used in teaching the patience of faith.

Considered a national lament, this prayer was prayed by someone at a time when Israel had suffered a defeat or a series of defeats. The nation's bewilderment over the humiliation of their setback is its burden. The writer's question is "Why has the great and awesome God of past victories not brought us similar current victories?"

We do not know what event or events form the background to the psalm. Consequently, dating the psalm is extremely difficult, if not impossible. The context suggests that Israel had a standing army, existed as an independent nation, and occasionally went to war against the hostile nations around her. These indications would require a date sometime during the monarchy. After being written, this song/prayer was probably used at junctures when the nation was concerned about the cessation of God's blessings upon them.

Underlying the psalm is the theology of the workings of God. The believer, sooner or later, must accept the truth that God does not always act in a public, demonstrative, clearly-observed way. When He works quietly and behind the scenes, we are put to the test to trust in Him even though we do not see His hand taking care of our affairs. At such times, we "must trust His heart," as someone has said, "even though we cannot trace His hand."

HE HAS WORKED BY MIRACLES (44:1–3)

¹O God, we have heard with our ears,
Our fathers have told us
The work that You did in their days,
In the days of old.
²You with Your own hand drove out the nations;
Then You planted them;
You afflicted the peoples,
Then You spread them abroad.
³For by their own sword they did not possess the land,
And their own arm did not save them,
But Your right hand and Your arm and the light of Your
 presence,
For You favored them.

Verse 1. The writer begins with the observation that God has worked miraculously and supernaturally in behalf of His people in the past. Verses 1 through 8 comprise a beautiful hymn of praise to God for defending Israel in their previous illustrious history.

He prays, **O God, we have heard with our ears, our fathers have told us the work that You did in their days, in the days of old.** He has been the recipient of marvelous stories that have been passed down by the forefathers, thrilling narratives that relate what God has done in the former days for His people.

Verse 2. Becoming more specific, he remembers and recounts what God did to bring Israel into the land of Canaan. **You with Your own hand drove out the nations; then You planted them; You afflicted the peoples, then You spread them abroad.** Emphatically, he says, "You, with Your hand, drove out the nations." In the conquest of Canaan God dispossessed the Canaanites, the Hittites, the Girgashites, the Amorites, the Perizzites, the Hivites, and the Jebusites (Deut. 7:1) before Israel so they could receive the promise that had been made to them. No specific battle is mentioned, but this verse and the next must refer to God's deliverance of Jericho and other cities into the hands of Joshua (see Josh. 6; 7).

Furthermore, he says, "You afflicted the peoples, then You spread them abroad." He "afflicted" or defeated the people of the land and drove them out into other lands beyond Palestine.

Verse 3. Any observant student of sacred history can see that God had fought their battles for them. **For by their own sword they did not possess the land, and their own arm did not save them, but Your right hand and Your arm and the light of Your presence, for You favored them.** The conquered cities and nations were not destroyed by the "sword" of Israel, but by the strong "arm" of their God. The Lord had spread Israel throughout the Promised Land as if He were planting a garden (see also Ex. 15:17; 2 Sam. 7:10; Ps. 80:8).

Mighty works had been performed for the Israelites because they were the objects of God's favor and grace, His chosen nation. He granted them His personal "presence," causing His face of blessing to shine fully upon them. Israel was chosen because of who God is, not because of the nation's character.

AN EXPRESSION OF FAITH (44:4–8)

⁴You are my King, O God;
Command victories for Jacob.
⁵Through You we will push back our adversaries;
Through Your name we will trample down those who
    rise up against us.
⁶For I will not trust in my bow,
Nor will my sword save me.
⁷But You have saved us from our adversaries,
And You have put to shame those who hate us.
⁸In God we have boasted all day long,
And we will give thanks to Your name forever. Selah.

Verse 4. The psalm moves from praising God for helping Israel in the past to a present statement of faith. **You are my**

PSALM 44

King, O God; command victories for Jacob. The Israelites of old had demonstrated faith, and those of the writer's time are following in their footsteps with the same type of faith, looking to God to be their sovereign Lord and great Commander.

Verse 5. They see God as their Warrior King. The writer says, **Through You we will push back our adversaries; through Your name we will trample down those who rise up against us.** Through God they will "push back" and "trample down" somewhat like a wild animal would when in the midst of conflict. Their aggressors are pictured as "adversaries" and as "those who rise up against" them.

God is in charge of their conflicts. He will choose the battles they will fight and will select the enemies they will overrun. In His strength, in His name, they will defeat their foes. The Israelites have placed themselves in God's hands.

Verse 6. The writer, like all true believers, can make a confession of faith. **For I will not trust in my bow, nor will my sword save me.** His faith is in God alone—not in the human arm or in military might, not in the "bow," the arrow, or the "sword."

Verse 7. God has been their deliverer in the past. He says, **You have saved us from our adversaries, and You have put to shame those who hate us.** God is the One who has brought about their conquests over those who opposed them. They have seen His might. He has completely routed their enemies, putting them to the "shame" of defeat.

Verse 8. Therefore, God has been their boast. They have been careful to give God the glory, dedicating themselves to giving thanks for the way He has given them victories and successes. **In God we have boasted all day long, and we will give thanks to Your name forever.** Their resolve is to praise Yahweh as their great Benefactor, and they have determined that this praise will continually rise up from their hearts and lips. The word for "boasted" (הָלַל, *halal*) comes from the word for "praise," not "brag." In God was their praise.

Selah most likely marks a pause for careful consideration.

Thus the first few verses of this prayer extol God for His miracles of the past. Bringing to remembrance such wonders bolsters anyone's faith and leaves him singing God's praises.

THE MATTER OF UNANSWERED PRAYERS (44:9–16)

⁹Yet You have rejected us and brought us to dishonor,
And do not go out with our armies.
¹⁰You cause us to turn back from the adversary;
And those who hate us have taken spoil for themselves.
¹¹You give us as sheep to be eaten
And have scattered us among the nations.
¹²You sell Your people cheaply,
And have not profited by their sale.
¹³You make us a reproach to our neighbors,
A scoffing and a derision to those around us.
¹⁴You make us a byword among the nations,
A laughingstock among the peoples.
¹⁵All day long my dishonor is before me
And my humiliation has overwhelmed me,
¹⁶Because of the voice of him who reproaches and reviles,
Because of the presence of the enemy and the avenger.

God has worked miraculously and providentially for Israel in the previous years. The writer has praised God for these glorious deeds as he lays the groundwork for a special appeal that he is eager to make.

As the psalm turns from Israel's past to the present, the writer wrestles with the silence and aloofness of God. He says, "Lord, I have a problem!" He wonders why he cannot see the mighty hand of God defending the Israelites in his day as He did in the past. "Where are the miracles I have heard about? Where is Your mighty power?" he asks. What he fails to see God doing becomes more and more detailed as the psalm unfolds.

Verse 9. It looks to him that God has turned away from them. **Yet You have rejected us and brought us to dishonor, and do not go out with our armies.** He thinks of God as rejecting His people, forcing them to face their enemies with merely their own

PSALM 44

strength; and this fact has resulted in their defeat.

Verse 10. It seems to him that God has brought about their downfall. **You cause us to turn back from the adversary; and those who hate us have taken spoil for themselves.** Because they have gone to battle without God's help, he argues, they have been beaten and embarrassed.

Verse 11. Using exaggerated emphasis that is characteristic of Hebrew poetry, he compares Israel to sheep being sent to the slaughter. **You give us as sheep to be eaten and have scattered us among the nations.** They were given to the enemy like "food" (מַאֲכָל, *ma'akal*) would be given to a wild animal. After being overcome, Israel's soldiers were scattered throughout Palestine, running for cover from the enemy. They were like people without a home.

Verse 12. By the use of another figure, he claims that God has sold them, as one sells people into slavery. **You sell Your people cheaply, and have not profited by their sale.** He depicts Israel as slaves being auctioned off to the highest bidder, declaring that God, the seller, made no profit from the sale. He was losing His worshipers and receiving nothing in exchange.

Verse 13. Furthermore, their defeat gives occasion for the enemy to laugh and make sport of God's people. **You make us a reproach to our neighbors, a scoffing and a derision to those around us.** Other nations are mocking Israel, saying with the most cutting jeer that they have no army. This part of the defeat hurts the most.

Verse 14. Israel is a reproach, a byword, throughout the land. **You make us a byword among the nations, a laughingstock among the peoples.** The word for "byword" (מָשָׁל, *mashal*) means "proverb" and suggests a comparison. The people near them are saying, "Israel is a classic illustration of a nation abandoned by her God." They have become the basis for the proverb "Who has been abandoned like Israel?"

The two Hebrew words translated "laughingstock" are "shaking [the] head" (מְנוֹד־רֹאשׁ, *m^enod ro'sh*). When Israel was thought of by the people, they would shake their heads in ridicule, dismay, or laughter.

Verses 15, 16. The embarrassment was unceasing. **All day**

long my dishonor is before me and my humiliation has overwhelmed me, because of the voice of him who reproaches and reviles, because of the presence of the enemy and the avenger. The Hebrew literally says, "The shame of my face covers me." It is an overwhelming embarrassment. Constantly humiliated, Israel is the object of criticism and the subject of derision. Enemies shake their heads and laugh to scorn God's chosen ones.

As an Israelite, the psalmist personally feels the shame of defeat. In addition, as the surrounding nations insult God's people, they dishonor God's name—and faithful Israelites resent such display of dishonor toward their God. The writer believes that "the reproaches of those who reproach You have fallen on me" (Ps. 69:9b).

WHAT IS HAPPENING? (44:17–26)

> [17] All this has come upon us, but we have not forgotten You,
> And we have not dealt falsely with Your covenant.
> [18] Our heart has not turned back,
> And our steps have not deviated from Your way,
> [19] Yet You have crushed us in a place of jackals
> And covered us with the shadow of death.
> [20] If we had forgotten the name of our God
> Or extended our hands to a strange god,
> [21] Would not God find this out?
> For He knows the secrets of the heart.
> [22] But for Your sake we are killed all day long;
> We are considered as sheep to be slaughtered.
> [23] Arouse Yourself, why do You sleep, O Lord?
> Awake, do not reject us forever.
> [24] Why do You hide Your face
> And forget our affliction and our oppression?
> [25] For our soul has sunk down into the dust;
> Our body cleaves to the earth.
> [26] Rise up, be our help,
> And redeem us for the sake of Your lovingkindness.

Verse 17. The psalmist takes his pain and disappointments to God. He asks God to tell him what is happening. Speaking for Israel, however, he pledges loyalty to God even though he and the people do not understand what He is doing. He says, **All this has come upon us, but we have not forgotten You, and we have not dealt falsely with Your covenant.** The plea for God to come to their rescue contains a reminder of their innocence and loyalty. Specifically, verses 17 and 18 mention their faithfulness to God's covenant, their commitment to His Word, and their loyalty to Him as the only true God.

Verse 18. Before God, he affirms their obedience to Him. **Our heart has not turned back, and our steps have not deviated from Your way.** The innocence that the psalmist claims is not absolute perfection or sinlessness, but an affirmation that he is unaware of any overt sins that would cause the afflictions that the Israelites had suffered. So far as he knows, there has been no national apostasy for which their present disasters would be a just punishment.

Verse 19. In spite of their obvious commitment to God, tragedies have beset them. He says, **Yet You have crushed us in a place of jackals and covered us with the shadow of death.** Their land is a deserted place because of the ravages of war. "A place of jackals" is a proverbial expression for a scene of desolation, a barren wilderness occupied by wild beasts (see Is. 13:22; 24:12, 13; Jer. 9:11; 10:22). Their country has been reduced to waste and devastation.

They were living in "the shadow of death" (צַלְמָוֶת, *tsalmaweth*). This word is sometimes translated "deep darkness"; it is the same word used in Psalm 23:4. It is used here to convey extreme darkness, a situation bordering on death.

Verse 20. If they are unfaithful to God, will He not make it known to them and rebuke them? **If we had forgotten the name of our God or extended our hands to a strange god....** "Surely," he maintains, "God would have stepped in with His rod of discipline if we had been rebellious to Him."

Verse 21. "Indeed," he further says, "had we departed from God, **would not God find this out? For He knows the secrets of the heart.**" God had not rebuked Israel for any sin. God knows the hidden thoughts of every heart; He knows their motivations and intentions. Thus the Heart-Knower would reprove Israel if their hearts were wicked.

Verse 22. In fact, their devotion has been demonstrated by their sacrifices. The psalmist says, **But for Your sake we are killed all day long; we are considered as sheep to be slaughtered.** Not only are the Israelites faithful in living for God, but they are figuratively enduring martyrdom for His cause. The Hebrew says, "Unto You we are [being] slain all day long." This expression of suffering is quoted in Romans 8:36, where Paul was reminding the Christians in Rome that they might have to face death for Christ's sake.

Verse 23. Having surveyed the condition of their hearts, the psalmist calls upon God to act: **Arouse Yourself, why do You sleep, O Lord? Awake, do not reject us forever.** He urges God to come immediately to Israel's defense. Anthropomorphically, applying human language to God, he speaks of God as being asleep. This figure of sleeping only suggests his perceived view of what God is doing. He feels deeply the need for God to act. In reality, he knows that the Keeper of His people has never dozed off as He has watched over them (see 121:3, 4).

Verse 24. The previous question about God's silence leads to another question: **Why do You hide Your face and forget our affliction and our oppression?** The psalmist uses the figure of God hiding His face to describe this apparent lack of attention. Since he thinks that God has not been working in their behalf, he says that God must be looking in another direction or has refused to see his needs.

Still another figure used is that of forgetting. "Why did You 'forget our affliction'?" he asks, as if the Lord has known about their trials but has let them slip from His mind.

God has been doing none of these things to Israel, but it seems to the psalmist that He has. This weary sufferer wonders in his prayer why God has not done more for His people.

Verse 25. These defeats have humbled them; they have brought them down to the dust in submission and mourning. He prays, **For our soul has sunk down into the dust; our body cleaves to the earth.** Their bodies join their souls in deep poverty of spirit. It is as if their bodies are lying prostrate in the dirt. Both expressions suggest oppression, embarrassment, and depression.

Verse 26. The final plea of the prayer is for God to come immediately to their support as their Redeemer, their only deliverer. He prays, **Rise up, be our help, and redeem us for the sake of Your lovingkindness.** Because of His "lovingkindness"—on the basis of who He is and the love He has for His people—the psalmist asks God to come to their rescue. He entreats God to be true to His character and save them.

A postscript: Did God answer this prayer? The psalm closes without indicating what God did. Our faith in God says that God answered it in His own time and in ways that are in accordance with His will and in harmony with the sincere faithful obedience of the ones who prayed it (Mt. 21:22; Mk. 11:24).

APPLICATION

Feeling Defeated?
The miracles of the plagues in Egypt (Ex. 7—13) and the crossing of the Red Sea (Ex. 14:21–31) were decisive and authentic, whether responded to by everyone or not. Each person who saw them either allowed them to humble his heart or harden it. They were events that drew a line and demanded, "You must get on one side or the other. Accept these wonders and believe in Yahweh as the true God, or reject them and rebel in your heart against the true God."

When God works silently, however, the evidence of His work is not as obvious. In a time of need, we may call out to God to assist us, but He may not seem to act. The classic illustration of God's silence in the Scriptures is Job. He prayed, yet no visible answer came. God was acting in Job's life, quietly and unobtrusively; but His actions were unknown to Job. We commend Job because he continued to believe even though he did not understand what God was doing with him.

Have you ever felt like this psalmist—that you were overrun because God did not go with you into battle, and you had to fight alone with your human strength? Have you ever said to God, "I really needed You; but as far as I can tell, You were not with me"?

All Christians on occasions are thrust into this type of trial. When these times come, remember the three ways that God works: by obvious miracles, by visible providence, and by silent providence.

Since He has given us His written Word, the age of miracles came to a close around the end of the first century (Heb. 2:3, 4; 1 Cor. 13:8). He will no longer make the sun stand still so that we can work longer for Him. The Scriptures imply that the day of miracles is past. The next time of miracles will be when Jesus comes again.

How then does He work today? He sometimes works by visible providence—by helping us in a way that is clear to all who have eyes to see. However, sometimes He works with His people by silent, invisible providence. During these moments we may wonder, as the psalmist did, if God is working in our lives at all.

Let us always remember that God is faithfully working in behalf of His children whether we see His hand or not. When you see His hand, rejoice in it; when you do not see His hand, trust Him!

Our Mandates and Mission

What should you do when you find yourself in a situation like the one in this psalm, a circumstance in which you cannot *see* God working? An answer is laid out by this psalm.

Pray. Thank Him for what He has done in the past for you and for His other family members.

Tell Him what you are going through. It is natural for a child of God to talk over his troubles with God.

Trust Him to see you through it. Remind yourself that God is working in your life even though you cannot see it.

The situation the psalmist was in was a tough and troubling time. He was walking with God in the dark. The biblical walk of faith includes walking with trust when we cannot see where we are going. When we are called upon to walk in the nighttime with God, let us not think that He has forgotten us or does not care for us.

The Theology of Suffering

When we are in the crucible of suffering, it helps to remember the different kinds of suffering that are mentioned in the Scriptures.

1. *The natural result of foolishness.* This type of suffering is illustrated in the parable and the proverb of poor investors (Mt. 25:14–30; Prov. 20:4).

2. *The God-allowed but Satan-sent persecution of believers.* This is illustrated by the troubles besetting the apostles in Acts.

3. *The God-sent punishment for disobedience.* This is illustrated by Korah and his rebellious company (Num. 16) and by Ananias and Sapphira (Acts 5:1–11).

4. *The God-sent discipline of believers.* This is illustrated by Moses' not being allowed to enter the Promised Land. This kind, like the one above, has a didactic purpose.

5. *The God-ordered suffering sent to edify but not caused by disobedience.* It does not aim at correction but at the glory of God and the building up of the saints. The man born blind (Jn. 9:3), the parable of the vine (Jn. 15:2), and Job illustrate this type.

6. *The suffering that results from the conflict between good and evil in this sin-cursed world.* As God's servants seek to do His will, they are opposed and hurt by sinful men. Joseph and Mary willingly yielded to God and became the parents of the Messiah; but when Jesus was born, His life was threatened by an insane Herod, causing Joseph and Mary to have to flee and lead a life of hardship in Egypt (Mt. 2). Even the innocent, such as the innocent babies killed by Herod, suffered as a result of the battle of righteousness and truth against evil.

The suffering being experienced by the psalmist in this psalm may have been the fifth type. God's silence did not mean that He had forsaken Israel; He was simply working out a part of His plan silently behind the scenes. Faithfulness to God is easy when a public victory is being celebrated and everyone can see what His mighty hand has done for His people. Faithfulness is more difficult—although sometimes it brings more glory to God—when a person trusts in Him and does His will even though he cannot see His hand or any immediate deliverance from the present suffering.

In the Midst of Suffering
When you are in the throes of pain, remember these statements:

When we cannot trace His hand, we can trust His heart. We will not always be able to see the actions of God. We know who God is and that we can trust in His goodness, even though we do not know what He is doing.

We should not doubt in the darkness what we have learned about God in the light. When we are enjoying His blessings and see how faithful He is, we are preparing for days during which we must believe even though we cannot see.

Being faithful is not always synonymous with being successful. Sometimes it will seem that we have been defeated. Witness Paul's preaching in Athens (see Acts 17:16–34). However, our business is to be faithful while we let God handle the results.

Perhaps thinking of these three statements will help us when we are walking by faith through the valley of the unknown.

When God Says No!
This psalm reminds us that God, for His own reasons, at times must say no to our prayers. In fact, the view that God will always say yes to our prayers is not a biblical teaching. Jesus said, "Whatever you ask in My name, that will I do" (Jn. 14:13). This implies that each request should be in harmony with God's will and not just some selfish whim.

Sometimes God says no because He has to. Why did He say no to the most fervent prayer ever prayed—the prayer of Jesus in the Garden (Mt. 26:39; Mk. 14:36; Lk. 22:42)? He had to (Jn. 12:27). There was no other way to save us. He will often have to say no to us for the same reason. If He always said yes to us, it could mean disaster for another child of His!

Sometimes God says no because it is best to. We may not be ready for the gift for which we have asked. It would not be for our good for Him to grant such a request. This is the confidence we have in God when we pray: we know that He will only grant what is best for us (1 Jn. 5:14).

Prayer would be a dangerous spiritual exercise if God granted every prayer that we pray. Most of the time we do not know what to ask of Him. We are like children in a superstore. They see toys, candy, and bicycles all around; and they just begin to ask for whatever is in sight, none of which they need. Wise parents respond to their requests by providing only what is needed and best. God has to deal with us in the same way.

Quietly Working

God's power was not always miraculously demonstrated in Old Testament times. Sometimes He chose to reveal His strength in providential ways. God did not rescue baby Moses from among the reeds in the Nile by a miracle; He did it with His providential oversight. He worked within the realm of nature, using Pharaoh's daughter to preserve Moses and give him the training needed for him to lead Israel out of bondage. Israel did not know what God was doing until eighty years later. We could call this action on God's part "His silent providence."

Today as well He works through His providence—through both His silent and visible providence. God's providing for us does not set aside the laws of nature, as His miracles did. Thus God's providence is not as flashy, decisive, direct, and confronting as His miraculous signs were. Through His providence, He moves in a somewhat mysterious way to perform His wonders.

This psalm highlights the miracles that God worked in the past. It does not mention His providence per se, but it implies it. The sweeping descriptions that are mentioned infer God's visible providence. Bringing Israel into a land which had standing grain, ripe and ready for them to eat (Josh. 5:12), is God's kind watch-care over His people. Indeed, back behind the scenes, undetected by the human eye and mind, were the silent actions of God. He has said no to our prayers, but invisible to us, He moves to accomplish His will in behalf of what is best for His children. Belief in this fact is a big part of what it means to walk by faith (2 Cor. 5:7).

The Mainspring of Life

Our thinking toward God will affect our attitudes and our actions, our will and our works, and our use of our tongues, talents, and treasures. Therefore, *the mainspring of life is our innermost thoughts about God.* If the source of the water, the spring, is poisoned, then the stream that flows out from it will be polluted.

One horrible result of God's being absent from the hearts of people is that they tend to abuse others. The unbeliever, rejecting his knowledge of right and wrong, devours others without thinking about his cruelty.

The key to proper living, then, is God and His will in the heart. More than facts are needed; the heart must have the love of God in it. When the heart is filled with the right beliefs, then the right attitudes and conduct naturally emerge from it.

PSALM 45

AN ODE TO A BEAUTIFUL WEDDING

The Superscription: For the choir director; according to the Shoshannim. A Maskil of the sons of Korah. A Song of Love. This robust title to the psalm includes five items of interest. First, it provides guidance **for the choir director** (לַמְנַצֵּחַ, *lamnatstseach*), the leader of one of the choirs for the temple.

Second, it says that the psalm is **according to** [or "upon"] **the Shoshannim** (עַל־שֹׁשַׁנִּים, *'al shoshannim*). The word "Shoshannim" is obscure to us but may mean "upon the lilies." It is the plural of *shushan* (שׁוּשַׁן) which means "lily." It may just refer to the tune to be used. This word appears in two other headings (69 and 80); and a variation of it, the singular form, is found in a third (60).

Third, the psalm belongs to **the sons of Korah** (לִבְנֵי־קֹרַח, *libney qorach*), a reference that indicates that it was written by one of the "sons of Korah" or that it was grouped with the songs used by them in the temple worship.

Fourth, the title says that this song is **a Maskil** (מַשְׂכִּיל) psalm, or a psalm likely used for "instruction." Fifth, it is said to be **a Song of Love** (שִׁיר יְדִידֹת, *shir y^edidoth*), which relates to the theme that the psalm presents.

No hymn book would be complete without a nuptial song. This psalm might be said to fill that role. It could be labeled "Wedding Music."

The message of it rejoices over the marriage of a king to a king's daughter. In the sense of its relation to a king, it would be classified as a royal psalm.

We do not know whose marriage the psalm was written to celebrate—whether it was Solomon's or someone else's. Possibly, it was read or sung as part of Israel's royal weddings.

As is true of the Song of Songs, this song reminds us of the beauty, dignity, and sacredness of human love. Interpreters often allegorize its images into a picture of God and Israel or Christ and the church. While it can be used to illustrate these divine relationships, the most obvious interpretation is that of seeing it as rejoicing over the wonder and joy of marital love in the context of a royal wedding.

Marriage was and is part of God's plan for the happiness of the family. In His infinite wisdom, He has made the home the cornerstone of society. Implied in this song is the truth that love, sex, marriage, the home, a lasting commitment between a man and a woman, and the sheer joy of a man and a woman being together in loving companionship are all gifts of God. He gave these blessings to us because He wanted us to live in an environment of fellowship, belonging, and acceptance, and to be encouraged and loved while we do His work. The presence of the home in this world indicates that God not only wanted to provide for our needs, but He also wanted to give us enjoyment and a haven of earthly love and peace.

A GOOD THEME (45:1, 2)

> ¹**My heart overflows with a good theme;**
> **I address my verses to the King;**
> **My tongue is the pen of a ready writer.**
> ²**You are fairer than the sons of men;**
> **Grace is poured upon Your lips;**
> **Therefore God has blessed You forever.**

Verse 1. The penman's heart tingles with excitement as he writes this psalm about the king's marriage. He says, **My heart overflows with a good theme**. The topic about which he is writing causes his heart to bubble with joy. The KJV says that his heart is "inditing [writing] a good matter." The Hebrew just has "My heart overflows" (רָחַשׁ לִבִּי, *rachash libi*). As he pens the words of his song, his heart rejoices over the lovely thoughts that the song will contain.

The way the psalm has been divided the first verse is the writer's introduction, and the last verse is his conclusion. Between these two bookends, he presents his message concerning the wedding. He refers to himself in both his introduction and conclusion.

He has a special person in mind as he records his words. He says, **I address my verses to the King**. His composition's central focus is the king, and he is ready and eager to put it together. He has much to say, and he wants to get started: **My tongue is the pen of a ready writer.** Words and sentences crowd into his mind, begging to be expressed. His fingers cannot record rapidly enough the beautiful words and pictures flooding his mind.

Verse 2. He describes the king as the most handsome of men. **You are fairer than the sons of men**, he says. In an ancient Semitic wedding, the man was emphasized more than the woman. Especially would this be true of the marriage of a king or a king's son. The guests at the wedding wait anxiously to see the bridegroom—how he would be dressed, how many attendants he would have, and how they would look.

His subjects look upon this bridegroom with love and thankfulness. **Grace is poured upon Your lips**, they say. The king's countenance radiates "grace" or favor and kindliness through his smile, his overall facial expressions, and his well-chosen words. Because of how he lives and who he is, he will be especially led by God. Indeed, it is as if his endowments from above have already been bestowed. **Therefore God has blessed You forever**, they sing. The bridegroom is admired by all. He is intelligent and gracious—because God has "blessed" him. As he continues in the path of goodness, God will continue to put His hand of favor on him.

FOR TRUTH AND RIGHTEOUSNESS
(45:3–7)

³**Gird Your sword on Your thigh, O Mighty One,
In Your splendor and Your majesty!**

⁴And in Your majesty ride on victoriously,
For the cause of truth and meekness and righteousness;
Let Your right hand teach You awesome things.
⁵Your arrows are sharp;
The peoples fall under You;
Your arrows are in the heart of the King's enemies.
⁶Your throne, O God, is forever and ever;
A scepter of uprightness is the scepter of Your kingdom.
⁷You have loved righteousness and hated wickedness;
Therefore God, Your God, has anointed You
With the oil of joy above Your fellows.

Verse 3. With the defense of the kingdom in mind, the king is described. He is asked to prepare himself for battle: **Gird Your sword on Your thigh, O Mighty One, in Your splendor and Your majesty!** As the leader of his people, he is to put on his sword and ride out arrayed in the armor and colors for battle.

Verse 4. Such a princely person is viewed as synonymous with victory. **And in Your majesty ride on victoriously**, the song says. He is encouraged to do what he has been appointed to do—to lead, defend, and sustain God's people in truth, meekness, and righteousness.

The king is God's earthly "chosen one" to lead His people in His will. **For the cause of truth and meekness and righteousness**, he is to go forth. God's people are to be meek, submissive to His laws. God's king in Israel is likewise to be committed to "truth" and "righteousness," and he is to direct his nation to be under God's leadership. Such obedience calls for a humble spirit. He has two supreme obligations: to make sure that God's people remain faithful to God and to see that they are not treated unjustly.

The focus of the celebration now dovetails into rejoicing in the king's strength. **Let Your right hand teach You awesome things**, they say. The expression "Your right hand" symbolizes the king's power and superb abilities. He will exercise his valor, and all will see and marvel at his talent and skill. They will look at his "right hand" and learn important lessons about how to lead a nation.

Verse 5. They will see how deadly his arrows are. **Your arrows are sharp.** Those who look at him in his regal power will conclude that anyone is foolish who ventures out to do battle with him. **The peoples fall under You; Your arrows are in the heart of the King's enemies.** They will be impressed by his strength, by the fact that he is a mighty warrior who will be difficult to defeat in conflict. He has been victorious over numerous nations and has successfully defended his kingdom from its enemies.

Verse 6. Embedded in this description of the king is integrity: **Your throne, O God, is forever and ever.** He is God's king; his standards are truth and righteousness; he is a leader of the submissive people of God. As God's earthly representative—the one whom God has appointed, a king who is committed to the truth of God—his throne is invincible. Its influence will endure "forever." **A scepter of uprightness is the scepter of Your kingdom.** The "scepter" that he holds in his hand, the sign of his royal authority, is moral correctness.

Verse 7. The truth will guide the king, and "righteousness" will be the standard by which he will rule in the affairs of his kingdom. It can be said of him, **You have loved righteousness and hated wickedness.** He is motivated by two emotions: love and hate. Because he loves righteousness and hates iniquity, God has chosen him to be His king. **Therefore God, Your God, has anointed You with the oil of joy above Your fellows.** By anointing him, God has separated him from his "fellows" and has given him unique and awesome responsibilities.

Verses 6 and 7 are quoted from the LXX in Hebrews 1:8, 9 and are applied to the Messiah. There can be no doubt about the application that is made in Hebrews, for the quotation is introduced with the identifying words "But of the Son He says, . . ." (Heb. 1:8). The psalm must be expressing the king's superlative qualities in poetic exaggeration and in terms of the ideal attributes of a king. As the writer gives his description, he prefigures in prophecy the King who will possess these traits in perfection, the coming Messiah.

If this interpretation of the way the passage is used in Hebrews is correct, then the earthly king, the dominant topic of the psalm, is being described in the elevated words of idealism. On the occasion of his wedding, he is being portrayed as a man of integrity and moral purity—the only kind of man God would choose as His king. The king described has the traits that God wants to exist in each person, especially in His king. However, on a higher level, the idealized picture of the king is a pictorial prophecy concerning the Messiah who would possess these traits in actuality, perfection, and truth.

THE BEAUTY OF THE BRIDEGROOM
(45:8, 9)

⁸All Your garments are fragrant with myrrh and aloes and cassia;
Out of ivory palaces stringed instruments have made You glad.
⁹Kings' daughters are among Your noble ladies;
At Your right hand stands the queen in gold from Ophir.

Verse 8. The bridegroom is wonderfully arrayed for his marriage. The song says of him, **All Your garments are fragrant with myrrh and aloes and cassia**. His festive clothes are saturated with costly perfumes brought from distant lands. "Myrrh" (מֹר, *mor*) is a resin product from Arabia; "aloes" (אֲהָלוֹת, *ᵃhaloth*) is the perfumed wood of an Indian tree; "cassia" (קְצִיעוֹת, *qᵉtsi'oth*) is a spice of cinnamon or the "koost" of India. As these oriental spices migrated, their names traveled with them into the Hebrew language; their original names are somewhat identical with the Hebrew words used for them. In addition to the spices giving their aroma to the occasion, gifts have been brought or sent to recognize the significance of the event.

The procession of the wedding party begins: **Out of ivory palaces stringed instruments have made You glad.** As the bridegroom moves with his entourage out of the palaces inlaid with ivory, he is greeted with music carefully chosen for this ceremony. "Stringed instruments" has been added by the translators as an interpretive reading of the text. No specific reference is made to "stringed instruments." The Hebrew simply says "has made you glad" (שִׂמְּחוּךָ, *simmᵉchuka*). The occasion, the circumstance, has brought great joy to the bridegroom.

Verse 9. Renowned people have come to be a part of the wedding: **Kings' daughters are among Your noble ladies; at Your right hand stands the queen in gold from Ophir.** Among these important guests who are present at the wedding are the "kings' daughters," "noble ladies," and other dignitaries, including "the queen." The NIV translates שֵׁגַל (*shegal*) "royal bride," while the NASB renders it "queen." The bride, the queen, stands at the bridegroom's right hand, resplendent with garments lined with gold from "Ophir." The aroma, the opulent circumstance, the ornate apparel worn by all, the gifts given, and the music in the air combine to make the celebration an elaborate and unforgettable event.

The wedding, the marriage of the king to a king's daughter, is one of the great celebrations of the nation. It captures the interest of each citizen and inspires the most detailed plans and decorations. We should allow the beauty of the king's wedding to remind us to make our marriage special—not only in its beginning, but also in its daily continuation.

With this psalmist, we can rejoice with the bride of a man who possesses these attributes that have been mentioned in an abundant measure. We can congratulate the woman who has become the wife of an honest man; just as we pity the woman who pledges her life to a man who is a stranger to the principles of moral truth and excellence.

INSTRUCTIONS AND GLORY
(45:10–15)

¹⁰Listen, O daughter, give attention and incline your ear:
Forget your people and your father's house;
¹¹Then the King will desire your beauty.
Because He is your Lord, bow down to Him.
¹²The daughter of Tyre will come with a gift;
The rich among the people will seek your favor.

> ¹³**The King's daughter is all glorious within;**
> **Her clothing is interwoven with gold.**
> ¹⁴**She will be led to the King in embroidered work;**
> **The virgins, her companions who follow her,**
> **Will be brought to You.**
> ¹⁵**They will be led forth with gladness and rejoicing;**
> **They will enter into the King's palace.**

Verse 10. The bride is receiving instruction, and she is asked to listen carefully to what she is being told. **Listen, O daughter, give attention and incline your ear.** Her life is about to change, and she should be aware of this dramatic transformation. She is given two instructions: to leave and to cleave. **Forget your people and your father's house.** Her "people" and her "father's house" are to be forgotten. In other words, she cannot look back with a longing heart at the family from which she came. This marriage will change her; she is becoming one with the bridegroom. Two people from two different homes are merging into a solemn union, and a new royal family is being born.

Verse 11. She is told to look to her husband as her head, giving him the appropriate respect. If this is done, she is told, **the King will desire your beauty.** Devotion to her husband will win and keep his tender affection, and her charms and graces will be his delight. She is told, **Because He is your Lord, bow down to Him.** She is to honor him as her head (see Eph. 5:23; 1 Cor. 11:1–4). Furthermore, she is to recognize him as her king.

Verse 12. As a faithful wife/queen, her reputation will spread far and wide. **The daughter of Tyre will come with a gift; the rich among the people will seek your favor.** She will receive the congratulations and applause of people and nations. Tokens of love and appreciation will come to her from afar.

Verse 13. The bride is described as the most attractive of all the lovely women. **The King's daughter is all glorious within; her clothing is interwoven with gold.** Lavishly attired, the bride is exquisiteness personified. Beauty radiates from what she is wearing, the personality and inner spirit she exhibits, and the arrangement and structure of the gathering.

Verse 14. The procession featuring the queen as its center will emerge and approach the king. **She will be led to the King in embroidered work; the virgins, her companions who follow her, will be brought to You.** In harmony with the custom of these times, she is led into the presence of the bridegroom, followed by virgins as her attendants.

Verse 15. As the queen's entourage takes its place, happiness and joy fill the air and the people present are caught up in the grandeur of the moment. **They will be led forth with gladness and rejoicing; they will enter into the King's palace.** It is a glorious occasion, and happiness and excitement characterize her entrance.

FOR GENERATIONS (45:16, 17)

¹⁶**In place of your fathers will be your sons;
You shall make them princes in all the earth.**
¹⁷**I will cause Your name to be remembered in all generations;
Therefore the peoples will give You thanks forever and ever.**

Verse 16. The psalm concludes with a listing of the rewards that will come to this royal marriage if the husband and the wife follow God's plan. **In place of your fathers will be your sons; you shall make them princes in all the earth.** The king is being addressed, as is indicated by the masculine pronouns. Thus these final words form a kind of benediction to the service.

Verse 17. The writer says that this song about the king's wedding will perpetuate the memory of the event from generation to generation. "Yes," says the writer, "**I will cause Your name to be remembered in all generations.**" Children will be born to him, and his sons are destined to become princes in the land. God intended that each marriage have an unending tomorrow to it. **Therefore the peoples will give You thanks forever and ever.** With endurance and perpetuity come blessings. Children and grandchildren come, bringing multiplied joys. With the passing of time, enduring distinction is given. An older couple is looked upon with respect and appreciation. The home that lasts will be crowned with the favor and approval of God.

APPLICATION

From a Wedding to a Home
The Scriptures sing of the sanctity and beauty of the home. The Book of Psalms would not be complete without a contemplation of the loveliness of love. Whenever a marriage is celebrated within the Scriptures, God's structure for the family comes through in what is said or implied.

Bursting out of this psalm, like the petals on a flower in the springtime, are foundations for the home. Some of them are merely implied; but whether by clear expression or by necessary inference, they shine through this festive, wedding event. The psalm describes the laughter, the rejoicing, the admiration, and the beauty of this social occasion that human beings find so exquisitely wonderful and so meaningful.

God and the Marriage
The first encouragement that emerges from this song is the admonition to make sure that God is a part of the marriage.

God created marriage. He made it for our happiness and as a basic structure for the family. There would be no wedding, were it not for God's design for the family.

God provides the opportunity for marriage. Behind the joy and the rejoicing is the loving grace of God. The king had been chosen by the Lord, and he was committed to being God's representative on earth. He was entering into marriage because God had given him the opportunity to do so.

God is willing to sustain our marriages. He will assist us in the maintenance that is necessary in order to have a good home.

Thus, indirectly stated, we see that a good marriage has God behind it and in it. He created it. He gives the opportunity for it, and He will help each couple who so chooses to make a good life together.

Integrity and Marriage
A good marriage must be based upon integrity. This essen-

tial quality begins with the husband.

Only integrity can make the marriage authentic. Truth and righteousness should kiss each other in the home, for the home is a place where promises are made and kept and where righteousness dwells. Without these two traits a marriage cannot be what God intended a marriage to be.

It will hold the marriage together. No lasting promise can be made without honesty of heart and soul. Love brings us to the relationship, but integrity keeps us in it and sustains the relationship.

It provides the foundation upon which trust can be built. Two cannot believe in each other unless they can trust each other; however, trust can only exist in an atmosphere of pure honesty.

A marriage without integrity is a relationship that is without the necessary cement to confirm it into a lasting relationship and without the energy to mend the weak places that appear.

A Lovely Wedding

Embedded in this psalm is the beautiful picture of the wedding occasion and what it means to have a lovely wedding. Marriage was intended by its Architect to be lovely, charming, and joyous.

A wedding is to be special. How unique a wedding is, whether it be the marriage of a king or the marriage of a common laborer! An authentic wedding is a once-in-a-lifetime event.

A wedding should be beautiful. At a wedding, we wear our best clothes, deck the wedding hall with flowers and lights, present gifts, and overlay the ceremony with our best wishes, laughter, and congratulations. This extravagance depicts our view of marriage; the wedding occasion should be a lovely event.

A wedding should be memorable. All of us look back on our weddings with joy and fondness. One thing every couple will remember as long as they have memory is their wedding. Since it is going to be a memory, it should be a beautiful memory!

Of course, a wedding does not have to be extravagant to be beautiful. Some of the most beautiful weddings have been simple, profound, and surrounded by the celebration of the two families that have produced it.

God's Great Plan for Marriage

Certainly the most important foundation stone for marriage is the inclusion of God's design for the home. Hints are given in the psalm as to what living should be like in the God-given marriage.

The husband is the head. God's plan is intimated by what has been said about the husband. One of William Shakespeare's characters stated that if two men ride one horse at the same time, someone will have to ride in front. The same truth applies to marriage. God has put it in His blueprint. The husband is commanded to lead—and he is charged to lead in sacrificial love, as Christ loved the church (Eph. 5:25). The wife is commanded to follow his leadership in loving submission, as unto the Lord (Eph. 5:22).

The wife is the queen. She provides the heart of the home. The wife does not take center stage in this psalm, but she is acknowledged as a beautiful centerpiece. The bridegroom has wooed her, and she has given her heart to him. They stand side by side as a wonderful unit, each complementing the other. They are two, but they are one. They walk together, though he is the head, and she is the heart.

God's will is the map and guide of the home. Only when the husband and the wife live to honor God's will do they find the meaning, peace, and future that they seek for their marriage.

God's design provides for our happiness and for the proper order of the home. Obedience to His plan is the avenue to marital success. Deviations from His instructions, whether through ignorance or rebellion, bring only frustration and tears.

Meant to Last

The home is to be characterized by longevity and permanence. In light of this fact, marriage should be viewed from different viewpoints.

Marriage is a birth. It is a covenant for life. It is not a "throw away" relationship, but a do-or-die promise made before God for life. A home is born to live and flourish.

Marriage is life. Every marriage should have an endless tomorrow in it. The commitment was never intended to be a brief fling. God ordained it to be a day-by-day loving and caring experience with each other, the children, and all the other relatives.

Marriage is historical. Every home will eventually have a wonderful past and a group of memories treasured by it, "a history of their home life." Pity the child who does not remember fondly his "growing up days." How sad for the couple who cannot have a happy stroll through their past experiences, joys and tears, together!

We can sum up a God-given home with three words: "life," "future," and "history"!

The Best Wish

The highest wish for young couples is this: "May you have a beautiful wedding—but even more, may you have a beautiful home."

Beyond the Psalm

This psalm is an ode to a beautiful wedding for the king. The outward splendor of this social event is portrayed in each line. We see the momentous occasion that was taking place for the bridegroom and the bride. For both, it was the end of an old life and the beginning of a new one. Above and beyond the wedding, we have seen pictures of the coming of the true King, the Messiah, who will reign forever.

Psalm 46

"A Mighty Fortress Is Our God"

The Superscription: For the choir director. A Psalm of the sons of Korah, set to Alamoth. A Song. This full heading mentions three characteristics of the psalm. These items are addressed to **the choir director** (לַמְנַצֵּחַ, *lamnatstseach*), a leader of one of the choruses for the temple. First, the psalm belongs to **the sons of Korah** (לִבְנֵי־קֹרַח, *libney qorach*), either because it was written by one of them or because it was part of the collection used by them. Second, it is **set to Alamoth** (עַל־עֲלָמוֹת, *'al ⁽ᵃ⁾lamoth*). The word "alamoth" means "damsels," a word that may suggest the use of soprano or female voices in singing the psalm. Third, the psalm is designated **a Song** (שִׁיר, *shir*), a general term that is applied in the Scriptures to secular as well as sacred songs. It is used thirty times in the titles to the psalms.

A beautiful psalm of confidence in God, this psalm has endeared itself to multitudes of distressed hearts. It tells the disturbed and troubled believer that regardless of what may happen in the world, he or she can trust in the protection and peace of God. Martin Luther's great hymn of faith, "A Mighty Fortress," was inspired by this psalm.

> We will not fear, for God hath willed His truth to triumph
>   through us:
> The prince of darkness grim—We tremble not for him;
> His rage we can endure, For lo, his doom is sure:
> One little word shall fell him![1]

---

[1] Martin Luther, "A Mighty Fortress," trans. F. H. Hedge, *Great Songs of the Church* (Abilene, Tex.: Abilene Christian College Book Store, 1973).

PSALM 46

The background of the psalm may well be God's miraculous deliverance of Jerusalem from Sennacherib, the great Assyrian monarch (2 Kings 18; 19; 2 Chron. 32; Is. 36; 37). The psalm does not provide extensive evidence upon which to make a determination, but it does contain some hints.

As Hezekiah, the king of Judah, tried to throw off his dependence upon Assyria, Sennacherib sent his army to beat him into submission. The Assyrian king had made his way across Judah, destroying forty-six walled cities. Apparently, he had agreed to spare Jerusalem if Hezekiah would submit to his rule and would express that submission by paying tribute to him once again. Hezekiah refused.

Sennacherib sent his forces to Jerusalem, demanding an immediate surrender. In a letter that was sent to Hezekiah, Sennacherib blasphemously denied the ability of Yahweh to deliver Jerusalem from his power (Is. 37:9–13). Hezekiah took Sennacherib's letter to the temple and laid it "before the Lord," appealing to God to show him what to do (Is. 37:14–20). In response, God's prophet Isaiah uttered a prophecy that promised that Sennacherib would be humbled and sent home (2 Kings 19:20–34; Is. 37:21–35).

Sennacherib's soldiers camped just outside of Jerusalem during the night, intending to take over the city the next morning. Amazingly, when morning came, 185,000 of Sennacherib's men lay dead (2 Kings 19:35; Is. 37:36). During the night, a sudden and mysterious visitation of death brought by an angel of the Lord had swept through their camp and destroyed them. Humiliated by what had happened, the Assyrian forces packed up and went home, leaving Jerusalem untouched.

A victory of this extent was a dramatic, persuasive, and visible illustration of how God comes to the rescue of His own! It brought forth shouts of thanksgiving and rejoicing and left lasting impressions in the minds of the people of Judah.

A few of the details in this psalm seem to point to this event. It may have been written shortly after this remarkable deliverance to portray love and appreciation for God because of His intervention. Even if this psalm was not written about this historical event, the Sennacherib encounter stands as a vivid illustration of what it envisions.

The psalm presents three comforting promises about life in three equal stanzas, each ending with "Selah." These truths relate to living by faith in the face of traumatic experiences.

Life consists of ups and downs. We enjoy the ups, but the downs sometimes shatter us. This psalm tells what the believer needs to know about the downside of life.

TURMOIL ALL AROUND (46:1–3)

¹**God is our refuge and strength,**
A very present help in trouble.
²**Therefore we will not fear, though the earth should change**
And though the mountains slip into the heart of the sea;
³**Though its waters roar and foam,**
Though the mountains quake at its swelling pride. Selah.

Verse 1. God is both His people's defense and offense, their stronghold and their strength. **God is our refuge and strength.** In times of adversity, He will sustain them internally by being their spiritual "strength" (עז, 'az) and protect them externally by being their divine "refuge" (מַחְסֶה, machseh).

He will be **a very present help.** The Hebrew phrase (מְאֹד נִמְצָא, nimtsa' me'od) literally means "He is found swiftly [or abundantly]." He is accessible, fully and immediately, in times of grave danger. Therefore, God's people have nothing to fear regardless of what may happen. God will always be more than sufficient for any of their trials.

Verse 2. Even in the most violent disasters, God will be a gracious, almighty help to those who trust in Him. A "therefore" is always apropos for God's people. **Therefore we will not fear.** This confidence can be theirs **though the earth should change and though the mountains slip into the heart of the sea.** This promise is sure, though the most reliable realities, the strongest material entities we see—the earth and the mountains—melt or crumble into the sea and disappear.

Verse 3. Nothing that happens to the sea, the land, or the mountains should shake our faith in God. **Though its waters**

roar and foam, though the mountains quake at its swelling pride. If the seas should rush out of their boundaries and the mountains bellow forth with volcanos and earthquakes, we can rest our hearts without anxiety in the kind superintendence of God.

Four expressions are used to show great and fearful calamities and catastrophic changes that cannot negate God's promises. We see four "possible eventualities" expressed with four transitional, NASB interpretative "thoughs": "though the earth should change," "though the mountains slip into the heart of the sea," "though its waters roar and foam," and "though the mountains quake at its swelling pride." Combined, these four phrases are saying that even if God's people experience earthquakes, landslides, ocean storms, and floods, He will protect them. Natural disasters are imagined to figuratively convey that God's people are safe in Him regardless of the storms that may assail them and regardless of the upheavals in nature or life that may confront them.

Implied in this first stanza is the truth that, individually and collectively, God's people will experience turmoil in the world. They cannot escape it. Part of earthly life is doing battle with the violent forces of hardship, struggle, and death. The earth, at times, may seem to be crumbling away from beneath the feet of the believer; the whole world may seem to be breaking up and falling apart. In addition, turmoil (though not mentioned specifically in this stanza) can come through unseen battles within. Whether the sweeping turbulences are visible and catastrophic or whether they take place within the secrecy of the soul, God will sustain His people. This fact is the divinely promised assurance that belongs to anyone who trusts in God.

Selah. Pause and think about this.

GOD IS YOUR ONLY REAL REFUGE
(46:4–7)

⁴There is a river whose streams make glad the city of God, The holy dwelling places of the Most High.

> ⁵**God is in the midst of her, she will not be moved;**
> **God will help her when morning dawns.**
> ⁶**The nations made an uproar, the kingdoms tottered;**
> **He raised His voice, the earth melted.**
> ⁷**The LORD of hosts is with us;**
> **The God of Jacob is our stronghold. Selah.**

Verse 4. Surrounded by an unpredictable world, God's people are set apart as God's possession and the object of His tender care. The Most High has consecrated and set apart Israel by His presence among them.

The writer says, **There is a river whose streams make glad the city of God, the holy dwelling places of the Most High.** God's people have no reason to fear, but have every reason to be "glad." God is among them, and His presence provides the highest security and joy.

God has assigned "a river" to flow through "the city of God" where the "holy dwelling places" are. "There is" was added by the translators for the sake of clarity. Jerusalem is the city of "God" (אֱלֹהִים, ᵉlohim), and the holy dwelling places belong to the "Most High" (עֶלְיוֹן, ʿelyon), the Supreme God, the one and only God.

We are not to think of this river as a literal one flowing through the physical city of Jerusalem; rather, it is a metaphor that suggests peace and tranquility coming to us, flowing out from the hand of God. The figurative "river" rushes out in various "streams," spreading God's calm throughout His city, the people He has chosen. To people in an arid land, flowing water is the supreme figure of abundance and provision. God's great comfort branches out to all the different areas of turmoil for His people.

Verse 5. We can be assured that His people will never fall. **God is in the midst of her, she will not be moved**. God's people will always be aware of His readiness to help them. Although "the city of God," which contains the holy dwelling places of the Most High, is threatened by the nations around, it is not dismayed by their threats. The city can calmly trust in the protection of the God who is "in the midst of her." God's presence means His protection.

God will be ever ready to deal with any enemy that approaches His people: Yes, **God will help her when morning dawns.** The phrase לִפְנוֹת בֹּקֶר (*lipnoth boqer*) literally means "to the turn of the morning." The help that would come "when morning dawns"—or, as the KJV has it, "and that right early"—may be a reference to the Assyrians who were found dead on the morning of their planned attack. On the other hand, it may just refer to the promise that God will not allow His people to suffer for a long period of time, even though they may have to suffer, metaphorically, through the night.

Verse 6. Nations may roar against God's people like angry waves of the sea tossing about. **The nations made an uproar, the kingdoms tottered; He raised His voice, the earth melted.** The kingdoms had "tottered" in the sense that they had been rising and falling. The kingdoms that were being invaded were falling, and the kingdoms that were making the conquests were excelling in power. Commotion and upheaval characterized the nations of the world.

In the midst of such national disturbances, God spoke and the earth "melted." At His word, the vicissitudes of the earth, as wide and violent as they were, passed away. The raging world became calm for the people of God.

Verse 7. The refrain of this verse pictures God as the sovereign Ruler of the universe. **The LORD of hosts is with us; the God of Jacob is our stronghold.** He is the almighty One, "the God of Jacob," the God of the nation of Israel. To have Him on one's side is to have a stronghold which cannot be broken into or overthrown by any force or enemy.

Selah. "Pause and reflect on this," the writer says.

HE IS OUR REFUGE (46:8–11)

⁸Come, behold the works of the LORD,
Who has wrought desolations in the earth.
⁹He makes wars to cease to the end of the earth;
He breaks the bow and cuts the spear in two;
He burns the chariots with fire.

> ¹⁰"Cease striving and know that I am God;
> I will be exalted among the nations,
> I will be exalted in the earth."
> ¹¹The Lord of hosts is with us;
> The God of Jacob is our stronghold. Selah.

Verse 8. In light of who God is, a special appeal to observe the works of God is made: **Come, behold the works of the Lord, who has wrought desolations in the earth.** The reader and the nations around are urged to look at what God has done, to consider His works, and to learn valuable lessons by viewing His wonders.

Verse 9. God has defeated the enemy of His people. **He makes wars to cease to the end of the earth; He breaks the bow and cuts the spear in two; He burns the chariots with fire.** He has overthrown nations and brought them to desolation. He has ended the attacks of heathen nations upon His people by breaking the bow and spear and by burning their chariots.

The writer may have been alluding to the great Assyrian army. The earth at that time had no greater war machine than the army of Sennacherib, the king who had threatened Jerusalem. His forces were feared throughout the nations, but God routed him decisively.

Verse 10. Because of His promises and His ability to keep them, God's people are told to relax. God says, **"Cease striving and know that I am God; I will be exalted among the nations, I will be exalted in the earth."** We can command our spirits to be calm and unafraid, using God's history and His present care as our reasons. God will not be overthrown by any person, nation, or force. He will be "exalted among the nations." Anyone who so chooses can see that God is the true and living God. The whole earth can observe that only God could have brought about what happened outside the walls of Jerusalem. So complete, so miraculous, and so decisive was this defense of Jerusalem that no one with an honest heart could fail to recognize the divine hand behind it. Anyone can see that there is no other God.

Verse 11. The writer closes his psalm with the same refrain that he used in verse 7: **The Lord of hosts is with us; the God**

of Jacob is our stronghold. The greatest news of all is that "the LORD of hosts," the almighty One, is with us. The God of Israel, the true and living God, is with us in times of trouble. No enemy is too strong for Him to overcome, no disaster is too cataclysmic for Him to stop, and no danger is too vicious for Him to prevent.

"The God of Jacob" has shown Himself to be stronger than the whole earth. The nations of the earth must learn that their strength cannot compare with His. God's people never need to fear when danger comes, for God is their refuge.

Selah. "Pause and think about this," the writer says.

APPLICATION

God, Our Strength

All recognize this psalm as a magnificent celebration of the believer's strength and security *in God*. Three truths confront us in it.

In the world we will have turmoil. This truth about life must be dealt with. Sometimes hardships will come quietly, without a lot of fanfare; at other times they will come in loud scenes of upheaval and volcanic-like explosions. When these trials come, we must remember that God is near and ever ready to assist us.

God is our only real refuge. No other refuge is strong enough, accessible enough, or large enough to provide the stronghold that all of God's people must have.

We must choose for Him to be our refuge. God will be our refuge *if* we choose Him to be. His help is available, but He will not force Himself upon us.

God alone is our protection from the hardships and difficulties of life. We cannot find real power and peace in political strength, well-armed military forces, the ingenuity of man, or any kind of human shelter. We rest in God, the mighty fortress!

Stronghold and Strength

God's presence in protecting His people is described by three metaphors with two explanatory phrases:

God is our refuge and strength,
A very present help in trouble (v. 1).

The LORD of hosts is with us;
The God of Jacob is our stronghold (v. 7).

The LORD of hosts is with us;
The God of Jacob is our stronghold (v. 11).

The figures are "refuge," "strength," and "stronghold." These three words are used as synonyms designating the origin and effectiveness of Israel's strength. As their strength, God was like a "refuge," where one could find rest and peace from the trouble around him. As their protection, He was their "stronghold." The "stronghold" or "fortress" was an isolated, elevated place where people built defenses against their enemies. God is like such a place—unreachable, impregnable, and secure.

Each of these metaphors is applied to God's people. When they were in distress, they especially required God's divine protection (Ps. 44:26; 63:7). They wanted Him with them at all times and in all places, but they experienced His help in particular when they were going through periods of anguish and trial (Ps. 23:4).

Beyond the Trouble

Beyond what we see in the tangible world are the will and the power of the God who made it. He is in charge. His presence means freedom from fear. He is to be worshiped and praised. His Word is mighty, final, and determinative.

When the rains of life come, He will be our shelter. When foes come against us, He will fight for us. When inner fears chase away our peace, His presence will calm us. The conclusion of this psalm must be our conclusion: Because we have God, we will not be afraid—regardless of what may happen to us or around us. No combined power on earth can give us the refuge that only God can give. True hope—real hope—is God.

Another Look at God
Who is God?

He is our salvation. No one can save us from our sins and mistakes but God. He is our only Savior. Anyone other than God who claims that he can save us is the worst type of fraud.

He is our offense. He shows us how to live in this world. We cannot figure it all out; so He lends us His almighty counsel and truth and gives us internal strength.

He is our defense. He protects us from enemies without and within. He stills the violent storm on the outside and quiets our raging fears on the inside.

He is our present help. He is always available and accessible. He is continually near, ready, and able to provide the strength and wisdom we need.

He is our peace. The end result of all this is that He makes, gives, and sustains our peace. Serenity can be ours even when the whole world is falling apart. We are hidden in God through Christ. God was here when nothing existed, and He will be here when everything has passed away.

God, then, is our all in all. With Him we have everything; without Him, we have nothing.

Why Should We Fear?
This psalm asks, "Why should the godly man be afraid?" (see vv. 1, 2). He has no reason to tremble because His God has His hand upon him, and His arms surround him.

Why should we fear external tragedies? Suppose the whole world falls down around us. The One who made it is still in control of all things, is He not? He is our refuge. The Almighty will not be affected by the collapse of the entire universe! He can hold it in the palm of His hand anyway; He can put it back together with one word.

Why should we worry about social upheavals? We do not want them to occur, especially if they should involve people in sin; but they cannot harm us as long as we have God as our fortress. With the whole world corrupt, God saved Noah and his family because they believed. He will do the same for us.

Why should we shiver in terror before inner turmoil? Great concerns come to our hearts. They are heavy, and they weigh us down. They cannot hurt us if we put our trust in God and follow His Word.

Nothing we see or will ever see is bigger than God. He has no big problems. The greatest tragedies we can imagine are only small, easily-fixed difficulties to Him. So, why worry?

Come and See

The writer asks the reader to "come and see" (see v. 8). He wants his readers to observe the works and actions of God in behalf of His people across the years. Why?

That we may know. We need to see who God is. We need to see His power, His wisdom, and especially His love. Such an observation will convince us that there is no God like Him.

That we may have confidence. When we see what He has done, we will know that He can do anything that needs to be done for us. There is no foe He cannot conquer and no circumstance He cannot rise above.

That we may be still. When we know who God is and have confidence that He can and will do whatever needs to be done for His people to deliver them and keep them safe for His service, we can relax and live life unafraid.

God wants His people to trust in Him and to be free from worry. When we are anxious, we are walking in fear, not in faith.

God and His People

The child of God is encouraged in the main by God, more so than by the commandments or the system of religion that he keeps. Think of God's relationship with His people. Beyond the commands, they see the Commander.

First, *He is "for us."* Even as parents are "for" their children, God is "for" us. He seeks our best interests and is on our side in the battles of life. He is both our coach and our best cheering fan.

Second, *He is "with us."* He stands beside us in the fight and in life. He is Immanuel, "God with us."

Third, *He is "in us."* He is in the midst of the city of God, sending out His streams of peace and mercy.

When dark days come and troubles descend, we think of God and our hearts are lifted. What greater encouragement could we have than knowing that God is for us, with us, and in us!

His Presence

Abundant living really stems from God's presence. His fellowship means power, peace, and pardon. Look at the all-inclusive nature of His being with us.

He is around us. He encircles us with His personality, wisdom, and power. We are hidden in His strength and love.

He is protecting us. God, the invincible God, is our shield. All the forces of the world, Satan, and evil cannot penetrate this shield.

Furthermore, *He is leading us.* We will never need to say to Him as Martha did, "Lord, if You had been here" (Jn. 11:21). He is always here with His children, leading them with His Word.

The only question I need to ask is this: Do I have the presence of God?

"Be Still"

The charge "be still" implies putting something in the place of something else. It means substituting the knowledge and love of God for all our questions and fears. Therefore, "being still" has important consequences for us.

It means "Quit fretting." Faith replaces fretting. Why should we be complaining when we have God looking after us?

It means "Quit fearing." Faith drives away fear. Behind fretting is fear. We do not need to be afraid even if the whole world crashes into little pieces.

It means "Quit fainting." Faith rebukes fainting. No true believer can give up or quit. Blush with embarrassment if you even think of taking off your armor. God is with us; and therefore we can boldly say, "Who can successfully come against us?"

PSALM 47

OUR GOD: THE KING OF KINGS AND LORD OF LORDS

The Superscription: For the choir director. A Psalm of the sons of Korah. The title gives guidance to (or **for**) **the choir director** (לַמְנַצֵּחַ, *lamnatstseach*), one of the chief musicians. It identifies this piece as **a Psalm** (מִזְמוֹר, *mizmor*) of praise that is either written by, for, or to one of **the sons of Korah** (לִבְנֵי־קֹרַח, *libney qorach*) or is one of the songs they collected and used.

Rejoicing over recent victories, this psalm gives glory to almighty God and pictures Him as the King of the earth. It is a hymn of praise and thanksgiving inspired by the kindness and grace of God.

Sigmund Mowinckel, a liberal Norwegian scholar, conjectured that this psalm should be labeled "an enthronement psalm." He translated the expression "God reigns" as "Yahweh has become king." He concluded that every year, following a Babylonian custom, Israel would symbolically enthrone Yahweh anew and celebrate, among other things, the military victories He had given them. Mowinckel has gained much popularity with his hypothesis. However, there is no evidence that Israel adopted such a festival from the Babylonians, nor do we find evidence that Israel ever had a festival similar to what Mowinckel described.

The psalm is a hymn of praise for the sovereignty and power of God. We cannot be certain about who wrote it, when it was written, or what event inspired its composition. A good guess is that it was written as a sequel to the previous psalm shortly after God delivered Jerusalem from Sennacherib's attack. If so, it may well be an extension of the rejoicing of the last verse of the previous psalm. If it is extolling God for the same deliverance mentioned in Psalm 46, it does so in a more general way. No clear allusions to the attack of Sennacherib are found in it.

Two golden themes run throughout the psalm: the kingship of God over all the earth and the victories He has brought to His people. Having enjoyed success in battle by the hand of the Lord, Israel used this hymn to praise God for what He had done for them and for His sovereignty over all the nations.

REJOICE IN THE LORD (47:1-4)

¹O clap your hands, all peoples;
Shout to God with the voice of joy.
²For the LORD Most High is to be feared,
A great King over all the earth.
³He subdues peoples under us
And nations under our feet.
⁴He chooses our inheritance for us,
The glory of Jacob whom He loves. Selah.

Verse 1. The writer urges each Israelite to rejoice in God with a fervent, high-spirited expression of gratitude. **O clap your hands, all peoples; shout to God with the voice of joy.** The admonition includes clapping the hands and shouting praises or thanksgivings to God with "the voice of joy." In Old Testament times these actions were typical ways of giving honor and acclaim to an earthly king. When Saul was appointed king, he was greeted with shouting and with the cry "Long live the king!" (1 Sam. 10:24). When the crown was placed upon the boy king Joash, the same cry was made; and in addition to the acclamation, the people "clapped their hands" (2 Kings 11:12). These two demonstrations are referred to figuratively in verse 1 of this psalm, as the people were being ask to acknowledge and celebrate Yahweh as the God of the nations.

Verse 2. Why should the Lord be praised? **For the LORD Most High is to be feared, a great King over all the earth.** God is to be adored because He is the "LORD Most High." This expression unites two names of God: "LORD" (יהוה, *YHWH*), the covenant God of Israel, and "Most High" (עֶלְיוֹן, *'elyon*), the sovereign God of the whole earth. With these appellations God is declared to be the Supreme God of the earth, the one and only God.

He is awesome, mighty, and flawless in His character. Indeed, He "is to be feared" (יָרֵא, *yare'*). The word "feared" is more like bowing in reverence than cowering in terror. The RSV has rendered this word "terrible." The greatest of all respect and honor are to be given to His great name and power.

He is the "King." His words and will are holy and binding upon all nations. He speaks, and a law is created; His majesty is unexcelled. All monarchs are puppet kings compared to His reign. Being the Creator, Redeemer, and Sustainer of the world, He is the Ruler of all the kings. The dominion of His kingship is universal, encompassing the whole "earth."

Verse 3. He is to be praised for what He has done. **He subdues peoples under us and nations under our feet.** He has overcome nations and peoples, political entities, and ethnic groups. Those who have disobeyed Him have been brought into submission to His plan for the world. The terms "subdues" (דָּבַר, *dabar*) and "under" (תַּחַת, *thachath*) suggest the Lord's overwhelming dominion that results from His actions.

Verse 4. In His grace, He gave Israel an inheritance. The writer acknowledges, **He chooses our inheritance for us.** He drove out the Canaanites and awarded their land to Israel, making the land **the glory of Jacob whom He loves.** These possessions and privileges He gave to His people because He had chosen to love Jacob uniquely.

Selah. The truth of what God has done should be carefully thought about.

GOD ASCENDS (47:5–7)

⁵God has ascended with a shout,
The LORD, with the sound of a trumpet.
⁶Sing praises to God, sing praises;
Sing praises to our King, sing praises.
⁷For God is the King of all the earth;

PSALM 47

Sing praises with a skillful psalm.

Verse 5. More reasons for praising God are given. **God has ascended with a shout, the LORD, with the sound of a trumpet.** He is pictured as "going up," as having "ascended with a shout." The verb translated "ascended" (עָלָה, '*alah*) means "to go up, to climb." It can be understood either to refer to God's going up to His throne after the battle is over or as "going up" to do battle. The latter view fits the technical use of the term in the Old Testament (Judg. 1:1; 1 Sam. 7:7). In light of the context of verses 3 and 9, it appears that we are to understand God's "going up" with "a shout" and "the sound of a trumpet" as His going into battle for Israel.

Verse 6. The call to praise becomes even more intense, being stressed by repetition. **Sing praises to God, sing praises; sing praises to our King, sing praises.** Yahweh has fought for Israel, and she is to give thanks to Him. God's people are to "sing praises to God," their "King" and the "King of all the earth." God is to be recognized as the Supreme King, a King whose sovereignty knows no boundaries. He is not only the King of Israel, but He is also the King of all nations. He created, owns, and controls the earth.

Verse 7. Because of His universal kingship, He should be the recipient of intelligent praise. **For God is the King of all the earth; sing praises with a skillful psalm.** The imperative "sing praises" (זַמֵּר, *zamar*) is repeated five times by the psalmist for the sake of emphasis.

Israel was also to sing to God "skillful[ly]" (מַשְׂכִּיל, *maśkil*) or "with instruction or understanding." True worship comes from the heart, the thinking part of the individual. We are to acknowledge in our praise that God is King over the populations of people and that He even reigns over the heathen, whether they know it or not.

GOD REIGNS (47:8, 9)

⁸**God reigns over the nations,
God sits on His holy throne.**

> ⁹**The princes of the people have assembled themselves as the people of the God of Abraham,**
> **For the shields of the earth belong to God;**
> **He is highly exalted.**

Verse 8. God rightfully claims the entire world as His domain. **God reigns over the nations.** In the psalmist's day, God manifested His kingly power over the heathen by subduing great numbers of them, making them subject to Israel.

His reign has width, but the width is conjoined with integrity and righteousness. **God sits on His holy throne.** No other throne can compare to His "holy [set apart] throne." From this eminence He exercises a just, righteous, divine rule.

Verse 9. He assembles the prestigious leaders of the earth to do His bidding. **The princes of the people have assembled themselves as the people of the God of Abraham, for the shields of the earth belong to God; He is highly exalted.** This line depicts God influencing "the princes" of the nations to be gathered to "the people of the God of Abraham." In this scene, both Jews and Gentiles are submitting to God's sovereignty, surrendering their "shields" and resolving to be under His leadership. "Shields" may even refer to the rulers of the earth who will yield to God's dominion. The point is that all will be honoring and exalting Him as the true God and He will be "highly exalted."

This part of the psalm portrays the invincible leadership that God will give to Israel. On a higher level, it foreshadows the time when citizens of every nation of the heavenly kingdom/church will praise God as brothers and sisters. This kingdom, the church, will be established by Christ's death and resurrection and by the coming of the Holy Spirit. Then the surrounding nations will join "the people of the God of Abraham" by obeying His gospel, entering the family of God, and giving thanks to Him for His salvation.

PSALM 47

APPLICATION

Continual Praise

One wonderful message in this psalm is that continual praise is part of the life of the believer. We know what God has done for us in the past; therefore, we gladly extol Him and ask Him to act for us in the future. We glorify His name while the battle takes place. When the battle is over and we are savoring the victory, we thank and praise the One who has given it to us. From beginning to end, we adore His name.

As this psalm is applied to the Christian, two words are obvious: "praise" and "persistence." A dominant thought in the Christian's mind is that his spiritual victories—past, present, and future—are gifts of God. He is aware of how dependent on God he has been, and he expresses his understanding of this fact in his daily and public thanksgiving to Him.

A Full-Orbed Answer

The Christian always has a three-part answer to the question "When should we praise Him?"

The first part of the answer is that we will praise Him *before a battle*. The appropriate way to prepare for any struggle is by praising God. We know the One who will fight for us. The great God who rules over all the nations and who has never lost a war will lead our campaign.

God has been good to us in the past. As we ask Him to fight for us, we will be grateful for the battles that He has already won in our behalf.

A second part of the answer to the question "When should we praise Him?" is also obvious: We will praise Him *during the battle itself*. While the struggle is going on, praises and thanksgivings ascend from our hearts to God. We fight with an attitude of thanksgiving.

The universal, sovereign King will always triumph, and all enemies of God will ultimately fail. Those who walk before God with blameless hearts, giving honor and glory to Him, will ultimately succeed. As we stand on the field of conflict, with our swords in our hands, let us have praises on our lips for God, our Leader and Commander in Chief.

Naturally, the third part of the answer is always the easy one: We are to praise Him *after the battle*. Praise flows freely from our lips in the calm of the victory as we rest from our conflicts.

Continual praise should rise from the believer—before the battle, during the battle, and after the battle. The trusting person has nothing that God has not given to him. God goes before him, is with him, and surrounds him as a great, impenetrable shield.

The Content of Praise

Why does this psalm urge us to praise God?

He is "the LORD Most High." He is the exalted and lifted up One, the Lord of lords and King of kings.

He is awesome. In fact, verse 2 says that He is "to be feared." He is entitled to supreme reverence because He is the only true God.

He is the King. His words and will are holy and are given to man for his meditation and guidance.

He rules the whole earth. He is the Creator, Redeemer, and Sustainer of the world. The dominion of His kingship is universal.

He is to be praised for what He has done. He has delivered and blessed His people. He gave Israel an inheritance, driving out the Canaanites and awarding their land to them.

It would be easy for the Christian to make a list of the reasons why he should praise the Lord.

"Worthy Art Thou"

This psalm begins where each worshiper should with a commitment to thanksgiving. The writer asks the reader to look at who God is and what He has done and then respond to what he sees with the appropriate adoration and praise.

God is the joy of the believer's heart. Anyone who reverently looks at God will see Him as our supreme Benefactor. Therefore, with the voice of joy, let us express our thanksgiving over who God is and what He has done for us.

He is to be feared. We see Him as God, the Lord Most High.

He is the King of all kings and Lord of all lords. He is the Sovereign over all nations and over all the earth. There is a reverence due Him that is due no other authority or ruler.

He is to be submitted to and obeyed. We see Him as our final authority. All true laws emanate from Him. We must bow before Him in humble obedience, recognizing Him as our only true Lord.

The question is not "Will we obey Him?" The question is "When will we obey Him?" One day all will submit to His sovereign will.

Who is God? He is our King, our Lord, and our Benefactor. He transcends all earthly authorities and obligations. We owe Him more than anyone can measure; He is absolute and unrivaled. Let us come before Him with thanksgiving, praise, and reverence.

The Nature of Praise

Think deeply about the character of true thanksgiving.

With joy. Part of the psalm may refer to the return of God and Israel from a victorious battle. God has given the victory and Israel knows it. Aware of what God has done, thanksgiving is given with gladness and singleness of heart.

With understanding. Praise should be given with skill or understanding. All true worship is done with the mind, as we consciously identify in our spirits God's gifts and give Him thanks.

With intensity. There is a depth of sincerity that should characterize our praise. Worship combines understanding and emotions in an intelligent, intense acknowledgment of who God is and what He has done for each of us.

Worship and praise of God is appropriate and right. Worship of God, the high moment of our lives, should receive the best of our thinking and our purest love.

God Is Supreme

In the final strophe of this psalm God is pictured as the greatest of all kings. Think of the nature and glory of His rule.

He rules justly. His throne is a holy throne. From Him come righteous, just, and truthful judgments. None of His verdicts can ever be tarnished with error.

He rules universally. All nations are under His dominion. The phrase that speaks of everyone becoming the people of Abraham probably prefigures the Gospel Age when all nations—Jews and Gentiles—will come under His leadership through the cross of Jesus. All shields of the earth will one day be placed at the foot of His throne.

He rules in majesty. He is high and lifted up by all His citizens. They adore and worship Him because of His love, beauty, and righteousness. He is the only perfect King, and He extends His scepter of truth to all who come to Him.

No wonder we can rejoice that God is our just, universal, and majestic King. Every believer will have an anthem of praise for Him in his heart.

God as King

This psalm—in a unique way—pictures Yahweh as King over all His people.

He is the King of kings. He reigns over all the peoples, nations, and territories of the earth. There is no space or inhabitants of the world over which He is not Lord. Some people realize that He is Lord, and some do not—but He is Lord, nonetheless. God, the greatest of all kings, reigns over the only true empire.

He rules in perfection and grace. He has never made a mistake in judgment. His directives are correctly and justly given. He guides us flawlessly with His Word and saves us perfectly with His grace. He rebukes when necessary and forgives graciously when we come to Him in penitence.

He provides our salvation as well as our sustenance. He saves us and keeps us saved, holding on to us while we hold on to Him. He has a spiritual reign over us in addition to His physical reign. His care covers the whole person—mind, body, and soul.

He is King forever. He will not reign as King today and then fade from power tomorrow. There is absolute certainty here. In fact, the reality of His reign is the only certainty there is.

No greater decision could ever be made than that of choosing God to be one's King. He is the greatest of all potentates, who is perfect in all His attributes. He will save us eternally, reigning over us forever.

Pursuing with Praise

As we go forth to battle, one of the unique characteristics about us should be the praise of our God.

David went before Goliath with five smooth stones; but when he spoke of what he was doing, he did not hold up the stones—he held up his true rock, Yahweh his God! He said to Goliath, "You come to me with a sword, a spear, and a javelin, but I come to you in the name of the LORD of hosts, the God of the armies of Israel..." (1 Sam. 17:45). The most obvious part of David's battle plan was God.

What Samson could not do with miraculous might for the nation of Israel, *Samuel* did with consecration to God and prayer. Before Samuel led the people to war, he conducted a revival. Before they sharpened their swords, they offered sacrifices to God (1 Sam. 7:10). The clearest thing about Samuel's leadership was his reliance on God.

Jehoshaphat was destined to confront the Moabites, Ammonites, and Meunites in a great battle (2 Chron. 20:1). The army that opposed him was vast, well-armed, strong, vicious, and intimidating. He gathered his nation before God and asked Him to deliver them. In the midst of that assembly, Jahaziel, the prophet, told them that they would receive the victory without raising a sword (2 Chron. 20:14-17). Jehoshaphat told the nation to trust in the Lord and they would see success. He sent the priests ahead of his army singing, "Give thanks to the LORD, for His lovingkindness is everlasting" (2 Chron. 20:21). When they arrived at the battlefield, the enemy had already been defeated by the Lord. No one can miss the place of praise in this victory.

It has been said that all great spiritual battles are won the day before in the closet of prayer. The great leaders are led by the Lord. They have gone out to do God's will, praising God as they have gone. They have gone in His name, in His strength and for His glory.

In this psalm we see the praise of God before the battle, during the battle, and after the battle. The victory is surrounded with the glory, grace, and grandeur of the Lord. The battle is won with songs of praise that acknowledge God's leadership and surrender to His will, not with swords of the flesh or human wisdom.

> Thus says the LORD, "Let not a wise man boast of his wisdom, and let not the mighty man boast of his might, let not a rich man boast of his riches; but let him who boasts boast of this, that he understands and knows Me, that I am the LORD who exercises lovingkindness, justice and righteousness on earth; for I delight in these things," declares the LORD (Jer. 9:23, 24).

PSALM 48

GOD AND THE CITY OF GOD

The Superscription: A Song; a Psalm of the sons of Korah. In its heading, this psalm is identified in three ways. It is called **a Song** (שִׁיר, *shir*), which must be the general term for a composition that is written to be sung. Second, it is called **a Psalm** (מִזְמוֹר, *mizmor*), a term that has to do with worship and is found in fifty-seven titles of the Book of Psalms. The word "psalm" must be more specific than the word "song." Third, the psalm is said to be of ["by," "for," or "to"] **the sons of Korah** (לִבְנֵי־קֹרַח, *libney qorach*). This designation could mean that the psalm was part of the collection of the psalms used by them.

This song is a hymn of praise to God for what He has done for the city of God, Jerusalem. Psalm 47 praises the God of Zion, but this Psalm (48) exalts the Zion of God.[1] It is the third in a trilogy of psalms (46—48) that give glory and thanks to God for some great deliverance.

Perhaps all three psalms were written to commemorate the salvation of Jerusalem from the planned attack of Sennacherib in 701 B.C. Verses 4 and 5 lend support to the supposition that this psalm was written about that attack. However, in light of verses 12 and 13, one might also wonder if this psalm could have been written to commemorate the rebuilding of Jerusalem by Nehemiah (Neh. 12:27). Absolute certainty may not be possible regarding the background of the psalm.

The glory of Zion, God's city, stands at the center of the psalm. Since God's dwelling place through the ark of the cov-

---

[1]Robert Alden, *Psalms: Songs of Devotion*, (Chicago: Moody Press, 1974), 1:117.

enant was in the temple in Jerusalem, the city received the magnificence radiating from His presence. The grandeur and power of God were shining on, in, and through the city. When Moses came down from Mount Sinai, his face shone; he had to cover his face with a veil because of its brilliant glow (Ex. 34:29–35). When one has been in the presence of God, he imbibes His glory.

However, a city—even Jerusalem, which had the temple of God—is not God. The recipient of His majestic beauty should not think that he is the originator of that splendor. Jerusalem was blessed because within that city was the Holy of Holies which the God of heaven had made His earthly sanctuary. The presence of God brought sovereignty and far-reaching beauty to that city.

This psalm was written to illustrate what God meant to His city and what the city meant to His nation. Furthermore, what God did for Jerusalem typifies what God does for all those who belong to Him.

THE BEAUTIFUL CITY (48:1–3)

¹**Great is the Lord, and greatly to be praised,
In the city of our God, His holy mountain.
²Beautiful in elevation, the joy of the whole earth,
Is Mount Zion in the far north,
The city of the great King.
³God, in her palaces,
Has made Himself known as a stronghold.**

Verse 1. The first line announces God's glory and greatness: **Great is the Lord, and greatly to be praised, in the city of our God, His holy mountain.** The Lord is "great," not weak or feeble, not inactive or dispassionate, as was the case with the pagan, lifeless gods. His power and love are seen in the significance He has given to "the city." He is the sovereign King, who is powerful, and transcendent. Having proven Himself to His people, He is to be highly exalted or "greatly to be praised" by them. They are to worship Him in Jerusalem, in the city that contains the temple where God has ordained that He should be worshiped. It is to be regarded as "holy" because it represents His abiding place.

Verse 2. Poetic exaggeration and plain facts are used to describe the loveliness of Zion. It is said to be **beautiful in elevation**. The hill of Zion had a physical elevation; but more than this, as the place chosen of God, it had a lofty position among the nations. In the eyes of a devout Israelite who understood its spiritual worth, it was **the joy of the whole earth**. Appeal and gladness were not inherent to Mount Zion; God brought grace and heavenly importance to it by His choosing it and by His continued presence in it.

It was to be regarded as **Mount Zion in the far north**. The word used (צָפוֹן, *tsapon*) can either be translated with the proper name "Zaphon" or with the word "north." The context must determine the translation. The temple's location may have caused the NASB translators to translate the word "north." Because Zaphon was to the Canaanites what Mount Olympus was to the Greeks—the place where they believed that their chief god of the pantheon, El, resided—some have translated it "Zaphon," using it figuratively for the true dwelling place of the true God.

Zion was not literally "in the far north" if viewed from the vantage point of the land of Palestine. The phrase "far north" (יַרְכְּתֵי צָפוֹן, *yark^{e}tey tsapon*) must be referring to the place where the pagan people thought the gods normally assembled. Thus in this psalm, "the far north" is applied to Jerusalem. The writer is saying that Jerusalem is the real "far north"—the actual place where the only real God reigns.

Zion rose prominently over the city and represented in truth everything (and far more) that the high hills of pagan idolatry signified in their false religions. This was the place God had chosen to reveal His presence among His people.

One can find higher mountains than Mount Zion, mountains that are more picturesque. However, God's choice of it as His dwelling place gave to it His greatness and fame and made it unlike any other mountain of Palestine.

The hill of Zion stands for the city itself—a part of the area standing for the whole area. It was **the city of the great King** because God had put His name on that city. Jesus must have appropriated this phrase in His reference to Jerusalem in Matthew 5:35.

Verse 3. The earthly king of Jerusalem has seen the Lord deliver His people. The king and the people know that **God, in her palaces, has made Himself known as a stronghold.** Within the walls and buildings that make up the city, praise is being given to God for what He has done for them. Perhaps this expression refers to the time when Hezekiah watched God protect Jerusalem against Sennacherib's army (see 2 Kings 19; 2 Chron. 32; Is. 37).

THE CITY STRIKES TERROR (48:4–8)

⁴For, lo, the kings assembled themselves,
They passed by together.
⁵They saw it, then they were amazed;
They were terrified, they fled in alarm.
⁶Panic seized them there,
Anguish, as of a woman in childbirth.
⁷With the east wind You break the ships of Tarshish.
⁸As we have heard, so have we seen
In the city of the LORD of hosts, in the city of our God;
God will establish her forever. Selah.

Verse 4. Verses 4 through 8 point to a sudden, remarkable redemption given by the Lord. The writer says, **For, lo, the kings assembled themselves, they passed by together.** "They" may refer to a coalition of kings that came against Jerusalem, or "they" may be used figuratively, indicating the vassal-kings or officers of Sennacherib. Isaiah 10:8 pictures Sennacherib as saying, "Are not my princes all kings?"

These kings, whoever they were, "passed by" in their expedition to conquer. They saw Jerusalem in the distance, and they knew that Jerusalem was too much for them. They decided against it and left it alone.

Verse 5. At the sight of the city, with its walls and towers, its hill of Zion, they resolved to retreat. **They saw it, then they were**

amazed; they were terrified, they fled in alarm. They concluded that the place was too strong for them to take, too powerful to be defeated. In this Hebrew sentence—made up of six words—there are four verbs, expressing the vivid action taking place. The picture of Jerusalem that they saw is figurative; they "saw" more than Jerusalem—they were viewing the wonders and workings of God in that city. They were "amazed" and "terrified"; consequently, "they fled in alarm." What they had seen of Jerusalem's God was enough for them, and they immediately left.

Verse 6. The kings' hearts melted before God's city. **Panic seized them there, anguish, as of a woman in childbirth.** Two striking figures are used to describe their reaction to what they had seen: the "anguish" of a woman in travail and a storm shattering the strongest ships (vv. 6, 7). The figure of a woman giving birth conveys that they were suddenly overwhelmed with pain. As they viewed God's power, they were instantly stricken with fear because they could see that the possibility of capturing the city was gone. It is as if they were seized with panic.

Verse 7. The second figure suggests the ease with which God repelled the enemies of the city. **With the east wind You break the ships of Tarshish.** The "ships of Tarshish" were the strongest and most admired among the seafaring nations. How sturdy and capable they were! However, they were easily destroyed by a strong "wind" at sea sent by Him. In a tempest on the open sea, even such a ship could lose its cargo and the people aboard, as is seen in the Book of Jonah. Furthermore, the vessel itself could be lost. The mighty ship would be like a tiny matchbox tossed about by the waves. The kings who sought to "storm" Jerusalem came face to face with a stormy wind sent by the Lord, and it blew them away. God can tear apart the strongest of ships with a mighty blast from His arsenal of weapons.

Verse 8. God's power had been manifested in behalf of Jerusalem. **As we have heard, so have we seen in the city of the LORD of hosts, in the city of our God; God will establish her forever.** His power is so much higher than the frail strength of mankind that one wave of His hand in the direction of Jerusalem was sufficient to deliver the entire city. Although enemies surrounded the city, one word from God melted them away. He removed their strength and caused their hearts to fail in the midst of the battle.

God had demonstrated in Jerusalem that He intended to protect His people and fulfill His will. The inhabitants of Jerusalem had heard about how He had protected His people in the past, but now they have seen it for themselves. This city has observed and felt the purpose of God. God continued to watch over His city until His divine will had been achieved through it.

Selah. This thought needs to be pondered.

THINKING OF HIS LOVINGKINDNESS
(48:9–14)

> ⁹We have thought on Your lovingkindness, O God,
> In the midst of Your temple.
> ¹⁰As is Your name, O God,
> So is Your praise to the ends of the earth;
> Your right hand is full of righteousness.
> ¹¹Let Mount Zion be glad,
> Let the daughters of Judah rejoice
> Because of Your judgments.
> ¹²Walk about Zion and go around her;
> Count her towers;
> ¹³Consider her ramparts;
> Go through her palaces,
> That you may tell it to the next generation.
> ¹⁴For such is God,
> Our God forever and ever;
> He will guide us until death.

Verse 9. The godly people of the city meditated on what they have seen and heard of God's mighty works. **We have thought on Your lovingkindness, O God, in the midst of Your temple.** Their contemplation inspires them to take comfort in His deeds, rejoice over them, and offer thank offerings for them. God's actions cause them to take note of how He has always dealt with

PSALM 48

His people. He has an uninterrupted history of being a refuge for them.

Verse 10. They recognized that God's gracious dealings are in harmony with His name. **As is Your name, O God, so is Your praise to the ends of the earth; Your right hand is full of righteousness.** The nations that attacked Jerusalem reacted to God with fear; the citizens of Zion burst forth in anthems of thanksgiving to Him. They rejoice so greatly that their praise can be heard or felt throughout the earth. As they thank Him, they declare that He is a God of holiness. In His strongest hand, His "right hand," are "righteousness" and truth. His strength is guided by His holiness. He rules with justice and love. Consistently, He brings victory to His people and vengeance upon their enemies; He is righteous and gracious.

Verse 11. Consequently, God's leadership brings joy, a joy that automatically spreads. This rejoicing of the citizens of Zion goes out from Jerusalem throughout Judah. Jerusalem, the place of God's abode and worship, is the point from which happiness in the Lord radiates out to all of Judah. The citizens of God's kingdom have been given innumerable victories, and gladness fills their hearts and spreads to the communities and regions around them.

It is time for praising God. **Let Mount Zion be glad, let the daughters of Judah rejoice because of Your judgments.** "Daughters of Judah" is an idiomatic expression for the villages of Judah. God's "judgments," His decrees of justice, have established His people by bringing defeat and subjugation to the opposing armies. This line is parallel to the previous one where the spread of the gladness of victory is emphasized.

Verses 12, 13. The inhabitants of Jerusalem are urged to walk around the city and survey it. **Walk about Zion and go around her; count her towers; consider her ramparts; go through her palaces, that you may tell it to the next generation.** They are to see how beautiful it is, how the walls are in place, how every part of it has escaped harm; not one mark has been left upon it. Because of God's presence within the city, it has resisted the most militant attack that men could bring against it. The purpose of their noticing the unscathed city is so that they could tell all future generations about God's goodness.

Verse 14. How then will God treat His people? What hope can they have for the future? **For such is God, our God forever and ever; He will guide us until death.**

When we realize that this God who rescued Jerusalem is the One who will be with us, we can rejoice—not only now, but from now on. God was not an impersonal force to Israel. He became Israel's God by demonstration. Knowing the facts about Him causes us to say, "He is God"; but knowing Him causes us to say in faith, "He is *my* God!" The people of the city had moved from fact to faith, from theory to trust. They were rejoicing in Him as their God at this time and in the prospect of His being their God throughout the future. If they were obedient to Him, He would always remain faithful to them.

The guidance God provides His people is continuous. "Guide" is not a noun, but a verb (נָהַג, *nahag*); it suggests that God is among us as our constant leader, providing the direction we need. We can count on this relationship with Him from now on—today, tomorrow, and forever.

APPLICATION

A Song and a Psalm

As its title intimates, this psalm has two characteristics: It is a song and a psalm. Perhaps those two terms mean that it is a song for joyfulness and a psalm for reverence. Whether or not the two words have these exact meanings, it is certain that the psalm does have these two traits.

What emotions should continually surge in the believer's spirit? Should he not be joyful and reverent? He should be rejoicing over the wonderful things God has done in his life; and he should have a respect for the great God who is almighty, righteous, and full of lovingkindness.

The Symbol of Jerusalem

Jerusalem is a personification of God's people and symbolizes that He dwells among His own. The city is a kind of synecdoche, a part standing for the whole. The one city, Jerusalem, stands for all of Judah, all of God's people. As God beautified, protected, and made glad this city, He was testifying to what He does for all of His people for all time. Jerusalem reflects God's glory, righteousness, eternal purpose, and what He means to those who put their trust in Him.

Being the People of God

What does God do for His people?

He beautifies them. His presence among them transforms them into a glorious city, a marvelous people.

He protects them. He has watched over Jerusalem and preserved her. The people who enjoy God's presence likewise enjoy His protection. God's fellowship enfolds them and gives them safety and security.

He makes His people glad. As they contemplate what He has done for them, they are filled with joy.

The City of God Today

A further application of this psalm for the Christian can be seen in the truth that the church today is the city of God (Eph. 2:19–22). What God did for His city in Old Testament times as He blessed Jerusalem, we can count on His doing for His people today as we live as His church.

The church is made up of His people. All Christians are living stones in the temple of God, the church (1 Pet. 2:5; Eph. 2:19–22).

He dwells within His church. In the Old Testament, we see a physical building that God used as His dwelling place; but in the New Testament, Christians are pictured as the dwelling place of God (1 Cor. 3:16).

He watches over His church. He places over His church the canopy of love, grace, and protection. One day His Son will come back to get His church (Eph. 5:26, 27).

God and Beauty

God and beauty go together. He decorates with His majesty whatever He touches. Everything and everyone connected with where He dwells is bathed in His glory. Whoever walks with God will be transformed by this association with Him. Living in the sunlight of His glory allows us to absorb His undiluted light and reflect it to others. No one can be in God's actual presence and be unaffected.

In God's Presence

What happens when one abides in the fellowship of God?

He takes on the glory of God. The city, Jerusalem, was glorious because God lived in her. The city was covered with His radiance. Moses' face shone because he had been in God's company.

He takes on God's character. By his walk with God, the Christian takes on His likeness and infinite goodness. It is only natural for the children of God, the people of the God of lovingkindness, to be people of lovingkindness. Like Father, like child.

He takes on God's purpose. Not only do we take on His character, but we also take on His eternal purpose. We become one with Him. His goals become ours.

He knows the peace of God. No harm can come to anyone who is in God's presence. God is his encircling shield. Being with God means that we are surrounded with His might and love.

Within the fellowship of God, one has all the great things of life—God's glory, His character, His purpose, and His peace! Think of what one misses when he is outside the life of God.

God, Our King

Yahweh, the King of His people, should be praised continually. Four elements of His greatness are detected in the first three verses of this psalm.

He gives significance to those who put their faith in Him. He stands above and beyond all other kings because He brings to His people worth and meaning. Jerusalem would have been just another city, but God's choice to put His name on it made it the greatest of all cities.

He beautifies whatever He touches. He took Jerusalem, an average looking city, and made it the envy of the nations of the world. He brought glory and holiness to it. God's glory flows out to those around Him.

He is the believer's stronghold. Those who trust in Him find Him to be their citadel of strength or fortress. They are safe from all enemies, not because of their military prowess, but because God is with them. He has never failed His people.

He brings gladness to His people. As they feel the warmth and comfort of His providence and provisions, they can do nothing but break out in rejoicing. Gladness resides in the hearts of those who faithfully serve Him.

One of the most natural things for the faithful child of God to do is to praise God. He is his great King. His greatness is unparalleled. He beautifies the place where He dwells. He is the refuge of His people. Consequently, He fills the trusting heart with gladness.

The Terror of the Face of God

Verses 4 through 8 of this psalm picture enemy kings looking at God. Terror filled their hearts.

They could see His great power. They knew that even collectively they did not have the strength that could be compared to His. Analyzing His might, they were amazed and overwhelmed by what they saw. They were terrified, and panic seized them.

They could see that He protects His own. They could observe that there was no doubt about God's acting in behalf of His people. He would defend them! He loved His people and He would go before them and fight their battles. At first, Sennacherib did not see it, but after he lost 185,000 men, he did!

They could see that He had a divine purpose. They could tell that He had a plan He would observe until it was fulfilled. God had established Jerusalem "forever." No enemy or group of enemies could thwart His holy design.

Any enemy who understands who God is will fear Him. One who sees God's great power, His desire to defend His own, and His dedication to His divine purpose will bow down before Him. Who would not be filled with terror in the presence of this God?

Let us remember that only the enemies of the Lord need to fear Him. His people can relax their hearts in His care and love Him.

The Contemplation of God

The last part of this psalm portrays God's people meditating upon God at the temple. What a wholesome and uplifting exercise it is to contemplate who God is and what He has done!

They remembered His lovingkindness. How kind and gracious God had been to them! He had always responded to their pleas and prayers with grace and mercy.

They remembered His righteousness. They had found that His right hand was full of righteousness. In His dealings with them, He had always acted in character. Their experience with God confirmed that the foundation of His character is truth and the core of His character is love.

They remembered that His judgments were just and right. All the decisions He had made were correct and appropriate. The villages throughout Judah were able to rejoice in the judgments of the Lord. They always found God to be faithful and true.

They remembered how He had blessed His people. He had continually dealt with them by the hand of grace. He had made them. They had become what they were by His hand, and they were currently living through His provisions.

He had directed them in the past. His Word had been the means of their success. Their resolve was that God would be their Lord for the rest of their lives.

The writer of this psalm urged everyone who read it to go look at Jerusalem and see how God had blessed it. The exhortation is "Go look at all the parts of Jerusalem. Count her towers. Consider her ramparts. Go through her palaces. See how everything is in place. No part of the city has become marred by the enemy." When one looks at the history of Jerusalem, he sees God.

As we meditate upon the name of the Lord, do we not see what they saw? We see His lovingkindness toward us, His righteousness, His faithful judgments, how He has always blessed us, and how He has guided us and brought us to where we are.

On our way to Jerusalem in 1999, Don Shackelford, one of our guides, reminded us that when a Christian sees Jerusalem for the first time, he weeps. It is such a moving experience for the believer to see it because of God's association with it. When we look at His city, we remember the way of God.

"For Such Is God"

What kind of God is God? His lovingkindness can be described in numerous ways. Verse 14 of this psalm looks at it from the standpoint of God's leadership of those who trust in Him.

God will take us up. This promise is an implication. When one comes to Him in faith and obedience, God takes him on as a project of His grace. He says, "As long as you follow Me with love and devotion, I will be responsible for you" (see Mt. 6:33).

He will continually guide us. The verb that is used suggests continuation. The idea is "I will be among you, constantly guiding you." God Himself, with His Word and His fellowship, will be our compass.

He will be with us until the end. The word "death" is in the text, but it figuratively points to the end, promising that God will be with us until we have gone through the wilderness of this world. The point is that God will stay with us until the journey is completed.

He is the eternal God. He will never pop into someone's life and give a momentary push and then disappear. He comes in to stay—to take us up, to guide us by walking beside us, and to see that we have made it to His eternal house.

Psalm 49

God or Gold

The Superscription: For the choir director. A Psalm of the sons of Korah. This subtitle addressed to **the choir director** (לַמְנַצֵּחַ, *lamnatstseach*) calls this piece **a Psalm** (מִזְמוֹר, *mizmor*). Further, it says it belongs to the collection that was written, gathered, or used by **the sons of Korah** (לִבְנֵי־קֹרַח, *libney qorach*). Beyond these indications of the title, we know little about who wrote the piece or when it was written.

This unique composition addresses the oft-discussed theme of man and money. Its major emphasis is encouraging the godly to make God their supreme object of devotion. It is a song of wisdom literature.

One notices that there is a similarity between this psalm and Psalm 37. The answer to the question "Why do the wicked prosper?" in Psalm 37 is that their prosperity is only temporary and will not last. In this psalm (49), the answer to the same basic question is taken further as the reader is urged to realize that riches cannot offer anything beyond this world. The inequities of life may never be fully understood during our earthly pilgrimage; but death gives equality to everyone, bringing the rich and the poor, the potentates and the paupers, down to the same level. When we understand that riches do not go with us beyond death, our tendency to trust in riches is rebuked, and our attitude toward them is brought into the proper focus.

The instructions given in this psalm help to clarify the nature of money, what it actually does for us, and the importance of a balanced understanding of it. Seeing material treasures for what they are helps us to put them in their rightful place and not allow them to interfere with the worship and service of God.

The psalm can be divided into three parts: a brief introduction stressing what the writer proposes to do (vv. 1–4), an affirmation concerning the tragedy of relying on wealth (vv. 5–12), and the future of those who trust in wealth (vv. 13–20).

THE PEOPLE AND THE PURPOSE (49:1–4)

> ¹Hear this, all peoples;
> Give ear, all inhabitants of the world,
> ²Both low and high,
> Rich and poor together.
> ³My mouth will speak wisdom,
> And the meditation of my heart will be understanding.
> ⁴I will incline my ear to a proverb;
> I will express my riddle on the harp.

Verse 1. "All" the people of earth are called upon to listen, since they will have to deal with the problem under discussion. The psalm begins, **Hear this, all peoples; give ear, all inhabitants of the world**. The total range of the earth's population is urged to take to heart what is said.

This instruction in song is directed to all "peoples," not just to the nation of Israel as is the case with most of the psalms. The word "world" (חֶלֶד, *cheled*) has to do with "time" and "transitory things." Anyone in this world is subject to the frail nature of this world's existence.

Verse 2. All social levels and economic strata are included among those being addressed: **both low and high, rich and poor together.** In Hebrew, two different pairs of words are used for the groups of mankind: בְּנֵי אָדָם (*bᵉney ʾadam*) and בְּנֵי־אִישׁ (*bᵉney ʾish*). They apparently are describing two different stations of life that parallel the phrase "rich and poor." The first pair describes plain, ordinary folks; and the second pair pictures the more elite. Most translations render the Hebrew phrase "both low and high" as the NASB has. Whether a person has riches in abundance or not enough money to buy daily bread, he is asked to receive the admonition this psalm gives. This wider outlook is necessary because the topic will relate to humanity in general.

Verse 3. He says, **My mouth will speak wisdom, and the meditation of my heart will be understanding.** The writer is giving out "wisdom" from God as is indicated by verse 4, where he commits himself to following what he is saying. He will be the Spirit's agent in making this wisdom known. Through his mind will be given divine guidance about money; from his heart will come clear "understanding" on how money is to be understood. The Holy Spirit will use the "meditation" (הָגוּת, *haguth*) or observations of his heart to reveal the truth contained in the psalm.

Verse 4. Thus the writer includes himself among those who must heed what is being said: **I will incline my ear to a proverb; I will express my riddle on the harp.** He stresses the importance of his theme by using four words to describe the lesson he wants to impart: "wisdom" (חָכְמוֹת, *chakmoth*), "understanding" (תְבוּנוֹת, *th^ebunoth*), "proverb" (מָשָׁל, *mashal*), and "riddle" (חִידָה, *chidah*). These words have basically the same meaning, with only shades of differences between them. The first two words, "wisdom" and "understanding," are plurals that convey the idea of "much wisdom" and "great understanding." The other two lean more toward how this teaching will be conveyed. It will be done by "a proverb" (a comparison) concerning "the riddle" (an enigma) of how riches and godly living go together.

The writer says that he will give special attention to this message; he will "incline [his] ear." That is, he will bend over to the message so he can hear it completely and thoughtfully, making sure that he does not miss any part of it. He is saying, in effect, "I realize that I must carefully ponder this matter. I urge you, my readers, to follow my lead." His presentation will be made in the form of a song "on the harp" so that all can easily meditate on it and remember the thoughts of it.

PSALM 49

MONEY IS LIMITED (49:5–9)

⁵Why should I fear in days of adversity,
When the iniquity of my foes surrounds me,
⁶Even those who trust in their wealth
And boast in the abundance of their riches?
⁷No man can by any means redeem his brother
Or give to God a ransom for him—
⁸For the redemption of his soul is costly,
And he should cease trying forever—
⁹That he should live on eternally,
That he should not undergo decay.

Verse 5. Poor people when in the presence of the rich and powerful may find themselves possessed by fear. As one of them, the writer exhorts himself to refuse to be intimidated by them: **Why should I fear in days of adversity, when the iniquity of my foes surrounds me**. As he encourages his heart, he refers to the persecutors near him as "iniquity at my heels" (עֲוֹן עֲקֵבַי, *ªwon ªqebay*). When he sees prosperous, ungodly people afflicting the righteous in order to gain more riches, he refuses to fret, for he knows that soon their wealth will slip from their hands.

Verse 6. Death and time will bring the rich man down to a lifeless body deteriorating in a grave. Indeed, **those who trust in their wealth and boast in the abundance of their riches** will be humbled. As surely as one puts his faith and hope in "wealth," he will be disappointed. Death will realign a person's misplaced trust. The rich man may put in his treasures the same confidence that the godly man puts in God; however, the stark implication is that this mistake will come back to haunt him. Money makes the worst master. It is fleeting and deceitful.

Verse 7. Sheer observation of what is going on around us indicates that money is limited in what it can do. A little thought will cause us to conclude that **no man can by any means redeem his brother or give to God a ransom for him**. A type of redemption is referred to in the Old Testament. For example, the firstborn son was "redeemed" with five shekels of silver (Num. 3:42–51). However, some things cannot be ransomed.

Through His death, Jesus, our Savior, made it possible for the sinner to be redeemed from the guilt of sin, but one cannot reclaim another from the clutches of death with money. All will one day die. The rich may brag about the goods they have laid up for later use; nevertheless, with all of their boasting, their riches cannot "redeem" them or anyone else from death. Regardless of how much they have amassed, they cannot buy a way to avoid the dark valley.

Verse 8. Some things are so costly that they cannot be bought with material possessions. **For the redemption of his soul is costly, and he should cease trying forever.** A person might as well quit trying to eliminate death. All of his efforts cannot change the fact that he will make an exit from this life.

Verse 9. The rich man may strain every muscle and stack up all his resources **that he [may] live on eternally, that he [may] not undergo decay,** but all such labor is expended in vain. The Grim Reaper makes its way into the luxurious mansions of the rich even as it enters the simple cottages and cardboard houses of the poor. Death does not respect any person's position, anyone's pocketbook, or any person's popularity. The end of life cannot be bought off, laughed off, ignored, or chased away. The appointment with the grave is one of life's inevitabilities.

MONEY IS ONLY TEMPORARY
(49:10–13)

[10]**For he sees that even wise men die;**
The stupid and the senseless alike perish
And leave their wealth to others.
[11]**Their inner thought is that their houses are forever**
And their dwelling places to all generations;
They have called their lands after their own names.
[12]**But man in his pomp will not endure;**
He is like the beasts that perish.
[13]**This is the way of those who are foolish,**
And of those after them who approve their words. Selah.

Verse 10. All are moving toward the cemetery, and anyone alert to the realities of life will be painfully aware of this fact. The observant man **sees that even wise men die; the stupid and the senseless alike perish and leave their wealth to others.** The "wise" men (חֲכָמִים, *ch^akamim*), the men conscious of the truth about life; the "stupid" (כְּסִיל, *k^esil*), the ones who refuse instruction and wisdom; and the "senseless" (בַּעַר, *ba'ar*), those who see themselves above rebuke (Prov. 12:1), will all descend to the grave and will leave all they have accumulated to others.

The mortality rate of human beings is 100 percent. Every day death comes to someone, and some day death will come to everyone. The richest man in the world will leave his money behind when he makes his exit. In this regard, the wealthiest and the most successful are no better than the most foolish and the biggest failures of the world.

Verse 11. However, the financially successful man may look beyond these facts and brag about what he has and the name he has made for himself. The writer says, **Their inner thought is that their houses are forever and their dwelling places to all generations.** These imprudent, rich people may vainly envision that they will live "forever." **They have called their lands after their own names.** When they do think of death, they may say to themselves, "The houses I have built will last, and my name will be passed on from generation to generation." They store up possessions and wealth. They spend and live luxuriously. However, regardless of what they own and what they have done, they will leave everything they own behind when at last their bodies enter the narrow graves they will borrow until the Resurrection. What they did upon this earth soon will be forgotten, and their names will fade from people's memories. Those who become self-confident about their power and what they have their names on are deluded and mistaken, and anyone who follows their example will live and die to regret it.

Verse 12. The absolute truth is that no person will remain perpetually on this earth. **But man in his pomp will not endure; he is like the beasts that perish.** The man who does not realize that he is born to die has not faced the truth about life. Human beings, from one viewpoint, are like "the beasts" of the field and forest. All the living creatures—including people—expire. A mere casual evaluation of the nature of things and living beings brings us to this realization.

Verse 13. Anyone who does not recognize the terminal nature of his body is unwise, foolish, and stupid. He has just buried his head in the sand. Indeed, **this is the way of those who are foolish, and of those after them who approve their words.** Anyone who follows after this thoughtless man is equally as foolish.

Selah. Certainly this is a truth that should be seriously pondered.

GOD, MY REDEEMER (49:14, 15)

¹⁴As sheep they are appointed for Sheol;
Death shall be their shepherd;
And the upright shall rule over them in the morning,
And their form shall be for Sheol to consume
So that they have no habitation.
¹⁵But God will redeem my soul from the power of Sheol,
For He will receive me. Selah.

Verse 14. Although this verse is difficult to translate, it surely pictures death as a "shepherd" watching over us; it is observing us and waiting for its turn to come to us. **As sheep they are appointed for Sheol; death shall be their shepherd.** Peering over their shoulders at all times is the "shepherd" of "death." One by one, all human beings will be led by that great superintendent to the grave, and their bodies will be kept by this overseer until God's appointed time of the Resurrection.

The good news is that the righteous will triumph in the time of God's choosing. **And the upright shall rule over them in the morning, and their form shall be for Sheol to consume so that they have no habitation.** The righteous will be granted victory over the wicked rich at death. No details are given, but a general belief in a future victory is alluded to. The faith of the righteous man is in God, and he knows that his God will see to it that his future is safe. The godly man does not trust in his money; he puts his faith in his Maker. The thought of trusting in God instead of material treasures is the heart of this psalm.

Verse 15. God will deliver the righteous man. The writer says, **But God will redeem my soul from the power of Sheol, for He will receive me. Selah.** Far beyond his mental capacity to understand, he believes that God will deliver him from the tomb and guide him into a greater joy and pleasure than the richest man could ever know in this life. This type of faith roots out fear and brings calm assurance to the heart.

DO NOT BE AFRAID (49:16–20)

**¹⁶Do not be afraid when a man becomes rich,
When the glory of his house is increased;
¹⁷For when he dies he will carry nothing away;
His glory will not descend after him.
¹⁸Though while he lives he congratulates himself—
And though men praise you when you do well for yourself—
¹⁹He shall go to the generation of his fathers;
They will never see the light.
²⁰Man in his pomp, yet without understanding,
Is like the beasts that perish.**

Verse 16. The man who has few riches may be prone to worry about the man who does have wealth. With this fact in mind, the psalmist advises, **Do not be afraid when a man becomes rich, when the glory of his house is increased.** We should not be upset or concerned when our neighbors succeed and become prosperous and we do not. We know that the inequity will be short-lived. He cannot take any of his possessions with him into the next world.

The rich man may say to himself, "You have done well. You are smart and intelligent—a self-made man." People around him may say, "He is an amazing person. Everything he's touched has turned to gold." His friends may bury his gold, treasures, and trinkets in the tomb with him when he is interred, but he will not be able to use them. They will only lie at his side throughout the remaining time the world stands or until they are stolen by the living.

Verse 17. A blatant certainty of life should be acknowledged by everyone: We will take nothing with us when we leave this world. **For when he dies he will carry nothing away; his glory will not descend after him.** Whatever "glory" man's wealth brings him in life will be left behind at death. However he may have enjoyed life, however he may cling to life, he must eventually join his forefathers in the grave. He will "descend" into the darkness of death, where no light from his riches will ever come. His glory will not descend after him in the sense that he will not enjoy the status, public recognition, or benefits that his riches brought him in this life.

Verse 18. The rich man is prone to haughtiness. Riches can generate pride. **Though while he lives he congratulates himself—and though men praise you when you do well for yourself.** The Hebrew has "he blesses his soul." He slaps himself on the back as he says, "You are really doing well." One can commend himself for the riches he has, and he can soak up the commendations of others for his achievements; however, he is forgetting that he will soon be a pauper, as penniless as a cow in the stall or a chicken in a cage.

Verse 19. The harsh fact is that soon he will not even be remembered. **He shall go to the generation of his fathers; they will never see the light.** He is going to where all his forebears have gone—to the world of the dead. The phrase "they will never see the light" could mean that the forefathers will never come back to this world or see the light of earthly life again. However, it could refer to the departed rich people, asserting that they will never come back here. Their opportunity for life here is over. The light of this life will never be theirs again.

Verse 20. Anyone who lives without the consciousness of the brevity and frailty of life is simply without understanding. The writer says, **Man in his pomp, yet without understanding, is like the beasts that perish.** Anyone who lives only for riches must be judged as without real "understanding" (בִּין, *bin*) about life. In this case, "understanding" refers to a realistic conclusion about earth-life that is based upon an unprejudiced observation of it. This type of insight comes from careful consideration. The writer has used a different word for "understanding" than the one he used in verse 3; however, both of them have basically the same meaning.

People come into this world to live and to die. We can make this journey "with understanding" or without it. The choice will be ours. One who chooses to live and die "without understanding" reduces his experience in this world to nothing more than the life the soul-less animals have.

Death brings to an end for him all of the pleasures and conveniences that his riches made possible, leaving him without any hope in eternity. The animals, the brute beasts, live for this world and this world alone; the same is true of the person who lives for wealth.

APPLICATION

To Control or to Be Controlled?

Part of our responsibility of living in this world is that of maintaining the proper attitude toward material possessions. They can control us, or we can control them; we can be their master, or we can be their slave. Each person decides what he or she will do regarding it.

Man and Money

This psalm opens with a call for all peoples, even all the inhabitants of the earth, to listen to this song about one's understanding of possessions. When the subject of money is broached, it is appropriate to call on everyone to listen, for the subject is relevant in scope to the whole human race. Every person on the earth has to answer the question "How will earthly possessions affect me?"

Drawing from this psalm, here are three observations and a conclusion regarding man and money.

Observation one: All will have to use money. It is inevitable. We confront its use almost daily. Some kind of medium of exchange goes with the territory of responsible living in this world.

Observation two: A decision concerning what part it will play in our lives will have to be made. Whether one is a rich man or a poor man, he will have to shape his attitude toward money. He must determine whether it will be used as a tool or will be his passion.

Observation three: Most will find this challenge difficult, if not overwhelming. All normal people struggle with this responsibility. Money walks close beside our selfish desires, our wants and likes; and the love of riches can quickly turn a good person into a bad one, a hero into a villain, a sensible individual into a vain one.

The conclusion: All need wisdom from God to know how to handle money. This psalm was written to present some necessary guidance from God regarding this challenge. All of us must incline the ear and listen closely to what this song of wisdom has to say. Only by seeking God's help can we avoid the mines that the devil has placed in the money-harbor through which we must sail.

Do Not Miss the Point

The major lesson that grows out of these truths about money is to trust in God, not in money.

A person's true life is made up of service to God, not what he owns. As our Lord said, "For not even when one has an abundance does his life consist of his possessions" (Lk. 12:15b). The value of a person's life is not determined by what he has, but by what he is.

An individual who makes his gold his god can only look forward to the miseries of the grave. His riches may bring him some good fortune in this world, but eventually he must go to another land where wealth is not used and only spiritual values are recognized.

If one has no understanding of himself as a human being, of his mortality, and of his need for God, he lives and dies "like the beasts that perish." The intention of this psalm is to instruct all people by giving them guidance. It does not suggest that having money is wrong; it only declares the tragedy of trusting in wealth. The difference between people and beasts lies in the degree of "understanding" people have chosen to have.

PSALM 49

Are we living with wisdom or without it? Do we live for God or for gold?

The Riches of This World

The nature of life compels us to consider and think deeply. Let us ask, "What are the facts about earthly wealth?" Three characteristics clamor for attention: Money influences everyone, it is limited in what it can buy, and its influence is temporary.

Money affects us all. It influences every person. No one can say, "I will never need to consider this problem. I will always be isolated from it because I'm poor." Earthly treasures are a perennial and universal influence on humanity. For this reason, keeping our thoughts in check concerning them is a daily chore.

Money is limited in what it can do. People tend to think of wealth as the answer to all their wants, dreams, and ills. This psalm says that we must not be misled by such a foolish idea.

Obviously, riches have a function, but it would be spiritual suicide not to realize that wealth has limitations. Mankind's ultimate folly is to seek eternal life through material possessions. Our Lord vividly taught this lesson in the Parable of the Rich Fool (Lk. 12:16–21). The needs of the soul cannot be supplied by earthly treasures in whatever form they may be acquired.

Earthly wealth is temporary. It is given to us for use only in this world. When our journey through this earth-life is completed, we must leave our riches behind.

Only by recognizing these truths can we keep the proper mindset toward money. Let us read this psalm often and imbibe its teachings to trust in God instead of in earthly possessions.

Money's Buying Power

One of the major thoughts of this psalm—the thought that money cannot prevent death—can be easily expanded into related truths.

> Money can buy entertainment, but not happiness.
> Money can buy food, but not an appetite.
> Money can buy medicine, but not health.

Money can buy a house, but not a family.
Money can buy quietness, but not peace.
Money can buy people, but not friends.
Money can buy glasses, but not eyesight.
Money can buy a Bible, but not salvation.

Money, the Great Deceiver
Sometimes in word and sometimes in action, people attribute a power to money that it does not and cannot possess. It is good, therefore, for us to ask, "What should I not do with money?"

We should not trust in it. This would be obvious to most people, but it is a truth that even good people forget. Our basic trust should be placed only in God. Those who boast in riches will one day see that they have trusted in nothing but dust.

We should not substitute it for spiritual values. Money cannot replace prayer, a study of the Scriptures, or walking with God. Money can be a means of service, but it has no character of its own. It takes its attributes from the hand that holds it or spends it. Those who have it determine whether it is good or bad by their use of it.

We should not envy those who have it. One day the rich will be brought down to stand alongside all others. Death is the great leveler. When we depart from this world, we leave every earthly thing we possess behind.

Our hearts should be devoted to God and should be somewhat indifferent to money. We are the servants of God, and money is our servant to use to His glory and in His work on earth.

Just God and the Soul
A time will come when only two realities will matter. At death everything will fade from the picture except God and the soul.

Death will show up our misdirected affections. If we have trusted in money, we will find that it makes a poor god. Confidence in anything or anyone will be destroyed at the hour of our departure from this world.

Death brings to us the realization that our relationship with God is of supreme importance. Eventually, life comes down to our being hidden in God through Jesus. Such is true for everyone at all times, but this truth does not become clear to many until death arrives and makes us look at the situation anew.

Death will work its reducing magic on all people, rich and poor. Death is impartial, treating everyone the same. Nothing earthly is allowed beyond death's door, and we will face God with only our spiritual values.

How wise we would be if we faced the truth today that at some time it will be just God and us—and not God, money, and us! If this is inevitably going to happen later, common sense says, "Why not recognize this truth and live in light of it now?"

Psalm 50
True Religion Before God

The Superscription: A Psalm of Asaph. Called **a Psalm** (מִזְמוֹר, *mizmor*) in its title, this composition is the first of twelve psalms that are said to be **of** ("by," "for," or "to") **Asaph** (לְאָסָף, *le'asap*) (50; 73—83). Only one (50) of the "Asaph psalms" is in Book II; the other eleven are in Book III (73—83). Asaph, along with Heman and Ethan, served as one of David's leading musicians (1 Chron. 6:39; 16:5). However, the title may not necessarily indicate the authorship. It may refer to the one who placed the psalm in the collection, the one or ones who made special use of it, or the style of the psalm.

Clearly, this psalm is a judgment-like song to call the nation of Israel to repentance. The time of its writing and the author are difficult to determine.

As his central theme, the writer discusses pure religion before God. In the fervency and rebuke of a fiery spokesman of God, he denounces the sinfulness of the nation and points to the way for a person or a nation to be pleasing to God.

The larger part of the psalm is cast in the form of God speaking to His people. As Judge, God brings His people before His searching eyes and announces His displeasure with them.

The scene is not that of the final judgment of all people; it is a dramatic portrayal of God's calling His chosen people into account for the way they were keeping their covenant with Him. The covenant concept especially surfaces in verse 5. However, the psalm is not just a depiction of judgment. The announcement of condemnation provides the framework in which important instructions are given on how to keep God's covenant.

The body of the psalm is comprised of two judgment-speeches delivered by the Lord. The psalm easily divides into three parts: an introduction to the covenant-lawsuit setting (vv. 1–6); verdict one: a rebuke for worshiping without sincerity (vv. 7–15); and verdict two: a severe reproof of those who claim to be in the covenant but live notoriously (vv. 16–23).

A CALL TO JUDGMENT (50:1–6)

¹The Mighty One, God, the LORD, has spoken,
And summoned the earth from the rising of the sun to its setting.
²Out of Zion, the perfection of beauty, God has shone forth.
³May our God come and not keep silence;
Fire devours before Him,
And it is very tempestuous around Him.
⁴He summons the heavens above,
And the earth, to judge His people:
⁵"Gather My godly ones to Me,
Those who have made a covenant with Me by sacrifice."
⁶And the heavens declare His righteousness,
For God Himself is judge. Selah.

Verse 1. In a brief prelude, a proclamation is made that announces that God is calling His people before Him in order to lay bare their sins. The whole earth is summoned to be witnesses of the event.

The voice behind the gathering of this court-assembly is the Lord Himself: **The Mighty One, God, the LORD, has spoken**. Three names of God are used in this first sentence: "the Mighty One" (אֵל, *'el*), "God" (אֱלֹהִים, *'elohim*), and "the LORD" (יהוה, *YHWH*). A similar use of these three names occurs in one other place in the Old Testament; it appears twice in Joshua 22:22. The mention of these names emphasizes the attributes of the One who is going to be pronouncing the divine verdict regarding His people. He is the Supreme-God, the Creator-God, and the Redeemer-God. He is the only true, almighty, and self-existent One.

God invites all **the earth from the rising of the sun to its**

setting, from the total land area covered by the track of the sun in its regular circuit, to listen to His decree about His people. These figurative expressions declare the far-reaching solemnity of the judgment that is about to be revealed.

Verse 2. The setting of the judgment is "Zion," or Jerusalem. **Out of Zion, the perfection of beauty, God has shone forth.** This assembly is to be where God is worshiped, "Zion," the place where His "beauty" and glory have long been beheld with awe.

Verse 3. The time of judgment is coming and will not be delayed. God is going to make known His sentence. The writer of the psalm says, **May our God come and not keep silence**. The dreaded moment of accounting must be preceded by the coming of the great Judge to His throne. As He comes, **fire devours before Him**. He comes forth in dazzling glory, with "fire" protruding before Him and a swirling tempest around Him. This imagery of His approaching the throne is similar to His descent to Mount Sinai to give His laws to Israel. Fire, smoke, and awesome reverence attended His descent (Ex. 20:18–25).

Verse 4. A broader group of witnesses are now called forth for the solemn occasion: **He summons the heavens above, and the earth, to judge His people**. Any legitimate trial must have witnesses, attorneys, and a judge. The "heavens" and the earth are asked to observe as God interrogates Israel, the nation bound to Him by a covenant. In fact, God will serve as both Plaintiff and Judge—as the One bringing the complaint and the deciding Judge.

Verse 5. With His own words, God sends out the injunction for the convening of even His faithful people: **"Gather My godly ones to Me, those who have made a covenant with Me by sacrifice."** The "godly ones" normally refers to God's loyal people (חֲסִידָי, *ch^asiday*). The word for "godly" comes from "lovingkindness," the great covenant-loyalty word. Are those being called for judgment being described in irony as "godly ones," or is this group the truly faithful who are seated as part of the vast array of witnesses? Perhaps they are being recognized for their faithfulness and are asked to observe the divine rebuke of the unfaithful in His nation.

This announcement of judgment is not the judgment of the

heathen; their time of judgment will come later. This event is the examination of God's people and them alone.

Verse 6. The august nature of the occasion is accented by the testimony of the heavens: **And the heavens declare His righteousness, for God Himself is judge.** The "heavens" confirm the "righteousness" of God, for they have continually observed this great attribute in all His verdicts and judgments. They were watching from above when the original covenant with Israel was made at Sinai.

Flawlessly righteous, God is preeminently qualified to be the Judge. He will speak, and His verdicts will be eternal. His divine words will rebuke and correct.

An event of this kind is necessary. God's people must be measured by the requirements of the covenant.

Selah. That is, with a pause in the psalm, the reader is urged to think about this.

"I WILL SPEAK" (50:7–15)

^{7}"Hear, O My people, and I will speak;
O Israel, I will testify against you;
I am God, your God.
^{8}I do not reprove you for your sacrifices,
And your burnt offerings are continually before Me.
^{9}I shall take no young bull out of your house
Nor male goats out of your folds.
^{10}For every beast of the forest is Mine,
The cattle on a thousand hills.
^{11}I know every bird of the mountains,
And everything that moves in the field is Mine.
^{12}If I were hungry I would not tell you,
For the world is Mine, and all it contains.
^{13}Shall I eat the flesh of bulls
Or drink the blood of male goats?
^{14}Offer to God a sacrifice of thanksgiving
And pay your vows to the Most High;
^{15}Call upon Me in the day of trouble;
I shall rescue you, and you will honor Me."

Verse 7. God, the Judge, calls for everyone's attention. He is ready to confront His people, and all are commanded to listen. **"Hear, O My people, and I will speak; O Israel, I will testify against you; I am God, your God."** Silence is necessary—for God's testimony against His people is of supreme importance. He is God and it is His right to describe the sins that they have committed. His words will be right, and His case will be presented accurately; therefore His judgment will have the most far-reaching import.

Verse 8. What accusations does God bring against His nation? His first criticism is that the people are not worshiping Him from their hearts. Their praise of Him consists only of externals—it is ritual without the heart, form without spirit. God says, **"I do not reprove you for your sacrifices, and your burnt offerings are continually before Me."** The people are not being chastised for failing to offer "sacrifices"; no indeed, they have given them. The law they were given required "offerings" from them, and they have kept that part of the law.

Verse 9. However, God does not want their oblations without their devoted obedience. He says, **"I shall take no young bull out of your house nor male goats out of your folds."** The deficiency in their worship is that they worshiped without an understanding of the meaning of their sacrifices and without taking to heart what they were doing. Because of this empty worship, their offerings have been repulsive to God. For purposes of sacrifice, God will not accept a young bull or a male goat from them. Our worship of God either brings Him great delight or great displeasure, depending on whether we worship with the sincerity of our hearts.

Verse 10. In one sense the sacrifices are meant for the worshiper, not for God, for He owns everything and has need of nothing from people. He says, **"For every beast of the forest is Mine, the cattle on a thousand hills."** The Hebrew has "beasts" (בְּהֵמוֹת, *bᵉhemoth*) in the second part of the verse; thus "cattle" is more of an interpretation than a translation. God did not need their "livestock," for He already owned them all. How could a man give God anything? He possesses all the domesticated animals of the earth, the beasts of the forests, fields, and hills.

PSALM 50

Verse 11. He not only owns everything, but He knows everything about His creation. No one needs to explain anything to God; He is omniscient, all-knowing. He sees every movement of even the smallest creature on earth. He affirms, **"I know every bird of the mountains, and everything that moves in the field is Mine."** No bird escapes His careful scrutiny, and no animal moves without His divine observation. Every action of His creation is under the intricate survey of His all-seeing eye.

Verse 12. He has no personal needs that a person could supply. God says, **"If I were hungry I would not tell you, for the world is Mine, and all it contains."** Our Creator is not sustained by food from the earth. It is an absurdity to think, as the heathen did concerning their gods, that sacrifices offered to God could in any way sustain Him. If God did get hungry, He would not tell any person about it, for He has created all things, possesses His creation, and owns all the food that the earth contains.

Verse 13. God, a spirit being, cannot be satisfied with or personally served by material things. Appropriately, He asks, **"Shall I eat the flesh of bulls or drink the blood of male goats?"** What shall God, a spirit, eat? Why would He seek physical food? If He needed it, He would not come to a man or woman for it, because He has a table set before Him filled with all the things of His creation.

Verse 14. What then should people do? What shall they give God? The answer is obvious: Let them **offer to God a sacrifice of thanksgiving and pay** [the] **vows** [made] **to the Most High**. The truth is that God accepts only one kind of sacrifice: the one given according to His will from a heart of joy, thanksgiving, and devotion to Him. He wants integrity and thanksgiving. He requires us to be faithful in keeping our word to Him. He seeks gratitude in the innermost being. The spirit of faith, love, and obedience, the involvement of the soul, would be the composite, required accompaniment of the sacrifice that God accepts. The "sacrifice[s]" and "vows" of the people were to be concrete expressions of their love and appreciation of God.

God is now referred to in a fourth way (see v. 1), as "the Most High" (עֶלְיוֹן, *'elyon*). He is the only true God.

Verse 15. In harmony with His great heart of compassion,

God says, **"Call upon Me in the day of trouble; I shall rescue you."** The God of Israel cares for His people. He has delivered them in their times of "trouble."

"And you will honor Me." He will inspire them to love and serve Him if they will open their hearts to His overtures of grace. When the proper response to God is made, He will answer their prayers, redeem them, and bless them. God will be honored by their relying upon Him. In return for His goodness, they will "honor" and praise Him with heartfelt joy for what He has done for them.

NOW, TO THE WICKED (50:16–23)

¹⁶But to the wicked God says, "What right have you to tell
   of My statutes
And to take My covenant in your mouth?
¹⁷For you hate discipline,
And you cast My words behind you.
¹⁸When you see a thief, you are pleased with him,
And you associate with adulterers.
¹⁹You let your mouth loose in evil
And your tongue frames deceit.
²⁰You sit and speak against your brother;
You slander your own mother's son.
²¹These things you have done and I kept silence;
You thought that I was just like you;
I will reprove you and state the case in order before your
   eyes."

Verse 16. In His judgment, God moves on from the sin of formalism, where one has outward action but no inner allegiance, to the sin of hypocrisy, where one professes religion with his lips but disregards it in his life. The persons who now come under God's condemnation are the Israelites who are blatantly wicked.

What indictments does He bring against them? **But to the wicked God says, "What right have you to tell of My statutes and to take My covenant in your mouth?"** An essential trait of

PSALM 50

the true religion that God holds before His people is purity in living. Therefore, He gives them a stinging rebuke about their failure to live according to His laws. They are teachers of His "statutes," but they are not living by those commandments. God will not permit His people to believe one way and live another way. God requires belief and behavior to match.

Verse 17. In this part of the psalm, God speaks to Israel with an even sterner tone. He accuses His people of open and willful transgressions. He says, **"For you hate discipline, and you cast My words behind you."** A heartless service of God eventually shows up in meaningless worship and an immoral lifestyle.

The wicked ones whom God is addressing think of themselves as belonging to the covenant. They know God's statutes (laws), and they teach others in Israel to live by them. However, when it comes to living by those commands themselves, they ignore the correction and despise the "discipline" (מוּסָר, *musar*) that these laws bring to them.

Verse 18. Furthermore, God condemns them not only for the sins of which they are guilty, but also for the permissive attitude they have toward others who engage in grievous sins. God says, **"When you see a thief, you are pleased with him, and you associate with adulterers."** The Ten Commandments are being abused and forsaken. They do not recoil in horror when they see someone stealing; rather, they find a sinister appreciation for these wicked actions. The Hebrew word רָצָה (*ratsah*) suggests that they delight in the wickedness of the wicked man.

The same type of response is made concerning adultery. As Israelites who are committed to God's covenant, they should be exhorting and teaching people to turn away from gross and terrible violations of God's laws. Instead, they gloss over the sins and practice the evil themselves. Simultaneously, while they do these horrible deeds, they pretend to be pious followers of the covenant. Their conduct is a plain and open insult to God.

Verse 19. To make matters worse, their tongues are given over to evil. God says, **"You let your mouth loose in evil and your tongue frames deceit."** They use their lips to tell lies, for manufacturing misleading innuendos, and to spew out falsehoods against others. The verb "frames" (צָמַד, *tsamad*) suggests "fastening together" as one would do while scheming or plotting. Thus it must be that the indictment is that their lips intentionally engineer deceit and falsehood.

Verse 20. The divine accusations in this psalm have moved from severe to the most severe, from bad to worst. God says, **"You sit and speak against your brother; you slander your own mother's son."** So vicious are they that they speak evil of their own kin, cutting down those whom one ordinarily would seek to defend and build up. Brother speaks against brother as slander is poured out against one's closest relatives. "You sit" (יָשַׁב, *yashab*) indicates a deliberate and settled practice of speaking evil against others.

Verse 21. God has given them space to repent and has not immediately condemned them for engaging in this type of corrupt living. He says, **"These things you have done, and I kept silence."** He has temporarily refrained from stepping in with His judgment. Apparently, the wicked used His "silence" to say that God condoned their actions. They failed to recognize that God's longsuffering never means that He is indifferent to sin.

He says, **"You thought that I was just like you."** Influenced by their sin, the hypocritical Israelites constructed a degraded view of God in their minds. In their twisted thinking, they pictured God as being like themselves, speaking one way but living another. They seemed to have concluded that God would be satisfied with their sacrifices and would overlook their atrocious actions.

God says, **"I will reprove you and state the case in order before your eyes."** Out of holiness and righteousness, God would declare plainly His "case" against them. The word for "in order" (עָרַךְ, *'arak*) is a word that means "to arrange or lay out in appropriate order." God will lay out His reasons for bringing them into judgment so that they will not misunderstand or misconstrue the event. Their sins and shortcomings will be brought into full view and sternly reproved and rebuked.

THE SALVATION OF GOD (50:22, 23)

[22]**"Now consider this, you who forget God,**

PSALM 50

> Or I will tear you in pieces, and there will be none to deliver.
> ²³He who offers a sacrifice of thanksgiving honors Me;
> And to him who orders his way aright I shall show the salvation of God."

Verse 22. As the psalm comes to its close, God offers an invitation to His people. He says, **"Now consider this, you who forget God, or I will tear you in pieces, and there will be none to deliver."** Israel is asked to "consider" (בִּין, *bin*) or understand what has been said. They are to take God's words to heart, reflect on them, and allow them to sink deeply into their minds and consciences. This process should bring them to repentance.

The fifth name for God in this psalm, אֱלוֹהַּ (*ᵉloah*), appears here. This name is found almost exclusively in Hebrew poetry. It is the singular of *ᵉlohim* and suggests that He is the true God. The plural form is thought to convey magnitude and majesty.

The people are given a vivid and pointed two-pronged warning. The first part stresses its severity: If God's correction is shunned, the people are told, they will be "torn to pieces" as a lion tears apart his prey. The second aspect of the warning emphasizes its eternal nature: When God brings His punishment upon a life, there is no escape. A time will come when no one, not even God, can save the rebellious person. No such person can be delivered from the sure and certain judgment.

Verse 23. However, God tempers His threat with mercy. He is ever the God of salvation to His people. **"He who offers a sacrifice of thanksgiving honors Me; and to him who orders his way aright I shall show the salvation of God."** The man who returns to Him, offers praise to Him from a sincere heart, and brings his life into harmony with His precepts can be saved. The Hebrew sentence does not have "aright," a word that has been inserted by the NASB because they have concluded that the word was implied. The literal reading is "He who orders his way." The word (שִׂים, *śim*) is "fixes" or "puts." The thought is "Whoever fixes or determines his way in God's way will have Yahweh's favor." Thus this psalm, spoken by God Himself, ends with a promise of "salvation" to those who will direct their lives into God's design for His covenant.

APPLICATION

What Is Pure Religion?

Using our Lord's judgment of His Old Testament people as an example, mark out the essential elements of pure religion before God. These determinations will be easy to make because sincere religion in God's sight is defined in this psalm by none other than God Himself. In His view, righteousness has two elements: worship from the heart and godly living. These two traits are inseparable. One without the other is insufficient and unacceptable to God.

A Divine Balance

One preacher used a physical illustration to communicate the essentiality of the divine balance between worship and work, between lips of praise and a life of obedience. As he preached to the congregation, he stood on one foot as long as he could. While standing on that one foot, he talked about faith and what it means. Finally, he could stand on one foot no longer and had to regain his balance using the other foot. He then stood on the other foot as long as he could, preaching this time on works and what they mean. He spoke for a few minutes in that stance, eventually losing his balance and having to catch himself again with the other foot. The congregation was able to anticipate what he said next: "I must have two legs on which to stand. Even so, God has given us faith and works. We must have both. Faith and obedience go together."[1]

This Psalm and Today

Can we not say that the lesson of this psalm is just as vital today as it was when given? The Old Testament context was that of animal sacrifices and temple worship, while the context for the Christian is the last days, the Christian Dispensation.

---

[1]Donald William, *Mastering the Old Testament* (Dallas: Word Publishing, 1986), 355.

The New Testament church worships through singing, preaching, prayer, communion, and giving as it looks to God in faith and love. Even though we live in a different dispensation from the time of this psalm, the lesson it gives is relevant and is repeated in the New Testament. Worshiping God from the heart and living out His words in our darkened world are mandated by both covenants.

If God called us before Him today for correction, what would He say? Would He rebuke us for our lack of heart in His worship and our lack of faithfulness in living out His will?

The Great Gathering

The most solemn assembly that one can imagine is the one which God will gather out of all the earth as He judges His people. On that occasion, what kind of Judge will God be?

He is the all-powerful Judge. We refer to Him as the mighty One, the almighty God. He has all power, and He will have no trouble convening the assembly and administering judgment.

He is a righteous Judge. All who know anything about God know of His righteousness. The foundation of His throne is holiness, and His actions are always in perfect accord with the ways of truth. We can be assured that His judgment will be a faithful and accurate judgment.

He will be a thorough Judge. He will judge our actions and our thoughts, down to our intention and imaginations. He knows everything about us, for He sees us from the inside out. No thought will be overlooked and no action missed.

He will judge regarding His covenant. The happy news for those who walk with Him is that His judgment will be according to His agreement with us. His relationship with His people is covenant based. Since He has never lied or failed to keep a promise, we can rest assured that His judgment will not deviate from the covenant-promises He has confirmed with us.

Answering to God will be the most significant event of all time. The entire world will be called upon to witness it. Nothing has ever happened on earth that supersedes in significance the moment when God calls His people before Him.

God in Three Dimensions

In the first line of this psalm God is referred to by three names. Each name points to a special characteristic of God.

He is the Creator-God. The word is *Elohim*, the name that is used of Him in the creation narratives of Genesis 1. He is the One who created mankind and created all things for them.

He is the Redeemer-God. The word is *Yahweh*, the name that suggests His covenant-keeping relationship with Israel.

He is the Supreme-God. The word is *El*, the name that pictures Him as the Almighty, the one and only God.

When these three names are brought together, we see the Creator, the covenant-keeping, Supreme God.

Serving God

What is God like? What is His nature, His essence?

In one sense, we cannot do anything for Him. He is God, and we are mortals. A human being is not able to give Him anything that He does not already have.

He is the self-existent One. He does not depend on man or any of His creation for anything. Amazingly, He does not even need our worship. Our devotion to God brings Him pleasure, but He does not need it. He is self-sufficient and self-sustained.

What, then, can we do for Him?

We can obey Him. His heart is pleased when we listen to His commands and sincerely obey them. What brings more pleasure to a father than his children following his guidance?

We can trust Him. Confiding trust grows out of confidence in and respect for God. When we trust Him, we are saying that we believe God to be trustworthy and reliable. This response is the highest compliment that we can give Him.

We can thank Him. The most helpless person on earth can say "thank you." Thanking God may be a small thing to do, but it brings great joy to our Father. Even God appreciates gratitude.

We can worship Him. He is our Creator, Sustainer, and Savior; and it is appropriate for us to acknowledge who He is in worship.

We can serve His creation. When we serve people, we are serving God. Jesus said that when we minister to the down and out, we have ministered to Him (see Mt. 25:31–46).

The Sins of God's People

Graphically and pointedly, verses 16 through 21 declare the sinfulness of God's people.

They were teaching the Word without living it. The people of God were interested in teaching the statutes of God, but they were not living by those precepts. They were shells, having a form but no spirit.

They were despising the discipline of God's Word. His Word brought the necessary correction to them, but they rejected and ignored it.

They were encouraging sin. Instead of rebuking sin, they cheered on those who were committing it.

They were offering their fellowship to evil people. They had daily, friendly, and approving associations with those who were living in adultery and engaging in other obvious sins.

They were slandering others. Their tongues were dedicated to evil instead of good. No one was immune to the venom of their gossip. When given the opportunity, they smeared their mud on even their nearest kin and dearest friends.

They pictured God as being like them. Through their despicable conduct, they were bringing the image of God down to their level. They were depicting God as if He were a sinful person.

These are terrible sins—because of their intrinsic nature and their horrible influence. With His divine eye, God had pierced the thin veneer of their superficial living and exposed what they really were. Let us look and listen. Do our faith and footsteps agree with each other?

The Worst Mistakes

No child of God can live without making mistakes (see 1 Jn. 1:8). The church is a hospital for sinners, not a museum that displays perfect saints; it is a place of Christian growth and not a place to showcase trophies of arrival. However, we should especially guard against three terrible failures.

Worship without heart. Our praise of God obviously should be sincere and full of devotion. Nothing hurts God more than a mannequin sitting in the worship service.

Living without guidance. When we ignore God's plain teachings on how He wants us to live, we deny His covenant.

Sinning without repentance. It is one thing to make a mistake; it is another to fail to correct that mistake. The worst mistake may be failing to correct a mistake that has been made.

These are tragic errors because they involve the heart. More than anything else, God wants our hearts. This is true because when God gets our hearts, He gets everything else.

The Evils of the Tongue

God has given people the awesome opportunity of communicating with Him and with one another. We figuratively summarize this privilege with the word "tongue." As James said, ". . . from the same mouth come both blessing and cursing" (Jas. 3:10).

The portion of this psalm that rebukes the ungodly for their misuse of their speech (vv. 16–20) confronts us with three great sins of the tongue.

Cursing. Nothing can be worse than using our lips to curse the God who created us and who sustains us. The action of using His name in vain or railing at Him receives a severe condemnation by the Scriptures and common sense (Ex. 20:7; Lev. 19:12; 24:15).

Lying. Using the tongue for deceitful purposes is another sin clearly rebuked by the Scriptures. Our lips were made to speak the truth of the Scriptures. The devil has commandeered our mouths for his mission when they spew lies, falsehoods, and error.

Slander. Destroying someone's reputation or spreading unproven rumors about someone also is reproved by God. Human respect and appreciation for the body of Christ should motivate us to carefully weigh our words about others before we speak them, asking, "Is it true?"; "Is it edifying?"; and "Is it encouraging?"

God has given most of us the ability to speak privately, conversationally, and publicly. This gift belongs only to people, and what a responsibility it brings! Let us put a watchman beside our lips to guard our words that they may be for edifying and encouragement and not for deceit and destruction. Before we speak, let us remember the words of our Lord: "For by your words you will be justified, and by your words you will be condemned" (Mt. 12:35).

"Saturday"
Perhaps a good place to end this study of Psalms 1—50 is with a meditation about "Saturday."

Following the crucifixion of Jesus, Matthew says, "Now on *the next day*, the *day* after the preparation . . ." (Mt. 27:62a; emphasis added).

We know what the disciples did on Friday, but where were they on Saturday? What was this historic Saturday like for them? On Friday, they stood in a huddle before the cross watching as their Messiah moaned and writhed in pain as the agonies of the crucifixion swept over Him. At the end of the day, they trudged to their homes completely numbed and confused by what they had seen.

The only reference to what happened on Saturday is a brief description of the Jews making the request for a guard to be placed beside the entrance to the tomb where Jesus had been buried. Nothing is said about what the disciples did on Saturday in the Gospels. Nevertheless, with our imaginations and with the implications of the facts that are given in the divine text, we can piece together what this unusual seventh day was like.

For some disciples, it was *a Saturday of mourning over unrealized dreams.* The death of Jesus had shocked them, and they were in a daze of doubt and quagmire of questions. Jesus had told them that He would arise from the dead on the third day (Mt. 16:21). They had heard His prophecy, but that prophecy had not soaked into their belief system. Now, having witnessed the Savior's execution, they were wondering what was happening to their world.

For others, it was *a Saturday of business as usual.* The guards who were placed by the tomb were just doing their duty as they had always done. They were soldiers fulfilling a charge, with no idea that they were watching the entrance to the tomb of the Son of God who had died for their sins. They had no notion that they were part of the greatest life-changing event that would break on the world the next day. They saw no farther than the command that they had been given. Saturday for them was just an ordinary day.

For still others, it was *a Saturday filled with glorious anticipation.* Surely some of the disciples were taking the prediction of Jesus seriously. Certainly, they remembered what He had said. If so, they knew that Saturday was "the day before." Jesus had said that three days after His death He would rise again. Saturday was "the day before" death itself would die.

This brief recounting of what the disciples did on Saturday raises a question for us: What is Saturday to us? You see, life to us in this world is similar to life on that Saturday long ago.

The psalms we have studied were expressions of life and worship to the Israelites on their "Saturday," as they waited for the coming of the Messiah. These psalms were lived during times of difficulties, questions, and struggles. Their challenge was to walk with God on "the day before" the Lord's Advent.

In another sense, today for us is "Saturday," "the day before." We are waiting for the return of Jesus. We have heard the promises from our Savior. He has said that He is coming again, and we hold that promise in our hearts.

How are we living on our "Saturday"? Are we living it as a day of unrealized dreams, as a day of business as usual, or as the day before the climax of history? The psalms we have studied have reminded us that we must walk with God while we wait for the big day. Let us live as if Jesus died yesterday, arose this morning, and is coming back tonight.

> Why are you in despair, O my soul?
> And why are you disturbed within me?
> Hope in God . . . (Ps. 43:5).

A FINAL WORD
PSALMS 1—50

An old story says that one day in ancient Greece Socrates was sitting beside the river, meditating. A passerby who was headed hurriedly toward a seemingly important destination saw him, went over to him, and asked, "How do I get to the great mountain, Mount Olympus, from here?" Socrates, responding as a philosopher, said, "If you will make sure that every step that you take is toward that mountain, you will soon arrive at it."

The sincere believer, as we have seen in these fifty psalms, is on a journey to God. His journey will not be completed with one step, with one decision, or during one day. The journey is always continual and upward. It involves a daily, conscious walking with our Father through Jesus. He has not promised us smooth sailing, but He has guaranteed us a happy landing. We may have to go through the wilderness of suffering and confusion on our way to that beautiful place. However, we can be confident of this truth: If we make sure that every step that we take is *toward* Him, one day, a day of His choosing, we will arrive at His eternal home.

From the Editor
Have You Heard...
About Truth for Today?

What are the big missionary needs of our time? Those who study missionary evangelism point to two paramount needs that are ever present in the mission field.

THE BIG NEEDS OF WORLD EVANGELISM

First, they tell us that educating and maturing the national Christian man so that he can preach to his own people in their own language is of supreme importance. Giving this type of assistance to the national man will help to make our missionary efforts more self-supporting and more enduring. We appreciate one of our own preaching to us, and so do other peoples of the world. When we consider the work "our work," we approach it with greater care and will sacrifice more for it. This principle holds true in all cultures.

Christianity can flourish in any nation and culture, in any time or circumstance, if we will let it. When it is established through national preachers, it is far more likely to grow and blossom in the lives of the national people and not become an effort that is totally dependent upon American support.

After the Restoration Movement began in America, it did not take the early preachers long to realize that they had to teach young men to preach if the movement was really to grow. Thus, very early in the history of the Restoration Movement, schools were established. Wisdom suggested that route.

Christians should be grateful for every mission effort that is going on, such as campaigns, medical missions, and television presentations. However, we must not overlook the surpassing value of providing educational opportunities overseas that will assist a man in becoming capable of preaching effectively to his own people. This approach is absolutely vital to the ongoing success of the overall missionary work of the church.

Second, those who have researched missionary evangelism tell us that we need to make available biblical literature that provides an understanding of the Bible on the level of the people. Those whom the missionary is seeking to teach need their own copies of the Bible and assistance in understanding the Scriptures. They require guidance so they can grow quickly and accurately in their comprehension of the Bible. (See Acts 8:30, 31.)

When Tex Williams, the director of World Bible School, was on Harding University's campus sometime ago, he spoke to students about mission work. As a guest lecturer, he told one of the mission classes that the greatest need of Africa is Christian literature. "Without this literature," he said, "they simply cannot become Christians and grow into Christian maturity as they should." There is possibly one exception to this principle. The exception would be places where there is the presence of well-grounded men of faith continually teaching and preaching. This exception obviously applies to only a few places around the world. Even then, biblical literature is needed to support the teaching done.

Let us all consider carefully these two obvious missionary needs. Our efforts must be geared to meeting them. Not to address them is to ignore the clear results of the research that has been done in mission evangelism.

ADDRESSING THESE NEEDS

An effort is currently being made to address both of these big missionary needs. It has been designated the Truth for Today World Mission School (TFTWMS). Started in 1990 as a work under the oversight of the Champions church of Christ in Houston, Texas, it has proven to be a wonderful way to combine three methods of evangelism and thus minister to these supreme needs.

HAVE YOU HEARD... ABOUT TRUTH FOR TODAY?

First, TFTWMS is a unique preacher school. An education in the Scriptures is mailed to the national preacher. The work started with 1,460 native preachers enrolled from 110 nations. Now literature is mailed to 40,000 people in 156 nations. These preachers were recommended to the school by World Bible School teachers, missionaries, campaigners, and the national preachers themselves. The school has enjoyed amazing growth.

Second, it is a printed preacher school. Every two months, the men enrolled receive the equivalent of three hundred pages of expository studies on the Scriptures. It is believed that the expository type of study crosses cultures better than other types of study. The materials sent give a thorough treatment of the New Testament book or Old Testament book being studied. It is designed to keep the national preacher enrolled in the school until he receives a study of each of the New Testament and Old Testament books, as well as *Cruden's Concordance, Smith's Bible Dictionary,* and several important special studies.

Picture two normal-sized books that are 150 pages in length, and you have the equivalent of the amount of material that is sent to these men every two months. The entire curriculum calls for these men to receive books that are 150 pages in size, that cover the entire Bible, and that include special studies on leadership, building sermons and Bible lessons, and soul-winning.

Third, in addition to sending expository studies to these men, a flexible, on-site preacher school is sometimes used as a follow-up to the printed material. This on-site school is literally taken to where the men are. Preachers and teachers go into a country and study with the national preachers in that location for two or three weeks. Students are provided with food and a syllabus for the classes they attend. They stay at that location day and night for the entire length of the school. They thus enjoy fellowship with other preaching brethren and are given opportunities to ask questions and receive feedback on problems they are facing.

The printed preacher school and the on-site school answer the big need of giving the national man an opportunity to prepare himself to preach to his own people in their own language. Since this work is accomplished to some extent through the printed page, it also answers the need of providing Christian literature for these teachers and preachers who are in desperate need of it.

THE STRONG POINTS

This unique missionary effort has strong points that should be immediately recognized. First, it provides an education to national men inexpensively. Expository materials can be sent to each of these men every two months in a cost-efficient way. Money for missions is hard to find or raise; what missionary money we have should be used to the maximum. TFTWMS sends an education to hundreds of national men with a small amount of money.

Second, the thrust of this work is to educate national men in their own land. Bringing these men to the United States for an education is very expensive. Often, when the national man tastes of the blessings of America, he does not want to return to his land. It is almost essential, therefore, that a way be found through which the national preacher can receive an education in his own country.

Third, this effort can reach out to hundreds of national men quickly. All of these men are in need of assistance now! How can we get it to them? This method is one of the most practical ways of immediately getting materials to them.

Fourth, it allows the national man to receive an education over a period of time. Because the education comes in the form of printed matter, they have access to the material for months and even years. These men need time to comprehend and assimilate the studies. The printed page offers them that opportunity. They can read and re-read it. They can easily store it. They can share it with others. It can be retained in their possession for as long as ten to fifteen years.

PICTURING THE EFFECTIVENESS

Picture 40,000 men (and thousands more as the work grows) in 153 nations of the world, going out to preach in their own languages to their own people. They are committed to Christ but have had little teaching upon which to build. Furthermore, these men will never have the opportunity to study in the United States to enable them to preach more accurately and faithfully. They have few books, if any. Picture yourself in this type of situation. What would you need?

Can you imagine how these men would be assisted if they received materials on every Old Testament and New Testament book? Can you imagine how encouraging it would be to them to be able to attend a two- to three-week preacher school in their community? Can you picture them in a school, taking several courses in Bible studies, having fellowship with other preachers, having opportunities to have their questions answered, and getting assistance regarding the problems they are facing? Can you not see how these opportunities would increase their effectiveness in leading souls to Christ and in edifying those who have become Christians?

HELPING THOSE WHO HAVE NOT HEARD

In order to help those who have never heard the gospel to become Christians, a special book was designed in 1998 by TFTWMS. It contains three hundred plus pages on how to become a Christian. The reader of the book is introduced to God, Christ, the Holy Spirit, the Bible, the earthly life of Jesus, the death, burial, and resurrection of Jesus, the establishment of the church, and how one can live for Christ today as a member of His church. Then, in the last two hundred pages of the book, there is a complete copy of the New Testament (NASB).

Thousands of these books have been sent to Africa, the Eastern European countries, India, and other places. The success rate has been very high—almost amazing. The book, 512 pages in length, can be printed and sent to someone in another country for $1.63. It is an attempt to bring together the very message that any Christian would want to provide for someone who has not heard the gospel.

Plans are being made every year to cover a large area of the earth with these books. Before printing, the book is culturally adapted for the specific area into which it is being sent.

HOW CAN YOU HELP?

Your help is needed to maintain this missionary effort that has become one of the largest, most cost-effective and productive efforts. Here is a two-part challenge for every Christian:

First, would you challenge the church where you worship and with whom you work to give a one-time contribution to this work? Even a small contribution will go a long way in providing teaching materials and on-site training for these national preachers.

Second, could you give a one-time contribution to this work? This contribution, of course, would have to be above and beyond your regular contribution to the local congregation of which you are a part. We are not asking anyone to interrupt his commitment to the work of the local congregation. The church needs more works, not fewer works. This effort is designed to strengthen every missionary activity and does not seek to detract from any one of them.

You would be surprised how much can be done if we all do a little extra. No one person has a lot of light, but if we put our lights together, we can have a big light that will reach out into all of the world. Would you decide today to dig a little deeper and give a little extra for this wonderful method of world evangelization?

CONTRIBUTIONS NEEDED

Contributions should be made out to Truth for Today World Mission School and sent to 2209 S. Benton, Searcy, AR 72143. Will you assist us in providing study materials for national preachers? This work is under the oversight of the Champions church of Christ in Houston, Texas.

Eddie Cloer